ESSENTIALS OF

PSYCHOLOGICAL

TESTING

BY

LEE J. CRONBACH

University of Illinois

HARPER & BROTHERS, PUBLISHERS

NEW YORK

To My Parents

Contents

CONTENTS

Preface

Texts in measurements reflect the trends in that field. Until recently, the problem of the instructor in psychological testing has been to acquaint his students with the instruments available, and textbooks have been essentially descriptive catalogs of tests. The years have seen such a multiplication of good and necessary devices that it is now hopeless to try to introduce the student to all the significant tests. Moreover, it is clear that more and more tests will be developed. In clinical psychology especially, there is a tendency to demand a great variety of tests rather than to seek a few best tests for each function. The clinician prefers to draw, from a huge armamentarium, the particular tools which best fit each individual client. In educational and industrial practice as well, we are learning that the test which best solves one problem may be of little value in other situations.

If we cannot introduce the student to all the tests he will use, the course in testing must have a different function. The obvious need is for a course which will present the basic principles of testing in such a way that the student will learn to choose tests wisely for particular needs, and so that he will be aware of the weaknesses of whatever tests he uses. Thus he will be enabled to cope with new tests as they emerge. It is well that experience and research on tests have unearthed a large vein of significant general principles.

While current textbooks should stress these general principles, specific tests need not be lost sight of. The student must surely know the tests most widely used and most widely cited in the literature, and a critical study of them is the best way to understand the principles. The student who understands how the Multiphasic differs from the Bernreuter is in a position to make sound decisions about any present paper-pencil test of personality. The student who can compare completely the Wechsler test with the Primary Mental Abilities battery applies every principle we know about intelligence testing. In choosing tests for study, emphasis has been placed on (1) tests having wide application, (2) tests which clearly illustrate significant principles either in the breach or the observance, and (3) tests which are prototypes of important techniques. Necessarily, many tests have been omitted, including some which are greatly respected. The space given to a test in this book is not in proportion to the goodness of the test. So that the student will have ready access to a wider listing of tests than we can discuss, a summary listing of tests accompanies many chapters. Even this listing has been selective. So that the student will have some idea whether a test merits further consideration for some purpose he has in mind, a column of critical comments has been added to each table. These comments are chosen from competent reviews of the test. No matter how careful one is in selecting such quotations, they cannot represent fully the thought of the reviewers. In many cases, it has been necessary to cite one out of several reviews of a test. Users of the book are therefore cautioned against treating these comments as final judgments; reference to the original source or to other similar reviews is required to obtain a full and balanced report on the test.

Testing has been furthered by two lines of emphasis in American psychology: one, the practical and clinical application of instruments; the other, the theoretical and statistical analysis of testing problems. So far have these two specialties drifted apart that the person trained in psychometric theory cannot accept some important instruments of the clinician, because clinicians often have faith in devices which do not satisfy the psychometric criteria. Yet if these devices were rejected, the clinician would be deprived of truly helpful tools. The other face of the picture is that the clinician is often dissatisfied with the precisely designed and statistically purified tests that come from the psychometric school, because they do not give the information he needs about his clients. Future research and courses in psychology must lead to a mutual understanding between these two equally necessary groups of specialists. To be welcomed, then, is any training which provides both with common basic concepts. On such a common course in principles of psychological testing, specialized study of industrial, clinical, or educational tests, and statistics, theory of measurements, and so on, may be founded. The clinician must know how the psychometrically trained specialist evaluates tests, but the test technician must see why tests he rates as poor do function, in practical conditions, better than the others he gives a clean bill of health. The obvious goal is to develop tests which merit the full approval of both groups, as few of our present devices do.

Every writer on testing faces the problem: How technical shall the presentation be? It is impossible to say some things that need to be said without resorting to statistics, and that means that the student must be able to grasp those statistics intelligently—hence a chapter early in the book on simple statistical methods, sufficient to give a little meaning to statements about correlation. In discussing reliability, and, even more important, validity, one can choose between superficiality and technicality. Even with ideal writing, topics such as these require energetic thinking. But a student of psychology is not equipped to read test manuals and research reports critically until he knows the principles included in this text. Some students will find parts of Chapters 4, 9, and 11 difficult and should be advised to postpone intensive study of them. Most students will find it valuable to return to Chapter 4 for review after covering the later chapters.

Factor analysis is a topic especially likely to seem difficult. Factor analysis is admittedly technical, but it is also so fundamental in the present and future of psychological testing that the student cannot dodge it. The emphasis on factor analysis provided in this text is the minimum that the student can know if he is to understand the new tests that are on the horizon.

One further explanation is required. The questions which stud the book are part of the text. They capitalize on our knowledge that the brain which works as it reads profits most. By thinking through the questions on each section, the reader sees how the principles apply and becomes aware of topics which need further thought. The questions do not always have specific answers. Frequently they are controversial, or can only be answered by a qualified "Yes, but—." The student who sees two sides to any of the questions can have confidence that he probably is doing good thinking.

Having these purposes in mind, the writer has done what he could to accomplish them. The work has been aided and improved by the careful criticisms of many friends. The writer is especially grateful to Irving Lorge, Walter L. Wilkins, Dorothy Knoell, and David Krathwohl for their careful reading and criticism of large sections of the manuscript. Many errors in particular chapters have been removed as a result of the helpful comments of Lewis M. Terman, K. J. Holzinger, and Quinn McNemar. The largest number of suggestions, and some of the most helpful, have come from the students on whom the materials were tried. Elizabeth Johnson, who took the major responsibility for clerical work on the manuscript, has been of great assistance.

As indicated within the text, several investigators have been kind enough to make unpublished materials available. The writer owes an especial debt to O. K. Buros, who went to great trouble to provide galley proofs of *The third mental measurements yearbook* so that up-to-date critical comments could be used. Thanks are also extended to the numerous publishers who gave permission to quote various materials.

Lee J. Cronbach

Urbana, Illinois
June, 1949

PART I
Basic Concepts

CHAPTER 1

Who Uses Tests?

"In the field of tests and measurements, we really have accumulated a vast amount of material—and I should say, reliable and valid material—on how to distinguish human ability. We know, for example, that we may find high mental ability at every socio-economic level. We know too (and we can demonstrate this with good statistical material) that children differ widely not only from one another but from their parents. We know that if we conduct a search for the kind of scientific and humane scholarly ability which we seek in high-school and college students, for example, we discover that Jefferson's ideal is sound—we will find such ability in every level of population, and one cannot tell, either, simply by looking at the parents or the success of the parents.

"Then, of course, everybody knows about what was done by social scientists in the two world wars. I do not see how we could have found good airplane pilots without our new and practical knowledge of vocational testing. I do not see how we can carry on good business and industrial enterprises from this time forward without using in guidance and counseling our testing knowledge.

"Again let us notice the practical social outcome. Let us take one very recent example. [The President's] Committee on Higher Education has just reported that, on the basis of adequate testing given really to millions of GI's, we probably could have twice as many men and women in college without diluting the mental ability at all. They just are not there now, not because of mental deficiency, but probably because of economic stringency" (2).[1]

That statement, delineating a few of the accomplishments of psychological testing and their significance for American life, was made by G. D. Stoddard. The comment was made in a radio discussion, in answer to a request from President Conant of Harvard to name any outstanding achievement of the social sciences in recent decades. The testing movement stands as a prime example of social science in action, since it touches on vital questions in all phases of our life. What is character, and what sorts of children have good character? What personality make-up promises that an adolescent will be a stable, effective adult? How can we tell which six-year-olds are ready to begin learning to read? Is this young man a good prospect for training in watchmaking, or should he go into a different vocation—say, steamfitting or patternmaking? Such are the problems to which testing, and research on individual differences, direct their efforts. In this book, we will survey the methods which have been and are being developed to solve these problems.

One way to get a quick overview of the region we are to explore is to find out what testers do. By meeting a few of the people who work with tests,

---

[1] Boldface numbers in parentheses refer to references at the end of the chapter.

we can get an impression of the variety of services tests perform, and of the way they fit into a psychological career. The people to be described are imaginary, each one being a composite portrait of many psychologists such as can be found in every part of the country.

Let's begin by calling on Helen Kimball. It's about eleven on a January morning, and we find her at her desk in the central administration building of the school system of Riverton, population 17,000. Miss Kimball is dark, attractive, 35ish. Her position bears the title, School Psychologist. The office in which we find her is unusually bright, with decorative pictures, drapes, and a table low enough to accommodate a child comfortably. On the table are spread out several objects: blocks, a cutout puzzle, a folder of pictures.

Miss Kimball apologizes for the disorder of the table as she greets us. "I just finished testing a boy and haven't had time to clean up the materials. Usually I keep just a toy or two on the table, to attract the interest of any child sent down to see me. These test materials are from two or three tests: the Cornell-Coxe Performance Scale (that's an intelligence test), a picture test for studying personality called the Thematic Apperception Test, and the Stanford-Binet." When we express interest in her case, and inquire about the reason for testing the boy, she outlines his background as follows:

Charles is a boy from a foreign home, middle-to-low economic status, who in the fourth grade suddenly is causing trouble after having been known as a friendly, successful pupil in other grades. His teacher reports that he has made almost no progress in school subjects since the start of the year, that he refuses her attempts to give him extra help, and that he has begun to disturb the class by hitting other boys, taking objects from the girls to annoy them, and similar misdemeanors. A check with the files showed that his previous teachers had made many favorable reports: "A fine worker. Does everything a little better than most other boys." "Learns new ideas quickly. Good at number work." But the objective tests given at the end of the third grade showed that he was not superior. In fact, in reading comprehension Charles was two months behind the average pupil of his class, and in arithmetic, his best score, he just reached the average. Probably the teachers were misled by his cheerfulness and industry into overrating his past learning.

"Now," says Miss Kimball, "they asked me to try to determine the causes of his problem. Teachers in each school check most of the cases; for instance, they give intelligence tests and reading tests, and make studies of most of the children the school needs to know more about. But Charles was sent to me because the teacher felt his behavior presented an especially serious problem. The school did have a mental-test record, because Charles' class was given the Kuhlmann-Anderson group intelligence test two months ago. Charles' IQ was only 65. But his teacher said Charles wouldn't work on the test. He did just a few items, then stopped and looked out the window; when she urged him to go ahead, he worked slowly, and didn't seem to be trying.

"So my first problem was to try to find out how bright Charles is, to learn what to expect of him. The Binet is our usual measure, and since we give it individually, most children coöperate well. When I gave the Binet this morning, Charles did about as well as most ten-year-olds; I haven't computed his IQ yet, but as I gave the test I got the impression it will come out about 90 to 100—just a trifle below average. Since that score might be affected by his schooling, as many of the questions deal with language, I also gave him the Cornell-Coxe scale, where he works with blocks, puzzles, and other tests not likely to be affected by schooling. But he did about the same as on the Binet, so apparently language difficulties aren't his big problem. I was pleased that he coöperated, since he'd had trouble before. He was eager to work, cheerful, and seemed pleased with his accomplishment. But of course we started out slowly, and I made a great effort to interest him in the 'games.'

"I did two other things with Charles. Usually we don't test so much in one day, but the school wants to make some decisions about Charles before mid-year promotions. So we broke off the testing and chatted awhile, then I gave him a vision test. I chose that because I noticed some squinting during the Cornell-Coxe, and the teacher had noted a few complaints of headaches. My vision tests aren't as precise as an oculist's, but they showed a little deficiency in one eye. Worse, though, is his coördination; the eyes don't work together, but instead look at slightly different parts of the page when he is reading. This probably can be corrected, but we'll need further visual tests to be sure. It would cause trouble in reading and lead to fatigue.

"Since the emotional problem seemed to be severe, from the reports of Charles' social behavior, I used my picture test. The child makes up stories about each picture, and the stories often reveal his worries and wishes. This test, too, I'll have to study in detail before drawing conclusions. But it shows Charles is greatly disturbed. Here's one picture, showing a boy huddled up in a corner. Charles makes up a story that the boy was playing with the others and they made him stop and go home. The other boys said he had a different way of playing that wasn't right. Several stories like that suggest that Charles is greatly worried about losing his friends, and about 'being different.' The test gives many other suggestions about Charles' problems, but I need to study the record before I make any definite analysis.

"Our next steps will be to check on the vision problem and to clarify the emotional difficulties. I'll have several conferences with Charles, helping him talk out his difficulties. Then we will see what can be done to help him solve them. The fact that he has normal mental ability is a real help, since we know he can do well if his adjustment improves. It will help to know that he is average rather than superior, as past teachers suggested. Maybe he's had to live up to too high a reputation. We may use further tests later, but so far they have helped to narrow our field of investigation, so that my conferences with Charles will be effective."

That cross section should give some idea of Miss Kimball's work. Not every case is just like Charles, nor are the tests the same for every case.

In contrast to this clinical approach, let's take a look at the work of a personnel manager for a department store. This is a store with about 350 employees, ranging from roustabouts to buyers and office personnel. Edward Blake, the personnel manager, is a heavy-set, graying man of forty-five, who seems interested in whatever we have to say to him. But there is also a briskness, a sticking-to-a-schedule. "The routines of the job? I don't do much testing myself; but I do interview everybody we hire. That helps the store, because every employee knows there's someone here in the office who has met him, and to whom he can take his problems.

"When an applicant comes in, we have him fill in a blank, and my assistant, Miss Field, gives each one a set of tests. The tests aren't quite the same for everybody. We give them all the Adaptability Test (a short intelligence test), since different jobs in the store call for employees of different caliber. Most applicants get a test of simple arithmetic—addition, percentages, discounts, and so on. For package wrappers and merchandise handlers, we use a simple test of motor ability, in which they have to place wooden cubes in a box as rapidly as possible. It doesn't predict who'll be the best employee, but it saves us from some lemons. For a few departments, we have trade tests, tests of information about the job. Some men claim to be shoe salesmen when they don't know a last from a counter. These tests check on the experience the applicant claims in his application blank.

"Whatever tests Miss Field gives are scored and recorded on the application blank. Then, when there is a vacancy, we pull out of the file the names of people who have the qualifications that job requires. I call in one or several of these people, interview them, and if I think they'll do, I hire them. The tests in our work are most useful to sort out the good and the poor prospects. Miss Field can give the tests very easily, and it saves us a lot of time we'd spend interviewing people who wouldn't be good workers. Of course, Miss Field does a nice job, making sure each person thinks we're interested in him, and sending each one away with a feeling that he's had a fair consideration."

Mr. Blake, of course, is a little different from this or that other personnel manager we might have talked to. But his work is fairly typical of that in businesses having substantial turnover. Perhaps the best contrast to him is Sam Garrett.

Sam is engaged in a research program which will eventually lead to a method for selecting airline pilots. Garrett's research agency is the national headquarters for investigations of airline personnel needs. Garrett, about 32, was hired as an assistant in this research just after he completed work for his doctor's degree in psychology. Before receiving his degree, he spent a large part of the war in the Air Force psychological program, developing tests for pilots. Just now he is setting up testing centers in various cities where prospective pilots can be given the experimental tests.

"Our tests are not being used for hiring yet," Garrett explains. "We work only with men who are going to be tried by the airlines. The pilots take our tests, and we will follow up in a year or so to see which men worked out well on the job. If we are right, we have a set of tests here that will select good pilots. But we're not sure unless we make some predictions and see how they work out. This set of tests is new. It includes some of the old stand-bys from the experimental psychology laboratory, like this coördination test. And many tests used during the war will be useful here. But our group of psychologists has been busy modifying old tests and inventing new ones, relying heavily on what we learned from wartime pilot selection. Nearly everyone in the group has a pet idea for a new type of test that might measure some important factor in pilot ability.

"We decided what to include by studying what makes a good pilot. We interviewed hundreds of pilots, CAA inspectors, and check pilots. We had them tell what caused accidents they knew of, what mistakes they had made, what things they knew made some men poor pilots. We also examined previous research on abilities. From the combined evidence, we got a list of the characteristics that seem to be most important in piloting. Then we found or designed tests which seemed to measure each characteristic. Our present list of 'critical requirements of the airline pilot's job' is (1):

" '1. *Judgment and Planning.* The ability to reason logically, to anticipate, and to use good judgment in practical situations.
" '2. *Pilot Information.* The possession of adequate knowledge of aero-equipment, principles of flight, instrument flying, navigation, and weather.
" '3. *Mechanical Relations.* The ability to visualize mechanical movements and to have insight into the operating principles of mechanical devices.
" '4. *Visualization of Movement.* The ability to visualize movements in the attitude of an object and to visualize the flight path of an airplane through space.
" '5. *Instrument Reading.* The ability to obtain data from instrument dials and scales quickly and accurately.
" '6. *Instrument Interpretation.* The ability to determine the attitude of an airplane from interpretation of the readings of instruments.
" '7. *Signal Reaction Time.* The ability to perceive a situation, decide quickly on the appropriate response, and make the correct movement.
" '8. *Coordination.* The ability to make smooth and precise movements.
" '9. *Orientation.* The ability to recognize landmarks from maps or photographs and to orient with reference to fixed positions in space.
" '10. *Personal Stability.* The ability to remain organized and to make appropriate responses to adverse or unusual situations.
" '11. *Attitudes and Interests.* The possession of personal attitudes and interests appropriate for an effective airline pilot.'

"The tests? Most of these things can be measured by printed tests—reasoning questions, questions of knowledge, tests showing pictures of the instrument panel and asking for interpretations. The mechanical relations test shows pictures of machinery and asks the man, for instance, how a wheel will turn when a certain gear moves. We have a few apparatus tests, which measure how well the applicant coördinates. Light signals indicate that he is to move certain controls, and the apparatus records how rapidly he responds. Sometimes he has to make several actions at once, which is pretty confusing to a man with poor aptitude and self-control. In addition, we examine the man's background, and interview him.

"These methods probably aren't the last word in pilot selection. We'll have to change some of these tests, and we'll have new ideas next year which will give us additional tests. But the research is progressing. The principal thing we're sure of now is that this job is too complicated to be predicted by just a single mental test of some sort. But with the right tests it can be predicted well enough that we should reduce crashes due to pilot error. Besides, the airlines will save a great deal of money if we can identify men likely to fail in training, since training a pilot is expensive."

That's the picture of testing in action. It doesn't yet cover the clinical psychologist in a hospital, the experimental psychologist studying a theoretical problem, the tester preparing standardized tests for school use, the vocational counselor, and many others. We haven't paid much attention to the Miss Fields who give most of the tests, in offices, clinics, schools, and industries. But from the portraits just presented we can draw some generalizations which warrant spending time learning about tests:

1. Tests play an important part in making decisions about people.
2. There is a great variety of tests, covering many sorts of characteristics.
3. Even for a single characteristic, such as mental ability, there are many tests which have different uses.
4. The significance of test scores is greatest when they are combined with a full study of the person, by means of interviewing, case history, application blanks, and other methods. Tests provide facts which help us understand people. They almost never are a mechanical tool which can make decisions for us.

SUGGESTED READINGS

Bordin, Edward S. "Self-conflict as a source of vocational maladjustment," in Burton, Arthur, and Harris, Robert E. (eds.), *Case histories in clinical and abnormal psychology.* New York: Harper, 1947, pp. 615–627.

Kutash, Samuel B. "Paresis," in Burton, Arthur, and Harris, Robert E. (eds.), *Case histories in clinical and abnormal psychology.* New York: Harper, 1947, pp. 366–380.

Shartle, Carroll L. "Occupations in psychology." *Amer. Psychologist,* 1946, 1, 559–582.

REFERENCES

1. Anon. *Brochure of the American Institute for Research, Inc.* Pittsburgh: Amer. Inst. Res., 1947.
2. Conant, James B., and others. "Prospects for the scientific study of human relations." *Univ. of Chicago Round Table,* 1947, No. 510.

CHAPTER 2

Purposes and Types of Tests

FUNCTIONS OF TESTING

Almost any task or action some men can and will do more skillfully than others. Since these individual differences are a principal problem in directing the activities of others, every leader, manager, teacher, social worker, and physician must be able to identify them. The purpose of every psychological test is to detect differences between individuals. This knowledge serves two functions: prediction and diagnosis.

Prediction

An attempt to predict underlies every use of testing. Whenever a test is given to two people, it tells about some difference between their performances at this moment. But the fact would be of no significance, would not be worth knowing, if from it one could not predict that these two people would differ in some future activity. Consider a test as abstract as flash recognition of letters. Some people recognize four letters in a brief instant; others react to five. This difference intrigues the curiosity, but it is an unimportant fact until it is related to some behavior it predicts. The psychologist interested in applications may be concerned with it because this behavior has much in common with airplane recognition and perception in reading. The theoretical psychologist is less concerned with immediate application of laboratory findings, but he too will consider individual differences in a predictive sense by inducing from them general laws about perception and recognition applicable to the future behavior of the individual.

Prediction is illustrated by clinical use of tests. A clinician gives a test of emotional adjustment to a client and finds that his score is far from the norm. Giving the test and using the results are based upon the assumption that atypical answers to the test predict that he will behave abnormally at some time in the future, unless corrective measures are taken. Prediction nearly always refers to some eventual overt behavior. The clinician would not be set to detecting emotional maladjustment if that were only some internal state of the subject, never to crop out. The significance of the entire problem hinges on the fact that answers given on the test permit one to predict deviant behavior which should be forestalled.

Prediction is the ultimate justification for the achievement test used for grading in school. It is used for prediction in two ways, although both teacher and pupil may overlook this fact in their concern with the grade itself. The grade is warranted primarily because it predicts the pupil's ability to carry on some future activity; if it does not predict that, grading is likely not to be worth the troubles it causes. Furthermore, test results should give the teacher a prediction that if she teaches another class by similar methods, she can anticipate similar results of instruction. Without its predictive function, grading would be an act of crying over spilt milk.

Prediction is most obvious in selection, when one chooses among many candidates for an assignment. Military selection has employed tests extensively at every stage of the induction and training procedure. Out of a vast number of recruits, tests quickly discard those who will be unlikely to adapt to the service, and identify the upper groups to be considered for training as specialists or officers. A further selection takes place at the end of training, when some men are passed for assignment to duty and others are failed and given less responsible work. Tests bear a major responsibility in military screening, since it is impossible to give personal attention to each individual, and decisions must be made rapidly and with finality. Industrial selection bears many of the characteristics of military processing.

1. Demonstrate that prediction is attempted in each of the following situations.
   a. A foreman is asked to rate his workers on accuracy and quality of work.
   b. Airlines require a periodic physical examination of pilots.
   c. A psychologist determines whether students are more "liberal" in their attitudes toward birth control after two years of college study.
   d. James receives a grade of C in algebra while Harry receives an A.

Diagnosis

Prediction emphasizes differences between individuals, or between an individual and some standard. A second function of testing, diagnosis, emphasizes differences among characteristics of the same individual. Diagnosis in guidance and individual case work identifies the particular strengths of the individual so that he may capitalize on them, or the particular weaknesses so that he may adapt to or correct them. The clinical psychologist diagnoses when he identifies the precise difficulty in a case of maladjustment. The school psychologist or counselor diagnoses cases of scholastic failure to determine appropriate action. Diagnosis involves prediction, since the test user must decide what behavior the present pattern of characteristics permits and how stable that pattern will remain.

The term "diagnosis," as used in this book, refers to the analysis and description of various aspects of behavior. This should be distinguished from the more restricted meaning of diagnosis as the process of placing the subject in a particular category, such as schizophrenic or psychopathic.

The principal difference between the diagnostic and predictive emphases in testing is that in diagnosis we must be more certain what a test score means. If we know that Test X predicts a given behavior, and that case 771 has a low score on Test X, we need know nothing about the reason for his low score in order to predict poor performance. But if diagnosis is sought, it is important to know what characteristics cause a low score on Test X, since the emphasis in diagnosis is on explaining the facts about one's case. If one knows what is wrong, one can plan a remedy, or soundly predict that the problem is incurable.

2. Describe one circumstance when a diagnostic approach would be used by each of the following persons.
   a. A girls' counselor in a college.
   b. An employment manager.
   c. A social worker dealing with children.
   d. A teacher of typewriting.
3. Show that each illustration given in answer to Question 2 involves attempted prediction.

Research

Attention should be drawn to research as a function of testing, even though research involves prediction and occasionally diagnosis. In the search for knowledge about human behavior, many questions arise which have only remote practical importance but which deal with fundamentals of biological or social science. Tests have frequently been designed to solve research problems, even though these tests have no everyday utility. One example of such a test was developed by Lewis. He played phonograph recordings of words backwards, in order to study the way people learn to recognize these strange sound patterns (3). Such tasks, just because they are novel, frequently make very good experimental test situations. Another type of research makes use of common tests but seeks scientific knowledge rather than application; an example is the study of differences between racial groups, in which psychological tests have been prominent.

WHAT IS A TEST?

A test may be defined as a systematic procedure for comparing the behavior of two or more persons. This is a broad definition, broader than that used by some other writers. The layman is apt to think of a test as a series of questions requiring a written or oral answer. Psychological tests are, however, extremely varied, and the range of stimuli adapted to testing is constantly growing.

The definition given here rules out one large class of procedures from consideration as tests. Interviewing is an important method of case study, but rarely is every individual treated in exactly the same way, and the emphasis is more upon study of the individual than upon comparisons. Occasionally standardized interviews have been used, in which a uniform set of questions is asked of all persons. Some of these interviews qualify as tests under the definition given above.

One would not consider as a test an informal method of forming an opinion about the individual, such as casual conversation. Even if a teacher calls on each member of a class in turn, asking questions about an assignment, such a procedure cannot be considered a test unless the questions are set and the performance of one pupil can be compared with normal expectation on the question he is asked. For a study of behavior to be a test, every person must be observed in the same way as those with whom he is compared. It is not necessary that results be reduced to scores. Some useful tests give verbal descriptions of the person rather than numerical scores.

The definition of testing suggested permits us to consider measurements using apparatus, systematic procedures for studying frustration, sets of questions for obtaining reports on personality, and collected records of performance in life situations. Thus a record of the production of a worker over a period of two weeks might be considered a test, if comparable records may be obtained for other workers. This broad definition is adopted because the principles of test construction, use, and interpretation to be studied in later chapters apply equally to all these types of measurement. Validity, objectivity, standardization, standard scores, and the like are broadly applicable concepts. It appears simpler to refer to all standard procedures as tests than to draw careful distinctions between tests, questionnaires, work samples, and observations. The reader is warned, however, that many definitions for "test" are in current use, so that it is important to use only one meaning in any context.

Tests, in this broad conception, need not be considered as measurements. Measurement attempts to assign a number, on a scale of equal units, to each person for each characteristic. Not only are psychological tests less perfect as measurements than measures used in other sciences, but many useful tests do not measure. One way to study a thing is to measure, but an equally helpful way is to describe it accurately. Tests of personality in particular often seek to describe a person rather than to reduce his behavior to a few scores. The measurement emphasis in psychology stems from two famous Thorndike dicta: "If a thing exists, it exists in some amount"; "If it exists in some amount, it can be measured." While these postulates set an excellent goal for psychology as an exact science, they have caused non-quantitative techniques to be slighted. Psychology must at present use both measurement and description. As in botany, geography, meteorology, and chemistry, descriptive methods may some day decline in emphasis as refined measurement can cope with more of our problems. It is likely, however, that some aspects of behavior will always remain beyond the reach of the measuring instrument.

4. Decide whether each of the following is a test in the sense defined above.
   a. A mark for a course is based on the average of the six tests given during a course.
   b. An anthropologist measures the skull dimensions of subjects.

    c. An inspector checks samples of the work produced by each punch-press operator and gives him a score on the quality of his work.

    d. A nursery school teacher rates children on sociability after observing the number of contacts each child makes with other children on the playground.

    e. Judgments on the physical skill of schoolboys are obtained by asking the coach to report his opinion of each.

    f. Foremen who have been given a course in industrial relations are asked to write out how they would solve a series of hypothetical grievance cases.

5. Compare the following definitions with that given in this text. What procedures if any are called tests in this text, that are excluded under each of the following definitions?

    a. "A situation in which a record of performance is secured directly, not by estimate" (2, p. 776).

    b. "The task, together with the means of appraising it, which defines an ability" (5, p. 62).

    c. "A psychological test is too often thought of simply as a measuring device. It is this and more. It is a standard situation in which to observe behavior" (1, p. 228).

CLASSIFICATION OF TESTS

There are numerous ways of classifying tests—according to form, purpose, content, and other characteristics. The simplest and most applicable grouping distinguishes between tests seeking to measure the maximum performance of which the subject is capable and those seeking to determine his typical behavior.

Tests of Ability

Tests of maximum performance are required in studying ability and capacity. *Capacity* is the person's hypothetical potentiality for acquiring a reaction, with training. One can never know what capacity is. Even if a person has reached a certain level after training, we cannot be sure that he would not do better with better training or motivation. *Ability* is more tangible; it may be defined as the person's performance on a task at present, with maximum motivation but without further training. Ability is never greater than capacity; how closely it approximates capacity depends upon the extent to which the subject's potentialities have been developed. Sometimes, too, emotional interference makes ability less than it could be, as in the case of stage fright.

Tests of maximum performance are tests of ability. Tests of ability to define words (vocabulary tests) have been used to predict school performance. Tests of ability to answer questions about a job (trade tests) have been used to distinguish between expert and less experienced workers. Tests of ability to respond instantly to a signal (reaction-time tests) have been used to weed out applicants who would make unsafe drivers. In each of these cases the tester seeks a measure of the best performance the person can produce. If this is obtained, a person who makes a poor score is known to be unsuitable for the purpose at hand, at least until he is given further training or treatment. As will be seen in Chapters 4 and 5, a principal problem with tests of this type is to make certain that the subject is doing his best. A good score does not guarantee, of course, that the person will be equally superior under everyday motivation.

Tests of Habitual Characteristics

Tests of typical performance are used in studying habits and personality. There is little value in determining how courteous an applicant for employment in a store *could* be when she wanted to; almost anyone of normal upbringing has the ability to be polite. But the test of a suitable employee is whether she maintains that courtesy in her daily work, even when she is not specially motivated or "on her best behavior." An inspector with proper vision and training should be able to detect defective parts. A test of his carefulness which determines how well he judges parts when trying especially hard would have little additional value. The difference between the good and poor inspector (of equal aptitude and training) is the extent to which the latter permits himself to be distracted and careless in run-of-the-mill duty. For cheerfulness, honesty, open-mindedness, emotional stability, and many other aspects of behavior there is almost no practical value in a test of ability, since most people can produce a show of the behavior when it is demanded of them. But persons who can act cheerfully, honestly, or impartially when they know they are being tested may not do so in other situations. The difference between the test of typical behavior and the test of maximum ability is that in the latter case the subject knows what is judged good and seeks to show good performance.

In many situations in which typical performance is studied the concept of "good" or "best" performance is inappropriate. Personality is usually analyzed in a descriptive way, with no attempt being made to consider one characteristic as ideal. Interest tests show this clearly. There is nothing good or bad about interest in, say, engineering. One who has this interest can use it, but one who has not finds other worth-while activities. In social relations, people show wide variations in dominance-submission, but one cannot say that any proportion of these qualities is best, since our world has places for all degrees of this behavior.

Testing of typical performance is difficult. It has been accomplished, with greater or less success, in a variety of ways. These methods may be divided into behavior observations and self-report devices.

Behavior observations are attempts to study the subject in action. Preferably he is unaware that he is observed; it is hoped that under such conditions a helpful sample of his typical behavior can be described. Behavior observations include both observations in standardized test situations and observations under "natural" conditions.

Test situations are usually employed for observing an aspect of behavior which could be seen only occasionally in everyday life. This technique has been used to determine typical reactions to frustrations. The person is started on a task and prevented in some way from succeeding at it. He may then react in many significant ways which give insight into his personality and emotional control. It is essential for the validity of test observations that the subject not know what characteristic is being observed. Sometimes the observer is concealed. At other times the subject is led to believe he is being tested on one behavior, when another is being observed. Reaction to frustration is frequently studied when the subject believes he is being tested for mental ability. His responses when frustrated by difficult questions are usually genuine and little disguised (4).

Field observations, where the subject acts in his normal situation, may call for elaborately standardized observations, or merely for ratings or judgments by persons who have had a good opportunity to observe the subject. Field observations are used in industry to study the production habits of workers, in preschools and on playgrounds to study social reactions of children, and in a variety of other situations. In baseball, for example, the batting average is essentially a score based on field observations, recorded systematically.

The *self-report* approach is based on the fact that the subject has had an unusually good opportunity to observe himself in a variety of situations, so that he can, if he wishes, give a helpful estimate of his behavior. Self-report tests consist of standardized questions for obtaining such estimates. The crucial problem in using self-reports is obviously that of obtaining honest analysis. If the person tries to give a "best" picture of himself instead of a typical one, the test will fail of its purpose. An added problem is that his view of himself is likely to be distorted to some degree, since one cannot be a truly detached and impartial observer of himself.

6. Classify each of the following procedures as a test of ability, a self-report test, an observation in a test situation, or a field observation.
   a. An interviewer from the Gallup poll asks a citizen how he will vote in a coming election.
   b. A broadcasting company wishes to know what program features appeal to different types of listeners. It presents a broadcast to a studio audience, who react to the broadcast by pushing signal buttons to indicate when they enjoy or dislike a part of the program.
   c. A test of "vocational aptitude" asks the subject how well he likes such activities as selling, poker, woodworking, and chess.
   d. An arithmetic test is given to a group of applicants for jobs as cashiers.
   e. Inspectors in plain clothes ride streetcars to determine whether operators are pocketing fares without "ringing them up."
   f. During an intelligence test, the examiner is alert for evidence of self-confidence or lack of self-confidence.
   g. In a test of "application of principles of science," students are told about a fire which breaks out when an oil stove is turned over, and asked to decide how to put out the fire and to tell why it should be done that way.
   h. In a test of "application of principles in social studies," students are told of

a conflict about admitting Negroes to a housing project, asked to state what they think the city council should do and to give reasons to support the choice.

Terms Used to Describe Tests

In addition to the classification just discussed, there are many bases for grouping tests to call attention to particular characteristics. Certain basic terms are used to describe tests, although not every writer uses these terms in the same way.

Objective tests are often distinguished from *subjective tests*. Objective procedures are those in which responses are scored or summarized in such a way that all judges would agree as to the score assigned or the analysis made for each person. True-false tests, arithmetic tests, and measures of speed of tapping are representative objective procedures. In subjective tests the opinions of the scorers are permitted to affect the score assigned. Typical essay examinations, ratings of quality of art or sewing, and estimates of personality characteristics from observation are subjective, at least to some degree.

Standardized tests are those in which the test procedure and content have been so fixed that subjects at different places and times may be compared. A standardized test usually but not always has *norms,* or standards of normal performance, for use in interpreting results. Standardized tests may be contrasted to *informal tests,* such as those made up by a teacher to test a particular block of assignments.

Performance tests are distinguished from *pencil-and-paper tests.* In a performance test the subject is required to demonstrate his skill by manipulating objects or apparatus. Among the performance tests which have been used for various purposes are assembling a jigsaw puzzle, constructing a bicycle bell from its parts, "inventing" a hat rack out of two sticks and a C clamp, and "sewing" a zigzag line on a card with a threadless sewing machine. Pencil-and-paper tests are those in which the subject answers questions by writing or drawing. The questions may be verbal or pictorial. A third variety, *oral tests,* should also be mentioned.

Group tests differ from *individual tests* in that group tests permit many subjects to be tested at once. This distinction refers more to the way in which the tests are commonly used than to differences in their structure. Group tests can be given to a single individual if that is desirable. Many individual tests require careful oral questioning or observation of reactions, in which case a tester cannot work with several subjects simultaneously. But some individual tests have been modified and simplified so that group administration is also possible. An example is the Rorschach test of personality. In the individual form of the test, a subject looks at a card bearing an inkblot, and states orally what the blot looks like to him. He is questioned about each response until the tester is sure just what the subject sees. In the group form, the blots are placed on slides and projected on a screen. Subjects write their responses, and individual questioning is omitted.

Speed tests are contrasted to *power tests* of ability. In speed tests (also called *speeded* or *time-limit tests*), the subject is required to complete as many problems or tasks as he can in a predetermined time. Some speed tests measure nearly "pure" speed, since the task is one the subject could surely solve if given enough time. Examples are the test, "Go over this page, crossing out as many *a*'s as you can before I call time," or the test, "In this row of circles, place just one dot in each circle; make as many dots as you can before I call time." Power tests, also known as *unspeeded* or *work-limit tests,* present a set of problems of increasing difficulty, the subject being required to do as many problems as he can. A test may measure power and speed in any mixture, depending on the difficulty of the items. To determine if speed is important, the tester must obtain data on the question: "Did the person have time to finish all or nearly all of the items he could have answered with unlimited time?"

Tests are also subdivided according to purpose. Psychological tests of maximum performance are referred to as mental tests, intelligence tests, aptitude tests, prognostic tests, tests of special abilities, psychomotor tests, achievement tests, etc. Formal definitions of these terms are not given here, but each type is treated at length in later chapters. Mental tests are tests of ability to perform mental tasks. The term "intelligence test," while not rigidly used, usually refers to procedures attempting to measure the general, over-all mental ability of the individual. Aptitude and prognostic tests predict performance or learning in a new situation; one might have an aptitude test for dentistry, or for carpentry, or for music. Special-ability tests attempt to measure some limited performance such as numerical reasoning or color vision. Psychomotor tests measure performance of adaptive physical activities; tests of coördination in skilled acts, speed of complex reactions, and steadiness are frequently used. Achievement tests are used to determine how much a person has learned from some experience such as schooling.

Because some writers prefer to restrict the term "test" to measures of ability, numerous other words are used to refer to devices for estimating typical performance. Self-report devices in particular are referred to by many names: "inventory," "questionnaire," "opinionaire," "checklist," "record," etc. These procedures have usually been thought of as "personality tests," and the various measures of personality have been classified as adjustment tests, character tests, attitude tests, interest tests, etc. Among personality tests, special interest attaches to the adjustment test. Adjustment tests attempt to measure the degree to which the subject has emotional conflicts, tensions, and unsatisfied needs. They are used in investigations of the mental hygiene of individuals or groups. Character tests are used to measure traits upon which society places a moral valuation, such as stealing, lying, and cheating. Attitude tests study the person's opinion regarding political and social policies and institutions; there are tests of attitude toward war, progressive education, Russia, one's job, and one's present teacher. Interest tests are similar to attitude tests, but stress liking for various sorts of activities.

Although some scheme of classifying tests is a convenience, all such divisions are arbitrary. One of the striking current trends is the breakdown of traditional division lines. As will be seen in later chapters, intelligence tests are being used to diagnose personality, and some of the newest tests of personality give useful estimates of intelligence. Even the distinction around which this book is organized, between tests of maximum and typical performance, is difficult to sustain for a few borderline tests.

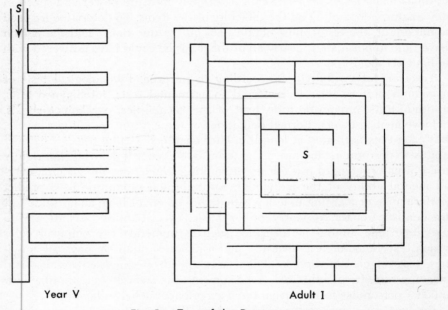

Year V   Adult I

Fig. 1.   Two of the Porteus mazes.

7. Judge each of these statements true or false and defend your answer.
   a. Batting averages are *objectively* determined.
   b. The 220-yard low hurdle race is a *standardized* test.
   c. A typing test which requires the typist to copy from a printed page as rapidly as possible is a *performance* test.
   d. A spelling test, dictated by the teacher and written by the pupil, is a *pencil-and-paper* test.
   e. A teacher has each member of the class read the same article in a current magazine. Time is called at the end of three minutes, and each pupil marks the place where he is reading. He then counts the number of words read and computes his reading rate in words-per-minute. This score is compared with a table of average reading speeds for typical magazine articles. This test is *objective*.

8. Classify each of the following tests, using as many of the descriptive terms discussed in the text as are clearly applicable.

    a. The Humm-Wadsworth Temperament Scale consists of several hundred printed questions, such as "Do you like to bet?" The subject answers each question by checking "yes" or "no." Answers are scored to indicate the extent to which he shows various trends in temperament.

    b. The Porteus Maze Test requires the child to trace the correct path through each of a series of printed mazes. The first mazes are very easy, with successive ones becoming more difficult. The child continues until he fails several trials at a particular maze. A failure is judged when he enters a blind alley.

Fig. 2.   The Tweezer Dexterity Test. (Photograph courtesy C. H. Stoelting Co.)

    c. In the Stenquist test booklet the subject marks illustrations of tools and mechanical objects to show which go together.

    d. The Bennett mechanical comprehension test presents questions about pictorial problems. A typical item shows two wagons poised on a stairway; the subject is to decide which wagon will roll down because of poor balance. Testing time is unlimited.

    e. In the Tweezer Dexterity Test the subject places pins in holes on a special board as rapidly as possible.

9. Would speed or power tests be most important to measure the skill of the following?

    a. typists.

    b. radio repairmen.

    c. dentists.

10. Can a subjective test be a standardized test?

11. Can an achievement test be an aptitude test?

12. Can a performance test be a group test?

REFERENCES

1. Bingham, W. V. *Aptitudes and aptitude testing.* New York: Harper, 1937.
2. Greene, Edward B. *Measurements of human behavior.* New York: Odyssey Press, 1941.
3. Lewis, Don. "The learning function." *Amer. Psychologist,* 1946, 1, 260.
4. McClelland, David C., and Apicella, F. S. "A functional classification of verbal reactions to experimentally induced failure." *J. abnorm. soc. Psychol.,* 1945, 40, 376–390.
5. Thurstone, L. L. *Multiple-factor analysis.* Chicago: Univ. of Chicago Press, 1947.

....

Interpreting Test Scores

RAW SCORES AND DISTRIBUTIONS

Meaning of a Raw Score

Most tests yield a numerical report of a person's performance. This may be reported in terms of the number of questions he answered, the time he required for the task, or some similar number. This number is his *raw score*. Because raw scores are readily available, and familiar from long experience in classroom tests, many people interpret them without realizing their limitations. A familiar example from the old-fashioned report card will demonstrate the problem.

Willie brings home a report showing that his average in arithmetic was 75, and his average in spelling was 90. His parents can be counted on to praise the latter and disapprove the former. Willie might quite properly protest, "But you shoulda seen what the other kids got in arithmetic. Lots of them got 60 and 65." The parents, who know a good grade when they see one, refuse to be convinced by such irrelevance. What do Willie's grades mean? It might appear that he has mastered three-fourths of the course work in arithmetic, and nine-tenths in spelling. But Willie objects to that, too. "I learned all my combinations, but he doesn't ask much about those. The tests are full of those word problems, and we only studied them a little." Willie evidently gets 75 percent of the questions asked, but if the questions are hard, the percentage itself is meaningless. We cannot compare Willie with his sister Sue, whose teacher in another grade gives much easier tests so that Sue brings home a proud 88 in arithmetic. It could be, too, that Willie's shining 90 in spelling is misleading. If the spelling tests deal with the very words assigned for study each day, and everyone but Willie earns 95 to 100, 90 is not so ideal.

Raw scores can indicate nothing of generalized significance until they are compared with some standard. Scores may be said to have an absolute meaning and a relative meaning. If a high jumper can cross the bar at 6 feet 3 inches, we have an absolute measure of what he can do. His performance takes on more meaning relative to the norm for his age, the performance of others in his group, or the world's record for high jumping. In mental variables, absolute meanings are uncommon. Willie's ability to spell 90 percent of his spelling words is an absolute and meaningful report—of his ability to spell *those* words. But it tells us nothing about his ability to spell words in general unless we know how common or difficult the test words were. If we standardize the list of words so that they are representative of the words he needs to spell in daily life, the report that he can spell 90 percent of them becomes an absolute measure of his ability to spell in general.

For an absolute measure one must have as a standard of reference some *true zero* of performance. Suppose Willie had earned a score of 10 percent in spelling. Does this mean that he knows only one-tenth of the words he should? No, for the teacher probably did not ask about the easy words, that Willie was sure to know. Even a score of zero on the test would not mean zero on knowledge of spelling-in-general. The difference between Willie with a score of zero and the model pupil who earns 100 is perhaps a difference in ability to spell only 20 words out of an active vocabulary of several thousand—if those 20 constituted the test. This interpretation is much more favorable to Willie. The same difficulty is less readily recognized in tests of intelligence. A raw score of 80 may seem to represent ability twice as great as the raw score of 40. Since the test does not include the items everyone can answer, perhaps the true ratio of performance, if every possible item had been used, would be 140 to 180, or 1040 to 1080. Even an infant, with his ability to recognize food and his mother, shows the presence of more than zero intelligence. Absolute zero, in any test of ability, is "just no ability at all."

1. Decide whether each of the following statements has absolute meaning—that is, whether one can make a meaningful interpretation of it without further data.
   a. Sarah can type 115 words per minute on typical business copy. yes
   b. Fred reads at the rate of 300 words per minute in the average college textbook. yes
   c. Morris earned a score of 84 on this mental test. no
2. How could one design a test which would give an absolute measure of the number of words a person knows, without asking about every word in the language?
3. Decide whether an absolute zero exists for each of the following variables, and, where possible, define it.
   a. Height. not an ability
   b. Ability to discriminate between the pitches of tones. no
   c. Speed of tapping. no
   d. Gregariousness, seeking the companionship of others.
   e. Rifle aiming.

Differences in raw scores do not represent absolute distances between individuals. Suppose Harry gets 110 points, Sam gets 120, and Jeff gets 130. Is Jeff as different from Sam as Sam is from Harry? Not at all, since the meaning of this difference depends upon the items in the test and the group studied. Any difference between raw scores can be stretched or reduced by introducing more or fewer items that discriminate between the persons involved. Suppose we add to the test ten items that Jeff can pass, but Sam and Harry cannot; the difference between Jeff and Sam has been stretched to 20 points. While absolute differences can be changed in this way, the ranks of the three men remain the same.

For this reason, raw scores are frequently converted into ranks, a kind of relative score, before use. Willie's report card (90 in spelling, 75 in English, 75 in arithmetic, and 86 in drawing) presents a very different picture if it reports his rank among 30 children (8 in spelling, 12 in English, 23 in arithmetic, and 23 in drawing).

4. If several pupils in Willie's class move away and are replaced with newcomers, will his raw scores probably change? His ranks? *yes*
5. If a different set of test questions had been used in English, would Willie's raw score change? His rank? *yes*
6. Alfred, a college freshman, is to receive guidance on his academic plans, and is given four tests of ability. Scores are presented in four different ways. Consider separately each row of scores, and interpret each set.

	Vocabulary	Verbal Reasoning	Non-Verbal Reasoning	Performance
Raw score	116	32	44	20
Percent of possible	77	73	80	67
Points above average	24	10	20	0
Rank among 260 freshmen	104	113	41	136

An Illustrative Mental Test

Before considering procedures for more systematic treatment of scores, let us examine a simple mental test. The Kent EGY ("emergency") Test is a short intelligence test, used when a quick estimate of ability is desired. The following questions are presented orally to each individual (5):

1. What are houses made of? (Any materials you can think of)
   One point for each item, up to four.
2. What is sand used for?
   Four points for manufacture of glass. Two points for mixing with concrete, road building, or other constructive use. One point for play or scrubbing. Credits not cumulative.
3. If the flag floats to the south, from what direction is the wind?
   Three points for north, no partial credits. It is permissible to say: 'Which way is the wind coming from?'
4. Tell me the names of some fishes.
   One point each, up to four. If the subject stops with one, encourage him to go on.
5. At what time of day is your shadow shortest?
   Noon, three points. If correct response is suspected of being a guess, inquire why.
6. Give the names of some large cities.
   One point for each, up to four. When any state is named as a city, no credit for New York unless specified as New York City. No credit for home town except when it is an outstanding city.
7. Why does the moon look larger than the stars?
   Make it clear that the question refers to any particular star, and give assurance that the moon is actually smaller than any star. Encourage the

subject to guess. Two points for "Moon is lower down." Three points for "nearer" or "closer." Four points for generalized statement that nearer object looks larger than more distant object.

8. What metal is attracted by a magnet?

Four points for iron, two for steel.

9. If your shadow points to the northeast, where is the sun?

Four points for southwest, no partial credits.

10. How many stripes in the flag?

Thirteen, two points. A subject who responds 48 may be permitted to correct his mistake. Explain, if necessary, that the white stripes are included as well as the red ones.

In this test, instead of one point for each question right, credits range from one to four points, depending on the quality of each answer. The total possible credit is 36 points. A person with a normal fund of information who can do simple thinking should do well on the test, but a mentally deficient person would earn a low score.

In the following sections we shall use a set of hypothetical scores on this test to illustrate the possible statistical procedures in test interpretation. Suppose that Mr. Gates, a psychologist attached to a criminal court, gives this test to prisoners to obtain a quick preliminary estimate of their ability. Men earn different scores, and soon Mr. Gates has a set of 45 scores, ranging from 15 points to 32 points. Mr. Gates could interpret each score by using a table of "norms" showing how men usually perform on the test. But if he has no such table, or wishes to compare each prisoner with the entire prisoner group, he will use some of the statistical procedures described below.

Distribution of Scores

In order to compare one man with a group, we need a simple method of summarizing the performance of the group. The usual first step is to make a *frequency distribution* by tallying how many people earn each score. In Computing Guide 1, the raw scores for Mr. Gates' prisoners are listed, and the procedure of tallying is illustrated. When a small group of scores is tallied, the distribution is irregular, but when large groups are studied, smoother frequency curves are obtained. It is convenient to smooth the distribution of scores, since minor irregularities are usually of no importance.

Figure 3 shows several frequency distributions in graphic form. These frequency distributions, like most distributions of test scores, are practically continuous. In everyday thinking, we speak of "bright," "average," and "dull" groups, but when ability is measured, these groups blend together and can only be distinguished by some arbitrary division. Suppose Mr. Gates calls men scoring 28 or over "superior" and speaks of men below 28 as an "inferior" group. Men on both sides of the border line are much nearer each other in ability than men having scores of 28 and 32, even though both the latter are classified as superior. Any attempt to classify normal subjects into types is only a crude way of reporting the actual individual differences. Distinctions of this sort are often made for practical purposes. Typists who can perform at a rate of 60 words per minute are accepted for employment while those at 58 are rejected. Soldiers who can meet fourth-grade standards are accepted as normal while those below this level are sent to classes for illiterates. An especially common situation in which the true continuity of life is replaced by dividing lines is the five-point grading system used throughout our schools. Classifications of this sort are artificial, no matter how helpful they may be. Other categories invented for convenient discussion are represented by the words "normal," "feeble-minded," "maladjusted," "neurotic," and "introvert." In every trait that has been studied, scores of people

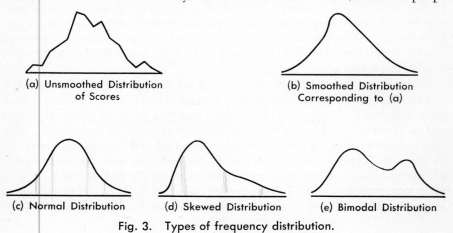

(a) Unsmoothed Distribution of Scores

(b) Smoothed Distribution Corresponding to (a)

(c) Normal Distribution

(d) Skewed Distribution

(e) Bimodal Distribution

Fig. 3.   Types of frequency distribution.

chosen at random are found to scatter gradually from one extreme to the other.

The _normal distribution_ is a basic concept in all statistical analysis, and helpful in interpreting most tests. A normal distribution is the bell-shaped curve illustrated in Figure 3(c). It is characterized by the concentration of scores near the average, and the symmetrical tapering toward each extreme. Normal distributions are generally found in measurements of biological characteristics, such as height and strength, of people chosen at random. Many mental tests also yield normal distributions.

A distribution which is not normal may be obtained when studying a selected group, even with a test which gave a normal distribution for an unselected group. Suppose curve (c), Figure 3, represents the distribution of mental test scores among unselected children. If the same test were given in a private school where only superior children are admitted, the curve of distribution might have the shape of curve (d). The average would of course be higher.

Changing the test items would also affect the shape of the distributions. Suppose most of the easy items were dropped from the test and many items were added which only the upper fraction of the group could pass. This would tend to wipe out the differences between poor and very poor children and would stretch out the curve at the upper end. The resulting curve would again be shaped like curve (d). This is known as a *skewed distribution.*

Bimodal distributions such as are shown in curve (e) are rarely encountered except where one is testing a mixed group, some of whom have been trained and some of whom have not. If typical adults were tested in speed of typing, a bimodal curve might be expected.

7. One could slice a normal distribution symmetrically into five parts, which would contain 7 percent, 24 percent, 38 percent, 24 percent, and 7 percent of the cases respectively. Grades are often so assigned: 7 percent A's, 24 percent B's, and so on. Sketch dividing lines cutting off roughly these percentages on a normal curve and on a skewed curve. Is an A as far above C as an F is below C? *yes   no* .
8. If intelligence is distributed on a continuous curve rather than by types which can be distinguished sharply, what implication does this fact have for identifying and planning for the feeble-minded?
9. Sketch a smoothed frequency curve for the distribution in Computing Guide 1. Is this distribution normal, skewed, or bimodal?

METHODS OF DESCRIBING RELATIVE PERFORMANCE

The performance of any man, in relation to that of the group, is indicated clearly if we locate his score against the frequency distribution. To make a permanent record of the man's standing is difficult, however, since the entire distribution can scarcely be placed in his file. Besides, we need a convenient method of recording his standing on every test he takes, so that his different abilities may be compared with each other. For this reason, most users of tests must either compute or make use of such statistics as the mean, median, and percentile ranks. In the following sections these concepts are presented briefly. Statistics texts give more complete discussions of the concepts and show other methods of computation.

Median and Percentile Score

Mr. Gates could record the rank of each man, and this would conveniently express his standing in the group. But if, on other tests, Mr. Gates has records of larger and smaller groups, the rank of 22 might sometimes be average, sometimes quite superior, sometimes quite poor. To eliminate this difficulty, interpretations are often based on *percentile rank, that is, the person's rank expressed as a percentage* of the group. Ranks are figured from the top of the group, rank 1 indicating the best performance, but percentiles are counted upward, the best performance being near the one-hundredth percentile. If a person falls at the 75th percentile, this means that 75 percent of the group is below him.[1]

---

[1] In exact computation of percentiles the case under consideration is divided in half in the following manner: Suppose that there are 50 cases; 31 fall below case A, and 18 are above case A. We consider that half of case A falls in each group, and the percentile rank is 31½ divided by 50, or 63.

1. Begin with the raw scores to be studied.

24 25 24 25 31 22 30 24 25 27 28 29 19 28 27
25 30 31 26 30 32 30 25 32 26 24 21 29 24 17
29 29 27 30 26 25 30 28 30 26 26 23 20 25 15

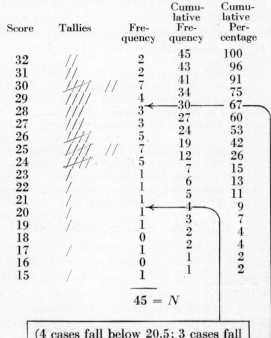

Score	Tallies	Frequency	Cumulative Frequency	Cumulative Percentage
32	//	2	45	100
31	//	2	43	96
30	//// //	7	41	91
29	////	4	34	75
28	///	3	30	67
27	///	3	27	60
26	////	5	24	53
25	//// //	7	19	42
24	////	5	12	26
23	/	1	7	15
22	/	1	6	13
21	/	1	5	11
20	/	1	4	9
19	/	1	3	7
18		0	2	4
17	/	1	2	4
16		0	1	2
15	/	1	1	2

2. Tally the number of cases with each score.

Write the number of tallies in the Frequency column.

3. Begin at the bottom of the column and add the frequencies one at a time to determine the cumulative frequency, the number of cases falling below each division point.

Divide the cumulative frequencies by N to determine the cumulative percentages.

$$45 = N$$

(4 cases fall below 20.5; 3 cases fall below 19.5, etc.)

(Two-thirds, or 67%, of the cases fall below 28.5; 67 is the cumulative percentage corresponding to score 28.5)

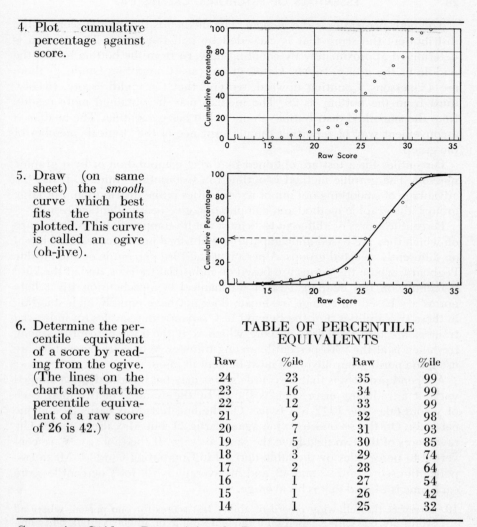

4. Plot cumulative percentage against score.

5. Draw (on same sheet) the *smooth* curve which best fits the points plotted. This curve is called an ogive (oh-jive).

6. Determine the percentile equivalent of a score by reading from the ogive. (The lines on the chart show that the percentile equivalent of a raw score of 26 is 42.)

TABLE OF PERCENTILE EQUIVALENTS

Raw	%ile	Raw	%ile
24	23	35	99
23	16	34	99
22	12	33	99
21	9	32	98
20	7	31	93
19	5	30	85
18	3	29	74
17	2	28	64
16	1	27	54
15	1	26	42
14	1	25	32

Computing Guide 1. Determining the Percentile Equivalents of Test Scores.

The 50th percentile is the *median*. The median is the middle score in the distribution, the score that is exceeded by half the group. The median is determined approximately by counting upward from the bottom to find the middle of the group. In Mr. Gates' group (see Computing Guide 1) there are 45 persons. Counting upward, we find that the middle score, twenty-third from the bottom, is 26. The median may be obtained more exactly from the smoothed distribution, along with other percentiles. The median is a convenient way of reporting the performance of the "typical" member of the group.

Percentiles for a test are obtained by direct computation or by a graphic method. The graphic method is outlined in Computing Guide 1. It has the advantage of smoothing out minor irregularities in the distribution. For large groups, the graphic method and computation give nearly identical results.

Percentile scores on different tests must not be compared unless the groups on which they are based are comparable. Published norms for tests are based on differently selected groups. A person at the 73rd percentile on the Purdue Pegboard, where the norms are based on industrial trainees, and at the 73rd percentile on the Bennett Test of Mechanical Comprehension BB, where norms are based on college freshmen, does not have equally high standing in these two abilities. For the Bennett test, separate percentiles for industrial trainees are also available. A score which is at the 73rd percentile among freshmen is at the 95th percentile among trainees. Wherever percentiles are used, the norm group involved must be kept in mind.

A second problem is that percentile scores may not be added and averaged without introducing error. This is shown by the example of two men, each of whom takes the EGY test twice. On the first test, Max earns 32 and Joe earns 29. On the second test, Joe again earns 29, but Max drops to 26. The raw scores of the two men have the same average. If the raw scores are converted to percentiles by the table derived in Computing Guide 1, Max's two percentile scores are 98 and 42, and his average is 70. Joe's percentile score each time is 74, and that is his average.

10. Interpret the following record of ability test scores for one person, where all scores are percentiles based on a random sample of adults: Verbal, 54; Number, 46; Spatial, 87; Reasoning, 40.
11. Determine approximately Alfred's percentile rank in each of the four tests he took (Problem 6, p. 22).
12. What is the median for Mr. Gates' group, estimated from the percentile table?
13. Raw scores usually change when a test is repeated, owing to chance errors of measurement. If each of the following persons changes two points up or down in raw score, on the EGY test, how much would his percentile scores change?
    a. A person with a percentile score of 54 on the first test.
    b. A person at the 98th percentile on the first test.
14. From the finding in Problem 13, what caution is suggested in interpreting percentile scores? When are differences in percentile scores least reliable?
15. The scores below are the times, in seconds, required by a group of persons to solve a puzzle. Prepare a table of percentile equivalents for this group.

52	34	41	42	46	45	27	48	35	35	38	29	54	36	33	30
48	39	44	36	36	34	51	40	30	33	37	41	56	32	48	35
37	28	28	45	31	39	31	27	35	36	34	42	38	33	33	31
39	28	36	33	37	36	34	54	34	32	33	38				

16. According to the table prepared in Problem 15, how much difference in absolute ability does a difference of 10 percentile points represent?

Mean and Standard Deviation

The second common system for describing distributions uses the mean and standard deviation. The *mean* (*M*) is the arithmetical average, obtained by adding all scores and dividing by the number of scores. The *standard de-*

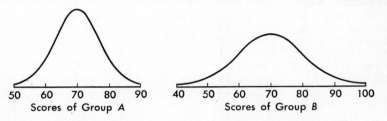

Fig. 4.   Distributions of scores of two classes on the same test.

viation (*s,* or s.d.) is a measure of the spread of scores. The variation of scores may be different on two tests even though the averages are the same. Figure 4 shows the smoothed distribution of scores of two classes taking the same test. Even though the groups are similar in mean ability, the distributions are not at all alike. Group B contains far more very superior and inferior cases. Group B has a larger standard deviation than Group A. A generally useful method of computing the mean and standard deviation is outlined in Computing Guide 2.

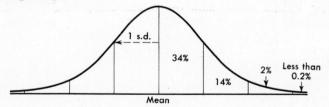

Fig. 5.   Percentage of cases falling in each portion of a
normal distribution.

If Mr. Gates followed this procedure, he could place in the record, along with each individual score, the information that the mean is 26.2 and the s.d. is 3.8. This, however, is fairly complicated to interpret, and the standard-score procedure presented below is more helpful. A particularly important use of the mean and standard deviation is for comparing one group with another. If Mr. Gates wished to compare EGY scores of habitual criminals

1. Begin with the raw scores to be studied.	24 25 24 25 31 22 30 24 25 27 28 29 19 28 27 25 30 31 26 30 32 30 25 32 26 24 21 29 24 17 29 29 27 30 26 25 30 28 30 26 26 23 20 25 15	

2. Tally the number of cases with each score. Write the number of tallies in the f (Frequency) column. Add this column to get N, the total number.

3. Select any score, usually near the middle of the distribution. Call this the arbitrary origin. (In the problem at right, 26 is used.)

Determine the deviation (d) of each score from the arbitrary origin.

[Score Tallies Frequency]

Score	Tallies	f	d	fd	fd^2
32	//	2	6	12	72
31	//	2	5	10	50
30	//// //	7	4	28	112
29	////	4	3	12	36
28	///	3	2	6	12
27	///	3	1	3	3
26	////	5	0		
25	//// //	7	−1	−7	7
24	////	5	−2	−10	20
23	/	1	−3	−3	9
22	/	1	−4	−4	16
21	/	1	−5	−5	25
20	/	1	−6	−6	36
19	/	1	−7	−7	49
18		0	−8		
17	/	1	−9	−9	81
16		0	−10		
15	/	1	−11	−11	121
		45 N		+9 Σfd	649 Σfd^2

Multiply, in each row, the entries in the f and d columns, and enter in the fd column.

Multiply the entries in the d and fd columns, and enter in a column headed fd^2. Add the fd and fd^2 columns.

4. Substitute the numbers in the following formulas:

$$c(\text{correction}) = \frac{\Sigma fd}{N}$$

$$M = A.O. + c$$

$$s.d. = \sqrt{\frac{\Sigma fd^2}{N} - c^2}$$

$A.O.$ is the midpoint of the score-interval selected as arbitrary origin.

$$c = \frac{9}{45} = .2$$

$$M = 26.0 + .2 = 26.2$$

$$s.d. = \sqrt{\frac{649}{45} - (.2)^2}$$

$$s.d. = \sqrt{14.42 - .04} = \sqrt{14.38}$$

$$s.d. = 3.8$$

Computing Guide 2. Determining the Mean and Standard Deviation.

with non-repeaters, the mean and standard deviation of each group would give a convenient basis for comparison.

The standard deviation has a definite relation to the normal distribution. If scores are normally distributed, the standard deviation is the distance from the mean to the "point of inflection" on the shoulder of the curve. This is the point where the curvature changes from convex (the hill-like portion) to the concave tail. This relation is illustrated in Figure 5. A second valuable property of the standard deviation is that very few cases fall more than three standard deviations from the mean if the distribution is normal. Two-thirds of the cases fall within one s.d. of the mean. If we know the mean and standard deviation, and can assume a roughly normal distribution, we can reconstruct the distribution curve from these facts.

17. a. In a normal distribution, what is the relation of the mean and median?
     b. What percentile rank corresponds to a score 2 s.d. above the mean? To a score 1 s.d. below the mean?
18. a. Compute the mean and standard deviation for the scores given in Problem 15, p. 28.
     b. How does the mean compare with the median computed previously?
     c. What is the approximate percentile rank for a score 2 s.d. above the mean in this distribution?
19. Assuming that scores are normally distributed on a test where the mean is 60 and s.d. is 8, interpret the following scores: Sara, 64; Harriet, 68; Charles, 87; Bob, 48.

Standard Scores

One method Mr. Gates can use for recording results is to convert raw scores into standard scores. The *standard score* for a case is his deviation from the mean, expressed in terms of the standard deviation. On the ECY test, a score of 30 is just 1 s.d. above the mean; $+1.0$ is the z-score corresponding to a raw score of 30. A z-score of -2.5 shows that a person is $2\frac{1}{2}$ s.d. below the mean. The computation of z-scores is illustrated in Computing Guide 3. The merit of the standard score is that if we know how many standard deviations from the mean a person falls on a given test, we can make a fairly accurate interpretation of his position in a group. In this sense, standard scores serve like percentile scores, but they have the additional advantage that they may be averaged and correlated without error.

Another type of standard score, the *T*-score, adjusts scores so that their mean is 50 and their standard deviation is 10. In *T*-scores, 60 represents a score 1 s.d. above the mean, and 25 is $2\frac{1}{2}$ s.d. below the mean. Computation of *T*-scores is also illustrated in Computing Guide 3. Other conversion formulas are also possible. The Army converted scores on its tests so that the mean standard score would be 100 and the standard deviation would be 20. Wechsler converts subtest scores on the Bellevue Intelligence Scale to standard scores with a mean of 10 and a s.d. of 3.

The student is warned of a possible confusion between standard scores

Begin with the distribution of raw scores to be studied and compute the mean and standard deviation by the procedure of Computing Guide 2.

To obtain z-scores, the mean is set equal to a z-score of zero. The z-score equivalent of other scores is obtained by the formula:

$$z\text{-score} = \frac{\text{raw score} - \text{mean}}{\text{standard deviation}}$$

If T-scores are desired instead of z-scores, the mean is set equal to 50. T-scores are computed by the formula:

$$T\text{-score} = 50 + \frac{10(\text{raw score} - \text{mean})}{\text{standard deviation}}$$

For the EGY scores,

$$M = 26.2$$
$$s = 3.8$$

Raw score 26.2 equals z-score 0.

To get z-score equivalent of 20:

$$z\text{-score} = \frac{20 - 26.2}{3.8} = \frac{-6.2}{3.8} = -1.6$$

Raw score 20 equals z-score -1.6.

To get z-score equivalent of 28:

$$z\text{-score} = \frac{28 - 26.2}{3.8} = \frac{1.8}{3.8} = 0.5$$

Raw score 28 equals z-score 0.5.

Raw score 26.2 equals T-score 50.

To get T-score equivalent of 20:

$$T\text{-score} = 50 + \frac{10(20 - 26.2)}{3.8}$$
$$= 50 + \frac{-62}{3.8} = 34$$

Raw score 20 equals T-score 34.

To get T-score equivalent of 28:

$$T\text{-score} = 50 + \frac{10(28 - 26.2)}{3.8}$$
$$= 50 + \frac{18}{3.8} = 55$$

Raw score 28 equals T-score 55.

Computing Guide 3. Computation of z-scores and T-scores.

computed by the method of Computing Guide 3 and "normalized scores," which also are identified by the names z-score and T-score. The normalized scores are computed by a different and more complex method, which will not be important to us in this book.

We can now review the methods available to Mr. Gates. If he wishes to record and report the performance of prisoner C. M., he can merely note the raw score of 24. He could make this more meaningful by reporting at the same time that the median is approximately 27. Or he could report it together with the mean (26.2) and the s.d. (3.8). If he wishes to convert to percentiles, he can report C. M.'s percentile score of 23, which is self-explanatory. If he prefers standard scores, he will record the z-score of -0.6 or the T-score of 44, either of which is readily interpreted.

20. With reference to Figure 5, interpret each of the following: a z-score of 3.0; a z-score of -2.0; a T-score of 40; a T-score of 65.
21. For the 1937 Stanford-Binet test, the mean IQ is 100 and the standard deviation is 16. Express in T-score form the following IQ's: 100, 84, 132, 150, 70, 105.

Comparison of Percentiles and Standard Scores

Both percentiles and standard scores are widely used, and under some conditions one may be translated into the other. The percentile score has these advantages: It is readily understood, which makes it especially satisfactory for reporting data to persons without statistical training; it is easily computed; it may be interpreted exactly, even when the distribution of test scores is skewed or bimodal. The disadvantages of percentile scores are these: They magnify small differences in score near the mean which may not be significant, and they reduce the apparent size of large differences in score near the tails of the distributions; they may not be used in many statistical computations. The advantages of standard scores are as follows: Differences in standard score are proportional to differences in raw score; use of standard scores in averages and correlations gives the same result that would come from use of the raw scores. The disadvantages are that standard scores cannot be interpreted readily when distributions are skewed, and that untrained persons are generally unable to understand them. Psychologists are increasingly urging that standard scores be used wherever possible. Testing experts believe that percentiles are too often misleading, and that if standard scores were consistently used non-statisticians would quickly learn to interpret them (11).

When the variable tested is normally distributed, standard scores may be converted into percentile scores and vice versa by means of the table of the normal curve (Table 1). This table is widely used in statistical work. It is based on the percentage of cases falling within each section of the normal curve, as shown in Figure 5. The table is symmetrical; a score 2 s.d. from the mean in either direction cuts off the same proportion of cases. The rela-

Table 1.   Relations Between Standard Scores and Percentile Scores, When Raw Scores Are Normally Distributed

Distance from Mean in s.d. (z-Score)	T-Score	Percentile Score	Percent of Cases in "Tail" of Curve	Percentile Score	T-Score	Distance from Mean in s.d. (z-Score)
3.0	80	99.9	0.1	0.1	20	−3.0
2.9	79	99.8	0.2	0 2	21	−2.9
2.8	78	99.7	0.3	0.3	22	−2 8
2.7	77	99.6	0.4	0.4	23	−2.7
2.6	76	99.5	0.5	0.5	24	−2.6
2.5	75	99.4	0.6	0.6	25	−2.5
2.4	74	99.2	0.8	0.8	26	−2.4
2.3	73	99	1	1	27	−2.3
2.2	72	99	1	1	28	−2.2
2.1	71	98	2	2	29	−2.1
2.0	70	98	2	2	30	−2.0
1.9	69	97	3	3	31	−1.9
1.8	68	96	4	4	32	−1.8
1.7	67	96	4	4	33	−1.7
1.6	66	95	5	5	34	−1.6
1.5	65	93	7	7	35	−1.5
1.4	64	92	8	8	36	−1.4
1.3	63	90	10	10	37	−1.3
1.2	62	88	12	12	38	−1.2
1.1	61	86	14	14	39	−1.1
1.0	60	84	16	16	40	−1.0
0.9	59	82	18	18	41	−0.9
0.8	58	79	21	21	42	−0.8
0.7	57	76	24	24	43	−0.7
0.6	56	73	27	27	44	−0.6
0.5	55	69	31	31	45	−0.5
0.4	54	66	34	34	46	−0.4
0.3	53	62	38	38	47	−0.3
0.2	52	58	42	42	48	−0.2
0.1	51	54	46	46	49	−0.1
0.0	50	50	50	50	50	0.0

tionship between the standard deviation and the percentage distribution of cases is valuable in the solution of many statistical problems. Whenever a variable is normally distributed, one may use Table 1 to reconstruct the distribution.

One of the most valuable methods for presenting test scores so that different tests may be considered simultaneously is the *profile*. A profile is a graph showing the subject's performance. In order to compare him on several tests, all scores are expressed as standard scores or percentile scores, using the same norm group. Illustrative profiles are found in Figures 30 and 39 in later chapters.

22. If a teacher wishes to keep records of class examinations in derived-score form, so that he can tell at a glance how well a person is doing and can average all tests equally in the final grade, should he use percentiles or standard scores?

23. In a certain college, all freshmen are given a "college aptitude test." The results are to be mimeographed and confidential copies given to all student advisers. Should the report use raw scores, standard scores, or percentiles?

24. The psychometrist giving tests for a Veteran's Counseling Center is asked to give a wide variety of tests to veterans needing counseling. After each man has taken from four to eight tests, results are to be placed on a standard report form so that performance on all tests can be compared by the counselor, in conference with the veteran. What problems will be encountered if all results are reported in percentiles? What problems will be encountered if all results are reported as standard scores? Can you suggest a suitable plan for report?

25. The American Air Force used a derived score called the "stanine" (stay-nine), in which 1 represented the lowest 4 percent; 2, the next 7 percent; 3, 12 percent; 4, 17 percent; 5, the middle 20 percent; and 6, 7, 8, 9 included corresponding percentages at the higher end of the distribution. Describe this system in terms of T-scores, using Table 1.

CORRELATION

Meaning of Correlation

Nearly all research on testing involves correlation. Correlation is a method of summarizing the relationship between two sets of data. It is the most common method for reporting the answer to such questions as the following: Does this test predict performance on the job? Do the diagnoses made from this test agree with diagnoses established by the case histories? Do scores made on this test a year ago agree with the scores the same people make now?

Correlation (r) may take any value from -1.00 to $+1.00$. If the standing of individuals in one test corresponds exactly to their standing in another, the correlation is $+1.00$. A correlation of 1.00 means that we could predict perfectly one test from the other. Psychological tests are rarely so accurate. If two variables are completely unrelated, so that one cannot be used to predict the other, the correlation is .00. Near zero correlation might be expected between speed of tapping and reasoning ability, or between ability to match colors and skill in archery. Where the degree of relationship is positive but imperfect, so that some prediction can be made, the correlation is expressed by some such number as .24, .63, or .87, depending on the extent of correspondence. Negative correlations are found when the relation between two variables is inverse, the person standing high on one test having a low standing on the other. A correlation of -1.00 is found between Number Right and Number Wrong on the same test, if everyone attempts every item. Negative relationships of intermediate size are sometimes found between aptitude and time required to do a job, or between somewhat opposite personality traits such as self-confidence and submissiveness.

Table 2 illustrates situations in which each degree of relationship is encountered. Correlations over .80 are uncommon. Correlations below about

.60 are frequently useful for establishing that a relationship exists, but when the relation is so imperfect one variable does not predict the other very exactly.

Table 2.   Variables Yielding Correlations of Various Sizes

r	First Variable	Second Variable	Reference
1.00	Length of side of square	Diagonal of square	
.93[a]	IQ on Stanford-Binet, Form L	IQ on Form M a few days later, children of uniform age.	10, p. 47
.88	IQ on Stanford-Binet, 1916 form	IQ on same test about 15 months later, for problem children.	1
.80	Raw score on Otis Self-Administering Test of Mental Ability	Age, for persons 7 to 17	7
.75	Interest scores of college seniors	Interest scores five years later.	9
.70	IQ on Henmon-Nelson group test for high-school seniors	Same, two years later	6
.65[a]	Score on a well-prepared one-hour classroom examination	Score on a similar test given shortly after	8, p. 472
.50	Score on essay examination in English literature	Score on objective test of same material	4, pp. 92–99
.45[a]	Intelligence test score	College marks	8, p. 848
.25[a]	Score on test of moral knowledge	Measures of actual conduct showing character	8, p. 168
.20[a]	IQ	School marks in foreign language	3
.15[a]	Intelligence	Composite index of bodily size	8, p. 183
−.20	Score on Linfert-Hierholzer infant tests at one year	IQ on Stanford-Binet at 4 years	2
−.50	Score on Otis Self-Administering Test of Mental Ability	Age, for adults from 20 to 92[b]	7

[a] Approximate; based on several correlations.
[b] There is little or no decline of ability in early adulthood, marked decline in later years.

26. What correlation would you anticipate between the following pairs of variables?
   a. Age and annual income of men aged 20 to 50.
   b. Age in January, 1930, and age in March, 1950.
   c. Scores on two intelligence tests, given the same week.
   d. Annual income and number of children, among married urban men.
   e. Maximum and minimum temperature in Wichita, each day for a year.

If two scores are available for each person in a group, a scatter diagram may be made to show their relationship. One axis for the diagram represents one score, and one represents the other. A point is plotted to show the scores of each person. A series of scatter diagrams representing different degrees of relationship is shown in Figure 6. If the two scores are highly correlated, the points fall close to a straight line, and the correlation is high. If the two scores have no relationship, a case having a given score on the first test may fall anywhere along the scale for the other test, and the scatter distribution will be nearly round.

A high correlation is often erroneously interpreted as showing that one factor causes the other. There are at least three possible explanations for a high correlation between two variables, A and B. A may cause or influence

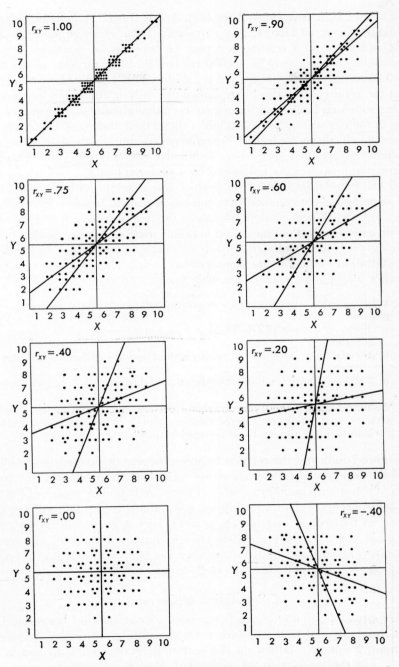

Fig. 6.   Scatter diagrams yielding correlations of various sizes.

the size of B, B may cause A, or both A and B may be influenced by some common factor or factors. The correlation between score on a vocabulary test and score on a reading test may be taken as an example. Does good vocabulary cause one to be a good reader? Possibly. Or does ability to read well cause one to acquire a good vocabulary? An equally likely explanation. But the results could also be explained as resulting from high intelligence, a home in which books and serious conversation abounded, or superior teaching in the elementary schools. Only a theoretical understanding of the processes involved, or controlled experiments, permit us to state what causes underlie a particular correlation. Otherwise, the only safe conclusion is that correlated measures are influenced by a common factor.

If the correlation is less than perfect, one measure, or both, is influenced by some factor not common between the measures. Random errors of measurement, which occur independently in the two measures, lower correlation. So do causal factors not measured in both variables. The correlation between intelligence and school marks is only moderate because many factors besides mental ability influence the marks one receives. These include pupil effort, teacher bias, previous school learning, health, and so on.

27. What possible causal relations might underlie each of the following correlations?
    a. Between amount of education and annual income of adults (assume that *r* is positive).
    b. Between average intelligence of children and size of family (assume *r* negative).
    c. Between Sunday-school attendance and honesty of behavior (assume *r* positive).
28. Account for the correlations in Table 2 in terms of possible causes. What common elements might lead to the relations found? What factors not common to both tests might reduce these correlations from 1.00?

Figure 7 indicates the relation between the size of a correlation coefficient and the accuracy of estimation of one variable from the other. If the correlation of a test with another variable is zero, prediction by means of the test is no more accurate than an arbitrary guess that every pupil will fall at the mean on the second variable (8, p. 594). Such a guess will be very wrong for most cases. As the correlation rises, estimation becomes more accurate, but errors are still substantial even when *r* is .90. A correlation of .50 permits predictions only slightly better than guessing.

Computation of Correlation

The *product-moment* correlation procedure outlined in Computing Guide 4 is closely related to the procedure for computing means and standard deviations. Points are tallied on the scatter diagram, and both means, both s.d.'s, and the correlation are computed. Variations in the procedure and checks are discussed in most statistics texts. Numerous forms have been pub-

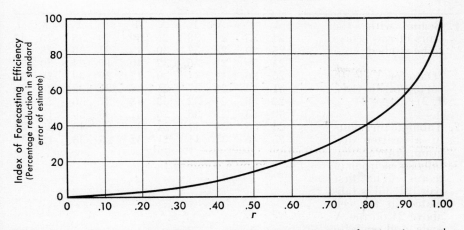

Fig. 7.   Index of forecasting efficiency, showing improvement of estimation as the correlation coefficient increases.

lished which reduce the labor of calculation. The product-moment method is generally employed for testing relationships, although other methods are more suitable for special problems, such as when regression lines are curved.

SAMPLING ERRORS

Although a full treatment of the topic requires more space than is available, attention must be drawn to the problem of sampling errors. Any score, and any average, percentile, or correlation, is an estimate. The score on a test would be different if we had tested the person at another moment. The average would be different if one or two different persons had been included in the scores averaged. Any statistic is only an approximation, since many factors determine the particular value obtained. This is especially true of norms, for when one attempts to state the average finger dexterity of typical ninth-graders, the attitude of typical Americans about tax reduction, or the normal percentage of maladjusted among unmarried women, what figure he reports depends upon which persons happen to constitute his sample. The reader of statistics must not take any number at its face value. It is necessary to realize that a different value—not much different, it is hoped—would have been obtained with other cases or if the test had been given at a different time. The experimenter usually guards against serious sampling errors by studying typical persons and by using a large sample. An average based on ten persons would change appreciably if only one member of the group were changed; an average based on five hundred would scarcely show the difference. Formulas for estimating the exact magnitude of sampling errors in correlations, means, percentiles, and other statistics are discussed in statistics texts.

1. Begin with the pairs of raw scores to be studied.

   (Data for X identical to scores in C. G. 1, 2)

2. Tabulate the points in a scatter diagram, entering one tally for each pair of scores. (The first pair [24–35] is tabulated in the cell above 24 on the X scale, and opposite 35 on the Y scale. This cell is outlined in the illustration.)

X	Y	X	Y	X	Y	X	Y	X	Y
24	35	27	38	26	39	29	35	20	42
25	39	28	37	30	39	24	38	28	37
24	39	29	36	32	40	17	24	30	39
25	36	19	34	30	42	29	38	26	37
31	43	28	37	25	38	29	38	26	39
22	38	27	32	32	43	27	36	23	37
30	43	25	38	26	37	30	39	19	29
24	35	30	41	24	36	26	40	25	38
25	40	31	41	21	32	25	33	15	31

Scatter diagram (Y axis 24–43, X axis 15–32) with computation columns:

Y	f_y	d_y	$f_y d_y$	$f_y d_y^2$	$\Sigma f_y d_x$	$\Sigma f d_x d_y$
43	3	6	18	108	15	90
42	2	5	10	50	8	40
41	2	4	8	32	9	36
40	3	3	9	27	5	15
39	7	2	14	28	9	18
38	8	1	8	8	-2	-2
37	6	0			3	
36	4	-1	-4	4	1	-1
35	3	-2	-6	12	-1	2
34	1	-3	-3	9	-7	21
33	1	-4	-4	16	-1	4
32	2	-5	-10	50	-4	20
31	1	-6	-6	36	-11	66
30		-7				
29	1	-8	-8	64	-6	48
28		-9				
27		-10				
26		-11				
25		-12				
24	1	-13	-13	169	-9	117
			$\overline{13}$	$\overline{613}$	9	$\overline{473}$
			N	$\Sigma f_y d_y$	$\Sigma f_y d_y^2$	$\Sigma f d_x d_y$

$N = 45$

f_x	1		1	1	1	1	1	1	5	7	5	3	3	4	7	2	2	45
d_x	-11	-10	-9	-8	-7	-6	-5	-4	-3	-2	-1	0	1	2	3	4	5	6
$f_x d_x$	-11		-9		-7	-6	-5	-4	-3	-10	-7		3	6	12	28	10	12
$f_x d_x^2$	121		81		49	36	25	16	9	20	7		3	12	36	112	50	72

$9\ \Sigma f_x d_x$

$649\ \Sigma f_x d_x^2$

3. Count the number of tallies in each column, and write it below the diagram in a row labeled f_x. Count the number in each row, and write it beside the diagram in a column labeled f_y.

4. Select an arbitrary origin for X and for Y, and determine the mean and standard deviation for each as in C. G. 2 (computation not shown).

correction — *mean* —

$A.O._x = 26.0$	$A.O._y = 37.0$
$c_x = .20$	$c_y = .29$
$M_x = 26.2$	$M_y = 37.3$
$s_x = 3.79$	$s_y = 3.68$

actual
standard deviation

5. In each cell of the scatter diagram, multiply the number of tallies by the value of d_x written below that column, and write the product in the cell. (In the outlined cell, for instance, there are two tallies, and d_x is -2; the product is -4.)

In each row, add the numbers written in the cells, and place in a column labeled $f_y d_x$.

Multiply each entry in this column by d_y and enter in a column labeled $f d_x d_y$.

Add the column $f d_x d_y$.

Substitute the numbers in the following formula:

sum *correction*

$$r_{xy} = \frac{\dfrac{\Sigma f d_x d_y}{N} - c_x \cdot c_y}{s_x \cdot s_y}$$

correlation

$$r_{xy} = \frac{\dfrac{473}{45} - .06}{3.79 \cdot 3.68}$$

$$r_{xy} = \frac{10.51 - .06}{13.94} = \frac{10.45}{13.94}$$

$$r_{xy} = .75$$

Computing Guide 4. Computing the Product-Moment Correlation Coefficient

SUGGESTED READINGS

Darley, John G. "Statistics and the understanding of tests," in *Testing and counseling in the high-school guidance program*. Chicago: Science Research Assoc., 1943, pp. 45–87.

Thorndike, Edward L. "The nature, purposes, and general methods of measurement of educational products." *Yearbk. nat. Soc. Stud. Educ.*, 1918, 17 (II), 16–24.

REFERENCES

1. Brown, Andrew W. "The change in intelligence quotients in behavior problem children." *J. educ. Psychol.*, 1930, 21, 341–350.
2. Furfey, P. H., and Muehlenbein, J. "The validity of infant intelligence tests." *J. genet. Psychol.*, 1932, 40, 219–223.
3. Greenberg, Jacob. The relation of mental ability to achievement in foreign languages. Unpublished Doctor's thesis, New York Univ., 1938.
4. Haggerty, M. E., and others. *Studies in college examinations*. Minneapolis: Univ. of Minnesota Press, 1934.
5. Kent, Grace H. "Emergency battery of one-minute tests." *J. Psychol.*, 1942, 13, 141–164.
6. Knezevich, Stephen J. "The constancy of the IQ of the secondary school pupil." *J. educ. Res.*, 1946, 39, 506–516.
7. Miles, Catherine C., and Miles, Walter R. "The correlation of intelligence scores and chronological age from early to late maturity." *Amer. J. Psychol.*, 1932, 44, 44–78.
8. Monroe, W. S. (ed.). *Encyclopaedia of educational research*. New York: Macmillan, 1941.
9. Strong, E. K., Jr. *Vocational interests of men and women*. Stanford Univ.: Stanford Univ. Press, 1943.
10. Terman, Lewis M., and Merrill, Maud A. *Measuring intelligence*. Boston: Houghton Mifflin, 1937.
11. Wolfle, Dael. "Standard scores and percentile scores." *Amer. Psychologist*, 1947, 2, 76.

CHAPTER 4

How to Choose Tests

WHAT IS A GOOD TEST?

When a teacher investigates the intelligence of her pupils, she wishes to use the best intelligence test available. An industrial psychologist hoping to select superior workers for a factory wishes to try the best possible test of intelligence. The clinical psychologist, studying a child who may be feeble-minded, wishes to use the intelligence test which will give the fairest results. It is not surprising, then, that the test user repeatedly asks, "What is the best test in this field?"

The purchaser of tests certainly has a confusing problem. He is faced with a choice among long tests and short tests, famous tests and unfamiliar tests, old tests and new tests, ordinary tests and novel tests. The catalogue of a leading test distributor offers 35 tests of general mental ability, and 18 tests of personality. Each of these tests was published by a person who thinks his test is in some way superior to the others on the market. He is frequently correct. Different tests have different virtues; there is no one test of any sort which is "the best" for all purposes. The teacher, the industrial psychologist, and the clinical psychologist need good tests of mental ability. But the test which serves one most usefully is probably not the best for either of the others.

Tests must always be selected for the particular purpose for which they are to be used. Some tests work well with children but not with adults; some give precise measures but require more time than can be allowed for testing; some give satisfactory general estimates of subjects but less detailed diagnosis of each individual than another test will. No test maker can put into his test all desirable qualities; a change in design improves the test in one respect only by sacrificing some other characteristic.

Not all published tests are good tests, however. Some have been published without adequate research and refinement. Some, even those having wide popularity, do not succeed in measuring what they were intended to measure. Some measure characteristics different from what their titles indicate. Test publication is a commercial activity, and, although most test authors and publishers maintain high standards, the description of a test furnished by the author usually advertises its favorable features. Since some published tests are nearly worthless, and others found useful for one task will not perform well in another situation, the user must be able to choose among tests intelligently. No list of "recommended tests" can eliminate the necessity for careful choice for the individual situation. Even in similar situations the same tests may not be appropriate. Different schools find different tests best. Tests which select supervisors well in one plant prove valueless in another. And clinicians choose different tests for each patient.

Any list of superior tests soon becomes outdated, so that it is necessary for the user of tests constantly to evaluate new developments. New tests are added, new uses of tests are discovered, and new findings about old tests are brought to light. Louttit and Browne found that of the nine psychological tests most used in clinics in 1935 only two remained when a second survey was made in 1946. Only two of the newcomers to the top nine were published later than 1935; the other five were available in 1935, but their usefulness had not been recognized (36). Buros, who established a "yearbook" of test reviews, comments as follows (9, p. 11):

"Instead of limiting the volume to reviews of new and recent tests . . . the decision was made to include old as well as new tests. Reviews of old tests may prove effective in eliminating from use many tests which were among the best in their day but are now outmoded and inferior to recently constructed tests. On the other hand, such reviews may result in increasing the use of old tests and testing techniques which compare very favorably with tests being currently published. The sale of outmoded and ever-decreasingly valid tests persists far beyond the sale of textbooks published in the same years. Despite the fact that tests have been on the market for five and fifteen years, there exists for probably ninety percent of the tests, a dearth of critical information concerning their reliability and validity. Appraisals and reappraisals of old tests are needed almost as badly as evaluations of new tests."

1. "Improving a test in one way weakens it in another." What advantage, and what disadvantage, comes from each of the following changes?
   a. Lengthening a test.
   b. Making it more interesting to children.
   c. Making it more diagnostic of strong and weak points.
   d. Giving it as an individual instead of as a group test.
2. This is a letter received by a psychologist from an industrial personnel manager hiring office and factory workers. How would you answer it on the basis of the paragraphs above, knowing that the tests mentioned are representative of their type?
   ". . . Just now we are planning the use of the following tests: Otis intelligence, Humm-Wadsworth Temperament Scale, and aptitude tests related to our openings, such as the MacQuarrie mechanical aptitude test. Does this seem to be a well-balanced testing schedule for industry? Are there tests that you think preferable to these?"

PRACTICAL CONSIDERATIONS IN CHOOSING A TEST

The most important factor in the suitability of a test is whether it does the job it is supposed to do. But in school, industrial, and clinical situations, the tester must bow to numerous practical considerations which limit the tests he can use. Of all the tests available, he must cross off those which are impractical before making a careful investigation of the validity of the remainder. Practical considerations never justify using a test which gives worthless information, but a technically sound test cannot serve where it is impractical. The most significant practical considerations are cost, time required, ease of administration and scoring, comparable forms, face validity and interest, user acceptability, and usefulness of results.

The _cost_ of the usual test is only a few cents, but when one is testing a large number of persons, a difference in cost may be important. Fortunately there is little relation between the cost of tests and their quality, so that even a limited budget permits the use of well-constructed tests. The cost is greatly reduced where it is possible to use an answer sheet and a reusable question booklet. Most tests intended for use with large groups are now published in this form. With young children or persons having little test experience, however, a separate answer sheet may prove confusing. In determining the cost of a test, one must consider not only the cost of the materials but also the cost of scoring. Cost must not be overweighted in comparing tests. Cost of tests is trivial compared to the cost which results from a wrong decision: training a worker who will not succeed on the job, or giving a semester's college education to a boy who will fail, or hospitalizing a soldier who becomes neurotic under the strain of combat. Even several dollars spent to reduce such errors are well spent.

3. Scates, in a careful cost accounting, found that purchasing, giving, scoring, and analyzing statistically the Stanford Achievement Test cost 56 cents per pupil at 1930 prices (40). This is a battery of ten group tests, requiring two and one-fourth hours of testing. Would costs be expected to run higher or lower in testing applicants for industrial jobs?

Time requirements of a test are frequently significant. Where only a limited time is available to obtain information, it may be necessary to use a short test rather than a longer one which would be more accurate. Sometimes several short tests give a more complete picture of the person than a single long one. The length of a test has an important effect on the coöperativeness of the subject. If a test begins to bore him, he is likely not to show his best ability and may develop antagonism toward the organization testing him. With subjects having high morale, on the other hand, even a very long test can be used.

Ease of administration and scoring must be considered, since some tests require the services of expertly trained testers and scorers. Unless such services are available, it will be impossible to use the tests validly. Even where skilled persons are available, it is sometimes wise to use simpler tests which others can give, conserving the time of the expert for other duties. In schools where classroom teachers can give the tests themselves, they often take a greater interest in the results than when "outsiders" must be called in. On the other hand, a testing program which requires that teachers score

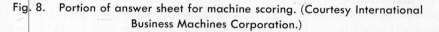

Fig. 8. Portion of answer sheet for machine scoring. (Courtesy International Business Machines Corporation.)

large numbers of papers becomes unpopular; tests that can be scored by clerks are more readily accepted.

Scoring is facilitated by efficient scoring stencils. The most useful design requires the student to mark his answer by checking or blackening one of several spaces; a punched-out key showing only correct answers is then superimposed for scoring. In large testing programs, the International Business Machines test-scoring machine is economical. It uses an answer sheet with spaces to be blackened to indicate correct answers. Electrical "fingers" in the machine sense where pencil marks appear, since the graphite in the marks carries electrical current. The total number of marks in the proper places is shown on a meter. The machine will report number of errors, rights-minus-wrongs, and other types of scores. With it one can score about 500 papers per hour. Military classification centers relied on the machines to speed processing of recruits.

Fig. 9. IBM test-scoring machine. (Photo, courtesy International Business Machines Corporation.)

Large school systems operate such machines for scoring of tests for the entire system. In most sections of the country, a test-scoring service is available where tests may be machine-scored for a moderate fee.

Comparable forms are helpful when tests are used for research or for measuring the effect of teaching or therapy. It is desirable to use equivalent tests before and after, rather than repeating the same test, in order to rule out the effect of memory. An equivalent form is also useful to confirm a test score which is possibly inaccurate owing to the emotional disturbance of the subject or some other unfavorable condition.

"Face" validity and interest are important in obtaining coöperation from the person tested. If the applicant for a job is given a test which seems to him silly or unrelated to the job, he is likely to be resentful. If he is not hired, he may excuse his failure by blaming the tests as unfair; such a report damages public relations and makes it harder to obtain job applicants. Some satisfactory workers have had little schooling and are distrustful of tests which probe their weaknesses. Catch questions and questions which seem childish are especially likely to arouse criticism. If a test is interesting, taking it is likely to be a pleasant experience. This not only tends to make the scores valid, but also helps establish good relations between the personnel worker and the subject.

The *acceptability* of a test to those who will use the results is equally important. Although fully trained psychologists will examine a test on a technical basis, other users of test results have strong prejudices. If a group of social workers is accustomed to and likes results from mental test A, when the psychologist decides to substitute mental test B he will encounter difficulty. Even if test B is more accurate than A, the social worker may disregard the results from B because it does not have his confidence. So important is user acceptability in working with teachers, industrial personnel men, physicians, and others that the psychologist must often use a test which would be his second or third choice. If he is certain that he should wean others from their initial preference, he must undertake a deliberate campaign in favor of the test he advocates.

One further practical consideration is the *usefulness of results* from a test. If results are couched in terms which require an expert interpretation, only the expert can use the scores, whereas another test may provide facts in a form useful to everyone working with the subject. Some tests give very limited information, which can be used only once, but a slightly more elaborate test will provide data to answer numerous questions in the future.

4. Decide which of the practical considerations mentioned above would be very important, which important, and which unimportant, in each of the following situations.
   a. The Army desires to test every man inducted during wartime to determine which ones may be feeble-minded.
   b. A college wishes to test every freshman during registration to determine which ones should enter a course in remedial reading.
   c. A court wishes a mental test to determine whether a prisoner is mentally defective.
   d. The Gallup poll wishes to determine the mental level of a cross section of the voting public while interviewing them (47).

TECHNICAL CRITERIA OF A GOOD TEST

Validity

The one indispensable characteristic of a test is validity. *A test is valid to the degree that we know what it measures or predicts*. There are two basic approaches to validity: logical analysis and empirical analysis. In logical analysis, one attempts to judge precisely what the test measures. In empirical analysis, one attempts to show that the test is correlated with some other variable, and therefore measures the same thing. Judgment leads to a psychological characterization of the test; e.g., "it measures speed of repetitive finger movement," or "it measures ability to visualize three-dimensional forms." An empirical analysis usually relates the test to a practical purpose: "The test measures aptitude for pharmacy" (i.e., it correlates with success in pharmacy).

Logical Validity

Every test is to some degree impure, and very rarely does it measure exactly what its name implies. Before the tester can understand test results, he must know whether his "intelligence" test is strongly influenced by how well the subject reads, whether his "scientific aptitude" test is heavily influenced by the subject's training in mathematics, and whether his test of "open-mindedness" is influenced by the subject's desire to make a good impression. One way to judge validity is to make a careful study of the test itself, to determine what test scores mean.

Logical analysis of a test aims at psychological understanding of the processes that affect scores. It does not stress validity for any particular purpose. If the user knows just what the test score tells about the subject, he can decide for which purposes it is appropriate. For this reason, the definition above has been given rather than the conventional "Validity is the extent to which a test measures what it purports to measure." Only empirical validity is concerned with the usefulness of a test for some single purpose.

Validity may be established deductively by showing that a test corresponds to the definition of the trait intended to be measured; or it may be established inductively by naming the traits represented in the items at hand. If we have a clear definition of a trait the test is supposed to measure, we can examine the items to see if they conform to that definition. For example, a test may attempt to measure knowledge of vocabulary. Before we can analyze it, we must know what is meant by "knowledge" and "vocabulary." If the tester then informs us that by "knowledge" he means "ability to give a definition," and that "vocabulary" refers to "words commonly used in seventh-grade textbooks," we can judge the test. If the test asks the student to give definitions of many words, and we find those words to be representative of seventh-grade textbooks, the definition describes the test.

But if the words are largely from science or are more difficult than those in seventh-grade texts, or if the items ask the student to match words with printed definitions, the score measures something other than what the definition implies.

Even when items relate to a definition, they may bring in irrelevant variables which make the test impure. The following five criticisms illustrate the types of weakness a careful analysis discloses.

1. The Relative Movement Test used by the Navy is intended to select men who, because of small-boat experience or aptitude, will be able to visualize how ships on various courses will move in relation to each other. The test consists of problems about "Ship A, one mile north of ship B, proceeding SW at five knots, etc." One landlubber of the worst sort was highly successful on the test because he could work the problems by geometry, while the mariners in the tested group were solving them by visualizing the sea situation. At sea, of course, the high-scoring men with sea experience could state almost without thinking where a given boat would be in fifteen minutes, whereas the mathematician, for all his high score, was completely at a loss. For some men the test was one of movement visualization, but he passed it on the basis of mathematical training. Many tests permit minor or irrelevant factors to influence the scores.

2. The Wechsler-Bellevue mental test designed for the Army required subjects to assemble cutout puzzles which formed objects. One cutout of a house seemed to have little relationship to ability. It was eventually concluded that this was due to a "cultural factor"; persons coming from regions where houses like the puzzle house were uncommon were handicapped on the test despite normal mental ability. The house item was replaced by a face to be assembled. Cultural factors make it difficult to obtain valid tests of intelligence.

3. Pitch discrimination is tested by Seashore and others by means of recorded sounds. The subject hears two successive tones and must tell whether the second is higher or lower than the first. On difficult items, it was found that some persons usually said "higher" while others were habitually biased toward "lower." Since this tendency affects the score the person receives, the test is not a pure measure of pitch discrimination. "Response sets"—personal habits of responding in borderline judgments—dilute some achievement and personality tests.

4. Traditional tests in school subjects have been criticized because they do not show the student's ability on all aspects of the course. If a course is supposed to teach historical facts and to develop ability to understand modern social problems, a test which asks only fact questions rewards memorization of facts but does not measure ability to apply those facts. Similar criticisms have been made of many testing and grading practices which test only some aspects of the variable under consideration.

5. The meaningfulness of any test score is also lowered by chance errors

of measurement. These are estimated by reliability formulas (see below).

Where an adequate definition of the function tested is not available, the test user studies the items to determine what definition they would fit. This is at best an uncertain process. A skillful analyst calls on a fund of knowledge about how people react and about factors found in previous studies of tests. Add to these keen observation and flexible thinking, and he is likely to know much about the test when he has finished.

But his final conclusion is at best only an enlightened guess, unless he can confirm his thinking by empirical studies of the test. This point cannot be too strongly emphasized. Over and over, it is found that tests which "ought to" predict some behavior do not. No test can be relied on for practical use until it has been validated empirically.

Attention must be given, not only to the content of items, but also to the form of presentation. This is demonstrated in studies of response sets. Most students tend to answer "true" rather than "false" when in doubt on a true-false test. This sometimes means that the student with little knowledge guesses correctly on true items but tends to guess wrong on false items. For one examination in psychology, three scores were obtained for each student: his score on the true items only, on the false items only, and on the total test. The reliability coefficients (split-half) of the three scores were .11, .72, and .62, respectively. (The meaning of this coefficient is explained on p. 66.) The correlations with a composite of other tests in the course were: true items, .22; false items, .67; total, .67. In other words, the false items alone tended to measure knowledge as well as the total test, but the true items were so much influenced by the habit of saying "yes" when in doubt that they were unreliable and invalid (12).

A *response set* is a habit which causes the subject to earn a different score from what he would earn if the same items were presented in a different form. Six types of response sets have been identified (15):

1. Tendency to gamble. When a subject does not know the answer to an item, he may leave it blank or may attempt to give an answer. This factor is eliminated only when every person attempts every item.
2. Different definitions assigned response categories such as "agree" or "like." Items like the following are common in attitude tests, where the subject is to mark each statement "agree," "uncertain," or "disagree."

   A   U   D   We cannot have lasting peace in a world where some nations are undemocratic.
   A   U   D   Compulsory military training is the best way to keep the United States safe from attack.
   A   U   D   The United States must not surrender to an international body its right to go to war.

Some subjects define "uncertain" very narrowly, using it only when they have absolutely no opinion regarding the item. Others consistently use "uncertain" for any statement about which they are not absolutely positive. With these different habits of responding, two subjects with the same beliefs would receive different scores.

3. Tendency to give many responses, when the subject is to check as many statements as he wishes. Some reasoning tests, for example, present a list of possible reasons and ask the subject to mark those which support a certain conclusion. A subject who marks a great many reasons is almost certain to include several poor ones, whereas the subject who stops after picking two or three best reasons will seem to show very accurate reasoning.

4. Bias, in which the subject tends to give one particular answer when in doubt. This has been illustrated above in regard to pitch tests and true-false tests. Similar bias is found in agree-disagree or like-dislike judgments.

5. Working for speed rather than accuracy. In any timed test, the subject sets himself a pace. If it is a fast pace, he takes chances of inaccuracy. If it is a careful pace, he may not complete as many items as he otherwise would. Sometimes a rapid pace will yield the highest score, and sometimes the slower pace will be rewarded.

6. Style of answer in essay tests. Everyone writing a free response has a choice of many styles: terse, elaborated, flowing, or outlined. Scorers are influenced by such factors.

These response sets appear to be personality characteristics. By influencing scores on tests of ability or attitude they dilute the degree to which scores depend on the variable to be measured. The multiple-choice item, with the subject forced to choose on every item, is the only form in common use for pencil-and-paper tests which appears to be free from response sets. This is one reason why it is being increasingly used in tests of knowledge, attitudes, interests, and personality. The following items illustrate the forced-choice technique:

Select the answer which best completes the statement:
   Magellan discovered: Cuba   the Philippines   Japan   India

Underline the adjective in each pair which best describes you:
   charitable—industrious   gloomy—careless

Which of the following would you prefer to do, assuming you had the needed abilities?
               Be a skywriter
               Write newspaper editorials
               Be a weather forecaster

Often, reconsideration is advisable when a subject's unusual response set may have lowered his score. This comment is made about one of the Differential Aptitude Tests (6, p. E-5):

"The *Clerical Speed and Accuracy* Test is designed to measure the student's speed and accuracy with simple number and letter combinations. It is the one test in the entire series which places a heavy premium on speed. As the test is scored, in fact, the student is not additionally penalized for any errors he may make, i.e., his score is the number of items correctly marked—wrongs are not subtracted. This scoring decision was based on research which indicated that in a task of the simplicity of this one, there are few, if any, errors made. . . . In interpreting Clerical scores of students whose other scores are high, it is vital that low scores be eyed suspiciously. With good all-round students, a low score on this test is just as likely to indicate the student's stress on correctness as it is to indicate real inability to work rapidly. The school ordinarily emphasizes accuracy rather than speed, and properly so; it is not surprising then that some good students will continue working in that way despite instructions to work rapidly. If Clerical Speed and Accuracy is considered by a counselor to be important for a specific good student whose score is low, it would be wise to retest him after re-emphasizing the importance of speed. (Forty-two pupils who scored high on the Verbal Reasoning and Numerical Ability tests and low on the Clerical Speed and Accuracy test, were retested after being urged to work rapidly. Their scores all increased appreciably.)"

5. A test of intelligence uses items like the following:

        sweet—sour .... SAME—OPPOSITE
        obscure—lucid .... SAME—OPPOSITE
        occult—mystical .... SAME—OPPOSITE

The student is directed to underline whichever word at the right is correct. What response sets is such a test subject to, if it is given with a time limit? How could a test calling for similar abilities be designed which would be less affected by response sets?

6. The Nelson-Denny Reading Test for high school and college contains a vocabulary section in which the subject chooses which of five words means the same as a key word. There are one hundred items. Ten minutes is allowed. The score is obtained by counting the number of correct judgments. With this knowledge, how can you explain the performance of a feeble-minded boy who reached a score of 25, better than 60 percent of other ninth-graders (15)?

7. Defend the statement: "In analysis of the psychological meaning of a test, the directions must be considered as part of the test."

How one proceeds in test analysis may be clarified by some examples. Figure 10 shows items from tests of intelligence and special ability. The top illustration, from one of Thurstone's tests based on factor analysis, represents a rather "pure" test. It seems to call for just one type of judgment, ability to visualize how a figure will look when rotated. In addition to "aptitude," however, observations show that work methods make some difference in the ease with which people obtain correct answers. Some think each item through carefully with a trial-and-error approach, mentally trying to turn the first figure into each position. Others first establish a generalization and try to apply it to each figure. The generalization may be incorrect, especially in persons having limited mental development or lack of experience in figure rotation; the subject who thinks "the loop must always be to the left" will make several errors. The person who has through some training

"In each row put a mark under every figure which is like the first figure in the row."

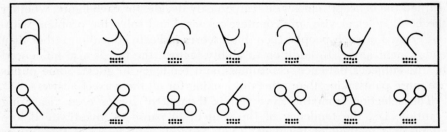

(From L. L. and T. G. Thurstone, *Chicago Tests of Primary Mental Abilities, Spatial*, Science Research Associates, p. 3. Copyright 1941.)

"Rank the diagonals *A, B, C, D, E, F* according to their length; that is, write 1 in the square corresponding to the longest diagonal, 2 in that corresponding to the next longest, and so on."

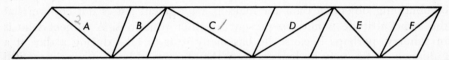

(From D. L. Zyve, *Stanford Scientific Aptitude Test*, Stanford University Press. Reduced about one-third.)

"Calculate the weight of a steel plate one foot square, $\frac{1}{2}$ inch thick, with a rectangular hole which measures 3 inches by 8 inches. Steel weighs 0.3 pound per cubic inch."

(A) 1.8   (B) 36   (C) 14.4   (D) 5.4   (E) 18

(From B. V. Moore, C. J. Lapp, and C. H. Griffin, *Engineering and Physical Science Aptitude Test*, The Psychological Corporation.)

"Read each statement and mark the answer space which has the same number as the answer which you think is BEST."

Farmers rotate crops because
1. Variety is the spice of life.
2. It confuses the plant pests.
3. It helps maintain soil fertility.
4. It gives the farmer a balanced diet.

(From L. M. Terman and Q. McNemar, *Terman-McNemar Test of Mental Ability, Form C*, World Book Company.)

"In each row, put an X in the box in the picture that is MOST DIFFERENT."

(From R. N. McMurry and J. E. King, *SRA Non-Verbal Form, Form AH*, Science Research Associates, items 43 and 44. Copyright 1947.)

Fig. 10.   Specimen items from tests of ability.

learned the concept "clockwise" can quickly decide, for each figure, whether the hook is "clockwise" or "counterclockwise" and solve the problem without error. For such people, then, high scores indicate education rather than endowment alone. In addition to ability factors, the test is also influenced by the subject's patience, carefulness, and tendency to guess. Some pupils are more painstaking than others in looking for *all* the correct answers.

The selection from the Zyve test is thought of by Zyve as measuring "caution, i.e., the tendency of the student to pause to investigate before adopting a method of behavior" (52). Subjects who guess at the answer will usually be fooled by optical illusions in the figure, whereas those who measure before answering should be more successful. Zyve feels that this attitude of depending on measurement rather than judgment is important for students of science. The test might measure "attitude *in taking the test* of obtaining objective data for making a judgment"; it is not certain that the same attitude would be present in other situations. A subject who is in a hurry, perhaps because he has many tests to take during a day at a guidance center, may be less accurate than he would be at other times. Still another factor affecting test score is the precision with which the subject measures. Some of the diagonals differ by only tiny amounts, so that even a person with a data-seeking attitude can obtain wrong answers unless he is also precise in measuring.

One of the most valuable ways to understand any test is to administer it individually, requiring the subject to work the problems aloud. A score for these experimental subjects can not be compared with the standard norms. But the tester learns just what mental processes are used in solving the exercises, and what mental and personality factors cause errors. A test of reasoning, for example, is clearly valid if all subjects who reason accurately get the right answers, but it is a poorer test if some persons fail only because they lack information required to solve the problems.

8. Analyze each of the other illustrations given in Figure 10 to decide what factors might affect the score of a college freshman taking the tests.

The name of a test is often misleading. Different tests of intelligence contain different sorts of items; therefore they must measure, in part, different things. Names are convenient, but the test user must be aware that the only way to know what he is measuring is to study the test items and the test structure. "Introversion" in one test is not the same as "introversion" in another. "Knowledge of arithmetic" in one test may involve speed in simple operations, but in another may require power of arithmetical reasoning.

A further problem in knowing what a test measures is that in different groups different factors account for individual differences on the test. A test calling for solution of scientific problems might measure intelligence in a group where the problems were unfamiliar. If some students had learned about the problems through science courses, differences in amount of science studied would be largely responsible for differences in score. A Japanese university includes in its entrance examination an American test of "ability to follow directions," with minor changes but still printed in English. Among American adolescents, the test shows differences in general mental ability. Among the selected group of Japanese, it becomes a measure of proficiency in English—which is important in Japanese higher education where students must read much material in English. The extent to which a factor influences differences in score is proportional to the range in that factor among the group tested. The Japanese vary more than the Americans in ability to read simple English. That ability has correspondingly high weight in the test when it is given to Japanese.

9. Steadiness is measured by having the subject put a stylus in a series of successively smaller holes without touching the sides. An electrical contact between the stylus and plate indicates an error. On a device similar to that in Figure 11, schizophrenics earned significantly poorer scores than normals (32). Why might this not indicate that these schizophrenics are less able to coördinate their muscles in hand movements?

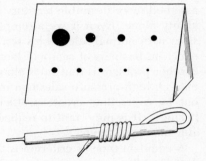

Fig. 11.   Steadiness test. (Courtesy Marietta Apparatus Co.)

10. A school system selects high-school teachers by a series of criteria, one of which is "knowledge of current affairs." It uses as a measure the *Time Current Affairs Test,* giving it to applicants before it is published in *Time* magazine, and without letting them know what test is to be used. Discuss the validity of the test in this use.
11. A set of red, blue, and yellow tags is provided to be sorted into red, yellow, and blue boxes. Number of cards sorted in two minutes is measured. Among the abilities required for a good score are understanding of directions, color discrimination, sustained attention, and motor speed. Which factors would influence scores most within each of the following groups: two-year-olds, six-year-olds, college students?

Empirical Validity

If a test correlates with some other variable of known validity, we can say that in part it measures the same thing. Empirical validity is studied by comparing test results with a *criterion* known to measure some characteristic of importance. For example, if we wish to know whether a test will identify successful salesmen, we might give it to new employees of a wholesale hardware concern and after six months correlate the test scores with the total amount of hardware each man has sold. The criterion, "amount sold in six months," is an index of success in selling. The size of the correlation indicates how well the test predicts this criterion. If the test does not predict, it is not a measure of "probable success in selling hardware" in this situation, and is invalid for selecting salesmen. It will be noted that empirical studies rarely clarify what psychological factors are represented in a test, but rather define the test's uses and limitations in practical terms.

The principal difficulty in empirical studies is the choice of a suitable criterion. If the criterion does not really represent "selling success," the test has not been given a fair trial. Let us look at the weaknesses of the criterion suggested. In the first place, it represents only the wholesale hardware business, so that at best we can judge the test for only this one use; additional empirical studies would be required if the test were being considered for hiring fire insurance, automobile, or machine-tool salesmen. Although amount sold appears to be a fair basis for judging success, it is probable that some men were assigned more desirable territory than others, so that sales would not reflect ability alone. Even if we attempt to control this by comparing each man's sales with normal sales in his territory, we have not considered the possible effect on business of seasonal factors, such as poor crops in one region. Still another problem is that sales alone may not be what we desire from a salesman. A high-pressure salesman may build up high total sales on a first trip but by overselling create problems which will eventually harm the firm's business. It is important to realize that even a criterion which looks reasonable may have faults.

A common type of criterion is the rating or grade. Aptitude tests are validated against marks earned in school. Industrial tests are validated against ratings by supervisors. These ratings are weak criteria, since the judge may not know the facts about the person, and different judges disagree. Methods of improving ratings are discussed in Chapter 18, but even the best ratings are only partially valid. When a test fails to predict a rating, one cannot say whether this is the fault of the test or of the rating.

Designers of new tests frequently validate their instruments by correlating them with established tests. Group tests of intelligence, for example, have frequently been correlated with the Stanford-Binet intelligence test, which itself has been thoroughly studied both empirically and logically. A test which shows a high correlation with the Binet test measures "whatever the Binet test measures" and may be relied upon for the same purposes. This procedure is often relied upon when no non-test criterion is readily available. Its weakness is that we must be very sure of the meaning of the test used as a criterion. There is little merit in showing that three questionnaires of "neurotic tendency" correlate highly, if scores on all the tests are determined mostly by the subject's ability to see through the purpose of the test and give "desirable" answers.

Table 3 shows the frequency with which various criteria are used in studies reported in one journal.

12. What are the weaknesses of the procedure described in the following quotation from a handbook on testing?

"Generally speaking, the validity of the test is best determined by using common sense in discovering that the test measures component abilities which exist both in the test situation and on the job. This common-sense approach to the problem of validity can be strengthened greatly by basing the estimate of the component of the job on a systematic observation of job analysis" (quoted in 37).

13. A test of preschool children is validated in three ways. (1) Intelligence is defined as ability to learn responses with which one has had no previous experience. The test items are examined and found to fit this definition. (2)

Table 3. Validating Criteria Used in Studies Reported in *Journal of Applied Psychology,* 1946–1947

Criterion	Frequency
Ratings by instructor or superior	14
Other test of same function	13
School or training grades	11
Clinical diagnosis	5
Laboratory or clinical measure of same function	2
Job turnover	2
Objective measure of job performance	1
School examination	1
Accident rate on job	1
Interview with subject	1

Scores on the test, given at age three, are found to be correlated with reading skill and vocabulary knowledge at the end of the first grade. (3) Scores on the test, given at age three, are found to be correlated with scores on the Stanford-Binet test given at age 16.

a. What possible uses of the test are warranted, on the basis of each of these studies?

b. Would it be possible for a test to show high validity by method (2), and not to be found valid by the other two procedures?

14. A "test of mechanical aptitude" is found to have a correlation of .65 with success of applicants in learning to operate and service a complex machine. Logical analysis shows that the test is only partly a measure of mechanical aptitude, but is also much influenced by various response sets, ability to understand the rather difficult vocabulary used in stating questions, and knowledge of arithmetic operations. Should it be used?

15. "Spelling ability has been found in many studies to be a good predictor of clerical ability. We have published a new spelling test. We may assume that it will predict clerical ability." What is the possible error in such a conclusion?

16. Criticize each of the following criteria.

a. Ratings of practice teachers by their supervisors, as an index of teaching ability.

b. Number of accidents a driver has per year, as an index of driver safety.

c. Number of accidents a driver has per thousand miles, as an index of driver safety.

17. A study-habits inventory asks such questions as "Do you daydream when you should be studying?"

a. What criterion would you use to determine empirically whether the inventory really measures study habits?

    b. What criterion would you use to determine whether the inventory predicts success in college?

    c. Which study would be best to show that the test is valid?

18. Criticize the procedure indicated in the following report of a study of success of teachers college students.

> "The correlation between all thirty of the [predictor] variables and the [school] superintendents' ratings was only .17, but that between the variables and marks earned during four years of college was .79. Since college marks were predictable on the basis of the thirty variables and . . . the superintendents' ratings were not, the marks were substituted for the ratings as a criterion of success" (cited in 19).

Validity coefficients are rarely as high as we would like. Table 4 lists typical validity coefficients of various sizes from studies reported in the past. Rarely does a validity coefficient rise above .70, although this gives far from perfect predictive accuracy. We would be better satisfied if our coefficients were higher, but any positive correlation indicates that predictions from the test will be more accurate than decisions made without data. Whether a validity coefficient is high enough to warrant use of the test depends on such practical considerations as the validity of methods already in use (such as interviewing), the urgency of improved selection, and the time and money available for testing.

In interpreting any correlation coefficient, the range of the group studied

Table 4.   Validity Coefficients of Various Sizes

Coefficient	Test	Criterion	Sample
.04	Otis Self-Administering (intelligence)	Rating of success	40 factory supervisors (39)
.18	How Supervise? (judgment)	Rating of success	40 factory supervisors (39)
.24	Cardall Practical Judgment	Rating of judgment	91 student retailing clerks (42)
.31	Seashore Musical Talent	Grades in applied music	59 women students in college of music (30)
.42	Otis Beta (intelligence)	Rating of success	297 supervisors, several plants (41)
.45	Bennett Mechanical Comprehension	Rating of success	297 supervisors, several plants (41)
.55	Ferson-Stoddard (law aptitude)	First-semester grades in law school	395 law students (20)
.57	ACE Psychological (scholastic aptitude)	Freshman marks	97 freshmen in junior college (34)
.59	Iowa Silent Reading, "rate of comprehension" score	Specially designed test of rate of comprehension	High-school pupils; number uncertain (7)
.66	Mental and psychomotor tests (combined)	Graduation or elimination from pilot training	1017 Air Force trainees (18)
.79	Mental and achievement tests combined with high-school grades	Freshman marks	97 freshmen in junior college (34)
.82	Orthorater, visual acuity both eyes	Clinical test of acuity	95 adults in industrial eye clinic (17)
.92	Revised Beta (non-verbal intelligence)	Wechsler test of mental ability	168 prisoners (35)

must be considered. The correlation is smaller in a selected group than in a group containing a wider range of ability. Perhaps the test How Supervise? which correlated only .18 with success in supervision (Table 4), would give a higher validity in selecting good supervisors from a random group of factory workers. The group tested, composed only of people already in supervisory work, had probably already been screened to eliminate men of very poor judgment. The effect of range is discussed at greater length in Chapter 11 (pp. 260 ff.).

A few current reports suggest a new concept of validity, called *factorial validity*. A test has high factorial validity if it is a pure measure of just one type of ability. Most mental tests used in school are far from pure; instead, they require a combination of many different abilities, such as verbal ability, reasoning, reading, mental speed, and so on. It is possible that pure tests, each measuring one ability, will eventually permit the tester to obtain better predictions (26). Pure tests are constructed on the basis of factor analysis, which will be discussed in Chapter 9. The most extensive discussion of factorial validity appears in a report on Air Force selection edited by Guilford (27).

19. In Table 4, what characteristics seem to be associated with tests having high coefficients?
20. What characteristics are associated with criteria yielding high coefficients?
21. How can you account for the low size of the first six coefficients, other than by assuming that the tests fail to measure what they are intended to measure?

Reliability

No test can have validity unless it measures accurately. The accuracy of measurement is expressed in the reliability coefficient. Any test score is a somewhat inaccurate measure, because many errors creep in when we take a small sample of a person's behavior. If we wish to measure ability to add, we present the subject with many items drawn from all the possible addition problems. We obtain a sample of his work on those items, at a particular time, assuming that this sample shows what his work will be like at other times. The measure obtained by a particular set of items will give an erroneous score if the combinations included happen to be those especially easy for the person. The sample of behavior will not be representative if we test him on an "off" day instead of taking our sample at a more favorable time. Such errors of measurement, together with all the small changes in score resulting from "lucky guesses" and the like, may result in a misleading impression of the subject. The reliability coefficient shows the extent to which errors of measurement influence scores on the test.

The complexity of factors which may influence scores on a test is indicated in Table 5, prepared by R. L. Thorndike. Reliability coefficients estimate the extent to which some or all of the factors in sections II, III, IV, and V of the table cause random changes in score.

Table 5.   Possible Sources of Differences in Performance on a Test
(**48**, pp. 102–103)

I. Lasting and general characteristics of the individual.
   A. General skills and techniques of taking tests.
   B. General ability to comprehend instructions.
   C. Level of ability on one or more general traits which operate in a number of tests.
II. Lasting but specific characteristics of the individual.
   A. Specific to the test as a whole (and to parallel forms of it).
      1. Individual level of ability on traits required in this test but not in others.
      2. Knowledge and skills specific to particular form of test items.
   B. Specific to particular test items.
      1. The "chance" element determining whether the individual does or does not know a particular
         fact.
III. Temporary but general characteristics of the individual (factors affecting performance on many or all
     tests at a particular time).
   A. Health.
   B. Fatigue.
   C. Motivation.
   D. Emotional strain.
   E. General test-wiseness (partly lasting).
   F. External conditions of heat, light, ventilation, etc.
IV. Temporary and specific characteristics of the individual.
   A. Specific to the test as a whole.
      1. Comprehension of the specific test task (insofar as this is distinct from I-B).
      2. Specific tricks or techniques of dealing with the particular test materials (insofar as distinct
         from II-A-2).
      3. Level of practice on the specific skills involved, especially in psychomotor tests.
      4. Momentary "set" for a particular test.
   B. Specific to particular test items.
      1. Fluctuations and idiosyncrasies of human memory.
      2. Unpredictable fluctuations in attention or accuracy.
V. Variance not otherwise accounted for (chance).
   A. Luck in the selection of answers by "guessing."

22. Locate each of the following sources of change in score in Thorndike's clas-
    sification.
    a. A student breaks his pencil and loses test time while obtaining another.
    b. An industrial worker who has been in this country a short time mis-
       understands an important phrase in the instructions for a performance test.
    c. A "hillbilly" is unable to answer correctly a question from an intelligence
       test about the purchase of a railroad ticket.
    d. A suspicious patient refuses to coöperate with a test and gives perfunctory
       answers.
    e. A student guesses at every item of which he is uncertain.

General Principles

   Before considering methods of estimating the reliability of a test, a few
general principles may be discussed. The principles are as follows:

1. The reliability coefficient depends on the length of the test.
2. The reliability coefficient depends on the spread of scores in the group
   studied.
3. A test may give reliable measures at one level of ability, and unreliable
   measures at another level.

The importance of lengthening tests is that, with every question added, the sample of performance becomes more adequate. One, and only one, addition problem is a very poor sample of a person's ability, since we are quite likely to hit on a number combination particularly hard or easy for him. If we ask more and more questions of the same general sort, we are far more likely to obtain a good estimate of his general ability on addition problems. Longer tests also are less influenced by guessing. If a test has only five multiple-choice items, a few people might get all the items correct by guessing, but in a fifty-item test, variations due to guessing tend to cancel out.

Suppose that a test has a reliability of .40. The Spearman-Brown formula, given at right, estimates the reliability of the score from a similar test n times as long.

$$r_n = \frac{nr}{1 + (n - 1)\, r}$$

where
r is the original reliability; r_n is the reliability of the test n times as long

To determine the reliability of a test twice as long as the original test, substitute in the formula $n = 2$, $r = .40$.

$$r_n = \frac{2(.40)}{1 + (1)\,.40}$$
$$= \frac{.80}{1.40} = .57$$

Suppose the original test is reduced to only half its original length. The reliability of the short test is computed using $n = \frac{1}{2}$.

$$r_n = \frac{\frac{1}{2}(.40)}{1 + (\frac{1}{2} - 1)\,(.40)}$$
$$= \frac{.20}{1 - \frac{1}{2}(.40)} = \frac{.20}{.80} = .25$$

Computing Guide 5. Use of the Spearman-Brown formula.

Short tests can be made more accurate by lengthening them. The Spearman-Brown formula, presented and illustrated in Computing Guide 5, estimates what reliability would be obtained if a test were lengthened or shortened. The formula assumes that when we lengthen the test we do not change its nature. Extreme increases in test length, however, introduce effects of boredom and actually reduce reliability. Unless one is careful, added items may not cover the same topic or ability as the original test.

The reliability of every score one intends to interpret needs to be studied. Because short tests tend to be unreliable, part-scores based on a few test items are of limited value. Unfortunately, many testers, knowing that a test as a whole is reliable, place faith in part-scores which are unreliable. Frequently authors fail to publish the reliability of subscores even though they advise the user to consider the subscores separately.

23. A spelling test of 30 words has a reliability of .80. What reliability might be expected if 90 words were used?
24. The California Test of Personality containing 144 items is reported to have a reliability coefficient of .933. What would be the approximate reliability of the subtest Sense of Personal Worth, which contains 12 items? (Use the formula, with $n = \dfrac{1}{12}$. This procedure underestimates the reliability because assumptions of the formula are not satisfied. The exact reliability of the subtest score has not been reported.)

Errors of measurement are most important when there are small differences in true ability among the people being compared. In hiring one person

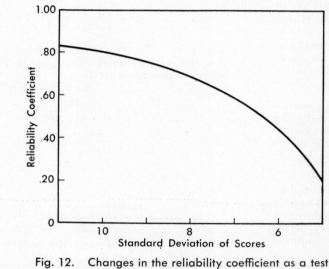

Fig. 12.   Changes in the reliability coefficient as a test
is applied to an increasingly uniform group.

out of a group of applicants, the final decision often hinges on a difference of a few points between the best and next-best man. Slight errors of measurement in such a case might result in hiring the poorer man. If one is screening general applicants for factory work merely to rule out the incompetent prospects, a less refined test will be satisfactory. An error of a few points in score cannot conceal the gross deficiencies in ability which distinguish the "hopeless" from the average run of workers. A test which has a satisfactorily high reliability coefficient for use with groups containing wide differences in ability may be unsatisfactory for comparing people in a highly selected group. Figure 12 shows how the reliability coefficient of a test drops when the test is applied to groups having a smaller range of differences. The drop in reliability indicates that, as the range decreases, a larger and larger percentage of the differences among individuals is due to errors of measurement.

25. A nationally known test of intelligence has a reliability of .82 for a representative population of college freshmen from all colleges. For this group the s.d. is 9.8. In a certain college which draws largely from superior high schools and has severe admission standards, the s.d. on this test is 7.6. If the test is equally reliable over the entire range of scores, what will its reliability coefficient be in this college? (Estimate from Figure 12.)

Because test reliability is usually reported as a single coefficient, it may be erroneously assumed that a test with a high coefficient is accurate for all types of people. But many tests are reliable only at certain levels of difficulty. The Gates Reading Survey Test, for example, is a reliable test, and gives good estimates of reading skill for pupils in most grades. But it attempts to measure pupils in any grade from third to tenth. When third-graders take the test, so much of it is difficult that they do a great deal of guessing. As a result, scores in the third grade give an inaccurate picture of individual differences. Tests, no matter how reliable, give inaccurate measures for pupils whose scores are near the chance level, and some tests give inaccurate measures of the extremely high ranges of talent.

Figure 13 shows a scatter diagram in which are plotted the scores of literate, non-defective Navy recruits who took a pitch-discrimination test twice. If the test is accurate, the two scores for each man should be nearly equal. The test consisted of 100 pairs of tones; in each pair, the man reported whether the second tone was higher or lower. A score of 50 would be obtained by pure chance. From the scatter diagram, high scores appear to be fairly reliable. Men scoring 85 on the first test fell between 72 and 95 on retest. But men scoring near the chance level (e.g., 55) scattered over a wide range on the retest (40 to 87). The upcurve of the regression line at the left is especially interesting. People with very low scores on the first test often did well on the retest. A score of 25 is so far below 50 that it probably did not occur by chance. Probably men with such low scores misunderstood directions on the first test and judged the *first* of the two tones as higher or lower. Following directions correctly on the retest would account for a shift from 70 items wrong to 70 items right (23).

A general rule of test selection is that the test must be appropriate in difficulty for the decision to be made. Figure 14 shows several distributions of test scores for the same group. Test A is very easy for the group; it gives a skewed distribution. It is probably unreliable for the group as a whole, since only a few points' variation would cause a subject to drop from the top of the group to the average. Furthermore, it does not distinguish between the persons tying at 100 even though they are probably not equally superior. The test may be quite satisfactory for measuring differences at the lower end of the group. Test B is difficult. The distribution is again skewed, but this time high scores are spread out and differences at the low end of the scale are too small to distinguish individuals reliably. A normal distribution, such as that for Test C, has the advantage of spreading out cases equally at both

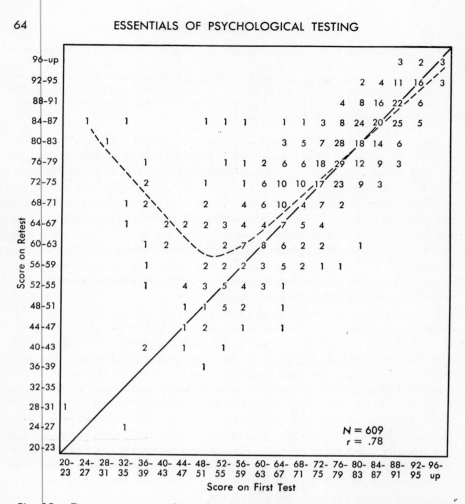

Fig. 13. Test-retest scores of naval recruits on a pitch-discrimination test (23).

ends of the scale. Under this condition, scores at the two ends are more likely to be equally reliable. For this reason, tests yielding roughly normal distributions are preferred where it is necessary to distinguish equally well at all positions on the scale. A normal distribution is not required for a test. Test D illustrates a type of distribution for a special purpose where only very coarse —but correct—grading was desired. The Army wished to screen all men having a mental age below 11 out of its induction line without giving a full mental test. A set of single-question tests was prepared, each question being one that the average person of mental age 11 could answer. Each man was asked one of the questions; if he failed, he was given another. Those who failed both were screened for further study (31). Such a test does not measure individual differences within either the passing or failing group, but it

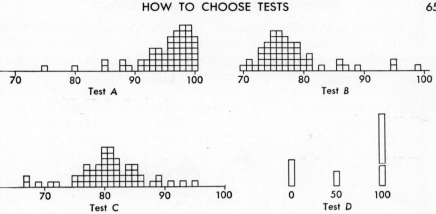

Fig. 14. Scores on several tests given to the same group.

gives an accurate measure at the one level where measurement is needed. Such tests are like the "go–no go" gauge used in industry to determine whether a part has been machined sufficiently.

26. Considering distributions A, B, and C in Figure 14, which would be most desirable to have in each of the following cases?
   a. A psychologist wishes to study the relationship between voting habits and an attitude test indicating liberalism.
   b. A college wishes to select those of its freshmen needing help in reading.
   c. Pupils to compete for national scholarships are to be selected.
   d. An employer wishes to select the best statistician from a group of applicants.
27. The California Test of Personality, Elementary, contains several subtests, one of which is Feeling of Belonging. A low score on this test is said to indicate maladjustment. According to the test manual, the percentile rank corresponding to each possible score is as follows:

Score 1 2 3 4 5 6   7   8   9 10 11 12
P.R.   1 1 1 1 1 5 10 15 25 40 65 90

   a. What is the shape of the raw-score distribution? What does this distribution imply regarding the usefulness of the test?
   b. How would a boy's standing in the group change if his score changed two points?
28. In World Series baseball, some pinch hitters reach batting averages as high as .750, whereas the best regular players rarely exceed .400 for seven games. How can this be explained? What principle regarding reliability does it illustrate?

Methods of Determining Coefficients

There are three types of reliability coefficient: the coefficient of equivalence, the coefficient of stability, and the coefficient of stability and equivalence. The coefficient of equivalence indicates how much scores fluctuate from form to form of the same test. The coefficient of stability measures the fluctuation on the same questions from one time to another. Both form-to-form and time-to-time fluctuations are considered in the coefficient of stability and equivalence, which is lower than the other two. When a "reliability coefficient" is reported, it is important to consider which type it is, since the three coefficients have different meanings (16; cf. Fig. 15).

The *coefficient of equivalence* indicates how precisely the test measures the person's performance at the particular moment. It estimates how much

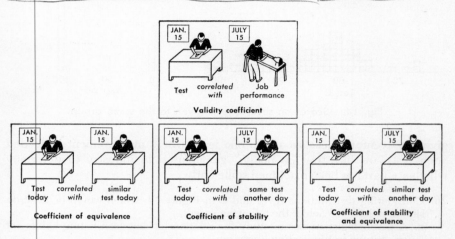

Fig. 15. Comparison of validity coefficient and three reliability coefficients.

his score would change if a different sample of questions testing the same ability had been used. This coefficient is usually estimated by the *split-half method*, as shown in Computing Guide 6, or by an alternate procedure using the Spearman-Brown formula. The split-half method gives misleading results unless the two half-tests are just as equivalent as parallel forms of the same test would be. The halves must have nearly equal standard deviations. The halves must be similar in content; it would not be fair to split an intelligence test containing some arithmetic questions so that most of those items fell into one half. It is common practice to compare the odd items (1, 3, 5, etc.) with the even items (2, 4, 6, etc.), but this may give halves which are not equivalent (14). A variation known as the *parallel-split* is recommended to make the half-tests more alike. A group of papers is analyzed to determine how many persons pass each item. Items are divided into two groups such that items in the two halves are matched in difficulty and in content. A second group of papers is then scored on the two half-tests and the formula of Computing Guide 6 applied (13).

The *Kuder-Richardson formulas* also estimate the coefficient of equivalence. The most widely used formula is presented in Computing Guide 7. This gives a good estimate when all the items in a test represent a single general factor (see Chapter 9). If the items in a test cover many different

1. In order to determine the reliability of a test by the split-half method, the test is divided into two halves, as nearly alike as possible in difficulty and content.

2. Each paper is scored on the two parts separately, so that one has an array of scores like that at right.

Name	Score		
	First Half (a)	Second Half (b)	Total (t)
Adams, J.	22	19	41
Allen, R.	30	22	52
Arthur, S.	25	27	52
Ashton, F.	16	18	34
etc..........			

3. The standard deviation of each column is computed, by the procedure of Computing Guide 2.

First half: $s_a = 3.0$
Second half: $s_b = 3.2$
Total: $s_t = 5.5$

4. The numbers are substituted in Guttman's formula (28):

$$r = 2\left(1 - \frac{s_a^2 + s_b^2}{s_t^2}\right)$$

$$r = 2\left(1 - \frac{9.00 + 10.24}{30.25}\right)$$

$$r = 2\left(1 - \frac{19.24}{30.25}\right)$$

$$r = 2\,(1 - .636)$$

$$r = 2\,(.364) = .73$$

s_a and s_b are the sigmas of the half-tests, and s_t is that for the total. r is the coefficient of equivalence (reliability).

The resulting coefficient is a serious underestimate if s_a and s_b are not nearly equal. In that case, a new split must be made.

Computing Guide 6. Determining the split-half reliability coefficient.

1. Before applying the Kuder-Richardson method to determine the reliability of a test, decide whether the test measures just one ability or calls for different abilities in different items. Unless all the items measure the same general ability, the method gives a misleading result.

2. Make a frequency distribution of scores and compute the standard deviation (s) by the method of Computing Guide 2.

For a particular 60-item test, the result may be:

$$s = 6.2$$

3. Make a tabulation of the number of people passing each item. This gives an array like that at the right. (The tabulation is usually made for a large number of papers—50 or more—but only 20 papers are used in this illustration.)

Item No.	Number of Persons Passing (out of 20)		p	q	pq
1	‖‖‖ ‖‖‖ ///	13	.65	.35	.23
2	‖‖‖ ‖‖‖ ‖‖‖ ///	18	.90	.10	.09
3	‖‖‖ ‖‖‖ ‖‖‖ /	16	.80	.20	.16
4	‖‖‖ ///	8	.40	.60	.24
5	‖‖‖ ‖‖‖ //	12	.60	.40	.24
6	‖‖‖ ‖‖‖ ‖‖‖	15	.75	.25	.19
7	‖‖‖ ‖‖‖ ‖‖‖ ‖‖‖	20	1.00	.00	.00
etc.	....				

$$\Sigma pq = 9.74$$

Compute p, the proportion of the group passing the item.

Determine q, the proportion of the group not passing, by subtracting p from 1.00.

Multiply p by q, and enter in the pq column. Add this column to get Σpq.

4. Note n, the number of items, and substitute in the formula:

$$r = \frac{n}{n-1}\left(1 - \frac{\Sigma pq}{s^2}\right)$$

$$n = 60$$

$$r = \frac{60}{59}\left(1 - \frac{9.74}{38.4}\right)$$
$$r = 1.01\,(1 - .254)$$
$$r = 1.01\,(.746) = .76$$

The resulting coefficient is a serious underestimate if the test is not a measure of a single general ability. The coefficient is a spuriously high estimate if the test is a speed test.

Computing Guide 7. Determining the reliability coefficient by the Kuder-Richardson method (Case III).

abilities, the estimate from this formula is low, sometimes much too low.

The coefficient of equivalence may also be estimated by the *parallel-test method*, correlating scores on two forms of the test given at the same time. This shows directly whether a different sampling of items would give the same picture of individual differences.

The *coefficient of stability* shows the extent to which scores on the particular test items are stable over a period of time. It indicates whether a sample of behavior taken at one time is typical of behavior at other times. It is estimated by the *retest method*, the same persons being given the same test on two different occasions, having had no opportunity between trials to study the material covered by the test. The retest method may contain a spurious factor due to carry-over from one trial to another. This is especially troublesome in tests of reasoning, for example, where the person may remember the solution to a problem so that it no longer tests his reasoning.

The *coefficient of stability and equivalence* measures fluctuations from day-to-day changes in the person and fluctuations due to the particular choice of items in the test. It shows the extent to which the test measures stable individual differences in the variables present both in the test and in its parallel form. It is estimated by the *delayed parallel-test method*. Two tests containing different questions, but supposedly equivalent, are given to the student on two occasions. The correlation between the two tests is taken as the coefficient.

Which method of estimating the amount of error in test scores is most suitable depends on the situation. In a speeded test, it is impossible to determine a coefficient of equivalence save by giving an immediate parallel test. The split-half and Kuder-Richardson methods must not be used. When this principle is disregarded, as it often is, and split-half methods are applied to speed tests, the resulting coefficients are grossly inflated. To show the size of this error, authors of one test computed the coefficients shown in Table 6, first by the proper parallel-test method, second by the inappropriate split-half method. The second set of coefficients is much higher. Some test manuals report only such spurious coefficients—the estimates are in error and give no useful information about the accuracy of the test.

If one considers that day-to-day variation is a source of error (as when trying to measure "intelligence," which is supposed to be constant), he will use a coefficient of stability or stability and equivalence. This is the case in most practical applications of tests. If the day-to-day fluctuations are considered to be "real" variables rather than error, a coefficient of equivalence is used.

The Detroit Beginning First-Grade Intelligence Test provides an example of both types of coefficient. The test is unspeeded, and may properly be split. The split-half coefficient is .91, which shows that the test is an accurate measure of beginning pupils. But when the retest method is used, the coefficient drops to .76 (correlation between scores at start of year and scores just four

Table 6. Inflation of Reliability Estimates When Split-Half Method Is Applied to a Speeded Test[a] (6, p. C–6)

Grade	Reliability Properly Determined by Correlating Two Forms	Estimates by Split-Half Method Obtained to Demonstrate Spurious Increase	
		Form A	Form B
8	.77	.990	.996
9	.83	.991	.989
10	.93	.996	.985
11	.86	.992	.993
12	.92	.996	.969

[a] One of the Differential Aptitude Tests.

months later). So pupils placed in a "fast" group or a "slow" group at the start of the year might shift in ability so rapidly that such a classification would be quite unjust a few months later. The test is accurate enough to measure what can be expected of pupils in the first weeks of school, but teachers must know that scores are unstable and that some pupils will change a great deal before the term ends.

The procedures for studying reliability are summarized in Table 7.

Table 7. Summary of Characteristics of Three Reliability Coefficients

Name and Method of Determination	Assumptions	Error When Assumptions Are Violated	Questions Answered by the Coefficient
Coefficient of equivalence			
Split-half	Halves must be equivalent.	Coefficient for speed tests falsely high. For other tests, coefficient is too low if halves are not equivalent.	How precisely does the test measure? How adequately does it sample all the items that might be included?
Kuder-Richardson	Test must measure a single factor.	Coefficient for speed tests falsely high. For other tests, coefficient is too low if items measure many factors.	
Immediate parallel test	Tests must be equivalent.	Coefficient shows degree of equivalence, rather than accuracy of either test.	
Coefficient of stability			
Retest after an interval	No opportunity for increasing ability by practice during interval.	Practice on function tested reduces coefficient.	How stable is measurement with the test?
Coefficient of stability and equivalence			
Parallel test after an interval	Tests must be equivalent. No opportunity for practice.	Coefficient underestimates accuracy of test if assumptions are violated.	How would the sample of behavior at one time correspond to results from a similar sample at another time?

Student	1	2	3	4	5	6	7	8	9	10	11	12	13	14	15	16	17	18	19	20	21	22	23	24	25	26	27	28	29	30	Score
A	+	+	+	+	+	+	o	+	+	+	+	+	o	o	+	+	+	+	o	+	o	+	+	+	+	o	+	+	+	+	24
B	+	+	+	o	+	+	+	+	+	+	+	o	+	+	+	+	+	+	o	+	+	+	o	+	o	+	+	+	o	+	24
C	o	+	+	+	+	+	+	+	+	+	+	+	+	+	o	+	+	+	+	+	o	+	+	+	o	o	+	+	+	o	24
D	+	+	+	+	+	+	+	+	+	+	+	o	o	+	+	+	+	+	o	+	+	+	+	+	+	+	+	+	+	o	26
E	+	+	+	+	+	+	o	o	+	+	+	+	o	o	+	o	+	+	+	+	+	+	o	+	+	o	+	+	o	o	23
F	+	o	+	+	+	o	+	+	+	o	+	o	o	o	+	+	+	+	+	+	+	+	o	+	o	+	o	+	o	o	19
G	+	o	+	+	+	+	+	o	+	+	+	+	o	+	o	o	+	+	+	+	o	+	o	+	+	o	+	+	+	+	24
H	+	+	+	+	+	+	+	+	+	+	o	o	o	o	o	+	+	+	o	+	o	o	+	+	o	o	o	+	o	+	15
I	+	+	+	+	+	+	+	+	+	+	o	+	o	+	+	+	+	+	o	+	o	+	o	+	o	o	+	+	o	+	22
J	+	o	+	+	+	+	+	+	+	+	+	+	o	+	+	+	+	+	o	+	+	+	+	+	+	o	o	+	o	o	24
K	+	+	+	+	+	+	+	o	+	+	+	o	+	+	+	+	+	+	o	+	o	+	+	o	+	o	+	+	o	+	24
L	+	o	+	+	+	+	o	+	+	+	o	o	o	+	+	+	+	+	+	+	+	o	o	+	+	+	+	o	o	o	21
M	+	+	+	+	+	+	o	+	+	+	+	o	o	+	o	+	+	+	o	+	o	o	+	o	+	+	+	+	o	o	19
N	+	+	+	+	+	+	o	+	+	+	+	+	o	+	+	+	+	+	+	+	+	o	+	o	o	o	+	o	+	+	24
O	+	o	+	+	+	+	+	+	+	+	+	+	o	o	+	o	+	+	+	+	o	+	o	o	+	+	+	+	+	o	21
P	o	+	+	+	+	+	+	+	+	+	o	+	+	+	+	+	+	+	+	+	+	+	o	+	o	+	+	o	+	o	27
Q	+	+	+	+	+	+	o	+	+	+	+	o	o	+	+	+	+	+	o	+	o	o	o	o	+	o	o	+	o	+	17
R	+	o	+	o	+	+	o	+	+	+	+	o	o	+	+	+	+	+	+	+	+	+	o	+	o	o	+	+	+	+	23
S	+	+	+	o	+	+	+	+	+	+	+	o	o	o	+	+	+	+	o	+	+	+	+	+	o	+	o	+	+	+	21
T	+	+	+	+	+	+	+	o	+	+	+	o	o	+	+	o	+	+	o	+	+	o	+	+	+	+	+	+	+	o	20
Number correct	18	14	20	17	20	19	13	16	20	19	16	9	4	14	16	16	20	20	9	20	11	14	10	15	11	9	15	17	10	10	

29. A test of 30 items is given to 20 students, with the results shown below. Each + indicates a correct answer, and each 0 an incorrect answer. Determine the coefficient of equivalence by the split-half method (odd-even) and by the Kuder-Richardson formula.

30. A teacher gives a standardized test of knowledge of scientific facts to her class in chemistry. Several students make scores lower than she had expected.
   a. She asks herself, "Could it be that I gave a form of the test which included many questions these particular pupils happened not to know? Would their scores have changed much if they had been asked other questions of the same type?" Which reliability coefficient is appropriate to answer this question?
   b. Suppose she asks, "Could the performance of these students be due to the fact that they were having an 'off' day? Does a pupil's score on tests of this type vary much from day to day?" Which coefficient is most helpful in answering this question?

31. Which of the factors in Table 5 would lower the correlation between test and criterion in each of the following situations?
   a. A test of high-jumping ability is used to select finalists in a track meet. The criterion is performance in the meet, two weeks after the trials.
   b. A pencil-and-paper test of mechanical ability is used to predict performance of mechanical trainees. Piecework earnings after training are used as the criterion.

32. The following quotation refers to hearing tests for children (29, p. 225):
   "It is certainly understood that physical and psychological changes taking place from day to day may make tests at two sittings less valid than a complete test at one sitting. Dr. Gardner observes empirically that he gets worse results on cloudy days than on sunny days."
   In what sense is the word "valid" used? Can you defend the contrary statement that scores at two sittings would be *more* valid than a complete test at one sitting?

Table 8.   Representative Reliability Coefficients

Test	Method	Coefficient	Sample
CEEB Scholastic Aptitude— Verbal	Odd-even	.96	500 applicants to colleges (11, pp. 29 ff.)
Kuder Preference Record (interests)	Retest (3 days)	.93 to .98	41 graduate students (51)
Adaptability Test (mental ability)	Parallel test, immediate	.89	548 adults (50)
CEEB Scholastic Aptitude— Verbal	Parallel test, varied time	.87	7396 applicants to colleges (11, p. 60)
Bernreuter, "self-confidence" score	Odd-even	.86	100 adolescent boys (22)
Kuhlmann-Anderson (IQ)	Parallel test (2½ yrs.)	.69	327 children in Grade I at first test (1)
Fels Parent Behavior Scales (ratings)	Two home visitors, one year apart	.61	Not reported (3)
Tests of cheating	Similar test (12 years)	.37	About 150 children in Grades VII–VIII at first test (33)

There is no single standard of what is an adequate reliability coefficient. Few tests approach perfect reliability. Sometimes short and unreliable tests are valuable for particular purposes, especially for making rapid judgments. Generally, higher reliability coefficients are obtained for ability tests than for measures of typical performance. Reliability coefficients reported for several tests are presented in Table 8.

The degree of reliability required varies with the purpose of the test. As with validity, the reliability desired is the highest we can get. Validity is the goal in testing. The *maximum* validity a test can have is the square root of the reliability coefficient.

Objectivity

In general, objective tests are to be preferred to those in which the opinion of the scorer influences the results, but subjectively scored tests are at times more flexible or better suited to a given purpose. This flexibility is especially advantageous in clinical work. Whenever one permits opinion to affect a test score, he makes it impossible to compare his results with those of other testers, and difficult to compare his subject with the normal person. Objectivity is always to be desired if it can be obtained without sacrificing the major purpose of the test.

Current practice in group testing favors the multiple-choice form. Although this measures recognition of correct answers rather than recall, it is satisfactory for many purposes. The College Entrance Examination Board, for example, reports that in a mathematics achievement test at the college level multiple-choice questions had reliability coefficients and correlation with grades in later mathematics essentially the same as those for free-answer questions (11, p. 61).

American practice, with tests designed to be used by different persons with the same results, is in interesting contrast to work in other countries, for example the Japanese Army procedures for selecting pilots. In addition to mental and psychomotor tests, an oral examination was given. Subjective judgment was used in evaluating test results. In the oral interview, an effort was made to avoid standardizing the questions and general approach, so as to observe applicants flexibly. Decision to admit the applicant to flying was based on an "artistic" judgment by the psychologist, rather than a numerical treatment of scores. Typical validity figures, using training records as a criterion, were reported as .40 to .65. "The validity coefficient for the final assessment was qualified by adding that this value was secured 'if Mr. Yoshino does it' (makes the final assessment). . . . Other 'experts' were not as good" (24). A similar impression was obtained by Fitts, who studied German psychological testing in World War II (21, p. 153):

"A marked characteristic of the German testing procedure was the emphasis on subjective evaluation of test data. German psychologists stated repeatedly that observations of the candidate's behavior during a test were more important than the actual score which he earned. . . . One man . . . said that the chief fault of inexperienced military psychologists was that they attached too much weight to objective scores and did not pay enough attention to the formation of an intuitive impression from observation of the candidate's reactions and expressions. Individual examiners were permitted and often encouraged to vary testing procedures and to emphasize their favorite tests."

Even in types of tests in which the subject must produce a free response, methods can be devised which permit fairly objective scoring. Ayres, in 1912, produced a guide for scoring pupil handwriting (Fig. 16). Samples of handwriting representing various levels of quality are given; the teacher compares the pupil's work to find the most similar sample (2). Product-rating scales have been used frequently in judging quality of cooking, shopwork, and other skilled work. Objective methods have not been completely successful in scoring free-response tests, but variation between scorers is re-

60	90
Four score and seven years ago our fathers brought for theupon this continent a new nation, conceived in liberty, and dedicated to the proposition that all	*Fourscore and seven years ago our fathers brought forth upon this continent a new nation; conceived in liberty*

Fig. 16.   Part of Ayres' scale for scoring handwriting samples. (Courtesy Russell Sage Foundation, publisher.)

duced by guides which show the approved scoring for representative answers. Noteworthy examples are the scoring manuals for the Stanford-Binet test of intelligence (45, 38) and the volume by Beck (5) on the Rorschach test of personality.

The importance of eliminating variation between scorers was established rather dramatically in a series of studies by Starch and Elliott (43, 44). They requested a large number of teachers to score a pupil's composition; the grades ranged from 50 percent to 98 percent. Teachers use different bases for judgment, and penalties of varying severity. Even in geometry, teachers gave grades ranging from 28 to 92 to the same paper. These results are extreme, since the teachers were given no instructions for grading, but they demonstrate that results will not be comparable unless scoring is standardized.

33. The question "Why should people wash their clothing?" is to be used in an oral intelligence test for adults, to test comprehension of common situations. Provide a set of scoring standards to indicate what should be considered correct. Make your list of characteristics of a satisfactory answer so clear that other scorers would be able to agree in scoring new answers.

Norms

The authors of most tests provide tables for interpreting a raw score in relation to "normal" performance. These tables are based on computations from scores on a *norm group*, or standardizing group. The data are usually presented as means, percentiles, or standard scores, so that the test user, knowing the score of a person, can determine how he compares with the standard group. *Age norms* indicate the average performance of persons of each age. *Grade norms* indicate the average performance of children in each grade. For personality tests and tests of mechanical ability, separate norms for men and women are usually needed, since their averages are different.

If a test is to be used only to establish individual differences within a group, norms are unimportant. Norms are of little use to the employment manager who wishes to hire the brightest 50 percent of a group of applicants. Norms are also of little value where a critical score is used (see Chapter 11). If a personnel manager knows from actual trial that persons with scores of 72 on test A make satisfactory punch-press operators, it is not necessary for him to compare applicants with national norms. Where only a single person is being tested, as in guidance and clinical work, it is extremely important that scores be interpreted in relation to good norms. A score which seems, at first glance, to be high may turn out to be only average when compared to a normal group of scores.

Whether norms are satisfactory depends on three questions: (1) Are the

Table 9.   Standardizing Samples Used by Authors of Representative Tests

Test	Type	Norms	Number of Cases	Nature of Cases
Wechsler-Bellevue	Intelligence, individual	Age; IQ	1751	White urban adults representative of all occupational levels; school children from normal and retarded groups
Henmon-Nelson	Intelligence, group	Percentiles by college years	5500	Students of colleges which admit high-school graduates without further selection
Terman-McNemar	Intelligence, group	Age; percentile	About 19,000	Random sample of pupils in 148 communities in 33 states plus 307 parochial schools near Philadelphia
Bell (adult)	Adjustment	Mean and sigma by sex	468	Adults from adult extension classes, YMCA counseling service, etc.; Los Angeles, Chicago, Boston, Madison, N.J.
Bernreuter	Personality	Percentile by sex, separately for h.s., coll., adult	121 to 651 per group	Details not reported
Minnesota Multiphasic	Personality	Standard score by sex	About 700	Healthy adult visitors to a Minnesota hospital
Progressive	Achievement, elementary	Percentiles by half-grades	Over 25,000	School children in many states

norms based on a sufficiently large group? (2) Is the standard group representative? (3) Does the standard group resemble the persons with whom we wish to compare our subject? The first two questions are general tests of the adequacy of published norms; the third depends on the immediate use intended. Table 9 lists the bases on which norms for several representative tests were established. The numbers of cases used by these authors differ greatly. If too few cases are used, the norms may be inaccurate owing to accidental selection of good or poor cases. With more cases, such variations should cancel out. No fixed number of cases is required for dependable norms; representativeness is more important than accumulating large numbers of cases which may not be representative.

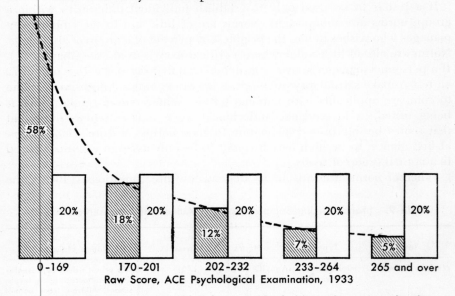

Fig. 17.   The importance of local norms. Shaded bars show score distribution for 40,299 freshmen in 203 colleges, according to national norms. Unshaded bars show distribution for 646 freshmen at the University of Chicago. (Data from **49**, p. 16.)

The norm group is representative if the persons included are typical of those on whom the test is to be used. If the sample is biased so that all types of people are not represented equally, the norms are of little value. If a test is intended for college students, it is fair to base norms on college students; but if the test is to be used with adults generally, the average of the college group would be an unfair standard of comparison. If college norms are to be used, it is important that all types of colleges be represented, that all geographical areas be represented, and that all types of students within the college be represented. Occasionally a test author makes the error of accumulating a large number of cases of the sort most readily available, and reports, perhaps, "The norms are based on scores of 2700 sophomores taking general psychology at four Western colleges." Norms such as these are useless unless the tester wishes to know how his cases compare with sophomore psychology students at Western colleges.

Even though a test has carefully prepared norms, the norms may not be adequate for a particular use. Norms for the Wechsler-Bellevue test of mental ability give helpful information about adults in general. But a boy who is above the average score for his age, when compared to people in general, may be below average among college freshmen. If we wish to predict whether he can succeed in college, we need to compare his score with Wechsler-Bellevue norms based on college students alone. Local norms are needed to predict success in a particular college (cf. Fig. 17). The Kuder Preference Record (1946 edition) provides norms based on a large group of high-school boys and girls. The interpretation of interest profiles of college freshmen, based on these norms, is complicated by the fact that non-academic high-school pupils drop out before reaching college so that the average college student probably has an "unaverage" profile. College norms for the test are in preparation. Local norms may be more useful than national norms for many problems. Sections of the country, schools, and ethnic groups vary widely in America. A person who is below the norm in a superior group may be able to compete successfully in a poorer group. If we wish to predict his standing, we must compare him to those with whom he associates.

Before we compare a pupil with a set of norms, we must consider the educational policies of the schools where the norms were obtained. In a school where some children enter before reaching the age of six, the reading and vocabulary norms for nine-year-olds will be relatively high, because some pupils will have had more schooling than nine-year-olds elsewhere who could not enter school until age six. In a school which promotes every child every year, the average performance of fourth-graders is likely to be lower than in a school which holds back the poorer students.

34. Discuss the representativeness of the groups used in standardizing each of the tests in Table 9.
35. In the freshman class of a particular college which admits all high-school graduates who apply, the median score is at the 65th percentile of the published norms for freshmen for the Henmon-Nelson test. What factors might account for this deviation?
36. Outline detailed plans for selecting a suitable norm group for a test of aptitude for engineering, to be used for vocational guidance in high schools and colleges.
37. A psychologist standardizes a primary intelligence test by testing every child entering the first grade in San Francisco during a particular year.
    a. For what purposes would these norms be valuable?
    b. Could equally satisfactory norms be obtained without testing every first-grader?

38. A "music aptitude" test measures such factors as tone discrimination. There is evidence that scores are increased by musical training. If the test is to be used for advising college freshmen whether to study music, what sort of cases should be used to establish national norms (25)?
39. How would you proceed to get an extremely representative sample of adult men in Chicago to use as a standardizing group for a mental test? Assume that you have sufficient research funds to pay each man $1.00 for taking the test.

Good Items

In creating a test, the test author tries to select items which will give reliable and valid results. Although the test user has no control over the test items, knowledge of the principles of item construction may help him to evaluate tests.

Good test items are unambiguous (with the exception of some personality tests where ambiguity is deliberate). There should be only one possible interpretation of the question, and if choices are offered in an ability test, competent judges should agree that there is only one acceptable answer. Questions should be stated so that the person knows what is wanted; all failures will then depend upon inability to answer, rather than lack of understanding of the tester's desires. "Catch questions" are undesirable.

Table 10. Percentages of Bright and Dull Children Passing Five Proposed Items for an Intelligence Test[a]

Item	Percent Passing, IQ Below 96	Percent Passing, IQ Above 105
1. Counting backward from 20 to 1 (Year VIII)	35	83
2. Drawing from observation an apple with a pencil through it (Year VIII)	62	57
3. Repeat six digits (Year X)	55	81
4. Binet's suggestion test, 1911 revision (Year X)	80	89
5. Drawing simple designs from memory (Year X)	45	70

[a] Data obtained by Terman in preparing his 1916 intelligence test (**46,** pp. 133–134). Percentages were computed for each test on children of the age at which the test is located.

Good test items measure what the tester wants to measure. This is the principal factor in logical validity of a test. With care the test maker can "purify" his test considerably. One important method of removing test items loaded with irrelevant factors is the *internal-consistency* test. If an item measures what the remainder of the test does, it should have a high correlation with the total test. A simple way of studying the item-test relationship is to select, in any group, a number of persons with high total scores, and another group with low total scores. It is customary to compare the top fourth with the lowest fourth of the group. The percentage of each group giving each answer is studied; if the item measures what the rest of the test measures, far more "good" students than "poor" ones should get the item correct.

An item which does not discriminate (i.e., where both groups are equally often correct) does not measure what the test measures. In Table 10, discrimination data for items of an intelligence test are shown. From these data, item 1 is excellent, but item 2 is quite unsatisfactory.

An even better procedure for selecting items is to test each item against a criterion of what the test is desired to measure. If such a criterion is available, the persons scoring high and low on the criterion are compared on every item.

Good items should have difficulty appropriate to the group tested. The best tests for measuring all levels within a group are those in which the average item difficulty is near 50 percent. Sometimes the test is made easier, so that subjects will not be discouraged by frequent failure. The items may range from a few very difficult ones to a few very easy ones. Items which practically no one passes are of little value, since they do not tell much about individual differences. Items which everyone passes give no information about differences; a few such items may be desirable to build morale and give the subject a "running start" in the test. Very difficult items are valuable to distinguish between superior persons, and easy items discriminate among people far below average.

40. In Table 10, are items 3, 4, and 5 good or poor, by the internal-consistency test?
41. Determine the discriminating power of items 1–10 from the data in Problem 29. Since few cases are available, compare the better half of the subjects to the poorer half.

SOURCES OF INFORMATION ABOUT TESTS

When confronted with a practical task, the tester must determine what tests are available and must select among them on the basis of the criteria just given. Accurate information about tests is therefore essential. For obtaining the names of tests of a particular type, catalogs issued by various publishers and distributors are helpful. These catalogs usually give brief descriptions of the test, and its cost. Many of the leading suppliers of tests are listed in Appendix B. Another important source of test listings is Hildreth's *Bibliography of mental tests and rating scales* (2nd ed.), published by the Psychological Corporation in 1939. A supplement was issued in 1945.

The manual of the test should provide the prospective user with the facts needed to judge its suitability. A satisfactory manual presents evidence of validity and reliability, describes the method of obtaining norms, and provides a basis for deciding what the test measures and how to interpret and use scores. Unfortunately many manuals do not give all these facts. When the facts are given, they are often given without comment, leaving the reader to decide whether the norm sample was adequate, whether the criterion for the validity study was suitable, and so on. Because considerable experience is required to judge the quality of a test with certainty, the user frequently wishes an expert opinion on the test. Buros' *Mental measurements yearbook* (9, 10) is the best single guide for the consumer of tests. Buros has enlisted the services of numerous specialists in testing, each of whom reviews tests with which he is familiar. The reviews are thoroughly critical, stressing differences between tests and limitations which must be considered in interpreting test scores. Each test is reviewed by several specialists wherever possible. Editions of the yearbook were published in 1938, 1941, and 1948; it is planned as a continuing project.

A few scattered sources also provide facts about tests of a particular type. Test users may wish to consult the following:

Review of educational research. "Psychological tests and their uses." National Education Association. Reviews new developments in testing over a three-year period; this feature is contained in the issues of February, 1941, February, 1944, February, 1947, and earlier.

Bennett, George K., and Cruikshank, Ruth N. *A summary of manual and mechanical ability tests.* Psychological Corporation, 1942. Reviews experimental studies on prominent tests in this field, and gives brief evaluations.

Moore, Herbert. *Experience with employment tests.* Studies in Personnel Policy No. 32. National Industrial Conference Board, 1941. Reviews tests of all types with emphasis on their significance for employment.

Borow, Henry, and Whittaker, Betty A. *Tests in industry.* Personnel Service Division, Pennsylvania State College, 1943.

Kaplan, Oscar N. (ed.). *Encyclopaedia of vocational guidance.* Philosophical Library, 1947. Contains descriptions of many tests, usually written by one of the test authors.

42. How acceptable is the point of view expressed in the following (quoted in 4)?
    "It is difficult to construct short tests that will be statistically reliable and valid. On the other hand, it is also difficult to validate a test that would be satisfactory to a psychologist while personnel work remains at its present level. It seemed logical, therefore, that it would be better to lean in the direction of the personnel supervisor's concept of a good test (short, no timing, self-administering, self-scoring, self-rating, easily interpreted, and practical) so that he would accept and use tests and thereby improve his personnel program sufficiently to make available better criteria by which tests can be validated."

43. List the facts which you would expect to be reported in the manual for a group test of intelligence which would help you decide whether to use it or a competing test.

44. "The time for each test (Stenquist Mech. Apt. I and II) is forty-five minutes, the reliability ranges between .67 and .84, and the validity between .66 and .84." How must this statement from a test review be supplemented to make it meaningful?

45. Two reviews are given in Buros' yearbook (10) for the California Capacity Questionnaire. Compare the reviews and attempt to decide why competent psychologists disagree in their evaluation of the test.

SUGGESTED READINGS

Bingham, W. V. "Selection of tests," *Aptitudes and aptitude testing.* New York: Harper, 1937, pp. 209–223.

Blommers, Paul, and Lindquist, E. F. "Rate of comprehension in reading; its measurement and its relation to comprehension." *J. educ. Psychol.*, 1944, 35, 449–473.

Cronbach, Lee J. "Response sets and test validity." *Educ. psychol. Measmt.*, 1946, 6, 475–494.

Ghiselli, Edwin B., Harrell, T. W., and others. Reviews of Pennsylvania Bi-Manual Worksample, in Buros, O. K. (ed.), *The third mental measurements yearbook.* New Brunswick: Rutgers Univ. Press, 1948, pp. 695–698.

Guilford, J. P. "New standards for test evaluation." *Educ. psychol. Measmt.*, 1946, 6, 427–438.

Jenkins, John G. "Validity for what?" *J. consult. Psychol.*, 1946, 10, 93–98.

Kent, Grace H. "The 'Andover' school-entrance test." *J. educ. Psychol.*, 1944, 35, 108–119.

Terman, Lewis M., and Merrill, Maud A. "Development and standardization of the scales—the selection of subjects," in *Measuring intelligence.* Boston: Houghton Mifflin, 1937, pp. 12–21.

Thorndike, Robert L. (ed.). "Problems associated with reliability and reliability determination," in *Research problems and techniques.* AAF Aviation Psychol. Prog. Res. Rep. No. 3. Washington: Govt. Printing Off., 1947, pp. 97–118.

REFERENCES

1. Allen, Mildred M. "Relationship between indices of intelligence derived from the Kuhlmann-Anderson intelligence tests for grade I and the same test for grade IV." *J. educ. Psychol.*, 1945, 36, 252–256.
2. Ayres, L. P. *A scale for measuring the quality of handwriting of school children.* New York: Russell Sage Foundation, 1912.
3. Baldwin, Alfred L. "The appraisal of parent behavior." *Amer. Psychologist*, 1946, 1, 251.
4. Baxter, Brent. "Reliability and validity of the Kopas Wage Earner Battery of Tests." *J. appl. Psychol.*, 1947, 31, 39–43.
5. Beck, Samuel J. *Rorschach's test. I: Basic processes.* New York: Grune and Stratton, 1944.
6. Bennett, George K., and others. *Differential abilities tests, manual.* New York: Psychological Corporation, 1947.
7. Blommers, Paul and Lindquist, E. F. "Rate of comprehension of reading; its measurement and its relation to comprehension." *J. educ. Psychol.*, 1944, 35, 449–473.
8. Bloom, Benjamin S. "Test reliability for what?" *J. educ. Psychol.*, 1942, 33, 517–526.
9. Buros, Oscar K. (ed.). *The 1940 mental measurements yearbook.* Highland Park, N.J.: The Mental Measurements Yearbook, 1941.
10. Buros, Oscar K. (ed.). *The third mental measurements yearbook.* New Brunswick: Rutgers Univ. Press, 1948.
11. College Entrance Examination Board. *46th annual report of the executive secretary.* New York: College Entrance Examination Board, 1946.
12. Cronbach, Lee J. "Studies of acquiescence as a factor in the true-false test." *J. educ. Psychol.*, 1942, 33, 401–415.
13. Cronbach, Lee J. "On estimates of test reliability." *J. educ. Psychol.*, 1943, 34, 485–494.
14. Cronbach, Lee J. "A case study of the split-half reliability coefficient." *J. educ. Psychol.*, 1946, 37, 473–480.

15. Cronbach, Lee J. "Response sets and test validity." *Educ. psychol. Measmt.,* 1946, 6, 475–494.
16. Cronbach, Lee J. "Test 'reliability': its meaning and determination." *Psychometrika,* 1947, 12, 1–16.
17. Davis, C. Jane. "Correlation between scores on Ortho-Rater tests and clinical tests." *J. appl. Psychol.,* 1946, 30, 596–603.
18. DuBois, Philip H. (ed.). *The classification program.* AAF Aviation Psychol. Prog. Res. Rep. No. 2. Washington: Govt. Printing Off., 1947.
19. Eckelberry, R. H., in book review. *Educ. Res. Bull.,* 1947, 26, 138–139.
20. Ferson, M. L., and Stoddard, G. D. "Law aptitude." *Amer. Law Sch. Rev.,* 1927, 6, 78–81.
21. Fitts, Paul M. "German applied psychology during World War II." *Amer. Psychologist,* 1946, 1, 151–161.
22. Flanagan, John C. *Factor analysis in the study of personality.* Stanford Univ.: Stanford Univ. Press, 1935.
23. Ford, Adelbert, and others. *The sonar pitch memory test: a report on design standards.* San Diego: Univ. of Calif. Div. of War Res., 1944.
24. Geldard, Frank A., and Harris, Chester W. "Selection and classification of aircrew by the Japanese." *Amer. Psychologist,* 1946, 1, 205–217.
25. Gilbert, G. M. " 'Aptitude' and training: a suggested restandardization of the K-D music test norms." *J. appl. Psychol.,* 1941, 25, 326–330.
26. Guilford, J. P. "New standards for test evaluation." *Educ. psychol. Measmt.,* 1946, 6, 427–438.
27. Guilford, J. P. (ed.). *Printed classification tests.* AAF Aviation Psychol. Prog. Res. Rep. No. 5. Washington: Govt. Printing Off., 1947.
28. Guttman, L. "A basis for analyzing test-retest reliability." *Psychometrika,* 1945, 10, 255–282.
29. Henry, Sibyl. "Children's audiograms in relation to reading attainment: I. Introduction to and investigation of the problem." *J. genet. Psychol.,* 1947, 70, 211–232.
30. Highsmith, J. A. "Selecting musical talent." *J. appl. Psychol.,* 1929, 13, 486–493.
31. Hildreth, H. M. "Single-item tests for psychometric screening." *J. appl. Psychol.,* 1945, 29, 262–267.
32. Huston, Paul E., and Shakow, David. "Studies of motor function in schizophrenia: III. Steadiness." *J. gen. Psychol.,* 1946, 34, 119–126.
33. Jones, Vernon. "A comparison of certain measures of honesty at early adolescence with honesty in adulthood—a follow-up study." *Amer. Psychologist,* 1946, 1, 261.
34. Leaf, C. T. "Prediction of college marks." *J. exp. Educ.,* 1940, 8, 303–307.
35. Lindner, Robert M., and Gurvitz, Milton. "Restandardization of the Revised Beta Examination to yield the Wechsler type of IQ." *J. appl. Psychol.,* 1946, 30, 649–658.
36. Louttit, C. M., and Browne, C. G. "The use of psychometric instruments in psychological clinics." *J. consult. Psychol.,* 1947, 11, 49–54.
37. Mosier, Charles I. "A critical examination of the concepts of face validity." *Educ. psychol. Measmt.,* 1947, 7, 191–206.
38. Pintner, Rudolf, and others. "Supplementary guide for the Revised Stanford-Binet Scale (Form L)." *Appl. Psychol. Monogr.,* 1944, No. 3.
39. Sartain, A. Q. "Relation between scores on certain standard tests and supervisory success in an aircraft factory." *J. appl. Psychol.,* 1946, 30, 328–332.
40. Scates, Douglas E. "Unit costs in the administration of a standardized test." *Educ. Res. Bull.,* 1937, 16, 38–45.

41. Shuman, John T. "The value of aptitude tests for supervisory workers in the aircraft engine and propeller industries." *J. appl. Psychol.*, 1945, 29, 185–190.
42. Smith, Leo F., and Hogadone, E. B. "Some evidence on the validity of the Cardall Test of Practical Judgment." *J. appl. Psychol.*, 1947, 31, 54–56.
43. Starch, Daniel, and Elliott, E. C. "Reliability of grading high school work in English." *Sch. Rev.*, 1912, 20, 442–457.
44. Starch, Daniel, and Elliott, E. C. "Reliability of grading high school work in mathematics." *Sch. Rev.*, 1913, 21, 254–259.
45. Terman, Lewis M., and Merrill, Maud. *Measuring intelligence.* Boston: Houghton Mifflin, 1937.
46. Terman, Lewis M., and others. *The Stanford revision and extension of the Binet-Simon Scale for measuring intelligence.* Baltimore: Warwick and York, 1917.
47. Thorndike, Robert L. "Two screening tests of verbal intelligence." *J. appl. Psychol.*, 1942, 26, 128–135.
48. Thorndike, Robert L. (ed.). *Research problems and techniques.* AAF Aviation Psychol. Prog. Res. Rep. No. 3. Washington: Govt. Printing Off., 1947.
49. Thurstone, L. L. *The primary mental abilities.* Chicago: Univ. of Chicago Press, 1938.
50. Tiffin, J., and Lawshe, C. H., Jr. "The adaptability test." *J. appl. Psychol.*, 1943, 27, 152–163.
51. Traxler, Arthur E. "A note on the reliability of the revised Kuder Preference Record." *J. appl. Psychol.*, 1943, 27, 510–511.
52. Zyve, D. L. "A test of scientific aptitude." *J. educ. Psychol.*, 1927, 18, 525–546.

CHAPTER 5

How to Give Tests

WHO SHOULD GIVE TESTS?

Tests should be given only by persons who will give them well. Some tests are sufficiently simple for any intelligent adult to give them successfully; others are so subtle that months of special training are required before the tester can do a fully effective job. In general, group tests require less training to administer than individual tests, although there are some exceptions. If the tester has no responsibility save to read a set of printed directions, any conscientious person should be successful. Where it is necessary to question the subject individually and to use follow-up questions when the first answer is unclear, great skill and experience are required.

The tester must take pains and precautions if he wishes to produce results which give every subject a chance to exhibit his ability, and which are comparable to results obtained by other testers. He must prepare for the testing by becoming thoroughly familiar with the test. If he makes errors in administering it, the scores will not be comparable to the norms. Even fairly simple tests usually present one or two stumbling blocks which can be anticipated if the tester studies a manual in advance.

The tester must maintain an impartial and scientific attitude. Testers are usually keenly interested in the subjects they work with, and desire to see them do well. As a result, beginning testers are tempted to give hints to the subject or to coax him toward greater effort. It is the duty of the tester to obtain from each subject the best record he can produce; but he must produce this by his own efforts, without unfair aid. The tester must learn to control both tendencies to give extra help directly and unconscious acts which may give the subject a clue. This is especially a problem in individual testing, where each question is given orally. On a mental-test item where the child is supposed to receive only one trial, he may give an answer which shows that he did not comprehend the question. The tester will often be tempted to repeat the question "since he could certainly have done it if he had understood what was wanted"; this must not be done, since the test directions permit only one trial. Adjustment may be warranted on some borderline decisions, however, such as the case in which the result is discarded, rather than scored as wrong, because an outside disturbance caused the child's failure. Help can be given the subject unconsciously by facial expression or words of encouragement. The person taking a test is always concerned with the question, "How am I doing?" and watches the examiner for indications of his success. Suppose he is given the problem: "Repeat backward 2–7–5–1–4." He may begin "4–1–7 . . ."; if the examiner, on hearing the "7," permits his facial expression to change, the subject may take the hint and catch his own mistake. The examiner must maintain a completely unrevealing expression, while at the same time silently assuring the subject of his interest in what he says.

Maintaining rapport with the subject is necessary if he is to do well. That is, the subject must feel that he wants to coöperate with the tester. A teacher who knows the child, or a counselor who has worked with an adult, can often secure more spontaneous and representative performance than a stranger called in to administer tests. Those who are acquainted with the subject, however, will be less impartial, and must be unusually cautious in following procedures. No rules can be given for the establishment of rapport, but testers with pleasing personalities will develop many techniques. The person who proceeds coldly and "scientifically" to administer the test, without convincing the subject that he regards him as an important human being, will frequently find it difficult to maintain coöperation. Poor rapport is evidenced by inattention during directions, "giving up" on a problem before time is called, restlessness, finding fault with the test, and similar symptoms. Additional suggestions for improving motivation will be made below. The reader who has not observed individual testing of children will probably be interested in the verbatim transcript of a test listed among the readings at the end of this chapter.

The characteristics usually required of a leader are helpful in testing. Poise, a clear voice, good diction, and a pleasant manner are assets to be cultivated by the tester. A tester who is shy may obtain poor results from a group test, until he overcomes his shyness by familiarity with the task.

PROCEDURE FOR TEST ADMINISTRATION

Conditions of Testing

The author of a test provides instructions for testers which must be followed uniformly. But many aspects of the test situation the manual does not discuss. The first of these is the physical situation where the test is given. If ventilation and lighting are poor, subjects will be handicapped. On speed tests particularly, their scores will be lower than they deserve if they do not have a convenient place to write, including sufficient space to spread out whatever materials they need. Subjects must be placed so that they can hear directions and see the gestures of the tester clearly. Very large rooms are generally bad for group testing, unless proctors are stationed to watch closely the performance of subjects. The large room has the disadvantage that a person may hesitate to ask a question about unclear directions which he would raise before a smaller audience. This may be solved by having him raise his hand so that a proctor will come to his seat and answer his question.

The state of the person tested affects the results obtained. If the test is given when he is fatigued, when his mind is on other problems, or when he is emotionally disturbed, results may not be normal for him. Occasionally it is necessary to test a person at an unfavorable time, as when psychological examinations must be given a criminal at the time of his trial, or when tests must be administered during Army induction procedures. In such cases, great care is required if rapport is to be established, and the possible invalidity of results must be noted. A more common illustration of this problem is the giving of tests to college freshmen. These tests, to be used in classification and guidance, are frequently given in the midst of a hectic week of orientation, college activities, establishment of new friends and living arrangements, and adjustment to a semi-adult world. Sometimes a freshman who later proves to be normally intelligent does very badly on placement tests because of homesickness, distraction, emotional exhaustion, or unidentified causes. Tests given under these conditions do have predictive value for most of the group, but many individual scores are untrue as a picture of the student. If a test must be given at a psychologically inopportune time, the only correct procedure is to maintain an adequately critical attitude toward results. Many times, however, testing can be improved by alteration of conditions. Spacing of tests to avoid cumulative fatigue, providing for adequate rest on the night before tests, and administering the program with a minimum of bustle and confusion are helpful.

The Army General Classification Test was often given just after induction when the men lacked sleep, were recovering from a farewell party, or felt ill from inoculations. In one study men who took a second form of the test after having familiarity with it and after becoming stabilized in Army routines raised their scores, some more than one standard deviation. The mean increase was 11.25 points (s.d. of scores = 20 points) (4).

Time of day may influence test scores, but it is rarely an important factor. When subjects are alert and eager, they are more likely to give their best results than when tired and dispirited. Evidence is adequate, however, that equally good results can be produced at any hour if the subjects want to do well. Fatigue apparently affects motivation rather than the ability one can summon up if he tries. The most thorough study was made by psychologists in the Army Air Force. Differences in scores earned at different hours were found to be negligible (10, p. 237). The cadets tested were extremely eager to make good showings, since their opportunity to become pilots hinged on the test results.

The health of the subject usually affects the efficiency of his activities, although here, too, good motivation may overcome handicaps. Since some persons in any large group will be in poor health, no matter when the test is given, the tester should note individuals in poor health so that test scores for them will be recognized as possibly invalid.

Control of the Group

No general rules need be laid down for individual testing, since the more complicated individual tests are learned under supervision, so that faulty procedures are corrected. For successful group testing, a few devices for keeping the group working as a unit are generally applicable. Group testing is essentially a problem in command. The subjects must do as the leader tells them, they must do it instantly, and every person must do the same thing. This attitude must be maintained, without interfering with the opportunity of individuals to ask legitimate questions. One person should be in command; he should be in front of the group, where he can see all members. He will find helpful the adage, "Never give an order unless you expect it to be obeyed." False starts, preliminary attempts to call the group to order while late-comers are still finding seats, and ineffectual gavel-rapping make it more difficult to secure real obedience when work begins. Commands and directions should be given simply, clearly, and singly. The speaker should have full attention before he starts to talk, so that repetition will not be necessary. A complex instruction: "Take your booklet, turn it face down, and then write your name on the answer sheet," will lead to misunderstanding and questions. It is better to break the instruction into unmistakable simple units: "Take your booklet." (Hold a sample up, and watch the group to be sure everyone has taken his booklet before proceeding.) "Turn it face down." (Demonstrate and wait until everyone has complied.) "Now take your answer sheet." (Exhibit a sample, and wait for compliance.) "Write your name on the blank at the top, last name first." By this technique, the subjects have a chance to ask questions whenever they are necessary. But the examiner should attempt to anticipate all reasonable questions by full directions.

Military techniques are effective for control of a group. When a military manner is assumed, however, it may enhance the "inhuman" character of the test situation and give some people the feeling that the examiner is not interested in their welfare. Effective control may be combined with good rapport if the examiner is friendly, avoids an antagonistic, overbearing, or faultfinding attitude, and is informal when formal control is not called for. After establishing control, for example, he may often relax his "command manner" and make informal comments about the test and its purpose; this does not interfere with his resuming formal control for the test proper.

The tester must take care to collect materials so that copies of questions will not be carried away. Persons not taking a test often wish to see copies of the questions, especially when some reward is attached to good test performance. The probability of questions being smuggled out is small, but this can be prevented if each student is given one and only one set of materials when the test begins, and if these are collected from him personally before he leaves.

Exceptional conditions arise which prevent uniform testing of all persons. Occasionally a person becomes ill during the test and must leave the room. Usually it will be possible to collect the materials, indicate that the test is invalidated, and provide for a make-up on another occasion, perhaps with a parallel test. The goal of the tester is to obtain useful information about people. There is no value in adhering rigidly to a testing schedule if that schedule will not give true information. Common sense is the only safe guide in the exceptional situation.

1. The ACE Psychological Examination uses a test booklet and a separate answer sheet, with a special soft pencil. Formulate a set of statements to be made by the tester who, with the assistance of proctors, must collect these materials from a group of 200 adults.
2. An employment office makes the practice of routinely testing all applicants on an intelligence test at the time their applications are filed. One man takes the test, together with several friends, and the group leave together. Ten minutes later he returns, greatly agitated: "Was I supposed to turn over the last page? I thought I had finished when I got to the bottom of page 9, so I looked back over my answers. I had plenty of time, and I'm sure I could have done well on the last page—my friends say the questions there were easy." What should be done in this case, if at the bottom of page 9 the booklet carried the printed statement "Go on to the next page."?
3. In testing a group of college freshmen to obtain information for use in guidance, the examiner finds that a Chinese student, newly arrived from China, is having great difficulty following directions because of unfamiliarity with English. The student asks many questions, requests repetitions, and seems unable to comprehend what is desired. What should the examiner do?
4. In the course of a clinical analysis of a preschool child who is in some way poorly adjusted, a report on a series of tests is requested. The psychometrist who gives the tests finds that the child is persistently negativistic and after coöperating reluctantly with two tests becomes inattentive and careless on the third. Assuming that the test results are needed as soon as possible, what should be done?

Directions to the Subject

The most important responsibility of the tester is giving the proper directions to the subject. The purpose of standardized tests is to obtain measurements which may be compared with measurements given at other times; *it is therefore imperative that the tester give the directions exactly as provided in the manual.* If the tester understands the importance of this responsibility, it is simple to follow the printed directions, reading them word for word, adding nothing and changing nothing. It is usual to provide for the subject to ask questions after the directions have been read. In answering such questions, the tester must not add to the ideas expressed in the standard directions, since such supplementation might give his group an advantage over groups not having such aid. The directions are part of the test situation; in many tests, including certain intelligence tests and projective tests of personality, the way the subject follows directions is intended to influence the score.

This advice is readily followed in most situations, but problems arise when subjects ask questions not provided for in the directions. Some are purely technical ("Do I need an eraser?" "Do we have as much time as we want for the test?"). Other questions that are particularly troublesome deal with matters not mentioned in the standard directions, answers to which would help the student to obtain a better score. Examples are: "Should we guess if we are not certain?" "How much is taken off for a wrong answer?" "Are there any catch questions?" "If I find a hard question, should I skip it and go on, or should I answer every question as I go?" The published directions to the test were evidently not adequate. If the tester refuses to give an answer to the question on guessing—and he must refuse if the scores are to be compared with norms—some subjects will guess and some will not. The directions are therefore standard in a verbal sense only, since procedure becomes unstandardized when members of the group interpret indefinite instructions in their own way. Investigators of aviation performance have pointed out the crucial importance of making sure that the task is clearly defined for the subject. In observing pilots' ability to execute a flying maneuver they found it advisable to tell the subject exactly how the performance would be scored. Otherwise, one pilot would keep his attention on maintaining correct altitude while another of equal ability would earn a different score because he concentrated on maintaining correct heading (7, p. 8). One can recommend that all tests should be provided with directions which leave no ambiguities for variable interpretation. The tester who must use a standard test for which directions are imperfect is faced with a dilemma for which no ideal solution exists.

The projective test is an interesting exception to the traditional psychometric pattern which defines the task very objectively. In this test the subject is given a very vaguely defined task, and the object of testing is to observe how he attacks it. For instance, he may be given an inkblot and told to report what it looks like to him. If he asks how many ideas to report or whether to use the same portion of the blot in two ideas or any other question, he is told, "That's up to you." Of course, the procedure for this test is standardized in its very vagueness, which is kept the same for all subjects.

5. The California Test of Mental Maturity consists of a series of 16 sections, each of which contains a different type of item. The sections are separately timed, each being about 3–5 minutes long. Is there any reason why a high school seeking data for guidance should not give pupils one or two sections of the test each day until all of it is taken, rather than giving it in just two sittings as the manual suggests?

6. "Exact timing of the tests is extremely important. Deviation of even five seconds can increase a score ten points. A score on an incorrectly timed test is valueless." This statement from the test manual refers to the two- and three-minute subtests of the SRA Reading Record. What does the test assume about the way in which eighth- to twelfth-grade pupils will use the working time allotted?

7. Some workers have tried to make the inkblot test more uniform by setting a

definite time, say, two minutes, for responding to each blot. What argument can be advanced against a worker's adopting such a procedure (1, p. 379)?

8. The ACE Psychological Examination (1939 edition) contained several sub-tests, each of which was preceded by practice exercises occupying a total of nineteen minutes. Says a reviewer, "Personal experience indicates that the time devoted to these might be reduced to about two minutes, thus saving about seven minutes, which would allow the test proper to be lengthened" (2, p. 200). Why may a tester not reduce the time for the practice exercise if he wishes?

Guessing

Because misunderstanding of the problem is common, we shall digress to consider the effect of guessing upon test scores. In every test, there are some answers of which the subject is not sure, although his doubt may range from slight lack of confidence in an answer to total ignorance. Some tests direct him to guess when in doubt; others direct him not to guess. The latter direction cannot be followed literally, since there are borderline items where he is neither totally sure nor totally guessing. Experimental studies show that if people know they will be penalized for wrong answers, some are hesitant to answer, but others answer freely even when in doubt (9). This difference in "tendency to gamble" is not eliminated by any change of directions or penalties. As the penalty becomes more severe, guessing diminishes, but the rash still take more chances than the timid.

Guessing affects the score received. If there is no penalty for wrong answers, the guesser receives a better score than the non-guesser of equal ability. It is common for the test constructors to compensate for success due to guessing by a formula for chance correction. If two-choice items are used, there is one chance in two of success by pure guessing, and the score is computed by the formula "Right minus wrong." For a multiple-choice item, the correction formula is "Right minus $\dfrac{\text{wrong}}{n-1}$," where n is the number of choices offered. Numerous technical flaws have been found in these formulas, but the most serious criticism is that they do not "correct for guessing." Guessing is not a matter of pure chance; the guesser should, on the basis of background and common sense, be able to guess the right answer on an aptitude or achievement test more often than if he decided his answer by a chance method, such as rolling dice. If a person guesses on 10 five-choice items, he will probably get at least three or four items right, instead of the two items chance would predict. But another person, who does not guess, will receive a score of zero on the same 10 items, so that the score depends less on knowledge than on the tendency to gamble. Individual differences in this tendency can be eliminated by directing everyone to guess, but guessing introduces large chance errors.

Empirical studies have been made of the reliability and validity of tests given with "guess" and "do not guess" directions. In general such evidence has shown statistical superiority for "do not guess" instructions. For individuals who are over-timid or who guess despite instructions, "do not guess" directions lead to invalid scores, but for the group as a whole these directions seem to give the most useful results. The problem of guessing is less important where the items are at a level of difficulty the person can cope with; chance errors in score are more numerous when many items require guessing.

9. Give a difficult five-choice test, such as the Nelson-Denny vocabulary test, to a friend with instructions to answer items only when fairly certain of the correct answer. When he has finished the test, provide a pencil of another color, and direct him to answer all the remaining items, making the best guess he can. Determine his raw score on each trial with and without correction for chance. Suppose the test were given with "do not guess" directions; how much would he gain or lose by guessing despite the directions?

10. In taking a true-false test scored "Right minus wrong," would a student be wise or unwise to give an answer to every question even when he is uncertain?

11. Some instructors advocate scoring tests by formulas which penalize guessing very heavily, such as "Number right minus twice number wrong." What effect would this have on validity of measurement $(3, 5)$?

12. Discuss the wisdom of the practice described in the following paragraph:

    A vocabulary test constructed for Air Force classification contains 150 five-choice items. The time limit is 15 minutes. The directions state: "This is not a speed test. Your score does not depend so much on how many items you try to answer as it does on how many you get right on each page you attempt."

    The test is actually a speed test, and the score taken is right minus $\frac{\text{wrong}}{4}$.

13. In the SRA Reading Record, Test 2 (Comprehension) presents 16 four-choice items about a paragraph just read. One item is "Methods of harvesting were entirely revolutionized in (a) half a century (b) a decade (c) 200 years (d) a century." In the eighth grade, norms are as follows: 14 right, 99th percentile; 13, 98th; 12, 92nd; 11, 84th; 10, 71st; 9, 67th; 8, 42nd; etc. Suppose that certain pupils, after answering eight items they can recall from the paragraph, use the remaining time to make a best guess on the other eight items. Estimate roughly how much these pupils will raise their percentile scores, if they have normal success in guessing.

MOTIVATION FOR TEST-TAKING

The efficiency of any performance depends upon the strength of the motivation; test-taking is no exception. It is a familiar experience in the home to find Johnny too tired to continue mowing the lawn, only to discover him fully recovered when a baseball game is proposed. This is not necessarily faking; we rarely use our highest level of output unless we have a great deal at stake. The purpose in ability testing is to determine the person's highest level of performance; to do this, it is important that he give as near to his maximum as we can induce him to give. Measuring weight is a simple matter —we place the subject on the scale, and a rather good measure will result no matter how he feels about the measurement. Measuring mental characteristics is quite another matter. The subject must place himself against the scale, and unless he cares what results, no measurement can be had.

Fortunately there are a number of positive motives to lead the subject to do as well as he can. At times, there is an expectation of direct reward from good test performance; this is true in industrial testing and in military classification. In such cases, performance less than one's best is uncommon. Rewards cannot ordinarily be provided, however, where they are not inherent in the purpose of testing. Definitive studies have not been made of the role of external rewards, such as promising a dollar to every person who does better on a test than he did the week before; one can guess that this would produce some changes, but such devices are impractical (8). Where no direct reward is offered, the subject usually is conditioned to good performance by his previous experience in a competitive world. He has been taught to try to surpass others; even where no results are to be published, the urge to "make good" is powerful. Social facilitation may also be helpful in some cases; when one is in the middle of a group, all devoting their efforts in the same way, he must be a rugged individualist indeed to take an attitude less serious than the others. The motivations of our competitive world are not accepted by all persons equally. Most middle-class children are imbued with the spirit of getting ahead through achievement. For them a mental test may be a challenging, exciting experience. Many lower-class children, according to cultural studies, care little about school and educational values; for them the test may be too unmotivated to do them justice.

Positive motivation itself may be harmful in tests where "typical" behavior is sought. As will be seen in connection with personality testing, the urge to "do well" may cause one to distort his answers to some types of tests.

The motivation most helpful to valid testing is a desire on the part of the subject that the score be valid. This is not the normal competitive set, where one desires a high score whether it is true for him or not. It is a scientific set, a desire to find out the truth even if the truth is unpalatable. Such a set, where the subject actually becomes a partner in testing himself, is not usually present in industrial, educational, clinical, and research testing. More nearly, an autocratic approach is followed, something like "Take this test and I shall decide what is to be done with you." Most testers would disclaim any intention of dictatorship, yet it is true that tests have most often been used for the private information of the tester, who then bases recommendations on them.

Coöperation between tester and subject is a not impossible goal. Where psychotherapy or counseling is based on diagnostic testing, where school administration is facilitated through results from standard tests, or where an employment manager must take responsibility for hiring the best-qualified applicants, responsibility will ordinarily not be transferred to the person tested. The point of view, however, that makes the subject a member of the tester's team (and vice versa) can be carried into practice in most situations by taking him into confidence as to the purpose of the testing and letting him feel that the test is an opportunity to find out about himself. The physician often finds it helpful to tell the patient what medicine he is being given and what good results are to be expected from it. If the person taking a test knows what it is measuring and why a fair measurement of that characteristic is to his advantage, he will have little motive to provide an untruthful picture. Perhaps the most "autocratic" of the current uses of testing is in industrial hiring—necessarily so, since the goal of testing is efficiency in industry. Yet the tests given in the hiring line are to the advantage of the person tested, and it will build good will if he knows it. The very facts regarding turnover that motivate the employer to screen applicants are facts which would reassure the worker if he knew them. If he does well on the test, he can have confidence of making good on the job. If he does badly, he would probably be laid off later, whereas the tests will make it possible for him to begin accumulating experience and seniority in another job for which he is fitted.

Indoctrination regarding the nature and purpose of tests is desirable before they are given. When tests are given without explanation, a sort of coöperation is obtained by virtue of the authority of the tester. Explanation makes clear what is to be done and why. An example of possible sound orientation procedure is the film *Cadet Classification* made by the Army Air Corps. Shown to soldiers before testing, the film would be an excellent introduction to the rather awesome array of tests given them. The film showed the tests, gave some insight into their purpose and the importance of following directions, and presented a dramatic scene in which Frank, who was classified by the tests as bombardier rather than pilot, was convinced that "a pilot who cracks up in training is one for the enemy; but a live bombardier over Tokyo is one for our side."

The College Entrance Examination Board, which obtains data to be used as a basis for admission to college, distributes to applicants a booklet of instruction and practice questions well in advance of the test. These questions give candidates an understanding of what is expected. They also reduce the element of surprise and misunderstanding of directions in the excitement of testing.

With young children and clinical cases, reliance on the tester's pleasing personality is more important, but with other subjects understanding the purpose of a test gives every motive to coöperate. If it is practical, a promise to discuss privately the subject's test results is of great motivating value.

14. How could a "coöperative" point of view in testing be adopted:
    a. By a school principal who wishes to divide his eighth grade into sections on the basis of intelligence?
    b. By a veterans' counselor who must approve the plan of a handicapped veteran to go to college and prepare for dentistry?
    c. By a consulting psychologist who is asked by a social agency to diagnose and report on a potential delinquent?
15. What explanation would you give the subject in each of the following cases?
    a. College freshmen are to be tested to determine which ones may fail because of reading deficiency.

b. At the end of a course in industrial relations for foremen, an examination on judgment in grievance cases is to be given.

16. Hebb and Williams devised a test to measure the intelligence of rats (6). The test consisted of a set of mazes to be run, success being scored if a direct path to the foodbox was taken. What problems of motivation would need to be considered in administering this test?

17. In prewar Japan, a young man's chance for success in life depended on his capturing one of the limited number of openings in the higher schools. These vacancies were filled on the basis of competitive examinations and other data. Magazines bearing such titles as *Student days, Examiners' circle,* and *Period of diligent study* were widely circulated. These dealt with topics of interest to candidates including information about test materials, although the tests themselves were of course guarded. Would such magazines increase or decrease the validity of test scores?

18. In planning a competitive mental test to be given all Japanese youth applying for higher schools, two policies appeared possible. One was to devise new types of test items each year, so that knowledge about previous examinations would be of no help. The other proposal favored using the same types of questions every year (for example, number series) but changing the items used. Discuss the relative merits of the plans from the point of view of the test maker, the student, and the person interpreting the results.

19. According to the motion picture "Personnel Selection," British soldiers to be classified were tested in groups. On one test, the agility test, however, each man was tested separately while his group of perhaps 20 others watched. The task called for running back and forth along a cross-shaped pattern, transferring rings from one post to another.

a. What effect on score would be expected from being tested in a group rather than without an audience?

b. What effect would be expected as a result of announcing each man's score at the end of his trial—to be applauded if good?

c. What advantage or disadvantage would a man have who comes last in the group?

It may seem surprising that there are motives which lead to lower, rather than higher, scores, yet this problem is not rare. Sometimes the subject wants to do well, yet earns an unduly low score; at other times he actually desires to do poorly. A common source of poor performance is anxiety and tension due to a strong desire to do well. When one is tense, he is likely to overlook errors that he would readily recognize otherwise. In psychomotor tests, tension leads to poor coördination and more erratic behavior than the best the subject is capable of. The subject who fears criticism of his answers may attempt to avoid it by being overcritical of himself. In individual mental testing, patients filled with anxiety frequently attack their own answers, finding fault with their statements or elaborating them to include all possible variations and qualifications. By this they may spoil an answer which would have received credit. Another familiar mechanism is blocking, where the subject delays his response perhaps through fear of criticism, perhaps through cautiousness and a desire to think through a problem before answering. Some deviation in the direction of cautiousness may be unimportant save as a mark of personality, but cautiousness rooted in emotional tension is likely to depress the score. It is this characteristic which makes it possible to use individual mental tests to diagnose personality deviations (see Chapter 7). It is impossible to remove personality factors from the testing situation, but the tester must do his best to minimize emotionality, while at the same time maintaining a high level of interest on the part of the subject.

When the subject develops fear of a test, not only are the results likely to be unfavorable, but the subject may develop permanently harmful attitudes. Every test is a threat, to some degree, to the pride and status of the subject; it is this quality which makes it challenging. But if one fears the damage the test may do, the pressure becomes highly unpleasant and he seeks an escape. one escape frequently encountered is refusal to respond. Some subjects will say "I don't know" rather than attempt an item where they fear failure. If one tries his best and is defeated, he must admit even to himself that he was incapable of success. If, however, he gives up, making only a half-hearted effort, he has protected himself, since he can rationalize: "I could have done as well as the others if I had tried, but I didn't care what mark I made." Such negativism may be accompanied by attacks upon the test or the examiner; if one rejects a test as "silly," "childish," or "unfair," he has excused himself for failure to perform well.

A test is necessarily a frustrating experience, since it is designed to include many items which the student will fail. Frustration usually disrupts behavior; the task of the tester is to make frustration mild. This can only be done where the threat implied in the test is minor. Few tests are life-or-death matters; but to the subject they may seem so. If a delinquent fears that his punishment will hang on the test results, if a child fears that a poor intelligence rating will disappoint his parents so that he may lose their affection, if a college girl fears that failure will force her to leave her campus friends and return to the farm, if a young man fears that a test will prove him insane, or if an unemployed man fears that he will be unable to get a job if he does poorly, he will be very conscious of the threat from the test. A striking example is the case of the young reserve officer, extremely eager to serve in time of war, who failed his physical examination twice because the importance of passing made him emotional—and the emotion always brought his blood pressure over the acceptable limit. A series of "reconditioning" treatments eventually made it possible for him to take the test calmly. (A more interesting solution was reported in another case, that of a flyer failed repeatedly owing to tension. The examining doctor, sure the young man was physically sound, finally gave up, saying, "I'm sorry, son, but you're out. Your blood pressure readings are just too high. But let's see, since you're washed out anyway, what your blood pressure really is." Relieved by a definite decision, even an adverse one, the young man took the next test calmly, made a satisfactory record, and was approved by the sympathetic doctor.) High blood pressure is more directly an emotional concomitant than is poor thinking, but the situations just described have their mental counterparts. Insofar as the tester can convince the subject that the tests will be used to help him, not to harm him, and that a failure will not debar him from his goals if he is later able to produce evidence of his ability, the validity of scores will be increased. Emphasis must be placed on the positive use of results. A job applicant fearful of failing an aptitude test can be given to understand how test scores may indicate what work he would succeed in. A patient fearing the verdict of a diagnostic test should understand that it will point the way to methods of curing him.

Cases may arise in which the subject frankly wishes to do poorly on a test. There are times when students try to limit their scores on mental tests because of a classification plan in which, it is rumored, the better students will be required to do more work. In military selection, as it becomes suspected that passing certain tests qualifies one for unpopular assignments, there is a temptation to fail them deliberately. Air Corps cadets reported (truthfully or not) having tried to do poorly on tests related to the post of bombardier, so that they would have a better chance of becoming pilots. Another motivation was that of the boy who deliberately failed his school subjects, so that instead of being promoted he would be kept in the grade where his less intelligent friends were to remain.

It is not possible for the tester fully to control motivation. The most helpful recommendation is that he should be aware of the motives in his group, counteract them as well as he can, and discount whatever invalidating effect they may have upon test score.

SUGGESTED READINGS

Biber, Barbara, and others. "Stenographic record of psychological examination," in *Child life in school*. New York: Dutton, 1942, pp. 631–639.
Bingham, W. V. "Administration of tests," in *Aptitudes and aptitude testing*. New York: Harper, 1937, pp. 224–237.
Herben, Mary S. "An analysis of rapport between adult and child, as shown in the psychological test situation," in Thomas, Dorothy S., and others, *Some new techniques for studying social behavior*. New York: Teachers Coll., Columbia Univ., 1929, pp. 161–198.
Lawson, Douglas. "Need for safeguarding the field of intelligence testing." *J. educ. Psychol.*, 1944, 35, 240–247.
Terman, Lewis M., and Merrill, Maud A. "General instructions," in *Measuring intelligence*. Boston: Houghton Mifflin, 1937, pp. 52–71.

REFERENCES

1. Biber, Barbara, and others. *Child life in school*. New York: Dutton, 1942.
2. Buros, Oscar K. (ed.). *The 1940 mental measurements yearbook*. Highland Park, N.J.: The Mental Measurements Yearbook, 1941.
3. Cronbach, Lee J. "The true-false test: a reply to Count Etoxinod." *Education*, 1941, 62, 59–61.
4. Duncan, Acheson J. "Some comments on the Army General Classification Test." *J. appl. Psychol.*, 1947, 31, 143–149.

5. Etoxinod, Count Sussicran. "How to checkmate certain vicious consequences of true-false tests." *Education,* 1940, 61, 223–227.
6. Hebb, D. O., and Williams, Kenneth. "A method of rating animal intelligence." *J. gen. Psychol.,* 1946, 34, 59–65.
7. "Psychological research on pilot training in the AAF." Staff, psychological research project (pilot). *Amer. Psychologist,* 1946, 1, 7–16.
8. Seashore, Harold G. "The improvement of performance on the Minnesota Rate of Manipulation Test when bonuses are given." *J. appl. Psychol.,* 1947, 31, 254–259.
9. Swineford, Frances. "Analysis of a personality trait." *J. educ. Psychol.,* 1941, 32, 438–444.
10. Thorndike, Robert L. (ed.). *Research problems and techniques.* AAF Aviation Psychol. Prog. Res. Rep. No. 3. Washington: Govt. Printing Off., 1947.

PART II
Tests of Ability

CHAPTER 6

The Binet Scale and Its Descendants

EMERGENCE OF INTELLIGENCE TESTING

Tests Before Binet

The outstanding success of scientific measurement of individual differences in behavior has been the intelligence-test movement. Despite the overenthusiasm and occasional errors that have attended their development, mental tests stand today as the most important single tool psychology has developed for the practical guidance of human affairs. Among mental tests, none has been more influential than that fathered by Alfred Binet, in its many forms. A history of mental testing is in large part a history of the Binet test, its antecedents and its descendants.

The first systematic experimentation on individual differences in behavior arose from the accidental discovery of differences in reaction time among astronomers. In 1796, an observatory assistant at Greenwich named Kinnebrook was engaged in recording, with great precision, the instant when certain stars crossed the field of the telescope. When Kinnebrook's results were found to be consistently eight-tenths of a second later than the observations of his superior, the Astronomer Royal, he was thought to have been incompetent in his work and was discharged. It was not until twenty years later that more careful study showed that the differences between observers were the result of the different speeds with which they could respond to stimuli. Only gradually did such differences come to be recognized as significant facts about human nature, rather than annoying errors contaminating scientific work.

Physiologists, psychologists, and anthropologists were stimulated by the scientific climate of the nineteenth century to make a great variety of measurements of human characteristics. Notable among these early workers was Galton, whose interest in differences among individuals was stimulated by Darwin's newly published theory of differences between species. Galton's studies during the latter half of the nineteenth century included numerous explorations of ways of measuring physical characteristics, sensory qualities such as keenness of hearing, mental imagery, and so on. These methods were not developed fully by Galton, but served as models for later tests. In addition, Galton's evidence that outstanding intellectual achievement was often found in successive generations of certain families emphasized that genius was not an accident or a gift of the gods, but rather an important phenomenon to be investigated scientifically.

At this time, psychologists were only beginning to apply objective techniques, and naturally turned their attention first to those things which could readily be studied in the laboratory. Wundt, with his laboratory in Leipzig, won a notable triumph in developing objective psychological laws comparable to those of physics. Necessarily, however, the search for such simple laws led him and his students to concentrate on simple phenomena. Moreover, since it was thought that the function of science was to analyze behavior into its simplest elements, a deliberate search was made for procedures having high logical validity, measuring very limited functions. While Wundt was not concerned with individual differences, his laboratory methods had a strong influence on early tests. As early as 1890, Cattell brought to the United States from Germany a collection of tests of such functions as sensory acuity, strength of grip, and memory. This development unfortunately met an early debacle when it was discovered that, while measuring "pure" characteristics, the new tests seemed to have no relation to significant human behavior. The crucial study was Wissler's work on test scores of Columbia students, reported in 1901. He correlated college marks with many of the Cattell tests, finding such negligible correlations as the following: reaction time, $-.02$; canceling a's from a printed page rapidly, $-.09$; naming colors, .08; auditory memory (recall of digits), .16 (48). Apart from the insignificant functions tested, low correlations were certain to result because of two principles mentioned in Chapter 4: brief tests are quite unreliable, and validity coefficients are always reduced when a group is highly selected. The disappointment which followed the Wissler study, however, delayed attempts to use measurement in applied psychology.

A third line of attack stemmed from abnormal psychology. The tests of Galton were a miscellaneous lot suitable to studying human variation in general; the psychophysical tests were selected because they were precise and suitable to the laboratory. In contrast, the tests of the early clinical workers were intended to serve a practical end. To study mental defectives and pathological cases, clinicians required tests of complex mental functioning. Numerous workers, notably Kraepelin in Germany, developed tests which were of value in distinguishing normal from abnormal subjects. Few of these tests, however, were perfected to the point of clinical usefulness.

The Binet Tests

Alfred Binet, a French psychologist, had become interested in studying judgment, attention, and reasoning. His interest in these more complex mental processes led him to try a greater variety of tests than his predecessors used. Binet was concerned with obtaining insight into real behaviors and did not restrict himself to "pure" measures. In studies published between 1893 and 1911, he explored in many ways the differences between bright and dull children. With little preconception regarding this difference, he tried tests including recall of digits, suggestibility, size of cranium, moral judgment, tactile discrimination, mental addition, graphology—and palmistry! As he found, with the earlier investigators, that the tests of sensory judgment and other simple functions seemed to have little relation to general mental functioning, he gradually formulated a description of intelligence as "the tendency to take and maintain a definite direction; the capacity to make adaptations for the purpose of attaining a desired end; and the power of auto-criticism" (41, p. 45).

The stage was set, then, for the call in 1904 to produce the first practical mental test. The schools of Paris became concerned about their many nonlearners and decided to remove the hopelessly feeble-minded to schools where they would not be held to the standard curriculum. Aware of the errors in teacher judgment, they wished to avoid segregating the child of good potentiality who could learn if he tried and the troublemaking child whom the teacher wanted to be rid of. Moreover, they wished to identify all the dull from good families whom teachers might hesitate to rate low, and the dull with pleasant personalities who would be favored by the teacher. Therefore they asked Binet to assist in producing a method for separating the genuinely dull from those who had adequate educability. Binet's scale, which drew on his earlier studies, was published in collaboration with Simon in 1905. In 1908, a revision was published. The tests were arranged in order of difficulty, so that a child passing those tests normally passed by ten-year-olds could be considered their mental equal in average performance. Still another revision was produced in 1911. The Binet scale, as it stood then, differs only in detail from the individual tests for children in widest use today.

At the time Binet's tests were made available, there was a great demand for objective methods of investigating psychological problems. American psychological research had been dominated for years by introspection and questionnaire techniques, both of which were as fallible as the judgment of the subject reporting. Binet's method, which was to a large degree impartial and independent of the preconceptions of the tester, was welcomed enthusiastically as a research technique and as a tool for studying subnormal children. In 1910, Lewis M. Terman began experimentation with the Binet tests and produced, in 1916, the Stanford Revision of the Binet Scale. He extended its application with normal and superior children. The Stanford-Binet had immediate popularity and became, rightly or wrongly, the yardstick by which other tests were judged. Although there had been various prior mental tests, the outstanding popularity of the Stanford test made its conception of intelligence the standard. The acceptance of the Stanford test was due to the care with which it had been prepared, its success in testing complex mental activities, the easily understood "IQ" it provided, and the important practical results which it quickly produced. Although many criticisms have been made of the test, it was and is an exceptionally useful tool.

Changes in individual intelligence testing since 1916 have been minor. A few new test forms were adopted, and several revisions of Binet's test were made by psychologists other than Terman, but all in all, present-day testing is traceable to the 1916 Stanford-Binet in form and conception. The student should not assume that other tests before and after Binet had no merit, merely because they failed to attain comparable prominence. It is probable that the early workers explored many leads which were worth exploitation and which have been unduly neglected. Binet himself (following the lead of earlier workers) made use of inkblots to study imaginative and perceptual processes, but this technique fell into obscurity from which it emerged only because Rorschach, twenty years later, independently revived the procedure. In his monograph, *The experimental study of intelligence,* Binet described the application of inkblot and imagery tests to his daughters, coming out with clinical, qualitative descriptions of the way their intelligence functioned which read as if taken from the most modern results of projective techniques (35, pp. 146–150). This lead, which psychologists are today pursuing, was neglected while the less informative plan of reducing all intelligence to a single score was adopted. The accidents of time and place play a large part in psychological history; there was, in 1905, a great practical need for a simple and objective way of comparing children, but no popular demand for diagnostic clinical tools.

The 1916 Stanford-Binet was replaced in 1937 when Terman and Merrill published Forms L and M of the Stanford-Binet. These tests improved on the construction of the former edition and offered the marked advantage of two comparable forms, so that the child could not increase his score on a re-test by remembering particular questions.

Other Developments

Other individual tests have been designed for special needs. Some tests have stressed "non-verbal" or "performance" items, which give a fairer estimate of intellect for children with language handicaps. Tests have been designed for special age groups, from preschool children to adults. One of the most significant of these is the Wechsler-Bellevue Intelligence Scale. This test, first designed for adults and now being extended to earlier ages, is discussed at length in the next chapter.

During the time of the emergence of individual tests, group tests also became widely popular. Several psychologists had devised experimental group tests prior to 1916, but it remained for World War I to give group testing its main impetus. When it became necessary to expand the Army at an explosive rate, the Army requested psychologists to provide a group test for inductees so that those who were promising could be given officer training, those who were unfit could be rejected, and others could be appropriately classified. In one of the major achievements of practical psychology, a group including Terman, Yerkes, and Bingham assembled (on the basis of test materials provided by A. S. Otis) a test which, after experimental revision, became famous as Army Alpha. Alpha was a test of ability to follow directions, simple reasoning, arithmetic, and information. It was a practical test, easily administered and highly useful to the Army, as Figure 18 suggests. It convinced people that adequate prediction of human success could be made by mass processing, so that following the war schools and industry demanded tests of this type. Alpha in a civilian revision and comparable group tests by Otis and others were widely applied. Tests being published today, and those used in World War II classification, differ only slightly from those

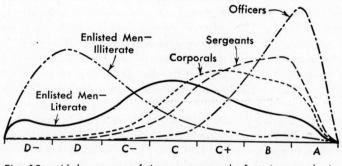

Fig. 18.   Alpha scores of Army personnel of various ranks in
World War I (49).

of the 1920 vintage. The principal difference is that care in construction has made the newer tests more reliable and provided better norms.

One major development has been the emergence of diagnostic mental tests, which seek to measure separately the various aspects of mentality instead of arriving at a single intelligence rating. The most complete development of this approach is found in Thurstone's Tests of Primary Mental Abilities. Thurstone has separated mental functions into such aspects as verbal, number, space, and reasoning, and has prepared separate tests of these abilities. While the many separate tests require more time than the usual test of general ability, they provide more information and will probably have practical importance. To date, they have been used principally for research.

The foregoing history is far too sketchy to do justice to the numerous contributors to present-day testing, or to indicate the serious and significant controversies regarding intelligence which were gradually resolved. The reader who wishes to trace the emergence of current concepts will find Peterson's book (35) especially helpful.

CHARACTERISTICS OF THE STANFORD-BINET SCALE

Assumptions About Intelligence

In the Binet scale, as in every test to be studied, one can trace how the investigator solved four problems which face every test designer. First, he must

decide just what he intends to measure. Second, he must invent or select
items which adequately serve that purpose. Third, he must find a measuring
unit in which to express results, since behavior rarely can be divided into
such countable units as inches, pounds, or light-years. Fourth, he must show
the validity of the test, usually by relating it to an external criterion. Knowing
how these were answered for the Binet test not only reveals wherein it made
a contribution but also throws light on its limitations.

The person making the first mental test is in the position of the hunter
going into the woods to find an animal no one has ever seen. Everyone is sure
the beast exists, for he has been raiding the poultry coops, but no one can
describe him. Since the forest contains many animals, the hunter is going to
find a variety of tracks. The only way he can decide which one to follow is by
using some preconception, however vague, about the nature of his quarry. If
he seeks a large flat-footed creature he is more likely to bring back that
carcass. If he goes in convinced that the damage was done by a pack of small
rodents, his bag will probably consist of whatever unlucky rodents show their
heads.

Binet was in just this position. He knew there must be something like intelligence, since its everyday effects could be seen, but he could not describe
what he wished to measure, as it had never been isolated. Some workers, then
and now, have objected to this circular and tentative approach whereby intelligence can only be defined after the test has been made. Tests are much
easier to interpret if the items conform perfectly to a definition laid down in
advance. When faculty psychology was in vogue, many separate tests were
designed for the separate mental faculties: reasoning, memory, attention,
sensory discrimination, and so on. None of these tests used singly, however,
was found to be useful. Terman explains this as follows:

"The assumption that it is easier to measure a part, or one aspect, of intelligence
than all of it, is fallacious in that the parts are not separate parts and can not be
separated by any refinement of experiment. They are interwoven and intertwined.
Each ramifies everywhere and appears in all other functions. . . . Memory, for example, cannot be tested separately from attention, or sense discrimination separately from the associative processes. After vainly trying to disentangle the various
intellective functions Binet decided to test their combined functional capacity without any pretense of measuring the exact contribution of each to the total product"
(45, p. 151).

We will see in later chapters how diagnostic tests have, in spite of this, obtained useful information about distinct aspects of ability. In Binet's time,
though, one of his great contributions was to abandon the idea of separate
functions for the concept of general intelligence. Having started with the
idea that some children were bright and some dull, he found quickly that
those who were best on tests of judgment were also superior on tests of attention, memory, vocabulary, and other mental activities. In other words, the
tests were correlated. This correlation shows that there must be some under-

lying unity among mental tests. This is what psychological testers mean by "general intelligence"; it is the factor which accounts for the correlation among mental tests.

Binet refined his idea of intelligence by trial and error. If color matching does not correlate with other estimates of mental ability, it must not be influenced by the common factor. If knowing certain information correlates with the tests of reasoning, both must be in part measures of intelligence. Out of a study of his best test items, Binet came to his famous description, quoted above. Binet also inferred that intelligence increases as one approaches maturity.

1. What do the following definitions of intelligence include that Binet's definition does not, and vice versa?
    a. "The ability to do abstract thinking" (Terman).
    b. "The power of good responses from the point of view of truth or fact" (E. L. Thorndike).
    c. "The property of so recombining our behavior patterns as to act better in novel situations" (Wells).
2. Would the same sort of test items be called for by these definitions?
3. Is previous learning included in intelligence by these definitions, and by Binet's?
4. Binet first sought to study brightness and dullness by comparing children of the same age whom their teachers considered superior or inferior. Might the children selected for him differ in any factors other than general intelligence?

Selection of Items

If we were testing high-jumping ability, we would ask a boy to jump over standards of varying heights, beginning with easy ones and increasing the height until we found the highest level at which he could succeed. The experimental psychologist uses the same device in measuring weight discrimination. The test begins with pairs of weights which are easily discriminated, and as the subject succeeds the difference in weights is reduced until he can no longer tell which is heavier. The Binet test adopts a similar "hurdle" pattern. It begins with items the subject is expected to pass. As the items become more difficult, the subject begins to fail, and the test is continued until we have discovered the most difficult mental hurdle he can get over.

Since mental ability is thought of as something that increases with age, a good test item is one that is passed by older children, but not by younger ones. We would reject a proposed exercise that 25 percent of children of every age can pass; although this item is difficult, it does not relate to mental development. Items for the Binet test and its revisions were tested by determining how many children at each age can pass them. How items are tested is illustrated in Figure 19, which is based on the standardization data for the 1937 test. Item A is a very good item, by the criterion of increase with age. It is rarely passed by those under 10, and is passed by almost all 16-year-olds. In contrast, item B is one of the least satisfactory items retained in the test; it shows very slight increases with age above 11. Items which showed even less relation to age were eliminated in making up the revision.

Binet's assumption, that a good item measures the same thing as other items, was also applied. Each item was correlated with the total scale (cf. Table 10). The correlations varied greatly; item A, just discussed, correlated .91 with total score of 13-year-olds, but the correlation for B was only .27.

Items are placed in the scale according to their difficulty for children at each age. A test which about 60 percent of 13-year-old children can pass is

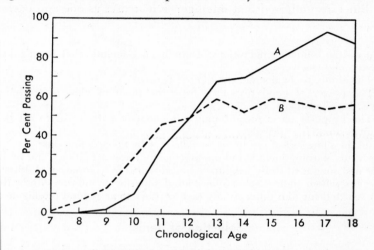

Fig. 19. Percentage of children of each age passing two Stanford-Binet items. (Data from **27**, p. 96.) A, Item from Form M, Year XIII—defining *connection, compare,* etc. B, Item from Form M, Year XIII—memory for details of story.

placed at Year XIII. Both item A and item B are placed at Year XIII. The percentage level used in placing a test varies from age to age. Tests passed by about 77 percent of two-year-olds are placed at Year II; tests passed by about 63 percent of eight-year-olds go into the Year VIII hurdle. Because adjustments are made to make the mean IQ 100 at all ages, all items placed at the same level are not exactly equal in difficulty.

5. Some nine-year-olds pass item A (Fig. 19). What tentative conclusion can be made about their mental age? Why is this conclusion merely tentative?
6. A Japanese investigator wishes to prepare a counterpart of the 1937 Stanford-Binet for Japanese children. In what ways would a mere direct translation of the test be unsatisfactory?

Description of Test

The child is given the Binet test by an experienced examiner, who gives each test in the precise manner called for by the directions (**44**). The examiner begins by establishing rapport, aided by the high interest value the "games" have for the younger child and the challenge of the test situation for the older child. The first tests tried are those for a mental level below that expected of the child; beginning with easier tests builds confidence. The *basal age*, the scale level at which the child can pass all the tests, is determined. Tests at each higher level are given, usually six at each level. The test is continued until the child fails all tests at some level.

In Forms L and M, tests have been prepared for levels of mental development from Year II to Superior Adult III. At the earliest years, ages two to five, there are six tests at each half-year of development. Above age five, hurdles are spaced one year apart; and above age 14, the levels have even wider spacing. No child takes the entire set of 129 tests. A nine-year-old would begin with tests for the eight-year level and, if he passed those, would continue until he could no longer succeed. Some nine-year-olds would be unable to go beyond the 11-year level, whereas others would still be passing a few tests at the 14-year level.

Administering the test requires a good deal of skill. The tester must exercise considerable judgment in obtaining from each child as clear answers as possible, without probing more than the standardized directions allow. Rapport is especially a problem with younger children, who are not habituated to tests or to tasks calling for sustained attention. One hour, more or less, is required for each test, although there is great variation from child to child.

Only those persons should give the Stanford-Binet who have been trained in its use and scoring. Terman suggests that an adequate training program calls for a general course in mental test theory, a second course in methods during which the student tests at least 25 subjects, and further experience in clinical courses where the student gives the test to various kinds of subjects. Training may be considered complete when the person has tested about 100 cases, beyond the 25 practice subjects.

The test includes a great variety of tasks. The range of mental abilities tapped is illustrated in Table 11. The following test, "Verbal absurdities," at Year IX, Form L, is representative (**44**, p. 108):[1]

"Procedure. Read each statement and, after each one, ask 'What is foolish about that?' If the response is ambiguous, say, 'Why is it (that) foolish?'
"(a) Bill Jones' feet are so big that he has to pull his trousers on over his head.
"(b) A man called one day at the post office and asked if there was a letter waiting for him. 'What is your name?' asked the postmaster. 'Why,' said the man, 'you will find my name on the envelope.'
"(c) The fireman hurried to the burning house, got his fire hose ready, and after smoking a cigar, put out the fire.
"(d) In an old graveyard in Spain they have discovered a small skull which they believe to be that of Christopher Columbus when he was about ten years old.

---

[1] Reproduced by permission of Houghton Mifflin Company.

Table 11. Representative Tasks from Stanford-Binet Test, Form L, Arbitrarily Grouped According to Behavior Called For

Year	Information and Past Learning		Verbal Ability	
II–6	*Points to toy object "we drink out of."	.69[a]	*Names chair, key, . . .	.41
	*Shows doll's hair.	.43	*Names objects from pictures.	.78
IV	*Shows "what we cook on" in picture.	.56	*Names objects from picture.	.74
VI	*Gives examiner 9 blocks.	.56	*Vocabulary: defines *orange, envelope.*	.65
VIII	*"What makes a sailboat move?"	.66	*Vocabulary: *eyelash, roar.*	.75
			*Finds absurdity in simple story.	.70
X			*Vocabulary: *muzzle, haste.*	.84
			*Names 28 words in one minute.	.46
XII			*Vocabulary: *skill, juggler.*	.79
			*Defines *constant, defend.*	.74
			*Finds absurdity in simple story.	.64
			*Completes "The streams are dry	
			there has been little rain."	.61
XIV			*Vocabulary: *brunette, peculiarity.*	.89
			*Defines *constant, defend.*	.83

* These tests are used if the scale must be abbreviated.
[a] Numbers are correlations of the test with the total test score, for pupils at the age level where the test is located (**27**, Table 53). The grouping of tests is based in part on McNemar's factor analysis (**27**, pp. 124–137).

"(e) One day we saw several icebergs that had been entirely melted by the warmth of the Gulf Stream."

The child passes this for two months' credit on his mental age score at Year IX if three items are solved satisfactorily. Four correct allow two more months' credit at Year XII.

Tests call for both verbal and non-verbal performances, simple memory and complex reasoning, familiar situations to which answers have been learned and novel problems where ability to adapt is called for. Those involving apparatus and pictures are used at younger ages, with an increasing

Table 11. (Continued)

Memory	Perception	Reasoning
*Repeats "4–7." .62	Formboard .46	
	Draws missing leg on man. .47 *Matches circles, squares. .72	"Why do we have houses?" .78
*Reproduces bead chain after seeing sample. .58	Finds missing part of picture of wagon. .46 *Finds unlike form in row of pictures. .73	Maze .60
Recalls story read by examiner. .70		*Tells how baseball and orange are alike and different. .75
*Reads paragraph aloud, recalls content. .49		*Finds absurdity in picture. (See Fig. 20.) .38
Repeats "4–7–3–8–5–9" .45		*Gives reason why children should not be noisy in school. .53
*Repeats backward, "8–1–3–7–9" .50		Describes picture; must make connected story .55
		Finds absurdity in picture. .60
		*Generalizes from paperfolding experiment. .75
		*Explains how to measure 3 pts. of water with a 7-pt. can and a 4-pt. can. .57 "Which direction would you have to face so that your *left* hand would be toward the east?" .57

reliance on verbal problems through the school ages, and more tests of abstract thinking at the upper end of the scale. In Table 11, representative tests are classified according to an arbitrary scheme. There is no evidence that scores on the items grouped together are determined by the same special mental ability, although some children show consistent weakness on verbal, reasoning, or some other type of problem. Most of the tests involve several types of performance; the maze, for example, calls for perception, reasoning, and comprehending verbal directions.

Responses are scored as objectively as possible, with the aid of the scoring guide. The guide may be illustrated with respect to the ten-year-level item reproduced in Figure 20. The absurdity, of course, is that the white man should not be shooting at the distant Indian when he is in immediate danger from the other two. The manual lists the following as acceptable answers: "He's just aiming at one Indian and the others could knock him over the head." "He's shooting at the Indian that's far away." There are five such samples given. Sample unacceptable answers include the following: "There's a hunting man, there's Indians there, they're going to kill him, he's standing there, he ain't running." "These are standing right by him letting him shoot the other fellow." "There's a man and he's dressed too modern to be in times

Fig. 20.   "What's foolish about that picture?"—a Stanford-Binet item (44).

of Indians—got too modern a gun" (44, p. 254). The principal difficulty in scoring this item occurs when a child does not explain clearly what he believes the absurdity to be. Skillful questioning is needed to obtain adequate elaboration in some cases.

7. Judge the following answers to the problem in Figure 20 right or wrong. (These answers are taken from the Pintner *et al.* "Supplementary guide" [36].)
    a. Three Indians are trying to hit this man on head when he tries to shoot them.
    b. This Indian (pointing to Indian in distance) trying to fight with white man (pointing).
    c. He hasn't a straight aim at the Indian; Indian will kill him, he should aim at first Indians, not back one.
    d. Indian has peculiar clothes. I should think man would be shooting at the nearest Indian.
8. Which of the terms introduced on pages 13 to 17 apply to Form L of the Stanford-Binet in whole or part?

What the Test Measures

A study of the items in Table 11, or, better, of the entire test, is the best way of understanding what a Binet IQ represents. Since most subsequent intelligence tests have been made to have high correlations with the Stanford-Binet, most statements about the meaning of "Binet intelligence" apply also to scores from other tests.

The reader will probably agree that most of the test items do fit Binet's definition of intelligence, in that they call for ability to maintain a definite set, adaptation, and self-criticism. That the items all measure some common element, which is named "general intelligence," is demonstrated by the correlations between each item and the total test. But a thoroughgoing analysis must do more than accept items because they include an element we wish to measure. An equally important question is: What elements affect the score that are not considered in the definition? Logical analysis plus various experimental studies have led to several general conclusions on this matter.

1. *The Stanford-Binet test measures present ability, not native capacity.* While it seems obvious that no test can measure anything but here-and-now behavior, there has been much confusion in the past thirty years because intelligence was thought of as hereditary. While there is necessarily an inborn potentiality, the test measures only present ability, which is affected by both innate factors and experiences. If a user wishes to infer that a difference between Binet test scores of two children represents an innate difference, he must assume that the two children have had much the same experience during their lives. If a child has had the same opportunity as normal children to acquire skills, information, and work attitudes called for by the tests, any failure to come up to normal performance must be due to his having failed to profit from his opportunities.

Binet himself never considered that his tests measured an innate capacity. While it is clear that for most children rank in intelligence is fairly constant because their environment is fairly constant, one must not assume that the IQ corresponds exactly to native capacity. The ability level can of course be changed by radical changes in environment, although we have found no general techniques for "mental orthopedics" (Binet's term) which will accelerate significantly the mental development of normal children from normal homes.

It is easy to list variations in experience that would make it easier for one child than another to pass the Binet tasks, even if they had equal native ability. Johnny was ill during much of the first grade; he is now a poorer reader than others. Freddie is only five, but his father has played number games with him so that he can count and add very well. Harold's mother did not like having her walls marked, so she refused to let Harold use pencils or crayons except under her supervision; Harold, at seven, doesn't seem to enjoy drawing and is clumsy at it. Sarah lived in a rural area, where she never saw trains or telephones, although their pictures were in her story books. Peter's parents are refugees; although both parents can speak English, they find it difficult and always use German at home. Frances has a set of children's puzzle books which include interesting puzzles, pictures containing absurdities, and pictures to compare to see if they are alike or different. Variations such as these are common in any group and may be counted on to raise or depress both test performance and school performance.

9. List for each of these children some of the tests in Form L which they would find easier or harder than children with "normal" experiences.
10. Which items in Table 11 depend upon previous school learning?
11. Which items would offer an advantage to a child from an upper-class home compared to a child from an impoverished working-class home?

2. *Stanford-Binet scores are strongly weighted with verbal abilities.* The great majority of test items call for facility in using and understanding words. If the child does poorly at these tasks, he probably will do poorly in other verbal activities. He may do badly on the test because of poor schooling, but this will also cause him to do badly in school in the future. The Binet test is an excellent measure of scholastic aptitude, of readiness to do the sort of tasks required in school. Since Binet originally sought tests which would identify superior and inferior pupils, as judged by their school performance, it is not surprising that the final test measures a general ability common in school work. If one were to examine intelligent acts outside of school, it might be found that verbal facility is not so widely important. The test is not a measure of all types of mental ability; various writers have commented on its underemphasis on insight, foresight, originality, organization of ideas, and so on. A high score on the test should not be interpreted as guaranteeing qualities which the test does not measure.

Table 12. Mean IQ's of Monolingual and Bilingual Children on the Binet Test and a Performance Test (12)

Test	Mean IQ for Monolinguals (N = 106)	Mean IQ for Bilinguals (N = 106)	Difference[a]
Stanford-Binet	98.7	90.9	7.8
Atkins Object-Fitting	89.0	97.5	−8.5

[a] Significance tests show that neither difference could be due to chance.

Among the pupils for whom this verbal loading causes the Stanford-Binet to give an unfair picture of intelligence as a whole are bilingual children, children from homes where experiences with English are limited, children with hearing deficiencies, and children who have had difficulty in reading. The examiner can often identify such cases by their relatively superior performance on items not stressing language. Table 12 compares the IQ's of children who speak only English, with bilinguals who speak a second language at home. Both groups were tested on the 1937 Binet and the Atkins

Object-Fitting Test, a performance test for preschool children which does not demand facility in English. It is evident that the bilingual group, which showed superiority on the non-verbal test, would be judged inferior on the Binet test.

12. Suppose one were faced with Binet's original problem, of deciding whether a pupil failing in school could profit from the regular curriculum. If the pupil is bilingual, which test would serve better?

3. *The Stanford-Binet score represents somewhat different mental abilities at different ages.* This is apparent from the shift of emphasis in Table 11. Early tests call for judgment, discrimination, and attention. Verbal tests and reasoning play a smaller part until later years. If all the tests measured general intelligence equally well, this would be no problem. From the evidence to date, the simple mental developments of early childhood predict only roughly the later emergence of verbal and higher mental abilities. While the early levels of the test are excellent in testing a child to be sure he is making normal progress, IQ's at preschool ages do not predict accurately the subject's later standing.

The clearest study on this comes from Maurer's work with the Minnesota preschool tests, which are similar to the early Binet levels. Maurer followed a group from preschool years to late adolescence, and retested them to determine what preschool test items had best predicted intellect at maturity. At maturity she used a group test, which is heavily weighted with verbal materials, but which is also highly correlated with both Binet scores and school success. She found that many items which correlated well with the total preschool scale were poor predictors of later development. Among the poor items were pointing out parts of the body, obeying simple commands, comprehension, and paper folding (28).

It is significant that functions tested during the stage when they are just emerging are poor predictors. That is to say, performance is unstable in the early portions of a learning curve. Anderson argues that vocabulary is a good test, at later ages, just because it is a learning based on a long period of environmental stimulation (2, p. 21). Maurer confirms this in her summary of the characteristics of good predictive tests for preschool ages (28, pp. 85–86): "[Good] tests for younger children make only minimal demands on language. They require perception of form and spatial relationships and the ability to reproduce them. They do not demand complex motor coordinations. They require controlled attention and ability to persist to a goal. Many of them are comparatively independent of training. Tests for older children [4–5 years] involve use of language in relationships which are not often practiced and constitute problem-solving situations involving the use of well-developed tools. Only two tests (response to pictures and naming colors) seemed to test skills in the early stages of formation."

4. *The test requires experiences common to the American urban culture,*

and is therefore of dubious value for comparing different cultural groups.
The Zuñi Indians, for example, have a coöperative society most unlike the
competitive attitudes we tend to encourage. Zuñi children have races. But a
child who wins several races is censured, as he has made others lose face.
Instead, he must learn to win some races, to show he is capable, and then to
hold back and give others an opportunity to win. In arithmetic, white teachers sent Zuñi children to the blackboard for arithmetic drills, with instructions to do a problem, then turn their backs to the board when finished. Instead, the pupils faced the board until the slowest had finished; then all
turned. This was to them simply courtesy; following the teacher's direction
would have been exhibitionism. It is easy to see why the typical American
speed test gives misleading results among the Zuñi. A Binet test fares no
better; the first subject may fail some items deliberately, because he fears the
next child will be unable to answer. All intelligence tests face the same problem; they are adequate for comparing persons with similar experience, but
white Americans would perhaps do badly on a test developed by a Zuñi
psychologist, using questions which differentiated between good and poor
Zuñis.

The influence of culture on performance is especially well shown by an
analysis of scores on the Goodenough Draw-a-Man Test in various Indian
tribes (17). In this test for young children, the child is asked to draw the
best man he can. Children of six Indian tribes were tested. The mean IQ
was computed by Goodenough's method, which scores the completeness
and realism of the drawing fairly objectively. For one group of Hopis, the
mean IQ for boys was 123; for girls, 102. Similarly, other Hopis and Zias
showed large differences favoring boys. For Navahos, on the other hand,
the mean IQ's were boys, 107; girls, 110. Anthropologists explained these
differences, pointing out, for example, that the Hopi boy is stimulated to
observe and work with his world, while girls' activities are limited to routine household tasks. Zia boys are encouraged to draw from infancy, whereas
girls rarely draw except in school. Boys are expected to paint animals on the
house walls at Christmas to encourage fertility, and to otherwise aid in
ceremonial painting. Girls paint only conventional pottery designs. In Nav-
aho tribes, however, boys and girls have similar experiences and opportunities to learn art. The Draw-a-Man showed correlations with the Arthur
Performance Scale ranging as low as .10 and .20, even though both are regarded as tests of intelligence in the white culture. Obviously, a test is indicative of innate aptitude only when all persons compared have similar
backgrounds.

5. *The Binet test does not give a reliable measure of separate aspects of
mentality.* Scores, however, are heavily influenced by abilities other than
general intelligence. It would be helpful if we could divide the Binet test
into segments and obtain separate estimates of verbal ability, information,
and so on. McNemar's factor analysis (27) effectively shows that this is not

possible. He finds that for the average Binet item, the general intelligence factor accounts for about half of what the item measures. The extent to which any item measures "general intelligence" is shown by the correlation between the test and the total score (Table 11). The other half of the variation between individuals is accounted for by miscellaneous knowledges and abilities which are irrelevant to the purpose of the test. Any particular specific factor is rarely found in more than one or two items; therefore it is not practical to identify these factors in separate scores. Since Binet and Terman deliberately sought a great variety of tests, so that no one subdivision of intelligence would have great weight in the final score, the Binet tests are necessarily unsuitable for diagnosing separately the various aspects of ability.

13. What sort of items have the greatest correlation with total test score at levels II–6 and IV? What does this suggest regarding the meaning of "general intelligence" in these scales?
14. What items have the greatest loading of "general intelligence" at the upper end of the scale? What is the meaning of "general ability" at that level?
15. Items having low correlations with total score are naming objects (II–6), repeating digits (X), and picture absurdities (X). What factors other than "general mental development" might influence these items?
16. The Stanford-Binet test has been criticized because it contains numerous items relating to death and other morbid subjects. What has this to do with the value of an intelligence test, so long as brighter pupils pass these items?

6. *The Binet score is influenced by the subject's personality and emotional habits.* In fact, Binet's description of intelligence involves persistence, flexibility of mental approach, and criticalness, all of which are regarded as important in clinical concepts of personality. Among the emotional habits which have an obvious effect on scores are shyness with strange adults, lack of self-confidence, and dislike for "schoolish" tasks. A self-critical person may say "I don't know" because he is dissatisfied with the best answer he can formulate; a person less sensitive to niceties may give an answer which is passable. A pedantic urge to accuracy may make it relatively easy to perform well on memory tasks. Inhibition and fear of being incorrect may cause failure on tasks requiring insight and imagination. No matter how careful a tester is, there is some danger that a child may fail an item even though he could have passed. One should therefore always bear in mind that the final test score shows how well the child functioned in comparison with others, in his present state, which may be markedly affected by emotional complications.

17. In indicating the importance of objective mental testing, Terman says, "I believe it is possible for the psychologist to submit, after a forty-minute diagnostication, a more reliable and more enlightening estimate of the child's intelligence than most teachers can offer after a year of daily contact in the classroom" (40, p. 204). In which of the following features does the advantage of the test over the teacher's report lie?

a. Freedom from personal prejudice.
b. Considering more aspects of intelligence.
c. Considering a basically different trait.
d. Observing capacity rather than level of actual performance.
e. Sampling behavior under a wide range of conditions.
f. Permitting an exact comparison from child to child.
g. Permitting an exact comparison of the child with a standard of normality.

Scoring System

Binet's plan of successive hurdles makes it possible to report mental development in a simple and easily comprehended score called the mental age. The *mental age* corresponds to the level on the scale at which the child can just pass the tests. Computation of mental age would be simple if the child passed all tests to a certain level and failed all tests after that level. Because the failures enter gradually, the mental age is determined by adding credits (usually two months per test) for tests passed at any level. Where test levels are two years apart, and six tests compose each level, each test counts four months; where levels are six months apart, each test counts one month. The total credit in months is converted into a mental age in years and months (written thus: 5–8 for five years, eight months).

Table 13. Binet Performance of Six Children

Child			Frank	Billy	Herbert	May	Bruce	Nancy
CA			6–4	6–2	8–0	5–3	8–6	10–3
Year	Number of Tests	Credit per Test (Months)	Number of Tests Passed by Child at Each Level					
V	6	2	6	—	—	6	—	—
VI	6	2	6	6	6	6	—	—
VII	6	2	4	4	4	5	6	—
VIII	6	2	1	4	6	2	3	—
IX	6	2	0	2	3	1	4	6
X	6	2		3	1	3	1	4
XI	6	2			0	1	0	0	4
XII	6	2			0			3
XIII	6	2						1
MA			6–10	8–2				

In Table 13, records of six children are reported. Frank shows very uniform ability; when he begins to fail, he fails nearly all tests at that level. His basal age is six. Four tests passed at Year VII add eight months' credit; one at VIII adds two months. His mental age (MA) is 6 years, 10 months. Billy has greater "scatter." His MA is figured as follows:

Basal Age		6 yrs.
VII	4 tests, 2 mo. each	8 mo.
VIII	4 tests, " " "	8 mo.
IX	2 tests, " " "	4 mo.
X	3 tests, " " "	6 mo.
Total		6 yrs., 26 mo.; 8 yrs., 2 mo. = MA

While mental age measures the pupil's performance, a measure of his brightness in relation to normal expectation for his age is helpful. Following a suggestion by Stern, Terman applied an intelligence quotient, or IQ, in his 1916 revision. This quotient is based on the definition of mental age. The average seven-year-old has a mental age of 7–0. A seven-year-old with a higher MA is superior, and one with a lower MA is inferior in mental development. The chronological age (CA) of the child is his age from birth. The IQ is the ratio of MA to CA, thus:

$$IQ = \frac{\text{Mental age}}{\text{Chronological age}} \times 100 = \frac{MA}{CA} \times 100.$$

For Frank, the CA is 6 years, 4 months, or 6.33 years. His IQ is 683 ($6^{10}/_{12} \times 100$) divided by 6.33, or 108. The IQ of the normal child is of course 100.

A special problem is presented in testing older adolescents and adults. The "developmental" idea of mental age is difficult to apply, since performance ceases to improve regularly as maturity is reached. There is almost no difference in test performance between 15-year-olds, 18-year-olds, and 21-year-olds, unless the test calls for items which added experience helps greatly in answering. Studies have shown that ability to adapt to new situations has reached nearly full development at age 16. By a series of interlocking definitions, the mental age and intelligence quotient of an older subject are determined as follows: If the true CA is greater than 13–0 (where gradual slowing of development begins), a correction is applied; the corrected CA is lower than the true CA. The mental age of the average adult is set at 15–0. It is impossible to define higher mental ages, attained by superior adults, as "the level attained by the average person at age —," because the average person never rises to these levels. Mental ages above 15 are arbitrary units designed to keep the distribution of intelligence quotients roughly constant into adulthood. The mental age for the older subject is found by adding to 14 (or lower), as a basal age, whatever credits he earns on the adult-level tests. This mental age is divided by the corrected chronological age; for persons over 16, the corrected CA is 15.

18. Compute the mental ages for the remaining four children in Table 13.
19. Compute the IQ's for the remaining five children in Table 13.
20. A 20-year-old passes the following tests: XIV, all; Av. Adult, 7 tests out of 8, credit 2 months each; Superior Adult I, 2 tests out of 6, credit 4 months each; Superior Adult II, 1 test out of 6, credit 5 months each. Find his IQ.
21. Find the IQ of a 40-year-old who passes the same tests as the subject in Question 23.
22. The statement, "The mental age of the average American adult is that of a 15-year-old" is frequently used in criticizing the quality of radio programs, the level of our civilization, or our political life. Discuss the validity of the argument. What practical implications may be derived from the facts about adult mental age?

CHARACTERISTICS OF THE IQ

IQ as a Measure of Rate

The intelligence quotient is a convenient way of summarizing performance from the test. It is particularly helpful because mental age is constantly rising, during the school years, whereas the IQ is more or less constant. While we shall examine the assumptions about IQ constancy in detail a few pages on, let us assume, temporarily, that the IQ of a child is actually fixed. Frank, whose age is 6–4 according to Table 13, is at present six months ahead of average test performance for his age; when he is 12 years old he will have increased his advantage proportionally. In the absence of further basis for prediction, we may assume that his IQ at that time will still be 108. His MA, when CA is 12, can be estimated by substituting in the equation, $IQ = \dfrac{MA}{CA} \cdot 100$. Then $108 = \dfrac{MA}{12} \cdot 100$, and the estimated MA is 12.96, or 13 years.

The IQ is useful in comparing children of different ages. Gain or loss, relative to the average, is shown in change of IQ. Generalizations can be established about the educational and vocational expectancies of children of different IQ's. Because it is easy to use, the IQ is often the only measure reported from the test. Users must remember that persons with the same IQ do not have the same present mental ability; they have only similar relative superiority. In any class, under-age children of superior ability are more like average children than they are like children of normal age with high IQ's. Only MA shows the present level of ability of the person. Two children of the same MA have the same general level of development, but they will differ in the direction of development. Table 14 shows the subtest performances of children with the same MA. Young, superior children pass different tests at Year IX than do older subnormal children.

Table 14. Relative Difficulty of Tests in 1916 Stanford-Binet for Children All Having an MA of 9 But Different IQ's
(29)

Year IX	Below IQ 70; CA 13 or Over (N = 48)	IQ 90–110; CA About 9 (N = 48)	Above IQ 140; CA 6–6 or Below (N = 22)
1. What is the date today?	71	63	26
2. Tells which of two weights is heavier.	47	47	91
3. Makes change.	83	67	31
4. Repeats four digits backward.	58	67	54
5. Uses three given words in a sentence.	83	65	68
6. Finds rhymes for day, mill, etc.	59	58	91

(23) Prepare a table or graph showing the probable MA's of the six children in Table 13 at the following ages: 4, 6, 11, 13.

24. Judging from Table 14, how does the mind of a child of IQ 150, CA 6, differ from that of the average nine-year-old?

Distribution of IQ's

Figure 21 shows the distribution of scores for a large group of persons from ages 2 to 18, used in standardizing the test. Scores approximate a normal distribution. The distribution centers around IQ 100, and deviate

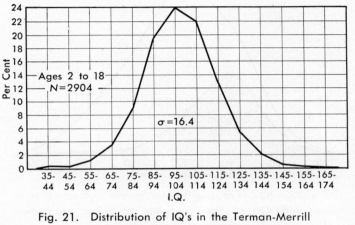

Fig. 21.   Distribution of IQ's in the Terman-Merrill standardization group (**44**).

IQ's are about equally common in the superior and inferior directions. The frequency of IQ's at each level is shown in Table 15. This table is the best single frame of reference for deciding how high, or how low, a given score is in relation to the population as a whole.

Comparison of cases with a normal group is frequently helpful. In prac-

Table 15.   Percentage Distribution of IQ's in Terman-Merrill Standardization Group (**30**)

IQ	Percent of Cases	Percent of Cases Falling in and Above Each Interval
150+	0.2	0.2
140–149	1.1	1.3
130–139	3.1	4.4
120–129	8.2	12.6
110–119	18.1	30.7
100–109	23.5	54.3
90–99	23.0	77.3
80–89	14.5	91.8
70–79	5.6	97.4
60–69	2.0	99.4
50–59	0.4	99.8
Below 50	0.2	100.0

tical situations, however, we must usually judge how a person will fit into a selected group. Selection begins by the time the child enters school, for many of the severely subnormal are institutionalized or cared for in the home. Through the grades a slow but continuous elimination process operates, especially where children are permitted to leave school to work. There

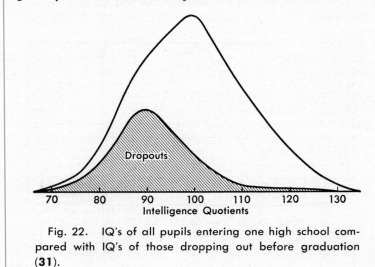

Fig. 22. IQ's of all pupils entering one high school compared with IQ's of those dropping out before graduation (**31**).

is less incentive for the superior child to leave school than for the child who is frustrated in school work. The end result is a gradual raising of the average level. Elimination is most severe at such breaking points as the beginning of high school or high-school graduation. The IQ range in high school is unlike the representative sample studied by Terman and Merrill, and college groups are even more highly selected. One of the many studies of the range of IQ's in high school showed the distribution in Table 16. Because a test other than the Binet was used, the norms are not precisely comparable to

Table 16. Distribution of Freshman IQ's in the High Schools of St. Louis, Missouri, in 1936 (**23**)

Henmon-Nelson IQ	Percent of 58,341 Pupils
140+	1
130–139	4
120–129	12
110–119	24
100–109	31
90–99	20
80–89	7
Below 80	1

those of Table 15. The median IQ was 106.8, and the dropping off of cases below 100 IQ is notable. Other evidence of selective elimination is provided by Figure 22, which compares the range of IQ's of 1146 pupils entering high school with those dropping during the course.

Since the range of abilities varies from school to school and from class to class, a final judgment of the pupil's standing must be based on local norms. Local norms change from time to time owing to population migration and changing school policies. At the college level, Traxler's data provide an important warning against overgeneralizing in interpreting an IQ. He studied data from 323 colleges, where the American Council test was given to all freshmen. After converting these scores to IQ's roughly similar to Binet IQ's, he obtained the results given in Table 17. Clearly, some students who would succeed readily in one college will be far below average if they unwisely select a college where the competition is stiffer (cf. Fig. 17).

Table 17. Median IQ's of Freshmen in American Colleges (47)

	Median IQ
Highest of 323 colleges	123
Median of all colleges	109
Median of four-year colleges	109
Median of junior colleges	105
Median of teachers colleges	105
Lowest of 323 colleges	94

25. The mental test scores of high-school students have, on the average, increased during the past twenty years, even though a constantly increasing proportion of the population has attended high school (14). How can this increase be explained?
26. Sketch a chart comparing the data from Tables 15 and 16, and discuss the extent to which the high-school group differs from a normal population.

Meaning of Particular IQ's

A frequent device is to label certain groups as "normal," "near genius," "feeble-minded," etc. This is fallacious, because there is no borderline at which genius, for example, suddenly appears. Some persons of IQ 110 make significant contributions, and some of IQ 160 lead undistinguished adult lives. Some adults of IQ 80 are incapable of adjustment to the world, and some of IQ 60 support themselves and make an adequate home. Some classifications of feeble-mindedness have been widely accepted as a starting point for thinking about the individual case. IQ's 60–69 may be labeled borderline; 40–59, morons; 20–39, imbeciles; and below 20, idiots. These are convenient, but it is wrong to think of them as rigid pigeonholes. Clinical disposition of a case is always based on a combination of mental test data with evidence on the person's functioning in social and practical situations.

27. Compute the mental ages of six-year-old children who are classified as idiots, imbeciles, and morons. What does this imply regarding the behavior to be expected from them?
28. Compute the mental ages of adults in each of these categories. Interpret the results in terms of the amount of care these adults will need.
29. In early psychological reports, a child having IQ 75 was sometimes referred to as having "three-fourths of normal intelligence." Why is this misleading?
30. Freeman (15) lists the imbecile range as 25–50, instead of 20–39 as reported above, based on Bernreuter and Carr's classification (4). Is there a way to decide which is correct?

An interesting basis for studying the human meaning of the high IQ is in the research by Catharine Cox Miles, who estimated the IQ of prominent historical figures from biographical data indicating their childhood development. "Voltaire wrote verses from his cradle; Coleridge at 3 could read a chapter from the Bible. Mozart composed a minuet at 5; Goethe, at 8, produced literary work of adult superiority" (11, p. 217). The minimum estimated IQ's which could account for the recorded facts about these men

Table 18.   Reference Points for Establishing the Meaning of an IQ

120	Needed to do acceptable work in a first-class college with normal effort (16, p. 261).
114	Mean IQ of children in Midwest city, from white-collar, skilled-labor families (18).
107	Mean IQ of high-school seniors (14).
104	Minimum IQ for satisfactory (i.e., average) work in high school, in academic curriculum (10).
100	Average IQ in unselected population (theoretical).
93	Median IQ of children in eight one-teacher rural schools in Texas (5).
91	Mean IQ of children in Midwest city, from low-income, socially depressed homes (18).
90	Adult of IQ 90 can assemble some parts requiring some judgment, can operate sewing machine where threading and adjusting machine is required (9).
	Child of IQ 90 can progress through eight grades with some retardation. With persistence may complete high school with difficulty (10, 42).
70	Adult of IQ 70 can set and sort type, do farm work (3).
	Child of IQ 70 will be able to attain fifth grade and may do average work there (42).
60	Adult of IQ 60 can repair furniture, paint toys, harvest vegetables (3).
50	Adult can do rough painting, simple carpentry, domestic work (3).
	Child above IQ 50 can profit from special classes in regular schools; need not be segregated (13)
40	Adult can mow lawn, handle freight, simple laundry work (3).

were: Voltaire, 180; Coleridge, 175; Mozart, 160; Goethe, 190. The true IQ might conceivably have been higher, but full evidence was not available.

This is perhaps a good place to comment on the reduction of IQ that occurs for unusually superior persons as they mature. It is mathematically possible for a six-year-old to reach an IQ well over 200, if he can pass tests through the 12-year level. When the same boy is 14, he may pass every item in the entire test, but his MA cannot exceed 22 years, 10 months. This "ceiling effect" makes the highest possible adult IQ 152. Chance errors will usually reduce the scores of even the highest adults somewhat below this. As a highly superior person reaches adulthood, then, his IQ declines, not because of less rapid development, but because of limits imposed by the test. Lest this be interpreted as suggesting that superior children lose their real superiority, attention may be drawn to Terman's studies in which he followed children of high IQ through early adulthood. Considering the group as a whole, these young adults were found to be in every way superior to average men and women of comparable age (43).

The meaning of the IQ is best understood by one who has great experience in observing children of known IQ in particular situations. A partial substitute for such a background may be gathered from the research literature, where various writers have established the IQ requirements of particular tasks. Many of these results are brought together in Table 18. These standards are not entirely trustworthy, since they are based on different tests and on different criteria. They are nevertheless worth study, since they challenge many preconceptions about intelligence.

31. If an IQ of 104 is demanded by the academic high-school curriculum, do such schools provide a suitable education for the majority of children?
32. What problems may be anticipated if economic trends cause most above-average high-school graduates to seek a college education?
33. The elementary school and the junior high school have been modified in the last 30 years, in the direction of a curriculum promoting rounded development in artistic, physical, and social skills—in contrast to the curriculum stressing memorization and skill in reading and arithmetic which was in effect when Terman (42) made his analysis of the educational expectancy of children with IQ 90 and IQ 70 (Table 18). Would this change in curriculum alter the expected educational progress of such children?

The Equivalence of IQ's

Although we have so far assumed that an IQ of a given size always represents equally high standing, it is now necessary to consider two limitations to this assumption. The first is that to some extent, Stanford-Binet IQ's are not comparable at different ages; the second, that IQ's from different tests are not perfectly interchangeable.

As we saw in Chapter 3, the most meaningful way to interpret a score is to study its relative position in the group. When the spread of IQ's at different ages is determined for the Stanford-Binet, it is found that there is some variation. On the whole, the standard deviation of the IQ is 16 or 17 points, but at a few ages Terman and Merrill found much higher or lower sigmas. In the standardization group, the standard deviation dropped to 14 at age 5, and 12.5 at age 6; it rose to 19 or 20 at ages 2½, 3, 12, and 15 (44, p. 40). These irregular fluctuations are probably due to peculiarities of the scale (27, p. 85). If a score two standard deviations below the mean represents the same degree of mental retardation at all ages, an IQ of 60 at age 3, 12, or 15 is equivalent to an IQ of 72 to 75 around age 6, and equivalent to an IQ around 67 at most other points on the scale. Further research on this problem is needed.

When we have learned what to expect of a child whose Stanford-Binet IQ is 80, we tend to transfer that expectation to another child for whom we have a Wechsler or Otis IQ of 80. This is not justified because different tests are standardized on different groups and IQ's are often computed by formulas different from the Binet procedure. Sometimes these differences are noteworthy. One group of college freshmen, for example, had a median Binet IQ (Form L) of 129, but on the Wechsler test their median was only 119 (1).

Error of Measurement

Naturally, no test score is completely dependable. The extent to which the IQ is affected by errors of measurement is shown by reliability coefficients. When the precision of the IQ is determined by comparing Form L and Form M IQ's obtained a few days apart, a correlation of about .91 is

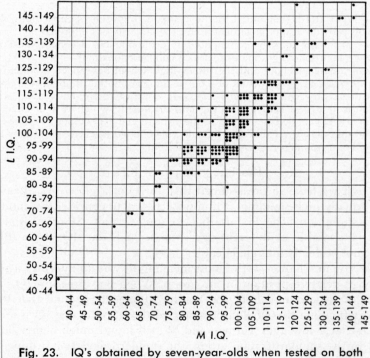

Fig. 23. IQ's obtained by seven-year-olds when tested on both forms of the Stanford-Binet (44).

obtained (44, p. 47). This establishes the Stanford-Binet as one of the most reliable of all tests. Even so, the average shift of IQ's from form to form is substantial: 5.9 for IQ 130, 5.1 for IQ 100, 2.5 for IQ's below 70. This means that an IQ of 130 may be 12 to 14 points from an estimate made for the same child a few days later, although such errors are infrequent. The best method for visualizing the error of measurement is to study the scatter diagram for seven-year-olds, reproduced in Figure 23. We see, first, that the test is more precise for low IQ's; changes below IQ 80 are slight. Next, we notice a few marked shifts, despite the general agreement between the two measures. For those with IQ 95–99 on Form L, the Form M estimates range from about 87 to about 112.

34. What range of Form M IQ's is found for children earning 130–134 on Form L?
35. There are 17 cases having Form L IQ's of 125 and above. Their median IQ on Form L is about 134. How many of them earned a higher score on Form M? How many shifted to a lower class-interval?
36. Twenty-one children had IQ's between 95 and 99 on Form L. What interpretation and recommendations would be made for them on the basis of this? Would the interpretation for any child be changed if his Form M IQ were used instead?
37. What is the largest change of IQ in the chart?

Figure 23 provides an illustration of the concept "regression toward the mean." A person's earned score on a test is his true score, plus or minus some chance error, The *true score* is the average we would get if we tested him over and over, ironing out the unpredictable variations. Of course "good luck" makes the raw score higher than the true score, and "bad luck" makes the raw score lower. Then if we find a person with a very high score, more likely than not part of that score is due to good luck. If we test him again, we can expect him to slip toward his true score, since chance rarely favors the same person continually. The general rule for regression is: scores above average will more often decline than increase on retesting; scores below average will tend to increase on retesting. When a person is found to have an IQ of 150, then, his "true" IQ is likely to be a few points lower. How far scores shift on retesting depends on the reliability coefficient.

Stability of Scores

A large number of studies have been made, especially with the 1916 test, to determine whether the IQ is "constant." If the IQ is fairly stable, educational and vocational courses can be plotted long in advance, but if the IQ changes from year to year, such long-range decisions will be undependable. Evidence from numerous studies with the Binet tests leads to the following general conclusions:

1. IQ's are generally stable, but the correlation is far from perfect.
2. Tests at early ages give less accurate predictions than tests given after age six.
3. Predictions are somewhat less accurate over very long time intervals than over shorter periods. R. L. Thorndike reviewed 36 correlations, and concluded that there was a regular trend. For immediate retests, $r = .89$; with a 20-month interval, $r = .84$; after five years, the correlation dropped to .70 (46).

Figure 24 shows what this instability means for individual cases. It demonstrates the change in scores found upon retesting of behavior-problem children with the 1916 revision. The average time between testings was 15 months. Brown comments on these data as follows (7, p. 348):

"Although the correlation between the ratings on one test and another on the Stanford-Binet is high, a large number of cases make considerable change, and from the clinical point of view these are often the important cases. One hundred eight cases or 15.2 per cent change eleven points or more. To say that the average change is about five points does not help a great deal, because in dealing with clinical cases one can never be sure that the particular case under observation may not be one that will show a large amount of change. It would seem advisable therefore to secure at least two ratings wherever an intelligence rating is especially important in disposing of the case or in making recommendations."

Another study of similar children over an even longer time found that 3 percent changed more than 30 IQ points and 10 percent changed 21 to 30 points (8).

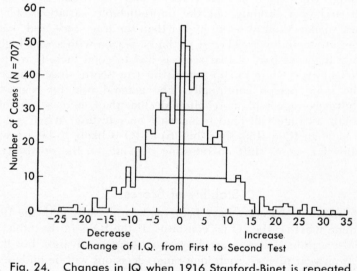

Fig. 24. Changes in IQ when 1916 Stanford-Binet is repeated after an average interval of 15 months (7).

Some shifts in IQ are due to errors of measurement, and some are due to major changes in the child himself resulting from physical disorders or recoveries, changed emotional adjustment, or a more stimulating environment. There is also evidence that the rate of mental development undergoes some change as the individual matures, even when external conditions seem fairly constant. For this reason, it is unsound practice to rely on mental tests given several years previously. Extreme reversals, from IQ 70 to IQ 120, are rare, but shifts of 20 IQ points are found for a few children in most large groups.

Scores of emotionally disturbed or uncoöperative children are especially untrustworthy. When the maladjustment is more than temporary, the child's IQ and his general performance will also be constant at a level below his capacity. But if the causes of emotional disturbance are remedied, drastic changes in IQ occur. Long-range planning on the basis of the IQ is justified so long as two cautions are observed: Interpretation must consider the elements in the child's background which would tend to raise or lower scores, and all judgments must be made tentatively, leaving the way open for a change of plans when evidence of change in development appears.

The case of Danny reported by Lowell, from which the following account is condensed, should make clear the hazards that await the psychologist who treats every IQ as immutable (26).

Danny R. was born January 15, 1929. He entered kindergarten at the age of five years and was found to be such a misfit in kindergarten that after a few weeks he was given a Binet test. The following are records of the four tests given before the end of Grade VI, with the date of test, mental age, and IQ.

```
2-2-34 MA   4 yrs., 2 mo. IQ   82
5-9-35 MA   6 yrs., 2 mo. IQ   98
6-8-37 MA   9 yrs., 4 mo. IQ  111
12-3-40 MA 15 yrs., 9 mo. IQ  132
```

The first Binet showed such mental immaturity that the child was excluded from kindergarten for a year. The next year Danny moved into another school district. This time, on a Binet, he seemed normal, so he was placed in the first grade in September in spite of his lack of social adjustment. The teachers complained that Danny seemed to live in a little world of his own, was noticeably poor in motor coördination, and had a worried look on his face most of the time. The mother was called in and only then was light thrown on his peculiarities.

The mother explained that while Danny was still a baby his father had developed encephalitis. In order for the mother to work, they lived in the grandparents' home, where Danny could be cared for. Danny's grandfather was a high-strung, nervous old gentleman who was much annoyed by the child's noise and expostulated so violently at times that Danny became petrified with fear. The grandfather's chief aim was to keep things quiet and peaceful at any cost. When Danny was excluded from kindergarten the mother took him from the grandparents' home.

The next few years were a period of educational, social, and emotional growth for the starved child. He amazed his teachers with his achievement. He became an inveterate reader and could solve arithmetic problems far beyond his grade level. He was under a doctor's care much of the time and was also treated by a psychiatrist because of his marked fears. He made friends with boys in spite of lack of physical prowess.

Except for cases of specific physical or psychiatric defects, it was once thought virtually hopeless to try to raise the IQ. In recent years, more and more studies have provided evidence that *radically* improving environments will raise the IQ in some cases. Not all these studies have been soundly conducted, but the general conclusion is certainly warranted that the IQ can often be changed if we try. When the IQ, i.e., present test performance, is changed, the person is presumably making better use of his capacity. No one claims that capacity itself is altered. The most striking recent claim is that of Schmidt, who reports gains in average IQ from 52 to 89 for children given special treatment (37). Many psychologists consider such marked changes improbable, and further investigation and confirmation of Schmidt's study is called for. Schmidt's work has received severe criticism for technical flaws in the research.

38. Do you think it correct to say that Danny's intelligence changed?
39. What explanation can you offer for the relative inaccuracy of prediction from preschool IQ's?

EMPIRICAL VALIDITY OF THE STANFORD-BINET

The Binet scale samples a variety of behaviors that are obviously important, and the score is a good predictor of future performance in the test itself. For practical use of the test it is important to know how closely the behaviors shown on it are related to external criteria. That is, how much are life success, school success, and so on influenced by "intelligence as measured by the Stanford-Binet test"?

School success is most easily and most frequently studied. In every case, one reaches the same conclusion. The Binet IQ predicts achievement sufficiently well to be useful, but many other factors influence achievement, so that predictions must be tentative. The following correlations, for all tenth-graders in one high school taking the subjects listed, are representative (6):

Form L IQ	with reading comprehension	.73
"	with reading speed	.43
"	with English usage	.59
"	with history	.59
"	with biology	.54
"	with geometry	.48

Correlations of the same magnitude are found at the elementary level.

40. From Figure 7, what improvement over chance prediction can be obtained using Binet IQ as a predictor of success in English or history?
41. The correlation of Binet IQ's with grades of medical school seniors was found to be only .15 in one study. The average IQ of these men was 131 (32). How can you explain the lowness of the correlation?

A vast body of literature shows mental ability to have significant relations to delinquency, vocational success, and so on. But it is recognized that intelligence is only one facet of individuality to be considered in a practical decision about a child or adult. One can neither predict behavior of a given case knowing only his IQ, nor make an intelligent prediction without using a good estimate of his mental ability.

DIAGNOSIS ON THE STANFORD-BINET

Children with the same MA are of course far from alike in mental development. This is shown by the fact that they pass quite different tests. The Stanford-Binet, as a varied standardized situation, brings to light far more individual differences than the single score represents. Experienced testers always study such differences, and many have tried to develop supplementary systems of scoring to report this information. In particular, many have hoped that the scatter of performance would have diagnostic value. The *scatter* is the range from the child's earliest failure to his highest success; it suggests whether all aspects of ability have developed evenly. After many studies of scatter, investigators now agree that it has no value as a score. All other attempts to obtain supplementary diagnostic scores from the Stanford-Binet have similarly failed.

The Binet test fails to yield diagnostic scores because it was designed to avoid permitting any factor save "general ability" to influence scores to a measurable degree. We cannot trace accurately the child's development in simple recall, for example, because the digit-span tests and others like them are not uniformly spaced at all levels of difficulty. Even within one year-scale, we cannot discuss the child's strengths and weaknesses with confidence, because tests grouped together do not have exactly the same difficulty. Nevertheless, the clinician is deprived of valuable clues if he does not study the pattern of test performance in detail.

One cannot measure a "verbal IQ" readily, but if a child has an unusual handicap or facility in verbal tests, the examiner has an excellent opportunity to note it. Deficiencies in information, arithmetic skill, and reasoning may also be noted. These indications, even if brought to light only in one or two subtests, provide profitable leads for further study and confirmation by reliable tests of the separate abilities.

The Binet also affords an excellent opportunity to see how the child works. The observer should note, for example, when an impulsive child uses trial and error in an attempt to "force" a solution instead of using reasoning. An inhibited child may refuse to take a chance on items where induction or imagination is called for and he cannot be positive that his answer is right. A distinction should be made between the child who is successful because of coaching, who does well on such teachable items as counting to 13 or saying the days of the week in order, and the more genuinely intelligent child who can make up a coherent story about a picture and tell what day of the week comes before Tuesday. There are great differences in the ways children fail, and the ways they react to failure. Some fail by not responding, while others give answers even to questions on which they are ignorant. Some do not know when their answers are incorrect, while others are clearly dissatisfied and aware they have met trouble.

The analysis resulting from a careful clinical study is illustrated by the tester's comments regarding John Sanders (CA 12.8; IQ 109), a normal adolescent (24, pp. 91–92):

"John showed a lively intellectual curiosity and was interested in a variety of things, but within each of these interests his attention seemed to be rigid and single-tracked. This lack of flexibility made it difficult for him to adapt to requirements when on unfamiliar ground. Upon encountering difficulties, he frequently demanded a pencil, because he could not 'see' the words or numbers; I have never tested a more eye-minded person.

"John's principal difficulties were on tests requiring precise operations, as in the use of numbers. With such tests he became insecure and often seemed confused, with slips of memory and errors in simple calculations. He asked to have instructions repeated, was dependent on the examiner, and easily discouraged. Although cooperative and anxious to do well, it was extremely hard for him to master a task (such as 'memory span') in which he was required to be exact by fixed standards. If this is also true outside the testing situation, it is not surprising that in his school work he has found great difficulty in learning to spell, in mastering the mechanics of English, and in learning a foreign language. We cannot tell from this test *why* he has had such unusual difficulty in this kind of learning. However, the supposition can be offered that in tasks involving an imaginative and analytic approach he imposes form upon himself; in tasks of the type which he finds difficult, form is imposed upon him from without. Resistance to such controls may account in part for the discrepancies between John's actual intelligence and his achievement in certain fields."

Clinicians find that the test directs attention to possible abnormal deviations. Schizophrenics in particular give certain distinctive responses (21, p. 984). Compared to normals of the same mental age, schizophrenics are superior in vocabulary, abstract words, and dissected sentences, but have much greater difficulty with bead chains, picture absurdities, memory for designs, and memory for stories (34). Because many normals also show these specific difficulties, the pattern of passes and failures cannot be relied upon as an absolute indicator of psychosis. As a preliminary indication to be checked with further tests, the Binet is of some value in psychiatric diagnosis for young subjects.

Still another technique of squeezing the test of its full contribution is to watch for indications of values, attitudes, and outlook on life. Strauss reports remarks of this nature (39). To the question on the 10-year-level, "What ought you to do before undertaking something very important?" delinquent mentally defective children answer, "Don't touch anything that doesn't belong to you," or "Run away from a guy who is going to take it. Go tell him nothing of the people that owns them." In defining *pity*, one of them answers, "Don't take pity on somebody, shoot them and kill them."

Essentially the Stanford-Binet is a standardized clinical observation. The fact that it also yields an IQ should not blind the tester to his obligation to report to those who will use the test everything he can observe. There is no adequate rationale for making and interpreting these observations, and they are necessarily tentative. But to avoid them because they are subjective is no more sound than if the clinician were to refuse to have a conversation with the child because it would not lead to a statistically manageable and reliable score. The Binet tester with adequate experience has a great advantage over the clinical interviewer because he can observe the child in a standardized situation and can compare what he does with the behavior of other children. The fact that the child does not think of a mental test as a situation revealing emotions and habits of work is a further asset.

42. What sort of report should be placed in the school files for a child who has been given a Stanford-Binet test?

EVALUATION OF THE STANFORD-BINET

The wide acceptance the Stanford-Binet Scale has had should not obscure the fact that the test has been found imperfect by many critics. Criticism attended Binet's first published scale and each subsequent revision. Criticism of even the 1937 revision ranges from minor suggestions regarding details to Stoddard's scornful statement, "The Iowa workers . . . feel that, over the years, the Stanford revisions have offered not very reliable measurements of functions not very close to intelligence" (38, p. 116). The wide acceptance the test has had reflects the fact that at each point in its development it was more serviceable than other available techniques. Its limitations are real, and better tests may supplant it some day.

The scale is not the most convenient intelligence test, because it requires a trained administrator and scorer, and much time per pupil. This lack of economy is compensated for by greater precision and greater variety of tasks than other tests offer, and by the wealth of observational data that can be obtained during testing. The test appeals to children, and is in that respect easy to give. The cumulated experience and research literature on the test make results more usable than those of any new test could be, which will make it difficult for even a better test to supplant the Stanford-Binet.

The test is accurate, except in those cases in which rapport is poorly established. The norms and the comparability of parallel forms are not open to serious question. The major controversies center around its validity, and it is of course not equally valid for all purposes. It yields a faulty picture of all-round ability for some children, but research has identified most of the factors which make the IQ misleading. If a worker draws false conclusions about the capacity of bilinguals, Negroes from an impoverished environment, or children rejected by their parents, the error lies in the interpreter. The test is not valid as a measure of capacity, unless a large number of assumptions about past experience are satisfied. As a measure of ability, the test serves very well. Some workers are critical because the test is heavily loaded with verbal tasks and tasks influenced by educational experience. This is a weakness for some applications, but for any attempt to predict the success of a child in school it is an advantage.

Many workers would prefer to have a diagnostic test which yields dependable scores representing the separate facets of mental development. They consider the Binet a hodgepodge, which of course it is. The difference between those who consider this an asset and those who wish to rectify it is in miniature the problem of all psychological research. In the history of psychology there has been a continual divergence between those who wish to measure precisely whatever they measure, and to know just what they are measuring even if it is of no practical importance, and those who wish to solve a practical problem by treating it as a complex whole with indefinable and inseparable elements. Binet's success, in contrast to his predecessors in mental testing, came because he found that in his time intelligence could not be successfully subdivided. Whether the later development of psychology has armed us with concepts and techniques which will make analytical tests feasible is now under investigation. The tests discussed in subsequent chapters are moving in that direction.

The age-scale method and the IQ, which have often been regarded as second only to the concept of general intelligence itself as a contribution of this test, are undergoing increasing criticism. The first limitation of the age scale is its inefficiency. Tests are presented in a "spiral" order, so that one goes through all types of test at one difficulty level, then mounts to another level and uses similar tests. If all tests of a given type, such as digit span, were given at once, testing time could be reduced. The pass-fail method of scoring is inefficient because it throws away information. There is a difference between the child who gets none of the verbal absurdities correct (p. 109) and the child who solves two of them; but by the hurdle system of scoring the child must pass three before the item adds to his score. Most critics of the Stanford-Binet have argued for a point system of scoring which would permit reliable measurement with fewer items. Numerous revisions using point scales have been produced, in which one or more points are allowed for each correct answer. Total point scores are converted into mental ages, so that the same interpretations are made as from the age scale.

Hutt challenges the basic notion of the test as a standard procedure. He contends that the patterns of success and failure of individuals cause frustration at different points, which makes their motivation different. He proposes instead to vary the test order with each subject by alternating easy and hard items and thus reducing the cumulative impact of failure at the end of the test. He hopes to obtain better diagnostic information. In an experimental trial with comparable groups, he found that his "adaptive" method yielded IQ's similar to the normal test, for very well adjusted children. The mean for very poorly adjusted children was 4.5 points higher with the adaptive method (22).

43. How could you decide whether Hutt's procedure is more valid than the standard method?
44. What arguments can be advanced against Hutt's proposal?

The attack on the IQ as a method of scoring has been based on many weaknesses. The variation in range of IQ's from year to year along the scale, the lack of comparability with tests of other functions, and the artificiality of the concept at adult ages have been pointed out. While the logic of the IQ is defensible, its popularity has led to a rash of quotients—achievement quotients, educational quotients, personality quotients, and so on—some of which are meaningless and all of which present statistical difficulties. Many workers who developed intelligence tests have devised synthetic IQ's which are not quotients at all and are called by that name only because test users have been accustomed to expect an IQ from an intelligence test. Because standard scores are not open to any of the above objections, and would permit direct comparison of standing in intelligence with standing in other abilities for which there are no quotients, most statisticians urge that standard scores be used with future tests, the IQ being discarded. Terman argues that although standard scores will do all the IQ does and are superior for research, teachers, social workers, and physicians have learned, over the years since 1916, what an IQ of a given size means (44, p. 27). This argument is a little weakened by the fact that an IQ of a given size has a different meaning on the 1937 test from what it had on the first test and a different meaning at different age levels of the 1937 test. But it is true that if we shift to standard scores it will take many years before the scoring is understood by as many people as can interpret at least crudely an intelligence quotient.

45. Prepare a table of T-scores (see p. 32) for the Stanford-Binet test at ages 8, 12, and 15, for a representative group of school children, using McNemar's data below (27, pp. 32–33).

Age	8	12	15
Mean MA	8.2	12.4	14.7
Standard deviation	1.2	2.3	2.7

46. If, in 1916, Terman had weighed the comparative advantages of introducing T-scores or IQ's, what arguments could have been advanced for the IQ?
47. With standard scores, how would adult performance be reported? Must any assumptions be made about the age when mental growth ceases?
48. If we had an accurate test, why could we not report color vision in terms of "color-vision age" and "color-vision quotient"?
49. The MA compares the subject to the group who are equal with him in mental development but not in age; the standard score compares him to those of his own age, but with different development. With which group will he most often be competing in life situations?

Another set of arguments has been set off by questions about the shape of the mental growth curve. The difference between MA 15 and MA 16 is quite small; people with either MA can do about the same things. The difference of one year in MA is quite large at early ages, in terms of what a child can do. Moreover, it is not accurate to assume that mental growth ceases utterly near age 15. Heinis proposed a scaling system in which equal score increments would represent equal amounts of mental growth. This in turn led to a "personal constant," or PC, which he would substitute for the IQ (19). Such methods appear to offer no advantage over the standard score for practical purposes.

Several revisions of the Binet other than Terman's have been developed. Characteristics of the most important ones are summarized in Table 19.

Table 19.　Representative Tests Derived from the Binet Scales

Test and Publisher	Author	Date	Age Range	Special Features	Comments of Reviewers[a]
Stanford Revision (Houghton Mifflin)	Terman	1916	3—adult	Introduced the IQ. Most widely used, 1916 to 1937	
Stanford Revision, Forms L and M (Houghton Mifflin)	Terman-Merrill	1937	2—adult	Parallel forms. Extended for higher and lower ages. Most widely used, 1938 to 1949	"Much superior to the old [1916] for survey purposes. . . . Many shortcomings for clinic use" (25).
Point Scale (Warwick and York)	Yerkes-Bridges	1923	3—adult	Subtests organized as point scale. Of mainly historical interest	
Tests of Mental Development (Educ. Test Bureau)	Kuhlmann	1939	3 months —adult	Uses Heinis' scaling and point scoring	"Rather intricate. . . . In the hands of qualified workers, highly reliable, stable, and accurate" (20).
Detroit Tests of Learning Aptitude (Pub. School Publ. Co.)	Baker-Leland	1935	4—adult	Tests grouped for diagnosis. Point scale	"Standardization is inadequate. . . . The whole interpretation lacks statistical foundation" (33, p. 129).

[a] The reader should refer to the source cited for a full statement of the reviewer's opinion.

SUGGESTED READINGS

Brown, Elinor W. "Observing behavior during the intelligence test," in Lerner, Eugene, and Murphy, Lois B. (eds.), "Methods for the study of personality in young children." Monogr. Soc. Res. Child Developm., 1941, 6, No. 4, pp. 268–283.

Doll, Edgar A. "Note on the age placement of year-scale tests." J. consult. Psychol., 1947, 11, 144–147.

Kent, Grace H. "Suggestions for the next revision of the Binet-Simon scale." Psychol. Rec., 1937, 1, 409–432.

Murphy, Lois B. "The appraisal of child personality." J. consult. Psychol., 1948, 12, 16–19.

Poffenberger, A. T. "The role of intelligence in adjustment," in Principles of applied psychology. New York: Appleton-Century, 1942, pp. 282–304.

Stoddard, George D. "The background of mental testing" and "Translations and revisions of Binet tests," in *The meaning of intelligence*. New York: Macmillan, 1943, pp. 79–99, 100–126.

Teagarden, Florence M. "The child's intelligence," in *Child psychology for professional workers*. New York: Prentice-Hall, 1940, pp. 387–428.

Terman, Lewis M. "The vocational successes of intellectually gifted individuals." *Occupations*, 1942, 20, 493–498.

REFERENCES

1. Anderson, Edward E., and others. "Wilson College studies in psychology: I. A comparison of the Wechsler-Bellevue, Revised Stanford-Binet, and American Council on Education tests at the college level." *J. Psychol.*, 1942, 14, 317–326.
2. Anderson, John E. "Freedom and constraint or potentiality and environment." *Psychol. Bull.*, 1944, 41, 1–29.
3. Beckham, A. S. "Minimal intelligence levels for several occupations." *Person. J.*, 1930, 9, 309–313.
4. Bernreuter, Robert G., and Carr, E. J. "The interpretation of IQ's and the L-M Stanford-Binet." *J. educ. Psychol.*, 1938, 29, 312–314.
5. Blanton, Annie W. "The child of the Texas one-teacher school." *Univ. Texas Bull.*, 1936, No. 3613.
6. Bond, Elden A. *Tenth grade abilities and achievements*. New York: Teachers Coll., Columbia Univ., 1940.
7. Brown, Andrew W. "The change in intelligence quotients in behavior problem children." *J. educ. Psychol.*, 1930, 21, 341–350.
8. Brown, Ralph R. "The time interval between test and retest in its relation to the constancy of the intelligence quotient." *J. educ. Psychol.*, 1933, 24, 81–96.
9. Burr, Emily T. "Minimum intellectual levels of accomplishment in industry." *J. person. Res.*, 1924, 3, 207–212.
10. Cobb, M. V. "The limits set to educational achievement by limited intelligence." *J. educ. Psychol.*, 1922, 13, 449–464, 546–555.
11. Cox, Catharine M. *Genetic studies of genius. II. The early mental traits of three hundred geniuses*. Stanford Univ.: Stanford Univ. Press, 1926.
12. Darcy, Natalie T. "The effect of bilingualism upon the measurement of the intelligence of children of preschool age." *J. educ. Psychol.*, 1946, 37, 21–44.
13. de Latour, Patricia M. The borderline child. Unpublished Master's thesis, Univ. of Otago, Dunedin, N.Z., 1944.
14. Finch, F. H. "Enrollment increases and changes in the mental level of the high school population." *Appl. Psychol. Monogr.*, 1946, No. 10.
15. Freeman, Frank N. *Mental tests*. Boston: Houghton Mifflin, rev. ed., 1939.
16. Gates, Arthur I., and others. *Educational psychology*. New York: Macmillan, 1942.
17. Havighurst, R. J., and others. "Environment and the Draw-a-Man Test: the performance of Indian children." *J. abnorm. soc. Psychol.*, 1946, 41, 50–63.
18. Havighurst, Robert J., and Janke, Leota L. "Relations between ability and social status in a midwestern community. I: Ten-year-old children." *J. educ. Psychol.*, 1944, 35, 357–368.
19. Heinis, H. A. "Personal constant." *J. educ. Psychol.*, 1926, 17, 163–186.
20. Hildreth, Gertrude. "The Kuhlmann Tests of Mental Development." *J. consult. Psychol.*, 1939, 3, 128–130.
21. Hunt, J. McV. (ed.). *Personality and the behavior disorders*. New York: Ronald Press, 1944.

22. Hutt, Max L. "A clinical study of 'consecutive' and 'adaptive' testing with the Revised Stanford-Binet." *J. consult. Psychol.*, 1947, 11, 93–103.
23. Johnson, George R. "High school survey." *Publ. Sch. Messenger*, 1937, 35, No. 4, 1–34.
24. Jones, Harold E., and others. *Development in adolescence.* New York: Appleton-Century, copyright, 1943.
25. Krugman, Morris. "Some impressions of the Revised Stanford-Binet Scale." *J. educ. Psychol.*, 1939, 30, 594–603.
26. Lowell, Frances E. "A study of the variability of IQ's in retest." *J. appl. Psychol.*, 1941, 25, 341–356.
27. McNemar, Quinn. *The revision of the Stanford-Binet scale.* Boston: Houghton Mifflin, 1942.
28. Maurer, Katherine M. *Intellectual status at maturity, as a criterion for selecting items in preschool tests.* Minneapolis: Univ. of Minnesota Press, 1946.
29. Merrill, Maud A. "On the relation of intelligence to achievement in the case of mentally retarded children." *Comp. Psychol. Monogr.*, 1924, 2, No. 10.
30. Merrill, Maud A. "Significance of IQ's on the revised Stanford-Binet scales." *J. educ. Psychol.*, 1938, 29, 641–651.
31. Mitchell, Claude. "Prognostic value of intelligence tests." *J. educ. Res.*, 1935, 28, 577–581.
32. Mitchell, Mildred B. "The revised Stanford-Binet for university students." *J. educ. Res.*, 1943, 36, 507–511.
33. Mursell, James T. *Psychological testing.* New York: Longmans, 1947.
34. Myers, C. Roger, and Gifford, Elizabeth V. "Measuring abnormal pattern on the Revised Stanford-Binet Scale (Form L)." *J. ment. Sci.*, 1943, 89, 92–101.
35. Peterson, Joseph. *Early conceptions and tests of intelligence.* Yonkers: World Book Co., 1925.
36. Pintner, Rudolf, and others. "Supplementary guide for the Revised Stanford-Binet Scale (Form L)." *Appl. Psychol. Monogr.*, 1944, No. 3.
37. Schmidt, Bernardine. "Changes in the personal, social, and intellectual behavior of children originally classified as feeble-minded." *Psychol. Monogr.*, 1946, 60, No. 281.
38. Stoddard, George D. *The meaning of intelligence.* New York: Macmillan, 1943.
39. Strauss, Alfred A. "Enriching the interpretation of the Stanford-Binet test." *J. except. Child*, 1941, 7, 260–264.
40. Terman, Lewis M. "The Binet-Simon scale for measuring intelligence: impressions gained by its application." *Psychol. Clin.*, 1911, 5, 199–206.
41. Terman, Lewis M. *The measurement of intelligence.* Boston: Houghton Mifflin, 1916.
42. Terman, Lewis M. *The intelligence of school children.* Boston: Houghton Mifflin, 1919.
43. Terman, Lewis M. *Genetic studies of genius. IV. The gifted child grows up.* Stanford Univ.: Stanford Univ. Press, 1947.
44. Terman, Lewis M., and Merrill, Maud A. *Measuring intelligence.* Boston: Houghton Mifflin, 1937.
45. Terman, Lewis M., and others. *The Stanford revision and extension of the Binet-Simon scale for measuring intelligence.* Baltimore: Warwick and York, 1917.
46. Thorndike, Robert L. "The effect of the interval between test and retest on the constancy of the IQ." *J. educ. Psychol.*, 1933, 24, 543–549.
47. Traxler, Arthur. "What is a satisfactory IQ for admission to college?" *Sch. & Soc.*, 1940, 51, 462–464.

48. Wissler, Clark. *The correlation of mental and physical tests.* New York: Columbia Univ., 1901.
49. Yoakum, Clarence S., and Yerkes, Robert M. *Army mental tests.* New York: Holt, 1920.

CHAPTER 7

··

Mental Diagnosis: The Wechsler Test

Whereas the Binet test was designed to yield a single measure of general mental ability, clinical users have long desired a test which would reveal more about the pattern of an individual's mental functioning. If it is possible to obtain reliable tests which will describe the person's particular strengths and weaknesses, as well as estimate his general level of development, such information will be of major value in guidance and in disposition of mental patients. The test which, at the present time, comes closest to an adequate diagnosis of mental abilities is the Wechsler-Bellevue Intelligence Scale. In this chapter we shall consider its characteristics, first as a general mental test, and then as a diagnostic instrument. This will provide an opportunity to consider the problems inherent in diagnostic testing in general.

CHARACTERISTICS OF THE WECHSLER TEST

Development of the Instrument

While the Binet scale contributed largely to the development of insight into mental abilities, deficiencies were found in the practical utility of the Stanford and other revisions. Those who used the test with adults were particularly troubled by the fact that they were planned for children. Wechsler's criticisms which led him to develop the Bellevue scale are worth quoting at length (17, pp. 15–18):

"The scales now in use fail to meet some of the most elementary requirements which psychologists ordinarily set themselves when standardizing a test. The first deficiency is that they have not been standardized on a sufficient number of cases. Indeed most of them were never standardized on any adults at all. . . .

"A more obvious shortcoming of the intelligence examinations now used for adults, and one that has often been noted, is the unsuitability of much of the material that forms part of the examinations. Many of the test items do not seem to be of the sort that would either interest or appeal to an adult. . . . To ask the average adult to say as many words as he can think of in three minutes, or to make a sentence of the words *to asked paper my teacher correct I my* and assume that he will be either interested or impressed, is expecting too much. The average child responds to such questions as a matter of course. The average adult will, as often as not, start wondering as to what possible purpose or meaning the tests can have. Such remarks as 'That's baby stuff,' 'Why do I have to do this?' and 'I never had that in school,' are very common, particularly among less alert subjects. . . .

"Apart from the matter of interest and appeal, there are other serious objections to the type of material generally employed in children's tests which make them

140

unsuitable for adult use. One of them is the fact that credit for correctness of response so often depends upon the individual's capacity to manipulate words (or objects), rather than upon comprehension of their meaning. . . .

"Another limitation to the use of tests on adults, originally standardized on children, is that many of these tests lay altogether too much emphasis on speed as compared to accuracy. . . . This is particularly true for older subjects who do badly on nearly all 'speed' tests. A number of explanations have been offered for this fact. The one which is of particular pertinence to our discussion is the possible influence of the different attitude which adults take toward set tasks or test situations. When you tell a child, 'Put these blocks together as fast as you can,' the chances are he will accept the instructions at their face value. One cannot be so sure of a similar acceptance in the case of the adult. He might be a type of individual characterizing the attitude, 'look before you leap,' or 'try to figure this thing out.' In that case his attitude might only serve to get him a lower intelligence rating."

1. Relate Wechsler's criticisms to the characteristics of a good test given in Chapter 4. To what extent do his criticisms refer to practical considerations, and to what extent to validity, reliability, and norms?
2. With reference to Table 11, identify several Stanford-Binet items open to one or more of Wechsler's criticisms.
3. To what extent do Wechsler's criticisms suggest that the Binet is a poor test for use with children?

Because of these difficulties, Wechsler determined to build a test appropriate to his needs. Just as Binet's interest in the failing school child helped to define his test, Wechsler's position as clinical psychologist in New York's Bellevue Hospital influenced his goals. Wechsler's duties included examination of criminals and patients who might be feeble-minded, psychotic, or illiterate. Whether these subjects were genuinely subnormal in intelligence was of major importance in deciding disposition. For Wechsler, as for Binet, the principal interest was in studying the average and below-average group; no particular effort was made to measure precisely the higher levels of adult mental ability.

It became particularly important for Wechsler, studying adults through very advanced ages, to establish a new approach to adult "normality." While adults do not grow in mental power through adulthood, it is not true that the average adult has at all ages the same mental power he had at 16. Wechsler's data from his test are presented in Figure 25. The average performance of adults begins to drop in the early 20's. If performance at age 16 were taken as normal, the average adult at age 50 would have an IQ of about 75, according to these data, since his performance is equal to that of a 12-year-old. This is a clear inconsistency, if IQ is to indicate deviation from the average.

Wechsler set about assembling appropriate test materials for his purposes. He is not very explicit about his theory of intelligence or the criteria used to select items. He subscribes to Binet's idea of a general or "global" ability, but he also recognizes that, in patients particularly, ability functions along some lines better than along others. Wechsler adapted from earlier tests a variety of items which he felt had been useful in understanding some of his patients. He was seeking items which, while falling within the area we identify as general intelligence, had sufficiently unique characteristics to silhouette different types of thinking or performance.

After considerable clinical trial, the first edition was published in 1939. Early in the war, the Army requested Wechsler to make a parallel form for its use. Form B was used extensively in Army hospitals, and considerable

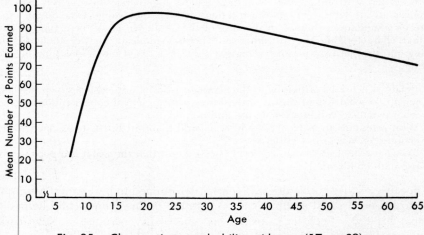

Fig. 25.   Changes in mental ability with age (**17**, p. 29).

research by Army psychologists has been published. In 1946, Wechsler published Form II of the test, which was substantially the same as Form B except for the discarding of experimental materials. The Wechsler test has received widespread use by clinicians, primarily with adult subjects. It is increasingly being applied to adolescents and is now being extended to make it appropriate for younger children.

Description

A detailed description of Form I, which has been most widely used, is the best means of introducing the test. Form II is the same in form but has different items. The Bellevue test is a point scale, in contrast to the age scale used by Binet. Each item is credited a certain number of points, the points earned being added to determine the score. The total number of points earned is converted, by norm tables, into a Wechsler IQ. Wechsler's test is divided into 11 subtests, each containing one type of item. This makes it possible to determine a separate diagnostic score on each type of behavior. Wechsler groups the subtests in two series, one of which yields a "verbal IQ," the other a "performance IQ." A total IQ is also used.

The Verbal scale includes tests of Information, Comprehension, Digit

Span, Similarities, Arithmetic, and Vocabulary. Vocabulary was originally considered an alternate test but proved so helpful that it is now generally administered as a regular part of the scale. The Performance scale includes Picture Arrangement, Picture Completion, Block Design, Object Assembly, and Digit Symbol. A brief description of each subtest follows.

Information includes such items as "What is the population of the United States?" "What does rubber come from?" and "How many weeks are there in a year?"

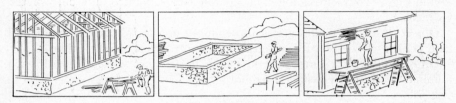

A. A Picture Arrangement item.

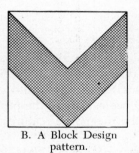

B. A Block Design
pattern.

C. An Object Assembly
item.

Fig. 26.   Representative materials from Wechsler performance tests.

Comprehension questions include "Why should we keep away from bad company?" and "Why are shoes made of leather?" The subject is expected to give a generalized, fairly direct answer.

In *Digit Span,* the subject is asked to repeat after the examiner three- to nine-digit numbers. These are given in hurdle fashion, and the test is stopped after two failures at any level of difficulty. The same type of problem is then repeated, with the subject required to give the numbers backward.

Similarities asks the subject to tell how the following are alike: orange and banana, air and water, poem and statue, etc.

Arithmetic is a test of numerical reasoning ability using simple verbal problems, such as "How many oranges can you buy for thirty-six cents if one orange costs four cents?" The subject is required to do the items mentally and receives no credit on an item where he uses more than a reasonable time.

Vocabulary requires the subject to define or explain such words as "diamond," "seclude," "pewter," and "chattel."

Materials for the Performance scale are illustrated in Figure 26. The pictures at the top are to be rearranged by the subject to make a meaningful story. Items of this type constitute the *Picture Arrangement* test.

In *Picture Completion,* the subject locates the missing part of a drawing of a familiar object.

Block Design requires the subject to produce such a complex design as (b) in Figure 26 by fitting together separate cubes, painted differently on the six faces.

Object Assembly makes use of three cutout objects, a manikin, hand, and face (c, Fig. 26). The subject must put them together, one at a time.

Digit Symbol is a timed test in which the subject writes beneath each number an arbitrarily assigned symbol.

4. Which subtests have the following characteristics?
   a. The score is affected by educational background.
   b. The test demands experiences found in the urban American culture.
   c. The test requires problem solving or reorganization of knowledge rather than mere recall.
5. How do the Wechsler test items differ from the higher levels of the Stanford-Binet?

After scoring responses according to Wechsler's guide, the examiner obtains the total score for each subtest. These are then translated into weighted scores to allow for the relative lengths of the tests. Since the weighted scores are standard scores, the mean always being 10, we can study the profile or pattern of the subject's performance. This is the diagnostic feature of the test.

The weighted scores for verbal tests and for performance tests may be combined and converted into the IQ's by reference to a table using the person's chronological age. Wechsler made no attempt to define mental age, since that concept is meaningless for adults. Instead, he defined the IQ in percentile terms. The median IQ was defined at 100, a value close to the 25th percentile was taken as IQ 90, and so on. Separate norm calculations were made for adults in different age ranges. A person who earns a total score of 70 points has a Bellevue IQ of 79 if he is 16 years old, 89 if he is 35 years old, 93 if he is 45, and 97 if he is 55. Tables are available for ages 10 to 59. IQ's may also be computed for more advanced ages.

Even more than the Binet test, the Wechsler provides opportunity for a standardized observation of behavior. The subject's personality characteristics are evident in his attack upon the performance items in particular. The Comprehension and Similarities tests of the verbal section are also informative, since the person's thinking habits are demonstrated. Projective content may be elicited by some of the questions. The boy who explains the similarity of praise and punishment with "They both come together. Whenever you get praised for something, then you get punished right afterward" reveals much about his morale and his relations to his parents. Such clues cannot be used except as a guide to further study and attempted confirmation.

The Wechsler test is comparatively simple to administer. The full test requires from 45 minutes to an hour. The directions are less complex than in the Binet, and the system of grouping similar tests reduces the task of the examiner. The ability of the examiner to establish rapport and his carefulness in following directions may influence the score greatly, so that skilled testing is required. In some of the verbal tests, the examiner must make rather sensitive judgments as to the correctness of an answer since it may be necessary to request the subject to elaborate his meaning. Answers that seem wrong may be correct when the subject explains himself. Subjectivity in scoring borderline answers is also a potential problem.

6. A 16-year-old earns a Stanford-Binet IQ of 79. What IQ's would be given by Terman to persons 35, 45, and 55 who passed the same subtests as he does?
7. Several experimental tests in the Army Wechsler have not been generally published. One was a maze test. What data would one obtain to decide whether the maze test should be made a permanent part of the Performance scale?
8. Wechsler standardized his test on a sample entirely composed of white persons. How would one interpret an IQ of 100 obtained by a Negro?
9. If you were working in New York City, attempting to establish norms which would be comparable to the performance of Americans in general, what factors would you have to consider in selecting cases? How could you proceed?

Reliability and Validity of the IQ

As one of the outcomes of the Wechsler test is an all-over IQ, it may be judged in the same manner as the Stanford-Binet. Reliability and validity coefficients have been reported from several studies, although the research is less complete than for the older test. The coefficient of equivalence, split-half, for 355 young adults, was .90 in one study. The stability of the IQ over intervals less than one year is indicated by two retest coefficients of .94 obtained for small groups (17). These studies suggest that error of measurement is usually small and that the Wechsler is as accurate as the Stanford-Binet.

Correlation with other tests is a favorite method of "validating" mental tests. The Stanford-Binet IQ and the Wechsler IQ correlate very highly. Studies reviewed by Rabin (11) and Watson (16) find correlations from .80 to .93 when the range of ability is not limited by pre-selection. Apparently the Wechsler correlates with Binet almost as well as two administrations of the same test correlate. But the fact that Wechsler IQ's are figured in a different manner means that a subject's Wechsler IQ will be quite different from his Binet IQ, even though his rank in his age group will be fairly similar on the two tests. An important finding is that the Verbal IQ usually correlates with the Binet and other tests far higher than the Performance IQ. For normal adolescents, the correlations with Binet IQ were: Full Scale, .86; Verbal, .80; Performance, .67 (5).

Few studies have related the Wechsler IQ to non-test criteria. With one group of college freshmen, the Wechsler Verbal IQ correlated .52 with marks, about the same as the Binet or the American Council group test for the same cases (1).

10. What do the high correlations between Wechsler and Stanford-Binet IQ's suggest regarding the importance of not using childish items with adults?

DIAGNOSTIC USE OF THE WECHSLER TEST

It was explained earlier that a profile could be obtained for the 10 or 11 subtests of the Wechsler. If each subtest calls for a different mental ability, an interpretation of the profile should be very informative. There are two basically different systems of interpreting the profile. One is the "signs" approach, which requires no assumptions about the logical validity of the subtests. The psychologist merely looks in the profile for peaks and valleys known to be common in certain types of cases. The other system is an interpretation in terms of the mental functions the tests are thought to measure.

Empirical Interpretation of Profiles

Most scientific progress begins with empirical observations. In clinical psychology somebody notices that mental patients behave differently in some respect, and gradually, as a result of much analysis, a theory to explain the difference evolves. When the results are merely empirical, they are little understood, but they are still useful. For instance, we know that some patients respond to brain surgery for the relief of psychosis but that others are not helped. A psychologist might try the Wechsler test with patients before operation (no one has) and find that patients who will recover do especially well on the Block Design test. This could not be immediately explained, but it could be put into use at once as a "sign" to help doctors decide whether to advise an operation. This is the way the diagnostic use of the Wechsler test has been built up, sign by sign.

Numerous studies have been made comparing the subtest scores of patients who have been classified by psychiatric examination. The full catalog of signs is far too long to describe here, but a few examples can be given. Verbal IQ is generally higher than Performance IQ for organic brain damage, schizophrenia, and neurosis, but lower for adolescent psychopaths and mental defectives (17). Given the problem, then, of a young criminal with a low IQ, we have a sign which helps us to decide whether he is feeble-minded or normally capable but performing badly because of emotional blocks. No final decision is made from one sign. For schizophrenia, Wechsler lists the following signs: Verbal higher than Performance, relatively high Information and Vocabulary, average to superior Digit Span and Block Design, average to poor Arithmetic, and low Object Assembly and Digit Symbol (17). Sometimes the signs are combined in complex formulas, as with Rabin's "schizophrenic index," the ratio of Information plus Comprehension plus Block Design to Digit Symbol plus Object Assembly plus Similarities (10). No one proposes that the Wechsler be substituted for other methods of clinical diagnosis; it merely sets up hypotheses which aid the clinician in thinking about his various data.

One feature of importance is the applicability of the Wechsler test to deterioration with age. Scores of older subjects decline especially on certain tests. This has been variously explained in terms of loss of mental speed, lack of continued practice on intellectual puzzles, and other factors. By including both tests which hold up with advancing age and tests which decline, the test makes it possible to estimate both an older subject's present level and the level of ability he had before deterioration set in.

Functional Interpretation of Profiles

In contrast to the strictly empirical approach, the functional approach requires the interpreter to know what mental functions each test requires, so that he can say what the peaks and valleys in the profile mean. This interpretation may be based on the profile alone, but far more information is obtained from a study of specific answers and of work habits in the performance tests. In the verbal tests, there are many opportunities to spot anxiety, ideas of reference, incoherence, pretentious verbosity, and other deviations from normal. In the performance tests, one watches for unplanned trial-and-error, sticky perseveration, blocking, and lack of critical evaluation. Rapaport illustrates "within test differences" (12, p. 40): "If a subject knows how many pints there are in a quart, but does not know what the Koran is, this will give us merely an idea of his range of information. But if he knows what the Koran is and asserts that a quart has four pints, we must consider the presence of a temporary inefficiency; and if he insists that the Capital of Italy is Constantinople, or that the Vatican is a robe, psychotic maladjustment will have to be considered."

What the tests mean is not reducible to such simple formulas as "low Vocabulary means poor ability to deal with symbols." Vocabulary is affected by the extent of the subject's past exposure to our verbal culture, including schooling, and his ability to express himself, which may be handicapped by emotional disturbance. It differs from Similarities in that Vocabulary can be passed on the basis of routine memory, whereas Similarities requires the subject to reorganize his information. This may explain the empirical finding that Vocabulary is higher than Similarities for cases with organic brain damage (13). All the elements that influence a particular test can be known only through great experience with the test. The most careful simple analysis is that of Rapaport and his co-workers, who group and characterize the tests as follows (12):

Verbal:
  Vocabulary—dependent on early education, resistant to deterioration.
  Information—indicates early environment, education; can be blocked by tempo-
    rary anxieties.
  Similarities—concept formation.
  Comprehension—requires judgment in reality situations, delay of impulses; re-
    flects emotional states.
Attention and Concentration:
  Digit Span—mainly a test of attention.
  Arithmetic—mainly a test of concentration.
Visual Organization:
  Picture Arrangement—calls for planning, anticipation.
  Picture Completion—concentration, appraisal of relationships.
Visual-Motor Coördination:
  Object Assembly—recognition of patterns, guidance of motor action.
  Block Design—differentiating a pattern into parts, reproducing it.
  Digit Symbol—psychomotor speed.

Another interesting classification, based on normal rather than clinical subjects, is schematically represented in Figure 27. The linguistic, clerical, and
spatial groups show correlations with aptitude tests designed to measure
these respective abilities, but the correlations are too low to permit using the
Wechsler subtests in vocational guidance.

	Spontaneous Responses	Reasoning	Usually Reflect Emotional Disturbance
Linguistic Tests	Information	Similarities	Comprehension
Clerical Tests	Digit Symbol	Arithmetic	Digit Span
Spatial Tests	Picture Completion	Block Design	Object Assembly
			Picture Arrangement

Fig. 27. Proposed classification of Wechsler subtests (after **4**).

It is difficult to describe just what any subtest means. Even within the same
subtest, questions differ psychologically. In Comprehension, for example,
some questions reflect knowledge of what to do in real situations and others
require ability to formulate rather abstract reasons for marriage laws or
taxes. Factor analyses show that the tests have different relations in different
age groups, and must presumably be interpreted differently at these levels (2).

Case 1 (17, p. 165)

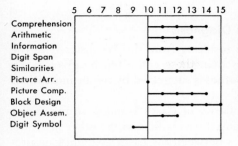

5 6 7 8 9 10 11 12 13 14 15

Comprehension
Arithmetic
Information
Digit Span
Similarities
Picture Arr.
Picture Comp.
Block Design
Object Assem.
Digit Symbol

Verbal IQ 120; Performance IQ 116

Analysis by Wechsler: "Male, age 25; college graduate, 'Y' secretary. Neurotic patterning: Verbal higher than Performance, high Comprehension and Information with relatively low Digit Span. Low Picture Arrangement and low Digit Symbol, Object Assembly less than Block Design. Negative sign: relatively good Arithmetic, but in this connection account must be taken of fact that subject is a college graduate with a B.S. degree." (D. Wechsler, *Measurement of Adult Intelligence*, Williams & Wilkins Company.)

Case 2 (7, p. 121)

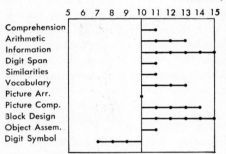

5 6 7 8 9 10 11 12 13 14 15

Comprehension
Arithmetic
Information
Digit Span
Similarities
Vocabulary
Picture Arr.
Picture Comp.
Block Design
Object Assem.
Digit Symbol

Verbal IQ 117; Performance IQ 112

Analysis by Knight *et al.*: "Male, age 26, engineering graduate who repeatedly attempted suicide. In the bright normal intelligence group. The scatter is very considerable, ranging over eight points; and while Information, Picture Completion, and Block Design are quite good, planning ability and judgment are quite impaired and psychomotor speed is poor. The patient's general mental efficiency is poor, with extremely poor learning efficiency. Comparison of the Information with the Comprehension score shows the impairment of judgment; comparison of Picture Completion with Picture Arrangement shows the impairment of planning ability. It is the extremely low Digit Symbol score which makes the scatter a psychotic one. This

impairment of psychomotor speed must be considered as probably indicating depressive trends." (*Bull. Menn. Clinic*, 1943, 7, 114–128.)

Case 3 (14, p. 617)

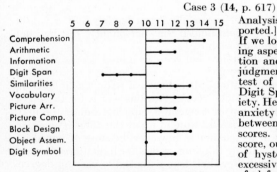

5 6 7 8 9 10 11 12 13 14 15

Comprehension
Arithmetic
Information
Digit Span
Similarities
Vocabulary
Picture Arr.
Picture Comp.
Block Design
Object Assem.
Digit Symbol

Verbal IQ about 112; Performance IQ about 116

Analysis by Schafer: [Sex and age not reported.] "This case is a conversion hysteric. If we look first at the scatter, its outstanding aspects are the impairment of Information and Digit Span; Comprehension, i.e., judgment, is well retained. Digit Span is a test of attention. As a test of attention, Digit Span is especially vulnerable to anxiety. Hence, our first inference is that intense anxiety is present; there is a 6 unit difference between the Digit Span and Vocabulary scores. In regard to the low Information score, our understanding is this: at the core of hysterical neurosis is a pathologically excessive use of repression as a mechanism of defense. Effects of repression become widespread, when knowledge, information . . . all may become dangerous to the hysterical adjustment and, therefore, have to be avoided; otherwise, these thoughts might, in some more or less distant way, touch upon the repressed ideas and thereby mobilize further anxiety. As a result of the widespread repression, the function underlying acquisition of information suffers, and the Information score becomes low. Analysis of verbalization shows that, in regard to the fire in the movie house, the subject would yell "fire" and run to the exit. The contrast of this impulsive response and the high Comprehension score indicates the characteristically hysteric-like affective lability. All these indications establish the diagnosis of hysteria." (By permission of the New York Academy of Sciences.)

Fig. 28. Bellevue test patterns and their interpretations.

Results of Diagnosis

Figure 28 presents three diagnoses resulting from the Wechsler-Bellevue test. Even more elaborate discussions than these can often be given when the clinician lists all the tentative hypotheses suggested by minor indications in the test.

Attention is called to the great similarity of Cases 1 and 2, so far as test scores are concerned. Yet one is diagnosed psychotic and the other neurotic. Probably each of the single differences between the cases (e.g., in Comprehension or Digit Symbol) is too small to be reliable. In each case the clinician reached the conclusion he did on the basis of the total pattern of scores, from study of detailed responses within the test, and perhaps from other knowledge about the case. Because it makes such demands for refined discrimination between very similar profiles, the Wechsler is not an easy tool to use for diagnosis. This is especially true because the profile is unstable owing to error of measurement. The test tempts the psychologist to make more definite diagnoses than its validity warrants.

11. Bill and John, two 15-year-olds, are referred to the school psychologist because both are failing in ninth-grade work, their courses being social studies, English, general science, and art appreciation. Both have IQ's of 93, but Bill has a Verbal IQ of 95 and a Performance IQ of 92, while John has a Verbal IQ of 87 and a Performance IQ of 106. How would the interpretations and suggestions for dealing with the two boys differ?
12. What limitations are imposed on the Bellevue test as a result of the attempt to make it a diagnostic measure?
13. What advantage would there be in using an "intelligence" test to diagnose abnormal personalities, over using a "personality" test having similar validity for that purpose? Would this argument hold if the "personality" test had definitely higher validity for diagnosing such cases?
14. What is the size of the usual difference between weighted scores Wechsler calls high and low, in Case 1, Figure 28?
15. Clinical psychologists frequently distinguish between a patient's "intellectual equipment" and his "functioning ability" (using various words for these concepts). Equipment is thought of, not as congenital capacity, but as the maximum intellectual power the person could summon up at this time. The equipment often does not function at its maximum, however, because of impulsiveness, inhibition due to anxiety, autistic thinking, and other limitations. In terms of this point of view, people fall below their true potential to varying degrees.
   a. In terms of these concepts, what does the Wechsler test reveal?
   b. In terms of these concepts, what does the Binet test reveal?
   c. Which of these concepts comes closest to "intelligence"?

PROBLEMS OF DIAGNOSTIC TESTING

Problems of Reliability

Having in mind the characteristics of the Wechsler test, we may now consider numerous problems of diagnostic testing which it illustrates. The considerations to be discussed here apply equally to many alleged diagnostic tests of mental ability, achievement, and personality.

Tests generally have great difficulty in providing diagnoses which are adequately reliable. The total score is often reliable, but decisions are made on the basis of subtests which are usually short. Every subtest is a test in itself and must demonstrate adequate reliability and validity. Moreover, since the diagnostic test is almost always intended to make important decisions about a particular individual, high reliability of subtests must be demanded. Unfortunately, many test manuals advise the user to interpret subscores without giving him data upon which to judge their dependability. The Wechsler test has had this fault, but the previously unpublished data in Table 20 indicate that many of the subtests are adequately reliable. These data are based on a selected group of patients; a study on a normal group is still needed. The coefficients were obtained by correlating Form I with Form II. A few of the tests are too inaccurate to be given weight in making decisions about a patient. Clinicians are often impressed by the successes of Wechsler diagnosis, so that they express little concern about reliability figures. It is far too easy, however, to remember one's successes and forget one's failures. Tests cannot be accepted on the basis of testimonials without controlled evidence.

Table 20. Coefficients of Equivalence for Subtests of the Wechsler Test, Based on 100 Cases with IQ 40 to 100

Subtest	Correlation Between Forms[a]	s.d.$_I$ (Raw)	Presumable Reliability in Unrestricted Group[b]	Probable Error of Weighted Score[c]
Information	.73	2.2	.86	1.1
Vocabulary	.68	1.4	—	—
Comprehension	.44	2.0	.78	1.4
Similarities	.55	2.2	.70	1.6
Digit Span	.63	2.4	.78	1.4
Arithmetic	.65	2.3	.79	1.4
Block Design	.80	2.7	.85	1.2
Digit Symbol	.81	2.1	.92	0.8
Picture Arrangement	.63	2.5	.76	1.5
Picture Completion	.34	2.5	.54	2.0
Object Assembly	.56	3.5	.54	2.0

[a] Correlations of Form I and Form II, computed by Wechsler (unpublished).
[b] Correction based on sigmas given by Wechsler (17, p. 222).
[c] A score for a subject is, in 50 percent of all cases, more than one probable error from his true score. The score is almost certainly within three probable errors of his true score.

For two scores to be compared with each other, as in a profile, the difference between them must be reliable. If two scores are highly correlated or if either one is unreliable, differences between them are likely to be due to chance. Bennett has produced a nomograph which reduces to simple terms the diagnostic power of any set of tests or subtests. Nearly everyone given two tests will be higher on one or the other. Bennett's nomograph, Figure 29,

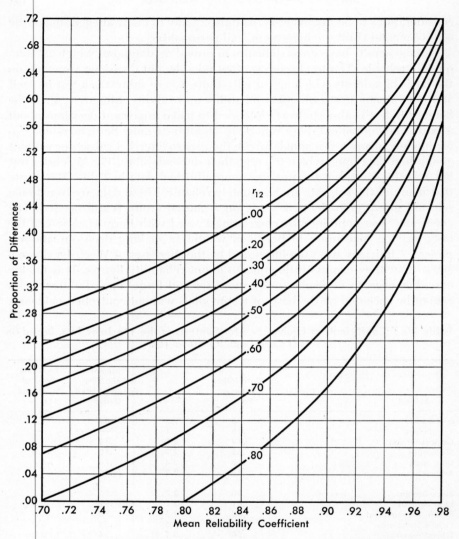

Fig. 29. Nomograph for evaluating reliability of tests intended for differential diagnosis (3). Find the average reliability of the two tests and locate this value on the horizontal scale. Find the correlation between the tests and locate the curved line for the value nearest to r_{12}. Move along this line until directly above the mean reliability coefficient. Note the corresponding value on the vertical scale, which indicates what proportion of differences in score are in excess of chance expectation.

indicates the percentage of such differences that are "real," i.e., likely to be found over and over if we retested the same person. Applying the nomograph to the difference between Comprehension and Information illustrates its use. The correlation of these two scores, from Wechsler's data, is .69; the reliabilities are .78 and .86. This means that 13 percent of the differences we find between the two tests are reliable, and that only the largest differences are trustworthy. Most persons showing a difference between the two scores might show the reverse difference on a retest. Whenever differences in a profile are to be interpreted, the subtests should be checked by the nomograph to see if they are precise enough to permit such discrimination. Few current diagnostic tests will bear this examination.

The nomograph shows that the higher the correlation between subtests, the less likely they are to give a reliable profile. If much of what two tests measure is the same, only a small portion of each test is left to carry the weight of diagnosis. This has an important bearing on diagnostic test construction. To yield a meaningful total score, the several parts should usually have a good deal in common; both Binet and Wechsler rely on this to measure general intelligence. It is not possible to eat one's cake and have it; the correlation among subtests which makes for good measurement of the common factor interferes with diagnosis. The easiest way to get a reliable diagnostic picture is to use tests which have very little in common; then the total is a poor measure of the general factor. For this reason, tests such as Thurstone's Tests of Primary Mental Abilities (p. 206), in which the subtests are relatively independent, may prove to be best designed for diagnosis but least satisfactory for a "global" estimate.

16. Case 1 in Figure 28 had a Comprehension score of 14. What can be said about his probable true score (cf. Table 20)?
17. The Kuder Preference Record "diagnoses" interests for the purpose of vocational guidance. Two of the scores obtained are Literary and Persuasive interests. Their intercorrelation for college students is .11 and their reliabilities are .93 and .90. What percentage of the subjects having differences between these scores really differ in the factors mentioned?
18. The Iowa Silent Reading Tests (Advanced) "diagnose" reading abilities. Two of the scores are Sentence Meaning and Paragraph Comprehension. Their intercorrelation is .48 and their reliabilities are .75 and .76.[1] How satisfactory is a diagnosis based on a comparison of these subtests?
19. Can you detect differences among the subtests of the Wechsler scale which would explain why some are more reliable than others? (The differences between tests in Table 20 cannot be entirely explained from a study of Form I, since different questions are used in the two tests.)

Validation of Diagnoses

It is especially difficult to validate diagnostic tests because criteria must be obtained for each type of judgment the test permits. A criterion is avail-

---

[1] Both reliabilities are great overestimates, since the tests are speed tests.

able for the Wechsler test because it could be applied to patients previously diagnosed by more complete methods. The usual method for demonstrating that a particular subtest predicts a given classification is to show that the mean score of patients of that type differs from normals or other patients on that subtest. Such evidence has been piled up, and tested by statistical means, for a great assortment of signs. It cannot be doubted that the Wechsler pattern is related to psychiatric diagnosis. Two cautions are important, however.

One is that signs must be confirmed by repeated studies before they can be trusted; even statistically significant differences may arise owing to accident, or to failure to equate the patients in different groups on age, education, and other factors. One strongly suspects that some of the signs discussed in the literature of the Bellevue test are mere chance findings due to accidents of sampling. Magaret and Wright, for example, found that several of the alleged schizophrenic signs were usually present in morons (9).

The second limitation of validation by mean scores is that the relationship, even though present, may be too low for individual predictions. Many studies agree with Wechsler that schizophrenics have, on the average, Verbal IQ's above their Performance IQ's. But when we look at Rapaport's data (12, Appendix II), we find that only 31 out of 72 schizophrenics have Verbal IQ's five points or more above the Performance IQ. Even among the fairly normal highway patrolmen used as a comparison group, 18 out of 54 showed this sign. Diagnosis based on multiple signs reduces errors of classification, but few patients show all the signs of their class. Levi set up two formulas for identifying psychopaths. But only 49 percent of psychopaths are identified by these tests, while 9 percent of the non-psychopaths show both signs (8). Since there are more normals than psychopaths, these signs would falsely label many adequately adjusted people.

Hunt and Stevenson comment on the falsity of attempts to set up standardized, mechanical diagnostic schemes which would eliminate "clinical judgment" (6, p. 29):

"Two things are wrong with this picture. In the first place all the statistical procedures involved in test validation are group procedures. They are based on a group tendency and allow for a margin of error which expresses itself as a dispersion around the central tendency. Ideally, this margin is never large for many cases. The statistician therefore writes it off as statistically unimportant, and the psychologist interested in group testing writes it off as operating expense. The clinical psychologist, however, is not dealing with groups, but with individuals, and they are individuals who usually come from the deviant group, the atypical persons to whom a group-validated test does not do justice. In handling these deviants, any standardized testing procedure frequently will yield erroneous results which can only be corrected by the psychologist's clinical evaluation. In the second place the goal of perfection has not been even approximated in many testing fields. Whatever dangers are inherent in applying group techniques to an individual are accentuated by the imperfection of most of our present techniques.

The fact that psychometrics has perfection as its goal may satisfy our super-egos, but it should not blind us to the practical fact that this goal is far away at present."

Attempted descriptions of mental make-up are almost impossible to validate. The interpretation is not capable of statistical evaluation by our present methods. Although there are certain starting points for interpretation, the clinician treats the same test profile differently in different cases. In one case, he makes allowance for a hearing deficiency; in another, for poor education or a foreign-language background; and in another, for the patient's manner in attempting the test. Although some published discussions imply that the profile alone yields an adequate description of mental functioning, the interpreter actually bases his analysis on everything he can observe about the person and every fact from the case history which would throw light on the test performance. Different clinicians probably notice different things and would make different reports about the same person. In validating a functional diagnosis we must study, not the validity of the test, but the validity of the diagnostician.

Clinical psychology is today moving slowly away from intuitive methods, but diagnosis is far from an objective, scientific level (15). It is still largely an artistic process, in which the psychologist relies on small cues that he himself is not always explicitly aware of, and combines his knowledge into a description that somehow seems to "fit." All the research on the Wechsler test suggests that there must be many errors in such a process. When we assume, for instance, that fumbling trial-and-error on the Block Design test implies similar behavior in problem solving outside the test, we are sometimes wrong. Undependable assumptions make diagnostic testing quite inadequate by the standards usually applied to validity. But we are at present faced with the choice between relying on these tests and assumptions, and trying to deal with people without even this partially trustworthy information. So long as the psychologist must make a diagnosis, he is wise to use the best indications he can get, no matter how imperfect they are. Erroneous conclusions from diagnostic tests need not be harmful because, if a patient is misclassified, further work with him will probably bring the error to light. There is no evidence to warrant relying on a functional interpretation of any current test as a basis for final decisions.

Defining Normal Performance

The profile method, which is inherent in all diagnostic testing, requires referring each subtest to a "normal" reference line. This reference line is usually the average or median of the standardization group on each test. A particular subject, however, must be diagnosed not as a specimen of "men in general" but as a member of some subclass, such as "40-year-old illiterates." The score on some verbal subtest that is merely normal in the standardization group may be exceptionally high compared to the average for illiterates.

No.	Test	Stand. Score
1	Rate: A + B	151
	Comprehension: A + B	190
2	Directed Reading	154
3	Poetry Comprehension	157
4	Word Meaning	150
5	Sentence Meaning	169
6	Paragraph Comprehension	160
7	Location of Information A. Use of Index	169
	B. Selection of Key Words	169

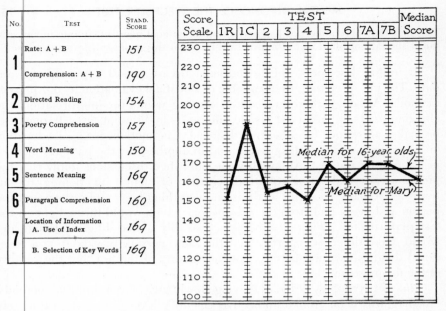

Profile of Mary Adams on Iowa Silent Reading Tests, New Edition, Advanced, plotted in normal manner.

No.	Test	Percentile
1	Rate: A + B	19
	Comprehension: A + B	59
2	Directed Reading	12
3	Poetry Comprehension	22
4	Word Meaning	3
5	Sentence Meaning	14
6	Paragraph Comprehension	20
7	Location of Information A. Use of Index	30
	B. Selection of Key Words	29

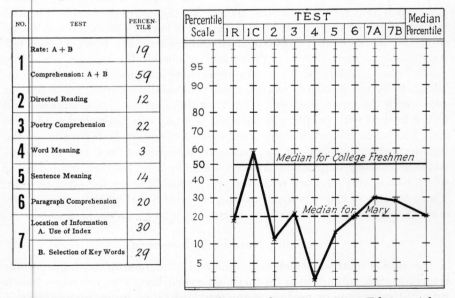

Profile of Mary Adams on Iowa Silent Reading Tests, New Edition, Advanced, based on percentiles for college freshmen. (Top profile reprinted by special permission from *Iowa Silent Reading Tests, New Edition, Advanced Test*. Copyright by World Book Company.)

Fig. 30. Effect of norm group on shape of profile.

If the profile were plotted against a norm line representing the average performance of middle-aged illiterates, an entirely different impression of the man would be gained. Wechsler guards against this error by his many studies of the normal performance of older subjects and other special groups, but other tests have made little allowance for shifts of the norm line.

The Iowa Silent Reading Tests provide an illustration of the effect on the profile of choosing a different norm group. This test is designed to give teachers or reading specialists a quick picture of the subject's proficiencies and deficiencies in separate aspects of reading. The published profile form is based on the performance of the average 16-year-old. When the test is used with college freshmen, however, it is far more important to know how a subject compares with a group like himself. Figure 30 shows the profile of a college freshman, Mary Adams, plotted on the usual profile sheet. A new profile is then shown, comparing Mary to the average college freshman. The difference in impression given by the two profiles is substantial.

20. What are Mary's strongest and weakest abilities, judged by the standard profile sheet? Judged by the profile based on freshmen? Which picture of Mary's reading skills is more accurate?

Norms for Diagnostic Batteries

One problem which does not affect the Wechsler test should also be considered here. Diagnosis is frequently based on a battery of tests, each of which was designed to measure some one function. If we know that a man is

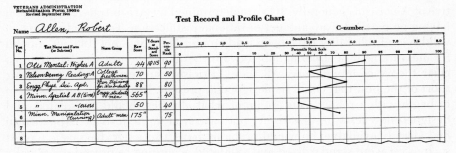

Fig. 31.   Record of a 21-year-old veteran, plotted on the profile sheet used by the Veterans Administration.

above average in finger dexterity, below average in general verbal intelligence, and at average in mechanical comprehension, we can make valuable suggestions regarding his educational and vocational plans. The difficulty is that "average" for each test is usually determined from a different group of cases. The shape of a profile is meaningless and misleading unless the reference line represents the performance of some clear-cut group. Until superior diagnostic batteries become available, we can obtain only faulty profiles.

Figure 31 shows the profile sheet used by the Veterans' Administration with records of performance on five widely used tests. The norm groups for each test are also indicated. In view of the fact that each test is standardized, not only on different men but on different types of men, the shape of the profile is of uncertain value. Competent counselors pay attention to the shift of norm groups, so that they avoid being misled; less trained workers, however, and the client himself, often fail to make due allowance for the incomparability of the tests. To avoid this difficulty we need batteries, every test of which is standardized on the same sample. Recent examples are the Differential Aptitude Tests, and the aptitude tests of the U.S. Employment Service.

SUMMARY EVALUATION OF THE WECHSLER TEST

Wechsler's test conforms well to the specifications he laid down. It is a practical test—not difficult to administer, easy to score, and informative. Wechsler's judgment, which led him to select certain subtests because he thought they permitted diagnostic insight, has been more than justified in use of the test. The opportunities for observation of behavior in both the verbal and performance sections are excellent.

At the same time, one can point to numerous shortcomings. Most of these arise from Wechsler's emphasis on clinical utility rather than upon any theory of mental measurement. The test consists of a random collection of items, most of them 20 or more years old. Although Wechsler collected norms conscientiously, and attempted some compensations for his failure to test subjects outside the New York area, his norms are probably not representative of Americans generally. IQ's are determined by an arbitrary computation having no particular advantages or rational justification. Technical reports on validity and reliability have been inadequate. The test is not difficult enough for measurement of superior subjects. Furthermore, the test was based on no clear theory of intelligence. All these criticisms suggest that the test is far short of the best that could be designed at present. If some worker now were to begin with a refined conception of what abilities should be isolated, and designed new tests for any ability not measured in the tests he happened to find already available, he would probably have a superior diagnostic tool. If such a test were standardized and validated according to procedures usually demanded in test research, it should be a major contribution to mental testing.

But such a test would differ from the Wechsler primarily in refinement rather than in general design. Many of Wechsler's subtests would be retained, since they do reveal significant mental characteristics. The Wechsler test at present gives a generally dependable IQ, useful in work with normal and abnormal adolescents and adults. Because the subject reveals himself in many subtle and detailed acts and remarks, the richest meaning of a Wechsler performance is apparent only to a skilled clinician. Most of the formulas and signs intended to permit mental diagnosis on the basis of simple combinations between scores are far from convincing.

Whether the Wechsler test is better or worse than the Stanford-Binet, for ages under 16, is at present a matter of personal preference. Gradually research will indicate which test serves best in school practice, in work with emotionally disturbed children, and for other purposes. Such evidence is not now available.

SUGGESTED READINGS

Hunt, William A., and Stevenson, Iris. "Psychological testing in military clinical psychology: I. Intelligence testing." *Psychol. Rev.*, 1946, 53, 25–35.

Rapaport, David. "The nature of intelligence," in *Diagnostic psychological testing*. Chicago: Yearbook Publishers, 1945, Vol. I, pp. 37–43.

Wechsler, David. "Selection and description of tests," in *The measurement of adult intelligence*. Baltimore: Williams and Wilkins, 3rd ed., 1944, pp. 73–101.

REFERENCES

1. Anderson, Edward E., and others. "Wilson College studies in psychology: I. A comparison of the Wechsler-Bellevue, Revised Stanford-Binet, and American Council on Education tests at the college level." *J. Psychol.*, 1942, 14, 317–326.
2. Balinsky, B. "An analysis of the mental factors of various age groups from nine to sixty." *Genet. Psychol. Monogr.*, 1941, 23, 191–234.
3. Bennett, George K., and Doppelt, Jerome E. "Evaluation of pairs of tests for guidance use." *Educ. psychol. Measmt.*, 1948, 8, 319–326.
4. Diamond, Solomon. "The Wechsler-Bellevue Intelligence Scales and certain vocational aptitude tests." *J. Psychol.*, 1947, 24, 279–282.
5. Goldfarb, W. "Adolescent performance on the Wechsler-Bellevue Intelligence Scales and the Revised Stanford-Binet Examination, Form L." *J. educ. Psychol.*, 1944, 35, 503–507.
6. Hunt, William A., and Stevenson, Iris. "Psychological testing in military clinical psychology: I. Intelligence testing." *Psychol. Rev.*, 1946, 53, 25–35.
7. Knight, Robert P., and others. "Comparison of clinical findings and psychological tests in three cases bearing upon military personnel selection." *Bull. Menninger Clin.*, 1943, 7, 114–128.
8. Levi, Joseph. "A psychometric pattern of the adolescent psychopathic personality," in *Abstracts of Theses, New York Univ. Sch. of Educ.* New York, 1943, pp. 65–68.
9. Magaret, Ann, and Wright, Clare. "Limitations in the use of intelligence test performance to detect mental disturbance." *J. appl. Psychol.*, 1943, 27, 387–398.
10. Rabin, Albert I. "Test-score patterns in schizophrenia and non-psychotic states." *J. Psychol.*, 1941, 12, 91–100.
11. Rabin, Albert I. "The use of the Wechsler-Bellevue scales with normal and abnormal persons." *Psychol. Bull.*, 1945, 42, 410–422.
12. Rapaport, David, and others. *Diagnostic psychological testing*. Chicago: Yearbook Publishers, 1945, Vol. I.
13. Reynell, W. R. "A psychometric method for determining intellectual loss following head injury." *J. ment. Sci.*, 1944, 90, 710–719.

14. Schafer, Roy. "The expression of personality and maladjustment in intelligence test results." *Ann. N.Y. Acad. Sci.*, 1946, 46, 609–623.
15. Schafer, Roy. "On the objective and subjective aspects of diagnostic testing." *J. consult. Psychol.*, 1948, 12, 4–7.
16. Watson, Robert I. "The use of the Wechsler-Bellevue Scales: a supplement." *Psychol. Bull.*, 1946, 43, 61–68.
17. Wechsler, David. *The measurement of adult intelligence.* Baltimore: Williams and Wilkins, 3rd ed., 1944.

CHAPTER 8

Other Tests of General Ability

It is the purpose of this chapter to acquaint the reader with the variety of tests available for measuring mental ability. In addition to the Binet-type scales and the Wechsler scale already discussed, there are numerous special-purpose individual tests, and group tests of equal variety. There is little merit in learning the characteristics of every test now on the market, so few specific descriptions will be given. The text will point out general features of each group of tests, with tables summarizing features of the most widely known or most characteristic ones.

PERFORMANCE TESTS

Purposes and Characteristics

In this chapter we are concerned with performance tests as they are used to study general mental functioning, rather than those which measure such more specific abilities as dexterity and spatial ability. Performance tests are employed widely, especially in clinical practice. They are ordinarily used in conjunction with verbal tests, since the difference between verbal and performance levels often throws light on deficiencies resulting from environmental handicaps rather than lack of potentiality. Performance tests are essential in the examination of persons with a language handicap due to foreign background, deafness, restricted education, or other causes.

Performance tests have already been encountered in Chapters 6 and 7, since they play a prominent part in the Binet and Wechsler scales. The tests most often used in performance scales are quite similar to those employed by Wechsler. In fact, a limited number of tasks have been used repeatedly in different scales, with or without adaptation. Among those most frequently encountered are the Manikin and other object assembly tests (found in the Wechsler-Bellevue), Kohs Block Design (from which Wechsler Block Design is adapted), formboard (in which the subject arranges cutout geometrical forms in corresponding holes or completes a picture puzzle); and Knox cube (in which the examiner taps on four blocks in irregular order and the subject must repeat the tapping pattern from memory). The contribution of investigators who assembled such tests into batteries was to standardize them on the same population, so that norms from test to test were comparable and the combined performance on all tests could be used to estimate general mental level.

Table 21.   Representative Performance Tests of General Ability

Test and Publisher	Age Level	Tasks Included	Special Features	Comments of Reviewers [a]
Arthur Point Scale of Performance Tests (Stoelting)	4½ to superior adult	10 subtests: form board, maze, block design, etc.	Can be given in pantomime. Easy to score. More satisfactory at upper levels of development than Cornell scale	"A good supplement to verbal tests of the Binet type" (Brown, 7, p. 202).
Cornell-Coxe Performance Ability Scale (World Book)	6–15	6 subtests: block design, digit symbol, cube construction, etc.		"Variety of tests not found in other performance scales. . . . Adequate age norms are not presented" (Whitmer, 7, p. 215).
✓ Goodenough Draw-a-Man (World Book)	3½–13½	Drawing a man	Can be used in many cultures. Requires no special materials	
Pintner-Paterson Scale of Performance Tests (Psych. Corp.)	4–16	15 subtests: form-board, manikin, picture completion formboard, etc.	Earliest elaborate battery. Widely used	
Wechsler-Bellevue Performance Scale (Psych. Corp.)	9-adult	Block design, picture arrangement, digit symbol, etc.	Comparable verbal scale (see Chap. 7)	"A valuable clinical instrument. . . . Patterns indicative rather than invariably diagnostic" (25).

[a] The reader should refer to the source cited for a full statement of the reviewer's opinion.

The psychologist has at his disposal an almost infinitely varied range of performance batteries. Some of the simplest present only one task. If more tests are required, as many as are desired may be added until the information sought is obtained. Tests vary in other characteristics also: Some are especially interesting for children; some make small demands on coördination and are superior for children with physical defects; some tap simple memory and perception, where others require systematic planning and reasoning; and so on.

Advantages

It has already been mentioned that performance tests provide essential information about children who have been handicapped on verbal tests. They also are helpful with children who, because of school failure, are discouraged in verbal tasks, but who have not been conditioned against the novel and intriguing manual puzzles. For a group of borderline mental defectives, ratings were obtained on how well they were able to adapt to society. Binet scores correlated only .57 with the ratings, compared to a correlation of .77 for the Porteus mazes (22).

The other major advantage of performance tests is the admirable opportunity they afford for clinical observation. The great variety of tasks, the high interest they usually elicit, and the variations visible at each step of the task make them far more helpful than verbal tests for studying some types of cases. Procedures for observation are not standardized but, as in the Wechsler test, call upon the tester to use his full alertness and insight to identify deviations which may have clinical meaning.

An important reason for including performance tests in studies of adults is that different mental functions decline at different rates after maturity is reached. Language tests and arithmetic tests remain stable well into the 30's, before slow decline sets in. But performance on non-language tests begins to decline in very early adulthood (26). This decline in perceptual and speed tests, and perhaps in all tests involving spatial reasoning, makes it important to include all types of tests in assaying the competence of a mature adult.

Performance tests have special importance in research attempting intercultural comparisons. Some performance tests have cultural loadings, but they are free from the most obvious influences of differences in educational opportunity and differences in verbal culture.

1. In what ways, if any, might cultural differences affect performance on each of the following tests?
   a. Formboard and puzzle cutouts.
   b. Wechsler Picture Arrangement (Fig. 26).
   c. Porteus mazes (Fig. 1).

Limitations

Performance tests have the practical limitation that they must be administered individually or in small groups, which is time-consuming. This may be converted into an advantage if the opportunity for observation is utilized. Competent observation, however, requires an observer with considerable clinical experience, which again raises the cost of testing.

Single performance tests are far from reliable. Each is a small sample of ability. Temporary response sets or work habits play a major part in determining score, and the habit which is rewarded in one test may lead to a low score on one scored differently. Reliability in performance testing is obtained by using batteries of tests, since the errors of measurement in many tasks tend to cancel each other when combined. One set of 13 tests gives the following reliability coefficients for 10-year-olds: .76 for boys; .54 for girls (11).

The "intelligence" measured by performance tests is not quite the same as that tested by the Binet and other verbal tests. In Wechsler's test, the correlation of Verbal and Performance scores was only .83 even after correction to compensate for errors of measurement. This correlation would be 1.00 if the two scores represented exactly the same ability. The relation of performance scores to Binet scores is illustrated in Figure 32, which shows scores of superior seven-year-olds on the Stanford-Binet, and a composite of the Pintner-Paterson, Porteus, and Healy Picture Completion tests. The most striking change indicated in the figure is that of Margaret. The precise cause of the shift is uncertain, but she is known to be greatly superior in academic skills, with a heavy build and a disinclination or inability to hurry, and great difficulty in social relations with adults.

The correlation of Binet IQ with performance IQ is always positive, but the tests do not measure entirely the same things. For children around age 13, one study found correlations of .55 (boys) and .67 (girls) between Binet IQ and six *selected* performance tests. But when the correlation was computed on a composite of fourteen run-of-the-mine performance tests, it dropped to .41 (boys) and .49 (girls) (11). Clearly, not all performance tests are equally

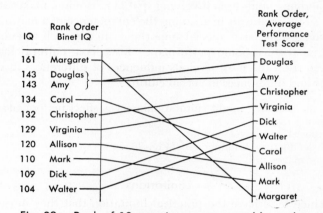

Fig. 32.   Rank of 10 superior seven-year-olds on the
Binet test and on a battery of performance tests (**6**).

good as measures of whatever the Binet test measures. Further light on the discrepancy between Binet and performance IQ's is obtained from results with a small number of canal boat children in England. These children live in an economically and educationally impoverished environment. The correlations found for them were: performance test vs. Binet test, .68; performance test vs. educational level, .26; Binet test vs. educational level, .58 (11). The important conclusion is that a performance test is not interchangeable with a Binet test. One need not argue which is truest; both may be accurate statements about different abilities. Prediction in situations requiring verbal facility will probably be highest if a verbal test is used. In many situations, including general adjustment to the community and to jobs, a performance score gives relevant information.

Some writers have questioned whether performance batteries measure general intelligence at all. Since subtest intercorrelations are low, it could be argued that they measure different highly specific aspects of perception and coördination. The lowness of the correlations, however, is readily explained on the basis of the unreliability of single tasks. Gaw found sufficient positive intercorrelation to support the view that performance tests do measure a general mental factor. But simple timed formboards, which emphasize speed rather than more intellectual operations, show little correlation with other mental measures (11). An American study by Morris tends to support this view (20). The common performance tests probably indicate general mental ability more with younger and inferior subjects than with superior and older individuals.

Fig. 33. Healy Pictorial Completion Test. (Courtesy C. H. Stoelting Co.)

2. Mental age scores for Dick (Fig. 32) range as follows: Stanford-Binet, 8–3; Pintner-Paterson, 12–6; Porteus Maze, 11–0; Healy P. C., 7–1 (6, p. 277). What must be considered as possible causes of these variations?
3. What justification can be offered for the common clinical practice of giving a verbal test as well as a performance test, even though it is known that the subject has a language handicap?
4. In view of the definitions of intelligence on page 107, do performance tests measure intelligence?

Illustrative Results

A sample of the information the performance test yields to a skilled tester and observer is indicated by the following record reported by Biber and her coauthors. Mark is nearly eight years old. With his Binet IQ of 110, his MA is 8–8. On the performance tests, he reaches 9–6 (Pintner-Paterson), 9–6 (Porteus), and 8–8 (Healy). This is the detailed record (6, pp. 527–528):[1]

"The most striking feature of Mark's examination was his extreme lack of confidence and his desire to do what was expected of him. This was manifested by his

---

[1] This quotation and Fig. 32 taken from *Child life in school, a study of a seven-year-old group* by Barbara Biber, Lois B. Murphy, Louise B. Woodcock, and Irma S. Black, published and copyright by E. P. Dutton & Co., Inc., New York. Copyright 1942, E. P. Dutton & Co., Inc.

constant reference to the examiner. Throughout all the tests, although he said little, it was evident that he was referring back to see whether the expression on the examiner's face indicated approval.

"In the Healy Completion the examiner noticed that once when she gave him a friendly smile he was content to leave an inferior solution, as if he were guided much more by his wish to please than by his own good intelligence. Although she busied herself with papers and tried to pay as little attention as is compatible with a test situation, it was impossible to prevent this. The directions in the Healy Completion to look the work over carefully and see if there are any changes to make seemed to imply criticism to Mark, and he removed a block which was correctly placed and substituted a blank. His first responses were all good. In this test, he placed the first three accurately; then, apparently, he began feeling anxious or uncertain, and the last three he placed were blanks. It seemed that he was using the blanks as a way of avoiding committing himself to a mistake, and that he felt that he would rather do nothing than to get the wrong result. This test was the most plainly motivated by his desire for approval, although there were indications of it throughout the other tests as well.

"In the Pintner-Paterson series, he seemed to be less conscious of the examiner, probably because he felt more sure of himself in these tests. When he was uncertain, as in the Ship and Triangle Tests [formboards], he would look up shyly as he worked. Several times he commented, 'That's easy.'

"The first part of the maze series he enjoyed, working quickly, accurately, and with ease. After his first failure in Year VIII [the mazes are scaled in difficulty], he seemed much more uncertain and slow. After practically every one he said, 'I'm not going to do any more of these.' With constant encouragement, he went on and completed Years X, XI, and XII, although he had four trials on Year XII. Toward the end of the series, there was little evidence of real effort on his part, but rather he seemed to be going through the motions because the examiner urged him on.

"Probably no test results on Mark are completely accurate because other factors besides ability are so definitely involved in his behavior. Difficulty did not stimulate him, as it did Douglas and Amy, for instance, but simply discouraged him and left him tense and uneasy. He was responsive to praise, but always with a questioning expression, as if he were trying to ferret out what one really thought of him. It was consistent with his total defensive attitude that he offered very little information during the test and several times he responded very shortly to questions that the examiner put to him."

5. What light do these observations throw on the interpretation of Mark's Binet IQ?
6. List several of the characteristics a tester should attempt to observe in giving an individual performance test.
7. In many clinical examinations, only part of a battery of performance tests is used, to save time. On what basis would you decide which subtests to retain?

TESTS OF EARLY DEVELOPMENT

Description

Much of the research on intelligence and personality has been done on children below the age of six. For such studies, as well as for clinical use, tests have been needed to measure the present development of a child and to predict his later standing. Numerous tests have been developed for comparing various aspects of child development. The aim in these tests has been to determine how far the child has progressed in the sorts of development normally taking place at his age. Little effort was made, in the beginning, to restrict infant and preschool scales to measures of intelligence. Workers have borrowed heavily from each other, and all scales have considerable resemblance. The discussion below centers on Bayley's definitive study, which dealt with most of the questions of importance in this area.

We cannot test a one-year-old on abstract thinking; we don't even know if he is doing it at this age. We cannot test the three-year-old on complex reasoning, because he has not developed adequate sustained attention and understanding of directions to attempt the problem. Investigators have concentrated on those aspects of behavior which can be identified objectively in the young child. Bayley's study (4) used a composite of 185 items from existing scales, of which the following are representative. The number in parentheses is the scale placement—the age in months at which the development is normally found.

(0.6)	Lateral head movements, prone.
(1.4)	Vertical eye coördination.
(3.0)	Reaches for ring.
(3.6)	Manipulates table edge.
(5.5)	Discriminates strangers.
(5.9)	Vocalizes pleasure.
(6.6)	Lifts cup by handle.
(8.6)	Says *da-da* or equivalent.
(9.3)	Fine prehension.
(9.9)	Rings bell purposefully.
(13.5)	Makes tower of two cubes.
(16.6)	Turns pages.
(20.1)	Square of triangle in Gesell formboard, reversed.
(21.5)	Names three objects.
(25.0)	Understands two prepositions.
(28.4)	Picture completion, one correct.
(34.6)	Copies circles, three trials.
(35.6)	Remembers one of four pictures.

8. Characterize the sorts of items used within each year level (assuming that those listed are characteristic).
9. How do the abilities tested in this scale differ from those tested in the Stanford-Binet?
10. To what extent would differences in experience give some children an advantage on the tasks listed?
11. How well do these items fit Binet's definition of intelligence?

Because the most observable developments in young children are in motor facility, scales have included many items of this type. Most writers make comments such as Boynton's: "When the Linfert-Hierholzer Scale attempts to measure intelligence in terms of the child's ability to follow visually a ball or to use a spoon in eating, or when Charlotte Bühler looks for intelligence in a child's smile or in the fact that he seeks a lost toy, it is apparent that the procedure involves matters which neither the layman nor the psychologist would regard as integral aspects of intelligence at a later age" (19, p. 629). The scales do, however, permit one to identify the child who is making less progress than others, in the sorts of development usually studied at these ages.

Table 22   Representative Tests of Infant Development

Test and Publisher	Age Level	Types of Performance	Special Features	Comments of Reviewers[a]
California First Year Mental Scale (Stoelting)	1 month to 18 months	Coördinations, vocalization, simple formboards, etc.	Standardized on same children at all ages	"Fairly accurate appraisal of child's status at time of testing. . . . Not a basis for predicting mental status after infancy" (Goodenough, 7, p. 205).
California Preschool Mental Scale (Univ. of Calif. Press)	1½ to 6 years	Manual facility, block building, language comprehension, recall, etc.	Yields MA, IQ, and profile of developments	"Good tests, inadequately standardized. . . . MA–IQ type of scoring seriously misleading" (Castner, 7, pp. 206–207).
Cattell Intelligence Scale for Infants and Young Children (Psych. Corp.)	2 months to 4½ years	Attention to test objects, manipulating cubes, pegboard, etc.	An extension of the Stanford-Binet, with some duplication	"Items very well adapted to infants. . . . Doubtful validity below 12 months" (Wellman, 8).
Linfert-Hierholzer (Williams and Wilkins)	1 month to 12 months	Coördination, reflexes, attention	Relation to later intelligence negligible	"Value now primarily historical" (Bayley, 8).
Merrill-Palmer Scale (Stoelting)	18 months to 71 months	Pegboards, information, block building, picture puzzles, etc.		"Predictive value very limited. . . . Outstanding merit is children's interest. . . . [Many] items test motor skills rather than insightful behaviors" (Bayley, 7, p. 228).
Minnesota Preschool Scale (Educ. Test Bureau)	1½ to 6 years	Vocabulary, drawing, response to pictures, digit span, etc.	Equivalent forms available	"Not very satisfactory with many children under three. . . . Most suited for children from 3 to 5 years of middle ability ranges" (Stutsman, 7, pp. 231–232).

[a] The reader should refer to the source cited for a full statement of the reviewer's opinion.

Limitations

Bayley's statistical findings are worth considerable attention, not only because of their direct value but because they represent a type of careful analysis of tests that should be made in other areas. The first finding to consider relates to reliability. One group of children was tested every month on her scale, and the split-half reliability coefficients shown in Figure 34 were obtained.

Bayley considers that the low reliabilities at ages 1–3 months and 12–15 months require special explanation. One reason is that more items enter scores at some ages than at others. Tests dependent on maturation she considers more reliable than those based on experience, which would explain higher reliabilities where tests of maturation predominate. A more widely applicable point is that at a level where a particular type of behavior is just

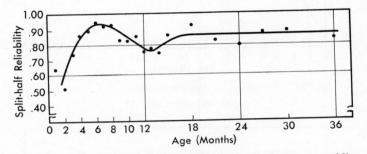

Fig. 34.   Reliability of Bayley's infant test at various ages (4).

emerging, the pattern is diffuse, varied, and inconsistent from time to time; measurement of such functions is therefore unstable. This accounts not only for the unreliability of neonate tests but for unreliability at the ages around 12 months where the child must first make adaptations to an adult examiner. Bayley's data illustrate that a test having satisfactory over-all reliability may be unreliable at certain levels or for certain groups.

12. How do Bayley's coefficients compare with the reliability of the Binet test for single-year groups (cf. p. 126)?
13. What implications does the unreliability of emerging behaviors have for testing each of the following?
    a. Social behavior of preschool children.
    b. Vocational interests of adolescents.
    c. Political attitudes.
    d. Skill of manual workers early in the training period.
    e. Relative popularity with boys, of girls in early adolescence.

The trend of mean scores with age rises in a fairly smooth curve. Figure 35, representing the standard deviations of scores at various ages, is more astonishing, especially as the same children were tested at different ages. The test apparently does not reveal individual differences equally at all ages. Bayley, in casting about for an explanation, studied the performance on different types of items. Items were classified in two subtests, one representing sensorimotor behavior (including simple vocalization) and one representing adaptive behavior (problem solving, imitation). The results plotted in Figure 36 were obtained. Babies differ in sensorimotor behavior most at age six months,

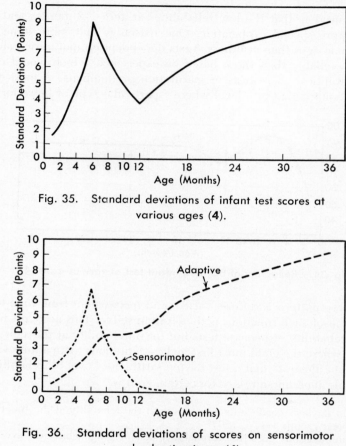

Fig. 35.   Standard deviations of infant test scores at various ages (**4**).

Fig. 36.   Standard deviations of scores on sensorimotor and adaptive items (**4**).

after which they become more alike. The rapidly developing infants have accomplished all they can in this type of development, and the slow ones catch up. As measured by this test, individual differences in adaptive behavior increase steadily with age, except near 12 months where the adaptive items contain a motor element. Essentially, the test seems to sample two different abilities, one of them being sensorimotor growth rather than intelligence. At different ages, the test measures different things.

There is no evidence that early development along non-mental lines is a good predictor of later mental prowess. Infant tests have been conspicuously non-predictive. Bayley makes the statement that mental test score at three years is better predicted by the education of the parents than by anything the child himself does during his first year (4, p. 73). Since we rarely care about preschool intelligence except on the assumption that it predicts later intelligence, this is a most serious limitation. Fortunately, adaptive and intellectual functions become easier to measure by age two to four, so that mental tests for the later preschool years have been somewhat successful.

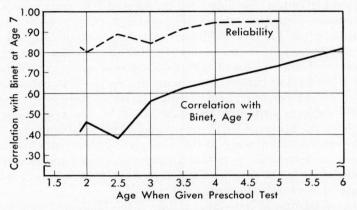

Fig. 37. Correlation of preschool tests with Stanford-Binet intelligence at age seven (12).

Honzik's data on the predictive value of infant tests show this rise in correlation (Figure 37).

Anderson states four precautions required with infant tests (3, p. 376):

"1. The earlier . . . the measurements are made, the less reliance can be placed on a single measurement or observation, if that measurement or observation is used for predicting subsequent development.

"2. The earlier . . . the measurements are made, the greater care should be taken to secure accuracy of observation and record and to follow standardized procedures.

"3. The earlier . . . the measurements are made, the more account should be taken of the possibility of disturbing factors, such as negativism and refusals, that operate as constant errors to reduce score.

"4. Since development is a timed series of relations or sequences, there are for many functions periods below which only a small portion of the function can be measured and above which a progressively larger portion can be measured. Hence, the possibilities of prediction are limited and progression with age is not an infallible indicator of the value of a measurement. Every effort should be expended to secure the most accurate and predictive tests by standardizing tests against multiple criteria [particularly measures of ability in later life] rather than against single criteria."

OTHER INDIVIDUAL TESTS

Individual mental tests for special clinical purposes have departed in several ways from the common tests so far described. Of these miscellaneous tests, only the Kent emergency tests are sufficiently prominent to require attention here. In contrast to the usual tests which require a large part of an hour, Kent designed her materials to fit into the clinical "emergency" where a rapid judgment must be made and a quick test would reduce error in judgment. Her set of five oral tests and seven written tests, each requiring about one minute, provides great flexibility and reasonable accuracy (16). The widely used EGY test was illustrated on page 22. The tests were helpful in many military situations, where large numbers of men were given quick psychiatric checks. Kent, in designing the battery, intended that the clinician choose whichever tests would be most helpful for each case; this contrasts to the usual psychometric plan of testing each person on the same items.

Tests used for the battery were generally designed to maximize opportunity to observe personal characteristics. In verbal tests, Kent recommends noting the subject's attitude to the examination, his spontaneity, his friendliness or hostility, his response to the examiner's personal approach, suggestibility, interest or indifference to the whole test and to particular materials, willingness or reluctance to hazard a conjecture, sensitiveness when forced to acknowledge that he cannot answer a question, suspiciousness, and change of attitude at any time in the test.

Another departure in individual testing is the "concept formation" test, a technique designed primarily to reveal the way in which a clinical patient thinks. Since this technique is more important as an observation than for measuring general ability, it is discussed in Chapter 19.

GROUP TESTS OF VERBAL INTELLIGENCE

Problems of Group Testing

Group tests are far more commonly used than individual tests because of their economy and practicality. Particularly in dealing with masses of subjects, whether in the Army, industry, schools, or research, group tests are essential. Furthermore, under favorable conditions they are as reliable and have as high predictive validity as do comparable individual tests. But they have certain limitations.

Group tests almost invariably make demands upon language. The questions are usually verbal, and even when they are not, the directions are verbal, with few exceptions. In addition to the bilinguals, ethnic groups, and the blind and deaf who have trouble on verbal individual tests, the group test handicaps those with partial loss of sight or hearing and those with reading difficulties. So much is this the case that a low score on the typical group intelligence test at the high-school level is as likely to represent ineffective reading as it is to represent low general ability.

Group tests are, with few exceptions, speed tests. This makes for uniform administration and permits good prediction in most situations. A few students, and many adults, tend to earn lower relative scores on speeded tests than they would if the same questions were given without time limit. Most tests combine power and speed, presenting items in order of difficulty so that each student encounters the items he can do. Table 23 indicates the effect on score when pupils are given added time on three typical tests. Evidently most pupils finished in the standard time all the items they could do. For occasional cases, of course, speed will still be the principal factor determining score. The current trend in making new tests is to provide ample time for nearly everyone to finish, or, if the test is speeded, to not chop the test into numerous subtests with time limits of five minutes or less.

Table 23.   Effect of Giving Pupils Additional Time on Group Intelligence Tests (10)

Age of Pupils	Number of Pupils	Test	Standard Time	Extra Time	Mean Points Earned in Standard Time	Mean Points Earned in Additional Time
9–10	223	Otis Alpha Non-Verbal	20 min.	30 min.	65.0	1.1
9–10	226	Henmon-Nelson	30 min.	20 min.	54.1	3.4
13–14	235	Otis Beta (verbal)	30 min.	15 min.	60.4	0.9

14. In the Air Force Qualifying Examination most applicants finished in 90 minutes, but a few kept working for 5 hours. What evidence would justify the decision to set a time limit of 3 hours on the test?

15. What arguments can you advance for and against the use of short, separately timed subtests in a 40-minute mental test?

Group tests rely on questions where the answer is a single response or a choice among alternatives. Such responses are objectively scorable, but in many ways less informative than the more varied responses obtainable on the usual individual test. The group test is somewhat limited in the sorts of abilities tapped—ability to invent solutions is notoriously unmeasured in the usual reasoning items. Tests often contain a few unsound items, in which a bright student can find a way to justify an answer other than the test maker's. Multiple-choice tests are more affected by chance than questions in individual tests, and response sets are found in some of the items used.

For some subjects, group administration does not yield the most favorable results. The skilled examiner, establishing rapport in an individual test, will overcome the inhibitions that prevent a timid subject from giving all the responses he can, but in the group test such rapport is hard to establish. Inquiry about ambiguous answers on an individual test may raise the score of a subject whose offhand answers are inadequate, but he gets no chance to explain himself in the group test. The group test is based on the assumption that every person understands the nature and purpose of the testing and wants to do his best; wherever these ideal conditions are not met results are invalid. In individual testing, the examiner can at worst usually recognize when the score does not do justice to the subject's ability.

Table 24.　Representative Group Verbal Tests

Test and Publisher	Grade Level	Special Features	Comments of Reviewers[a]
ACE Psychological Examination (Educ. Testing Service)	High school, college	L (linguistic) and Q (quantitative) scores. Primarily for college guidance (see Table 28)	"A well-planned hour test" (R. L. Thorndike, 7, p. 201). "No evidence as to the validity of Q and L scores" (Dunlap, 7, p. 200).
Army Alpha: First Nebraska Edition (Sheridan)	High school, adults	Early forms once used widely in research. Revision gives verbal, number, and relationships scores	
Army General Classification Test (U. S. Army; Civilian form, Sci. Res. Assoc.)	High school, adults	Used in World War II. Norms for vast number of adults	
California Test of Mental Maturity (Calif. Test Bureau)	Kgn.–1; 1–3; 4–8; 7–10; 9-adult. Various short forms	Yields diagnostic profile showing MA in separate tasks. "Language" and "non-language" IQ's	"The *unabbreviated* batteries are among the very best. . . . Language enters both IQs" (Kuhlmann, 7, p. 209). "Doubtful whether two tests of memory are sufficient and whether there are enough subtests in other groupings for differential judgment" (Garrett, 8).
Henmon-Nelson (Houghton Mifflin)	Grades 3–8; 7–12; college	Easily administered 30-minute test	"Serves [for] preliminary rapid exploration and rough classification" (Anastasi, 7, p. 221).
Kuhlmann-Anderson (Educ. Test Bureau)	Overlapping forms, grades 1–12	Variety of test materials, scaled over continuous range. Relatively hard to administer	"Relatively less dependent upon reading skill than most other group tests" (Marzolf, 8).
Ohio State University Psychological (Sci. Res. Assoc.)	Grades 9–college	Unspeeded test of verbal abilities	"[Yields] best predictions now available for an over-all academic aptitude instrument at the college level" (Guilford, 8).
Otis Quick-Scoring (World Book)	Grades 1–4; 4–9; 9–college[b]	Easily administered 30-minute test	"Otis tests among the easiest and most economical to score. . . . Hazardous to attempt prediction in individual case [in grades 1–4]" (Kuder, 8).
Terman-McNemar (World Book)	Grades 7–12	Measures verbal abilities	"Restriction to verbal materials has had the effect of narrowing and purifying the function measured" (R. L. Thorndike, 8).

[a] The reader should refer to the source cited for a full statement of the reviewer's opinion.
[b] These forms are known as Alpha, Beta, and Gamma. Numerous other tests by Otis are similar. Wonderlic has prepared a revision for industrial use.

"Group" tests are frequently administered individually. In educational, vocational, and adjustment counseling a group test will often provide the desired data. Since group tests can be given by less skilled testers than individual tests require, they are advantageous.

Characteristics of Group Tests

Table 24 lists the features of a number of group tests. Because of their wide sale to schools, it has been profitable to design group mental tests with greater care than is true for most psychological tools. The better tests have been carefully standardized, and some provide comparable forms for use at all school grades from primary to high school. Items have usually been carefully selected, and directions and manuals worked out so that tests can be used without psychologically trained personnel.

The common tests are heavily verbal. While several of them include problems requiring reasoning about numbers or geometric forms, verbal items account for the bulk of the variation in scores. This is warranted by the fact that verbal items generally correlate well with other sorts of items. Nearly all group tests are thought of by their designers as scholastic aptitude tests. Even the Army, in Army Alpha and the Army General Classification Test, sought to predict which men could most readily learn new duties. Since school demands verbal facility at every turn, this justifies the usual verbal loading of tests.

The majority of current tests are adequately reliable. In one tabulation of coefficients of equivalence from common tests, nearly all have coefficients between .88 and .94 (19, pp. 631–632). Authors of group tests have often violated the rule that split-half methods must not be used with speeded tests (p. 69). As a result, the reliabilities claimed for some tests are illegitimate. Only tests which nearly all pupils finish can be studied by the split-half method.

One caution must be repeated: Different tests of the same function are not interchangeable. Not only have authors used different standardizing groups, but they converted scores to "IQ's" which resemble Binet IQ's only in having a mean of 100. If persons with Binet IQ's of 123 took nine different group tests published before 1924, they would earn the following average IQ's on the different tests: 124, 124, 127, 128, 131, 138, 138, 143, 149 (18). While more recent tests have been based on larger norm groups. the IQ still rises or falls according to what test is given. In one recent study, over 2200 nine- and ten-year-olds took four accepted group tests. The number of pupils receiving IQ's below 80 was as follows: on the Henmon-Nelson test, 119; Kuhlmann-Anderson, 53; Otis Alpha Verbal, 47; Otis Alpha Non-Verbal, 68. The differences in the proportion of high IQ's were even more marked, but partly explained by the fact that the two Otis tests were too easy to test the full ability of the better pupils (10). How one person's tested IQ varies is illustrated by the scores earned by an adolescent boy during a three-year period (Table 25).

Table 25.   Intelligence Test Results for John Sanders[2]
(14, p. 90)

	John's	
Test	CA	IQ
Kuhlmann-Anderson	12.1	101
Terman Group Test A	12.6	119
Terman Group Test B	12.7	100
Stanford-Binet (1916)	12.8	109
Kuhlmann-Anderson	14.1	91
Terman Group Test A	14.5	113
Terman Group Test B	14.6	112
Terman Group Test B	15.1	115

Group verbal tests do not differ very much in over-all character. The differences that lead the tester to choose one test rather than another relate to the convenience of a test in a particular situation. Carefully prepared group tests have comparable reliabilities and validities, and tests for a given age test about the same functions. The lengths of the tests vary from 15-minute tests used in rough classification in industry to the 2-hour tests used to meas-

56. 6, 4, 7, 5, 8, 6, 9, ... What number should come next?
(1) 7, (2) 10, (3) 8, (4) 6, (5) 11.......... [1] [2] [3] [4] [5]

57. Which word does not belong with the others? 1 apparatus,
2 foundation, 3 equipment, 4 device, 5 appliance. [1] [2] [3] [4] [5]

58. Inconsequential means about the same as: 1 sorry, 2 incorrect,
3 useful, 4 unimportant, 5 necessary........ [1] [2] [3] [4] [5]

59. 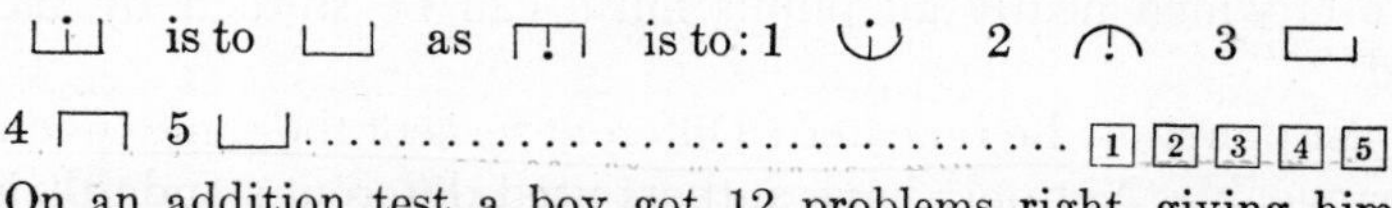 └┴┘ is to └─┘ as ┌┬┐ is to: 1 ∪ 2 ∩ 3 ⊏
4 ┌─ 5 └─┘............................... [1] [2] [3] [4] [5]

60. On an addition test a boy got 12 problems right, giving him
an accuracy of 75%. How many problems did he *miss?*
(1) 8, (2) 9, (3) 6, (4) 4, (5) 3............ [1] [2] [3] [4] [5]

61. The United States entered the World War in: (1) 1914, (2) 1915,
(3) 1916, (4) 1917, (5) 1918................ [1] [2] [3] [4] [5]

Fig. 38.   Items from Henmon-Nelson Test of Mental Ability,
High School Examination.[3]

ure college aptitude. In general, longer tests are required for fairly homogeneous groups or for refined measurement. Another major difference between group tests is in convenience of administration and scoring. The quick-scoring features of the recent tests are greatly appreciated where large numbers

[2] See also p. 132.
[3] From the *Henmon-Nelson Tests of Mental Ability*, Houghton Mifflin Company.

1946 Revision

CALIFORNIA TEST OF MENTAL MATURITY—ADVANCED SERIES
Devised by Elizabeth T. Sullivan, Willis W. Clark, and Ernest W. Tiegs

Name *Harold Brown*   Occupation or Grade *L 10 (10.4)*

Date *Jan. 15*   Age *15*   Last Birthday *Nov. 10 (182 Mo.)*   Sex: Ⓜ F

Teacher or Examiner *Miss Ross*   School or Organization *Lincoln High*

TEST FACTOR	Possible Score	Score				
1. Visual Acuity	40	38	0 28 29	Low Average	⊗ High	40
2. Auditory Acuity	15	14	0 9 10	Low Average	⊗ High	15
3. Motor Co-ordination	20	12	0 10 11	Low Average ⊗	18 High	20

DIAGNOSTIC PROFILE
(Chart scores here)

TEST FACTOR	Possible Score	Score	Mental Age	Percentile Rank
A. Memory	53	38		30
4. Immediate Recall°	33	22		
5. Delayed Recall (p. 16)	20	16		
B. Spatial Relationships	45	22		30
6. Sensing Right and Left°	20	14		
7. Manipulation of Areas°	15	3		
8. Foresight in Spatial Sit'n°	10	5		
C. Logical Reasoning	60	30		60
9. Opposites°	15	8		
10. Similarities°	15	8		
11. Analogies°	15	5		
15. Inference (p. 14)	15	9		
D. Numerical Reasoning	45	21		50
12. Number Series°	15	7		
13. Numerical Quantity°	15	9		
14. Numerical Quantity	15	5		
E. 16. Vocabulary	50	17		80
Total Mental Factors (A+B+C+D+E)	253	128		60
F. Language Factors (5+14+15+16)	100	47		70
G. Non-Language Factors (Total Mental Factors Minus F)	153	81		50
Chronological Age		182		
Actual Grade Placement (Grade pupil is in)		10.4		

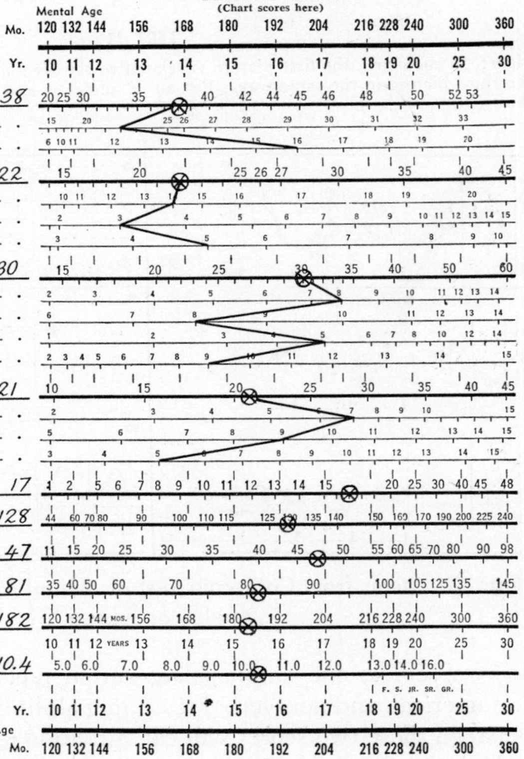

°Non-Language tests.

SUMMARY OF DATA

	Score	M. A.	÷ C. A.°	= I. Q.
Total Mental Factors	128	193	182	106
F. Language Factors	47	202	182	111
G. Non-Language Factors	81	184	182	101

*Age 16 and older, divide by 192 months.

Fig. 39. Profile sheet for California Test of Mental Maturity.

of papers must be processed in a short time. A third feature to consider in choosing a test is the suitability of the norms for the use the tester has in mind. This is not highly important, however, as local norms based on the group with which the subject will be working are generally more informative in the types of processing where group tests are used.

Few group intelligence tests make any attempt to yield diagnostic scores. One major exception, the Primary Abilities tests, is treated in Chapter 9. Most group tests yield only a single score, recognizing that reliable measures can rarely be obtained in subtests requiring less than 15 minutes. A few tests

TEST 11.

Directions: In each row, the first picture is related to the second. Find a picture that goes with the third picture in the same way. Put an ✕ under it and write its number on the line to the right.

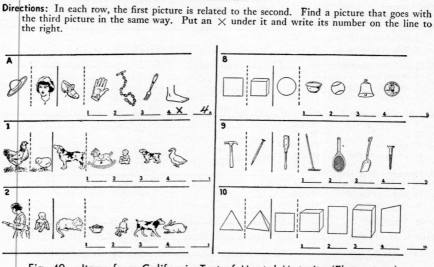

Fig. 40. Items from California Test of Mental Maturity (Elementary), Analogies subtest.[4]

provide two scores, one emphasizing verbal factors and one emphasizing spatial, numerical, and non-verbal reasoning abilities. Sometimes the discrepancy between these two scores will call attention to a subject having a reading handicap or a language deficiency.

The California Test of Mental Maturity (CMM) series is particularly interesting in view of its attempt to make an intensive diagnosis of mental ability. It contains a variety of objective subtests which yield an IQ of satisfactory reliability. In addition, the CMM yields separate "Language" and "Non-Language" IQ's. The reliabilities of the long form for the Advanced test are .945 for the Language score, and .935 for the Non-Language score. The two scores correlate .63, which shows that somewhat different abilities

---

[4] Fig. 39 from the *California Test of Mental Maturity, Advanced Series;* Fig. 40 from *ibid., Elementary Series.* Both are published with permission of the California Test Bureau, Los Angeles, California.

are measured in them. This diagnosis is further broken into a profile showing ability in different areas, as illustrated in Figure 39. Care is needed in interpreting the profile to avoid giving undue weight to fluctuations due to chance. While the five "factor" scores have adequate reliability and measure fairly distinct abilities, attempts to interpret the profile on single subtests (such as Manipulation of Areas) are most inadvisable. These subtests are brief and therefore not reliable; strength or weakness on any single test is not significant unless it is confirmed by further observation. Since nearly all the tests involve more than one type of ability, users must study the content of the sections of the tests rather than interpret weakness in "memory" or "logical reasoning" at face value.

16. What evidence would help you decide on the "true" number of cases having IQ below 80 in the group of 2200 discussed above?
17. What is the best estimate you can make as to John Sanders' "true" IQ?
18. In common usage, is "scholastic aptitude" identical to "intelligence"?
19. One section of the Ohio State Psychological Examination is a test of reading comprehension. Can you justify including this section in a test of scholastic aptitude?
20. There are three major quick-scoring techniques. The Henmon-Nelson test uses a booklet sealed at the edges. After the subject has marked his test, he tears open the booklet and finds that each answer has been transferred to a sheet where printed squares indicate the correct answer, so that the score may be counted directly. The Ohio State test uses a pinprick method of transferring marks from the front sheet to a concealed, pre-keyed second sheet. Holes punched through marked spaces on this inner sheet represent correct answers. The IBM answer sheet, described on page 46, is the third method. Papers in this form may be hand-scored with a punched-out key. Consider the relative advantages of these three devices with respect to the following characteristics:
    a. Ease of changing an answer after marking it.
    b. Possible inaccuracy in obtaining scores.
    c. Speed and convenience when the subject scores his own paper.
21. There has been a trend recently toward short tests. For example, a 15-minute test (SRA Verbal Form) has been derived from the ACE test, which requires about an hour. What limitations does such a shortened test have, compared to the long form?
22. Describe the abilities required by the Henmon-Nelson test (Fig. 38).
23. Suppose that some subtest scores in the profile, Figure 39, change two points up or down on retest. This is not unlikely on multiple-choice items. How great a change might this make in the profile of "factor" scores? Of scores on single subtests?
24. The subtest reproduced in Figure 40 is titled "Reasoning-Analogies." What other mental functions seem to be involved in this test, and would in part account for differences in score?
25. The Analogies subtest is included in the CMM score Non-Language Factors. Why have some writers criticized that score as not being free from the influence of language abilities? Does this influence impair the usefulness of the non-language score?
26. What interpretation would be made if a child has a Non-Language IQ of 120, Language of 90? What interpretation would be made if the Language IQ were 120, Non-Language 90?

27. In the CMM Elementary test, pupils listen to a story about "The Pack Train." In the story, a man goes to a mining camp by pack train, passing a glacier and being threatened by a grizzly bear. After hearing the story, pupils go on to take other sections of the test. After an elapsed time of 25 minutes, the pupils are asked questions about the story. What does the test measure besides general ability in "delayed recall"?
28. What interpretations about Harold Brown are suggested by his CMM profile, when you bear in mind the nature and reliability of the subtests?
29. One of the subtests of the Tanaka group intelligence test (Japanese) requires the subject to cross slanting lines, making X's as rapidly as he can, thus X X X X X / / / / / /. Such a subtest is rarely used in American intelligence tests. On what basis could the inclusion of such a test be criticized? What argument or evidence would justify including this subtest in a general mental test?

Empirical Validity

Because group tests were first thought of as substitutes for the Stanford-Binet test, their correlations with that test are an important evidence of validity. If the correlation is high, they measure the same thing as the Binet. Representative correlations with the Binet test actually found are as follows: CAVD, .87; Detroit Advanced First Grade, .85; and ACE, .58–.62 for college freshmen (19, 2). These correlations are based on typical school populations. Comparable evidence for clinical groups and for industrial workers is lacking. In clinical work, individual tests are preferred over group tests. Although individual tests are less convenient, they provide more information. In industrial work, they are rarely considered, and validity is judged by the value of the group test in predicting a job criterion.

A second line of evidence is to determine whether the group test principally measures speed. Apparently, from the studies available, speed of work is not the principal element causing high or low scores on most group tests (5, 10). But speed tests may be undesirable, even when speed is a minor factor. The Ohio State Psychological Examination was given to groups twice, one form timed and the other untimed. The correlation with college marks was .53 without time limit, .46 speeded (27). More recent forms of the test, unspeeded, have even better validity.

Table 26.   Relation of Reading Ability to Group Test IQ's (9)

Reading Ability of Pupils, Compared to Those of Equal MA	N	Mean IQ on Binet Test	Mean IQ on Haggerty Group Test	Difference
Very superior readers	36	94	114.5	+20.5
Superior readers	224	92	109	+17
Retarded readers	100	107	99	−8

The correlation of mental tests with tests of achievement is high. With measures of reading, total score on CMM correlates .70–.78 for children, and language score correlates .80–.84. The non-language part correlates .36 to .56

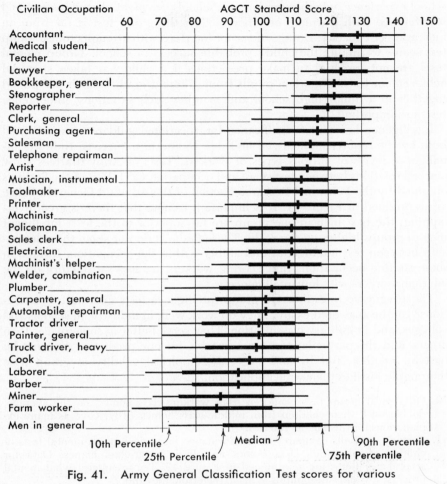

Fig. 41. Army General Classification Test scores for various occupational groups (after **23**).

(24). Poor reading lowers group test performance (see Table 26). Correlations between intelligence tests and standardized tests of school knowledge include .82 (Detroit Alpha), .75–.85 (National Intelligence), and .78 (Kuhlmann-Anderson) (19, pp. 631–632; 1). Apparently, group tests reflect school achievement (this is not a question of prediction, since both tests were administered at the same time). Kelley estimates that for children what one group verbal test measures is 95 percent the same as what another such test measures, is 92 percent the same as what typical reading tests measure, and is 90 percent the same as what is measured by the typical informational school achievement test (15, p. 208). This overlap is probably less for out-of-school adults. The implication of this finding is that for pupils with deficient school experience, whether due to poor schools, frequent absence, emotional interference with learning, or other factors, the group test is far from an indication of capacity. But this does not interfere with attempts to use group test scores to predict the child's probable success in school. Group mental tests are not essential to make predictions if a child has taken standard achievement tests. But when pupils from different grade schools are pulled together in a junior high school and in other such situations, intelligence tests are important.

Intelligence has direct significance for vocational guidance, as indicated both by the reports summarized in Table 18 and in numerous studies of intelligence levels of various types of workers. Tests of Army draftees show marked relations between test score and occupation (23). Part of the findings obtained by the Personnel Research Section of the Adjutant General's Office are reproduced in Figure 41. It is important to note that there is great overlapping; the best men in one group are far superior to the least intelligent men in groups higher on the scale. These findings do not show the relationship between test intelligence and ability within the occupation. In fact, in some routine occupations high-scoring workers are less satisfactory on the job than workers with low intelligence.

The pragmatic question: Do group intelligence tests give useful predictions? can be answered easily. They do work well, in industry, in schools and colleges, and in military classification. They serve better in some places than others, and the particular test most suitable for one prediction may not be best for another. But by and large, the empirical validity of group tests thoroughly justifies their wide application.

30. On typical group tests, children from working-class homes, on the average, do less well than children from middle-class homes (10). Give as many explanations for this fact as you can.
31. A study by Eells compares the performance on typical group mental tests of children from middle-class homes and from lower-class homes. Data for several test items are reproduced in Figure 42. Try to suggest what mental processes would cause pupils to make the errors they did.
32. What differences between lower-class children and middle-class children appear in the data of Figure 42?
33. According to Army Alpha results, white adults in certain Southern states earned, on the average, lower scores than typical adults from certain Northern and Western states. Give as many possible explanations of this fact as you can.
34. Outline an intelligence testing program for use in a public elementary school, considering such questions as: How often should every child be tested? Should all testings be based on the same series? What provision should be made to allow for the fact that group test IQ's may be seriously wrong for some pupils?

A Form for Examining Tests

There is little purpose in attempting to describe here the details of specific tests, since the interests of readers will vary widely. But every reader should

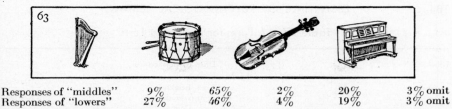

Responses of "middles"	9%	65%	2%	20%	3% omit
Responses of "lowers"	27%	46%	4%	19%	3% omit

From Otis Alpha Non-Verbal Test. Directions given orally: "Find the three things that are alike and draw a line through the one that is not like these three."

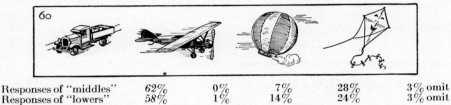

Responses of "middles"	62%	0%	7%	28%	3% omit
Responses of "lowers"	58%	1%	14%	24%	3% omit

From Otis Alpha Non-Verbal test. Directions same as above.
(This and the above reprinted by special permission from *Otis Alpha Non-Verbal Test, Form A.* Copyright by World Book Company.)

A fire always has	wood	coal	gas	warmth	furnace	
Responses of "middles"	18%	9%	1%	69%	2%	0% omit
Responses of "lowers"	22%	22%	7%	38%	7%	4% omit

Which month comes just before March?	April	September	May	February	August	
Responses of "middles"	12%	0%	1%	85%	0%	2% omit
Responses of "lowers"	15%	5%	7%	62%	7%	4% omit

(This and the above from the Henmon-Nelson *Tests of Mental Ability, Elementary,* Houghton Mifflin Company.)

"Find the word in the last of the list which tells what kind of a thing the first word in the list is."

	salmon	meat	water	swim	fish	food	
Responses of "middles"		12%	0%	1%	75%	10%	2% omit
Responses of "lowers"		15%	3%	10%	47%	17%	8% omit

(From the Kuhlmann-Anderson Test, by permission of Educational Test Bureau.)

"Mark under the R for rights, and under the L for lefts."

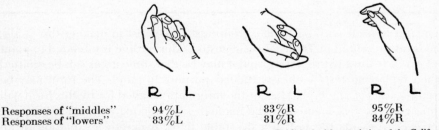

	R L	R L	R L
Responses of "middles"	94%L	83%R	95%R
Responses of "lowers"	83%L	81%R	84%R

(From the *California Test of Mental Maturity, Elementary Series.* Published with permission of the California Test Bureau, Los Angeles, California.)

Fig. 42. Responses of nine- and ten-year-olds from two social-status classes on intelligence test items (**10**). Items selected for this figure are not entirely representative of the findings on the basis of all test items included in the research.

Table 27. A Form for Analyzing Tests

Title: Date of publication:

Authors: Cost, booklet:
                                          answer sheet:

Publisher:

General purpose of test: Time required:

Group to which applicable: Forms:

Mental functions represented in each score reported (from logical analysis):

What author intended to measure; basis for selecting items:

Basis for scoring (correction formulas, empirical weighting, etc.—if any):

Evidence of empirical validity (criterion, number and type of cases, results):

Comments regarding validity for particular purposes:

Evidence of equivalence of scores (method of determining, number and type of cases, results):

Evidence of stability of scores (method of determining, number and type of cases, results):

Norms (type of norms reported, sample on which determined):

Comments regarding adequacy of reliability and norms for particular purposes:

Practical features of importance:

Comments of reviewers:

General evaluation:

References:

---

acquaint himself with particular group tests. To assist in making this study, the form presented in Table 27 is suggested. This outline is intended to point out every feature worth noting, and it may be that some items can be omitted when reviewing tests with a particular purpose in mind. The form may be used for tests of any type. Most of the information called for by this form will appear in the test manual, if the manual is an adequate one. The manual, however, presents the test in a favorable light. A careful evaluation of all claims made is essential to bring to light the limitations of the test. Sources such as Buros will also be helpful, and both research and experience with the test contribute to evaluation.

To demonstrate what a complete test analysis is like, the author has made

Arithmetic

    1. How many pencils can you buy for 50 cents at the rate of 2 for 5 cents?
        (a) 10   (b) 20   (c) 25   (d) 100   (e) 125

Completion. Select the first letter of the word which fits the following definition.

    The thin cutting part of an instrument, as of a knife or sword.
        A   B   D   H   W

Figure Analogies. Decide what rule is used to change Figure A to Figure B, apply this rule to Figure C, and select the resulting figure from the five at the right.

A	B	C	1	2	3	4	5

Same—Opposite. Select the word that is the same or the opposite of the word at left.

    ancient   (1) dry   (2) long   (3) happy   (4) old

Number Series. Select the next number for the series at left.

10	8	11	9	12	10		9	10	11	12	13
							(a)	(b)	(c)	(d)	(e)

Verbal Analogies.

    cloth-dye   house-   (1) shade   (2) paint   (3) brush   (4) door

Fig. 43.   Sample items from subtests of the American Council
Psychological Examination.

Table 28.   An Analysis of the ACE Test

Title: American Council on Education Psychological Examination for College Freshmen

Authors: L. L. and T. G. Thurstone	*Date of Publication:* see "Forms"
Publisher: Educational Testing Service	*Cost, booklet:* 8¢ answer sheet: 2¢
General purpose of test: to measure aptitude of college freshmen	*Time required:* 1 hour, plus administration time
Group to which applicable: college students	*Forms:* new form each August. (Another form for high school. SRA Verbal Form and Thurstone Test of Mental Alertness are similar, shorter.)

Mental functions represented in each score reported (from logical analysis):
    L, linguistic ability—Includes vocabulary knowledge and ability to reason with words; speed of reading may be important.
    Q, quantitative ability—Includes skill and speed in arithmetic problems, reasoning with numbers, and a difficult non-verbal reasoning section.

Table 28. (Continued)

Total score—Influenced both by past school learning and ability to attack unfamiliar problems. Speed is important.

What authors intended to measure; basis for selecting items:
Scholastic aptitude, with especial reference to college curricula.
Items chosen by factor analysis and preliminary trial, those having suitable difficulty and discrimination being retained.

Basis for scoring (correction formulas, empirical weighting, etc.):
Score is number right.

Evidence of empirical validity (criterion, number and type of cases, results):
Numerous studies in various colleges show correlations with marks around .50.
But some studies fail to support belief that Q best predicts engineering and science courses, or that L best predicts work in more verbal subjects (17).
Comparison with Rorschach for 80 college girls shows that test reflects personality factors. Girls with L higher than Q have greater spontaneity; those with higher Q have tendency toward precision, control (21).
Correlation of ACE with Binet Form L is .60, for 112 superior college freshmen (2).

Comments regarding validity for particular purposes:
Estimates probable college success as well as any mental test; Ohio State test equally suitable. Owing to greater difficulty, ACE is superior to general-purpose tests with college groups. Owing to lack of correction formula, it tends to reward hasty workers. Slow workers earn low scores, no matter how capable they would be with longer time. Low scores should be considered as indications that student will do poorly unless given special help (perhaps remedial work in reading or arithmetic); low scores are not necessarily a sign of basic inaptitude. ACE probably not suitable for non-academic prediction. Further research on significance of Q and L scores is required.

Evidence of equivalence of scores (method of determining, number and type of cases, results):
Correlation between forms not published.

Evidence of stability of scores (method of determining, number and type of cases, results):
$r = .83$, for 286 college women tested as freshmen and seniors.
Marked gains in score during freshman year (13).

Norms (type of norms reported, sample on which determined):
Each summer, national percentiles and means for all cooperating colleges for previous year's test are published, without identifying colleges by name. The 1946 norms were based on 86,212 cases in 317 colleges. Preliminary norms, estimated from results with previous form, are published when each new form is released.

Comments regarding adequacy of reliability and norms for particular purposes:
Reliability is quite satisfactory for college groups. Few other tests are equally reliable for superior students. One-year lag in publication of norms causes no serious difficulty. Test should be interpreted with reference to local norms, since demands of different colleges vary. Separate norms by divisions of the college or university should be collected.

Practical features of importance:
Adapted to machine scoring, which is essential for rapid processing of freshmen. Requires painstaking administration, owing to numerous timed subtests. New forms each year eliminate much practice effect, leaking of questions in advance.

Comments of reviewers:
"This is perhaps the test that one is likely to recommend to anyone who is looking for a 'good' intelligence test to give to a group of college freshmen. . . . Division of the score into a Q and an L score needs considerable study before its full significance is apparent" (Commins, 8).

"Constructed with high quality of workmanship. . . . Avoids the overweighting of one fundamental resource (verbal ability) to the neglect of others that may be relatively more important in specialized curricula and courses. . . . The 'quantitative' part is a conglomerate factorially. . . . It is the reviewer's belief that the factors measured, except for the numerical, should be assessed by means of power tests" (Guilford, 8).

General evaluation:
An especially useful test for its purpose. Must not be treated as an all-purpose mental test. Persons with low scores must be studied carefully.

---

such a report on the American Council Psychological Examination. Figure 43 illustrates the types of items composing the subtests of the ACE test.

GROUP NON-VERBAL TESTS

Non-verbal group tests have not been widely used in this country. It is rare that one has occasion to test an entire group of persons who are linguistically handicapped. Such situations do arise, as in military processing of illiterates or in special schools for "non-academic" pupils. It is possible that non-verbal tests deserve wider application in industry than they have received.

The most widely known non-verbal test is Army Beta, which was used in World War I for those cases in which the verbal test, Alpha, was considered inappropriate. Directions were in pantomime, which removed the effect of differences in language ability from the score. In World War II, the Group

Table 29. Representative Group Non-Verbal Tests

Test and Publisher	Age Level	Typical Tasks, Special Features	Comments of Reviewers[a]
CMM Non-Language (Calif. Test Bureau)		See Table 24	
Cattell Culture-Free Test (Psych. Corp.)	MA 12 to superior adult	Classification, figure series, etc. Nearly unspeeded. Supposed free from school influence. Range covers superior groups	"Relatively uninfluenced by cultural factors, highly saturated with general intelligence" (Shipley, **8**). "Little evidence to show test free from over-all cultural influence" (Wechsler, **8**).
Chicago Non-Verbal (Psych. Corp.)	Age 6 to adult	Digit symbol, block counting, etc. Can be used with pantomime directions	"Not reliable enough to use in comparing a child with his classmates. . . . Norms tentative" (Bernreuter, **7**, p. 211). "Wider range of mental functions [than competing tests]" (Pignatelli, **7**, p. 212).
Pintner General Ability Tests: Non-Language (World Book)	Grades 4–9	Paper folding, reasoning with forms, etc. Pantomime directions possible	"Well constructed. . . . Best test in its field" (Whitmer, **8**).
Revised Beta (Psych. Corp.)	Age 16–60	Maze, digit symbol, picture completion, etc.	"Most of the subtests measure the same things that verbal tests do except that the subject is given pictures and symbols, not words" (Wechsler, **7**, p. 242).
SRA Non-Verbal Form (Sci. Res. Assoc.)	Adolescents and adults	Picture classification (see Fig. 10)	

[a] The reader should refer to the source cited for a full statement of the reviewer's opinion.

Target Test filled the same function. There have been a variety of civilian non-verbal tests, each offering new item forms, superior standardization, or other minor changes. Most recently, non-verbal materials have been used as sections in diagnostic or semi-diagnostic batteries. Thus, the CMM Non-Language section is a largely non-verbal test and can be given separately, but it is more often given as part of a general mental test. Some other tests having non-verbal sections are listed in the next chapter.

Development of non-verbal tests has been hampered by the difficulty of eliminating language completely, since directions are difficult to pantomime. Another is that most non-verbal items do not call for very complex mental processes. With the exception of "spatial" items which measure ability to perceive relations among forms, most non-verbal items are too easy to measure superior adolescents and adults. Some recent tests have demonstrated ingenious solutions to this problem. But if "higher intelligence" involves ability to do abstract thinking, it is hard to conceive of an adequate high-level test that does not involve vocabulary and concepts.

Table 29 lists several current non-verbal tests. These are primarily used for clinical purposes. If a pupil is a poor reader, he will do badly on most verbal tests; if he does much better on a non-verbal test, he is a good prospect for remedial reading, since his problem seems to be a verbal handicap rather than lack of mentality. Delinquents who have done badly in school may show significantly better performance on non-verbal tests than on verbal tests; such a finding dramatically changes the treatment one would prescribe. Like performance tests, non-verbal tests are important in intercultural comparisons.

On the whole, the empirical validity of non-verbal tests has been only moderate. They do not correlate highly with verbal tests or with school success. This is to be expected, but a test which is not known to correlate with some other variable has little practical value. Criteria of success outside of school might correlate with non-verbal tests, but evidence has not been presented to establish this as a fact.

35. In a Veteran's Counseling Center, adults with varying educational backgrounds and vocational goals must be given advisement. Prepare what you consider a minimum list of intelligence tests needed to cope with all non-psychiatric cases.
36. Prepare a minimum list of intelligence tests needed by a school psychologist who is expected to diagnose any pupil, age 6 to 16, whose behavior or schoolwork is considered unsatisfactory.

AN EVALUATION OF INTELLIGENCE TESTING

Now that the reader is acquainted with the range of approaches used in studying general intelligence, it is appropriate to ask how adequate these mental tests are. Tests of general intelligence have been found useful in all types of psychological practice and research, but for some problems our present armamentarium is far from ideal.

One great gap is in tests of high-level general mental ability. The Wechsler test and the Binet tests have low ceilings, and are undependable in distinguishing between the superior and the very superior within, for example, college-graduate populations. The way to distinguish between the high grades of ability is to introduce more difficult items, but this is usually accomplished, as in the ACE test, by adding items depending upon advanced education rather than items calling for superior adaptive ability. It is hard to invent a test item which only one person in a thousand can pass, unless it calls for experiences that only highly educated people have. There is need for high-level tests in selecting graduate students and in choosing among employees in such superior groups as junior executives and engineers.

A second major limitation is the scholastic emphasis of present tests. Efforts to test types of thinking characterized by logic, accuracy, and knowledge have been very successful. There has been little success in testing the types of thinking which distinguish the novelist from the engineer or the clinical case worker from the museum curator. This is probably of minor importance at younger ages where all abilities seem to be highly correlated, although even here we must occasionally overlook a child of high potential along lines not stressed in our tests. In vocational guidance, we have little basis for judging which man will be most insightful, most creative, and most original, except to assume that these traits are correlated with high vocabulary or ability to solve analogies.

We also need better non-verbal tests. Non-verbal tests are much the same, and few of them require above-average-adult thinking. If one can have high mental ability, all tasks considered, without having exceptional verbal ability —as Thurstone's studies discussed in the next chapter imply—many people have been rated unjustly by our present tests. Mental tests do not have to be verbal. The stress in our culture on verbal education as the key to advancement has set the pattern for our tests. But the opposite situation is found in Japan. The written Japanese language is so difficult that it requires most of six years of schooling to become literate. Most Japanese, before the war, left school at the sixth or eighth grade, so that only the privileged elite developed their verbal abilities fully. To test school children and prospective employees, Japanese psychologists were forced to make nearly all their group tests non-verbal, since differences in verbal ability primarily reflected education. American testers have tended to assume that verbal differences should be stressed in tests, a statement which is unarguable only so long as the performances to be predicted are verbal in nature.

As against these persistent stumbling blocks, attention may be drawn to the steady progress that has been made in efficient test design, to the great growth in awareness of limitations of tests which has improved interpretation, and to the recent emergence of tests which call the clinician's attention to how the subject thinks, rather than how many points he can earn. More effective diagnosis of the facets of mental ability is promised by emerging research reported in the next chapter. We have come a long way from Wissler's trying to correlate college success with speed of canceling a's, and from Binet's wondering whether phrenologists had anything to contribute to the identification of mentally inferior children. The user of today's tests can be sure that the people they select for him will be a clearly superior group. The fact that the tests sometimes do injustice to an individual is a problem to which, in a democracy seeking to give everyone the opportunity he needs for development, we must give conscientious attention.

SUGGESTED READINGS

Bennett, Mary W. "Introduction," pp. 241–250, in "Factors influencing performance on group and individual tests of intelligence: I. Rate of work." *Genet. Psychol. Monogr.*, 1941, 23, 237–318.

Biber, Barbara, and others. "Performance tests," in *Child life in school.* New York: Dutton, 1942, pp. 273–297.

Canady, Herman G. "The methodology and interpretation of Negro-white mental testing." *Sch. & Soc.*, 1942, 55, 569–575.

Hamlin, Roy. "The role of intelligence in manipulative tests." *Amer. J. ment. Def.*, 1943, 48, 162–168.

REFERENCES

1. Allen, Mildred M. "Relationship between Kuhlmann-Anderson Intelligence Tests and academic achievement in grade IV." *J. educ. Psychol.*, 1944, 35, 229–239.
2. Anderson, Edward E., and others. "Wilson College studies in psychology: I. A comparison of the Wechsler-Bellevue, Revised Stanford-Binet, and American Council on Education tests at the college level." *J. Psychol.*, 1942, 14, 317–326.
3. Anderson, John E. "The limitations of infant and preschool tests in the measurement of intelligence." *J. Psychol.*, 1939, 8, 351–379.
4. Bayley, Nancy. "Mental growth during the first three years." *Genet. Psychol. Monogr.*, 1933, 14, 1–93.
5. Bennett, Mary W. "Factors influencing performance on group and individual tests of intelligence: I. Rate of work." *Genet. Psychol. Monogr.*, 1941, 23, 237–318.
6. Biber, Barbara, and others. *Child life in school.* New York: Dutton, 1942.
7. Buros, Oscar K. (ed.). *The 1940 mental measurements yearbook.* Highland Park, N.J.: The Mental Measurements Yearbook, 1941.
8. Buros, Oscar K. (ed). *The third mental measurements yearbook.* New Brunswick: Rutgers Univ. Press, 1948.
9. Durrell, Donald D. "The influence of reading ability in group intelligence measures." *J. educ. Psychol.*, 1933, 24, 412–416.
10. Eells, Kenneth C. Social-status factors in intelligence-test items. Unpublished Doctor's thesis, Univ. of Chicago, 1948.
11. Gaw, Frances. "A study of performance tests." *Brit. J. Psychol.*, 1925, 15, 374–392.
12. Honzik, Marjorie P. "The constancy of mental test performance during the preschool period." *J. genet. Psychol.*, 1938, 52, 285–302.
13. Hunter, Elwood C. "Changes in scores of college students on the American Council Psychological Examination at yearly intervals during the college course." *J. educ. Res.*, 1942, 36, 284–291.
14. Jones, Harold E., and others. *Development in adolescence.* New York: Appleton-Century, copyright, 1943.
15. Kelley, T. L. *Interpretation of educational measurements.* Yonkers: World Book, 1927.
16. Kent, Grace H. "Emergency battery of one-minute tests." *J. Psychol.*, 1942, 13, 141–164.

17. MacPhail, Andrew H. "Q and L scores on the ACE Psychological Examination." *Sch. & Soc.*, 1942, 56, 248–251.
18. Miller, W. S. "The variation and significance of intelligence quotients obtained from group tests." *J. educ. Psychol.*, 1924, 15, 359–366.
19. Monroe, W. S. (ed.). *Encyclopaedia of educational research*. New York: Macmillan, 1941.
20. Morris, Charles M. "A critical analysis of certain performance tests." *J. genet. Psychol.*, 1939, 54, 85–105.
21. Munroe, Ruth L. "Rorschach findings on college students showing different constellations of subscores on the A.C.E." *J. consult. Psychol.*, 1946, 10, 301–316.
22. Porteus, S. D. "The validity of the Porteus maze." *J. educ. Psychol.*, 1939, 30, 172–178.
23. Stewart, Naomi. "AGCT scores of Army personnel grouped by occupation." *Occupations*, 1947, 26, 5–41.
24. Strang, Ruth. "Variability in reading scores on a given level of intelligence test scores." *J. educ. Res.*, 1945, 38, 440–446.
25. Watson, Robert I. "The use of the Wechsler-Bellevue Scales: a supplement." *Psychol. Bull.*, 1946, 43, 61–68.
26. Weisenburg, Theodore, and others. *Adult intelligence*. New York: Commonwealth Fund, 1936.
27. Workman, B. E. "The work-limit method vs. the time-limit method in the construction and administration of college ability tests." *Ohio Coll. Assn. Bull.*, 1932, No. 79, 963–973.

CHAPTER 9

Thurston – Luther 9

Factor Analysis: The Sorting of Abilities

In previous chapters, attention has been given to measures of general mental development. Within those tests, however, there were many attempts to break down this all-over rating to describe the particular tasks at which the subject is best and poorest. General intelligence by no means tells the whole story about a person's endowment. He has certain knacks or talents which set him apart from those of equal general ability; these specific aptitudes are of great importance in guidance and personnel selection.

Aptitude tests first appeared in hit-or-miss fashion, as a psychologist interested in a particular performance such as music, typewriting, or assembly of small parts developed a device which he hoped would fit his needs. Often these tests failed to predict the task under consideration and though often labeled as "aptitude" or "prognostic" tests were essentially general intelligence tests. Recent studies are beginning to provide a more systematic method of studying aptitudes. Instead of cataloging all the specific tests that have been tried, it will be profitable to consider the major independent abilities in broader groupings.

Factor analysis is the tool used in sorting out the abilities of man. It helps separate special aptitudes from general intelligence and permits grouping of tests which overlap. Understanding factorial thinking is essential, as it underlies a large amount of current test construction. Because factor analysis is a difficult topic, only the simpler aspects of the method can be presented here.

THEORY OF FACTORIAL ANALYSIS

Interpreting Sets of Correlations

Conclusions about what a test measures are readily drawn from its correlations with other tests. A table of intercorrelations permits us to study the relations among a set of tests. Any correlation indicates that tests possess a common element. The common element that causes tests to be correlated is a *factor*. Binet applied such reasoning when he decided that his tests, all having a substantial relation to each other, must all be influenced by the same common factor, general intelligence. Gaw used the same reasoning to conclude that different performance tests measured the same thing (see p. 165). Wissler, who found that his tests had very small intercorrelations, concluded correctly that they had very little in common and therefore represented different abilities (see p. 102). The factor concept can be illustrated by means of a series of problems.

Table 30 presents correlations among three Navy classification tests. One should arrive at two conclusions from these data: (1) Because the correlations are generally positive, the tests must be affected by some common characteristic. (2) Tests A and B appear to have more in common than either has in common with test C. The reasonableness of such a result is clear when we find that A is the General Classification test, B the Reading test, and C the Arithmetic Reasoning test. Probably the common element in all three tests is general ability, schooling, and past learning. But the two verbal tests would certainly have more in common than either would have in common with a test strongly influenced by aptitude or training in mathematics. A formal factor analysis goes beyond this inspection and estimates how much each test is influenced by the common factors.

Table 30. Intercorrelations of Three
Tests for Navy Recruits (3)[a]

	A	B	C
A		.81	.69
B			.69
C			

[a] To simplify tables, each correlation is presented only once. The correlation of A with B (or B with A) is .81. Symmetrical entries could be made below the diagonal if desired.

Table 31. Intercorrelations of Four Attitude Tests Given to Young
Adults (14)

	Family	Law	Education	Economic Conservatism
Attitude Toward Family		.39	.30	.08
Attitude Toward Law			.40	.19
Attitude Toward Education				.09
Economic Conservatism				

A different factor description is needed for the attitude tests whose intercorrelations appear in Table 31. This time there is no substantial common element in all four tests. "Economic conservatism" seems to be nearly independent of the other three variables. "Family," "Law," and "Education" scores have positive intercorrelations and may be said to reflect a common factor. Frequently it is desirable to guess at the nature of the underlying factor and to name it. The correlations suggest that those who are critical of the family are also critical of the legal system and of educational institutions. Those who favor one of these tend to favor the others. Therefore, a proper name for the common factor might be "social conservatism," or "acceptance of present social institutions." In Table 31 the correlations are lower than in Table 30. The relatively low intercorrelations show that in addition to the common factor each of the first three tests includes some trait not common to the other tests.

Table 32.   Intercorrelations of Six Navy Classification Tests for Recruits (3)

	General Classification	Reading	Arithmetic Reasoning	Mechanical Aptitude	Electrical Knowledge	Mechanical Knowledge
General Classification	.81		.69	.60	.53	.49
Reading			.69	.56	.51	.46
Arithmetic Reasoning				.61	.47	.41
Mechanical Aptitude					.53	.55
Electrical Knowledge						.78
Mechanical Knowledge						

1. Table 32 presents correlations between tests of the Navy classification battery. Does there appear to be a single common factor among all these tests? If so, what might be its psychological nature?
2. Which pairs of tests seem to have the greatest common element, or overlap?

FACTOR THEORIES OF INTELLIGENCE

Factor analysis has clarified theoretical and practical problems. It helps to reduce duplication in testing programs where tests with different names actually measure the same trait. It reduces a conglomerate of psychological tests to ordered families. In one famous study, Thurstone found that most of the individual differences affecting scores on 56 mental tests could be expressed in terms of only 9 factors (8). Perhaps the greatest contribution of factor analysis has been to bring system to the study of the nature of intelligence.

Intercorrelations permit us to identify three types of elements in tests: general factors, group factors, and unique factors. A *general factor* is a factor present in all the tests in a given set. A *group factor* is a factor present in several, but not all, of the tests under consideration. A *unique factor* is a characteristic which influences score on only one of the tests (Fig. 44). General factors are present for the tests in Tables 30 and 32, but in Table 31 the general factor is negligible. A group factor is found among three tests in Table 31. Every test is probably influenced by some unique factor, but the Economic Conservatism score in Table 31 most clearly illustrates a test with a large specific content. In recent studies of the organization of abilities, the central question has been to identify the general, group, and unique factors in ability tests.

In the days of "faculty psychology" men were described as possessing good or poor memory, reasoning, imagination, and so on. These powers were thought of as largely independent of each other, but of course tests of the same function were expected to have a great deal in common. This was a

Suppose we have just one test, which we will represent by a diamond shape. Then we cannot assume the presence of common factors with other tests. We will use an unshaded area to represent unique factors.

Now suppose a second test is added. Then the following patterns are possible. The shaded area represents a general factor, common to both tests.

All factors may be unique.	There may be both general and unique factors.	The tests may measure the general factor and nothing else.

The possible patterns are even more varied if we add a third test. This time a general factor, present in all three tests, is shown by a heavily shaded area, and group factors are shown by lightly shaded areas.

All factors may be unique	There may be group and unique factors.	There may be general, group, and unique factors.	There may be only general and unique factors.

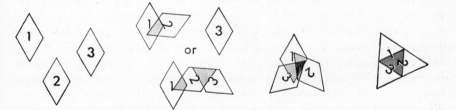

With three tests, it is also possible to have general and group, but no unique factors; group factors alone; or a general factor alone. These are unlikely.

Fig. 44. Possible factorial relations among tests.

group-factor theory, a theory that abilities fall into groups which are largely distinct from each other. Studies like those of Wissler tended to break down this theory by showing that even tests within the same group did not measure the same ability. If different memory tests measure entirely different things, we must retreat to a theory of unique abilities. The problem then would be to catalog, as independent abilities, such traits as memory for digits, memory for poetry, memory for designs, and so on. There would, of course, be an overwhelmingly long list of such subdivisions. Binet led a march away from the unique and group theories of mental organization with his search for a general, pervading "intelligence." As we have seen, this was justified by his evidence that a large number of tests dealing with significant abilities had a considerable common element. While the concept of intelligence as a general characteristic found in most mental performances has been of great usefulness, it has never been entirely satisfactory. Binet's test and every other have shown that mental development is not uniform, that no test is a pure measure of general intelligence alone. Recent research has emphasized a search for these other elements which affect test performance, in addition to Binet's general factor.

The theory of general intelligence has been most effectively stated by Spearman. He conceived of abilities as divisible into g (the general factor) and many unique factors found only in single tasks. Many investigators, especially in England, have used factor analysis in order to discover the nature of g by identifying tests saturated with it. According to Spearman (16, p. 411): "The g proved to be a factor which enters into the measurements of ability of all kinds, and which is constant for any individual, although varying greatly for different individuals. It showed itself to be involved invariably and exclusively in all operations of eductive nature, whatever might be the class of relation or the sort of fundaments [content] at issue. It was found to be equally concerned with each of two general dimensions of ability, Clearness and Speed."

Spearman's theory has been modified to account for the fact that some sets of mental tasks have common elements not present in other tasks. The Holzinger-Spearman method, known as "bi-factor" analysis, seeks to divide a set of tests into their general, group, and unique components (10).

A competing theory holds that it is most efficient to describe intelligence as broken into psychologically separate bundles of aptitudes, which can be separately measured. This theory does not require the clusters to be entirely independent. Although the theory superficially resembles faculty psychology, it accepts none of the faculty psychologists' ideas as to the nature and source of abilities. This group-factor emphasis is represented by Thurstone's "multiple-factor" techniques (19). The relations between the general and group theories of ability will be clarified in the sections to follow.

3. In different methods of interpreting performance, the Wechsler test yields information about a general factor, about group factors, or about unique factors present in only one subtest. Demonstrate the truth of this statement.
4. Confidence may be manifested in a variety of situations: making a speech to a women's club, taking one's car apart to repair it, piloting a fighter plane, going to a show instead of cramming for a test, and so on. Give three alternative explanations of the nature of confidence: one in which it is considered as a general factor, one in which it is divided into group factors, and one in which it is considered as a number of highly specific factors. Which theory do you think is most adequate?
5. If confidence is to be measured for selecting future fighter pilots, how would a psychologist test confidence for this purpose if he believed it to be a general trait? How would he proceed if he considered confidence to be specific to a particular situation?

Patterns of Factors

Before studying the evidence from factor analysis, it will be helpful to note two of the kinds of factor descriptions theoretically possible. Hypothetical correlations are used in the following illustration.

Table 33 gives intercorrelations for five tests and shows two ways of de-

Table 33.   Factorial Descriptions Appropriate for a Set of Five Tests

			Correlations		
	1	2	3	4	5
1		.60	.50	.35	.20
2			.30	.25	.10
3				.35	.20
4					.50
5					

A. Bi-Factor Structure					B. Multiple-Factor Structure				
	Factors[a]					Factors[a]			
Test	a	b	c	Unique	Test	a'	b'	c'	Unique
1	xx	x		U_1	1	xx		x	U_1
2	x	x		U_2	2	x		x	U_2
3	xx			U_3	3	xx	x		U_3
4	x		x	U_4	4		xx		U_4
5	x		xx	U_5	5		x		U_5

[a] Entries in the factor description indicate which tests are influenced by each factor; x indicates a moderate influence, xx indicates a marked influence. The complete factor pattern of any test is determined from the correlations by complex statistical procedures not discussed in this book.

scribing the tests factorially. The first pattern is a bi-factor description. According to Table 33A, Test 1 is made up of a heavy loading of the general factor (a) plus some of a group factor (b), and its unique factor (U_1). Mathematically it is equally sound to divide the tests according to the factor plan shown in Table 33B. This is a multiple-factor design and groups the tests in such a way that no general factor is reported. This time, Test 1 is found to contain two group factors (a') and (c'), and its unique factor (U_1).

The investigator in any study chooses whether he prefers to use a bi-factor or a multiple-factor description (or one of the several alternative methods such as those of Kelley and Hotelling). The choice is determined in part by the data and in part by the description that would be convenient for a particular purpose. The problem is not discussed fully here, but two basic principles are:

1. A general factor can always be obtained, if desired, when all the correlations in a matrix are positive.

2. One type of factor solution can be converted into another by appropriate algebraic methods (9).

This means that one can sometimes prove the absence of a general factor.

If the correlations permit a general factor, we may isolate it or not as we choose. For sets of positive intercorrelations, neither factor description is more "right" than the other. The difference between them is one of emphasis and convenience.

How Factor Analysis Groups Tests

A simple example of how factor analysis permits regrouping of tests will clarify its application. Peterson factored the Navy classification scores from the General Classification, Reading, Arithmetic, Mechanical Knowledge, and Mechanical Aptitude tests (13). These were tests designed by psychologists to measure each recruit on the types of abilities most important in placing him in a suitable berth. Because classification interviewers wished diagnosis of strengths and weaknesses, tests were broken into many subscores. There were twelve scores which had been used separately or considered for such use. The results of a multiple-factor analysis are found in Table 34.

Table 34. Factor Analysis of Navy Classification Test Scores (13)

| Test | Subdivision | Factor Loading[a] | | | |
		I	II	III	Unique
Reading	Reading	.70	0	0	x
General Classification	Opposites	.76	0	0	x
	Analogies	.73	0	0	x
	Series Completion	.68	0	x	x
Arithmetic Reasoning	Arithmetic Reasoning	.56	0	x	x
Mechanical Knowledge	Tool Relations	0	.69	0	x
	Mechanical Information	x	.59	0	x
	Electrical Comprehension	x	.67	0	x
	Mechanical Comprehension	x	.64	0	x
Mechanical Aptitude	Block Counting	0	0	.61	.64
	Mechanical Comprehension	0	x	.52	x
	Surface Development	x	x	x	.65

[a] x indicates factor loading between .20 and .50; 0 represents negligible loading, below .20.

The analysis shows only three common factors in the twelve tests. This of itself does not prove that there are only three abilities involved; perhaps each test makes a unique contribution, measuring an important independent factor. But the unique-factor loadings are too small to warrant using any tests to measure unique factors except Block Counting and Surface Development. Peterson, then, showed that most of the measurement in the twelve scores can be reduced to five scores which provide the same information without duplication. Factor I, Factor II, Factor III, and two unique factors are warranted. If a reliable test for each factor is designed, seven scores could be eliminated from the record a classification interviewer need think about. Peterson recommended that GCT and MK not be broken into subtests, since

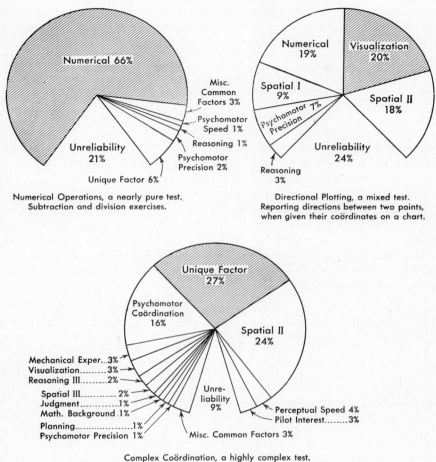

Numerical Operations, a nearly pure test.
Subtraction and division exercises.

Directional Plotting, a mixed test.
Reporting directions between two points,
when given their coördinates on a chart.

Complex Coördination, a highly complex test.
Job replica apparatus test.

Fig. 45. Tests of different factorial purity. Factor loadings were determined by analysis of a complete battery of AAF classification tests (**7**, pp. 828–831). The most prominent factor in each test is shaded.

the subtests within each measured nearly the same thing. The logic is identical to that introduced in Chapter 7, when it was pointed out that subtests having high correlations are rarely suitable for diagnosis.

The reader may be puzzled by the factor weights in Table 34. The weights for Block Counting, for example, add to over 1.00. It is necessary to explain that the weights, as written, do not represent the percentage breakdown of the tests. If the factors are uncorrelated, that breakdown is represented by the equation:

$$1 = f_1^2 + f_2^2 + f_3^2 + \ldots + U^2 + (1 - r_{11})$$

f_1, f_2, etc. are the factor weights for the various common factors, U is the unique-factor weight, and r_{11} is the coefficient of equivalence (reliability). If the reading test has a reliability of .85 (1), it breaks down as follows:[1]

> 15% unreliability, or error of measurement $(1 - .85)$
> 49% Factor I, probably scholastic ability $(.70^2)$
> 36% unique factors (remainder: 100% minus 15%, 49%)
> 100%

The percentage of the reliable portion of the test that is accounted for by the most prominent factor is called the saturation or purity of the test. For the Reading test, 49 percent out of 85 percent (the reliable portion) represents Factor I. There is 58 percent saturation $(49 \div 85)$.

Many investigators are seeking to develop saturated tests of various mental factors. It is contended that combinations of such pure tests permit more accurate predictions than tests which are impure. Figure 45 shows the factorial make-up of three tests tried by the Air Force. In this study a tremendous number of factors were isolated mathematically. Some tests, such as Numerical Operations, were found to be quite pure, whereas others combined a great many different abilities.

6. In Table 33A, describe the factor composition of Tests 2, 3, 4, and 5.
7. In Table 33B, describe the factor composition of Tests 2, 3, 4, and 5.
8. Diagram the factor structure of Tables 30 and 31, according to either the bi-factor or the multiple-factor pattern. Do not attempt to determine factor weights.
9. Compute the percentage contribution of each factor to the Reading test, assuming a reliability of .75 instead of .85.
10. What tests could be discarded, among the five in the Navy battery, without losing any factor now being reliably measured?

A Typical Factor Analysis

Factor analysis has been applied to aptitude, attitude, and personality variables. In the following section, an elaborate study of tests of mechanical ability is presented which both illustrates the results to be obtained by the method and leads to helpful conclusions regarding mechanical aptitudes.

This study was made by Harrell in an attempt to clarify the nature of "mechanical ability" (8). In 1940, when his work appeared, there were many tests for selecting workers for mechanical jobs, based on many assumptions about the nature of mechanical abilities. Were these tests, including measures of motor speed, coördination, visual perception, mechanical knowledge, and so on, measuring the same thing? If not, how many basically different sorts of ability were represented in the tests? Harrell gave 31 tests to 91 cotton-mill machine fixers, and supplemented the tests with other data. He

---

[1] Peterson's three factors have small intercorrelations (.19 to .31), but the formula for uncorrelated factors may be used here, since the Reading test contains only one of the factors.

Table 35. Factor Loadings of Mechanical Ability Tests **(8)**

		\<Factor Loadings\>				
Variable	Type of Performance	I Per- ceptual	II Verbal	III Youth	IV Agility	V Spatial
1 Youth		−.012	−.038	**.630**	.023	.068
2 Schooling		−.059	**.456**	.058	−.047	.079
3 Inexperience, Mech.		.033	−.177	**.618**	.061	.082
4 Minn. Spatial, acc.	Puts cutouts in holes	**.392**	.282	−.043	−.194	−.178
5 " " , speed	" " " "	.251	.043	.058	−.018	.275
6 " Assembly	Puts together mechanical devices	**.415**	−.190	−.026	−.163	**.383**
7 " Paper Form Board	Visualizes cut-up forms (Fig. 50)	.228	.052	.142	−.176	**.517**
8 " Interest Blank		.016	.149	.267	−.005	−.007
9 " Routine assembly	Same as 6, without novelty	**.624**	−.026	.068	−.004	.154
10 " Routine stripping	Same as 9, taking objects apart	**.457**	.001	−.090	.091	.044
11 Whitman pinboard, preferred hand	Puts pins in holes	.295	−.036	.193	**.357**	−.125
12 Whitman pinboard, non-pref. hand	" " " "	−.005	−.185	−.160	**.380**	.042
13 Whitman pinboard, both hands	" " " "	−.076	−.187	−.013	**.505**	.137
14 Whitman pegboard	" pegs " "	**.384**	.059	**.450**	.270	−.063
15 Whitman pegboard, disassembly	Removes nuts from bolts	.123	−.006	−.135	**.426**	.072
16 Whitman pegboard, assembly	Puts nuts on bolts	.319	.007	−.055	**.378**	−.130
17 Whitman Peg sorting	Sorts colored pegs into boxes	**.392**	.110	**.383**	.065	−.051
18 O'Connor Wiggly Block	Puts together cutout block	.230	−.050	−.073	.060	.332
19 Crockett assembly	Puts nuts on bolts	.248	−.018	−.174	**.430**	.058
20 " Block packing	Puts blocks in box	.128	−.002	.113	**.384**	.146
21 " Block laying	Puts blocks in row	−.078	−.150	.200	.180	.212
22 MacQuarrie Tracing	Traces narrow path	.167	.094	.336	.134	.065
23 " Tapping	Makes dots rapidly	−.015	**.367**	.121	.322	−.001
24 " Dotting	Makes dots precisely (Fig. 47)	−.111	.035	.117	**.501**	.043
25 " Copying	Copies figure by coördinates (Fig. 48)	−.015	.109	.007	.035	**.494**
26 " Location	Locates items by coördinates	.049	.305	.129	−.059	**.352**
27 " Block counting	Counts hidden blocks (Fig. 48)	.045	.077	−.008	−.062	**.540**
28 MacQuarrie Pursuit	Traces line through tangle pattern (Fig. 48)	−.080	.058	−.077	.077	**.515**
29 Stenquist I	Identifies tools	**.397**	.179	.009	−.003	.222
30 Thurstone Spatial Relations A	Identifies rotated figures (Fig. 10)	.238	.004	.001	.010	.327
31 Thurstone Spatial Relations B	Identifies rotated figures	−.066	.117	−.065	−.026	**.487**
32 Thurstone Punched holes	Visualizes paper folding	−.134	.086	−.054	.034	**.585**
33 " Opposites	Verbal opposites (Fig. 43)	−.044	**.547**	−.014	.047	.234
34 " Analogies	Verbal analogies (Fig. 43)	−.048	**.480**	.033	.014	.271
35 " Completion	Vocabulary (Fig. 43)	.046	**.561**	−.071	−.073	.244
36 Poor general rating		−.155	−.257	.321	−.028	.180
37 Poor mechanical rating		−.082	−.196	**.491**	−.043	−.020

Loadings of .35 or over in boldface type.

then obtained the 666 intercorrelations for 37 variables. This overwhelming array of data is in striking contrast to the results of the factor analysis, which reduces this mass of data, two pages hence, to only two brief sentences. The virtue of factor analysis is its ability to extract the significant elements from such a table of intercorrelations.

The factor loadings for the tests are reproduced in Table 35. The factor analysis was made by a multiple-factor method, since the absence of a general factor is suggested by the original correlations. The analysis shows five common factors. The factors themselves are somewhat correlated. Factors II, III, and V are influenced by a common element, probably general mental alertness. Factors I, IV, and V have some factor in common, probably motor

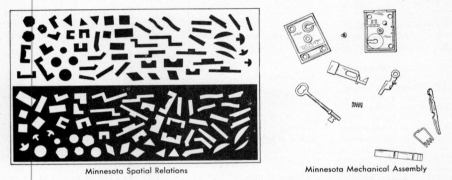

Minnesota Spatial Relations   Minnesota Mechanical Assembly

Fig. 46.   Tests measuring Factor I, Perception. (Courtesy, Marietta Apparatus Co.)

speed. The problem of factors which are only partly independent may be clarified by an analogy. Each factor represents a cluster of tests like a human family—all closely related. But different families in a tribe also may have some relationship—less close than within the family. Then, of course, there may be tribes with no common blood between them.

Factor I was found to be present particularly in test 9, routine assembly; 10, routine stripping; 6, assembly; 29, Stenquist I; 4, spatial relations accuracy; 17, peg sorting; and 14, peg sticking. Harrell identifies the probable meaning of this factor by the following reasoning (8, p. 22):

"None of the tests with high factor loadings are verbal. This factor seems to be Thurstone's perception (P) factor, even though none of the Thurstone perceptual tests are present in the above list. Thurstone writes that: 'The tests that call for this ability require the quick perception of detail in either visual or verbal material. . . .' One reason for deciding that this is not essentially a manual factor is because Factor IV is definitely manual. The Factor I identification tests differ from those of Factor IV in that they demand more discrimination and are less routine."

Factor II had its highest loadings in test 35, completion; 33, word opposites; 34, word analogies; and 2, schooling. This was identified as a verbal factor.

Factor III appeared in three non-test variables (1, youth; 3, inexperience;

and 37, poor mechanical rating) and two tests (14, peg sticking; and 17, peg sorting). The reasoning used by Harrell to describe this factor calls attention to significant elements in test validity (8, p. 23):

"The two variables with the highest weights, Youth and Inexperience, identify this factor as Youth (Y). The high loadings in the two tests may be due to a youthful willingness to follow directions, or to a deterioriation with age. The former explanation is preferred. Why just these two tests and no other should be highly weighted with Y may be understood by remembering that sticking and sorting the pegs according to their colors impress the machine fixing subjects as more childish than other tests. It looked fairly sensible, for example, to the machine fixers to put together a spark plug or a pair of calipers and there the older fixers would cooperate, but they could not understand why they should hasten to put red pegs in one tray and purple pegs in another tray. The younger fixers, however, were more impressed with the entire testing program and could not be dissuaded from believing that their responsiveness would influence their future chances of promotions."

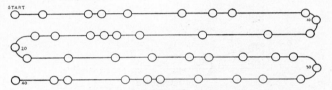

Fig. 47. MacQuarrie Dotting subtest, a measure of Factor IV, Agility. (By permission of California Test Bureau.) The subject dots as many circles as he can in the time allowed. (Shown here one-half size.)

Factor IV included test 13, pinboard with both hands; 24, dotting; 15, taking nuts off; 20, block packing; 12, pinboard with non-preferred hand; and 16, putting nuts on. This factor involves manual dexterity or agility.

Factor V is found in test 31 and 32, spatial tests; 27, block counting; 7, paper formboard; 28, pursuit; 25, copying; and 6, assembly. Nearly all these are pencil-and-paper tests requiring perceptual reasoning. This is recognized by Harrell as Thurstone's spatial factor (S), which Thurstone relates to "tests which require the subject to think visually of geometrical forms and of objects in space."

To summarize: The 37 scores yielded 5 group factors—visual perception, verbal, youth, manual agility, and spatial. There are two more pervasive group factors overlapping and linking these, namely, general mental alertness and motor speed.

The usefulness of such factor analysis is in giving a clearer picture of what tests are measuring. While this analysis does not bring out the importance of unique factors, it does suggest which tests tend to duplicate measurement of the same factors. Thus Harrell points out that each factor present in the more cumbersome apparatus tests is also measured by some pencil-and-paper test.

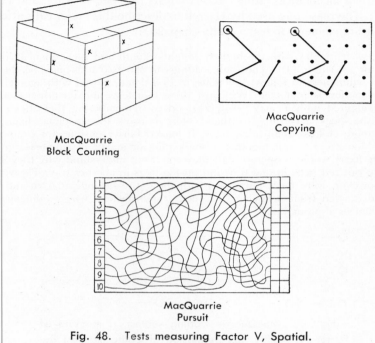

MacQuarrie
Block Counting

MacQuarrie
Copying

MacQuarrie
Pursuit

Fig. 48.   Tests measuring Factor V, Spatial.
(By permission of California Test Bureau.)

11. Suppose you wished to assemble a battery which included one test to measure each of Harrell's five factors as "purely" as possible. Which of the 37
tests would you use?
12. Describe each of the following tests in terms of Harrell's factors: Minnesota
Paper Form Board (7), interests (8), dotting (24), and location (26).
13. Putting nuts on bolts (16), and removing them from bolts (15) seem to be
fairly similar tasks. Can you explain why they have different factor composition?
14. After having the workers assemble novel tools (6), Harrell had them repeat
the procedure which was now familiar (9). Account for the shifts in the
factor loadings.
15. Describe in words the difference between Factor I (Perceptual) and Factor
V (Spatial).
16. The MacQuarrie subtests measure at least two different factors. What does this
suggest regarding the use of this test for vocational guidance?
17. Which tests have low weights in all five of Harrell's factors? What does this
indicate about their possible usefulness for measuring mechanical aptitudes?

PRIMARY MENTAL ABILITIES

Thurstone's Investigations

Having seen how Harrell divided the heterogeneous domain of mechanical ability into the most commonly measured factors, we are now in a posi-

tion to examine comparable work with mental tests. Factor studies of intelligence were begun by Spearman and his associates in England. An American pioneer in this area was T. L. Kelley, whose *Crossroads in the mind of man* (11) outlined the practical possibilities of factor analysis which are now beginning to be exploited. An extensive study by Spearman and Holzinger spent many years in the search for unitary mental traits. These and other ground-breaking studies have received less attention than the work of Thurstone; the claims and possibilities of factor analysis are best illustrated in his work, however.

Thurstone was interested in grouping the many types of exercises used in intelligence tests, to determine what major sub-abilities were to be found. His procedure was to give a large number of mental tests to the same subjects, compute intercorrelations, and make a multiple-factor analysis (18). The first study, which yielded nine factors, has since been supplemented by many similar analyses. Several of the factors have been found repeatedly, leading Thurstone to conclude that there are seven major types of ability which account for most correlations among mental-test items. These factors are Spatial (S), Perceptual (P), Number (N), Verbal (V), Word Fluency (W), Memory (M), and Reasoning (R). In addition, various minor factors, found in only a few test exercises and difficult to isolate and identify, have been suggested. One important factor found in studies other than Thurstone's is a speed factor; the speed element was held constant in Thurstone's studies, but would otherwise have accounted for part of the intertest relationship.

Thurstone followed his preliminary investigations with attempts to construct tests which would measure the separate primary abilities. Several batteries for different age levels have been produced, in which each test is saturated with only one of the major factors. These tests yield a diagnosis or breakdown of mental development, usually into six scores (P has been omitted). Since time must be allowed for a reliable measurement of each factor, the battery is long. The basic set of tests for ages 11 to 17 requires nearly two hours. This set of tests is compared with other differential batteries in Table 45. More recently, brief editions claiming to measure factors in only five minutes each have been placed on the market. No acceptable evidence of reliability is available and some of the tests are probably undependable.

Although verbal tests form a cluster in a set of heterogeneous tests, when a large battery of verbal tests is factored it breaks down into many sub-clusters. Each domain has been found to consist of many abilities, so that it is necessary to speak of "the verbal abilities," "the number abilities," and so on. Occasionally such refined analysis carries implications for vocational guidance and selection. Bechtoldt has analyzed the perceptual domain, which is relevant to mechanical tasks and visual inspection jobs. He found the following somewhat distinct abilities in such a battery: ability in choice-discrimination tasks, facility with familiar symbols, facility in associational recognition, facility in restructuring perceptual material, and facility in organizing simultaneously presented stimuli during distraction, etc. (1). A psychologist trying to identify superior inspectors could not use just any perceptual task to measure the perceptual element in job success. The element important in a particular inspection process might be any of Bechtoldt's factors, so that tests measuring each factor would probably have to be tried.

The Primary Abilities

While factor names are as descriptive as possible, the only way to understand the meaning of a factor is to study the types of test exercise where it appears. The following section describes the major Thurstone factors, with reference to Thurstone's tests and Wright's factor analysis of the 1916 Stanford-Binet (24).

The verbal factor V is found in the usual vocabulary tests, and in tests of comprehension and reasoning. Wright found verbal loadings in Binet vocabulary, comprehension, verbal absurdities, dissected sentences, and other tests. Among the items Thurstone uses to measure V are:

Today much of our clothing is designed to make a fashionable appearance rather than for

                          style   protection   children   sale   dresses

Synonyms: quiet   blue   still   tense   watery

The word-fluency factor W, which is only moderately correlated with V, calls for ability to think of words rapidly, as in anagrams and rhyming. The distinction between V and W is shown in two synonym tests tried by Thurstone (19, p. 3). A test requiring the subject to select the correct synonym from several choices was saturated with V but not W; a test in which he rapidly supplied three synonyms for each of a list of easy words measured W, not V. In the primary abilities tests, one W exercise requires the subject to list four-letter words beginning with c as fast as he can.

The spatial factor S was mentioned in connection with Harrell's study. S tests deal with visual form relationships. In the Binet, spatial loadings appeared in the ball-and-field test, copying a diamond, drawing a design from memory, and induction from observed paper-cutting. One of Thurstone's S tests is illustrated in Figure 10.

The number factor N appears in simple arithmetic tests. Tests of arithmetical skill are more saturated with N than tests of arithmetical reasoning. Counting from 20 to 1 and repeating digits backward are among the Binet items with number loadings.

The memorizing factor M appears in tests which call for rapid rote learning. One way to test this is to present nonsense material (such as first-last name pairs) for a short study period, then to test recall after an interval.

Reasoning, *R*, occurs in tests requiring induction of a rule from several instances, as in number series and in drawing conclusions from syllogisms. Many Binet items contain reasoning factors. Considerable loadings in reasoning factors were found for the ball-and-field test, verbal absurdities, interpretation of pictures, and other tests. The reasoning cluster is complex and has not been thoroughly studied. The primary abilities tests make use of such items as the following:

> *Letter series* (Mark the letter which comes next):
>   abxcdxefxghx . . .   hijkxy
> *Letter groupings* (Mark the group that is different):
>   AAAB   AAAM   AAAR   AATV

Another of the tests is "Pedigrees," illustrated in Figure 49.[2]

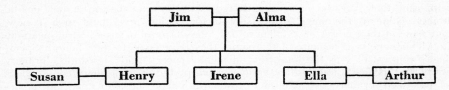

This chart tells you that Jim and Alma were married and had three children, Henry, Irene, and Ella. Henry married a girl named Susan, and Ella married a man named Arthur.

Now answer these questions by consulting the chart.

Irene's brother is
Jim   Henry   Arthur   Ella   Susan

How many children has Alma?   1 2 3 4 5

Irene's brother-in-law is
Henry   Susan   Ella   Arthur   Jim

Fig. 49.   Pedigrees, a test of factor *R*.

18. Which of the primary abilities seem to be represented in each of the following tests: ACE Psychological (pp. 185 ff.), SRA Non-Verbal (p. 52), and Henmon-Nelson (p. 176)?
19. Four scores in the primary abilities tests for ages five and six (*V*, *P*, *Q* [similar to *N*], and *S*) are added to obtain a total "intelligence quotient," representing "general learning ability." In what ways does the meaning of this score differ from that of other intelligence ratings for school ages? Which type of information about the pupil is most "valid"?
20. This statement comes from the manual for one of the primary abilities series: "Word Fluency. This factor involves the ability to think of isolated words

---

[2] From the *Chicago Test of Primary Mental Abilities*, Science Research Associates, Chicago.

with little concern for their meaning. It is important in school courses where written assignments are stressed, and in occupations requiring creative writing or reporting."

a. What evidence is required to demonstrate that the second sentence is true?

b. Describe a school assignment where W, rather than V, might be important.

Are Primary Abilities "Real"?

Throughout the history of factor analysis, there has been considerable debate regarding the reality of mental factors. Much of this debate is due to misunderstanding of the differences between systems of analysis, or of the statistical methods involved. Wolfle, who summarizes the development of factor analysis, makes this comment (23, p. 26):

"Thomson, Thurstone, and Tryon have repeatedly criticized the naivete of supposing that every factor necessarily represents an ultimate and unitary mental ability. None of the major students of factor analysis ever held such a view, but some of their critics have fallen into the easy error of accusing both Spearman and Thurstone of it because of the names they have given to their factors. Spearman's concept of g as the total fund of mental energy, and Thurstone's 'primary traits' and 'primary abilities' are easily misinterpreted. The ordinary connotations of the word 'primary' are such as to foster the belief that Thurstone has, or believes he has, isolated the basic and ultimate causes of differences in ability."

Factor analysis is in no sense comparable to the chemist's search for elements. There is only one answer to the question: What elements make up table salt? But in factor analysis there are many answers, all equally true but not equally convenient. The factor analyst may be compared with the photographer trying to picture a building as revealingly as possible. Wherever he sets his camera, he will lose some information, but by a skillful choice he will be able to show a large number of important features of the building.

Primary traits are not indivisible. They are merely families in which many interrelated abilities can be found. Their diagnostic importance lies in the fact that the separate families are less highly correlated than are tests within any one family. On this point hinges one of the major misunderstandings regarding factor analysis. Multiple-factor analysis has not disproved the existence of a general ability. On the contrary, Thurstone's factors are themselves correlated (Table 36). More and more studies now show that a gen-

Table 36.   Intercorrelations of Six Primary Abilities for Eighth-Graders (21, p. 37)

	N	W	V	S	M	R
N		.47	.38	.26	.19	.54
W			.51	.17	.39	.48
V				.17	.39	.55
S					.15	.39
M						.39
R						

eral factor may be extracted from such tests as those yielding the primary-abilities theory. Thurstone speaks of the primary factors as "different media for the expression of intellect" (20, p. 3). Whether the general factor is as prominent among adults as among children is still unsettled (2, 5, 22).

The factor analysis of a test will be somewhat different when based on different groups of subjects. Harrell's peg-sorting test might measure peg-sorting skill in a young group, but when older subjects were included most differences were accounted for by motivation. One must be particularly hesitant about assuming that a test measures the same factors in widely different groups, such as normals and psychotics (21, pp. 2 ff.).

One major question relates to the validity of the primary abilities for guidance and other practical application. There is little evidence today which permits practical interpretation of a Primary Mental Abilities (PMA) test profile. Those who claim that factor V predicts linguistic subjects, N predicts mathematics, and S predicts art or architecture have leaped to conclusions. Thurstone does declare that the tests have been used for over half a million cases in Chicago high schools and have been useful in understanding pupils. Says he, "It requires often considerable insight of the examiner to relate the mental profile to the circumstances of each case, but there is no question but that the profile is more helpful than the IQ in the interpretation of educational and behavior problems" (20, p. 10). This is an encouraging statement, but at present there is no published research to assist a counselor in making inferences about, say, a pupil with poor M and high R, or low V and average W. Adoption of the tests in school or industry is probably premature.

Some critics of factor studies have been disappointed because not all factors seemed to measure practically significant mental abilities. Kelley has expressed a fear that some of the factors are "mental factors of no importance" (12). Probably the correct position to take is that factor studies clarify what present tests measure. They cannot identify factors not built into the original tests. They cannot guarantee to produce factors of practical importance. But by clarifying the nature of tests they permit the psychologist to decide whether he is satisfied with the present content of his instruments. Too, the sorting out of primary abilities directs research to the question: For what are these particular human talents useful, and how can we capitalize on them?

One of the many studies of the relation between factored abilities and school performance is that of Swineford. Her work was based on a bi-factor analysis, which led to separate estimates of the general, verbal, and space factors. The correlations of these factors with high-school marks were as shown in Table 37. The column headed "Multiple Correlation" shows the degree of prediction possible by the best combination of the three scores. It may be concluded that factors V and S add little to the prediction based on general mental ability alone. A similar study by Shanner, with a set of

Table 37.   Prediction of Marks from Factor Scores (17)

Subject	N	General[a]	Verbal	Spatial	Multiple Correlation
General science	110	.74	.19	.21	.74
Biology	36	.65	.11	.07	.66
English	110	.53	.39	−.08	.64
English	40	.65	.11	.13	.66
Civics	35	.56	.30	.05	.69
Art	108	.68	.16	.24	.69
Algebra	50	.54	−.03	.12	.57
Geometry	36	.54	.11	.14	.55
Mechanical drawing	14	.85	−.47	.78	.87

[a] The test for g included items resembling Thurstone tests N and R, in addition to general-factor loadings from the verbal and spatial tests.

Thurstone's tests, showed correlations of only moderate size between ability scores and achievement tests, and some of them in directions contrary to expectation. (Example: N with advanced French, .34; with algebra, .12; with general science, −.32 [15].) A large number of studies at the college level give similar results (6). One of the more informative correlates seven PMA scores (R is broken in two parts and W is not tested) with grades for home economics students, and also correlates the grades with the Pressey and Otis tests, both of which are brief measures of general ability. The following listing includes all correlations over .30 (and the highest correlations for the art course):

Art: Inductive, .26; S, .25; V, .24.
Chemistry: N, .46; deductive, .43; inductive, .37; Pressey, .38; Otis, .37.
English composition: V, .55; Otis, .54; Pressey, .48.
Home Econ. 101 (Personal Problems): V, .50; inductive, .35; P, .31; Pressey, .41; Otis, .48.
Home Econ. 109 (Nutrition): V, .37; N, .33; deductive, .33; Pressey, .41; Otis, .43.

The best combination of two or three primary factor scores should predict grades a little better, in most subjects, than the short general mental test. The improvement of correlation is quite small, however, especially in view of the longer testing time used. All studies of prediction indicate that in its present stage of development the factorial approach has not produced tests which are superior to non-factorial diagnostic tests for practical purposes.

It was once hoped that only a few scores would be needed to describe fully the significant abilities of men. This hope has been dashed by increased experience with factor studies. According to Davis (4, p. 59):

"The results of testing hundreds of thousands of men in the armed forces and of analyzing these data suggest to many psychologists that the number of basic mental abilities may often have been underestimated. From factorial analyses of many different matrices of intercorrelations obtained as a result of testing aviation cadets in AAF classification centers, factors that have been mathematically determined have been named as indicated in the following list.

Carefulness	Numerical
General reasoning I	Perceptual speed
Integration I	Pilot interest
Integration II	Planning
Integration III	Psychomotor coordination
Judgment	Psychomotor precision
Kinesthetic motor	Psychomotor speed
Length estimation	Reasoning II
Mathematical background	Reasoning III
Mathematical reasoning	Social science background
Mechanical experience	Spatial Relations I
Memory I	Spatial Relations II
Memory II	Spatial Relations III
Memory III	Verbal
	Visualization

"There is no objective method of determining whether the names attached to the factors discovered in the analyses are accurate descriptions of the mental abilities represented by the factors. In any case, . . . the number of basic mental abilities may be much larger than was formerly believed."

21. Which correlations in Swineford's study were most changed by adding V and S as predictors?
22. Are there any areas of mental ability, which might yield additional factors, which would not have been included in studying aviation classification but might be important in other studies of talent?
23. How closely do the Thurstone factors correspond to the definitions of intelligence given in Chapter 6 (p. 107)?
24. According to the manual, the PMA tests for ages five and six should be given at the start of the first grade. "The tests may be given at the end of the kindergarten year, but mental growth is so rapid at this age that more valid measures can usually be obtained at the time of entrance to first grade."
    a. Why would mental growth affect validity, as well as level of scores?
    b. In view of the quoted statement, are scores obtained early in the first grade likely to be trustworthy?

SUGGESTED READINGS

Crawford, Albert B., and Burnham, Paul S. "Unitary traits and primary abilities," in *Forecasting college achievement. Part I.* New Haven: Yale Univ. Press, 1946, pp. 170–215.

Guilford, J. P., and Zimmerman, Wayne S. "Some AAF findings concerning aptitude factors." *Occupations,* 1947, 26, 154–159.

Holzinger, Karl J. "Why do people factor?" *Psychometrika,* 1942, 7, 147–156.

Thurstone, L. L. "Testing intelligence and aptitudes." *Hygeia,* 1945, 53, 32–36 *et seq.*

REFERENCES

1. Bechtoldt, Harold P. "Factorial investigation of the perceptual-speed factor." *Amer. Psychologist,* 1947, 2, 304–305.

2. Clark, Mamie P. "Changes in primary mental abilities with age." *Arch. Psychol.*, 1944, No. 291.

3. Conrad, Herbert S. *A statistical evaluation of the Basic Classification Test Battery (Form 1).* O.S.R.D. Rep. No. 4636; Publ. Bd. No. 13294. Washington: U.S. Dep. Commerce, 1946.

4. Davis, Frederick B. *Utilizing human talent.* Washington: American Council on Education, 1947.

5. Garrett, Henry E., and others. "The age factor in mental organization." *Arch. Psychol.*, 1935, No. 176.

6. Goodman, Charles H. "Prediction of college success by means of Thurstone's primary abilities tests." *Educ. psychol. Measmt.*, 1944, 4, 125–140.

7. Guilford, J. P. (ed.). *Printed classification tests.* AAF Aviation Psychol. Prog. Res. Rep. No. 5, Washington: Govt. Printing Off., 1947.

8. Harrell, T. W. "A factor analysis of mechanical ability tests." *Psychometrika*, 1940, 5, 17–33.

9. Holzinger, Karl J., and Harman, H. H. "Relationship between factors obtained from certain analyses." *J. educ. Psychol.*, 1937, 28, 321–345.

10. Holzinger, Karl J., and Harman, H. H. *Factor analysis.* Chicago: Univ. of Chicago Press, 1941.

11. Kelley, Truman L. *Crossroads in the mind of man.* Stanford Univ.: Stanford Univ. Press, 1928.

12. Kelley, Truman L. "Mental factors of no importance." *J. educ. Psychol.*, 1939, 30, 139–142.

13. Peterson, Donald A. *Factor analysis of the new U.S. Navy Basic Classification Battery.* O.S.R.D. Rep. No. 3004. Princeton: CEEB, 1943.

14. Rundquist, E. A., and Sletto, R. F. *Personality in the depression.* Minneapolis: Univ. of Minnesota Press, 1936.

15. Shanner, William M. "A report on the Thurstone tests for primary mental abilities," in *1939 achievement testing program in independent schools and supplementary studies. Educ. Res. Bull.* No. 27, 1939, pp. 54–60.

16. Spearman, Charles. *The abilities of man.* New York: Macmillan, 1927.

17. Swineford, Frances. The nature of the general, verbal, and spatial bi-factors. Unpublished Doctor's dissertation, Univ. of Chicago, 1946.

18. Thurstone, L. L. *Primary mental abilities.* Chicago: Univ. of Chicago Press, 1938.

19. Thurstone, L. L. *Multiple-factor analysis.* Chicago: Univ. of Chicago Press, 1947.

20. Thurstone, L. L. "Psychological implications of factor analysis." *Psychometric Lab. Rep.* No. 44. Chicago: Psychometric Laboratory, 1947.

21. Thurstone, L. L., and Thurstone, Thelma G. *Factorial studies of intelligence.* Chicago: Univ. of Chicago Press, 1941.

22. War Manpower Commission, Division of Occupational Analysis. "Factor analysis of occupational aptitude tests." *Educ. psychol. Measmt.*, 1945, 5, 147–155.

23. Wolfle, Dael. *Factor analysis to 1940.* Chicago: Univ. of Chicago Press, 1940.

24. Wright, Ruth E. "A factor analysis of the original Stanford-Binet Scale." *Psychometrika*, 1939, 4, 209–220.

CHAPTER 10

Tests of Special Abilities

This chapter describes tests of special abilities widely used in vocational guidance and industrial selection. The purpose in describing these tests is to acquaint the reader with the variety of tools that have been explored and the ingenuity used in designing tests. No particular test or group of tests is of outstanding importance. The tests are grouped according to the following categories: spatial and perceptual abilities, psychomotor abilities, mechanical knowledge, artistic abilities, and sensory acuity and discrimination.

SPATIAL AND PERCEPTUAL ABILITIES

Spatial and perceptual tests have already been encountered in Thurstone's and Harrell's factor analyses, and as parts of many tests of general mental ability. Spatial tasks are illustrated in Figures 10 and 48, and in Figure 50 in this section. Tests of spatial abilities require the subject to reason about forms, or to recognize relations between them. Some tests are two-dimensional, and others require the solution of three-dimensional problems. Both pencil-and-paper and apparatus tests are used.

Spatial abilities have been considered important in engineering subjects such as mechanical drawing, descriptive geometry, architecture, and the like. Such a factor might be important in shop training and industrial jobs which call for judgment rather than mere manipulation. Validation studies, some of which are listed in Table 38, show that spatial ability is a useful predictive factor, but it alone rarely accounts for the major differences among students or workers. Such tests must be combined with other predictors.

A widely known apparatus test of spatial ability is O'Connor's Wiggly Block. This test consists of a large block ($9 \times 9 \times 12$ inches) which has been separated into nine longitudinal segments by wavy cuts with a jig saw. The parts are scattered in front of the subject, and the time he requires to assemble them is noted. The test was reported by O'Connor as a measure of "spatial visualization." Differences in the way the subject attacks the test appear to be of major importance in determining the score. Some people use a sheer trial-and-error approach, trying to assemble the block with great haste. Others study the pieces deliberately and then assemble the block. Some begin well, but are so concerned when unable to find the right block for a particular spot that they become disorganized. All these characteristics suggest that perhaps the test reveals behaviors which would be significant

Table 38. Empirical Validation of Spatial Tests

Test and Publisher	Sample	Criterion	Correlation of Test and Criterion	Remarks and Reference
Wiggly Block (Stoelting)	Engineering students	Grades in descriptive geometry	.30	Test described in text (22).
Mann Staticube (Missouri Educ. Test Co.)	Engineering students	Grades in descriptive geometry	.63	Pencil-paper test with high difficulty. May overlap with intelligence tests (3).
MacQuarrie Mechanical Ability (Calif. Test Bureau)	Dentistry students	Grades in "technique" courses	.25 to .46[a]	See Fig. 57, 58 (23).
MacQuarrie: Location subtest	Adding-machine operators	Production on work sample	.31	Other subtests less effective, except Tracing (r = .38) (28, p. 149).
Minnesota Paper Form Board (Psych. Corp.)	Apprentice pressmen	Ratings of skill, compared to others of equal experience	.58	Job requires fine perceptual judgment and mechanical adjustments (9).
Minnesota Paper Form Board	Lampshade sewers	Production speed	−.04	(28, p. 221)
Minnesota Paper Form Board	Merchandise packers	Production speed	.48	(28, p. 221)
Minnesota Paper Form Board	Pull-socket assemblers	Production speed	.05	(28, p. 221)

[a] Where more than one correlation is given in tables of this type, several estimates have been made.

on the job—but these are significant in the realm of personality, not ability. Since ability cannot be measured without some control of personality factors, scores on the Wiggly Block do not measure aptitude alone. It does provide an interesting opportunity to observe personality. Remmers and Smith (22) have been critical of the reliability of the Wiggly Block, which ranges (retest method) in the .70's for the three trials recommended by O'Connor. A total

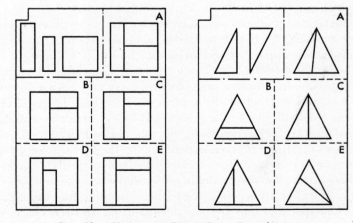

Fig. 50. Minnesota Paper Form Board items.

of *ten* trials would be reliable enough for guidance. Reliability is a common problem in psychomotor testing. Puzzles, where luck plays a part, are especially likely to be unreliable tests.

Perceptual tests emphasize rapid observation rather than reasoning. Perceptual tests have not been prominent in practical selection, although in a few fields perceptual abilities may be important. These are thought to include factory inspection jobs, aircraft recognition, bombardiering, and radar operation. Perceptual factors have also been studied intensively in research on reading, and perceptual tasks are used to diagnose poor readers or to determine whether pupils entering school have adequate ability to learn to read.

A special type of perceptual test is used for measuring "clerical aptitude." In the Minnesota Clerical Test, which is typical, the subject goes through a list like the following, noting errors as rapidly as possible:

$$79542_____79524$$
$$5794367_____5794367$$
$$\text{John C. Linder}_____\text{John C. Lender}$$
$$\text{Investors Syndicate}_____\text{Investors Syndicate}$$

A factor study shows this ability to be distinct from other perceptual abilities involving judgment of forms (34). Validation studies of perceptual tests are illustrated in Table 39.

Table 39. Empirical Validation of Perceptual Tests

Test and Publisher	Sample	Criterion	Correlation of Test and Criterion	Remarks and Reference
Minnesota Clerical Test (Psych. Corp.)	Groups of clerical workers	Supervisors' ratings	.28 to .42	Criterion believed unreliable (21, p. 208).
Minnesota Clerical	Punch-card operators	Volume of errorless production	.24 to .33	Correlations based on parts of test (28, p. 143).
Minnesota Clerical	Coding clerks	Volume of errorless production	.38 to .46	Correlations based on parts of test (28, p. 145).
Speed of identification (Air Force)	Bombardier students	Graduation-elimination	.14	(8, p. 264)
Visual section in Reading Aptitude Tests, Primary form (Houghton Mifflin)	First-grade pupils	Reading achievement at end of year	.60	Tests of orientation, visual pursuit, memory for forms. Visual, auditory, and other tests combined correlate .75 with criterion (17).
Lee-Clark Reading Readiness (Calif. Test Bureau)	First-grade pupils	Reading achievement at end of year	.49 to .68	Intelligence test correlates only .40 with criterion. Test calls for matching letters (15).

1. What characteristics of the jobs involved might account for the variation of validity coefficients for the Minnesota Paper Form Board from .58 to −.04 (Table 38)?

2. How might the tenth trial on the Wiggly Block reflect a different characteristic of the subject than the first three trials?
3. Under what circumstances might a test such as the Minnesota Clerical have low correlations with production among workers already successful in an occupation, and yet be highly valid for selecting new employees?

PSYCHOMOTOR ABILITIES

Grouping of Psychomotor Abilities

If one defines *psychomotor* to refer to all tests demanding mind-muscle coöperation, many sorts of test are included. We will concentrate attention here on tests useful for vocational selection. These tests deal with speed, simple reactions, and coördination, as well as perceptual factors.

Many people have investigated whether there is a general motor ability running through all skilled behaviors. Studies show that various significant motor behaviors are largely independent. A number of factor analyses now suggest the following list of group factors in psychomotor tests (7, 10, 20, 33, 34):

Spatial
Perceptual
Manual dexterity (Harrell's "agility")
Stereotyped rapid movement ("aiming")
Steadiness
Strength

There are other important elements each found in only a few psychomotor tests. In this chapter, it is convenient to group psychomotor tests as follows: speed and simple reaction time; steadiness and simple controlled movement; choice reaction time; and complex coördination. Tests grouped together are not necessarily highly correlated. Psychomotor tests are largely independent, so that when selecting workers one must find a particular performance test similar to whatever task one is investigating. One cannot rely on a few "primary" psychomotor abilities to include all important factors.

Speed and Simple Reaction Time

Among the methods used to determine the speed of simple reactions are tapping tests. These may use an electrical circuit, the subject tapping a key as rapidly as possible, or may use a pencil-and-paper form such as the Mac-Quarrie tapping test in which the subject places three dots in each printed circle as rapidly as possible. Speed tests generally measure finger, hand, or hand-and-forearm movements.

A slightly more complicated test of speed is the Minnesota Rate of Manipulation Test. This uses a board, containing rows of two-inch holes, and a number of loosely fitting round blocks. The subject places the blocks in the holes as rapidly as possible. Since everyone can do the task, differences in score are almost entirely attributable to speed. In the turning test, the same equipment is used, but the subject turns each block over in its hole. The correlation of placing and turning scores, similar as the tasks appear to be, is only .57 (36).

Reaction time is tested by special timing equipment. The subject may be required to throw a switch as soon after a light flashes as possible, or to step on a "brake" in response to a signal. For the refined measurements of reaction time required in experimental psychology, quite elaborate devices have been developed.

Tests of speed predict performance in extremely simple activities. There is little relation between speed of simple and complex reactions, or between simple reaction time and reaction time when judgment is required. Validity data are reported in Table 40.

Table 40.   Empirical Validation of Motor Speed Tests

Test and Publisher	Sample	Criterion	Correlation of Test and Criterion	Remarks and Reference
Minnesota Rate of Manipulation (Educ. Test Bureau)	Packers of facial tissues	Ratings of speed on job	.66	Based on three part scores combined (36).
Minnesota Manipulation	Can packers	Production speed	.35, .22	Based on separate part scores (28, p. 227).
Minnesota Manipulation	Pull-socket assemblers	Production speed	.09, .19	Based on separate part scores (28, p. 227).
Disk-setting, similar to Minn. Manipulation	Adult women	Ratings of skill in packaging, etc.	.56 to .77	Median, .67 (32).
Dotting, similar to MacQuarrie Tapping	Adult women	Ratings of skill in packaging, etc.	.31 to .83	Median, .64 (32).

Steadiness and Simple Controlled Movement

Steadiness is required where one must hold a posture or must trace a pattern accurately. Postural steadiness has been tested by the *ataxiameter*. One such instrument consists of a small balanced platform on which the subject stands; movements of the platform are recorded automatically. Arm steadiness is tested by measuring the subject's ability to hold a stylus outstretched in a small aperture without touching the sides of the hole. The stylus and hole are connected electrically, and each contact is registered on a counter. A test of hand steadiness requires the subject to move a stylus along a groove with narrowing walls.

Aiming also may be measured by a stylus-and-hole apparatus. The subject is required to thrust the stylus into progressively smaller holes without touching the sides (Fig. 11), or into holes momentarily uncovered by a rotating shutter.

4. Decide which type of steadiness test would be most promising for selection of operators for each of the tasks listed below. If none of these tests seems fully suitable, attempt to describe one more comparable to the job.

a. A jigsaw operator is to move a board, about eight inches square, so that a curved pattern is cut out.
b. A rifleman must hold his sights steadily on a target while resting on an elbow in prone position.
c. A pistol marksman must hold his sights steadily on a target while standing.
d. An engraver must follow a pattern with great precision using a small power tool.

Various measures test coördination or dexterity. The simplest coördinations require ability to use opposing muscles or two parts of the body coöperatively. Pursuit rotors have been a popular coördination test. In one common pursuit device, a small disk is set in a phonograph-like turntable. The subject is given a stylus and must follow the disk as it traces a circular or eccentric path. Electrical connection between the stylus and disk makes it possible to record the total time the subject holds contact.

The Two-Hand Coördination (or "lathe") Test is more complicated. The subject must follow a slowly moving disk with a pointer mounted in a carriage. By turning one handle with his right hand, he can move the pointer in

Table 41.   Empirical Validation of Tests of Simple Coördination

Test and Publisher	Sample	Criterion	Correlation	Remarks and Reference
Steadiness, hand[a]	Dentistry students	Four-year dentistry grades	.04	(11)
O'Connor Finger Dexterity (Stoelting)	Dentistry students	Dentistry grades	.15	(11)
Finger Dexterity	Dentistry students	Dentistry grades, all courses	.20, .30	r's range .00 to .38 for specific courses (21).
Finger Dexterity	Pull-socket assemblers	Production speed	—.09	(28, p. 235)
Scott Three-Hole (Stoelting)	Girls in training	Ratings as power-sewing-machine operators	.54	(Cf. Table 43.) Any single test practically valueless in eliminating failures (31).
MacQuarrie Test of Mech. Ability: Dotting (Calif. Test Bureau)	Punch-card operators	Volume of errorless production	.19 to .27	Other subtests gave lower correlation: Tapping, .19; Copying, .15; Pursuit, .12, etc. (28, p. 143).
MacQuarrie: Tracing	Adding-machine operators	Production in work sample	.38	(28, p. 148)
MacQuarrie: Dotting	Adding-machine operators	Production in work sample	.18	(28, p. 148)
Pegboard (USES)	Can packers	Production speed	.45	(28, p. 148)

[a] Steadiness tests are published by Stoelting and other firms.

one coördinate; by turning another handle simultaneously with his left hand, he can obtain movement in the perpendicular direction. Both hands must be used constantly to pursue the disk on its irregular path. Total time of contact is recorded.

Dexterities are measured by devices emphasizing both speed and accuracy. The O'Connor Tweezer Dexterity Test is one of the most widely known examples (Fig. 2). The subject is given a trayful of pins to be set rapidly in holes by means of tweezers. Finger dexterity is tested by tasks requiring the subject to screw nuts on bolts, or place pegs in holes.

Validities of tests of steadiness and simple movements are illustrated in Table 41.

Choice Reaction Time

Few skilled jobs call for simple instantaneous reaction where the subject can set himself and know in advance what reaction will be signaled for. Instead, the locomotive engineer, the gunner, and industrial control operators must make instant choices among the responses open to them to select the one most appropriate. Tests of complex reaction time present series of signals, with the subject to make the response associated with each signal. An example is the Discrimination Reaction Time test used by the Air Force. Two green and two red lights are mounted in a square pattern before the subject, together with four switches. The subject is to consider any pair of lights that flashes as if it were an arrow, the red light being the head. If this "arrow" points upward, for example, the uppermost switch is to be thrown as quickly as possible. Problems are presented in rapid succession.

Complex Coördination

With complicated machinery to be managed by simultaneous control of levers, pedals, and wheels, the operator must perform complex acts of skill. A conspicuous example is the task of piloting an airplane. The pilot must manage controls for rudder, elevator, and tail surfaces simultaneously, perhaps moving them in different directions and at different speeds. To test aptitude for this task, the Air Force used a Complex Coordination Test in which the subject, responding to light signals, was required to make the three types of motion used in piloting (Fig. 51).

This task represents the "job miniature" or *job replica* test. There is reason to believe that a different complex coördination test must be devised for each job. To make the test for pilots as much like the job coördination as possible, the equipment used and the motions required resemble the job as much as possible. In this case, the test equipment consists of a "stick" which moves like that in the plane, and foot rudder controls. The stimulus is a panel of lights which partially duplicates the type of signal given by turn and bank indicators. The advantages of replica tests are that they tend to require the same aptitudes as the job itself, that they appeal to applicants as realistic, and that they avoid the danger and expense of a tryout on the actual equipment. The name "miniature," although widely used, is misleading. Unless a replica is built to the same scale as the job equipment, and requires the same actions, it is not likely to measure the job aptitudes.

Another type of work sample uses equipment just like that on the job.

Fig. 51. SAM Complex Coördination Test (Mashburn), a job replica used in pilot selection. Note arrangements for group administration of a psychomotor test. Counters before the examiner record each man's performance. (Courtesy USAF.)

Sometimes special performance tasks are designed which duplicate one specific segment of the job to be predicted. An example is the Metal Filing Worksample, intended to measure that skill used in dentistry. This isolates one element of the job and measures it directly.

Complex coördination tests are of considerable value, provided they truly resemble the job to be predicted. The Metal Filing Worksample correlated .53 with grades in dentistry courses (1). The I.E.R. Trimming Test,[1] in which one cuts between a pair of narrowing lines with scissors, correlated .69 with ratings of power-sewing-machine trainees (31). The Hand-Tool Dexterity Test,[2] requiring operations on bolts and nuts with wrench and screwdriver, correlated .46 with performance of machinists (4).

General Considerations

The essential feature of a good psychomotor test is that it measure exactly the abilities called for by the job. In other areas where there is a large general factor there are usually many adequate tests, but in the psychomotor area the test that serves best on one problem may be quite unsatisfactory in predicting the next job. Table 42 presents Air Force data on this type of test. Validities are the correlations between test score and success in completing a particular type of training. The tests are not interchangeable. They meas-

---

[1] Publisher: C. H. Stoelting Co.
[2] Publisher: Psych. Corp.

ure different things, according to the intercorrelations. The Complex Coordination Test, good as a predictor of pilot success, is no good as a predictor of bombardiering; and so on.

Table 42.   Intercorrelations of Psychomotor Tests for Aircrew Candidates (8, pp. 92 ff.)[a]

	Complex Coördination	Two-Hand Coördination	Rotary Pursuit	Choice Reaction Time	Aiming Stress	Finger Dexterity	Validities		
							Bomb.	Nav.	Pilot
Complex coördination		.46	.30	.27	.14	.22	.13	.31	.40
Two-hand coördination	.46		.37	.25	.17	.25	.12	.29	.35
Rotary pursuit	.30	37		.22	.23	.26	.14	.12	.26
Choice reaction time	.27	.25	.22		.11	.19	.25	.41	.28
Aiming stress	.14	.17	.23	.11		.19	.00	.09	.12
Finger dexterity	.22	.25	.26	.19	.19		.15	.22	.15
Steadiness	.12	.07	—	.00	—	.16	.02	—	.02
Rudder control	.32	.30	.32	.07	—	.11	—	—	.30

[a] Data are combined from several tables. All correlations are based on large numbers of cases. Dashes indicate data not available. Validities differ slightly from those in Table 49; these differences are the result of basing the calculations on different samples.

The reader will have noted that psychomotor validity coefficients are generally disappointingly low, but psychomotor tests improve prediction when combined or added to batteries of other types of tests. Some of the validity coefficients are low because the criteria are inaccurate measures of success.

5. Which of the validity coefficients in Table 42 appear to support the principle that tests which require the same motor skills as the job are superior predictors?
6. What hypotheses can be advanced to explain the low correlation of the steadiness test with bombardier and pilot success, since it is obvious that steadiness is needed in both jobs?

Because of the number and diversity of manual tests, there is little value in a summary table of selected tests. The reader is referred to Bennett and Cruikshank, who review over 100 tests of manual and mechanical abilities. They arrive at the following general conclusions (3, pp. 4–5):

1. For vocational selection the motor tests should measure as nearly as possible the movements required on the job. Thus for routine motor tasks the miniature test, built to duplicate the movements required by the performer on the regular test, is probably best.
2. The test should, in most instances, involve a sufficiently large unit of work to measure fatigue and endurance rather than momentary capacity.
3. The test should be administered at the time of applicant selection. As yet no adequate study has been made which would lead us to believe that long-range prediction for motor tasks is entirely satisfactory.
4. For some skilled motor performances, requiring a diversity of motor op-

erations, some of the more complex manual tasks may probably be used with good success.

5. Vocational guidance (not selection) on the basis of motor skill alone is quite deplorable, except in the case of individuals who have gross incapacitating motor disabilities which may prove a deciding factor in vocational selection.

6. Sufficiently inclusive norms have not been obtained for tests which are probably very useful. This means that the user of tests for applicant selection should be constantly checking on the standards for the job in question.

If a test is supposed to measure aptitude, it is important to obtain a stable measure, characteristic of the person over a period of time. Unstable scores are obtained if we apply a psychomotor test without giving the subject a chance to learn the task in preliminary trials. On complicated testing devices, a subject cannot show his full ability until he has become familiar with the reaction required. Wulfeck gathered data with the Two-Hand Coördination Test. Ten subjects, selected on the basis of high or low initial ability, were given 10 trials on the equipment each day for 10 days. Subject A, who spent 81.5 percent of his time on target in six preliminary trials, learned very rapidly, reaching 99 percent "on target" on the third day. Subject C, beginning at 77.1 percent on target, learned steadily, reaching 99 percent on the fourth day. Subject Z, with the very low score of 52 percent before practice, rose even more rapidly, passing subject C on the second day and maintaining a 100 percent score on the fourth day and after. All other members of the "poor" group reached 96 percent or better on the fourth day. Since both the "good" and "poor" subjects showed nearly perfect ability on the task after becoming familiar with it, the first trials apparently measured their facility in adjusting to the new task, rather than their motor coördination. Wulfeck recommends that in such motor tests a minimum of 20 trials be used, the score on the last 5 trials being used as an index of ability (35).

7. Experimenters wish to study the effect of vitamin lack on motor performance. They plan to test a group, then alter the diet, and test again after some time. Would it be desirable to offer training on the tests before the first measurement?

8. a. Under what circumstances would measuring fatigue or endurance (2 in the numbered paragraphs above) lower the validity of a psychomotor test?
   b. Under what circumstances would it be desirable to measure endurance?

9. Psychomotor tests of school children and adolescents have not been found good predictors of later vocational success in mechanical work. What explanations can be advanced for this (3, pp. 10–11)?

10. In view of the low correlations between psychomotor tests, can such tests be helpful for guiding junior-high-school boys who are considering learning a trade?

11. Psychologists are now seeking pencil-paper tests of psychomotor abilities to

replace expensive apparatus tests. What types of apparatus test will be easiest and which most difficult to replace?

Psychomotor tests may be used fairly only to compare people at the same point on the learning curve. What a man does when he first tries the task does not always correlate highly with scores he earns later in the practice series (10, 26, 27). Scores tend to be more reliable after he has had practice on the task sufficient to remove the element of problem solving (26, 27). For most jobs, it is more important to know what coördination or speed the applicant can display after training than how fast he can adapt to a new task. Only where cost of training is high does the employer worry about speed of learning. The purpose in selection is to get workers who will produce well at the end of training.

In line with the evidence that good predictors resemble the job, J. L. Otis found that tests which predict quality on a job well may be poor predictors of speed (19). Correlations of predictive tests for sewing-machine operators are shown in Table 43, with both speed and quality criteria. Otis points out that workers suitable for a shop stressing quality may lack aptitudes needed in a shop seeking high volume of production. The user of psychomotor tests must have clearly in mind the nature of the job he wishes to predict. There is no all-round superior worker. (On some jobs, even intelligence is a liability because brighter workers dislike routine.)

Table 43. Prediction of Quality and Quantity of Work of Sewing-Machine Operators (19)

Test	Correlation with Quality Criterion (N = 52)	Correlation with Speed Criterion (N = 52)
Minnesota Clerical, Names	.36	.08
Minnesota Clerical, Number	.26	.22
Poppelreuter Tracing (time score)	−.31	.45
Poppelreuter Weaving	.27	.21
Paper folding	.30	−.10
Minnesota Spatial Relations (time)	.24	.28
Minnesota Paper Form Board	.32	.17
O'Connor Tweezer Dexterity	.07	.46
O'Connor Finger Dexterity	.20	.27
Minnesota Manipulation	.08	.31
Otis Self-Administering (IQ)	.17	.11
Tests with correlations in boldface, combined	.57	.64

MECHANICAL KNOWLEDGE

Information

Performance tests deal mostly with manipulation and motor speed. Tests of mechanical knowledge test information and problem-solving ability. They may be regarded as achievement tests, if the subject has learned to do the problem through experience and training. When such tests are used to classify applicants, it is assumed that those who have no mechanical background failed to acquire it because of lack of interest. A man making a poor score is therefore considered a probable poor job risk, even if his trouble is lack of background rather than poor capacity. Stenquist found it helpful, in guiding adolescent boys, to determine their knowledge of tools. A set of pictures of tools and machines is presented in his test, together with questions about their purpose or operation.

12. What assumption is made about the experience of junior-high-school boys, in using the Stenquist test as a measure for vocational guidance? What additional data should be used in deciding whether a boy will do well in shop work?

The U.S. Employment Service has done much to develop *trade tests,* for use where knowledge about only one job is important. These tests measure

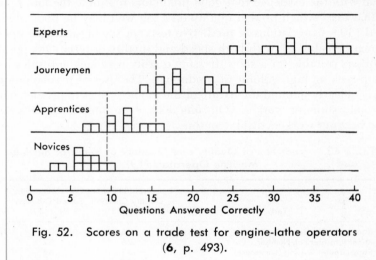

Fig. 52.   Scores on a trade test for engine-lathe operators
(**6,** p. 493).

knowledge about the job and are essentially short interviews. Many men who claim experience in a trade fail on the questions. During wartime, such a screen used in an employment center eliminated men who might otherwise have been shipped across the country to a plant where skilled men were needed. Trade questions are selected by analysis of job processes and tools. Questions are tested to eliminate any which would be unfair because of regional differences in methods of work or vocabulary. Three criterion groups are tested: expert workers, beginners in the trade, and workers in closely related trades. The items which discriminate are retained. Items from several tests are (28, pp. 45–47):

(Carpenter) What do you mean by a "shore" in carpentry? *Ans.* Upright brace.
(Plumber) What are the two most commonly used methods of testing plumbing systems? *Ans.* Water, smoke, peppermint, air (any two).

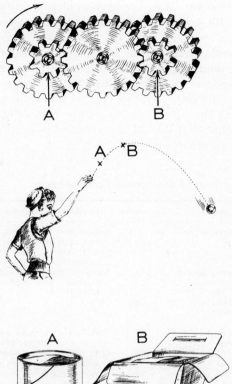

Which gear turns slower?
(If equal, mark C.)

At which point was the ball going
faster?
(If equal, mark C.)

In which container will the ice
cream stay hard longer?
(If equal, mark C.)

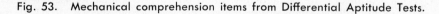

Fig. 53.   Mechanical comprehension items from Differential Aptitude Tests.

(Asbestos worker) In stitching canvas covering over pipes, where is the seam run?
   Ans. Out of sight, back or top of pipe (either).

A good trade test discriminates between novices, apprentices, journeymen,
and experts. In Figure 52 we see how a test of engine-lathe operators functions. Such a distribution of scores permits one to classify a new applicant
with little error; a score of 22 almost certainly indicates a journeyman.

Comprehension and Reasoning

   The Bennett Test of Mechanical Comprehension has been widely used. It
has three forms, and, in addition, items have been adapted for military
classification tests and for other aptitude tests. Bennett claims that "the problems have been selected in such a way as to minimize the effect of training

and formal knowledge" (3, p. 39). Emphasis is on application of principles rather than specific verbal learnings. Illustrative mechanical comprehension items are shown in Figure 53.

The Stenquist Assembly test is a performance test of knowledge or insight into mechanical problems. The tests, which range from third grade to adult levels, present simple mechanical devices: clothespin, push button, hinge, caster, etc. The parts of these devices are to be put together by the subject. The test was improved and issued as the Minnesota Assembly Test (Fig. 46), which uses a wider variety of objects. Table 44 reports validity coefficients for tests of comprehension and knowledge.

Table 44. Empirical Validation of Tests of Mechanical Comprehension

Test and Publisher	Sample	Criterion	Correlation	Remarks and Reference
Cox Mechanical Aptitude: Models (N.I.I.P.)	Engineering students	Engineering grades	.41 to .42	Subject must explain action of hidden mechanism, seeing only its effects (5).
Stenquist Mechanical Aptitude (Picture) II (World Book)	Engineering students	Engineering grades	.43	Stenquist Picture I and Assembly give negligible r's (13).
Bennett Mechanical Comprehension (Psych. Corp.)	Machine-tool operators	Ratings of proficiency	.64	(4)
Stenquist Assembly I (Stoelting)	Junior-high-school boys	Ratings by shop teacher	.77	(29). Lower r's found by later investigators (20).
Stenquist Picture II	Junior-high-school boys	Ratings by shop teacher	.64	(29). Lower r's in other studies (20).
Minnesota Assembly (Marietta)	Junior-high-school boys	Carefully scored quality of shop products	.55	Criterion correlates only .21 with IQ (20, p. 204).

13. From a study of the items, what would you say that tests of the Bennett type measure?
14. What features of the Bennett test would improve or impair its usefulness for predicting college engineering grades? For predicting success of naval recruits in learning maintenance of Diesel engines?
15. What does the Minnesota Assembly Test measure? Is it a test of innate ability or of knowledge?
16. Tiffin speaks of the Minnesota Assembly Test as follows (30, pp. 110–111):
"One criticism that has been leveled against this type of test is that persons tested are likely to vary in their familiarity with the various items, and hence the test is likely to measure this familiarity rather than mechanical ability. In spite of the validity of this criticism from a theoretical viewpoint, the fact remains that, in practical situations, the test has shown itself to be a serviceable measuring scale. This fact, rather than a theoretical criticism, is the basis upon which it should be evaluated."[3]

_____

[3] Reproduced by permission of Prentice-Hall, Inc., from *Industrial psychology*, Second Edition, by Joseph Tiffin. Copyright, 1942, 1947, by Prentice-Hall, Inc.

Do such theoretical criticisms have any importance for psychologists engaged in selection of employees?

17. a. The Purdue Assembly test is designed to include mechanisms using each important mechanical device: gears, levers, rack-and-pinion, etc. Does such a test assume that mechanical aptitude or comprehension is a single general ability, or that it is a group of specific abilities?
   b. If the latter theory is true, what implications does it have for selecting an employee for training in a skill such as watch repairing?
18. Boys surpass girls on the Bennett test (2). How may this finding be explained?
19. Mellenbruch reports validity coefficients ranging from .50 to .60 for his Mechanical Aptitude Test, which is somewhat like Stenquist's picture test. The criteria used are teacher's ranking of engineering drawing trainees (women), experience in mechanical activities, Stenquist scores, and scores on the Air Force Mechanical Information Test. What other validity studies are needed to support the recommendation that those scoring low on the test should not be hired for mechanical work or should be placed only in routine mechanical jobs?

ARTISTIC ABILITIES

Since general mental ability is no guarantee of success in artistic endeavors, much study has been directed toward identifying talent in art. A variety of tests of artistic aptitude have been proposed, which illustrate how special abilities are investigated. If one is to measure "aptitude for art" he must analyze the work of the artist to determine what that calls for. Having made such an analysis, he must design tests for the abilities involved. The tests must not depend on special training, since this would give an untrue picture of a person with little talent who had begun artistic training. The tests, of course, are refined and validated in the usual ways, with the added problem that there is no completely adequate criterion for judging superiority as an artist.

Different analysts have considered different abilities. The Meier Test of Art Judgment, the Lewerenz Test of Fundamental Abilities in Visual Art, and the Horn Art Aptitude Inventory are among the promising preliminary attempts in this field.[4]

The Meier test, as its name implies, studies the extent to which the subject is a good judge of aesthetic qualities. As such, it measures taste rather than ability in using art media. Pairs of pictures are presented in which some one characteristic has been altered markedly in composition, shading, or technique (cf. Fig. 54). The subject decides which of the two presentations is the more pleasing; if he agrees with "experts" who have taken the test, he gets a high score. Two further tests are planned, to measure "creative imagination" and "aesthetic perception."

The Lewerenz test is a battery of measures to indicate likelihood of success in drawing and painting. Among the aspects of artistic ability measured

---

[4] Publishers: Univ. of Iowa (Bureau of Educ. Research and Service), Calif. Test Bureau, Rochester Athenaeum, respectively.

Fig. 54.   Item from the Meier Test of Art Judgment.

are preference for designs, drawing a sketch to fit a pattern, locating proper positions of shadows, art vocabulary, reproducing a form (vase) from memory, correction of perspective, and color matching.

Creative and artistic abilities at a fairly high level are tested by the Horn Art Aptitude Inventory, designed for estimating the probable success of applicants to art school. Most of these persons will have had previous art training. The test has three parts: a scribble exercise to build confidence, a "doodle" exercise calling for simple compositions, and an imagery test. In the imagery test, the subject is given several cards, each bearing a pattern of lines. Around this set of lines, he is to sketch a picture (Fig. 55). The pictures are judged by art instructors as to imagination and technical drawing quality. Using careful scoring directions, competent judges can attain a correlation of .86 between independent scorings. A correlation of .66 is reported between freshman grades in art and scores at the beginning of the year (14). Further validation is in progress. The currently popular theory that ability and personality are in truth inseparable is well demonstrated by this test. Hellersberg has taken the Horn test, aptitude measure though it is, and used it to diagnose personality (12). Her method is to interpret the test as a projective technique (Chap. 20).

The prediction of artistic success is only in the beginning stages. Reliabilities and validities of tests are far too low to permit final judgment of talent from test scores. Two studies have pointed the way for further investigations in this field. Meier, reviewing extensive biographical and experimental studies, concluded that artistic talent lay in six traits: fine eye and hand coördination (craftsman skill), energy and concentration, intelligence (or some factors within it), perceptual facility (keenness of observation), creative imagination, and aesthetic judgment (16). It has long been thought

Fig. 55. Specimen item from Horn test of art aptitude, showing stimulus lines and two drawings based on them.

that the artist differs from other intelligent people in personality, perhaps more than in "aptitude." Roe has opened this area to testing with the Rorschach test (Chap. 20). She found that there is no one artistic personality, nor do successful artists seem to have "creative" personalities. It is true, however, that the style and character of pictures an artist produces are in many cases related to his personality structure (24).

20. What criterion would the Meier test be expected to predict better than the Horn test would, and vice versa?
21. What aspects of art ability if any do not appear to be measured by any of the tests described?
22. How could one obtain evidence whether the Meier test reflects native capacity rather than experience with art?

23. In view of the limited reliability and validity of art aptitude tests, in what way may they be used for guidance in the public schools at present?

SENSORY ABILITIES

Tests of simple sensory judgments and acuity have played a large part in experimental psychology and the development of test methods. From a practical point of view, only tests of vision and hearing are widely important. Only a cursory survey of the major types of vision and hearing tests can be offered here.

Vision

Because of the importance of visual skills in reading and industry, much research on vision has been done by medical and psychological investigators. The most refined measurement procedures are used by oculists, but many simpler techniques are used in school and industry. The range of visual abilities measured is impressive, and directs attention to the fact that most seemingly obvious psychological variables break down, when scrutinized, into many specific elements.

Accommodation, the ability to form a sharp image of the object seen, is tested most simply by the familiar Snellen and broken-circle charts. Convergence, the ability to use the two eyes together, is tested in several ways, the most common of which employs a binocular viewer. Special test cards permit the tester to determine whether the eyes are used together. These variables in turn are frequently subdivided. Near-point accommodation may not correspond to far-point vision. The two eyes must be tested separately, since they are often different. The eye muscles may work skillfully in horizontal tracking but coördinate poorly in vertical movements. And so on. The Telebinocular, which has been popular as a screening test for children, reports a total of 11 different scores. The Orthorater, designed for military and industrial use, analyzes vision into 12 separate scores. Both the latter tests use stereoscopic lenses to measure depth perception and coördination.[5]

Color vision has been the subject of many tests. While original interest in color vision stemmed from theoretical problems, tests have been important in military selection and in some industries. The Ishihara test has been widely used; it consists of plates in which greenish-yellow numbers are embedded in a yellow-orange field. A person who cannot distinguish the green and orange tints sees both areas as uniformly yellowish and cannot identify the numbers. Furthermore, a pattern of blue-green spots in red-orange background will catch the eye of the red-green-blind person, and cause him to report a different number, whereas the totally color-blind person will report no number at all. Various refinements of this technique, known as the pseudo-isochromatic test, have been developed. Other techniques require sorting or matching of colored wools or tiles.

---

[5] Publishers: Keystone View Co., Bausch and Lomb, respectively.

24. a. What criteria might be used to determine whether the Telebinocular test is valid?
   b. What criterion would be most suitable to determine the usefulness of the test for the routine screening of school children to locate visual defects? (Cf. 18.)

Hearing

Ability to hear is tested both in terms of general lack of deafness and in terms of a wide variety of specific abilities such as pitch discrimination. The common method for testing general acuity is the audiometer, an electronic

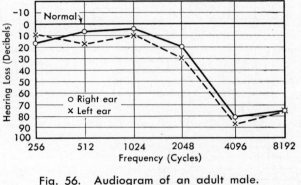

Fig. 56.   Audiogram of an adult male.
(Courtesy J. Donald Harris)

instrument which produces tones of any desired frequency and loudness. The faintest tone the person can hear at each frequency is determined. This test again illustrates how abilities can be broken down into finer subdivisions. The audiogram in Figure 56 is not an unusual type. As the heavy line shows, this subject has normal hearing in the frequency range near 1000 cycles. He probably hears a radio or speech as loud as does the person next to him. But his hearing loss in the high frequencies is severe, even though he may think of himself as having perfect hearing. He will lose some of the high-frequency sounds that help make consonants intelligible, he will miss some of the "brilliance" of orchestral music, and he will be a failure at some military duties where detection of high-frequency sounds is important.

Good hearing alone, however, does not mean that one will be superior in all hearing tasks. Military research established a need for special tests of ability to hear through noise. Communication in airplanes requires understanding of speech in the presence of a high noise level. Some persons with good general hearing could not do this.

Seashore's so-called Measures of Musical Talent (RCA) measure separately sensitivity to pitch, intensity, time, timbre, tonal memory, and rhythm. Pitch is tested by a series of paired tones, the subject judging whether the second tone is higher or lower than the first. Similar devices are used to de-

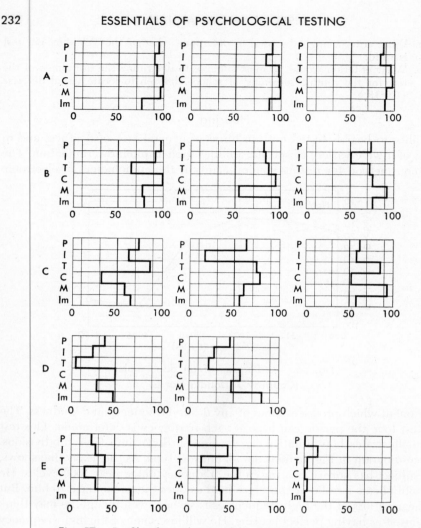

Fig. 57. Profiles from the Seashore Measures of Musical Talent. Profiles are rated A, safe; B, probable; C, possible; D, doubtful; E, discouraged, in terms of prognosis of success in the Eastman School of Music. Letters at the left of the profile signify the tests given: pitch, intensity, time, consonance, memory, and imagery.

termine the smallest difference to which the subject can react correctly in each aspect of hearing. The pitch, tonal memory, and intensity scales, which have satisfactory reliabilities, are good examples of tests having high logical validity. The tests have been used extensively to eliminate from musical training those whose scores were exceptionally low, or to advise students in the choice of musical instruments according to their pattern of aptitudes. Several Seashore profiles are shown in Figure 57.[6]

25. What conclusion can be drawn about an adolescent who does exceptionally well throughout the Seashore battery? Should such a person plan on a musical career?
26. An 11-year-old girl takes the Seashore test and does badly on pitch and rhythm. What assumptions are being made if the psychologist advises her mother that she should not take piano lessons?
27. What aspects of musical ability are most likely to account for the difference between a gifted conductor and a merely adequate conductor? Can such abilities be tested?

DIAGNOSTIC TEST BATTERIES

The desire to use a few dependable tests for guidance in a wide range of situations has led to the development of several diagnostic batteries for measuring abilities. A diagnostic battery is a set of tests having comparable norms and usually organized in an easily administered series with uniform style. Such batteries may be contrasted to collections of tests prepared by different authors and standardized on different populations, on which counselors have previously been forced to rely.

Table 45. Batteries for Differential Testing of Abilities

Test and Publisher	Age Range	Scores Reported	Special Features
Differential Aptitude Tests (Psych. Corp.)	Grades 8–12	Verbal reasoning, number, abstract reasoning, space relations, mechanical reasoning, clerical, spelling, language usage	Designed for guidance. Norms based on large numbers of representative pupils
Guilford-Zimmerman Aptitude Survey (Sheridan Supply Co.)	Adolescents and adults	Verbal reasoning, numerical, perceptual speed, spatial orientation, spatial visualization, mechanical knowledge	Adapted from Air Force tests. Authors hope to combine pure tests to predict various activities. Thirteen more tests planned
Primary Mental Abilities (Sci. Res. Assoc.)	5–6; 7–11; 11–17[a]	Verbal, word fluency, number, space, reasoning, memory	Intended for research on mental abilities
Yale Aptitude Battery (Yale Univ.)	College freshmen	Verbal, linguistic, verbal reasoning, quantitative reasoning, mathematical aptitude, spatial visualization, mechanical ingenuity	For college guidance. Various tests correlate high with certain courses, low with others
USES General Aptitude Test Battery (USES)	Adults	General intelligence, V, N, S, P, clerical perception, aiming, motor speed, finger dexterity, manual dexterity	Designed for placement of workers. Not released to testers generally. Based on extensive validation research with workers

[a] Various sets of the tests for adolescents have been published. The principal difference is in the length and reliability of the measures.

[6] By permission from *Psychology of music*, by Carl E. Seashore. Copyrighted, 1938, by McGraw-Hill Book Co., Inc.

Five rather different batteries are described in Table 45. The tests in some sets are selected for a practical purpose, each test being supposed to predict certain types of performance. Other batteries, constructed along factorial lines, depend more on test purity and logical validity than upon demonstrated empirical validity. In due time we may anticipate that pure, psychologically valid tests can be developed which will have empirical validity adequate for vocational and educational guidance.

There are too many uncorrelated special abilities for us to measure all the significant ones with a single battery. One encouraging fact is the finding of the U.S. Employment Service that jobs fall into "families" having similar requirements. Within jobs of broadly similar type and occupational level, persons qualified for one job also can succeed in other jobs. This means that tests might conceivably be validated on job families rather than single jobs. Unfortunately, even the best such attempt to date, a general battery for clerical workers, is quite inadequate for guidance. Correlations with success on different jobs are all positive, but often much too low. Correlations with criteria include .64, comptometer operators; .39–.48, coding clerks; .20, hand transcribers; .12, bookkeeping-machine operators (28, p. 154). Evidently each job has large specific elements. Conditions under which correlations under .50 have practical value are discussed in the next chapter.

28. In the extensive Minnesota investigations of mechanical ability, Paterson and his co-workers assumed a "theory of unique traits" which they describe as follows (20, p. 14):

> "According to this theory, the difference between individuals of two occupational classes can be expressed in terms of quantitative differences in a few traits. The difference between a machine tender and a farm hand, for example, is a matter of differences in a few particulars such as physical strength, ability to resist monotony, scope of attention, mechanical aptitude, and intelligence. Similarly, these and other capacities may serve to distinguish the machine tender from the tool maker, the tool maker from the foreman. . . ."

Under the theory, one would identify the limited list of unitary traits, make a test for each, and analyze each job to see which traits it demands. How well does this theory hold up, in terms of present knowledge about aptitudes?

SUGGESTED READINGS

Bennett, George K., and Cruikshank, Ruth M. *A summary of manual and mechanical ability tests.* New York: Psych. Corp., 1942.

Bennett, George K., and Fear, Richard A. "Mechanical comprehension and dexterity." *Person. J.*, 1943, 22, 12–17.

Long, W. F., and Lawshe, C. H., Jr. "The effective use of manipulative tests in industry." *Psychol. Bull.*, 1947, 44, 130–148.

Seashore, Carl E. "Principles of guidance in music," "Measures of musical talent," and "Analyses of talent in a music school," in *Psychology of music.* New York: McGraw-Hill, 1938, pp. 286–320.

Walther, Leon. "Technopsychology in a Swiss industry." *Person. J.*, 1929, 8, 1–18.

REFERENCES

1. Bellows, Roger M. "The status of selection and counseling techniques for dental students." *J. consult. Psychol.*, 1940, 4, 10–16.
2. Bennett, George K., and Cruikshank, Ruth M. "Sex differences in the understanding of mechanical problems." *J. appl. Psychol.*, 1942, 26, 121–127.
3. Bennett, George K., and Cruikshank, Ruth M. *A summary of manual and mechanical ability tests.* New York: Psych. Corp., 1942.
4. Bennett, George K., and Fear, Richard A. "Mechanical comprehension and dexterity." *Person. J.*, 1943, 22, 12–17.
5. Brush, Edward N. "Mechanical ability as a factor in engineering aptitude." *J. appl. Psychol.*, 1941, 25, 300–312.
6. Burtt, Harold E. *Principles of employment psychology.* New York: Harper, 2nd ed., 1942.
7. Buxton, Claude. "The application of multiple factorial methods to the study of motor abilities." *Psychometrika*, 1938, 3, 85–93.
8. DuBois, Philip H. (ed.). *The classification program.* AAF Aviation Psychol. Prog. Res. Rep. No. 2. Washington: Govt. Printing Off., 1947.
9. Hall, O. Milton. "An aid to the selection of apprentice pressmen." *Person. J.*, 1930, 9, 77–81.
10. Harrell, T. W. "A factor analysis of mechanical ability tests." *Psychometrika*, 1940, 5, 17–33.
11. Harris, Albert J. "The relative significance of measures of mechanical aptitude, intelligence, and previous scholarship for predicting achievement in dental school." *J. appl. Psychol.*, 1937, 21, 513–520.
12. Hellersberg, Elizabeth F. "The Horn-Hellersberg test and adjustment to reality." *Amer. J. Orthopsychiat.*, 1945, 15, 690–710.
13. Holcomb, G. W., and Laslett, H. R. "A prognostic study of engineering aptitude." *J. appl. Psychol.*, 1932, 16, 107–116.
14. Horn, Charles A., and Smith, Leo F. "The Horn Art Aptitude Inventory." *J. appl. Psychol.*, 1945, 29, 350–359.
15. Lee, J. Murray, and others. "Measuring reading readiness." *Elem. Sch. J.*, 1934, 34, 656–666.
16. Meier, Norman C. (ed.). "Studies in the psychology of art. Vol. III." *Psychol. Monogr.*, 51, 1939, No. 5.
17. Monroe, Marion. "Reading aptitude tests for the prediction of success and failure in beginning reading." *Education*, 1935, 56, 7–17.
18. Oak, Lura. "An appraisal of the Betts Visual Sensation and Perception Tests as a sorting device for use in schools." *J. educ. Psychol.*, 1939, 30, 241–250.
19. Otis, Jay L. "The prediction of success in power sewing machine operating." *J. appl. Psychol.*, 1938, 22, 350–366.
20. Paterson, Donald G., and others. *Minnesota mechanical ability tests.* Minneapolis: Univ. of Minnesota Press, 1930.
21. Paterson, Donald G., and others. *Student guidance techniques.* New York: McGraw-Hill, 1938.
22. Remmers, H. H., and Smith, J. M. "Reliability and practice effect in the O'Connor Wiggly Block Test." *J. appl. Psychol.*, 1936, 20, 591–598.
23. Robinson, J. Ben, and Bellows, Roger M. "Characteristics of successful dental students." *J. Amer. Ass. colleg. Registr.*, 1940, 16, 109–122.
24. Roe, Anne. "Painting and personality." *Rorschach Res. Exch.*, 1946, 10, 86–100.
25. Seashore, Carl E. *Psychology of music.* New York: McGraw-Hill, 1938.

26. Spence, Kenneth W., and others. *The effect of massing and distribution of practice on the Rotary Pursuit Test scores.* Washington: CAA, 1945.
27. Spence, Kenneth W., and others. *The effect of massing and distribution of practice on the S.A.M. Complex Coordination Test.* Washington: CAA, 1945.
28. Stead, Wm. H., and others. *Occupational counseling techniques.* New York: American Book Co., 1940.
29. Stenquist, John L. *Measurements of mechanical ability.* New York: Teachers Coll., Columbia Univ., 1923.
30. Tiffin, Joseph. *Industrial psychology.* New York: Prentice-Hall, 2nd ed., 1947.
31. Treat, Katharine. "Tests for garment machine operators." *Person. J.,* 1929, 8, 19–28.
32. Walther, Leon. "Technopsychology in a Swiss industry." *Person. J.,* 1929, 8, 1–18.
33. War Manpower Commission, Division of Occupational Analysis. "Factor analysis of occupational aptitude tests." *Educ. psychol. Measmt.,* 1945, 5, 147–155.
34. Wittenborn, J. R. "Mechanical ability, its nature and measurement." *Educ. psychol. Measmt.,* 1945, 5, 241–260, 395–409.
35. Wulfeck, W. H. "Learning the two-hand coordination test." *J. appl. Psychol.,* 1942, 26, 41–49.
36. Ziegler, W. A. *Minnesota Rate of Manipulation Tests, Manual.* Minneapolis: Educ. Test Bureau, 1939.

CHAPTER 11

Problems in Prediction: Prognostic Tests

PROCEDURES IN PREDICTION

When we must predict success in task X, we would like to look in a publisher's catalog, find a test labeled "Test of Aptitude for Task X," and begin using that test for selection. Unfortunately, the procedure required to establish a prediction program is much more complicated, because of faulty labeling of tests and the difficulties inherent in practical prediction. As previous chapters have shown, tests of intelligence measure different things, tests of mechanical abilities vary widely in content and psychological meaning, and even narrow subdivisions of ability may be represented by several tests which do not correlate highly with one another. Not all tests claimed to measure aptitude in a given area have been tested for empirical validity, and no one knows how well any test will work in a particular practical situation until he tries it out.

The counselor, employment manager, or administrator setting up standards for screening or providing for individual differences can accept no test on face value. As will be seen, he cannot accept a test solely on the basis of research conducted elsewhere. Sooner or later, nearly every test worker must make validity studies to determine whether his prediction methods are working. While the practicing tester may limit his studies to relatively simple checking, it is important to know the full procedure for validation research, since this establishes the basic logic of any study of prediction.[1]

To establish a testing program for prediction one chooses a number of tests for trial, determines their effectiveness experimentally, and devises a plan for using test scores in making decisions. One procedure relies on crude trial and error: the experimenter assembles a "shotgun" battery of all kinds of tests in the hope that one or more of them will prove effective. This method was more common in earlier years and is declining as we understand better why some tests are valid and others are not. Psychologists developing test batteries for guidance or selection today devote considerable thought to the characteristics of the job and the establishment of adequate criteria, as well as to the search for promising tests.

The stages in prediction research are as follows:

---

[1] The ensuing discussion is centered around employee selection in industry, primarily to simplify the explanation. The reader can paraphrase the procedures to apply to military, school, or clinical problems.

1. Job analysis, to determine what characteristics make for success or failure.
2. Choice of possibly useful tests for trial.
3. Administration of tests to an experimental group of workers.
4. Collection of criterion data showing how the experimental group of workers succeeded on the job.
5. Analysis of relation between test score and success on job, and installation of most effective selection plan.

Job Analysis

The first stage in establishing a prediction or selection program is to analyze the job to be predicted. This analysis attempts to determine what abilities and habits contribute to or limit success in the job. No machine-like procedure of checking off one by one all possible factors has ever been found successful. Instead, the psychologist studies the task with whatever insight and psychological knowledge he can muster. Analysis is in large measure an art. In this stage, one is looking for hunches worth pursuing by formal research methods. No prediction research can establish relations between tests and performance unless the experimenter is capable of forecasting what tests will be worth trying. The great number and variety of tests discourages a blind trial-and-error procedure.

One frequent approach to job analysis is to compare good and poor employees. Simple studies of such men often permit one to define the essential difference between good and bad performers. Such evidence does not, however, directly justify using tests of this ability for selection, since the good workers might have acquired their superior characteristics on the job after hiring.

In order to make a successful analysis, one must first of all have wide background in psychology. Understanding of motivation, motor habits and the organization of abilities, and knowledge of the multitude of tests now available for use are required. Detailed motion analysis will reveal what dexterities or coördinations are important. Analysis of the stimuli to which a worker responds may suggest that certain specific perceptual or sensory abilities are needed for success. Study of workers in training is helpful, since their difficulties in learning may show what aptitude is needed to avoid failure. Studies of prediction for other jobs are helpful, since they draw attention to tests worth trying, and sometimes suggest that certain tests may be eliminated without further trial. No routine or stereotyped approach is likely to be successful, however. The analyst must take off from the experience of others, but unless he brings in new hypotheses he is unlikely to find a better method of predicting than his predecessors. The history of testing shows many instances in which psychologists, merely trying over the same tests others had used before them, overlooked major aspects of the job which were not tested by the familiar instruments.

Form ES-267
(Rev. 2-44)

WAR MANPOWER COMMISSION
BUREAU OF MANPOWER UTILIZATIO
WORKER CHARACTERISTICS FORM

Budget Bureau No.11 RO-83.2
Approval Expires Feb.28,1946

Job Title ___LOUVER CLEANER___   Schedule No. ___Example___

Indicate the amount of each characteristic required of the worker in order to do the job satisfactorily by putting an X in the appropriate column. Following are the definitions of each level:

O - The characteristic is not required for satisfactory performance of the job.
C - A medium to very low degree of the characteristic is required in some element or elements of the job.
B - An above-average degree of the characteristic is required, either in numerous elements of the job or in the major or most skilled element.
A - A very high degree of the characteristic is required in some element of the job.

When in doubt between A and B, rate B; when in doubt between B and C, rate B; when in doubt between C and O, rate C. If some characteristic not on this list is required, write it in, rate it, and define it briefly at the bottom of the form.

O	C	B	A	CHARACTERISTICS REQUIRED	O	C	B	A	CHARACTERISTICS REQUIRED
	X			1. Work rapidly for long periods.		X			26. Arithmetic computation.
	X			2. Strength of hands.		X			27. Intelligence.
	X			3. Strength of arms.		X			28. Adaptability.
	X			4. Strength of back.		X			29. Ability to make decisions.
	X			5. Strength of legs.		X			30. Ability to plan.
X				6. Dexterity of fingers.		X			31. Initiative.
	X			7. Dexterity of hands and arms.		X			32. Understanding mechanical devices.
	X			8. Dexterity of foot and leg.		X			33. Attention to many items.
	X			9. Eye-hand coordination.		X			34. Oral expression.
X				10. Foot-hand-eye coordination.		X			35. Skill in written expression.
	X			11. Coordination of both hands.	X				36. Tact in dealing with people.
		X		12. Estimate size of objects.	X				37. Memory of names and persons.
		X		13. Estimate quantity of objects.	X				38. Personal appearance.
	X			14. Perceive form of objects.		X			39. Concentration amidst distractions.
X				15. Estimate speed or moving objects.			X		40. Emotional stability.
	X			16. Keeness of vision.			X		41. Work under hazardous conditions.
	X			17. Keeness of hearing.		X			42. Estimate quality of objects.
X				18. Sense of smell.			X		43. Unpleasant physical conditions.
X				19. Sense of taste.	X				44. Color discrimination.
X				20. Touch discrimination.	X				45. Ability to meet and deal with public.
		X		21. Muscular discrimination.					46. Height.
	X			22. Memory for details (things).					47. Weight.
	X			23. Memory for ideas (abstracts).					48. _____
	X			24. Memory for oral directions.					49. _____
	X			25. Memory for written directions.					50. _____

DEFINITIONS FOR ADDITIONAL CHARACTERISTICS:

7-6307 bu-wp

Fig. 58. The form has been filled out for the occupation of louver cleaner. A louver cleaner cleans and adjusts electrolytic cells used in magnesium processing. (Courtesy U.S. Employment Service.)

A job analysis should be highly specific. One should not state that successful workers have "mechanical ability"; one should instead define the ability as "knowledge and ability to apply principles of gears," or "speed in routine two-handed manipulation, not involving much finger dexterity or thinking."

Such breakdowns permit one to try the most appropriate test. The analysis should include as many characteristics as can possibly be detected in the worker. It is certain that some of these will be minor, and may not be important enough to test experimentally. Having a full analysis, however, permits the investigator at any time to reconsider his basis for prediction and introduce some of these additional elements. The analysis should not look only for "mental abilities." Instead, it should range over the entire field of abilities, habits, personality characteristics and interests, previous experiences, knowledge, physical characteristics, and so on.

The worker characteristics form of the U.S. Employment Service is designed to record the characteristics most often found in job analysis. Naturally, additional job specifications must be added for individual jobs. The form shown in Figure 58 has been filled out for the occupation, louver cleaner. This rating of characteristics is based on the judgment of a field analyst and is subject to experimental validation through the use of tests of the abilities rated A or B. Although traits are listed on the form in generalized terms, they are defined in the analyst's manual, e.g., "Dexterity of fingers: ability to manipulate small objects by rapid and/or accurate movements of the fingers" (20, pp. 175–183).

1. Which of the characteristics listed in Figure 58 may actually be composites including several abilities, in terms of the findings reported in previous chapters?
2. Prepare a list of the probable factors composing aptitude for one of the following jobs: making pie dough, operating a calculator of a particular type, taxi driving, or school teaching of some one type.
3. For many jobs requiring long training, e.g., physiotherapists, it is undesirable to take girls into training who will probably marry and drop out. What characteristics might distinguish between probable marriers and non-marriers?

Choice of Tests for Trial

Knowing the characteristics important in a job, the investigator must then find tests to measure each. He must make a choice between seeking one test which is a composite of the job requirements and seeking a group of tests, each of which is a pure and independent measure of one of the characteristics. The former method, which usually leads to tests of the job-replica type, is suitable only if the investigator is willing to go to the trouble of designing a new test for the job. The composite test has distinct disadvantages:

1. In employee placement or in guidance it is more economical to use a few tests which give information about many jobs than to have a separate test for each job.

2. If one function of testing is to place the worker in the most suitable job of several available, a test which includes characteristics of more than one job will be non-distinguishing.

3. Work samples must be revised, restandardized, and revalidated when

any change in the nature of the job is made. A battery of tests may often be revised to fit minor changes in the job by altering or adding only one test.

Despite these objections, the complex work sample usually is better than the pure test, because well-designed job replicas give the best validity coefficients.

Assuming that the investigator decides upon using many tests, each for a particular function, he must then choose between using available tests and constructing new ones. Insofar as the job under consideration uses abilities or traits already measured in published tests, such tests should be tried. Naturally, not every test with a relevant name will be suitable; the investigator must consider the difficulty of the test, its appropriateness to the intelligence and education of his subjects, and the like. If the job calls for an ability only partly similar to available aptitude tests, it is more desirable to make a new test to measure the ability the job requires than to obtain a pale distorted image of it from a less direct measure. Without condemning the useful Bennett Test of Mechanical Comprehension, we can use it to illustrate this point. The items measure some general factor, but there are also group and unique factors among its items, which are drawn from all portions of physics and mechanics. To select men for advanced electrical training, background and comprehension are significant; but it is probable that Bennett's items dealing with electricity will give better correlations than his items on forces, motion, and buoyancy. Inclusion of the latter items might, in fact, dilute the test so that it will fail to select good workers, whereas the electrical items alone, or a longer test of such items, would predict adequately.

Unless there is a close psychological correspondence between an available test and the job, a new test of the ability must be constructed. Even if the test items are appropriate, the structure of the test may make it unsuitable. A timed test, of excellent items, might predict badly on a job in which speed was insignificant. The solution is to use the test but to discard the author's time limits. If a job calls for bimanual speed, perhaps packing small objects with both hands, it would probably be sounder to restandardize the Minnesota Manipulation test for two hands than to use the standard (one hand) directions.

There is no simple answer to the question of published versus homemade tests. Tests with a wide range of usefulness are of distinct advantage in educational guidance, and to a lesser extent in employment work. Counselors would prefer to predict all jobs with a few tests. But the test which fits a specific job usually has significantly higher validity than the test for general use.

4. The Army and Navy tended to employ classification batteries made up of tests of general aptitudes likely to be found in several jobs, while the Army Air Force screened its candidates through tests many of which were related only to one particular aircrew job. Explain this difference in terms of the classification problems of each service.

5. What practical conditions would a department store consider in deciding whether to make a special test for each type of clerk or to use a published test for salespeople in general?

Experimental Trial

The crucial step in prediction research is experimental trial of the instruments chosen after job analysis. One must give the tests to typical *applicants* and observe the correspondence of test scores to success. In practical work there is unfortunately much pressure to do without experimental study. When the psychologist reports to his boss that he believes test D will eliminate poorer employees, the boss is far more anxious to install the test and benefit from it at once than to withhold judgment during weeks or months of study. Full experimental trial is indispensable. No hypothesis can be trusted until tested, because there have been many instances in which "likely" tests proved to be of no value in selection. The non-psychologist may propose to use the test to eliminate poor men, and to conduct research on the survivors to determine the relation between test and performance. A good test, however, might not predict which of the acceptable men would do well on the job, even though it could weed out the failures. (Example: An audiometric test would rule out some people as music students; but within a selected group, all of whom could hear, it would not predict success.) It will become clear later, too, that only trial on an unselected group can accurately establish critical scores, weightings of tests, and correlations. So important is experimental trial on an unselected population that the AAF went to the trouble to validate its selection methods by sending 1300 men, a random sample of all eligible soldiers, through training for flying, even though it knew in advance that the majority of these men would be failures (8, pp. 181–258).

The tests should be given with the same motivation that would exist in their practical use. One will try more tests than he can use in his final prediction battery, since some will probably not be helpful and will have to be eliminated. This makes the trial battery long in many cases, so that special care must be given to maintaining coöperation from the subjects. Sometimes one test can be studied at a time, but sooner or later the entire selection battery must be validated on a single group.

The Criterion

After having given his tests, the experimenter waits for the emergence of evidence of good and poor job performance. The experimental group is treated in the same way as other workers, being given normal training and duties. After a suitable interval, data on success are obtained. Among the criteria often used are quantity of production, quality of production, turnover, and opinions of foremen or supervisors. As was explained on p. 56, it is important that the criterion possess a high degree of validity. A test which can predict quality of work will seem to be a poor test, if it is judged by a criterion which does not fairly indicate quality of work. The criterion must cover all important aspects of the job.

Criteria may be based on output, field observations, or ratings. The criterion must have high reliability. An adequate number of observations, representative of normal performance, is required. Achievement tests may be the criterion, in which case they must meet the usual requirements of objectivity, stability, and validity. Ratings are particularly common criteria and are subject to many errors. Methods of making ratings more dependable are discussed in a later section (pp. 397 ff.).

It is frequently impossible to obtain a single perfect measure of success. One reason for this is that different workers seem best at different times. Sometimes the fastest learner, who does well at the end of a short training course, does not give as good final results as a learner who continues to gain in ability after he starts work. Sometimes the worker who possesses good learning ability, and so makes good grades in training, lacks temperamental qualities for ultimate success on the job. Sometimes the requirements for success are not the same for all workers in the same field. Teachers, for example, may be successful in different ways: One may develop into a friend and counselor for youth; one may stimulate independent and courageous thinking in the few brightest pupils; another may have excellent results in overcoming the blockings that cause failure among poor students. No one of these teachers is best, but all are necessary types. It is impossible to find a single criterion that is adequate for comparing these different types of teaching success.

More and more attention is being given to establishing many criteria for success in the same job. This is particularly important for high-level jobs; there are a great many patterns of success among officers, executives, consulting engineers, or artists. If it is possible to predict the particular strengths and weaknesses of an applicant, the employer has an excellent basis for placing him in the particular responsibility where he will be successful. This is exemplified in a study, by the writer, of the success of students seeking Doctor's degrees in education. In this already highly selected group, preliminary results show no way of predicting success or failure in doctorate research in general. But appropriate methods do identify specific characteristics, which knowledge may be used to help the student set up a research problem on which his aptitudes and personality assets will be helpful. One of the few completed studies using more than one independent criterion is that of Otis, reported on p. 223.

6. List several independent (non-duplicating) criteria which might be used to evaluate teacher success.
7. List several independent criteria to consider in judging branch managers of an equipment firm. Branches are responsible for both sales and service.

A striking study by Lennon and Baxter inverts the normal procedure and determines what aspects of the criterion can be predicted by available tests (13). Each item on a 90-item check list applied to clerical workers was correlated against a revision of Army Alpha and an aptitude test requiring alphabetizing, number checking, coding, digit counting, computation, and reading of tables. For some aspects of job performance, correlations with the predictors were high, but other qualities were not predicted. Check-list items dealing with understanding of the work, quantity and speed of work, performance of multiple tasks, and avoidance of duplication of effort were well predicted. Items dealing with errors in work, typing, shorthand, grammar, orderliness, and "personality" were not predicted successfully. Some of the results are shown in Table 46. This study shows why it is difficult to predict such a composite criterion as "supervisor's rating of all-round performance."

8. What procedure might be suggested for selecting clerical workers, in view of Lennon and Baxter's findings?

Table 46.　Percentage of Office Workers Having High and Low Aptitude Scores Rated as Having Particular Characteristics (13)

Characteristic	Learning Ability Test		Clerical Aptitude Test	
	High 27% (N = 58)	Low 27% (N = 58)	High 27% (N = 58)	Low 27% (N = 58)
His working instructions have to be repeated frequently	7	12[a]	5	5
Has made helpful suggestions about work handled	31	29	38	22[a]
Often does necessary but unrequested work on his own initiative	37	26[a]	39	25[a]
Checks his work for errors before releasing it	51	45	52	48
Sometimes forgets matters which should receive prompt attention	5	7	7	7
Is inclined to sacrifice accuracy for speed	4	3	6	5

[a] Difference between low and high group is probably a true difference, rather than the result of chance in sampling.

When records have been collected to show which workers are most successful, the final procedure in a selection study is to process the data and determine which tests were the best predictors. Before discussing the detailed processes of analyzing prediction data, it will be best to see the entire research process in perspective by examining an actual study.

Development of an Aptitude Test

One use of the procedures just outlined is to develop prognostic tests. In earlier chapters emphasis was placed on tests likely to have value in making a wide range of predictions. Because there are many jobs which these measures of basic abilities do not predict, it is also necessary to design special tests for specific jobs. The development and characteristics of prognostic tests are well illustrated by the E.R.C. Stenographic Aptitude Test.

Prediction of success in learning shorthand is of importance because many girls undertake the study and quite a few fail. A test which could be given before training would save time and money spent in stenography courses, and permit girls to select a more appropriate vocation. Moreover, available tests of general intelligence and other abilities have never been effective in predicting failures in shorthand. Deemer therefore decided to develop a new test, geared specifically to the problem of predicting success in learning stenography. The abilities to be built into the test would be those important in stenography, even if they were of no significance anywhere else in business or education.

A job analysis was made. The analysis was based, in this case, upon a study of the shorthand systems and the nature of the job, rather than upon observation of stenographers. The resulting list of abilities was as follows (7):

"*During dictation*: The more efficient stenographer will probably be superior to the less efficient in:
"1. Ability to listen to what is being said during dictation, i. e., facility with which she attaches meaning to each word dictated.
"2. Ability to write correct outlines fluently and rapidly.
"3. Ability to hold a number of words in mind while writing others.
"4. Ability to be 'behind the dictator' without becoming flurried.
"5. Knowledge of symbols for complete words. The less efficient stenographer will have to compose more outlines sound by sound during dictation.
"6. Thoroughness in checking, during pauses in dictation, the outlines just written.
"*During transcription*: The more efficient stenographer will probably be superior to the less efficient in:
"1. Ability to judge from the length of her notes where to begin the letter on the page.
"2. Ability to produce letters which are neat and clean.
"3. Ability to read the outlines she has written.
    a. To call up the word or words for which an outline stands, either by recognizing the outline as a whole or by deciphering the outline sound by sound.
    b. To choose, when necessary, the word that fits the context.
"4. Ability to spell the words.
"5. Ability to type the words accurately and rapidly.
"6. Ability to judge how far ahead to read before beginning to type."[2]

This list of abilities was reviewed in the light of previous studies of shorthand aptitude. It was reduced by eliminating aptitudes which all girls might be expected to possess to an adequate degree, by eliminating those abilities which would be learned in training, and by combining some abilities. The preliminary forms of the test were then designed, using the following exercises:

---

[2] From W. L. Deemer, Jr. *E.R.C. Stenographic Aptitude Test, Manual*, p. 1. Reproduced by permission of Science Research Associates. Copyright 1944 by Walter L. Deemer.

I. *Speed of writing.* Girls were required to copy the Gettysburg Address in longhand as rapidly as possible. This may be considered a complex coördination test, duplicating many motor elements of shorthand writing.

II. *Word discrimination.* In this test, girls choose which of two words best fits a particular context, as in "We are satisfied that our (**personal personnel**) is completely loyal to the firm." This simulates the problem in shorthand of choosing the correct word when an outline fits more than one word. This is a complex intellectual action involving verbal intelligence, vocabulary, and spelling.

III. *Phonetic spelling.* Girls are to write, correctly spelled, the words represented phonetically by *oshen, akshn, vejtabl, bleef,* etc. This simulates the problem in shorthand of recalling the entire word from a phonetic symbol.

IV. *Vocabulary.* The subject is required to choose the best synonym for a word presented in a sentence, e.g., "His **associates** [**enemies, employees, colleagues, pets, relatives-by-marriage**] fear him."

V. *Sentence dictation.* In this test, the tester reads aloud sentences of varying length which the subjects take down. The sentences increase in length, so that the subject must eventually carry many words in mind. The following sentence, for example, is read in 24 seconds, and 48 seconds more are allowed for girls to finish writing it: "Because of your error in filling our last order we were unable to meet the demand of our customers for holiday flowers and thus lost money and good will."

The next stage in the study was to try the preliminary forms of the test. Some items proved ambiguous, too easy, or too hard and were removed. Thus, in Test V, sentences of 15 words or less were found to be so easy as to have no discriminating power and were dropped. The final form of the test for validation was then prepared.

Validity was determined by administering the test to 500 students entering shorthand classes. During the next two years, various measures of achievement were collected. Table 47 reports validity coefficients obtained for the total test score. These validity coefficients are high enough to justify using the test at least to identify girls likely to have difficulty in the course. Since a coefficient of .65 means that many false predictions will be made in individual cases, a school may prefer to use the test to point out those who should have special attention from the teacher rather than arbitrarily to bar girls with low scores from trying shorthand.

Table 47. Correlation of Scores on E.R.C. Stenographic Aptitude Test with Various Criteria, for 500 Shorthand Students (**7**)

Criterion	Correlation
Accuracy of transcription after one year of study: dictation at 60 w.p.m. or less	.54
Accuracy of transcription after two years of study: dictation at 80 w.p.m. or less	.65
Accuracy of transcription after two years of study: dictation at more than 80 w.p.m.	.70
Accuracy of transcription after two years of study: dictation of material, the shorthand outlines for which had not been studied (80 w.p.m.)	.58
Accuracy of transcription after two years of study, shorthand notes being transcribed two weeks after dictation (90 w.p.m. or less)	.65
Rate of transcription at end of two years of study	.35

9. What abilities listed in the job analysis are not represented in the final test?
10. What forecasting efficiency corresponds to a validity coefficient of .70?
11. Says Deemer's manual, "No reliability coefficients are reported for this test because it is felt that they add nothing to the reported validity coefficients. If the validity coefficient is satisfactory, the reliability coefficient must be satisfactory." Although the latter sentence is defensible, one sometimes wishes reliability data also. What important questions about Deemer's test would be answered by reliability coefficients for subtests and total score?
12. What explanations can be offered for the failure of the validity coefficient to reach 1.00? What does this imply regarding ways to improve the prediction in further studies?

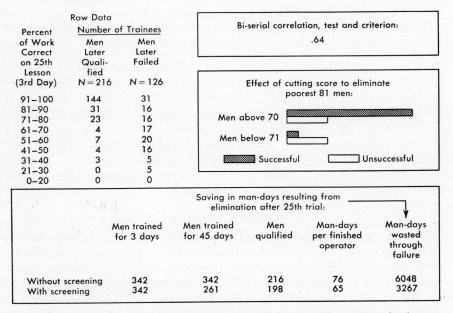

Percent of Work Correct on 25th Lesson (3rd Day)	Raw Data Number of Trainees	
	Men Later Qualified $N = 216$	Men Later Failed $N = 126$
91–100	144	31
81–90	31	16
71–80	23	16
61–70	4	17
51–60	7	20
41–50	4	16
31–40	3	5
21–30	0	5
0–20	0	0

Bi-serial correlation, test and criterion: .64

Effect of cutting score to eliminate poorest 81 men:

Men above 70

Men below 71

Successful   Unsuccessful

	Saving in man-days resulting from elimination after 25th trial:				
	Men trained for 3 days	Men trained for 45 days	Men qualified	Man-days per finished operator	Man-days wasted through failure
Without screening	342	342	216	76	6048
With screening	342	261	198	65	3267

Fig. 59.   Three methods of reporting the effectiveness of a proposed selection plan for Morse code receivers (data from **11**). Men were given repeated lessons in code-voice training. It is proposed that men having difficulty on the twenty-fifth trial, on the third day, be dropped from the program, which requires a total of 48 days.

TREATMENT OF DATA IN PREDICTION STUDIES

There are many methods of organizing data from prediction studies. The reader who surveys the literature will be impressed with the variety of reports used, but dismayed by the difficulty of comparing results from studies presented in different ways. Often an investigator deliberately chooses the form of report which, while truthful, places his selection battery in the most favorable light. The reader must be able to compare different methods of reporting similar data, to avoid being misled by dramatic rephrasing of the same facts. The widely used methods of reporting prediction studies are as follows:

1. Correlation. A test having a high correlation with a criterion is a useful predictor; one with low correlation usually is not.
2. Screening effectiveness. Such a report indicates the number of successful employees earning good and poor scores on the selection test, compared to the number of unsuccessful employees earning similar scores.
3. Benefits. In this method, attention is focused on the net gain, in dollars and cents, from employing only selected men. This method usually compares the turnover cost of failing employees and superior employees, or the labor cost per unit produced by each group. Where man-hours are precious, savings may be reported in those terms.

All of these methods are legitimate, and in business the third may be the only relevant indication of the merit of a selection plan. On the whole, however, correlation is a preferable method for reporting validation research. It has the advantage of permitting comparison of the results of different studies, and of giving a figure which can be placed on a scale from zero to perfect forecasting efficiency (p. 39). The second method has the advantage of easy interpretation and is more suitable than simple correlation wherever there is a curvilinear relation between test and criterion. Special problems in this method of analysis are discussed in Chapter 14.

Multiple Correlation (comparable money terms)

Where a single correlation is to be predicted, one seeks the tests having the highest correlation with the criterion. Better prediction is obtained by basing the prediction on several tests, since the job usually calls for many abilities. *Multiple correlation* is a statistical technique for determining how to combine tests to get the best possible prediction and to estimate what correlation the composite score will have with the criterion. Formulas for multiple correlation are given in most statistics texts.

Table 48.   Effect on Multiple Correlation of Adding Tests
to Battery (**17**, p. 83)

Tests	Correlation with Criterion (Shop Performance of Junior-High-School Boys)	Multiple Correlation of Criterion with First Test, First Two Tests, First Three Tests, Etc.
Paper Form Board	.43	.43
Stenquist Assembly	.26	.44
Steadiness	.29	.53
Card sorting	.27	.563
Tapping	.18	.580
Link's Spatial Relations	.36	.594
Packing blocks	.28	.5953

To obtain a high multiple correlation, tests are sought which have a positive correlation with the criterion and low correlations with each other. There is little value in combining tests of the same ability; this is merely equivalent to making the original test more reliable. But if a new test measures a component of the job-criterion not estimated by the first test, it will improve the multiple correlation appreciably. The example in Table 48 shows not only that prediction improves when we combine several tests with low validity. It also shows that the multiple correlation reaches a ceiling very rapidly, so that adding tests beyond the first three or four is rarely valuable. More elaborate prediction batteries are worth while only when each added test measures a new factor.

One can often afford to discard tests from a trial selection battery even though they have positive correlations with the criterion. A study with the MacQuarrie test, which has seven subtests, illustrates this point. The test was used to predict ratings of radio assemblers in training. The best correlation obtainable by weighting all seven subtests was .46. By combining the four best subtests—Tracing, Location, Copying, and Blocks—a multiple correlation of .44 was obtained. The four best tests are as useful in this prediction as the entire set requiring about twice as much time (10).

A third illustration may be given to show how little value there is in extending a battery by adding even reliable tests, if they duplicate abilities already measured. The following correlations between tests and elimination from flying training were found by the AAF (8, p. 194):

Pilot stanine (i.e., composite score on selection battery)   .653
Stanine plus Qualifying examination   .655
Stanine plus Qualifying plus General Classification Test   .655

Critical-Score Method

In contrast to the prediction formula by means of which one sets up a composite score on all tests, the critical-score technique is much simpler. A *critical score*, or cutting score, is the score at which the number of probable failures becomes so high that persons below that level are poor risks. To use more than one predictor, a multiple screen is set up, so that a person falling below the critical score on any test is eliminated.

Establishment of a critical score is illustrated by the data in Figure 60. The investigator here obtained IQ's from the Terman Group or Otis Self-Administering mental tests, which are nearly equivalent, for 1146 pupils in one high school. Over a period of years, he accumulated records of their passing and failing, as plotted in Figure 60. From these data, one may advise an entering pupil whether he has a good chance of passing the course. If one chooses to screen out pupils who have one chance in three of failing, IQ 92 will be used as a cutting score for admission to algebra, and IQ 80 for admission to English.

The peculiar effectiveness of the critical-score method is shown by Tiffin's data on paper-machine operators (23). The Bennett test was only a fair predictor, judged by the correlation of .47 with foreman's rating. But the data shown in Figure 61 indicate that the test is quite effective in one way: Anyone who is very bad on the test is very bad on the job. Evidently, mechanical comprehension is a necessary but not sufficient condition for being a good operator. A cutting score of 30 will eliminate five very poor men, at no cost in

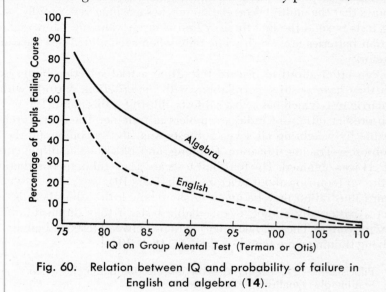

Fig. 60.   Relation between IQ and probability of failure in
English and algebra (14).

good men. Any higher score begins to take a toll of both good and poor men. (In practice, more cases are required to establish a cutting score than are available here.)

13. What cutting scores would be used if we wished to admit pupils to classes when they have an even chance of passing (Fig. 60)?
14. What assumptions are made if cutting scores based on Figure 60 are applied in other schools?
15. What effect would raising the cutting score for code learning to 90 have on the screening effectiveness of the proposed elimination plan (Fig. 59)? How many man-days would be saved?
16. Under what circumstances is it practicable to use a severe cutting score rather than a lenient one?
17. Determine the median rating of men falling in each interval, 0–30, 31–40, 41–50, 51 and over, from the data in Figure 61. What effect would a cutting score of 50 have on the quality of employees hired?

Results of screening are often described in terms of "misses" and "false positives." The aim in screening is to detect probable failures. Since one is looking for symptoms of failure, the medical terminology of "false positive" applies when one labels a person as a probable failure though he would not actually fail (see Fig. 62). If the screening system accepts a man who later fails, that case was a "miss" for the system. The best selection system reduces both false positives and misses, but a deep cut leads to many false positives and few misses, while a shallow cut is likely to increase the number of misses. Which type of cut is best depends upon the relative seriousness of false positives and

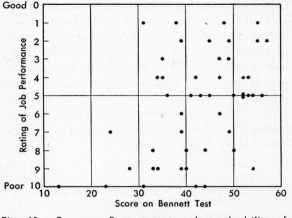

Fig. 61.   Score on Bennett test and rated ability of paper-machine operators.[3]

misses, and whether we can afford to discard many applicants in processing.

18. Which would be preferable, false positives or misses, in each of these situations?
   a. Candidates for admission to teacher training are screened for ability.
   b. It is important to hire skilled sheet-metal workers to fill vacancies, during a time of tight labor supply. Men cannot be trained on the job.
   c. In inducting soldiers, screening is used to determine which should be checked individually by psychiatrists.
   d. A company wishes to hire mechanics and put them through an expensive training program; success cannot be observed until the end of the course.

In guidance the above plans for screening are modified. Since factors not measured in tests must be considered to do full justice to the results, counselors prefer to use tests as a basis for discussion and judgment, rather than to employ arbitrary cutoffs. Many personnel workers selecting or placing workers use tests as a source of information rather than adopting cutting formulas; selection is based on a final subjective judgment. Some doubt is cast on the wisdom of such a selection procedure, except where personnel workers are extremely compe-

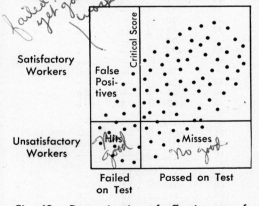

Fig. 62.   Determination of effectiveness of a critical score.

[3] Reproduced by permission of Prentice-Hall, Inc., from *Industrial psychology*, Second Edition, by Joseph Tiffin. Copyright, 1942, 1947, by Prentice-Hall, Inc.

tent, by results found in Navy classification. Trained enlisted classification specialists interviewed each man, having available his test scores, a life history, and other data. The interviewer gave a final rating as to the man's probable success in training school. Men sent to electrician's mate school had varying success in the school. A combination of two tests (Electrical Knowledge and Arithmetic Reasoning) correlated .50 with success in training. Interviewer's rating, based on tests plus judgment, correlated only .41 with success. In other words, judgments departing from the test recommendation reduced the correctness of prediction (6). This finding was confirmed in Air Force research.

19. What factors outside the test must ordinarily be considered in deciding which of two men with equal test scores should be hired for a civilian job comparable to electrician's mate trainee?
20. A high-school boy has equal scores in two test batteries, one supposed to predict success in electrical work, and one to predict success in work with Diesel engines. If the tests are equally valid, what non-test factors would be considered in advising him which type of training to enter?

Illustrative Results

When research on validation is completed, one has a selection program to put into operation. Tables 49 and 50 illustrate the selection program installed by the Army Air Force, which used a multiple-correlation method, and the

Table 49.   Validity Data and Combining Weights Used in the AAF Classification Program of November, 1943 (**8,** pp. 99, 101)

Test	Correlation with Criterion[a]			Relative Weight		
	Bomb.	Nav.	Pilot	Bomb.	Nav.	Pilot
Printed tests:						
Reading comprehension	.12	.32	.19	8	2	—
Spatial orientation II	.09	.33	.25	—	10	5
Spatial orientation I	.12	.38	.20	—	9	6
Dial and table reading	.19	.53	.19	14	18	4
Biographical data—pilot	—	—	.32	—		15
Biographical data—navigator	—	.23	−.03	—	9	—
Mechanical principles	.08	.13	.32	—	—	8
Technical vocabulary—pilot	.04	.10	.30	—	—	13
Technical vocabulary—nav.	.04	.22	.09	—	—	—
Mathematics	.10	.50	.08	—	18	—
Arithmetic reasoning	.12	.45	.09	8	12	—
Instrument comprehension I	—	—	.15⎫	—	—	9
Instrument comprehension II	—	—	.35⎭			
Numerical operations, front	.13	.26	.01	—	—	—
Numerical operations, back	.11	.28	.02	—	—	—
Speed of identification	.09	.19	.18	—	—	—
Apparatus tests:						
Rotary pursuit	.14	.10	.21	12	—	4
Complex coördination	.18	.24	.38	12	—	17
Finger dexterity	.16	.20	.11	19	6	—
Discrimination reaction time	.22	.36	.22	27	6	4
Two-hand coördination	.12	.26	.30	—	11	4
Rudder control	—	—	.42	—	—	12

[a] The criterion is graduation or elimination from training.

Table 50.   Multiple Cutoff Plan for British Army Classification[a] (3)

"Family" of Duties	Matrix[b]	Bennett Mechanical Comprehension	Arithmetic	Verbal	Clerical	Agility[c]	Other Tests
1. Driving	4	3 −	Any	Any	4	4	Assembly[d] over 23
2. Maintenance	3 −	3 +	3 −	Any	Any	Any	Assembly over 40
3. Signaling	3 −	3 −	3 +	3 +	3 −	4	Morse[e] over 50
4. Construction	4	4	4	4	Any	4	—
5. Clerks, storekeepers	3 −	4	3 −	3 +	3 −	Any	—
6. Other mobile (combat)	Any	Any	Any	Any	Any	3 −	—
7. Other domestic, administrative	Any	Any	Any	Any	Any	Any	—

[a] Each score indicates the lowest test grade usable in each classification. Grades range from a high of 1 to a low of 5.
[b] A non-verbal test of general ability.
[c] A test of general bodily coördination and speed.
[d] A test resembling the Stenquist Assembly test.
[e] A test of perception of dots and dashes, resembling the Seashore rhythm test.

program of the British Army, which used a multiple cutoff plan. The AAF tried numerous tests, chosen on the basis of a job analysis. These were tested experimentally on successive classes of air cadets, the battery being revised as new and better tests were found. The same tests were used to predict success as pilot, bombardier, and navigator, using a different combining formula for each job. Table 49 indicates the weighting plan. In selecting bombardiers, for example, discrimination reaction time and finger dexterity counted very

heavily; reading and arithmetic had only a small weight. Composite scores could also be computed for such specialties as fighter pilot, bomber pilot, mechanic-armorer-gunner, and radar observer. Figure 63 shows representative validity data, gathered over a two-year period. The correlation of pilot aptitude rating with graduation-elimination was .45, but this coefficient would be higher if men with low composite scores had not been eliminated before entering elementary training.

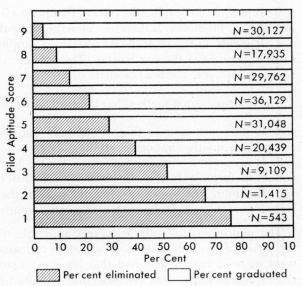

Fig. 63.   Elimination of cadets from elementary pilot training in relation to pilot aptitude score (8, p. 134)

The British plan, instead of combining scores into a single composite, employed separate hurdles or cutting scores for each test in each division of the service. For men who qualified for several classifications, assignment was made on the basis of preference and the current needs of the various branches.

21. What abilities counted more heavily in the bombardier-prediction score than in the other two predictions?
22. How do you account for the different weights assigned the first two tests in navigator prediction, in view of their similar validity coefficients?
23. Which of the three aircrew jobs has the smallest psychomotor component, according to the prediction weights?

Comparison of Multiple-Screen and Multiple-Correlation Methods

The essential difference between the two plans for organizing predictive data is that one yields a composite score and one does not. Figure 64 outlines graphically the difference in the assumptions made under the two plans. The multiple-correlation method has these advantages:

1. It indicates the rank, in all-round ability, of men who pass the screen. This is useful in identifying men requiring special assistance during training, or for singling out superior men for special responsibility.

2. For a particular man, it permits a comparison of his probable success in various specialties, instead of merely eliminating the assignments in which he would fail.

3. It permits combining the tests in that proportion which gives the highest correlation. Prediction is therefore more accurate than with a multiple cutoff.

4. It yields, in the multiple correlation, a simple estimate of the efficiency of prediction from the test battery. The formula also indicates the contribution of each test to the final prediction.

The multiple cutoff method has these advantages:

1. It does not assume that strength in one ability compensates for inadequacy in another important ability.

2. It is easier to compute and easier for the layman to understand than a composite formula. It is usually easier to administer.

3. Retaining the scores of separate tests in the record permits more effective guidance or placement than an undifferentiated composite or average.

The multiple cutoff plan is more compatible with recent thinking about the value of multiple criteria. If a person can succeed on a job in different ways, it need not be assumed that his special strengths and special weaknesses cancel each other. In selecting potential symphony conductors for training, most people would agree that intelligence and pitch discrimination are requisites. But if tests were used, a battery combining these two pre-

Suppose an intelligence test and a coördination test both predict a certain job, as indicated by the following data:

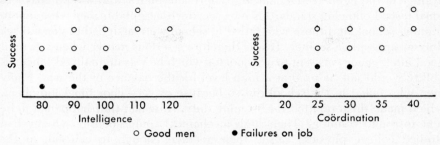

Then suppose six new applicants are being considered, whose scores are as follows:

IQ 80	IQ 100	IQ 90	IQ 90	IQ 100	IQ 110
Coörd. 20	Coörd. 30	Coörd. 25	Coörd. 40	Coörd. 30	Coörd. 35

Multiple-screen method of selection

The scatter diagram shows that men with IQ 80 or 90 tend to fail on the job. Also, men with coördination of 20 or 25 tend to fail. It is therefore decided to screen out all applicants with IQ below 100, or coördination below 30.

This is how the six men are judged by this method:

Multiple-correlation method of selection

The statistical computations of this method set up a prediction formula for combining the scores. In this problem the formula might be *IQ + 4 times Coördination*.

This formula is applied to each man, with these results:

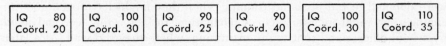

Combined Score 160	Combined Score 220	Combined Score 190	Combined Score 250	Combined Score 220	Combined Score 250

The men with the poorest composite scores are eliminated:

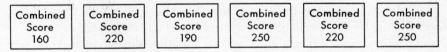

When the fourth man is hired, it is assumed that his superior coördination makes up for his lack of intelligence. On some jobs this assumption is unsound.

Fig. 64. Comparison of multiple-screen and multiple-correlation methods.

dictive scores would pass an exceptionally brilliant thinker who could not tell when the musicians were in key.

At one time during World War II, the Navy desired to train men to operate anti-submarine listening gear. By the usual research procedure, psychologists established a prediction formula: Men were screened on general intelligence; and within the surviving group, predictions were based on the average of the Bennett Mechanical Comprehension test and several Seashore tonal tests. Following standard Navy procedure, acceptable men were sent to training school, and those who failed in school were assigned to general sea duty as apprentice seamen. It was therefore a serious matter when a man of good intelligence was sent to a school for which he was unqualified, since his ability would not be used at a high level for the balance of the war. Many men who failed in the school did so because of very poor tonal judgment, which made them unfitted for listening duty. How had they happened to be sent to sound training? Their high mechanical comprehension (many had studied college physics) raised their average enough to conceal, in the formula, their weakness. Such men, despite an adequate "average" ability, were doomed to fail in sound training when they might have been good in engineering, radar maintenance, or navigation. In fact, a few were salvaged by school officers and sent to other training, where they did well. At a later date, further research led to a multiple-screen selection procedure.

Unless used wisely, the prediction-formula procedure can lure a tester into the ancient error of adding 3 pigs and 2 wheelbarrows, and taking the answer "5" seriously.

PRINCIPLES OF PREDICTION

Anyone selecting aptitude tests has to evaluate studies of validity reported in the literature. These studies follow the general plan outlined earlier in the chapter, but to interpret the results correctly one must be aware of several statistical principles. This section presents the most important of these.

What Is an Acceptable Validity Coefficient?

As validity coefficients for various tests have been presented in past chapters, the reader has probably been mentally classifying them as "good" or "poor." Many tests, especially of special abilities, do not seem very satisfactory at first glance. But, in one sense, a test has a satisfying validity coefficient if it is better than other tests for the same purpose. A correlation of .70 is far short of perfect, yet Deemer's shorthand test is a substantial achievement, simply because it yields a better prediction than previous tests for stenography. Probably the only fair standard for an acceptable validity coefficient is the question: Does the test permit us to make a better judgment than we could make without it—sufficiently better to justify its cost?

Psychologists have now abandoned their insistence on validity coefficients of .70 or .80 for all tests. While we would be pleased to reach these or better levels, the experience of 30 years of practical testing shows that we very often cannot attain such standards. It has been found repeatedly that coefficients as low as .30 are of definite practical value (cf. Table 49). Occasionally, a test with much lower validity is promising for further development, if it measures what no other test does.

The evaluation of validity coefficients for industrial and military testing is now made in terms of selection cost (1). A test which substantially increases the proportion of good employees is a test worth using. But the validity of the test must be balanced against attrition, the number of potential good employees discarded in screening. The point may be illustrated with reference to Figure 61. If paper-machine operators rated 6 or below are considered undesirable, the Bennett test will sort out poor employees. Of the present employees, 19 (40 percent) are poor. If we had refused to hire any man with a Bennett score below 31, only 15 men out of 43 (35 percent) would be poor. A cutting score of 40 would pass 27 men, of whom 5 (19 percent) would be poor. A cutting score of 50 passes just 11 men, but only 9 percent of them are poor. With different cutting scores, then, we can increase the percentage of satisfactory employees from 60 to 91. But the attrition is tremendous. With a cutting score of 50, it would be very difficult to find enough suitable employees, since we would have to process four times as many applicants to obtain the same number of operators. Whether this can be done depends upon the labor supply. A low cutting score on the Bennett test would be helpful in times of tight labor supply, since it would drop out four failures at no cost in good men. In times when applicants are plentiful, the test could be used with a very high cutting score, since it is certainly desirable to upgrade the working force until 91 percent are satisfactory.

Two other factors are considered in addition to labor supply. One is the possibility of placing rejected applicants in other jobs. This is especially important in military processing, where nearly every man must be used. Since every man is to be placed, there is nothing to lose if tests having very low but positive validities are used in assigning men. The other factor to consider is the cost of hiring unsuitable workers. If hiring and training cost is low, there may be little value in screening employees even when a validity coefficient is .70. A test with a validity of only .10 or .20 may be important if it saves thousands of dollars otherwise wasted in training an inept flier or rehabilitating a man who develops a predictable combat neurosis.

Taylor and Russell have developed tables showing the relations between validity coefficient, selection ratio (percentage of applicants to be hired), and improvement in percentage of satisfactory employees (22). Tiffin's chart based on these tables shows this relation graphically (Fig. 65). The chart is based on a situation in which 50 percent of employees are satisfactory before introduction of a proposed selection test. It is seen from the chart that if we can afford to hire only 30 percent of those tested, a test with a validity coefficient of .50 will cut the number of failures in half. Even a test with a validity of .20 will eliminate eight failures out of every hundred men hired.

The following comment by Tiffin is a good summary of the point under consideration (23, pp. 69–70):

"Psychologists dealing with vocational guidance and individual consultation are usually more interested in making accurate individual predictions than in making group predictions. Most of these psychologists have tended, therefore, to evaluate a test almost entirely in terms of its validity coefficient. They have stressed the fact (which is unquestionably true for individual prediction) that there is no substitute for high validity: that if two tests have been validated against the same criterion, and one has a higher validity coefficient than the other, there is no way to make the one having the lower validity serve as well. The main point

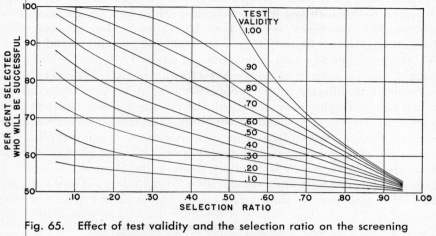

Fig. 65. Effect of test validity and the selection ratio on the screening efficiency of an employee selection test.

of the above discussion is that in group testing, where one is interested in average rather than individual results, one can make the test with the lower validity perform as well as the other by sufficiently reducing the selection ratio. In other words, in group testing, a reduction of the selection ratio is a substitute for high validity. . . . A reduction in the selection ratio can be utilized whenever two or more employees are being placed on two or more different jobs, and if tests of some validity are available for each of the jobs."[4]

In evaluating a validity coefficient to decide whether a test is worth using, one must ask the following questions:
1. Is the decision being made one of crucial importance to the individual, so that an error in prediction will be very damaging to him?[5]
2. Can we afford to hire, and later discharge or transfer to other duties, men who prove to be unsuccessful?
3. Is it important to hire every applicant who will be satisfactory, even though this also involves hiring many men who will fail?
4. Does this test measure an ability which is already fairly well measured by other tests or procedures already in use?

---

[4] This quotation and Fig. 65 reproduced by permission of Prentice-Hall, Inc., from *Industrial psychology*, Second Edition, by Joseph Tiffin. Copyright, 1942, 1947, by Prentice-Hall, Inc.

[5] The questions are so worded that an answer of "no" indicates that tests of relatively low validity are likely to be helpful.

5. Is the validity coefficient much lower than the reliability coefficient of the test? (If not, lengthening the test should raise validity.)

6. Is administration of the test difficult and costly?

24. In the light of the foregoing questions, how satisfactory is Deemer's validity coefficient of about .65?

25. In one pilot-selection study, the predictive validity of pencil-and-paper tests was .64 (elimination-graduation criterion). The coefficient is raised to .69 when apparatus tests are added (8, p. 193). Is such a small increase worth while, in view of the questions listed above?

26. The USES General Clerical Battery is intended to guide workers into appropriate clerical positions (20, p. 154). A very low selection ratio may be used, since a particular unemployed worker may be directed into any one of hundreds of job families. Assume a selection ratio of .10.

   a. What improvement in success of workers recommended will result if the test is used to select card-punch-machine operators? The validity coefficient is .39.

   b. What improvement will result if the test is used to select bookkeeping-machine operators? The validity coefficient is .12.

Prediction as a Function of Criteria and Training

The size of a validity coefficient is limited by the reliability of the criterion. Therefore in many studies improvement in validity coefficients is obtained by refining the criterion rather than by continued development of the predictors. An example of the effects of better criteria is shown in Figure 66. When Navy classes in ship's engine operation were given no standard achievement tests, school grades had rather small correlations with predictive tests. But when two highly valid achievement tests were used in allotting school grades, the classification tests were much better predictors. It is to be noted that the earlier grades were influenced most by the abilities measured in the Arithmetic test. When a valid measure of job knowledge and skill was developed, the prediction relied most heavily on Mechanical Knowledge and Mechanical Aptitude factors. The tests that predict a valid criterion may be different from those predicting an invalid criterion.

When a prediction study is made, it is assumed that all cases included in a particular correlation have been given similar treatment in all stages of the study. They must have the same training, the same incentive, and the same type of grading. Otherwise, the correlation will be reduced even if the test predicts well how each man responds to whatever experiences he receives. Variation in grading from instructor to instructor has been one major source of difficulty in predicting college grades. A study of prediction of success in 20 nursing schools gave multiple correlations of disappointing size, from .26 to .50. When computations were based on one school at a time, validities jumped markedly (as high as .80 in school A; as high as .77 in school K). The authors traced the low correlations in combined samples to variation in grading policies of the schools (24).

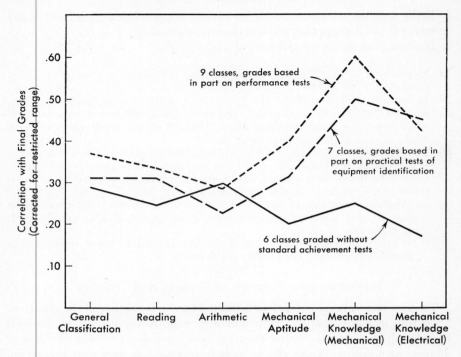

Fig. 66. Correlations of Navy classification tests with grades in Basic Engineering School, before and after introduction of standard achievement tests (**21**, p. 307).

If there is variation in the training given different men, their final scores will not be predicted accurately. Figure 67 illustrates this problem. The data plotted are the scores of two classes of student torpedomen on a prediction test and an achievement test. Since actual scores of all men are not available, these scores are hypothetical data based on a study reported by the staff of the Bureau of Naval Personnel (21, p. 308). For the entire scattergram, the correlation is positive but low. It is apparent that Class 2 had poorer instruction, since men of the same aptitude earned poorer scores than similar men in Class 1. Within either class, the correlation is high, and final scores can be predicted in either class with an error of five points or less.

Restriction of Range

It was mentioned in Chapter 4 that tests predict less accurately when they are applied to a homogeneous group. Validity coefficients rise when a test is applied to a group with a wide range of ability, and drop when the test is used on a restricted, preselected group. Many studies are based on selected groups. Deemer, for example, did not test how well his instrument predicted shorthand learning of all girls. Instead, it was tried on girls already planning to take the course. Probably many of low aptitude were not included, since girls entering a shorthand course have normally already successfully completed some work in typing. If Deemer's test, then, were applied to an entirely unscreened group, a higher coefficient would result. On the other hand, it would yield a lower validity coefficient if applied to a single class, all of whom had about equal intelligence.

The effect of screening upon validity coefficients is illustrated by the AAF study referred to earlier. The validity coefficient of the battery for pilot selection was in the neighborhood of .37 for men normally passing the screen. When, for experimental purposes, a completely unscreened group was sent to pilot training, the failure rate rose enormously. In this group, the validity coefficient rose to .66 (8, pp. 103, 193).

Investigators are frequently perplexed when a variable listed in the job analysis fails to predict the criterion of success. The job analysis may have been correct in listing the ability as essential to the job, yet selection may have reduced its significance as a predictor. If one is to continue to draw his sample from a similarly selected group, this variable will not help in prediction. But if prediction on a less selected group becomes important, the variable which was once of no value may turn out to be a good predictor. For example, intelligence tests have consistently been poor predictors of success in teaching. The explanation is obvious: Nearly every teacher has survived years of schooling with at least adequate grades, so that every teacher has a fair to superior degree of intelligence (Fig. 68). Among those so selected, differences in tested intelligence play little part in determining success as teachers. Granted that an intelligence test will not help a school system hire teachers, an intelligence test is still a major factor in advising a girl in high school whether she is likely to be able to complete a teacher-training course.

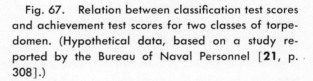

Fig. 67.   Relation between classification test scores and achievement test scores for two classes of torpedomen. (Hypothetical data, based on a study reported by the Bureau of Naval Personnel [21, p. 308].)

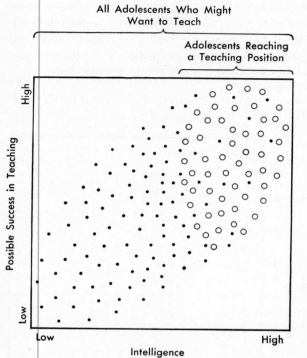

Fig. 68. Hypothetical data illustrating the effect of preselection upon correlation. Dots show scores to be expected if every ninth-grader interested in teaching later enters the profession. Circles show scores of persons likely to survive gradual elimination as a consequence of low school marks.

27. Preselection operates on some characteristics and not on others in any situation. If one were considering the probable success in industrial jobs of graduates from an engineering school, what characteristics would have a restricted range owing to preselection? What characteristics would probably not have been so restricted?

Contamination of Criteria

It is important to guard against contamination of criteria, which spuriously raises correlations. Wherever ratings are used as criteria, there is a possibility that teachers, foremen, or other judges are influenced by partial knowledge of the prediction test scores. Teachers may be influenced in their grading by knowledge of a pupil's IQ. A foreman may rate a man higher than his performance warrants, because he knows the man has considerable experience. These influences raise the correlation between grade and intelligence or rating and experience. The only way to eliminate contamination is to keep test data secret until all criterion scores have been collected.

28. In each of the following situations, trace the way in which contamination might occur, and suggest an improved procedure to avoid it.

a. A psychologist administers aptitude tests to entering college freshmen, and from the results predicts each student's success. Success is determined after two years by noting which students have been dropped from school by the school guidance committee for unsatisfactory work. The predictions are kept in a locked file and not made available until the two years have passed. The psychologist is a member of the committee, but did not discuss the predictions.

b. Test data on pupils' intelligence, mathematical ability, and other facts are made available to science teachers so that they can do better teaching. Learning in science, which was to be predicted, is judged not by ratings but by an objective test of ability in science given at the end of the course.
c. Tests for selecting salesmen are being tried experimentally. Because they are considered probably valid, the results are given to the sales manager for his guidance in assigning territories to the salesmen in the experimental group. After a year of trial, each man is judged by the amount of his sales in relation to the normal amount for his territory.
d. Flight instructor's ratings are used as a basis for promoting men from primary to advanced training. It is desired to check the validity of these ratings as predictors of success in advanced training. Advanced training is taken at the same field, with a different instructor. This man's judgment supplies the criterion.

Necessity for Confirmation of Findings

When an investigator has once obtained a satisfactory validity coefficient, he tends to install his program and stop research. Other workers, reading his report of the study, may accept his test as valid and put it to work in their own situations. This is unsound. In the first place, any validation results are influenced by chance, and correlations will fluctuate from sample to sample. As a result, the test which proves best in one sample may prove not to be the best predictor in another similar sample. Even when the results are based on a large sample, the particular critical score or the particular weights most effective in a multiple correlation are certain to change when a new group is tested. If the same formula is applied in other groups, the correlation is sure to drop. Moreover, the supply of men and conditions of training change from time to time in any situation where prediction is attempted. It follows that the investigator must redetermine the validity of his prediction technique periodically.

This problem is illustrated by data selected from a study of the success of recruits in a Navy radio school (9). Instead of making only one study and relying on the resultant correlation, the investigators tested successive companies of men. It is apparent from Table 51 that different tests would have seemed valid in different companies, if any one had been used as the sole experimental group. The most striking difference is in the electricity test. The

Table 51. Change of Validity Coefficients from Group to Group **(9)**

| | | | | | Correlation with Grades | |
Company	Number	Test	Mean	s.d.	Mathematics	Radio Lab.
A	94	Mental ability	51	11.2	.50	.60
		Mathematics	35	10.0	.68	.73
		Electricity	95	6.8	.19	.38
B	100	Mental ability	53	10.6	.61	.40
		Mathematics	34	11.3	.82	.54
		Electricity	87	11.3	.25	.69
C	100	Mental ability	56	10.1	.41	.20

experimenters traced the shift in correlation to the fact that Company A was composed of recruits having some electrical experience, whereas Company B included many men with little electrical background.

If a battery selected for a given situation must be rechecked from time to time, we surely cannot expect the battery used in one situation to work without modification in a different situation. If the second situation is much like the first, the tests useful in one place should prove valid in the other. If the situations differ appreciably, it may be necessary to introduce new tests or to change the weights assigned. In using the findings of research in another situation, there is no substitute for confirmatory research in the new situation.

29. What selection or classification scheme would probably have been used if only Company A had been studied? If only Company B had been studied?
30. Which shifts in correlation (Table 51) can be explained in terms of change in the range of talent from group to group?

SINGLE-PURPOSE APTITUDE TESTS

One by one, we have considered the various important types of ability tests. General mental ability, which was first considered, is a factor found to influence success in almost every job. Attention was next directed to tests intended to measure each of the widely important special abilities; they also are likely to be valuable in prediction in many situations. To complete the picture of ability tests available for predictive uses, it remains only to survey the tests designed for prognosis of specific single activities. Deemer's stenographic test is an example of this type. Complex coördination tests also are useful only for predicting very limited performances.

Table 52 contains a representative listing of the prognostic tests which have been described in the literature. Tests have been designed for prognosis in most secondary-school subjects and for many college subjects, in an at-

Table 52.   Representative Prognostic Tests

Test and Publisher	Content and Special Features	Validity Coefficient[a]	Comments of Reviewers[b]
Prognostic Tests for Academic Subjects:			
Iowa Placement Examinations (Univ. Iowa)	Mental operations and knowledge like that used in the course. Separate tests for foreign language, chemistry, etc.	.50–.60 with marks in the individual course	"Higher prognostic validity for that purpose than general intelligence tests. . . . Distinctive advance in psychometric procedures" (16, pp. 228–229).
Lee Test of Algebraic Ability (Pub. Sch. Publ. Co.)	Arithmetic, proportions, number series, formulas	.71 with achievement test	"Undoubtedly of some value in detecting ability in algebra. . . . Would be much better if each subtest not quite so homogeneous . . ." (Wilks, 4, p. 280).
Symonds Foreign Language Prognosis (Teachers Coll., Columbia Univ.)	Knowledge of English grammar, exercises in learning Esperanto	.60 with achievement tests	"Hardly more than a linguistically weighted intelligence test" (Kaulfers, 4, p. 157).

Table 52. Representative Prognostic Tests (Continued)

Test and Publisher	Content and Special Features	Validity Coefficient[a]	Comments of Reviewers[b]
Tests for Professions and Vocations:			
Engineering and Physical Science Aptitude (Psych. Corp.)	Mathematics, spatial, mechanical comprehension, vocabulary, etc. Designed for war-industry trainees	.73 with grades in war-emergency training	"Should be validated in terms of the situation in which it is to be employed. . . . User will find it necessary to prepare norms based on his local group" (Fredericksen, 5).
Stanford Scientific Aptitude (Stanford)	Various types of judgment, reasoning, carefulness. Supposed to select research workers	.74 with ratings of science students	"The test is not valid. . . . Zyve's coefficients are almost certainly spurious" (16, p. 238. See also Crawford, 4, p. 453).
Medical Aptitude (Assn. Am. Med. Coll.)	Verbal abilities, with emphasis on scientific content. Test not released. One annual nation-wide testing for prospective medical students	.37 with freshman medical grades;[c] higher r expected in unscreened group	
Aptitude for Nursing (Geo. Washington Univ.)	Information, reading, memory, verbal; nursing content	.64 with first-quarter nursing grades (18, p. 245)	
Detroit Clerical Aptitudes (Pub. Sch. Publ. Co.)	Handwriting, checking, arithmetic, alphabetizing, etc.	With marks: bookkeeping, .56; shorthand, .37; typing, .32	"Basically, the test measures factors common to intelligence tests and speed tests" (Lorge, 4, p. 434).
Iowa Legal Aptitude (U. Iowa)	Verbal abilities with legal materials	.42–.77 with law-school grades (1)	
Other Prognosis Tests:			
Tests for radio telegraphers (U.S. Army, unpub.)	Discrimination of code patterns, learning of a few code characters	.25, .33 with time required to attain code speed of 16 w.p.m. (19)	
Combat Information Center (tactical direction) Aptitude (U.S. Navy, unpub.)	Translation of polar coördinates to grid, scale reading, relative movement	.40–.55 with success in CIC training (21, p. 115)	

[a] From test manual unless otherwise indicated.
[b] The reader should refer to the source cited for a full statement of the reviewer's opinion.
[c] Computed by tetrachoric method from data reported by Moss (15).

tempt to improve upon the correlations of .40–.55 that can be obtained using general mental tests. Tests for vocational guidance and for selection among applicants for training have sought to measure the abilities required for particular occupations, especially at the professional level. Except in the field of medicine, however, such tests have had limited usefulness. Several tests were designed for selection of men for military specialties which cannot be predicted by the general classification tests.

On the whole, standardized prognostic tests for special purposes have declined in use. For guidance in a high school, it would be impossible to give every pupil a test for every subject offered, and prognostic tests have had validities only slightly better than those for more general tests. Most counselors find that a test profile describing such abilities as verbal, arithmetic reasoning, and mechanical comprehension is more useful than one producing scores such as "aptitude for engineering" or "aptitude for woodworking." Prognostic tests geared to a particular subject or occupation have an advantage when many people are to be considered for that one performance, and where the performance to be predicted involves special factors not measured in tests otherwise available. Therefore, prognostic tests help the shorthand teacher identify which pupils are likely to need special instruction, assist medical schools to select desirable entrants, and aid the Navy in selecting radar operators. But a counselor, helping a young man choose a vocation, will ordinarily map out his abilities with tests measuring widely important factors, rather than employ test after test for single vocations. Only in the final stages of guidance, when choice has narrowed to a few vocations, are specialized prognosis tests efficient.

Prognostic tests for national use have one severe limitation, namely, that the requirements for success in an activity may be different in different situations. Perhaps Latin courses seem likely to be uniform enough so that a test which predicts performance in Massachusetts would predict equally well in California. But Kaulfers points out that the validity of a prognostic test in a foreign language depends on the type of course offered, and that the available tests are appropriate only for a now-obsolescent grammar-translation type of course. He adds, "Foreign language prognosis tests of the [conventional] type are usually excellent means for reducing foreign language enrollments in non-functional courses taught by teachers incapable of adjusting either method or content to the needs, interests, and abilities of children" (4, p.158).

Over and over, prognostic tests with general names have been found not to cover validly all the situations covered by such a name. This has been most clearly proved by the many studies of "aptitude for selling," for which a test would indeed be desirable if practical. Say Kornhauser and Schultz, reviewing the literature (12): "It is abundantly clear from these and other investigations that effective selection procedures must be worked out in relation to the particular type of selling; there are at present no *general* 'sales ability' tests. Where psychologists have carried on thorough and continuous research, however, to develop tools which may aid management in selection of specific sales personnel, definite results of value have been achieved."

Since it is not practical here to summarize the many investigations of prognosis for various purposes, Table 53 has been prepared to draw the reader's attention to sources where summaries of prognostic studies may be found.

31. The aptitude tests in the Iowa Placement Examination require about 40 minutes each. The usual general ability tests for college freshmen require about one hour. Discuss the way in which the Iowa tests could be most effectively

Table 53. References Summarizing Research on Prognosis

Performance Predicted	Author of Summary, and Reference	General Findings
Clerical work	Bills-Hammitt *Natl. Bus. Educ. Q.,* 1936, 4, No. 3, 26–30 Osborne *Natl. Bus. Educ. Q.,* 1945, 13, No. 4, 19–28	General mental tests helpful in selection of employees; shorthand demands special abilities not tapped by general tests.
Dentistry	Bellows *J. consult. Psychol.,* 1940, 4, 10–15 (Anon.) *Vet. Admin. Tech. Bull.,* 1947, TB 7–44	Five essential areas; college aptitude, ability in science, interests, spatial ability, eye-hand coördination.
Law	Adams *Educ. psychol. Measmt.,* 1943, 3, 291–305; 1944, 4, 13–19	Iowa Legal Aptitude Test plus pre-law grades yields validities as high as .77.
Music	Bienstock *J. educ. Psychol.,* 1942, 33, 427–442	Results are not conclusive, and present methods are inadequate for predicting individual achievement. Tests are useful in a negative way, to prevent failures.
Reading, beginning	Robinson-Hall *Bull. Ohio Conf. Reading,* 1942, No. 3	Readiness tests are fairly valid, but no better than intelligence tests or ratings based on study of each child.
College grades	Segal *U.S. Off. Educ. Bull.,* 1934, No. 15 Durflinger *J. Amer. Assn. Coll., Registrars,* 1943, 19, 68–78	Ability tests, achievement tests, and high-school marks all correlate .50–.55 with college marks. Multiple r's reach .60–.70.
School success, all levels	Eurich-Cain *Encyclopaedia of Educ. Res.,* 1941, pp. 833–860	

used, considering who should take the tests, and what judgments would be based on the data.

32. Which of the prognostic tests in Table 52 would be expected to have high correlations with group tests of general intelligence? What does this imply regarding the usefulness of these tests?
33. Do you agree with Kaulfers that courses should be tailored to student aptitudes, rather than designed to fit a limited group of pupils who can be preselected?

SUGGESTED READINGS

Bellows, Roger M. "Procedures for evaluating vocational criteria." *J. appl. Psychol.,* 1941, 25, 499–513.

Paterson, Donald G., and others. "The criterion of mechanical ability," in *Minnesota mechanical ability tests.* Minneapolis: Univ. of Minnesota Press, 1930, pp. 144–202.

Stalnaker, John M. "Personnel placement in the armed forces." *J. appl. Psychol.,* 1945, 29, 338–345.

Tiffin, Joseph. "General principles of employee testing," in *Industrial psychology.* New York: Prentice-Hall, 2nd ed., 1947, pp. 46–80.

Toops, Herbert A. "The criterion." *Educ. psychol. Measmt.*, 1944, 4, 271–297.

Van Dusen, A. C. "Importance of criteria in selection and training." *Educ. psychol. Measmt.*, 1947, 7, 498–504.

REFERENCES

1. Adams, William M. "Prediction of scholastic success in colleges of law. I." *Educ. psychol. Measmt.*, 1943, 3, 291–305.
2. Berkson, Joseph. "Cost utility as a measure of the efficiency of a test." *J. Amer. statis. Ass.*, 1947, 42, 246–255.
3. British Information Service film, "Personnel classification," 1944.
4. Buros, Oscar K. (ed.). *The 1940 mental measurements yearbook.* Highland Park, N.J.: The Mental Measurements Yearbook, 1941.
5. Buros, Oscar K. (ed.). *The third mental measurements yearbook.* New Brunswick: Rutgers Univ. Press, 1948.
6. Conrad, H. S., and Satter, G. A. *The use of test scores and Qualification Card ratings in predicting success in electrician's mate school.* O.S.R.D. Rep. No. 5667, 1945.
7. Deemer, Walter L. *E.R.C. Stenographic Aptitude Test, manual.* Chicago: Science Research Assoc., 1944.
8. DuBois, Philip H. (ed.). *The classification program.* AAF Aviation Psychol. Prog. Res. Rep. No. 2. Washington: Govt. Printing Off., 1947.
9. Frandsen, Arden N., and Hadley, J. M. "The prediction of achievement in a radio training school." *J. appl. Psychol.*, 1943, 27, 303–310.
10. Goodman, Charles H. "The MacQuarrie test for mechanical ability: I. Selecting radio assembly operators." *J. appl. Psychol.*, 1946, 30, 586–595.
11. Keller, Fred S., and Jerome, Edward A. *Progress in receiving International Morse code.* O.S.R.D. Rep. No. 5366. New York: Psych. Corp., 1945.
12. Kornhauser, Arthur W., and Schultz, Richard S. "Research on selection of salesmen." *J. appl. Psychol.*, 1941, 25, 1–5.
13. Lennon, Roger T., and Baxter, Brent. "Predictable aspects of clerical work." *J. appl. Psychol.*, 1945, 29, 1–3.
14. Mitchell, Claude. "Prognostic value of intelligence tests." *J. educ. Res.*, 1935, 28, 577–581.
15. Moss, F. A. "Report of the Committee on Aptitude Tests for Medical Schools," *J. Ass. Amer. med. Coll.*, 1942, 17, 312–315.
16. Mursell, James T. *Psychological testing.* New York: Longmans, Green, 1947.
17. Paterson, Donald G., and others. *Minnesota mechanical ability tests.* Minneapolis: Univ. of Minnesota Press, 1930.
18. Paterson, Donald G., and others. *Student guidance techniques.* New York: McGraw-Hill, 1938.
19. Staff, Personnel Research Section, Classification & Replacement Branch, AGO. "Personnel research in the Army: IV. The selection of radio-telegraph operators." *Psychol. Bull.*, 1943, 40, 357–371.
20. Stead, William H., and others. *Occupational counseling techniques.* New York: American Book Co., 1940.
21. Stuit, Dewey B. (ed.). *Personnel research and test development in the Bureau of Naval Personnel.* Princeton: Princeton Univ. Press, 1947.
22. Taylor, H. C., and Russell, J. T. "The relationship of validity coefficients to the

practical effectiveness of tests in selection." *J. appl. Psychol.*, 1939, 23, 565–578.

23. Tiffin, Joseph. *Industrial psychology*. New York: Prentice-Hall, 2nd ed., 1947.
24. Williamson, E. G., and others. "The selection of student nurses." *J. appl. Psychol.*, 1938, 22, 119–131.

CHAPTER 12

Measures of Achievement

FUNCTIONS OF ACHIEVEMENT TESTS

Achievement tests attempt to determine how much a person has learned from some educational experience. This chapter will demonstrate the variety of tests which have been devised and call attention to the many uses they have over and above the traditional assignment of marks. Most achievement tests are prepared for local purposes, but some have been standardized for widespread use. Although standard achievement tests have real merits, they are best adapted to fairly standardized types of education.

Perhaps the best way to see the value of carefully prepared, standardized tests of achievement is to examine their use in a somewhat unfamiliar situation. The Navy has long operated, with notable success, an immense program of vocational education. Navy recruits receive training in a variety of skills needed to maintain a complex fighting force. When civilians with educational and psychological training entered the service during World War II and were given responsibility for some Navy schools, one major change they proposed was the development of standard achievement tests for most service schools. The history of this program is given in a report by the Bureau of Naval Personnel (28, pp. 287–354). The advantages the Navy found may be summarized as follows:

1. Tests aided in standardizing the instruction of all schools preparing men for a given duty. Although objectives of instruction and curricula were standardized, individual schools had been deviating by neglecting or over-emphasizing certain topics. Any deviation would be reflected in scores on the test lower than in other schools. The tests therefore forced teachers to do as the course planners intended.

2. The tests provided a basis for suggesting curriculum revision and improving instructional methods. If certain learnings were found not to be mastered in the time allotted, it was possible to reconsider the length of the course or the emphasis placed on these outcomes in the course. Without such tests, instructors often assumed that, having "covered" a topic, they had taught it as well as possible. Test results were of great interest to instructors and often caused them to seek help from supervisors or specialists to improve their teaching. The tests helped to make teachers self-critical.

3. Some tests required that the student demonstrate job skills rather than merely give back verbal answers. Such tests directed the attention of instructors to the importance of teaching the behaviors the course was in-

tended to produce. Reliance on the lecture-discussion method of teaching declined. A definite improvement in the effectiveness of training was found.

4. In the absence of tests, grades had been assigned to students on the basis of subjective impressions, or, at best, with the aid of teacher-made tests. Such marks were unreliable, failed to give attention to all significant aspects of the course, and were subject to bias. Even objective tests, when made by teachers without special training, have generally been poor measuring instruments. Careful preparation of tests increased the probability that each man would be rated fairly and accurately.

5. Tests which placed emphasis on all significant aspects of the course made sure that all-round achievement would be considered and deficiencies noted. In the Basic Engineering school, before standard testing, grades were strongly influenced by performance in mathematical aspects of the course, probably because this ability was easy to test. Examinations were altered to place emphasis on mechanical understanding. As a result, attention was drawn to men who, despite skill in arithmetic, were poor in other essentials.

6. Standard tests permitted analysis of grading standards and reduced variations due to generosity or severity of graders. When considered in relation to aptitude scores, achievement scores identified classes which failed to make adequate progress (Fig. 67). When marks were based solely on standard tests, grades given at different places represented the same degree of proficiency.

7. Motivation of students and instructors was improved by developing rivalry based on a fair standard. Showing a man the particular ways in which he needs further skill is an excellent way to motivate study.

8. More accurate final marks were a better criterion against which to validate proposed selection tests. Accurate marks were more useful in making subsequent administrative decisions about men.

Nearly all the above purposes and advantages have their counterpart in public schools and colleges, because the same problems are present. Marks are unreliable, and may emphasize some aspects of the course to the exclusion of others. Different instructors in the same department grade differently and teach with different effectiveness. Teachers often depart from planned curricula. But to some extent, the outcomes which were virtues in military training are *undesirable* in general education. These difficulties will be discussed in the next section.

One significant contribution of standardized tests has been to break down the "time-serving" concept of education. While a person's standing in school is still usually judged by the number of years he has put in, or the number of courses he has passed through, this system is being increasingly criticized. In one study, thousands of college students took standardized tests of knowledge in various fields; it was found that many college seniors knew less than the average high-school senior (18). A person who has spent four years in high school or college may not have acquired an education during that time. Tests are therefore being given increasing weight as evidence of educational development. Following World War II, high-school diplomas have been issued to many veterans who did not complete high school but who demonstrated satisfactory educational development on standard tests. College credit was also allowed on the same basis, on the reasonable argument that a man who could do well on a standard test in English did not need to serve time in a freshman English course. This use of carefully prepared standard tests appears likely to increase.

Achievement tests have clinical and predictive uses, apart from their more common function of appraising learning. Tests of achievement are often superior predictors of work in future courses. They may be used in hiring employees, examples being the usual civil service examination and the arithmetic tests used in stores and offices. They provide valuable insight into many clinical cases. A delinquent, for instance, may turn out to have excellent achievement in school subjects even when teachers have given him low grades. Achievement tests are also useful in evaluating and diagnosing mental deterioration from organic or emotional causes, in making recommendations regarding the feeble-minded, and so on.

DIFFICULTIES OF ACHIEVEMENT TESTING IN SCHOOLS

Historical Background

Examinations have been used always, but standardized tests are a comparatively modern innovation. Fifty years ago teachers around the country taught in their own ways, set their own expectations of their pupils, and assigned grades independently. If the average fourth-grader in Mill Corners could outread sixth-graders down the road at Pinetown, that fact was never brought to light. Parents and employers looked at the performance of school graduates and, according to their dispositions, were pleased or displeased with the results. There was no sound basis for judging whether the school had taught as well as might reasonably be expected. The first systematic comparison of school attainment was made by an educational crusader, J. M. Rice, in 1897. Rice was convinced that the pressure for perfection in certain types of achievement was leading to faulty emphasis in education, and prepared a test of spelling ability to determine what results could be expected. His test was given in twenty-one scattered cities and showed that, regardless of the time devoted to spelling, the test scores of eighth-graders were about the same in all cities. He showed further that although children in some cities were superior in spelling during early grades, presumably because of stress on that subject, such differences vanished by the end of schooling (25). It is ironical that Rice hoped by such evidence to show that the time spent on formal learning could be reduced, saving more time for an enriched curriculum. Instead, the testing movement which he fathered became a factor tending to hold the schools to limited curricula.

Educators were quickly impressed with the advantages of determining when schools were "up to standard," and tests of reading and arithmetic were prepared and widely used. Tests in other subjects followed rapidly. At the height of the enthusiasm for standard tests, in some cities every pupil was given a nationally distributed examination each June in nearly every course he studied.

Despite the marked benefits conferred by tests, similar to those discovered in the Navy program outlined above, the testing craze eventually produced serious dislocations in the school program. The tests became a taskmaster which everyone in the school found himself trying to serve. When good standing on the final test in June became the goal of the entire year's work, useful classroom activities which would not raise test scores received scant encouragement. The harmful influence on the school program of tests used unwisely will be outlined in detail in the following sections. Because of increased recognition of these problems, there has been a swing away from mandatory testing since about 1930. Standardized tests are still used in most school systems, but they are used in moderation. In sound practice, evaluation of a pupil or a teacher is never based on these tests alone; instead, the tests are treated as one source of data to be linked with many other facts in making a final evaluation. Tests made by the classroom teacher to fit his class are now regarded as an indispensable and valid type of measurement; at one point in the not-distant past, they were regarded as inferior substitutes for the standard test, then considered to be the "true" yardstick of attainment.

Problems of Validity

Sampling of Content

Standard tests have not always given valid measures of the content areas they dealt with. If a test purports to show how much Theodore has learned in French, but asks questions involving French words Theodore has not studied, the resulting measure may be quite unfair to him. The necessity of fairness is nowhere greater than in standardized tests, since these tests are used to compare schools using different textbooks and covering somewhat different material.

This has led to considerable attention to problems of sampling in achievement tests. The only fair test of factual knowledge in an entire area is one which weights equally all significant topics in the area. A history test which emphasizes political and military history is fair only if that is the sort of history the school desires to teach. A test can present only a sample of the items taught in spelling, history, arithmetic, or grammar. When a sample is taken, chance in sampling is likely to give some pupils or schools an advantage through the inclusion of items on which they happen to be superior. One of the major advantages of the objective test over the essay test is that, by including more questions, the objective test reduces the probability that a poor student will earn a high score by a lucky break in the selection of questions.

Sampling was seriously faulty in early achievement tests. Often they tested spelling words someone believed pupils "ought" to know, rather than words actually being taught in school. A test in history, based on facts chosen from only one textbook, would apparently measure a significant sample of historical knowledge but in truth would be a most unfair test. To guard against invalidity due to poor sampling, recent tests of knowledge and skill are based on careful consideration of curricula. The test designer looks at many courses of study to decide what topics to cover. A sampling plan is used to draw items equally from all significant topics. Such a test will still give a low score to a class which has placed its entire emphasis on one or two topics and mastered them thoroughly. But these students do have a low mastery of the total field as taught in most schools.

Curricular Validity

In one sense, a test which is a fair sample of the content of a field is a valid test. In another sense, it may be quite invalid. When a test is to be used to judge the effectiveness of a learning experience, it is important that it have curricular validity. A test has *curricular validity* if it measures fairly the extent to which pupils have learned what the curriculum was intended to teach them. A designer of a standard test cannot adapt his test to local needs. But teachers must often adapt their courses to fit the problems in a particular school or community. Different knowledges in science, for example, are important for pupils who will later become Ford factory workers, Minnesota dairy farmers, students at M.I.T., or housewives. If each of these groups studied a different science curriculum and mastered it, some groups would do badly on a standard test of science knowledge because it would ask what they had not studied. A test which does not fit the course gives a misleading answer to such common questions as "How effective has the teaching been?" and "Which pupils have failed to learn what has been presented?"

Measurement of Appropriate Behaviors

It is fallacious to measure all achievement in terms of factual knowledge and a limited group of skills. If you ask a teacher why he is teaching his course, he will list a large number of objectives. The geometry teacher, for example, would deny that the purpose of his course is to transmit a certain number of theorems, a few practical principles, and some skills with ruler and compass. Instead, he would speak of developing habits of reason-

ing, skill in identifying assumptions, skeptical attitudes regarding unveri-
fied conclusions, and so on. Yet in most subjects traditional achievement
tests have stressed specific facts and skills to the exclusion of the more important outcomes of the course. In a series of studies of college and high-
school teaching, Tyler and his co-workers identified a large number of purposes schools claimed to hold. These aims may be grouped as follows
(adapted from 24, 26):

1. Functional information. Not mere rote knowledge, but knowledge
   that can be applied to new situations where it is relevant.
2. Thinking skills and habits.
3. Attitudes and social sensitivity. (Tolerance, scientific spirit of inquiry, appreciation of music, etc.)
4. Interests, aims, purposes. (Vocational goals, wise use of leisure, etc.)
5. Study skills and work habits.
6. Social and personal adjustment.
7. Creativeness.
8. Physical health.
9. A functional philosophy of life.

In order to obtain evidence of pupil growth in these qualities, it is necessary to define them in terms of behavior. How does a person act who has
ability to draw sound conclusions from scientific data? How can we recognize pupils who have "a functional philosophy of life"? Some objectives
are easier to translate into behavior terms than others, but when such a
translation has been made, it is possible to gather data, by tests or observations, to show changes in pupils. "Skill in interpretation of data," for example,
is shown by certain definite actions. If we give a skilled person a table or
graph related to a topic he has not studied, he does certain things. He identifies major trends. He disregards fluctuations that are probably due to variations in sampling. He reports that factor A and factor B change together,
not that factor A causes factor B. These and other interpretation skills can
readily be tested, because we have defined precisely what actions give
evidence that the subject possesses the desired skill.

1. For one of the following courses, try to list all the important objectives.
   a. Study of literature in the junior high school.
   b. A course to train union officials for collective bargaining.
   c. A course to train junior executives in human relations.
2. Would the purpose of a course in "European history since 1815" be the same in
   an American and a Russian university? Could the same test validly be used for
   both courses?
3. Define each of the following objectives in terms of specific behaviors.
   a. "To train young people for wise parenthood."
   b. "To increase appreciation of good literature."
   c. "To prepare young people for the duties of citizenship."

Facts and skills loom so large in the usual classroom that teachers and test designers have often emphasized them out of proportion to other types of outcome. Although it is important to measure gains in knowledge and skill, a pupil may earn a high score on a test covering only memory-type material and yet have made little progress toward understanding of the course. A course in cooking presumably is supposed to improve ability to cook. But when one teacher tested a college class on their knowledge of scientific principles underlying cookery, and also had them cook food, the quality of cooking correlated only .25 with the verbal knowledge (3, p. 60). In 14 college courses Tyler correlated tests supposed to measure different types of learning outcomes. The correlations (corrected for errors of measurement) were small: knowledge of facts vs. application of principles, about .45; knowledge vs. inference, .35; application vs. inference, .40 (17).

Studies of forgetting give weight to the argument that changes in thinking and attitudes, as well as knowledge, should be measured. These studies show that facts which are little understood are quickly dropped from the mind. Attitudes and changes of thinking habits are usually found to be much more lasting. Tyler gave a zoölogy test to one college class before they studied zoölogy, at the end of the course, and again after another year in which they studied no zoölogy. The results in Table 54 indicate that the lasting changes were primarily in ability to apply principles to new problems and to draw conclusions from data.

4. In a certain course, the correlation between a factual test and a test of ability to apply knowledge to new situations is .40. Assume that grades are assigned as follows: 10 percent A, 20 percent B, 40 percent C, 20 percent D, and 10 percent F. What grades will A students on the first test receive if the second test is used as a basis for grading? (Use the scatter diagram on p. 37.)

Table 54. Improvement in Abilities in Zoölogy, Measured at the End of the Course and One Year Later (after 33, p. 76)

Type of Examination Exercise	Mean Score			Percent of Gain During Course Which Was Later Lost
	Beginning of Course	End of Course	One Year Later	
Naming animal structures pictured in diagrams	22	62	31	77
Identifying technical terms	20	83	67	26
Recalling information				
a. Structures performing functions in type forms	13	39	34	21
b. Other facts	21	63	54	21
Applying principles to new situations	35	65	65	0
Interpreting new experiments	30	57	64	25[a]
Average, all exercises	24	74	63	22

[a] *Gain* over scores at end of course.

Testers have sometimes confused ability (maximum performance) with typical performance. Many students who pass examinations by showing that they know what should be done may not do the right thing when the problem arises in life. It is easy, for example, to prepare a true-false test for a course in "how to study." After exposure to a few lectures on principles of study, most students know what good study habits they should have and can answer the test. But the gap between what students know about study and what they do about it is large. The need for testing typical behavior is great, yet most achievement tests have stressed abilities produced on demand. Tests of typical behavior are needed to evaluate the effectiveness of courses teaching handwriting, leadership or personnel management, resistance to propaganda, accuracy in arithmetic, and many other objectives. Some devices for testing typical behavior are described in Part III.

Some tests of achievement permit irrelevant variables to affect the score. Reading ability affects scores on almost all achievement tests. This is difficult to avoid, but a valid measure of knowledge is not obtained if a person who knows a fact misses an item about it because of verbal difficulties. Sometimes the verbal factors play a large part in the test. The Navy Mechanical Knowledge Test contained four types of item: mechanical facts, tested verbally; mechanical facts, tested pictorially; electrical facts, tested verbally; and electrical facts, tested pictorially. The intercorrelations in Table 55 show that in this case similarity of content produced lower correla-

Table 55. Correlations of Tests Having Similar Form, and Tests Having Similar Content (Navy Mechanical Knowledge Test) (8)

	Correlation	Correlation Corrected for Unreliability
Tests similar in form, different in content:		
Verbal tests: mechanical vs. electrical	.63	.79
Pictorial tests: mechanical vs. electrical	.64	.86
Tests similar in content, different in form:		
Mechanical: verbal vs. pictorial	.61	.71
Electrical: verbal vs. pictorial	.51	.74
Tests different in both form and content:		
Mechanical verbal vs. electrical pictorial	.49	.63
Electrical verbal vs. mechanical pictorial	.45	.59
Kuder-Richardson reliability coefficients:		
Mechanical verbal	.89	
Mechanical pictorial	.82	
Electrical verbal	.71	
Electrical pictorial	.67	

tions than similarity in form. In other words, the form of the items largely determined the score received. Another study made at a naval training center provides even stronger evidence that the verbal element in tests is frequently undesirable. Training of gunners had been validly evaluated by scores made in operating the guns. To obtain a more economical substitute, verbal and pictorial tests were developed. Identical information was tested in the two forms, the same question being asked in words alone or by means of pictures supplemented by words. Questions dealt with parts of the gun, duties of the crew, appearance of tracers when the gun was properly aimed, etc. The pictorial test had a correlation of .90 with instructors' marks based on gun operation whereas the validity of the verbal test was only .62. The verbal test was in large measure a reading test; it correlated .59 with a Navy reading test, while the picture test correlated only .26 with reading (30). Obviously, scores on verbal achievement tests should be viewed with suspicion for pupils who are poor readers.

Another variable which reduces validity of achievement tests is the speed factor. Time limits are often needed for administrative convenience, but when speed becomes a major element in determining a person's score, the score is likely not to represent his attainment accurately. Speed is a legitimate element in achievement tests only when speed is an objective of the course. Speed is relevant and important in tests of typing attainment or reading facility, or tests of arithmetic for use in hiring cashiers. Speed is irrelevant if we wish to know how large a pupil's vocabulary is, how much science he knows, or how accurately he can reason. In most achievement tests a speed loading can be justified only if the test is to be used empirically to predict success in a task where speed is helpful, or if data are available to prove that scores on the speeded test correlate very highly with scores on the unspeeded test. Speed tests have limited validity for describing the knowledge of individual pupils, since a few well-informed pupils are slow workers.

Recognition and Recall

Because only objective tests can be depended upon to compare pupils tested in different places, multiple-choice and other recognition items are necessarily given great emphasis in standard testing. This has been a source of concern to many teachers who felt that only tests requiring free responses could measure adequately what they were teaching. Recognition of right answers is easily tested by objective items, but where the purpose of teaching is to produce ability to recall or invent new solutions, teachers tend to prefer free-response tests. The English teacher often prefers to have her students judged on a sample of their free writing, rather than on tests of the copy-reading type where the student merely identifies errors. The mathematics teacher has felt that his students should be required to solve problems, rather than merely to select alternatives in what one writer calls "place-your-bet" questions.

Considerable research has been done to determine if objective tests are adequate. The findings have been consistently favorable to the use of well-constructed objective tests. When a multiple-choice test is made up of correct answers, together with incorrect alternatives chosen from among the wrong answers *given by students* who have answered the same questions with free response, the multiple-choice test has a high correlation with the free-response test. One would think that ability to generalize from data could be tested only by requiring that the student form his own generalizations. But a test carefully prepared by Tyler requiring undergraduates to identify the best and poorest generalizations from a set of data correlated .85 with ability to draw generalizations directly from the data. Ability to plan an experiment is a creative function; yet a recognition test calling for choice among alternative plans correlated .79 with ability to make plans without suggestions (33, pp. 27–30). Tharp found correlations as high as .84 between ability to pronounce French, tested by a sample of the student's speech, and score on a recognition test (29). Other studies have shown that recognition tests in writing and mathematics are valid tests (cf. p. 73).

There are probably many places where only a free-response test is a good measure. If Tyler's study of ability to plan experiments were repeated with a group of graduate students, all of whom had overlearned the verbally stated principles of scientific method, probably all would do well on any reasonable objective test. But even among such students there is marked variation in inventiveness in attacking new problems. Similarly, Tharp's test sorted students accurately on French pronunciation. But it is doubtful if, in an advanced group, fine discrimination between those with authentic and those with false accents could be obtained save by a test of performance. While good objective tests are dependable for surveys of most abilities and for marking, free-response tests are also widely used. Because these are difficult to score, they can only be standardized by the adoption of uniform scoring guides.

5. Distinguish, in each of the following types of learning, the relative importance of recall or invention, and recognition.
   a. Learning to interpret children's problem behavior in terms of probable causes.
   b. Learning to play bridge.
6. Discuss the following point of view:
   "I view with some misgivings the purely utilitarian course in 'Communications' which has been substituted for the traditional freshman composition course at S—. Students' needs in this course, we are told, are ascertained by the administration of 'batteries of tests.' I venture to assert that nothing will be learned from these tests which a skilled teacher would not find out from a single theme and a half-hour interview; and that these would be better for the student psychologically, as motivation for the course, than the 'batteries of tests'" (11).

Technical Accuracy

Although it should be obvious that a test is invalid if the keyed answers are incorrect, some published tests contain a serious proportion of errors. These errors result from inaccurate editing, ambiguities, and oversimplification of technical problems to fit the objective-item form. Diamond made a thorough criticism of 16 published tests in science. While some were completely free from error, in other tests the number of errors of fact or theory rose as high as 9 per 50 items (9).

Meaningfulness of Grade Norms

Educational tests have commonly been standardized in terms of grade norms. A pupil's raw score is translated into a "grade equivalent," so that the standing of a superior sixth-grader may read as follows:

Reading	9.7	History	9.2
Math	9.0	Geography	8.6
English	8.7	Spelling	7.7
Literature	10.3	Total	9.1

This means that, for example, his ability in mathematics equals that of the average beginning ninth-grader. Such reports are misleading unless the user is aware of the pitfalls in grade norms. The difficulties are three in number:

1. Grade norms are based on more or less representative samples of pupils throughout the nation. Some sections of the country are far superior to others, owing to differences in pupil ability, differences in the quality of teachers, and differences in expenditures for education and the resulting program. No teacher or superintendent from a superior school can take pride if his group merely reaches the national norms; no one from a handicapped school district should be condemned if his group cannot attain the national average. The only fair basis for comparing schools is to judge each school against schools of similar type and resources. Rarely are published norms based on such meaningful segments as "New England public elementary schools, in cities with population 2000 to 10,000" or "Southern rural elementary schools."

2. Norms are not "standards." It is a common mistake to assume that all pupils in the ninth grade should reach the ninth-grade norm. This is of course a fallacy; in the standardizing sample, 50 percent of the pupils fall below the norm. Furthermore, the test shows only what schools are doing at present. It is highly unlikely that the schools are doing so well that the national average represents what pupils could attain with the best teaching methods. The teacher whose class reaches the average has no cause for complacency. There is much room for the development of better educational methods.

3. Grade norms are based on grossly unequal and artificial units of measurement. It looks as if the pupil is greatly superior who reaches the "ninth-grade level" in geography when he is only in Grade VI. But in many standard tests this difference in score represents very little gain, because the average pupil increases his ability only slightly from Grade VI to Grade IX. In other tests, this difference in "grade level" is merely an arbitrary assumption based on extrapolation rather than upon testing of pupils in higher grades.

"Ninth-grade levels" in different subjects are not equally hard for sixth-graders to reach. The pupil who is "two years beyond his grade" in a subject may sometimes be markedly superior; at other times this represents a standing equaled by a large proportion of his class. Moreover, a two-grade superiority in one subject is not at all equivalent to a two-grade gain in another. The profile of grade scores may give a very different picture of strengths and weaknesses than a profile of scores comparing the pupil to other sixth-graders.

As in the case of the IQ (see p. 135), it is probably wise to replace grade norms with derived scores of the standard-score type. Some standard tests now give norms in the form of percentile scores in each grade, the Progressive Achievement Tests being an example. Percentiles within a single grade group do not permit a comparison of pupils in different grades, but this is rarely needed.

Harmful Effects in the Educational Program

It has been mentioned that the very powers sought in standardized testing have been a two-edged weapon, damaging the educational program as much as helping it. The essential difficulty is that *achievement tests determine the curriculum.* Both college students and younger pupils devote much of their time to trying to determine what will be tested, so that they can study that material and neglect anything else. Students use different study methods, concentrate on different materials, and have different accomplishment when objective tests replace essay tests (22). The teacher too is driven by the test to direct his energies into the paths they dictate. A chemistry teacher considering the modification of his course to stress applications and reasoning rather than technical formulas is deterred if he fears that his class, and hence his teaching, will "look bad" when a standard test at the end of the year asks about the formulas. The writer recalls visiting a rural school which was alarmed because all the boys, upon finishing the compulsory eighth grade, immediately left school to work on the farm. The principal believed they should stay in high school, but the boys considered school a waste of time. A look at the "literature book" for Grade VIII supplied one clue to the difficulty. Pupils were being held to selections about a Hindu boy and his village, mountain climbing in Tibet, and other topics of remote interest. When the teacher was asked why she did not encourage the boys to develop their language skills on bulletins from the agriculture extension service and other materials that the boys would consider valuable, her answer was ready: "I know this book isn't good, and the boys don't like it, but I have to teach it because it prepares pupils on topics covered in the standard test given at the end of the year by the — Office" (an agency supervising the schools). While hesitancy in this situation related primarily to desire to avoid criticism, in other cases tests have directly forced schools to follow rigid curricula laid down from above. This was considered essential in Navy training where every man must serve in the highly standardized fleet, but in general education it is deplorable. Many schools have in the past been unable to modify their curricula because graduates were forced to pass traditional college entrance examinations if they wished to go to college. Such tests have been liberalized in recent years to permit more flexibility in lower-school curricula. Tests encourage sound teaching and sound study attitudes only when they measure all the behaviors the teacher wishes to develop, and nothing else.

When tests have been used to determine whom in the group to find fault with, they have bred considerable ill will. A whip motivates, but it builds tension. Teachers have, in some cases, been discharged because standard tests made their work look poor. Promotion of pupils from grade to grade has sometimes rested on the standard test, with no consideration given to the remainder of the school record. The administrator who introduces tests can make them an ally of teacher and pupil, a way for both to determine how to improve themselves. But if he is not careful, he will arouse anxieties which reduce the morale and effectiveness of the organization.

A common error in applying standard tests has been to employ the norms without considering what might reasonably be expected in terms of pupil ability. Since intelligence varies from person to person and group to group, one can only judge whether progress is adequate by comparing the person or group with others of similar potentiality. A common method for making this comparison is the *accomplishment quotient* (AQ). The AQ is the ratio of "educational age" to mental age. Alice, a nine-year-old with MA 12, reaches the achievement norm for eleven-year-olds. Her AQ is 92 ($11 \div 12$). This is an ingenious procedure for identifying those who are "underachieving" and "overachieving," but it has led to so many unreasonable results that the AQ is in growing disrepute. The weaknesses arise from the limitations of grade norms and from unsound statistical assumptions (13, p. 251). Alice, for example, can scarcely be expected to be three years ahead of her grade in history if she hasn't been exposed to sixth-grade history, so she is no underachiever. Because of these limitations the accomplishment quotient should be discarded and replaced by a comparison showing how the pupil's learning compares with that of other pupils of similar aptitude or initial ability. Such comparisons are usually based on local norms, but national norms of this type can be prepared. The procedure by which any teacher can make such an analysis is described by Trimble and Cronbach (32).

7. What effects, good or bad, would the practices described in the following paragraph have on the education of the pupils?
"The New York State Education Department, better known as the Regents, administers uniform examinations, also better known as the Regents, semi-annually to all high-school students pursuing key subjects. To prepare their students for this ordeal, many teachers abandon the regular textbook in favor of a special booklet containing a review of the subject and a reprint of recent Regents' examinations. The general practice is to begin the review about four to six weeks in advance of the big test, although some teachers start Regents preparation as early as the first day of the term" (2).

8. What effect would the above practices have on the validity of comparisons of different schools on the Regents' tests?

9. What arguments can be advanced for and against the policy of a county school superintendent who gives a standardized battery of achievement tests in every elementary school under her jurisdiction, and reports the standing of each school in each subject to the local newspapers?
10. Why was each of the difficulties discussed in the foregoing section less significant in the Navy than in public school testing?
11. In prewar Japan and Germany, the schools were held to curricula rigidly laid down in the national education ministries. It has been the policy of the occupation in both countries to encourage local initiative in revising courses of study and trying new methods of teaching. The purpose is to eliminate stereotypy and thought control, to encourage independent thinking of pupils, and to develop programs adapted to local needs and interests as well as national policies. Some leaders propose that psychologists and educators develop standardized tests for important types of learning, to be made available to schools through the national and regional ministries. The aim of such tests would be to promote a high standard of teaching. Discuss whether the proposal should be adopted.
12. "As a general rule, no achievement test printed or revised more than five years ago, or any other test more than ten years old, should be used" (34, p. 26). Why do you think a writer on educational evaluation would make this statement? Do you agree?

TYPES OF ACHIEVEMENT TESTS

Among the myriad standard achievement tests, a few broad types appear. Some tests measure achievement in a single subject, such as history or science. Batteries of achievement tests have also been prepared, especially for the elementary grades. Such batteries consist of several subtests, each measuring an area of learning. Since the subtests are standardized together, the test tells how a child's knowledge in one subject compares with his ability in other areas. The areas most commonly measured at the elementary level are reading, spelling, grammar, history-civics, and the like (see Table 56). Tests for high schools and colleges have also been prepared to give a picture of growth in all areas, but on the whole, single-subject tests have been more widely used than batteries of subject tests.

If one's purpose is to determine how much science a student considering a premedical course knows, his general competence is of more interest than his mastery of a particular segment of science. A few recent test batteries for high school and college have attempted to measure general educational growth without regard to narrow subject-matter divisions. The tests of General Educational Development (G.E.D.) of the U.S. Armed Forces Institute are an example. These have been used widely to decide which veterans have learned enough while out of school to receive a high-school diploma, even though they never "completed" high school. The test battery measures mathematical ability and English expression by more or less conventional tests, but its measures in science, social studies, and literature are novel. Instead of testing what facts a man knows in science, or what works of literature he happens to have encountered, these are "tests of interpretation" in the three fields. Passages similar to those in college science texts are presented and questions are asked to determine how well the man comprehends them. Similarly, he is required to interpret social science materials and passages from literature. Such a test draws on knowledge, but does not require a man to remember specific detailed facts. Since the test resembles the task of college work, it should be a good predictor of success in college (6).

In contrast to survey tests which estimate the person's general attainment in an area, some diagnostic tests have been prepared, notably for reading and mathematics. A diagnostic test attempts to determine, not the level attained, but the specific strengths and weaknesses of the student. Diagnostic tests focus on the process by which the subject responds, rather than the product. Diagnostic procedures in reading will be described below. Diagnostic procedures are sometimes used in any teaching, whether of music, piloting a plane, winding armatures, or clinical psychology. The teacher cannot teach effectively unless he knows just what is wrong with the student. But since the intra-individual comparison is stressed rather than comparison with others, diagnostic methods have rarely been standardized.

Most published tests have measured knowledge, neglecting other behaviors. Among the most promising developments in achievement testing are several new measures of other objectives, notably ability to apply principles, reasoning skills, and ability to interpret data. In addition to these, some schools have used interest tests and attitude tests (Chaps. 15, 16) to study pupil progress.

Tests of ability to apply principles are unique in that they ask the pupil not to state or recognize a fact, but to solve a new problem where that principle is relevant. If a pupil can determine the correct solution to a "life" situation, not previously studied, and defend it with a sound scientific principle, it is certain that he understands the principle. The most complex and highly developed tests of ability to apply principles in science and social studies are those of the Progressive Education Association, made under Tyler's direction (26). Examples, related to most school subjects, are presented in *The measurement of understanding* (16). Few standardized tests have employed this technique as yet, but the following illustrations are taken from instruments developed by the Cooperative Test Service:

"The walls of a living room which is to have indirect lighting should be finished in
"1. a glossy, rather dark paint
"2. a rough, rather dark wallpaper
"3. a rough, brightly colored wallpaper
"4. a shiny white paint
"5. a rough, cream-colored stipple or wallpaper"[1]
"*Experiment.* Coal gas which has not been previously mixed with air is burned at a gas jet (no. 1). At a similar jet (no. 2) the coal gas is mixed with air before it is burned.

---

[1] From the Cooperative General Science Test, Revised Series, Form Q.

"*Probable results* (Mark those which explain the result. . . .)
"1. Incomplete combustion leaves some uncombined carbon in the flame.
"2. The presence of nitrogen retards combustion.
"3. Particles of uncombined carbon glow when heated. . . ."[2]

The essential point in tests of this type is that the question must present a problem unfamiliar to the student, without telling him what principle to use.

Tests of reasoning ability are used in intelligence tests, but certain types of reasoning are directly taught in school and can be tested as achievements. Particularly in courses stressing propaganda analysis, scientific thinking, or logical proof, learning can only be measured by presenting the pupil with arguments to be analyzed. The Nature of Proof tests of the Progressive Education Association are an example (26, pp. 126–154). A typical problem describes a news report regarding deaths from typhoid in a town where water was polluted. A conclusion is suggested that the sickness of one man living on the stream above the town caused the widespread illness. Students are then given many reasons (taken from previous student papers) which they are to judge as supporting the conclusion, contradicting the conclusion, or irrelevant. "Good doctors should be available when an epidemic hits a small town" is irrelevant. "Typhoid fever germs are active after being carried for about half a mile in clear running water" is necessary in proving the conclusion. After studying and marking the reasons, the student decides whether the conclusion was proved. A number of separate scores are obtained from the complete set of several problems. Scores include "number of accurate conclusions," "number of irrelevant reasons called supporting," and so on. This is consistent with the belief that reasoning ability is not a unit, but includes many different behaviors. Reliability coefficients for the Nature of Proof scores range from .82 down to .20 (26, p. 517), which indicates that the present form of the test is not adequate for diagnosis of logical thinking. It can be a useful teaching instrument, since it focuses attention of pupil and teacher on an important type of behavior.

The third important new test is Interpretation of Data, a PEA instrument.[3] Exercises require the student to make inferences and interpretations from tables, charts, maps, and other forms of presentation. Data deal with a wide range of interesting and unfamiliar situations, from baseball averages to diet. Students are given numerous suggested interpretations, which they rate as "true," "probably true," etc.

13. If admission to college depends in part on a test which stresses knowledge of historical facts, what sort of course could a teacher give high-school seniors which would improve their chances of passing? What sort of social studies course could he give if admission is based on the G.E.D. tests?

14. The G.E.D. tests require up to two hours to obtain a single score, whereas the

---

[2] From the Cooperative Chemistry Test for College Students, Form 1940.
[3] Now published by the Educational Testing Service.

Progressive Achievement battery obtains about 20 scores in two hours. Are these equally good measurement practices?

15. Discuss the argument: "The USAFI tests of interpretation are measures of intelligence and reading ability rather than educational development."

16. Would the Nature of Proof test be valid as a measure of intelligence of adolescents?

Table 56.   Representative Achievement Test Batteries

Test and Publisher	Grade Level	Content	Comments of Reviewers[a]
Cooperative Tests (Educ. Testing Service)	High school; college	English, lit. comprehension, lit. acquaintance, social studies, nat. sciences, math., contemporary affairs	Eng.: "Excellent for survey. . . . Not individually diagnostic" (Leonard, 5). Lit. comp.: "Question whether test measures anything of consequence" (Roberts, 5).
Metropolitan Achievement Tests (World Book)	Grades 1; 2–3; 3–4; 4–6; 7–8.	Reading, vocab., arith. fundamentals, history, spelling, etc.	
Progressive Achievement Tests (Calif. Test Bureau)	Grades 1–3; 4–6; 7–9; 9–13	Vocab., reading, math. reasoning, math. fundamentals, language	"Diagnostic features excellent. . . . Conform with the best practices in test construction and standardization" (Witty, 5). "Among the best of their type. . . . Scarcely fulfill all the claims made for them" (Odell, 4, p. 38).
Stanford Achievement Tests (World Book)	Grades 2–3; 4–6; 7–9	Reading, language, arith., soc. science, spelling, etc.	"[Certain portions] not surpassed as tests of skill subjects. . . . Subtests covering content fields not abreast of curricular changes" (Preston, 5).
Iowa Tests of Educational Development (Sci. Res. Assoc.)	High school	Social concepts, background in science, writing, quantitative thinking, interpretation of reading materials, etc.	"Probably best battery available for use in senior high school" (Chauncey, 5). "Intended to measure relatively permanent changes in broad aspects rather than specifics" (Hanna, 5).
U.S. Armed Forces Institute Tests of General Educational Development (Educ. Testing Service)	High school; college	Mathematics, expression, interpretation of reading in soc. studies, etc.	"Quality of items high. . . . Absence of validity data deplorable. . . . One chief question is whether tests measure academic achievement independent of general intelligence or general reading ability" (Conrad, 5).

[a] The reader should refer to the source cited for a full statement of the reviewer's opinion.

READING TESTS

Reading deserves special attention in a book of this type for two reasons. First, reading tests have been developed in greater number and variety than any other type of achievement test and demonstrate numerous problems in test construction. Second, they are probably used more widely in guidance and clinical practice than other achievement tests.

Definition of Abilities

At a glance, reading seems like a clearly defined skill which could be readily measured. Actually, no area illustrates more clearly than reading that tests having the same name measure quite different behaviors. Different authors disagree on what is included in the area and on the most useful definition of rate, comprehension, word knowledge, etc. for testing purposes. One author examined 24 reading tests and found that between them they measured 48 different skills (31). This does not mean that reading is a complex of so many specific abilities, however. One test claimed to measure several "entirely different" reading skills, but the correlation of scores showed that these different abilities were actually the same function measured over and over under different names (14). One way of clarifying which reading abilities are truly different is factor analysis. In 25 tests of reading and study skills, the following common factors were found: tendency to read carefully (an attitude or response set), inductive reasoning, rate of reading, verbal ability, vocabulary, rate for unrelated facts, and chart reading (14). In view of the variety of test content the person who needs a test of reading must be careful to define what reading ability he wishes to measure, and must turn to dependable sources (4, 5, 20, 31) for a trustworthy analysis of possible tests.

Survey Tests

Survey tests are ordinarily intended to represent, in one to three scores, the subject's general level of reading development. They are used to screen people who could be helped by remedial teaching, to predict success in courses, and to check whether poor reading explains a subject's poor performance on a group mental test.

Reading development includes both speed of reading and comprehension, and a useful test must consider both these elements. Most testers have tried to develop tests which can measure independently the two aspects of performance, and they have been largely unsuccessful. This problem occurs in most testing, but rarely is it so easily recognized as in reading: When an act contains several integral aspects, one cannot divide the act into fragments for testing purposes. This principle has been illustrated in Binet's finding that significant intellectual performances could only be measured by complex tasks, and in the finding that complex coördination tasks resembling a job are often better predictors than any combination of elemental dexterities.

In theory, the way to separate speed and comprehension is to hold one constant while the other is measured. Speed can be minimized by giving a test without a time limit; the subject's understanding of what he reads should be a pure measure of comprehension. Rate is much harder to measure. Every person has a variety of reading rates, changing with his purpose and the material read. Good readers tend to shift their speed as difficulty increases whereas poor comprehenders seem to use a rather unvarying rate (1). The problem for the tester is: How can we have every student read the same passage with the same degree of concentration and the same effort to comprehend? Rate of reading can be raised so easily by becoming superficial that the final result is ambiguous unless effort to comprehend can be controlled. The usual technique to control comprehension is to require the subject to answer questions about what he has read, or to cross out absurdities as he reads. The former technique is employed in the Iowa Silent Reading Test and the Nelson-Denny test. The Nelson-Denny method is illustrated in Figure 69. The score is the number of questions answered correctly in a set time.

The government of Henry the Seventh, of his son, and of his grandchildren was, on the whole, more arbitrary than that of the Plantagenets. Personal character may in some degree explain the difference; for courage and force of will were common to all the men and women of the House of Tudor. They exercised their power during a period of one hundred and twenty years, always with vigour, often with violence, sometimes with cruelty. They occasionally invaded the rights of the subject, occasionally exacted taxes under the name of loans and gifts, and occasionally dispensed with penal statutes; Nay, though they never presumed to enact any permanent law by their own authority, they occasionally took upon themselves, when Parliament was not sitting, to meet temporary exigencies by temporary edicts. It was, however, impossible for the Tudors to carry oppression beyond a certain point, for they had no armed force, and they were surrounded by armed people. Their palace was guarded by a few domestics, whom the array of a single shire, or of a single ward of London, could with ease have overpowered. These haughty princes were therefore under a restraint stronger than any which mere law can impose.

1. With whom is the paragraph chiefly concerned? 1. The Tudor Kings. 2. The Plantagenet Kings. 3. The palace guards. 4. The London populace. 5. The English people.
2. How were new laws secured when Parliament was not sitting? 1. They were made by a single London ward. 2. Old laws were revived. 3. They were made by the army. 4. The King issued an edict. 5. They were made by the Princes' council.
3. Under what guise were taxes sometimes collected? 1. Fines. 2. Loans. 3. Tariffs. 4. Commissions. 5. Sale of public offices.
4. What personal trait was always displayed by the rule of the dynasty discussed in the paragraph? 1. Cowardice. 2. Deceit. 3. Vigour. 4. Vacillation. 5. Forbearance.

Fig. 69.   Specimen item from Nelson-Denny Reading Test[4]

In the Iowa test, the student reads first for a set period of time, which yields his rate score, and then turns the page and answers the questions, which give a comprehension score. The absurdities technique is represented by the following item from the Dvorak–van Wagenen test:

Directions: Read each paragraph carefully, find the word in the last half that does not fit in with the meaning of the rest of it, and make a cross through it.

Mrs. Glenn has been buying a lot of new furniture for her house. Yesterday the furniture truck came with a new table, a new hat, and several new rocking chairs.

Reading survey tests have the following weaknesses:

1. The scores on rate and comprehension are often interdependent, so that the pupil can raise one at the expense of the other. When only a single "rate

---

[4] M. J. Nelson and E. C. Denny, *Reading Test for Colleges*, Houghton Mifflin Company.

of comprehension" score is obtained, the score is influenced by the subject's tendency to read cautiously which will raise or lower his score relative to others.

2. Tests supposed to measure comprehension are often heavily speeded, so that they are strongly influenced by rate of reading. Such tests are of little value for diagnosing, although they are good predictors.

3. The reading test covers only a selected range of content, yet reading ability varies somewhat with different materials. Some people can read history well but not science; some do well on stories, poorly on textbooks. The survey test includes a sample of a broad or narrow type of content; the way the content is selected makes the test more useful for predicting some types of performance, less useful for others.

4. Many tests measure only a limited type of comprehension. The skilled reader must not only be able to make sense of sentences, as in the cross-out item illustrated above. He must also be able to take the main idea from a long passage, put together ideas in separate sentences, follow a logical argument, and so on. Some reading tests measure only the simplest type of comprehension, whereas others demand deep and thorough interpretation. A survey test cannot measure all types of comprehension separately, which makes it important to use a test measuring the type of reading with which one is concerned.

17. Examine the questions used in the Nelson-Denny selection (Fig. 69), and decide what mental activities each calls for. Justify or criticize this meaning of comprehension in a survey test for college readers.
18. As an evidence of validity, the Nelson-Denny manual reports a high correlation of the test with freshman marks. Does this demonstrate that the test is valid?
19. Could a student attempt to answer the questions by reading the questions first and looking up the answers, rather than first reading through the whole paragraph? Would this procedure affect the score obtained?
20. For what predictive and guidance purposes would it be most desirable to have each of the following tests?
    a. A test of ability to read selections drawn from college textbooks in a variety of fields.
    b. A test of ability to read selections drawn from college textbooks in physics and mathematics.

Diagnostic Methods

A diagnostic achievement test at its best is an impressive tool. With or without such tests all teachers must at times study their students to determine why they are having difficulty. The diagnostic test tries to increase the efficiency of diagnosis by bringing to the teacher's aid all the insights available from research on learning failures. An ideal diagnostic achievement test calls the teacher's attention to every aspect of the reading process wherein the pupil might have stumbled. By checking off one at a time the many sorts of possible error, the teacher is left with a picture of the specific weaknesses that must be remedied before the pupil can make normal progress.

Such a diagnostic procedure must be based on extensive research to determine what types of errors are made. Once the errors are listed, it is necessary to devise test procedures to reveal clearly which errors the pupil makes. Diagnostic methods have been standardized for arithmetic and a few other school subjects, but they have reached their highest development in reading. Reading specialists have available a great variety of diagnostic techniques, and a few of these have been organized into batteries sufficiently simple for classroom teachers to use. The two most widely known methods of individual diagnosis are the Monroe-Sherman tests, which include both aptitude and achievement measures, and the Durrell Analysis of Reading Difficulty. The latter will be described here.

Durrell bases his tests on study of the reading errors made by 4000 school children. His tests provide an opportunity to observe the child at work in oral and silent reading, and in special tests. In this respect, they are like the observations of performance discussed later in the chapter. The first tests deal with oral reading. The tester notes the time required to read the standardized paragraphs, and notes whatever errors occur. Silent reading is then checked on a set of paragraphs of equal difficulty to the oral series. Questions are used to check recall, and the teacher observes such reading habits as visible lip movement. A flash-exposure device is used to show words briefly; this indicates perceptual habits and errors. Finally, there is a phonetic inventory for children who have difficulty in word perception. The analysis is not a mechanical device—it calls for great skill and keenness of observation by the tester. In the oral tests, the tester must record phrase reading, hesitation on words, mispronunciation, omission of words or syllables, ignoring of punctuation, and enunciation. The virtue of the test is that it presents materials of standardized difficulty, and that the check list of errors calls the tester's attention to all the significant facts that may be noted.

The type of information that comes from a careful diagnosis is illustrated by Durrell's report on Anthony, age 9–8, in the fourth grade. His Binet MA was 9–4, and his IQ was 97, but his general reading achievement was at the low second-grade level.

"On the Durrell *Analysis of Reading Difficulty,* Anthony made a low second-grade score on oral-reading tests, but seemed quite unable to keep his attention on silent reading. He did poorly on quick perception of words, and had no method of word analysis. He read a word at a time in a strained voice and a monotone. He was markedly insecure in his reading and repeated words continually. He was unaware of the errors in his reading, indicating a lack of concern about meaning. When his errors were corrected in his oral reading, his comprehension was excellent.

"The silent reading was marked by a high rate at the expense of mastery. He skipped all the hard words; as a result his recall was scanty and inaccurate, although he did the best he could with it. Strictly speaking, he did not read silently at all, since his reading was accompanied by constant whispering of the words, vague sounds being given for the difficult words. His eye movements in silent reading were irregular and unrhythmic, with seven to ten per line and many regressive movements" (10, p. 333).

Another group of diagnostic tests is much simpler, being intended for group administration. These contain subtests presumed to measure various types of reading ability. Performance is represented as a profile showing the relative strengths and weaknesses of the pupil. The Iowa Silent Reading Test is among the most prominent of these tests. It reports nine scores, based on these subtests:

Rate of reading. The pupil reads two short articles, marking his place when a signal is given. He then answers simple questions on the passages. Both rate and accuracy scores are reported.

Directed reading. The pupil answers questions about paragraphs by indicating the place in the paragraph where each question is answered. This and following tests are separately timed, with most pupils having insufficient time to finish.

Poetry. The pupil reads poetic selections and answers questions about their meaning.

Word meaning. Four lists of words are presented, in social science, science, mathematics, and English. With each word is presented five alternatives, the pupil choosing the best synonym. This test is conducted in four 90-second sections, the pupil going from one list of words to the next when time is called. One score is obtained on the section.

Sentence meaning. The pupil reads sentences dealing with the meaning of words and simple information, marking each true or false.

Paragraph meaning. The pupil reads paragraphs and answers questions about each. Items call for both direct memory and recognition of central thought.

Use of index. An abbreviated index is presented, and the pupil reports which pages of the book would contain answers to certain questions.

Key words. The pupil indicates what words he would seek in an index in order to obtain information about such questions as, "What is the value of our annual supply of mineral products?"

21. Reliabilities of the subtests for the Iowa test are not reported except by split-half methods which are incorrect for speed tests. What possible fallacy is involved in interpreting a profile without knowing the reliability of subtests?
22. In what ways would the test be more or less satisfactory if all parts except "Rate of reading" were given with no time limit?
23. Since the entire Iowa test requires more than one hour to give, it is sometimes desired to omit certain sections. Which parts would be most valuable to help plan remedial training for a college student having difficulty due to slow reading?

Table 57 lists a small sampling of the great variety of reading tests on the market. Not only do the tests vary in design, but the authors of tests have widely differing opinions as to the most useful subdivisions of the reading act for testing purposes. McCullough, Strang, and Traxler list 17 questions that need to be answered in choosing a group reading test for school use, and make it clear that several tests do not measure up to these criteria (20, pp. 133 ff.). They go on to say, "There has yet to be constructed an entirely satisfactory silent-reading test, and it is quite possible that when such a test does appear, no one will buy it except for use in clinical situations. A truly adequate test would have to be too long, with too many parts to score and too many kinds of material, for any school to find time to use it on a school-wide basis."[5]

24. If survey tests give an inadequate description of reading difficulties, and if

Table 57.   Representative Reading Tests

Test and Publisher	Grade Level	Time	Scores Reported	Comments of Reviewers[a]
Cooperative Reading Comprehension (Educ. Testing Service)	7–12; college	40 min.	Vocabulary, speed of comprehension, level of comprehension	"The level of comprehension score is not complicated by rate except for certain students. . . . Advantages of such a score in clinical work, instruction, and research are obvious" (Stroud, 5).
Diagnostic Reading Tests (Educ. Rec. Bureau)	7–13	For survey, 40 min.	Survey: rate, comprehension, vocabulary. Diagnostic: vocabulary, in five areas; comprehension, silent and auditory; rate for stories, soc. studies, science; word attack	
Durrell Analysis of Reading Difficulty (World Book)	1–6	About 50 min.	Tester notes speed and specific errors in oral and silent reading, flash perception, phonetics	"No reliability coefficients. . . . Little concerning validity is cited. . . . Author correctly emphasizes usefulness of test for standard observation of errors" (Tinker, 4, p. 341).
Dvorak-van Wagenen Diagnostic Examination of Silent Reading Abilities (Educ. Test. Bureau)	4–6; 7–9; 10-college	About 2 hrs.	Rate of comprehension; ability to perceive relationships; vocabulary, in context and isolated; six other scores	"Reliability of some of the parts low and intercorrelations high" (20, p. 132).

[a] The reader should refer to the source cited for a full statement of the reviewer's opinion.

[5] This statement was written before the appearance of the Diagnostic Reading Tests, on which two of these authors collaborated.

Table 57.   Representative Reading Tests (*Continued*)

Test and Publisher	Grade Level	Time	Scores Reported	Comments of Reviewers[a]
Gates Reading Tests (Teachers Coll., Columbia Univ.)	Various[b]	35–60 min.	In survey test for grades 3–10: level of comprehension, vocabulary, speed	Primary: "Test exercises reasonably valid. . . . Can be used for general survey or diagnostic purposes" (Gray, **5**). Survey: "Most valuable survey-type reading test at present time. . . . Where further diagnosis is desired, may be supplemented" (Holberg, **5**).
Gray Oral Reading Paragraphs (Pub. Sch. Publ. Co.)	1–8	About 10 min.	Tester notes speed and specific errors made	"Observations may have considerable diagnostic value" (Kopel, **4**, p. 368).
Iowa Silent Reading, new edition (World Book)	4–9; 9–13	49 min.	Rate, comprehension, word meaning, paragraph meaning, five other scores	"Primarily a survey test. . . . Rate of work affects scores on all parts. . . . Merits attention and study" (Booker, **4**, pp. 347 ff.). "Appears to reward pupil who reads superficially and parrots glibly" (Davis, **5**).
Monroe-Sherman Group Diagnostic Aptitude and Achievement (C. H. Nevins Co.)	Age 8–15		Paragraph meaning, speed of reading, word discrimination; seven scores on visual, auditory, motor aptitudes	
Nelson-Denny (Houghton Mifflin)	High school, college	30 min.	Vocabulary, paragraph meaning	
Sangren-Woody (World Book)	4–8	27 min.	Word meaning, rate, fact material, total meaning, central thought, following directions, organization	"Admirably suited both for diagnostic purposes and comprehensive survey" (Liveright, **4**, p. 364).

[b] Gates has produced a great variety of tests adapted to specific purposes and particular grade levels.

diagnostic tests are too complex for widespread use, how can reading tests be used most effectively in the school?

25. In what respects is a group of the Iowa type inferior to an individual test for diagnostic purposes?

26. The following paragraph is from the manual for the SRA Reading Record:

"Reliabilities were computed on the record for one thousand ninth- and eleventh-grade students. The median reliability for these two homogeneous groups is: Test 1, .79; Test 2, .75; Test 3, .86; Test 4, .96; Test 5, .86; Test 6, .83; Test 7, .96; Test 8, .79; Test 9, .78; Test 10, .75; and Total, .93. In terms of these correlations, the scores on the record are reliable enough for individual as well as group diagnosis. Individual students may be guided into advanced reading or placed in remedial classes with the assurance that such decisions are based on accurate facts about their reading skills."[6]

To interpret the above facts one also needs to know that each subtest is timed, and that the separate tests presume to measure separate aspects of reading, even though their correlations are "moderate to high." Reliabilities were determined by the split-half method. What facts about reliability have been ignored, in judging this test to be accurate enough for individual diagnosis?

TESTS OF SKILLS IN PERFORMANCE

It is important in vocational courses and in employment to measure skills. All courses teach skills (reading, interpretation of data, etc.), but skills are particularly central in typewriting, comptometer operation, shopwork, blueprint reading, dressmaking, music, and so on. Measurement of maximum ability to perform is based on the principle of the worksample.[7] One either obtains a sample of the subject's product and rates it, or observes and judges his performance as he works.

Product Rating

For product rating, we must compare similar specimens of the best work of each subject. Sampling is a difficulty, since a single object may not represent the learner fairly. To compare several people, it is desirable to have

		1	2	3	Score
Appearance	1. Shriveled		Plump and slightly moist		1.
Color	2. Pale or burned		Well browned		2.
Moisture Content	3. Dry		Juicy		3.
Tenderness	4. Tough		Easily cut or pierced with fork		4.
Taste and Flavor	5. Flat or too highly seasoned		Well seasoned		5.
	6. Raw, tasteless, or burned		Flavor developed		6.

Fig. 70. Score card for rating sample of cooking.[8]

them work on similar material. One standard test in stenography accomplishes this with a recorded dictation which the subject must take down and transcribe. This method holds constant not only the difficulty of material, but also the speed of dictation and clarity of speech. McPherson standardized a test in simple woodworking by requiring each boy to construct a wood block like a model. The block was designed to demand use of saw, drill, and

---

[6] From G. T. Buswell, SRA Reading Record, Examiner Manual, p. 3. Reproduced by permission of Science Research Associates. Copyright 1947, by Science Research Associates.

[7] Many of the methods described can also be applied to the study of typical behavior, if test motivation is absent. Methods discussed in Chapters 18 and 19 deal primarily with typical performances.

[8] Clara M. Brown and others, Food Score Cards, University of Minnesota Press.

chisel. Scoring was done objectively by imposing a plastic pattern on the block to check dimensions (21).

Objectivity in scoring is aided by a check list or rating scale. This forces all judges to notice the same features of the sample and to use a comparable numerical scale. Two product rating forms are illustrated in Figures 16 and 70.

Tests of Performance

Tests of performance, or worksamples, are needed for skills where a sample of the product is not an adequate index of ability. The standard typing test in civil service practice is such a test, indicating both speed and quality of performance. Some tests may use regular factory or shop equipment, while others use special apparatus. Use of normal equipment is illus-

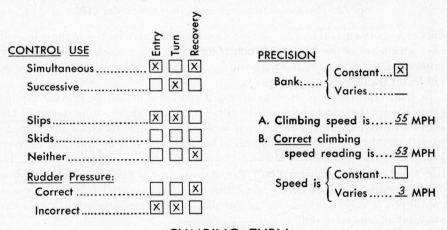

CLIMBING TURN

This is a maneuver that calls for proper coördination of all controls.
A. SPEED is the most common speed shown by the indicator during the turn.
B. The "Correct climbing-speed reading" during the turn is determined from the air-speed indicator in the same way as the climbing speed in a straight climb.

Fig. 71.   Portion of Ohio State Flight Inventory, used for recording performance in a climbing turn (23).

trated by a test of ability of packers in a cannery. Production on the job could not be used as a test, because of variable factors from day to day and because the job was normally affected by teamwork. For test purposes, one conveyor belt was set aside and one worker at a time assigned to it. A count was made of the number of cans he packed per hour (27, p. 86).

In worksamples, as in some psychomotor tests, it must be recognized that a score represents only maximum ability at the present point in a learning

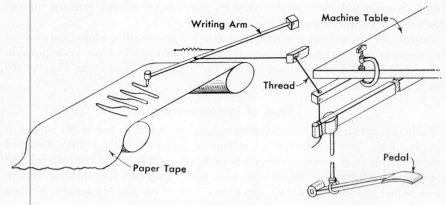

Fig. 72. Schematic diagram of Lindahl's recorder (**19**).

curve. A score earned by one worker on a machine may be the highest he will ever attain, since he has had much training; another worker, with a lower numerical score, may in the long run be a better worker, in view of his present lesser training or experience.

Special equipment is used to obtain a worksample where regular equipment cannot be used, because of either cost or danger. It is essential for every submarine crewman to learn to use the escape hatch of his ship, in case it should sink in shallow water. The only sure test of ability is to have him try to use it, but it is obviously impossible to make the test at sea. To test (and to train) crewmen on shore, a deep tank is used in which a replica of the escape hatch is built. Since this is in all essential features like sea conditions, a valid worksample can be obtained to determine when a man has attained an adequate skill.

Motion pictures have occasionally been tried as a method of obtaining worksamples of ability to observe. Ability of aerial navigators was tested by showing them a motion picture, taken from a plane, which showed a view of the ground and of the essential instruments. Aided by a map, students were to make a plot such as they would in flight. Like many worksample tests, this proved to have little reliability and was not adopted (7). Low reliability is characteristic of worksamples where one error may disturb the entire sequence of performance. All worksample tests must represent normal conditions of work and a large enough sample of performance must be obtained. Motion-picture techniques were successful in obtaining reliable measures of many skills important in the Army Air Force. These successful tests, however, usually included a large number of short, similar items, rather than a few complex sequences of performance (**12**).

Evaluation of performance is aided when an objective record is made of what the subject does. Check lists or rating scales are helpful, especially to record how the man performs, his style and methods of work, and what errors he makes. Such a record permits concentration on weaknesses in later training. An example of such a check list is the Ohio State Flight Inventory, designed to aid in research on pilot training. While the pilot followed a prescribed maneuver, the instructor riding with him checked his procedures on a form such as that shown in Figure 71. In all, 640 items were to be checked (23).

At times a performance is too rapid or too subtle for an observer to identify the correct and incorrect actions. Psychologists have found mechanical recording devices helpful for measuring and teaching such skills. An example from industrial training is provided in Lindahl's study of disk-cutter operation. The difference between good and poor performers was found to lie in the speed with which they went through each phase of the cycle of operation. The operation called for pressing a pedal to drive the cutting wheel, and releasing it for a new cut. Lindahl devised the recording device shown in Figure 72, which yielded records such as that in Figure 73. These objective records showed not only

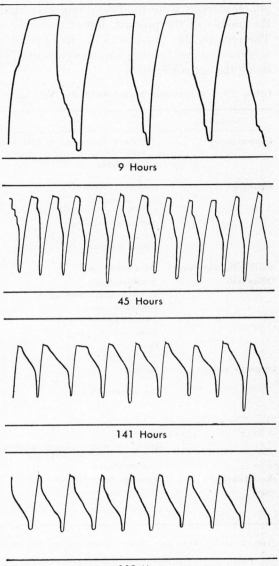

9 Hours

45 Hours

141 Hours

239 Hours

Fig. 73. Improvement in the foot-action pattern of a trainee (**19**). The record at the top shows long pauses between strokes, uneven speed during the cutting (downstroke), and jerky foot action at the end of the stroke. All these faults were eliminated in the final record.

which workers were the best producers, which could have been judged by the quality of the product, but also exactly what errors each was making. The records also provided a means of teaching the worker what errors he was making and helping him recognize the "feel" of the pedal when he was doing the act correctly.

Table 58.   Achievement and Aptitude Tests Used in R. H. Macy & Company, Inc.[a]

Category	Test	Remarks
General ability	Wonderlic adaptation of Otis Self-Administering	For non-executives
	Mental ability	Difficult one-hour test for prospective executives
Arithmetic	Fractional arithmetic	Problems related to salesclerk's duties
	CMC arithmetic	More difficult test of fundamentals for merchandise control clerks
	Arithmetic reasoning	For supervisors, and senior positions in merchandise control
	Mental Arithmetic	For tellers in Depositor's Account Division
Merchandise Knowledge	Wine and liquor	For salespersons in liquor department
Office skills	Thurstone typing	Rough-draft typing and tabulation
	Bureau of Adjustments typist	For workers filling in small forms
	Blackstone typing	Simple copying for junior-typists
	Stenography	
	Comptometer adding	Adding long columns on comptometer
	Filing	Alphabetical filing test for experienced filers
Language ability	Spelling	For typist correspondents and secretaries
	Correspondent's test	Worksample; subject writes letters answering inquiries from customers, following directions indicating proper content for letter. Graded on composition and grammar.
	Speed and accuracy; same-different; comparison of signatures and printed names	Tests of clerical perception and accuracy for various jobs
Manual ability	Minnesota Rate of Manipulation	For kitchen employees
Vision	Ishihara color vision	For guards and stockmen handling colored merchandise (e.g., men's ties)

[a] Information supplied by Patricia Scharf, of Macy's Personnel Division. All tests except the Wonderlic, Thurstone, Blackstone, Minnesota, and Ishihara were specially constructed by Macy's.

27. Outline a plan for obtaining product ratings and performance observations for each of the following situations. In each case, discuss the relative merit of the two procedures.
    a. Testing a boy's knowledge of how to wire batteries in series.
    b. Testing the improvement in technique of a concert violinist.
    c. Testing ability to operate a calculating machine for all types of operation.

ACHIEVEMENT TESTS IN EMPLOYMENT PRACTICE

Achievement tests for hiring employees are quite varied, since each one must deal with the skills or knowledges of a particular job. Except in the clerical field, standard tests are rarely used. So long as the requirements of jobs in several places are similar, there is no reason why achievement tests for specific jobs should not be standardized. A few such tests have made their appearance, an example being the series of Purdue Vocational Tests,[9] dealing with machine shop, electricity, and industrial mathematics. The tests are more precise and more difficult than simple oral trade tests.

The wide range of achievement tests usable in hiring and promotion is illustrated by the list of tests used by one organization, R. H. Macy & Company. The tests used in that store are summarized in Table 58. Noteworthy are the variety of tests and the adaptation of the tests to the specific demands of jobs. Such tests can be used for placing an applicant in the most suitable job, which is an advance over the policy of hiring "typists" and placing them at random in clerical jobs without further testing of specific abilities.

28. Classify the tests in Table 58 as to whether they measure aptitude or achievement.
29. Some clerical aptitude tests include a vocabulary section. What advantages would there be in measuring "office vocabulary" rather than vocabulary in general? Which of the following words would be most suitable for an "office vocabulary" test: *beneficial, indemnity, allegro, lament, kingly, itinerary?* (All words from SRA Clerical Aptitudes Test.)

ACHIEVEMENT TESTS IN THE SCHOOL PROGRAM

In view of the dangers found in indiscriminate use of standard achievement tests, it is important to formulate a policy to guide the sound use of tests in schools. In recommending the use of standard tests, there are four questions to be answered: When should they be used? What should they test? Which tests should be chosen? How should the results be used? Of these, the fourth is paramount.

The proper function of a test in school is to improve the educational program. It may do so by helping plan what learning experiences a pupil needs, by indicating ways in which teaching can be improved, or by building attitudes in pupils and teachers which will promote better teaching. McConn reviews and discards all proposed purposes of testing in schools save one, guidance of the pupil (15, pp. 443–478). Guidance is conceived, however, not in narrow vocational terms, but as the problem of finding out all about the pupil so that his growth can be promoted.

Once this point of view is accepted, several corollaries follow. If tests are for guidance, they are initial, not terminal, parts of the educative process. There is little merit in testing after it is too late to profit from the results. For this reason, more and more schools are using achievement survey tests at the beginning of the school year. When suitable tests are given and the results placed in the hands of every teacher, they provide a sound basis for planning the year's work. Under this point of view, there is no argument against testing again in June to determine improvement, but in fall testing the emphasis

---

[9] Publisher: Science Research Associates.

is placed on diagnosis and guidance rather than marking and recrimination.

If tests are used for guidance, they are used *for* the pupil rather than *on* him. They become a means for him to assess his weaknesses, and are a more effective argument for his taking certain courses or changing certain habits than pressure from the teacher. In such testing, it is important to minimize elements of marking, "competition," and imposition from above. In the most successful programs, the pupil takes the tests because *he* wants to know the results.

It then follows that the tests to be used have to measure something of importance. Some schools will seek to measure acquisition of subject matter. Others will be more concerned with general educational development, defined less in terms of knowledge than in terms of skills such as interpretative reading and interpretation of data. Probably there are few objectives so widespread that all pupils should be tested on them at the high-school level. This means that in addition to every-pupil tests, tests will be needed in specific subjects, such as foreign language, and in vocational skills. Probably the tests to be used in school-wide testing will deal with the objectives which are the major concerns of the school: command of the English language, desirable citizenship attitudes, critical thinking, and the like.

Increasing attention should be paid to specific performances—success on particular items, or particular subskills in complex tests. Attention to *what* is missed, rather than *how much*, is a step toward eliminating the error.

Interpretation is likely to be adequate only when tests are comparable. Comparable tests measure growth from year to year, and compare the pupil's development in various types of behavior. For this reason, series of tests such as those of the Cooperative Test Service or the Iowa Tests of Educational Development are more adequate than tests of single objectives, independently standardized. At the elementary level, achievement batteries have comparability from score to score, but often use unsound grade norms.

Use of achievement tests has been unhealthy in the past when they have forced schools into training rather than educating pupils. So long as tests are considered in the light of the pupil's past development and as a guide to his future progress, they need have no harmful results. In many respects, they will have to be modified to meet these new demands adequately. Tests of limited validity may serve tolerably as impartial marking instruments. But when a test bears the responsibility of describing what a pupil knows and can do, and what he needs to attain, it will have to meet a high standard of validity. It is in this direction that improvement is to be anticipated.

SUGGESTED READINGS

Durost, Walter N. "What constitutes a minimal school testing program?" *Educ. psychol. Measmt.*, 1947, 7, 45–60.

Lindahl, Lawrence G. "Movement analysis as an industrial training method." *J. appl. Psychol.*, 1945, 29, 420–436.

Raths, Louis E. "Evaluating the program of Lakeshore School." *Educ. Res. Bull.*, 1938, 17, 60–80.

Simpson, Ray H. "The critical interpretation of test results in a school system." *Educ. psychol. Measmt.*, 1947, 7, 61–66.

Thorndike, Robert L. (ed.). "Problems in determining an adequate criterion," in *Research problems and techniques.* AAF Aviation Psychol. Prog. Res. Rep. No. 3. Washington: Govt. Printing Off., 1947, pp. 29–56.

Tyler, Ralph W. "The relation between recall and higher mental processes," in Judd, C. H., and others, *Education as cultivation of the higher mental processes.* New York: Macmillan, 1936, pp. 6–17.

REFERENCES

1. Blommers, Paul, and Lindquist, E. F. "Rate of comprehension of reading; its measurement and its relation to comprehension." *J. educ. Psychol.*, 1944, 35, 449–473.

2. Brickman, William W. "Preparation for the Regents' Examination." *Sch. & Soc.*, 1946, 64, 263.

3. Brown, Clara M. *Evaluation and investigation in home economics.* New York: Crofts, 1941.

4. Buros, Oscar K. (ed.). *The 1940 mental measurements yearbook.* Highland Park, N.J.: The Mental Measurements Yearbook, 1941.

5. Buros, Oscar K. (ed.). *The third mental measurements yearbook.* New Brunswick: Rutgers Univ. Press, 1948.

6. Callis, Robert, and Wrenn, C. Gilbert, "The GED Tests as predictors of scholastic success." *Educ. psychol. Measmt.*, 1947, 7, 93–100.

7. Carter, Launor F. (ed.). *Psychological research on navigator training.* AAF Aviation Psychol. Prog. Res. Rep. No. 10. Washington: Govt. Printing Off., 1947.

8. Conrad, H. S. *Statistical analysis for the Mechanical Knowledge test.* O.S.R.D. Rep. No. 3246. Princeton: CEEB, 1944.

9. Diamond, Leon N. "Testing the test-makers." *Sch. Sci. and Math.*, 1932, 32, 490–502.

10. Durrell, Donald D. *Improvement of basic reading abilities.* Yonkers: World Book Co., 1940.

11. Frederick, John T. "I've been reading." Chicago *Sun Book Week*, Feb. 16, 1947, p. 4.

12. Gibson, James J. (ed.). *Motion picture testing and research.* AAF Aviation Psychol. Prog. Res. Rep. No. 7. Washington: Govt. Printing Off., 1947.

13. Greene, Edward B. *Measurements of human behavior.* New York: Odyssey Press, 1941.

14. Hall, William E., and Robinson, Francis P. "An analytical approach to the study of reading skills." *J. educ. Psychol.*, 1945, 36, 429–442.

15. Hawkes, Herbert E., and others (eds.). *The construction and use of achievement examinations.* Boston: Houghton Mifflin, 1936.

16. Henry, Nelson B. (ed.). The measurement of understanding. *Yearb. nat. Soc. Stud. Educ.*, 1946, 45 (I).

17. Judd, C. H., and others, *Education as cultivation of the higher mental processes.* New York: Macmillan, 1936.

18. Learned, William S., and Wood, Ben D. *The student and his knowledge.* New York: Carnegie Foundation for the Advancement of Teaching, 1938.

19. Lindahl, Lawrence G. "Movement analysis as an industrial training method." *J. appl. Psychol.*, 1945, 29, 420–436.

20. McCullough, Constance M., and others. *Problems in the improvement of reading*. New York: McGraw-Hill, 1946.
21. McPherson, Marion W. "A method of objectively measuring shop performance." *J. appl. Psychol.*, 1945, 29, 22–26.
22. Meyer, George. "The effect on recall and recognition of the examination set in classroom situations." *J. educ. Psychol.*, 1937, 27, 81–99.
23. National Research Council, Committee on Selection and Training of Aircraft Pilots. *History and development of the Ohio State Flight Inventory, Part II*. Washington: CAA, 1945.
24. Raths, Louis. "Basis for comprehensive evaluation." *Educ. Res. Bull.*, 1936, 15, 220–224.
25. Rice, J. M. "The futility of the spelling grind." *Forum*, 1897, 23, 163–172, 409–419.
26. Smith, Eugene R., Tyler, Ralph W., and others. *Appraising and recording student progress*. New York: Harper, 1942.
27. Stead, William H., and others. *Occupational counseling techniques*. New York: American Book Co., 1940.
28. Stuit, Dewey B. (ed.). *Personnel research and test development in the Bureau of Naval Personnel*. Princeton: Princeton Univ. Press, 1947.
29. Tharp, James B. "A modern language test." *J. higher Educ.*, 1935, 6, 103–104.
30. Training Aids Section. Ninth Naval District Headquarters, Great Lakes, Ill. A comparative study of verbalized and projected pictorial tests in gunnery. Unpublished. 1945.
31. Traxler, Arthur E. *The nature and use of reading tests*. Chicago: Science Research Assoc., 1941.
32. Trimble, H. C., and Cronbach, Lee J. "A practical procedure for the rigorous interpretation of test-retest scores in terms of pupil growth." *J. educ. Res.*, 1943, 36, 481–488.
33. Tyler, Ralph W. *Constructing achievement tests*. Columbus: Ohio State Univ., 1934.
34. Wood, Hugh B. *Evaluation of pupil growth and development*. Eugene: Univ. of Oregon Coop. Store, 1940.

PART III

Testing of Typical Performance

CHAPTER 13

Problems and Practices

THE MEANING OF "TYPICAL BEHAVIOR"

To solve many of their most vital problems, psychologists must draw conclusions about the typical behavior of individuals. Abilities and capacities define limits of performance, but what one actually does is rarely motivated to the point where he uses his utmost quantity or quality of performance. One characteristic, for example, which cannot be defined in terms of ability is character; nearly everyone exposed to a culture for a reasonable period knows what is the approved course of action. In order to study character formation or to use character as a guide in employment, we must in some way find out whether the individual habitually, characteristically, typically chooses the "good" action.

"Typical behavior" is an elusive concept because behavior in a given situation is not the same on all occasions. If the worker who works at 80 percent of his ability today would do so tomorrow and every day, it would be easy to describe him. Typical behavior, however, is an abstraction. It is doubtful if one ever has a truly typical day. Typical behavior could be described as an average or composite of many single behaviors, as when one judges punctuality by noting the number of tardinesses in a month. But no single event is typical of the person's punctuality, so that simple testing is difficult.

Behavior is determined by the interaction of the person and his environment. One can rarely be certain that behavior seen in one situation will also occur in another. We find more consistent behavior if we define the trait to be measured very narrowly, so that variation in situation would be slight; for example, we might study "punctuality in reporting to the office during the autumn." The alternative is to think about the subject's behavior in a hypothetical "normal" situation, as we often do in describing cheerfulness, neatness, or submissiveness.

To observe typical behavior, one must in some way obtain a sample of all relevant situations and of all times when the situation arises. No one act can be taken as typical, since it is influenced by mood, immediately preceding experiences, details of the surroundings, and other factors. Even if we should happen to observe the person in an act that is typical for him, there is no way to be sure of this typicalness except through further observations.

When we assume that we are measuring typical behavior, we often ignore the fact that behavior shows cycles and trends (6). Suppose that, in a series of observations, we find the subject to be quarrelsome. It does seem that this is typical for him, but perhaps he is in a continuing state of irritability due to some worry, and some months earlier or later he would be found well-adjusted socially. In this case, it could be contended that the sample was insufficient to study typical behavior, and that the period observed was a mere temporary deviation. Yet the deviation was real, and the behavior reported was typical for the subject during that time.

It follows that careful attention must be paid to definition in thinking about typical behaviors. One can only be sure what is meant by a "typical behavior" (or trait) when the observer specifies the range of time represented in the data, the range of situations represented, and the degree of motivation to "good" performance present. While these are rarely considered explicitly, it is often possible to find them implied in the nature of the tests used. Fortunately, personality and work habits seem rather stable, which gives hope of useful observation.

1. Define the range, in time and situations, of the "typical behavior" which you think should be studied to answer these questions?
   a. How well does each of these supervisors handle grievances?
   b. Does a study of the "100 Greatest Books" make an adult more rational in his daily life?
   c. Does viewing a film on nutrition improve housewives' practices in menu planning?
   d. Do graduates of the modern elementary school write legibly?

TYPES OF MEASURES

Measures of typical behavior are subdivided into self-report procedures and behavior observations. In each of these procedures, there are inherent assumptions and problems.

Self-Report Tests

Self-report devices have come into prominence because of the practical difficulties in making sufficient observations to determine typical behavior. While the experimenter can rarely follow his subject about in his many activities, there is one person in a position to see how the subject acts, namely, the subject himself. If we could enlist him as an observer, we would overcome the limitations of cost and privacy.

Self-report devices usually ask the subject to look back upon his past and from his memories to answer whatever questions concern the investigator. Rarely, an inquiry employs a diary technique, in which events are recorded as they occur. Another variant of the self-report requires the subject to state only how he feels or acts at a given instant. This involves no error of memory, but increases problems of sampling, since a particular instant may give a poor sample of behavior over a period. Among the uses of questions of this sort are the public-opinion polls ("How would you vote if the election were held today?"), sociometric investigations ("Choose the three people you would like to have on a committee with you"), and verbal substitutes for behavior observations ("What did you have for lunch today?"). Questions of preference ("Would you prefer to write a best-seller or own a successful night club?") are self-report devices asking for a prediction of behavior in hypothetical situations no one can observe.

Most self-report tests rely on a person's insight into himself. Personality, adjustment, attitudes, and interests have been studied by such questions as "Do you usually daydream?" and "Do you like mysteries?" The crucial assumptions involved are that the subject is willing to tell the truth to himself and to the investigator, and that the subject can determine the truth. There is little direct evidence that subjects can be relied upon to tell the whole truth about their personalities. On the other hand, there is considerable reason to suspect that they sometimes conceal evidence they consider damaging, and psychoanalytic studies call attention to repression, whereby we conceal from ourselves memories which would be unwelcome. An adult, asked to give information regarding his own character, might be expected to suppress or even fail to think of events he has been ashamed of. A boy taken with the glamour of engineering as a profession may report great interest in engineering and engineering activities, even though he really lacks interest in all save the drama and prestige of engineering.

Subjects are able to falsify self-reports. If a subject tries to make his score look "better" than the truth, he can do so. Students took the Humm-Wadsworth Temperament Scale with instructions to be truthful, and again with instructions to assume that the record would be used in considering them for employment. Scores on the test changed markedly in the seemingly desirable direction with the second directions, and correlations between the two testings ranged from −.03 ("Normal Component" score) to +.61 (Paranoid score) (13, p. 119). Olson found marked changes of score between anonymous and signed responses to the Woodworth-Mathews Personal Inventory (10). Fosberg gave the Bernreuter Personality Inventory with three sets of directions: (a) standard, (b) to give the best possible picture of oneself, and (c) to give the worst possible. The correlations of scores were standard with "best," .11; standard with "worst," −.30; "best" with "worst," −.83 (3). It is therefore agreed that self-report tests are undependable unless full coöperation is expected, or unless controls are used to detect or prevent faking. Typical control methods are discussed in connection with the Minnesota Multiphasic Personality Inventory (p. 319) and the Jurgensen Classification Inventory (p. 325).

The self-report test suffers from problems of communication. Questions are not likely to prove reliable or valid if they mean different things to different subjects. Yet the words used, the responses required, and the very nature of the task are left open to interpretation in most current self-report tests. The subject is told, in one set of words or another, to report his typical behavior. He is, however, sophisticated enough to know that he has no typical behavior, but only a range of behaviors that come out in different situations and moods. "Do you usually seek suggestions from others?" is a fairly clear question; but most people would have to answer, "Sometimes I do, but not always." This might be further qualified: "I do on difficult problems"; "I do if someone is around whose ideas are especially good"; "I don't if I'm supposed to make the decision myself." These could be called quibbles, but they are questions the subject must face in answering. Since he cannot average his memories to determine what percentage of the time he has sought suggestions, the question is likely to be answered offhand. If one person defines "usually" to mean "with very few exceptions" and another defines it as "fairly often; at least in difficult situations," they are answering different questions and their responses are not comparable. Another example of ambiguous content in an apparently clear item is the Kuder Preference Record question: "Do you like to operate an adding machine better than [two other activities]?" Many students say that they enjoy this activity, but would be dissatisfied with a job if they had nothing to do but operate an adding machine. It is impossible to qualify items to eliminate such problems of interpretation. It appears that in the presence of ambiguities, differences in final score are strongly influenced by such response sets as a habit of saying "yes" when in doubt, or of using the "?" or "indifferent" response for unclear items (2). Most self-report tests employ such words as "always," "frequently," "usually," and "often." That these words are ambiguous was shown by Simpson, who asked subjects to indicate the frequency, in percent of all occurrences, that would be required to justify the use of each word. Table 59 shows the meaning of each word, as defined by his subjects (12).

Table 59. Range of Meanings Assigned to Words Commonly Used in Personality Tests (12)

| Word | Answer Given When Asked to Indicate What Percent of All Occasions Is Indicated by the Word | |
	Median Answer	Range of Answers of Middle 50 Per- cent of Subjects
Usually	85	70–90
Often	78	65–85
Frequently	73	40–80
Sometimes	20	13–35
Occasionally	20	10–33
Seldom	10	6–18
Rarely	5	3–10

To some extent, investigators have been able to avoid the criticism that self-reports are inaccurate by justifying their techniques empirically. One who wishes to consider himself healthy may overrate his health in answering "Is your health better or poorer than the average for your age?" Another person with only minor ills may exaggerate them, perhaps without conscious intention, to get sympathy or justify self-pity. This question would not obtain valid facts about health. But if it can be established that clinically diagnosed neurotics reply "poorer" more frequently than do normals, this answer may be diagnostic even when it is "untrue"—in fact, it may be diagnostic just because it is untrue.

Empirical uses of self-reports are necessarily valid. The report itself is a behavior; one obtains a direct record of response to a standardized stimulus when he asks a verbal question. Empirical scales, according to Meehl, take the "attitude that the verbal type of personality inventory is *not* most fruitfully seen as a 'self-rating' or self description whose value requires the assumption of accuracy on the part of the testee in his observations of self. Rather is the response to a test item taken as an intrinsically interesting segment of verbal behavior, knowledge regarding which may be of more value than any knowledge of the 'factual' material about which the item superficially purports to inquire. Thus if a hypochondriac says that he has 'many headaches' the fact of interest is that he *says* this" (7, p. 9).

The usefulness of empirical tests depends primarily on the adequacy of the experimentation by which the scale has been validated. Manifest absurdities in empirical treatment of self-reports suggest that the original validation was not based on an adequate sample. Allport, for example, protests against a scale in which the word association "green" to the stimulus "grass" is scored +6 as a sign of "loyalty to the gang" (1, p. 329). Loyal boys might have given this response often in the sample test, but it is implausible that this would be found in further studies. Large and representative samples are crucial in establishing empirical keys.

In view of the difficulties encountered, self-report tests, especially those not based on empirical validation, have been severely criticized. Much work has been done to find acceptable substitutes, and it is probably fair to say that *self-report methods should never be used where acceptable substitutes are available.* Because self-report tests can be short and inexpensive and because they frequently have crude validity for the mass of subjects even when invalid in individual cases, they are unlikely to be completely replaced.

2. Distinguish in each of these cases whether the investigator is assuming that self-reports are truthful.
   a. The clinical symptoms of condition *x* are determined by observation. A list of symptoms (swollen feet, rash, etc.) is prepared. This list is used in many localities to determine how frequent condition *x* is. Each subject is asked to check whatever symptoms he has.
   b. There are three general stages in social development in which a child names as favorites (*a*) other children without regard to sex, (*b*) persons of his own sex exclusively, (*c*) persons of the opposite sex. The investigators ask a child to name his favorite playmates as a means of determining his level of development.
   c. A psychologist administers a check list to a group of applicants, in which each checks the adjectives he considers as describing himself. The success of

these men is observed, and a list is made of the characteristics checked by the successful applicants but not by the others. This check list is then given to further applicants, and those who check the same characteristics as the previously successful men are hired.

3. List several situations in which signed self-reports are likely to be truthful.

Observations

Among the techniques in which actual behavior is observed in order to deduce typical behavior, three types may be noted: observations in natural situations, observations in standardized situations, and projective methods. These categories overlap, but a distinction calls attention to special purposes and problems. Observation in the natural situation calls for studying actions under everyday conditions, covering a narrow or wide range of the subject's life. One may study work habits by observing the worker at his bench day after day, or one may study flying performance by observing the pilot as he handles his plane. A broader range of situations would be involved in studying the social behavior of a child, which could be done by having each teacher report observations made in classes and on the playground. Standardized observations are made in situations so planned that every subject undergoes approximately the same experiences. If every person works under the same conditions, what each does will be primarily a reflection of his individual characteristics. In projective tests the subject is turned loose in an unfamiliar situation where he presumably has no specific habits for behaving; what he does in this "unstructured" situation tells a great deal about his deep-lying behavior tendencies.

A crucial problem in observing behavior is to make sure that the act of observing does not distort the behavior. Just as the presence of a traffic cop at an intersection raises drivers from their habitual level to nearly their best ability, so the presence of the judge or observer may cause the subject to try harder. This effect seems to occur even when no reward or punishment is involved. Roethlisberger and Dickson attempted to study typical work output under a variety of conditions at a Western Electric manufacturing plant (11). Relay assemblers were placed in a small experimental room where they could be observed and their output recorded in great detail. In successive periods various rest pauses were introduced, to test the effect on production. As each change was introduced, no matter what it was, production for most workers climbed. Finally, in the twelfth and thirteenth periods, the rest pauses and privileges were removed, and production per hour still was as high as under the "best" working conditions. Another striking change was that absenteeism changed from 15.2 days per year per worker before entering the study to 3.5 days per year after workers were placed in the test room. The investigators were forced to abandon their study of rest pauses as a single variable, since the morale of the workers—as a result of being more closely singled out for study, of being better acquainted with their supervisors, and of feeling personal responsibility for their rate of output—basically altered their performance.

Distortion due to judging is reduced when the judging is a regular part of the work procedure. Ratings by foremen are probably based on typical behavior in the plant, for the foreman is usually present; how the man would act if the foreman were not provided is not in question. Wherever the rater can be a normal member of the group, his presence will have little distorting effect on results. These distortions may be minimized by concealing the observer as by the one-way vision screen employed for studying infants (4), by giving the observer an ostensible reason for being present, as in studies of adolescents where adult observers participated in their picnics (9), or by establishing familiarity through a long series of preliminary observations.

The standard observation has definite advantages over observations made in normal random conditions. Fair comparisons between men are impossible if the normal situations under which they work are unlike. Watching salesman A deal with prospect X, and salesman B with prospect Y, is likely to be misleading if the prospects differ in temperament and approachability.

Standardized observations reveal behavior typical of non-test situations only when the subject is unaware that he is being observed. This is hard to manage, but one can often assume that the subject does not know what characteristics are being observed. This is illustrated in a stress investigation. Aircrewmen were asked to observe a pattern of five planes in a short exposure on a motion-picture screen, and to record the locations of the planes. Successive items were shown with shorter exposures, until it was impossible to observe and record in the time allowed. A few easy items, with ample time, were spread through the test. Decline in score on these items was taken as a measure of disturbance due to frustration (5). Since the subjects thought they were being tested on perceptual ability, it is unlikely that they recognized that the frustration was planned to observe their resistance to it. This test was not used practically, so that evidence of empirical validity is lacking.

4. If a subject suspected that the recognition test was a frustration experiment, how would he probably behave?
5. Is the observation of actual driving usually required of applicants for drivers' licenses a test of typical behavior?
6. Devices have been invented to record whatever changes are made in the setting of a radio or television dial. By installing a large number of these in coöperating homes, broadcasters might obtain precise data on when programs gain or lose listeners. Do you think the typical tuning behavior of the set owner would change when he knows this device is added to his set?

Projective tests attempt to avoid the systematized behaviors subjects use to conceal their individuality. Children are easily observed in daily life, because they are relatively naïve and have not yet learned that it is desirable to draw a curtain over their personalities. As maturity increases, one represses more and more of his thoughts and controls his actions. By adulthood, one has a series of etiquettes, customs, and clichés in which he can hide himself. Applicants for secretarial positions display an astonishing similarity of words, smiles, and actions during an interview. Insofar as they can guess what is expected of an ideal applicant, they act that role. Yet the goal of the interviewer is to determine not ability to assume a mask but underlying personality. The problem of the tester is to penetrate the façade in a short time. The ideal answer may be to present a situation so novel that the subject has no idea what disguise to assume. This should reveal his "basic nature." Projective tests attempt to permit this type of observation. Because these tests seek to uncover personality structure rather than specific isolated habits, Murphy makes this extreme statement about one of them: "The Rorschach should predict a specific future behavior better than does the study of past specific behavior, except when the new behavior is essentially a repetition of the old" (8, p. 675). Owing to the newness of projective techniques, it will be some time before practical uses are fully developed.

SUGGESTED READINGS

Cowell, Charles C. "Play behavior and personality analysis." *Educ. Res. Bull.*, 1937, 16, 182–186.
Symonds, Percival M. "Significance of the diagnosis of conduct," in *Diagnosing personality and conduct.* New York: Appleton-Century, 1931, pp. 3–22.
Vernon, Philip E. "The attitude of the subject in personality testing." *J. appl. Psychol.*, 1938, 18, 165–177.

REFERENCES

1. Allport, Gordon W. *Personality: a psychological interpretation.* New York: Holt, 1937.
2. Cronbach, Lee J. "Response sets and test validity." *Educ. psychol. Measmt.*, 1946, 6, 475–494.
3. Fosberg, Irving A. "An experimental study of the reliability of the Rorschach technique." *Rorschach Res. Exch.*, 1941, 5, 72–84.
4. Gesell, Arnold, and others. *An atlas of infant behavior.* New Haven: Yale Univ. Press, 1934.
5. Gibson, James J. (ed.). *Motion picture testing and research.* AAF Aviation Psychol. Prog. Res. Rep. No. 7. Washington: Govt. Printing Off., 1947.
6. Hersey, R. B. *Workers' emotions in shop and home.* Philadelphia: Univ. of Pennsylvania Press, 1932.
7. Meehl, Paul E. "An investigation of a general normality or control factor in personality testing." *Psychol. Monogr.*, 1945, 59, No. 4.
8. Murphy, Gardner. *Personality.* New York: Harper, 1947.
9. Newman, Frances B. "The adolescent in social groups." *Appl. Psychol. Monogr.*, 1946, No. 9.
10. Olson, W. C. "The waiver of signature in personal reports." *J. appl. Psychol.*, 1936, 20, 442–450.
11. Roethlisberger, Fritz J., and Dickson, W. J. *Management and the worker.* Cambridge: Harvard Univ. Press, 1939.
12. Simpson, R. H. "The specific meanings of certain terms indicating different degrees of frequency." *Quart. J. Speech*, 1944, 30, 328–330.
13. Tiffin, Joseph. *Industrial psychology.* New York: Prentice-Hall, 2nd ed., 1947.

....

CHAPTER 14

Self-Report Techniques: Personality

HISTORICAL AND THEORETICAL BACKGROUND

History of Personality Questionnaires

Self-report techniques have a long history. Medicine has long used the patient's report of his symptoms for diagnosis and evaluation of treatment. In psychology, almost the entire development of modern hypotheses about personality hinges on self-report. Freud, for example, based his findings and theories almost wholly on interviews, reports of dreams, and other introspective data. Attempts to reduce personality to psychometric terms grew out of the need for mass-processing methods capable of more speed and standardization than clinical interviews permitted. As in the case of intelligence testing, World War I brought into prominence the possibilities of group procedures for obtaining self-reports.

Essentially, a personality questionnaire is a standardized interview. The sensitivity of individual questioning is sacrificed for speed. The first important questionnaire was Woodworth's Personal Data Sheet, widely used in processing World War I recruits. The Personal Data Sheet (45) was a collection of questions about symptoms considered significant by psychiatrists (daydreaming, enuresis, etc.). Woodworth's scale was found useful for detecting maladjusted soldiers, and was especially valued because adequate individual interviews were totally impracticable.

Following World War I, enthusiasm for mental testing led to a demand for equally promising tests of personality. A swarm of instruments for probing the individual were devised, many of them adapting Woodworth's questions. Each test consisted of a collection of questions presumed to measure one aspect of personality. Among the supposed traits often investigated were neurotic tendency, introversion-extroversion, and dominance. Items were chosen which, by definition, were related to each trait: "Do you worry . . . ?" would show neurotic tendency: "Do you lead . . . ?" would show dominance. In some cases the assumption that the items all related to a single trait was checked by internal-consistency tests or an outside criterion. Woodworth, for example, used only items which were checked twice as often by known psychoneurotics as by normals. The Bernreuter Personality Inventory, published in 1931, was intended to serve all functions of previous tests, being constructed by pooling items from tests by Thurstone, Laird, Allport, and others. Separate scores were obtained for the traits—neurotic tendency, introversion, and dominance—the previous authors had sought to measure, plus self-sufficiency. Because it appeared to offer a considerable amount of information about the individual, the Bernreuter test was widely accepted. Although there have been recent innovations in the design of personality tests, these newer ideas are only beginning to be widely used. Most current personality testing in schools and industry is done with devices like Bernreuter's.

The results of questionnaires were not always satisfying. Because they were introduced at a time when intelligence tests were being used to "make psychological measurement scientific," personality tests were expected by many to contribute a high level of accuracy to studies of personality. The fact that these devices could yield no more than an interview and would usually yield less only gradually became apparent. With this realization, uncritical use of questionnaires began to decrease, and more thoughtful bases for their construction were generally adopted.

One major line of attack was improved definition of traits to be tested. Research since 1931 has been largely directed at replacing the traits arbitrarily assumed by early investigators with traits representing genuine and significant aspects of personality. One approach to this is factor analysis. Flanagan's factor analysis of the Bernreuter test (see p. 316) broke the ground in this area. Recent studies have provided lengthy lists of fairly pure traits which may be tested.

Some of the most promising recent instruments have placed their emphasis on scores claiming empirical validity, making psychological interpretation of scores a secondary consideration. This is the case with the Minnesota Multiphasic Personality Inventory (MMPI) and the Humm-Wadsworth Temperament Scale. Items were selected, not because they fitted a definition of a trait, but because experimental trial showed that mental patients gave responses different from those of normal adults. Scores on these tests indicate how far the subject deviates from normal in such directions as "paranoid," "hysteroid," or "manic." The manic key is simply the group of items that persons classified as manic answer differently from normals. This is the same procedure that Woodworth originally used to choose his items, but which was largely neglected in subsequent questionnaires.

Although faith in personality questionnaires, except as "preliminary interviews," had somewhat declined by 1940, interest has been revived by their excellent service during World War II. Industries, anxious to expand their working forces rapidly without hiring misfits, made much use of the tests and reported satisfactory results, although scientific evidence of validity was scant. In the armed services, rapid screening devices were necessary, and for this purpose two new questionnaires were widely used. The Cornell Selectee Index and the Shipley Personal Inventory were found to be rapid and efficient tools in military processing.

In virtually every walk of modern life, personality and mental hygiene are crucial. Maladjusted parents make for maladjusted children. Teachers with inadequate personal adjustment are unsatisfactory. Employees who grumble or are temperamental cause undue trouble. In most chronic illnesses, doctors now recognize a psychological element. In these and all the other areas where doctors, psychologists, and social workers would like to identify, diagnose, and assist the emotionally immature person, a rapid group test could be of untold value. As present techniques become more valid, they will aid in solving major social problems.

1. Which of the following investigators assumed that self-reports are truthful: Woodworth, Bernreuter, Hathaway and McKinley (MMPI)?

The Trait Theory of Personality

Nearly all the prominent questionnaires have sought to describe the individual in terms of traits. If a test is to be a measuring stick, assigning a rank or score to the individual, there must be a characteristic or dimension in which this variation takes place. The desire for linear measures analogous to those for size, temperature, and reaction time led psychologists to postulate that personality had dimensions or traits. A *trait* is a tendency to react in a defined way in response to a defined class of stimuli. Traits are familiar in everyday thinking; nearly all the adjectives which apply to people are descriptions of traits: happy, grouchy, conventional, stubborn, and so on. Traits are elusive in scientific analysis, however, and can be defined and measured only at the risk of some ambiguity.

The postulate that traits exist is based on three facts: (1) Personalities possess considerable consistency; a person shows the same habitual reactions over a wide range of similar situations. (2) For any habit, we can find among people a variation of degrees or amounts of this behavior. (3) Personalities have some stability, since the person possessing a certain degree of a trait this year usually shows a similar degree next year.

These facts lead one to consider personality traits as habits, capable of being evoked by a wide range of situations. It would be tedious to catalog a series of traits such as "habit of bowing politely when meeting a pretty woman of one's own age on the street on Sunday," "habit of bowing politely when meeting a not-pretty woman . . . ," etc. Therefore traits are sought which describe consistent behavior in a wide range of situations. Any value of the trait approach to personality depends on the hope that it will describe economically the significant variations of behavior, neglecting unduly specific habits. Since the English dictionary offers no less than 17,953 adjectives describing traits, the problem of economy is a serious one (3).

A trait is a composite based on many specific behaviors covered by the trait name. To say that a boy is perfectly honest gives information which definitely predicts his behavior in any situation involving honesty. In most cases, however, the person possesses an intermediate degree of the trait in question; he is honest in some situations but not others. Two people possessing the same composite score in a trait may not be alike in personality. We might say that a boy is "50 percent honest," implying that there is an even probability of honest or dishonest behavior. But the description would conceal the fact that he is perfectly honest in money matters and perfectly dishonest in situations in which grades are the reward; the description in terms of his hypothetical trait "general honesty" is an imperfect basis for prediction. The extent to which a trait gives good descriptions depends upon the extent to which the behaviors collected under the trait definition are coherent and present in the same person. Traits have therefore been defined most often by internal-consistency tests. A group of items or test situations is collected which may relate to one aspect of behavior, and the degree of relation is tested empirically by the method presented on p. 78. Items which do not correlate with the composite are dropped. The trait is, in the end, defined by the items retained in the test.

2. Show how the trait "stubbornness" might be present in some situations and absent in others for the same person, even though both actions are typical for him.
3. An investigator believes that leaders can be characterized by the trait "autocratic-democratic." Outline the procedure needed to make a self-report test, if he decided to choose his items
   a. By definition.
   b. By internal-consistency tests.
   c. By correlation with an external criterion.

Traits having different names may not be genuinely different. "Introversion" was postulated as a trait after clinical studies showed that certain behaviors such as isolativeness, interest in ideas, and shyness were often present together. "Neurotic tendency" attracted interest as a result of studies which

Table 60.   Intercorrelations of Bernreuter Scores for Adolescent
Boys, Corrected to Remove Spurious
Elements (14, p. 44)

	Neurotic Tendency	Self-Sufficiency	Introversion	Dominance
Neurotic Tendency		−.39	.87	−.69
Self-Sufficiency			−.33	.51
Introversion				−.62
Dominance				

showed the neurotic pattern to contain certain recurrent symptoms. Both were widely used to describe personality, until the Bernreuter scale showed correlations between the two of .96 (this containing a spurious element because both scores were based on the same questions). Flanagan applied factor analysis to the four scores from Bernreuter's test, using a group of 305 adolescent boys. The correlations shown in Table 60 indicate that the scores overlap greatly and are certainly not reporting four independent traits. Flanagan found that two factors were sufficient to account for the major differences between individuals reported in these four scores. He therefore proposed two new scores, to represent the two traits the Bernreuter test could distinguish. His scores, called Self-Confidence and Sociability, are nearly independent ($r = .04$). One may have high confidence with or without sociability. The old "neurotic tendency" is about the same as low confidence; "self-sufficiency" is merely a combination of high confidence and low sociability; and so on (14).

A more basic approach to trait identification considers the intercorrelations between single items. Items having substantial correlations are brought together to form broader traits. Cattell, from factorial studies, considers that 12 such traits have been identified (10). Guilford has published several questionnaires measuring such presumably homogeneous traits. His Inventory of Factors S-T-D-C-R, for example, breaks the familiar introversion-extroversion into social introversion, thinking introversion, depression, cycloid tendencies, and rhathymia (happy-go-lucky disposition). Some of these scores are correlated, so that the traits are not independent (18). The Guilford list has been simplified by Thurstone into a set of seven "primary" traits which most often affect scores in current self-report tests. These seven aspects of temperament are: reflective (thinking introversion), friendly, emotionally stable, masculine, ascendant (leadership), active, and impulsive (42).

"The normal personality" presents troublesome problems of measurement. It is comparatively easy to identify abnormals, since they tend to fall into distinct syndromes or patterns of personality. In most traits, the deviate at either end of the normal distribution is well characterized by his score. He exhibits the trait in unusual degree and in a large number of situations. Intermediate positions, falling toward the center of the distribution, tell the investigator little except that the subject is not a deviate. Every normal personality has its unique characteristics. Even a person who is "normal" in all the traits we measure has individuality. Reducing his performance to a single index of normality, we lose patterns which make him different from his also-normal neighbors.

Allport has criticized the entire trait approach on this ground (2, pp. 248–257). Suppose that honesty were statistically coherent, so that the correlations between different types of honesty were substantial. This might be explained in terms of differences in moral upbringing which make some people well-behaved throughout their lives. But there are other organizing patterns underlying honesties which make their correlations less than 1.00. One man may act from need; he will take money to feed his family, but will not cheat or lie. Another man may be prudent rather than honest; he will be as honest as he must to avoid being caught. Another may define honesty in a limited way; he would never steal, but he thinks it right to operate a business on the principle of "buyer beware." These men are all honest to an intermediate degree; they are all more or less "normal." The problem in studying personality is to detect the true patterns behind behavior. Although the trait method will not do this, there is probably no solution but the trait approach for studying personalities in the mass.

4. Some testers treat Flanagan's two scoring keys as supplements to the four supplied by Bernreuter, and report all six scores to describe an individual. Discuss the advisability of this practice.
5. Do you think that most introverts are emotionally maladjusted? What does this answer imply regarding the correlation of the N and I scales?
6. What is a "desirable" score on a test such as the Bernreuter?
7. What does it mean to say that Henry falls at the 50th percentile in Sociability?
8. "Adjustment" inventories ask the person to indicate his worries or symptoms. The number of such symptoms is taken as his score. What meaning should be attributed to a median score on such a test?

SIGNIFICANT SELF-REPORT TESTS

To understand how psychologists have designed self-report tests, and to interpret the evidence on validity, we shall need to know a few tests in detail. The following section describes the Minnesota Multiphasic, which represents unusually careful test design and seems useful for studying abnormal subjects; and the Bell and Bernreuter inventories, which have been widely used and for which much evidence on validity has accumulated. Other tests to be described are important, not because they are widely used, but because they have unique and promising features. The Allport-Vernon Study of Values, Jurgensen's Classification Inventory, the Shipley and Cornell inventories for military use, the Rogers test for children, and the PEA Interest Index fall in this group.

Bell Adjustment Inventory

The Bell Adjustment Inventory is simple in design and intended for use with normal groups rather than for clinical analysis. The inventory has two forms, one for students in high school and college, the other for adults. The student scale yields separate scores for home, health, social, and emotional adjustment. Items, answered "yes," "no," or "?," include

Do you get discouraged easily?
Are you subject to eye strain?
Would you feel very self-conscious if you had to volunteer an idea to start a discussion among a group of people?

Questions retained in the scale are those found to differentiate between students known to be maladjusted and students considered normal by judges who know them well. The principal use of the test is to identify those who should be offered counseling. While "problem cases" who cause trouble for teachers are easily recognized, students who are withdrawn, shy, and internally upset may not attract the attention of observers. An adjustment inventory brings to light many of these cases.

Bernreuter Personality Inventory

The Bernreuter test has been referred to at several other places in this chapter. It was first designed for use with college students and has been extended to pupils in schools, employees, and other groups. It provides a description of personality which, if valid, would be of interest in case studies and research. The Neurotic Tendency score is a convenient index of self-reported maladjustment.

The test consists of questions much like those of other inventories: e.g., "Do you daydream frequently?" The test seems primarily to measure self-confidence and sociability. Scoring is relatively complex, particular answers being given weighted credits. For the item on daydreaming, "yes" is credited 3 points, "no" is credited -5, and "?" 0, in the Self-Confidence score. Other credits are assigned to the same answers in each of the other keys.

9. Since "neurotic tendency" and "maladjustment" are measured by similar items, the Bell and Bernreuter inventories may be used to identify the same types of students. What practical considerations would be important in choosing between them, if they are equally reliable, and validity in the situation under consideration has not been determined?

Minnesota Multiphasic Personality Inventory

The self-report test most promising for diagnosing abnormal personality patterns in the clinic is the MMPI. This test consists of 495 questions to be judged "true," "false," or "cannot say." Typical items are

I think most people would lie to get ahead.
A windstorm terrifies me.
My hardest battles are with myself.

These items were administered to diagnosed psychiatric patients and to normal adults, principally visitors to a large city hospital. Responses were compared, and any answer given more often by one of the psychiatric groups than by normals was placed in the appropriate scoring key. The classifications scored are hypochondriasis (Hs), depression (D), hysteria (Hy), psychopathic deviate (Pd), masculinity (Mf), paranoia (Pa), psychasthenia (Pt), schizophrenia (Sc), and hypomania (Ma). The higher a subject's score in a classification, the more his answers resemble those given by that type of patient. Any standard score greater than 70 is taken as an indicator of significant abnormality.

Some errors common to self-report tests are controlled by a set of scores known as ?, L, K, and F. The "?" score is based on the number of times the person replies, "cannot say." Excessive evasion of questions of course makes it impossible to compare a count of the subject's reports of his symptoms with the replies of the psychiatric group. Profiles showing high "?" scores are recognized as invalid. There are some test items so extremely worded that a person who denies having these symptoms is almost certainly not evaluating himself frankly. The L (lie) score is based on a count of these improbable answers; a high L score indicates that answers are untrustworthy, but need not indicate deliberate lying. The K score is based on the finding that some normal people earn scores above 70 in significant columns. A list of items checked by these "false positives" was studied and built into the K correction key (29, 31). A person who earns a very low K score is likely to have been unusually severe in describing himself while taking the test; apparently, excessive frankness causes some normals to earn "abnormal" scores. One who habitually gives himself the benefit of the doubt earns a notably high K score. The F (false) score is a count of replies given by the subject which are given by others extremely rarely. This count reveals careless sorting, misunderstanding, or other invalid answers.

The operation of these keys is shown in a study in which psychologically trained persons attempted to "fake" in answering the test so as to appear psychoneurotic or psychotic. In attempting to give answers like neurotics, these experts succeeded (their mean Hs was 99; mean D, 108; mean Hy, 87; mean Pt 86), but their mean K was 44 whereas real neurotics averaged 51, and their mean F was 74 compared to 67 for true neurotics. In simulating psychotic answers, they also succeeded fairly well (mean Pa, for example, was 97), but mean F at 80, mean L at 60 signaled that something about the responses was untrustworthy (16).

Although the test has been used successfully with clinical patients, it has not been found trustworthy with college students. Many college students earn scores which would usually be indicative of abnormality, although these students are known to be adequately adjusted. This is a further example of the undesirability of blindly applying a test validated on one population to a different type of group.

The MMPI is quite similar to the earlier Humm-Wadsworth Temperament Scale. This scale has been less widely investigated than the Minnesota because commercial restrictions limit its availability. It has had wide application in industry. The temperament scale reports scores based on a psychiatric theory of the components of personality. It employs a check score to identify undependable self-report. Both the MMPI and the Humm-Wadsworth employ ingenious correction formulas to compensate for a subject's tendency to give a favorable or over-frank self-report (31, 23).

10. Under what circumstances might a person wish to convince a tester that he is psychotic, so that his scores would be falsely high?

11. A client coming to a social agency shows these MMPI scores:

Hs	D	Hy	Pd	Mf	Pa	Pt	Sc	Ma
43	45	50	50	50	68	42	67	69

How would the interpretation be affected if the "control scores" were as follows:

a. ?, 72; L, 50; K, 50; F, 50.
b. ?, 50; L, 73; K, 50; F, 50.
c. ?, 50; L, 50; K, 72; F, 50.
d. ?, 50; L, 50; K, 35; F, 50.

12. How could one restandardize the MMPI so that it would correctly locate persons with mental hygiene problems among entering college freshmen?

The type of report of which the MMPI is capable is indicated in the following analyses. The first is that of an 18-year-old boy, committed from a juvenile court after arrest for homosexual practices. The MMPI was administered individually, the examiner reading the items aloud, since Earl's mentality was limited. The scores, plotted in Figure 74, are discussed as follows (9, pp. 494–495):

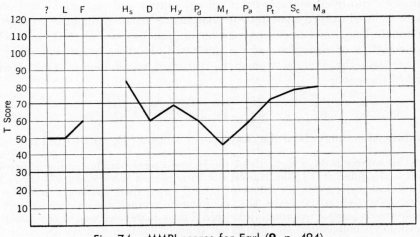

Fig. 74.   MMPI scores for Earl (9, p. 494).

"The validity scores are conventionally acceptable, with 50 T-scores for ? and L, and 60 for the F scale. The latter score shows a slight tendency toward carelessness or lack of comprehension, but not so great as to invalidate the scale. It can be seen that—with the exception of the masculinity-feminity scale (Mf)—all the scores lie toward the maladjustment end of the distribution; but hypochondriasis, psychasthenia, schizophrenia, and hypomania are all beyond the 70-point customarily regarded as indicative of maladjustment. The hysteria score is approximately at 70. This is a non-specific record and serves best to point up areas of maladjustment rather than specific psychiatric entities. The high Hs, Hy, and Pt indicate a neurotic trend; Sc, Ma (and also Pt) a schizoid trend. These trends in part characterize the subject's personality structure. Earl complained of periodic headaches and dizziness and had been observed by other inmates to 'black out.' These experiences . . . are probably reflected in the Hs and Hy scores. His history of shyness and solitariness [had] already been noted. The hypomania score (Ma) accounts for his minor periods of overproduction and temporary enthusiasms. It is interesting to note in passing that despite Earl's arrest and commitment for homosexual activities, and certain feminine secondary sex characteristics, his interests —as measured by the Mf scale—are not feminine."

In this case, the MMPI did not provide a specific diagnosis, though it was useful in establishing severe maladjustment and throwing doubt on the importance of Earl's sexual irregularities. The final diagnosis, based on encephalogram and clinical analysis, was intracranial brain damage, probably following birth injury, complicated by a completely unfavorable environment.

One can proceed beyond a general estimate of adjustment to a description of the subject's traits, if one is willing to assume that self-reports are true self-descriptions. Verniaud tested women optical workers and found that over 77 percent of her group exceed the norm in Hypomania, Psychasthenia, Paranoia, and Psychopathic Deviate. She interprets this as an expectation that these workers would be "restless, full of plans, alternating between enthusiasm and over-productivity in energy output and modes of depression, more inclined toward anxieties and compulsive behavior than the average individual, disinclined to concentrate for long periods on one task, somewhat oversensitive or suspicious of the good-will of others, somewhat more inclined than the average woman to disregard social mores." One woman earned these scores:

?	L	F	Hs	D	Hy	Pd	Mf	Pa	Pt	Sc	Ma
50	53	50	41	42	52	67	63	67	60	58	68

Additional findings about the case were as follows (43, pp. 610–611):

"This woman is 34, a high school and business school graduate. She is married, with a daughter of 12. She started out as a clerical worker, worked up to the position of secretary to the editor of a local newspaper, advanced from this to newspaper reporter. However, she was put to reporting women's affairs, had no chance to do general reporting as the men did, and after two years left to work for a clothing manufacturer. She started out as his bookkeeper, but also went out into the plant to do cutting. She disliked the bookkeeping, 'loved' the cutting. . . .

"She is now supervisor of the polishers. By the shift foreman's report, she has transformed the polishing room from one of their major headaches to a 'bangup' job. She is exacting to work for, unpredictable as a person. She likes to do 'screwball' things. Once she emerged from the polishing room with the red polishing compound smeared on hands and arms to the elbows, waved them in the investigator's face, saying 'Blood!' During the holidays, when you heard a jingle, you knew that the supervisor of polishers was going through. She had tied bells to her shoes."

13. Under what conditions may a person have deviate scores on MMPI and yet not need clinical attention?
14. What assumptions are made if a psychologist applies MMPI to adolescent boys coming before the juvenile court?
15. Would it be legitimate to correlate scores on MMPI with job success, to see if it would be a helpful selection device?
16. If, as some psychologists predict, a new set of diagnostic categories comes into use for describing patients, what steps will be required to adapt MMPI to the new system? Assume that the changes are fundamental, such as replacing paranoia and schizophrenia with four new categories.

Study of Values

A unique instrument which has been primarily a research tool is the Allport-Vernon Study of Values. It is based on the conception of Spranger that there are six basic types of men: theoretical, whose interest is truth ("His chief aim in life is to order and systematize his knowledge"); economic, whose interest is in the useful, the practical affairs of the business world; social, who values love of people; political, primarily seeking power; religious, who works for unity, "seeks to comprehend the cosmos as a whole"; and aesthetic, who stresses form and harmony. The subject is asked to indicate which of two activities he would prefer—for example, "Would you prefer to hear a series of popular lectures on (a) the progress and needs of social service work in the cities of your part of the country or (b) contemporary painters?" The former is scored for Social value, the second for Aesthetic. A profile of six scores is obtained.

The test is at times valuable in academic and vocational guidance because it is based on a set of variables which cut across the categories of more common interest tests. Some "theoretical"-type persons, for example, find little satisfaction in the day-by-day routines of some positions in industrial chemistry, yet enjoy teaching chemistry.

17. A psychology major, who has a keen interest in psychology courses, wishes guidance toward a particular vocation.
    a. What suggestions might be considered if he shows a high score in Theoretical value?
    b. What vocation in psychology would be most appropriate to each of the other values?

Rogers Test of Personal Adjustment

In contrast to the trait approach taken by the bulk of tests, the Rogers test for children and the PEA test for adolescents operate on a theory of personality as a complex whole. In the usual test, a response is treated as if it had the same emotional import for all subjects. Yet "I find it hard to make new friends" may, in one person, be a sign of anxiety, and in another person may be evidence of mature and calm insight into his limitations. By considering self-descriptions in relation to the subject's stated aspirations, Rogers obtains a richer picture than any study of self-description alone can provide. Necessarily, the more complex interpretation is difficult to objectify.

The test has the additional advantage of format and questions that appeal to children. Questions deal with the child's fantasies, wishes, opinions of himself, and affection for others. This is an example:

Peter is a big, strong boy who can beat any of the other boys in a fight. Am I just like him? Do I wish to be just like him?

The child answers by checking a scale from "yes" to "no." There are separate forms for boys and girls.

Although scores are obtained on the test, an analytic study of items is required to obtain a clinical picture of the child. A diagnosis reported in the manual reads: "On this test Edward shows evidence of a great deal of maladjustment. His outstanding difficulty is his lack of adjustment to other boys and girls. He evidently has no friends, is not well liked and lacks ability in games. He also feels inadequate personally. He thinks he is lacking in brains, strength, and looks. He covers his feelings of inferiority with an extravagant, boasting attitude. He also indulges in a great deal of day-dreaming. He seems most attached to his mother, and may be somewhat jealous of his father and brother, although the evidence here is contradictory. He is to be regarded as a personality problem of a very serious sort."

18. What "traits" are discussed in the description of Edward? How does it happen that so many facts are reported from a test of about 50 items, whereas other longer tests report fewer traits?

Interest Index

A similar clinical treatment has been developed for the Interest Index, 8.2a, 8.2b, and 8.2c, developed for the Progressive Education Association. This is included here rather than in the chapter on interest tests because its primary use is for description of personality. The test, for high-school pupils, has the advantage that students tend to be more frank in expressing interests than in describing symptoms. Among the items to which they respond "like," "indifferent," or "dislike" are the following:

To write stories.
Having people take me for older than I am.
Pretending to be the hero or heroine in a movie.
Helping to get meals ready at home.
Dancing or singing or telling stories to amuse a group.

These items are grouped into a large number of categories, ranging from overt interests such as "Mathematics" to categories based on psychiatric theory such as "Acceptance of own impulses," "Solitary," and "Fantasy life." The scores are used as a basis for interpretation of the personality as a unit. This interpretation, which is a subjective synthesis of all the facts brought to light by the test, considers adjustment less as a count of symptoms than as a relation between desires and activities. The psychologist in one case gleans sufficient material from the test, without having seen the boy himself, to fill nearly six printed pages. The final summary is (38, p. 383): "In conclusion, one may say that Lyle probably does not get into open clashes with adults and is very likely to be academically a good student. His age-mates may elect him to class offices, but probably few of them, if any, accept him as a real member of the group. A number of youngsters are apt to be annoyed with him and make him the butt of their jokes. Lyle's main difficulties seem to be that although or because he has accepted prematurely the standards and values of a certain group of adults—his own emotional development has been warped and arrested."

19. Consider the following tests: MMPI, Bell, Bernreuter, Allport-Vernon, Interest Index.
   a. Which ones would give the most useful information to a high-school counselor? How could the information be used? Disregard ease of administration.
   b. Answer the same questions from the point of view of the personnel manager of a moderate-sized office.
   c. Answer the same questions from the point of view of a clinical psychologist attached to a juvenile court.
20. What "traits" are discussed in the portrait of Lyle based on the Interest Index? Why would not a test scored for these traits serve the same function as the index?

Classification Inventory

The MMPI sorts out abnormal personalities by a direct empirical method, rather than through descriptive traits. Jurgensen has approached employee selection in a similar manner (26). His Classification Inventory is also noteworthy in its use of the forced-choice technique. Jurgensen obtains a large number of self-reports about irritations and preferences. One item, where the subject indicates which alternative is most, and which least, irritating, is

People who (a) Laugh at you
            (b) Are sarcastic to you
            (c) Gossip about you.

There are no standard keys for the test. A new key is made in each employment situation where the test is to be used. The test is given to employees known to be good or poor on a particular job, and a key is made up of those responses which differentiate good and poor workers. The test must be validated anew in each new application.

21. What advantage, and what disadvantage, comes from making a new key for each selection task, rather than establishing general keys for nation-wide use for such occupations as salesman, accountant, etc.?
22. Assume that a descriptive inventory gives reliable scores on five traits.
   a. How could an industrial psychologist using such a test determine what score or score-pattern indicates probable success on a particular job?
   b. If this method, and Jurgensen's, gave equally good validity coefficients, which type of test would be preferable in a personnel program?

Other Tests

Several devices were developed during the war for the identification of possibly unstable recruits. The two most widely used were the Shipley Personal Inventory (PI) and the Cornell Selectee Index. Each has been used in a variety of editions. They are noteworthy because they were generally found to be reliable despite their brevity, and because several studies have shown satisfactory validity (20, 37).

The PI is in many ways like the Classification Inventory. It uses forced choices, such as

(a) I wish I didn't have so many aches and pains.
(b) I wish I wouldn't keep changing my mind.

Choosing between undesirable alternatives is much less open to falsification or ambiguity than the usual single question. Even a psychologically sophisticated subject often cannot guess the "good" answer. The PI also reflects the trend toward empirical keying of items. In the example above, one choice is scored as indicating maladjustment, not because it is a well-known symptom of disorder, but because that response is given more often by deviates than by normals.

Rapport is a serious problem with forced-choice tests. Guilford is very critical of the PI because some examinees in Air Force testing resented the forced choice. "Some of the items appear unsuitable for use in the selection program, because they present a choice between an acceptable and unacceptable response (e.g., 'I get embarrassed easily'—'I seldom get embarrassed'), or because both items are socially unacceptable and of the type of 'Have you stopped beating your wife?' (e.g., 'Our family scraps often came after someone had been drinking'—'Drinking never was the cause of our family scraps')" (17, p. 607).

Facts about the more widely known tests of personality are summarized in Table 61.

Table 61. Representative Personality Questionnaires

Test and Publisher	Age Level[a]	Number of Items	Variables Scored; Special Features	Comments of Reviewers[b]
Allport Ascendance-Submission (A–S) (Houghton Mifflin)	Men; women	34	Dominance	"Very doubtful that scale can be employed without verification, supplementary information" (Humm, 7, p. 50).
Allport-Vernon Study of Values (Houghton Mifflin)	College and adult	45	Six value types identifying evaluative attitudes	"Validity fairly good. . . . Social value score unreliable, ambiguous. . . . With suitable caution, can be recommended as . . . having considerable value" (Meehl, 8).
Adams-Lepley Personal Audit (Psych. Corp.)	Adult	450	Impulsiveness, irritability, tolerance, etc.	"Claims made for this instrument go beyond the data" (Symonds, 8).
Bell Adjustment Inventory (Stanford)	Grades 9–16; adult	140	Adjustment: home, social, job, etc. Items selected by external criterion.	"Useful in a personnel program" (Darley, 7, p. 52). "Can be recommended to the clinician" (Beck, 7, p. 53).[c]

[a] Semicolon indicates separate forms of test.
[b] The reader should refer to the source cited for a complete statement of the reviewer's opinion.
[c] Body of text carries more complete reports on validity of these tests.

Table 61.   Representative Personality Questionnaires (Continued)

Test and Publisher	Age Level[a]	Number of Items	Variables Scored; Special Features	Comments of Reviewers[b]
Bernreuter Personality Inventory (Stanford)	Adolescent and adult	125	Self-confidence, sociability, etc.	"No convincing evidence of validity" (Maller, 7, p 189).[c]
California Test of Personality (Calif. Test Bureau)	Grades Kgn.-3; 4–8; 7–10; 9-coll.; adult	96 to 180	Self-adjustment, social adjustment. Twelve subscores.	"Subtest reliabilities far too low. . . . Validity entirely unestablished" (Shaffer, 8).
Classification Inventory (C. E. Jurgensen)	Adult	288	Keys prepared to select good employees on particular jobs	
Cowan Adolescent Adjustment Analyzer (Cowan Res. Proj., Salina, Kans.)	Age 12–18	90	Areas of adj.: fear, family emotions, maturity, etc.	"Despite weaknesses, one of the better tests for adolescents, used by a qualified child psychologist in the clinical situation" (Snyder, 8).
Humm-Wadsworth Temperament Scale (D. G. Humm)	Adult	318	Hysteroid, manic, epileptoid, etc. Wide use in industry.	"Room for more studies on reliability, validity. . . . Found it very useful in industrial situations, particularly on supervisory level" (Meltzer, 8).[c]
Interest Index 8.2a, b, c (Prog. Educ. Assn.)	High school	600	Numerous interest categories. Clinical interpretation possible.	
Inventory of Factors S-T-D-C-R (Sheridan)	Adolescent and adult	175	Five aspects of introversion. Based on factor analysis. Two other inventories in this series.	"A distinct advance in test construction but [lacking] in validation data, . . . a test for the experimenter rather than for the practical tester in clinic or factory" (Eysenck, 8).
McFarland-Seitz Psychosomatic Inventory (Psych. Corp.)	Adolescents and adults	92	Neurotic tendency; stresses physiological symptoms.	"Unusually high validity. . . . Possible distorting factors" (Mosier, 7, p. 77).
Maller Character Sketches (Teachers Coll., Columbia)	Grade 5-college	200	Six aspects of adjustment. Indirect questions.	
Minnesota Multiphasic Personality Inventory (Psych. Corp.)	Adult	495	Nine clinical categories. Empirical construction. Scales to detect invalid responses.	"As a general screening test, very valuable in psychiatric clinics. . . . No great reliance may be placed in the belief that the subscales measure what their titles suggest" (Rotter, 8).[c]
Pintner Aspects of Personality (World Book)	Grades 4–9	105	Ascendance, introversion, emotionality. Worded for children.	"No reason for believing teachers can safely depend on an individual's score. . . . As a clinical tool, very satisfactory" (Louttit, 7, p. 56).
Rogers Test of Personality Adjustment (Association Press)	Age 9–13. Boys; girls	Six sections	Inferiority, social adjustment, family adjustment, daydreaming. Stresses clinical analysis.	"In our clinic the most satisfactory method of personality measurement" (Louttit, 7, p. 94).

23. Consider the method of item selection and keying for the tests discussed in the text.
    a. Which tests use items selected by an external criterion of the trait measured?
    b. Which tests use items selected by an internal-consistency test only?
    c. Which tests use items selected to fit the definition of the trait, without direct empirical checking?

Comparison of Tests

The tests described above differ in at least the following respects:

Purpose: clinical description (MMPI, Rogers) or screening (Bell, Shipley PI).

Theory of personality: explicitly assumed types (Humm-Wadsworth, Allport-Vernon), defined traits (Bernreuter), personality as an integrated whole (Rogers, Interest Index), or no particular theory (Jurgensen).

Length: 20 items (PI, short form) to 500 items (MMPI).

Control over response sets, honesty: control scores (MMPI, Humm-Wadsworth), forced choice (Allport-Vernon, Jurgensen), study of responses item by item (Rogers), or no control (Bell, Bernreuter).

RELIABILITY AND VALIDITY

The Stability of Personality

All personality tests assume that habits are stable, at least over significantly long periods. Retest correlations with personality tests are generally high for all traits studied, even with long intervals between the tests. These correlations are, however, smaller than those obtained from immediate retests or parallel tests administered consecutively, which shows that some change occurs. Maller states that some personalities are organized more stably than others, so that it is possible to obtain stable measures for some persons but not for all (28).

Description of Personality

The most ambitious purpose of personality tests has been to describe individuals. Tests which give only one score have been intended for screening and prediction, but other tests yield several scores describing personality, or even complete portraits of cases. To study validity of descriptions, possible criteria are other self-report tests, data from normal behavior and standardized observations, or clinical reports based on detailed case studies.

Comparison of different self-report indices can yield only negative evidence of validity, since two tests might agree, yet both be invalid. There is general consistency among self-report tests of the same function, as would be expected from their duplicating content. This correspondence is not perfect. Correlations between four tests supposed to measure introversion are shown in Table 62. These tests do not measure the same thing. The names given to traits by test authors cannot be trusted; what a test measures can be understood only in terms of detailed study of the items or an outside criterion.

Table 62. Intercorrelations of Four "Introversion" Scores for 172 College Students (15)

Name of Test	Bernreuter	Laird	Marston	Northwestern
Bernreuter	.80[a]	.47	.37	−.09
Laird	.47	.55	.30	.10
Marston	.37	.30	.84	.25
Northwestern	−.09	.10	.25	.62

[a] Italicized figures are split-half reliability coefficients.

Attempts to describe clinical patterns of personality have been most often based on the MMPI. The authors of that test have found marked differences between patients diagnosed by psychiatrists in various categories. Meehl made blind analyses of test records of independently diagnosed patients. The test score permitted him to classify those with abnormal patterns correctly as psychotic, neurotic, or conduct disorders in about 60 percent of the cases (30). Less favorable results were obtained by Benton and Probst, who made a study of 70 patients. Psychiatrists rated the degree to which each patient, by his behavior, showed each deviate trend reported by the MMPI. This is a direct test of the MMPI as a descriptive tool. They found a significant degree of agreement between test and rating on Pd, Pa, and Sc, but small or zero agreement on Hs, D, Hy, Mf, and Pt (6). Further study of the test will be needed before descriptions made by it can be depended upon. The recent K correction should increase the accuracy of the test.

For normal subjects, clinical criteria are rarely available. Ratings of behavior by acquaintances are frequently used as a criterion, and usually show small positive correlations between test scores and opinions of judges. One of the highest sets of validity coefficients from ratings is reported for the Guilford inventory. Scores of 50 adult students of psychology were correlated with ratings made by close acquaintances. Correlations for five aspects of introversion (see p. 317) were .70 for factor S, .60 for D, .48 for R, .20 for C, and .08 for T (18). The low correlations for C and T are partly due to invalid ratings.

In a few studies, descriptions from personality tests of normals have been compared with extensive case material from other sources. Sheviakov used this method to validate the clinical interpretation of the Interest Index for Lyle. The results showed that the descriptions were far better than a blind guess, but not adequate as a basis for action without further verification (38). To validate the Humm-Wadsworth profile, subjects were rated on each component of personality by the test and also from a case history. Almost incredible validities, from .83 to .92, were reported (24). It is unfortunate that published confirming studies under independent investigators are not available as a basis for judging the test. It is to be noted that validities are much lower, according to the published data, for cases with extreme response biases, such as a tendency to say "no" in answering questions. When these cases are identified by a control score and dropped out, the validity coefficient rises, e.g., from .85 to .94 (22). No data have been published indicating the validity of extreme scores after correction for response sets, a procedure only recently introduced.

Screening of Maladjusted Cases

In industry, the armed services, and some school and clinical situations, self-report tests might be helpful in screening. Since screening is a "pass or fail" operation, validity is best judged on the *false positive* and *pickup* rates.

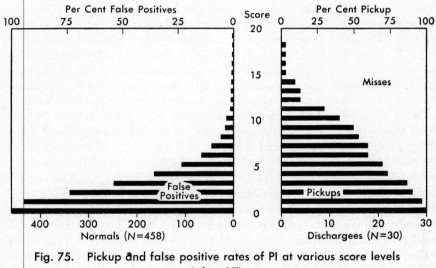

Fig. 75. Pickup and false positive rates of PI at various score levels (after 37).

A test identifying probable deviates must not screen out too many normals (false positives) since the burden of examining further so many men is troublesome. At the same time, the test must pick up nearly all the deviates. For practical work, as distinguished from research, it is necessary to determine the efficiency of selection rather than whether a significant positive relation between test and criterion is present. Evaluation must consider the *number* of false positives rather than the percentage of such errors. In large populations, a small rate of error may force the psychiatrist to study an unnecessarily great number of cases (39).

Hunt and Stevenson discuss at length the military problem of screening and the importance of adjusting the critical score in the light of practical conditions. They conclude that self-report tests have proved much more successful in military screening than in similar civilian situations (25). The following studies are typical of the results found.

Figure 75 shows results with the short form of the Personal Inventory applied to recruits. These data show how test results correspond with the judgments of psychiatrists who examined all men. More unfit men than normals make high (undesirable) scores on the test. Out of 30 dischargees, 12 made a score above 9, but only 13 normal men out of 458 were falsely screened by this cutting score. This cutting score, however, would miss 18 dischargees. A deeper cut, screening men at 5 and above, catches 21 of the unfit men, but the price of this better identification is that 108 false positives must also be individually examined. Such a screening device will always miss a few men, but it is clearly more effective than no device at all. The cutting score used will depend on the importance of eliminating nearly every unfit man at this stage of processing, and on how many men the psychiatrists have time to interview.

24. What percentage of dischargees have scores of 12 or over? Of 3 or over? What percentage of non-dischargees have these scores?
25. In selecting men for responsible duty, as in submarines, what cutting score would be best, assuming that the test measures a factor important on the job?

A study of marine recruits used an inventory of 52 items, constructed to meet the needs of the specific situation. The inventory, together with one of the Kent "emergency" mental tests, was used to provide information to the psychiatrist interviewing the men. With this plan, it was possible to process 400 men in 2½ hours with only 2 psychiatrists. Although the investigators feel that their criterion was somewhat contaminated by factors not experimentally controlled, the inventory did identify potentially unsuccessful men. The test was given to about 3500 men. About 600 out of 900 who failed training (66 percent pickup) had scores of 9 or over; such a cutting score would yield about 250 false positives (10 percent) (32).

An adaptation of two short questionnaires given 2081 Seabees successfully identified 281 cases later adjudged as presenting neuropsychiatric conditions by psychiatrists, missed 16 who came to the psychiatrists' attention through difficulty on duty, and falsely screened 244 men judged normal upon further study (20). This means that the tests permitted psychiatrists to omit individual interviews with 1540 men—not a trifling saving.

Attempts to screen students to find those requiring counseling have been more disappointing. Darley, for example, tested over 800 students at the University of Minnesota. Each student was interviewed repeatedly during the year by a counselor, after which a diagnosis of the kind and extent of maladjustment was made. The Bell Adjustment Inventory had identified correctly 40 students having problems relating to home adjustment, but missed 41, and produced 73 false positives. On emotional adjustment, there were 32 hits, 75 misses, and 42 false positives (11). In a study of the Bernreuter test at the University of Iowa, an exceptionally good criterion was used—observation records on 81 girls gathered continually during the year. Of 16 girls at the maladjusted extreme on the Neurotic Tendency scale, only six were considered actually maladjusted, whereas two of those least maladjusted, according to the test, were rated maladjusted on the criterion. The Self-Confidence scale was more successful. Ratings agreed with test scores for 10 of 10 girls showing extreme lack of confidence on the test, and for 6 of 8 whose test scores showed high confidence (13).

Although errors are too frequent to warrant trust in these devices as screening tools, scores have a validity better than chance. Many studies have found relations such as those reported by Stogdill and Thomas. They found that the *mean* scores of students reporting voluntarily for counseling were significantly deviant on both Flanagan keys for the Bernreuter. The correlation of Self-Confidence scores for men with ratings on degree of maladjustment was .59. Overlap in scores between normal and counseling groups was too great for screening validity, and correlations with ratings were of negligible size in a group of probationary students referred for assistance (40). The test is more likely to be valid in groups seeking assistance than in groups who are uncoöperative. Despite its lack of precision in individual measurement, the Bernreuter test describes tendencies in groups sufficiently well so that several writers have endorsed it for research use (41). An invalid test, however, may conceal relationships which it would be important to discover.

Identifying problem cases by self-report methods at earlier ages has proved even more difficult. Investigators who compare groups of known delinquents with normals find some differences in scores, but the scores of the groups overlap so much as to discourage use of the tests for screening (5, 9). Wittman and Huffman, for example, found about 20 percent of delinquent boys show poor emotional adjustment on the Bell test, but that 15 percent of non-delinquent boys do equally poorly (44).

Studies of the value of personality tests for screening of undesirable employees are at present inadequate for a final judgment of the method.

Two studies offer promise in the application of tests to abnormal patients. Hathaway applied the Bell, Bernreuter, and Humm-Wadsworth tests to nine cases of "constitutional psychopathic inferiority." The Bell inventory gave no useful indications, but scores on the other tests showed suspiciously "supernormal" patterns for these cases. Such psychopaths were expected to be uninhibited and lacking in feeling of inferiority. On Bernreuter scale N they scored in the highest 10 percent, some going "off the scale" in the direction usually considered *good* adjustment. On the Humm-Wadsworth the group was average or better on every component. Hathaway considered this positive evidence in favor of test scores, clinically interpreted (21). Neymann and Kohlstedt prepared a yes-no questionnaire and applied it to diagnosed schizophrenics and manic-depressives. The distribution was bimodal, with

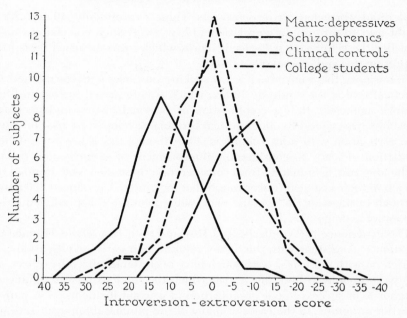

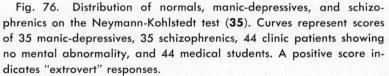

Fig. 76. Distribution of normals, manic-depressives, and schizo-phrenics on the Neymann-Kohlstedt test (**35**). Curves represent scores of 35 manic-depressives, 35 schizophrenics, 44 clinic patients showing no mental abnormality, and 44 medical students. A positive score in-dicates "extrovert" responses.

little overlap of the two groups. Schizophrenics ranged from −1 to −50, while manics ranged from −6 to +50. Ninety-three percent of the patients were correctly classified (34). A repetition of the study produced similar re-sults, shown in Figure 76 (35). The difference between the psychotic groups is significant and suggests that test scores may aid in classifying psychotics, but not necessarily in screening them from unselected groups.

Prediction of Success

Self-report personality tests have been used to predict such performances as school grades, success in industry, and success in selling. Attempts to pre-dict school grades by self-report tests have been completely unsuccessful. An occasional study finds a correlation as high as .40, but the consensus is that a particular personality trait may be helpful or harmful in attaining good marks, depending on the way that trait is organized into the total personality.

Prediction of pilot success by personality inventories was not generally successful. Nearly every published test was tried on at least a small group, and the correlations with graduation were small. Of all tests, the highest cor-relations were obtained for the Humm-Wadsworth scores Hysteroid and

Epileptoid, corrected for response sets. These r's were only .19 and .22, but might add to a multiple correlation (17, p. 583). Such correlations do not consider the significant *patterns* of scores which form the usual basis for interpreting this and several other tests.

In business, there have been a few striking successes with the method. One practical tool is the Aptitude Index, which was designed for use in life insurance agencies.[1] It is a combination of personal history and personality questionnaire, scored by an empirical formula developed by trial on agents. The correlation with sales volume is .40. Although this is low for individual prediction, it leads to considerable improvement of average sales per man in the long run. Eliminating from consideration those men who dropped from the job in their first year, it was found that men rated A produced 206 percent as much business as the average man, while men rated E produced only 41 percent of average (27).

The experience of Wonderlic and Hovland with Household Finance Corporation is consistent with this. They report: "Our early investigations were carried on with published tests which have been standardized by others. . . . We were unable to find any test in which the total score was significantly prognostic of success in our organization to warrant its inclusion as part of a selection program. In the cases of many of the purchasable personality tests, results were obtained which ran counter to expectations. Clerical workers seemed to be more aggressive than salesmen, salesclerks were higher than managers" (33, p. 60).

They describe a procedure of selecting a new set of items which distinguished between good and poor employees. This new scale, they report, is definitely helpful in selection. Validation figures are not available. They point out that whereas measuring the most favorable personality pattern for their particular work has been successful, it would be necessary for any other organization to develop its own test by empirical studies in its own plant. This is also the argument behind Jurgensen's test.

In contrast to this, some attempts have been made to suggest to counselors the personality patterns appropriate for given vocations. Thus Harmon and Wiener suggest the use of the MMPI in veteran's counseling (19). High Hs, D, and Hy, they suggest, may show unwillingness to take dirty or heavy jobs, and desirability of avoiding stress. High Pa and Sc indicate the desirability of relatively routine work. Such recommendations are based on the assumption (often incorrect) that the person who has a high Paranoid score has paranoid behavior; and so on. Thinking of this type is most helpful when tests are used as Moore suggests (33, p. 32): "They provide leads for the interview, so that the astute examiner may use them as starting points to disclose attitudes, values, feelings, and meaningful experiences. They open the possibility of discussing issues to which the candidate has given some con-

---

[1] Publisher: Life Insurance Agency Management Association.

sideration, which may lead to the disclosure of significant experiences and attitudes that are destined to affect activity in future work. Their most reliable value is in their aid in spotting those with extreme tendencies. . . . However, to infer that the presence of these tendencies is a guarantee of adequacy or trouble is to make an assumption that has not been supported by any type of follow-up study."

Several studies of marital happiness have used personality inventories. Adams, for example, tested students before marriage, and measured their marital happiness by a questionnaire after they had been married six months or longer. For 100 couples, the Terman Prediction Scale, which is a self-report device, correlates .32 (men) and .38 (women) with happiness (1). Personality traits measured by the Personal Audit had no predictive value.

26. How might lack of self-confidence help one student to attain high marks, yet be a drawback to another?
27. How adequate is a validity coefficient of .30–.40 for advising a particular couple whether to marry?

Conclusion

There are few hotter arguments in testing today than whether self-report personality measures should be trusted. It is clear that the hopes originally held for them have not been fulfilled, but they have not proved worthless in all situations. The range of opinions currently held is represented by these two quotations. Patterson, who made a careful study of the literature on the Bernreuter test, which of all tests has been most widely studied, insists (36): "It must be concluded that the results of studies using the Bernreuter Personality Inventory are almost unanimously negative as far as the finding of significant relationships with other variables is concerned. . . . It is no doubt largely due to the nature of the questionnaire approach, which appears to be a fruitless technique for the study of personality."

While test manuals and advertisements still make extreme claims for some self-report tests, such claims are rejected by most psychologists. Baker, discussing the diagnosis of children, represents the cautious position taken by those psychologists who, in good faith, uphold use of the tests (4, pp. 379–380): "It is generally known that children's problems are so close to their lives that they can scarcely refrain from answering what applies to them. This situation is similar to the quite universal tendency of most individuals to unburden themselves about their problems even to strangers if they are encouraged to talk about themselves. As such tests are becoming more practical and cover more areas, their uses are certain to increase when economy of time and usefulness become more apparent. It should be understood that they are not an end in themselves but should be the basis for further interview by trained workers."[2]

---

[2] From Baker: *Introduction to exceptional children.* Copyright 1944 by The Macmillan Company and used with their permission.

Much of the difficulty in personality testing has no doubt arisen from inadequate preparation of instruments and inadequate theories of personality. Certainly there is a wide range of value from the best self-report tests to the poorest. With more careful research and critical application of tests, this technique should be increasingly helpful, provided the following principles are kept in mind:

1. A "poor" score on a personality inventory probably indicates a person who should have further attention; a "good" score does not guarantee the presence of "good" qualities.

2. A test may be assumed to be valid with a particular group only when validity has been proved by experimentation on such subjects. Tests standardized on college students are unlikely to work without change for employees, patients, or soldiers. Empirically developed scoring is far superior to scoring keys constructed in an armchair.

3. A self-report test can never be used as a final basis for any decision in counseling or disposing of an individual. It performs its most useful function in suggesting to the psychologist possible facts about the individual to be confirmed by further study of him.

4. Tests having control scores to identify unusual response sets, or tests using a forced-choice design, are generally superior.

5. Results are far more trustworthy if the subject desires to give a true picture of himself.

28. Among the studies cited above reporting positive validity, which were based on tests designed for the particular sort of prediction being made? Which were based on tests designed for use in many different situations?
29. How would self-report tests be useful in a college guidance program?
30. What factors made for the unusual usefulness of self-report tests in military processing?

SUGGESTED READINGS

Harmon, Lindsay R., and Wiener, Daniel N. "Use of the Minnesota Multiphasic Personality Inventory in vocational advisement." *J. appl. Psychol.*, 1945, 29, 132–141.

Hunt, William A., and Stevenson, Iris. "Psychological testing in military clinical psychology: II. Personality testing." *Psychol. Rev.*, 1946, 53, 107–115.

Maller, J. B. "Personality tests," in Hunt, J. McV. (ed.), *Personality and the behavior disorders.* New York: Ronald Press, 1944, pp. 170–213.

Shaffer, Laurance F., and Spencer, Douglas. Reviews of California Test of Personality, in Buros, O. K. (ed.), *The third mental measurements yearbook.* New Brunswick: Rutgers Univ. Press, 1948, pp. 55–58.

Sheviakov, George V., and Block, Jean F. "Evaluation of personal and social adjustment," in Smith, Eugene R., Tyler, Ralph W., and others, *Appraising and recording student progress.* New York: Harper, 1942, pp. 349–402.

REFERENCES

1. Adams, Clifford R. "The prediction of adjustment in marriage." *Educ. psychol. Measmt.*, 1946, 6, 185–193.

2. Allport, Gordon W. *Personality: a psychological interpretation*. New York: Holt, 1937.
3. Allport, G. W., and Odbert, H. S. "Trait names: a psycho-lexical study." *Psychol. Monogr.*, 1936, 47, No. 1.
4. Baker, Harry J. *Introduction to exceptional children*. New York: Macmillan, 1944.
5. Bartlett, Edward R., and Harris, Dale B. "Personality factors in delinquency." *Sch. & Soc.*, 1936, 43, 653–656.
6. Benton, Arthur L., and Probst, Kathryn A. "A comparison of psychiatric ratings and Minnesota Multiphasic Personality Inventory scores." *J. abnorm. soc. Psychol.*, 1946, 41, 75–78.
7. Buros, Oscar K. (ed.). *The 1940 mental measurements yearbook*. Highland Park, N.J.: The Mental Measurements Yearbook, 1941.
8. Buros, Oscar K. (ed.). *The third mental measurements yearbook*. New Brunswick: Rutgers Univ. Press, 1948.
9. Burton, Arthur, and Harris, Robert E. (eds.). *Case histories in clinical and abnormal psychology*. New York: Harper, 1947.
10. Cattell, Raymond B. *The measurement of personality*. Yonkers: World Book Co., 1947.
11. Darley, John G. "Tested maladjustment related to clinically diagnosed maladjustment." *J. appl. Psychol.*, 1937, 21, 632–642.
12. Ellis, Albert. "The validity of personality questionnaires." *Psychol. Bull.*, 1946, 43, 385–440.
13. Feder, D. D., and Baer, L. Opal. "A comparison of test records and clinical evaluations of personality adjustment." *J. educ. Psychol.*, 1941, 32, 133–144.
14. Flanagan, John C. *Factor analysis in the study of personality*. Stanford Univ.: Stanford Univ. Press, 1935.
15. Gilliland, A. R. "What do introversion-extroversion tests measure?" *J. abnorm. soc. Psychol.*, 1934, 28, 407–412.
16. Gough, Harrison B. "Simulated patterns on the Minnesota Multiphasic Personality Inventory." *J. abnorm. soc. Psychol.*, 1947, 42, 215–225.
17. Guilford, J. P. (ed.). *Printed classification tests*. AAF Aviation Psychol. Prog. Res. Rep. No. 5. Washington: Govt. Printing Off., 1947.
18. Guilford, J. P., and Martin, Howard. "Age differences and sex differences in some introvertive and emotional traits." *J. gen. Psychol.*, 1944, 31, 219–229.
19. Harmon, Lindsay R., and Wiener, Daniel N. "Use of the Minnesota Multiphasic Personality Inventory in vocational advisement." *J. appl. Psychol.*, 1945, 29, 132–141.
20. Harris, Daniel H. "Questionnaire and interview in neuropsychiatric screening." *J. appl. Psychol.*, 1945, 30, 644–648.
21. Hathaway, S. R. "The personality inventory as an aid in the diagnosis of psychopathic inferiors." *J. consult. Psychol.*, 1939, 3, 112–117.
22. Humm, Doncaster G., and Humm, Kathryn A. "Validity of the Humm-Wadsworth Temperament Scale." *J. Psychol.*, 1944, 18, 55–64.
23. Humm, Doncaster G., and Humm, Kathryn A. "Compensation for subjects' response-bias in a measure of temperament." *Amer. Psychologist*, 1947, 2, 305.
24. Humm, Doncaster G., and others. "Combination scores for the Humm-Wadsworth Temperament Scale." *J. Psychol.*, 1939, 7, 227–253.
25. Hunt, William A., and Stevenson, Iris. "Psychological testing in military clinical psychology: II. Personality testing." *Psychol. Rev.*, 1946, 53, 107–115.
26. Jurgensen, Clifford E. "Report on the 'Classification Inventory,' a personality test for industrial use." *J. appl. Psychol.*, 1944, 28, 445–460.

27. Kurtz, Albert K. "Recent research on the selection of life insurance salesmen." *J. appl. Psychol.*, 1941, 25, 11–17.

28. Maller, J. B. "Personality tests," in Hunt, J. McV. (ed.), *Personality and the behavior disorders*. New York: Ronald Press, 1944, pp. 170–213.

29. Meehl, Paul E. "An investigation of a general normality or control factor in personality testing." *Psychol. Monogr.*, 1945, 59, No. 4.

30. Meehl, Paul E. "Profile analysis of the Minnesota Multiphasic Personality Inventory in differential diagnosis." *J. appl. Psychol.*, 1946, 30, 517–524.

31. Meehl, P. E., and Hathaway, S. R. "The K factor as a suppressor variable in the Minnesota Multiphasic Personality Inventory." *J. appl. Psychol.*, 1946, 30, 525–564.

32. Miles, Dwight W., and others. "The efficiency of a high-speed screening procedure in detecting the neuropsychiatrically unfit at a U.S. Marine Corps recruit training depot." *J. Psychol.*, 1946, 21, 243–268.

33. Moore, Herbert. *Experience with employment tests.* Studies in Personnel Policy No. 32. New York: Natl. Indl. Conf. Board, 1941.

34. Neymann, Clarence A., and Kohlstedt, K. D. "A new diagnostic test for introversion-extraversion." *J. abnorm. soc. Psychol.*, 1929, 23, 482–487.

35. Neymann, Clarence A., and Yacorzynski, G. K. "Studies of introversion-extraversion and conflict of motives in the psychoses." *J. gen. Psychol.*, 1942, 27, 241–255.

36. Patterson, Cecil H. "The relationship of Bernreuter scores to parent behavior, child behavior, urban-rural residence, and other background factors in 100 normal children." *J. soc. Psychol.*, 1946, 24, 3–50.

37. Shipley, W. C., and Graham, C. H. *Final report in summary of research on the Personal Inventory and other tests.* Applied Psychology Panel, Project N-113, Report No. 10. O.S.R.D. Rep. No. 3963; Publ. Bd., No. 12060. Washington: U.S. Dept. Commerce, 1946.

38. Smith, Eugene R., Tyler, Ralph W., and others. *Appraising and recording student progress.* New York: Harper, 1942.

39. Stalnaker, John M. "Personnel placement in the armed forces." *J. appl. Psychol.*, 1945, 29, 338–345.

40. Stogdill, Emily L., and Thomas, Minnie E. "The Bernreuter Personality Inventory as a measure of student adjustment." *J. soc. Psychol.*, 1938, 9, 299–315.

41. Super, Donald E. "The Bernreuter Personality Inventory: a review of research." *Psychol. Bull.*, 1942, 39, 94–125.

42. Thurstone, L. L. *The dimensions of temperament.* Report No. 42, the Psychometric Laboratory. Chicago: Univ. of Chicago Press, 1947.

43. Verniaud, Willie M. "Occupational differences in the Minnesota Multiphasic Personality Inventory." *J. appl. Psychol.*, 1946, 30, 604–613.

44. Wittman, Mary P., and Huffman, Arthur V. "A comparative study of developmental, adjustment, and personality characteristics of psychotic, psychoneurotic, delinquent, and normally adjusted teen-age youth." *J. genet. Psychol.*, 1945, 66, 167–182.

45. Woodworth, R. S. *Personal Data Sheet.* Chicago: Stoelting, 1918.

CHAPTER 15

Self-Report Techniques: Interests

NEED FOR INTEREST TESTING

An interest may be defined as a tendency to seek out an activity or object, or a tendency to choose it rather than some alternative. Knowing the interests of an employee helps us predict whether he would be satisfied if transferred to a new type of work; knowing the interests of a juvenile delinquent suggests activities which might keep him satisfied at home; and knowing the interests of a pupil helps the teacher to suggest projects, topics for writing, and social experiences which he will pursue more eagerly than others.

Interests can rarely be determined adequately by a direct question. There would be no need for tests if one could obtain from a subject a valid list of his major preferences. The question "Would you like to be a physician?" does not help greatly to determine whether a boy should consider medicine as a career. Apart from the usual problems of obtaining honest self-report, answers are often misleading. Frequently the response is to the symbol rather than the activity; medicine is respected, and the boy may feel that he should like anything respectable. Answers are often based on ignorance or superficial understanding of the activity. Girls may reject teaching for no better reason than that they think correcting papers would be tedious, little realizing the numerous other activities in a school day. Some boys choose law because it calls for public speaking, ignoring the long hours of isolated research and thinking called for. Counselors encounter numerous students and employees who are vocationally misplaced even though they had thought they would be interested in the work and enjoyed much of their training for it. Having made a choice, one often tends to defend that choice as correct; thus many people continue in activities, not facing the fact that they wish they had chosen differently. Under such circumstances, a simple question will not reveal the true interest pattern. Therefore, interest tests seek reactions to a mixed list of activities, some apparently remote from the interest under discussion. By such indirect approaches insight into true interests is obtained.

EMPIRICAL CONSTRUCTION OF INTEREST TESTS

Assumptions and Procedures

One of the two most widely used tests of interests is the Strong Vocational Interest Blank, first published in 1927. It is a superior example of the empirically constructed interest test.[1] Strong's empirical test may be contrasted to Kuder's Preference Record discussed below, which describes directly what the subject likes.

Strong's test makes use of the fact that people in a particular occupation have roughly similar interests. It is then assumed that a person having the same pattern will find satisfaction in that field, but that one having dissimilar interests will not be happy in it. For example, Strong identifies the interests which are characteristic of practicing engineers. In giving the test to college students, those who have interests similar to adult engineers are advised to consider engineering as a vocation, and those who have low scores in "engineering interests" are advised that they may not enjoy the work of the engineer.

The second assumption necessary to the Strong blank is that interests are fairly constant. The test is ordinarily given to late adolescents and young adults, and an attempt is made to predict what occupations the subjects will find satisfying as a lifetime activity.

The test was constructed by listing questions on hundreds of activities both vocational and avocational. Most items require a "like-indifferent-dislike" report regarding activities or topics: biology, fishing, being an aviator,

Table 63.   Determination of Weights Used for Strong's Engineer Key (21, p. 75)

First 10 Items on Vocational Interest Blank	Percentage of "Men-in-General" Tested			Percentage of Engineers Tested			Differences in Percentage Between Engineers and Men-In-General			Scoring Weights for Engineering Interest		
	L	I	D	L	I	D	L	I	D	L	I	D
Actor (not movie)	21	32	47	9	31	60	−12	−1	+13	−1	0	1
Advertiser	33	38	29	14	37	49	−19	−1	+20	−2	0	2
Architect	37	40	23	58	32	10	+21	−8	−13	2	−1	−1
Army officer	22	29	39	31	33	36	+9	+4	−13	1	0	−1
Artist	24	40	36	28	39	33	+4	−1	−3	0	0	0
Astronomer	26	44	30	38	44	18	+12	0	−12	1	0	−1
Athletic director	26	41	33	15	51	34	−11	+10	+1	−1	1	0
Auctioneer	8	27	65	1	16	83	−7	−11	+18	−1	−1	2
Author of novel	32	38	30	22	44	34	−10	+6	+4	−1	1	0
Author of technical book	31	41	28	59	32	9	+28	−9	−19	3	−1	−2

planning a sales campaign, etc. The list of questions was given to successful members of a particular profession, and the interest pattern for that profession was determined by comparing the responses of the group with those of unselected men of similar age. A weighted scoring key was then prepared to give each person a score reporting how his interests correspond with those of the professional group.

[1] An impression of the amount of effort involved in thorough and painstaking test construction may be obtained from Strong's report that over $45,000 was spent, and blanks from over 23,000 people were obtained, in the course of his research (21, p. x).

Table 63 illustrates the plan by which the key was constructed. On each item, the percentage of men-in-general giving each answer was compared with the percentage of men in the occupation giving the answer. Engineers dislike "Actor" more often than other men; therefore, response D was assigned a positive weight in the engineer scale. The weighting is proportional to the difference; liking to be author of a technical book is especially significant of engineering interests. In contrast to the engineers, 40 percent of artists respond "like" to "Actor." The weights of "Actor" in the artist scale are 2 for L, 0 for I and −1 for D (21, p. 73).

Strong developed keys for 39 occupations (printer, musician, etc.). A blank for women was also devised, which can be scored for nurse, stenographer, dentist, and 15 other occupations. Keys for masculinity-femininity, occupational level (professional, skilled, unskilled, etc.), and maturity of interests have also been prepared. The scores on each variable are converted into grades A (70 percent of successful men in the occupation fall in this group), B, and C.

1. Estimate the approximate weights for the chemist scale, on the item "Actor," if responses of chemists are as follows: 16 percent L, 34 I, 50 D.
2. Estimate the weights for the musician scale of "Actor," if responses of musicians are 34 percent L, 48 I, 18 D.
3. Suppose you wished to make a key for the Strong blank for women to measure interest in being a mother, i.e., to predict whether a girl will enjoy raising a family. Outline the steps you would follow to prepare the scale, with especial attention to the persons you would use as a basis for the key.
4. Each of the following assumptions is implied in the construction or in some uses of the Strong test. For each one, state a contradictory hypothesis that might be reasonable.
   a. One is not likely to succeed in an occupation unless the work is interesting to him.
   b. One is not likely to succeed in an occupation unless his interests are similar to those of most other men in the profession.
   c. Success and interest in the school subjects required for preparation for a profession are not an adequate basis for predicting satisfaction and success in the profession.
   d. The interests leading to success in a vocation in 1930 will also be the interests associated with success in 1950.

A Typical Strong Scale

The meaning of Strong test scores may be understood more thoroughly by examining a particular scale, say, "psychologist." Strong prepared his key from responses of 192 members of the American Psychological Association. Since full membership in this association was then restricted to persons who had demonstrated ability in psychological research, these men were presumably successful psychologists. The usual key was prepared which assigned weights on the basis of the extent to which the psychologists differed from unselected men. Among the weights are:

	L	I	D
Author of technical book	4	−4	−4
College professor	4	−3	−4
Employment manager	1	0	0
Social worker	0	1	−1
Undertaker	−4	0	1
Zoölogy	4	−3	−4
Musical comedy	0	0	0
Interviewing prospects in selling	−3	−1	3
Opening conversation with a stranger	−1	1	0
Expressing judgments publicly without regard to criticism	−1	0	1

5. At the time of Strong's study, the American Psychological Association included most teachers and research workers, but did not include a large proportion of clinical psychologists and applied psychologists.
   a. What limitation does this place on the interpretation of scores on the Strong "psychologist" key (7, p. 11)?
   b. Would it be advisable to make a new key, using as a standardizing group both academic and applied psychologists? [Research on new keys for the psychological profession is in progress.]
6. Psychologists are generally required to do considerable mathematical work in their research, yet liking for mathematics is assigned a weight of zero in the Strong scale. How can this seeming inconsistency be explained?
7. "An A rating in psychologist with B+ in physician and dentist should suggest a different preparation and career than an A rating in psychologist with B+ ratings in engineer, production manager, and carpenter" (21, p. 54). What differences in advice are justified in these cases?

The Global Interest Chart

For guidance, the total picture of the subject's interests must be obtained, rather than scores merely in the one or two occupations he considers himself interested in. Obtaining a complete profile on the Strong test is laborious and expensive. Fortunately, factor analyses have shown grouping among interests, so that one can score the student for broad groups and then consider specific occupations in a few keys only. Clusters of interest found in the Strong test for men are (21):

Group I, Creative-scientific: Artist, psychologist, architect, physician, dentist.
Group II, Technical: Mathematician, physicist, engineer, chemist.
Group III: Production manager.
Group IV, Sub-professional technical: Farmer, carpenter, printer, mathematics-science teacher, policeman, forest service.
Group V, Uplift: YMCA physical director, personnel manager, YMCA secretary, social science teacher, school superintendent, minister.
Group VI: Musician.
Group VII: Certified public accountant.
Group VIII, Business detail: Accountant, office man, purchasing agent, banker.
Group IX, Business contact: Sales manager, real-estate salesman, life insurance salesman.
Group X, Verbal: Advertising man, lawyer, author-journalist.
Group XI: President of manufacturing corporation.

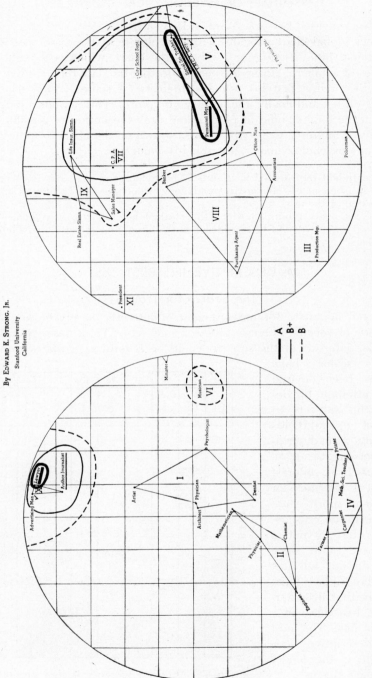

Fig. 77.   Global interest chart for Strong Vocational Interest Blank for Men. (Reproduced by permission of Stanford University Press.)

Strong has provided keys for groups I, II, V, VIII, IX, X.

Strong's global chart provides a simple picture of the major patterns of occupational interests. Figure 77 shows the chart, which is thought of as two faces of a sphere. Strong advocates locating the data for a student to be guided by circling first his primary interests (A scores), then secondary interests (B+), and finally, the tertiary (B) scores. This permits a judgment based on the total significant pattern and draws attention to possible combinations of interests. Curves have been drawn on the chart to indicate the ratings of a psychology major, tested in his senior year.

8. If the student represented in Figure 77 has done good academic work and has been satisfied in his courses in psychology, what possible vocational aims are suggested by the test?
9. There are many groups in which this student has low scores. Which of these lacks of interest would be significant in deciding against certain psychological positions?

A DESCRIPTIVE INTEREST TEST

The Search for Traits

It is not adequate for measurement of interests merely to catalog the thousands of specific interests a person may have. Yet a description of the particular interests of the subject would be helpful in working with him. Several scales have therefore been devised which attempt to describe the subjects in terms of general fields of interest. As in descriptive personality tests, traits (such as "interest in clerical activities" or "interest in sports") are the basis for description. Strong's test is not a descriptive scale since scores do not tell just what the subject likes, but only that his interests are like those of a group of men. The most useful descriptive interest scale is the Kuder Preference Record.

Kuder's test, like

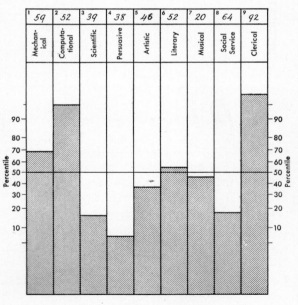

Fig. 78. Kuder Preference Record profile of Mary Thomas.

Strong's, is primarily intended for vocational guidance. He began by listing a large number of activities from work, school, and recreation. An analysis of correlations was then made to determine which of these interests were found together. The test includes seven independent clusters or areas of interest. Two additional scales were added which partly overlapped two of the original ones. The final profile describes the subject in terms of his interests in mechanical, computational, scientific, persuasive, artistic, literary, musical, social service, and clerical activities. The scores are presented as a profile, such as the one illustrated in Figure 78.[2] Each Kuder item has the form of a forced choice among three possible activities, the person being required to select the one he likes least and the one he likes most. An example is

 a. Develop new varieties of flowers.
 b. Conduct advertising campaign for florists.
 c. Take telephone orders in a florist shop.

A person who chooses "a" as most liked receives credit under Scientific and Artistic; choice of "b" is scored as Persuasive; and choice of "c" is counted as Clerical.

Interpretation of Scores

Kuder profiles are interpreted on their face value. A person who shows high interest in Clerical and Computational (as in the profile of Mary Thomas) would be expected to enjoy positions demanding such activities. The low-interest areas are also important, since the person might dislike work demanding considerable activity of this type. In Mary Thomas' case, the interest test was very useful. She was majoring in child development in college at the time she took the test. Her grades were mediocre, and her work with children neither especially good nor unsatisfactory. When questioned regarding her choice of major, she explained that she had set her heart on work in an orphanage. This desire had arisen in childhood when she read a book about a woman who helped orphan children, and this had seemed to her a "wonderful" thing to do as a lifework. The low Kuder scores in Persuasive and Social Service activities suggested a tendency to introversion; the high Mechanical, Computational, and Clerical scores suggested a liking for routine rather than creative activities. When questioned about office work, she enthusiastically described her enjoyment of previous summer work as a file clerk; her duties apparently had consisted solely of alphabetizing folders, yet she had "just loved it." Moreover, she had done well in secretarial training courses. Evidently both ability and interest fell in the same area, one she had not considered as a vocational goal.

Data have been gathered to show which interests are prominent among

---

[2] The Profile Sheet for the Kuder Preference Record for Women, Science Research Associates. (Adapted by permission.)

persons successful in a given occupation. From the average scores for an occupation listed in Kuder's manual, the student can determine, as in the Strong test, whether he has the normal interests of those successful in a chosen occupation. Kuder is now releasing formulas for computing, from the nine descriptive interest scores, occupational interest scores similar to Strong's. These formulas are based on differences between men (or women) in an occupational group and men (or women) in general.

10. What tentative conclusions can be drawn about a college man with the following percentile scores: Mechanical, 50; Computational, 30; Scientific, 70; Persuasive, 98; Artistic, 70; Literary, 90; Musical, 50; Social Service, 40; Clerical, 15?
11. A boy who is majoring in business administration shows high interests in Persuasive and Social Service. He is near average in Clerical and Computational. He has a high score (78th percentile) in Scientific, which is not usual among business managers. What suggestions do these findings justify?

Comparison of the Strong and Kuder Tests

The Strong and Kuder tests, both widely used, illustrate the practical problem of choosing between tests having similar purposes. The practical differences between the tests are small except for cost of scoring. The tests require about the same time and both are easily administered. The test materials are comparable in cost. Scoring the Strong test on all possible occupations requires much clerical work. The charge of 70¢ per person made by one agency for complete scoring service indicates the order of magnitude of the cost. The Kuder test may be scored by the subject himself in a few minutes, so that scoring cost is negligible. Several investigators have urged a simple, unweighted scoring for the Strong blank, and offered evidence for its adequacy, but Strong considers these proposals unsound (14, 23).

Which test gives the most useful information depends upon one's purpose. The Kuder focuses attention on the nature of the activities enjoyed, whereas the Strong focuses on the persons to whom one is similar. The logical validity of the Kuder is accordingly high, since a high mechanical interest score indicates self-reported liking for the activities listed in the Mechanical scale. The case for the Strong test rests on empirical validation, since a high score on the Carpenter scale does not mean one would like all the activities of the carpenter.

How students rate the tests is indicated by reports of 50 high-school seniors (boys) who took seven interest inventories. The Kuder test was overwhelmingly judged easiest to comprehend, easiest to mark, and mechanically attractive. On the question, "In which did you find the items of greatest interest?" 17 said Strong and 9 chose Kuder; the Gentry and Cleeton tests were chosen by 11 and 10 boys respectively. The crucial question was "Which yielded results which were most satisfying to you?" There was little uniformity of choice; Strong received 15 choices, Gentry 13, and Kuder 10 (**13**).

The empirical test is somewhat more indirect and subtle. It is probably easier to fake high interest in an area on a descriptive test than to guess how responses are scored on the empirical test. This gives the empirical test an advantage when self-report is likely to be false (18).

The tests apply to the same age range. The Strong blank for women uses different questions from the blank for men, whereas the Kuder uses the same questions but bases profiles on separate norms for each sex. Because the Strong test for women is less complete than that for men, Darley advocates the use of the men's blank for prospective "career women" in college (7, p. 13).

Most interests measured by both tests have correlations near .60 (25). The correlations are in themselves some evidence that the tests are valid, since tests made by very different techniques give similar pictures of the individual. At the same time, there is evidence that scores with similar names are not always interchangeable. Whereas Kuder Scientific scores showed marked agreement with Strong Chemist, Engineer, and Dentist, there was almost no correspondence of Kuder Artistic and Musical with Strong Artist and Musician, respectively (26). Interest tests can only be validly interpreted by a person who has studied each blank carefully to learn its idiosyncrasies.

12. Compare the extent to which the two tests are subject to response sets.
13. Which test would be most useful for counseling a group of high-school students with both professional and non-professional interests?
14. Which test would give you the most assistance if you were seeking vocational guidance (now or at an earlier age)?
15. It is desired to use an interest test for helping college freshmen make vocational plans. Among the training programs offered are veterinary medicine, dietitian, and others not directly represented in the Strong and Kuder keys. How could each test be extended to assist students in judging whether they would like these fields? Which test seems to be more adaptable?

Other Interest Measures

In addition to vocational guidance, interest tests may be used for other purposes. Interest items commonly play a part in personality and adjustment inventories. Several of the tests described in the previous chapter are essentially measures of interest, notably the Allport-Vernon test and the Interest Index. They are used, however, to obtain information about basic personal characteristics. Pressey, in his Interest-Attitude Test, determined which items were checked by subjects in varying age groups and, by scoring the items marked by older subjects, obtained scores which represent "interest maturity."

16. How might an interest test be used to distinguish, among prospective teachers, those likely to be traditional subject-matter teachers from those likely to

emphasize the development of the pupil as a person? Outline a plan for research to develop such a procedure (5). Why might such a test be more successful than a questionnaire on educational beliefs?

17. How could a psychologist design empirically a key for the Kuder or Strong test to measure the "emotional adjustment" of subjects?

Several investigators have sought to avoid the errors of self-report by measuring what the subject knows about each area, assuming that one acquires more facts about topics which interest him. The validity of such measures has generally been unsatisfactory, but in a few cases promising results were obtained. The Cooperative Test Service suggests using scores on its Contemporary Affairs tests as interest indicators. Knowledge of current developments in politics, social-economic, science-medicine, literature, fine arts, and amusements was found to correspond to Strong test scores, college majors, and other interest indicators (12). AAF experience with a similar technique is reported on p. 351.

PREDICTIVE VALIDITY OF INTEREST SCORES

Stability

When the reliability of interest scores is studied by immediate retests, coefficients are high, as would be expected from the large number of items used. A more important question is the stability of scores, since, when we measure the interests of a student as a method of vocational guidance, we assume that he will have similar interests when he becomes a worker. Scores on the Strong test are fairly stable. Strong gave his test to Stanford seniors, and again 10 years later. Correlations between scores were sizable: .77 for Physician, .51 for Personnel Manager, .68 for Sales Manager, .79 for Lawyer, etc. (21, p. 361). The interest profiles for individuals were frequently very stable; correlations between profiles ranged from .25 to .96 (median .75). Only about 3 percent of all A ratings changed to C, and vice versa. For high-school students, correlations between scores in tenth and twelfth grades were somewhat lower, the average correlation being .57 (3). Although scores are fairly stable, interests depend in part on maturity. Darley feels that if allowance is made for the fact that interests are still changing, the Strong test may be used effectively by age 15 (7, p. 28). Strong states that scores are dependable after age 17 (21, p. 57).

Fewer data are available on the more recent Kuder test, but one study of adults tested 15 months apart showed correlations as high as .93 (Musical) and as low as .61 (Social Service); median, .83 (24).

Validity for Vocational Guidance

The evidence that interest test scores do discriminate between men in various occupations is partial evidence that interests are a sound basis for guidance. Both the Strong and the Kuder tests have been studied sufficiently to verify that the majority of successful men in an occupation have corresponding scores on the interest tests. The validity of a scale, however, depends upon its interpretation. Not all engineers have the same interest. Estes and Horn made new keys for the Strong test which distinguished between advanced students in civil, mechanical, electrical, chemical, and industrial engineering. The correlations between scores on these special

Table 64.   Representative Interest Tests

Test and Publisher	Age Level	Scores Reported, Special Features	Comments of Reviewers[a]
Brainard Occupational Preference Inventory (Psych. Corp.)	Adolescents and adults	Seven fields; commercial, personal service, professional, etc. These further subdivided into areas (e.g., dairying)	"In the hands of qualified counselors, can be useful. . . . Too much has been sacrificed to convenience. . . . Entirely too brief" (Manuel, 2).
Dunlap Academic Preference Blank (World Book)	Junior high school	Literature, history, etc. Predicts school achievement	"Uses not adequately investigated. . . . Probably not usable for describing individual interests. . . . Constructed with unusual care" (Cronbach, 2).
Interest Index 8.2a, b, c (Prog. Educ. Assn.)	Adolescents	Liking for sports, fantasy, etc. Clinical analysis of personality is made (cf. pp. 324 ff.)	
Kuder Preference Record (Sci. Res. Assoc.)	High school, college	Computational, literary, etc.	"Quick and economical point of departure in helping students select occupations" (Berdie, 2).
Lee-Thorpe Occupational Interest Inventory (Calif. Test Bureau)	Adolescents	Artistic, business, occupational level, etc.	"Acceptable largely because of the possibilities of using test items as leads in interviewing. . . . Scores are of limited value due to lack of research" (16).
Pressey Interest-Attitude Tests (Psych. Corp.)	Grade 6 to adult	Emotional maturity, measured by empirical key	"Promising. . . . Valuable clues for investigation through interviews" (Spencer, 1, p. 86).
Strong Vocational Interest Blank (Stanford)	Adolescent and adult men; women	Empirical keys for interests similar to engineers, farmers, etc.	"Undoubtedly of value" (4, p. 459). "No adequate information on validity [of women's blank]" (Strang, 1, p. 462).

[a] The reader should refer to the source cited for a full statement of the reviewer's opinion.

keys and Strong's Engineer key included .71 (electrical), −.09 (civil), and −.63 (industrial) (11). Merely identifying the student as belonging in a broad vocational-interest type does not guarantee that he will be equally satisfied by all jobs within that area. At the same time, engineering jobs are enough alike so that a mechanical engineer would presumably like civil engineering better than journalism.

Interest scores have been correlated with self-estimated interests. On the Kuder categories, correlations between scores and self-estimates were in part as follows : Scientific, .48; Musical, .58; Social Service, .39; Persuasive, .62, average, .52 (6). This is perhaps most significant as evidence that self-reports in response to varied items give a picture that differs appreciably from responses to occupational labels.

The only way to really determine whether guidance based on interest tests is sound is to follow persons given such guidance until they have become settled in their work, and then to measure their job satisfaction. No such studies have been made. The nearest approach to such evidence is Strong's follow-up of college graduates. Some of these men changed occupation within 10 years after graduation. Strong shows evidence for the following statements: Men who remain in an occupation for 10 years average higher scores for that occupation than for any other; men continuing in an occupation have higher scores in that interest than men who try the occupation and change; men who change from one occupation to another change to one in which their interest scores are about as high as for the first choice. Interest scores in college have a clear relation to vocation chosen (21).

Carter reviews a number of scattered studies with imperfect criteria and concludes (4, p. 32): "In summary, one may say that there are very few careful studies which furnish clear-cut evidence of the validity of interest inventories for the prediction of vocational choice, but that this is due in part to the complexity of the problem. There are a variety of reports indicating that the majority of practical workers have confidence in the tests. The available heterogeneous array of evidence tends to show that the inventories are sufficiently valid for use, but the nature of vocational choice is such that no single quantitative test of validity is at present feasible."

Interest tests in no way represent ability or aptitude. They deal with only one of many factors leading to success in a job.

18. Do you agree with the following statement?
> "Insofar as stated choice of occupation by groups of individuals (high school girls) may be considered a true criterion of interest, the lack of relationship between statement of occupational choice and interest scores . . . may be considered evidence of the lack of validity of the interest inventories" (15, p. 89).

Validity for Academic Prediction

Although the Strong and Kuder keys have low correlations with grades, they measure a factor of undeniable significance in school success. Several studies have shown that they improve the prediction obtainable from intelligence measures alone. Segel found definite correspondence between interests and *differences* in achievement between different courses. The correlation of Strong Engineer interests and mathematics-marks-minus-history-marks was .61 (20). Correlations between interest scores and grades in engineering and dentistry are low, but in one study of dental students 92 percent of those with A and B+ ratings were graduated, compared with 67 percent of B's and 25 percent of C's (21, p. 524).

Greater success in predicting grades has been obtained with specially constructed keys. There is a "studiousness" key for the Strong blank, based on items which distinguished good and poor achievers (27). Mosier's findings illustrate results with this scale. Studiousness scores and grades correlated .47 for students in liberal arts, .24 for engineering students, and only .05 for business administration majors (17). Evidently such a score can be used to improve prediction, but its validity must be tested in each new situation. A similar technique has been applied to the Kuder test (9). Dunlap has devised a test for predicting junior-high-school grades by selecting interest items which correlate with achievement in specific subjects. Separate keys predict grades in literature, reading, social studies, and so forth. Correlations range from .50 to .70 (10).

Validity for Employee Selection

Strong has made numerous comparisons of interest scores for insurance agents with their success. The correlations are about .40, when success is judged either by ratings or by business produced. Men with A scores in interest produce, on the average, $169,000 per year of new policies, whereas C men average only $62,000. A few C men, however, are unmistakably successful (21, pp. 486–500). A number of minor studies have found small correlations between interest scores on the Strong test and criteria of success in other vocations.

Some efforts have been made to design prediction keys based on items which discriminate between good and poor workers. One of the few studies to show promising results obtained significant differentiation between good and poor salesmen of accounting equipment and between good and poor servicemen for that equipment (19).

Davis speaks highly of the Activity Preference Blank used by the Adjutant General's Office for personnel classification. While this test was thought to be proof against false self-report, an information test of interests was perhaps even better. The Air Force General Information Test (see Table 49) measured aviation interest by testing the candidate's knowledge about flying. Such tests, used for predicting success in pilot training, says Davis, "were so satisfactory as to imply that this approach to the measurement of vocational interests should be more widely used than it has been." The correlation of this test with graduation from training (.51) was higher than for any other single test used in the entire AAF selection program (8, pp. 54–56).

19. What might account for the fact that some men succeed as insurance salesmen whose interests are very different from insurance salesmen in general?
20. How would Strong's correlation be expected to change if data were gathered

on an unselected sample of men, rather than those who were actually engaged
in insurance selling at the time of the study?

GUIDANCE USES OF INTEREST TESTS

Interviewing

Few counselors today are satisfied to make arbitrary predictions on the
basis of interest tests. Matching a young person to a vocational goal is a
highly individualized process in which temperament, previous experiences,
and the entire picture of interests must be considered. The counselor ordinarily uses one or more interviews to formulate vocational plans. In this
interviewing, interest tests have proved valuable. An interest test is, in fact,
an interview, presenting the student with hundreds of questions such as the
counselor might otherwise ask. The pencil-and-paper questioning conserves
the time of the counselor for less routine work.

Having before him the interest test, the counselor can focus the interview
on areas where clarification is needed. Discrepancies between reported interests and vocational aims are frequently observed; many men seeking
guidance indicate engineering occupations as a first choice, while showing
on the test a great dislike for computational activities. Questioning the client
as to the sort of engineering he envisions will help to bring to his attention
the unrealistic nature of his plans. The interest test also assists in overcoming the inertia of the client who "has no idea what he'd enjoy." After expressing in the test his interest in a variety of specific activities, he has a
basis for considering possible vocations calling for those activities.

Use for Academic Guidance

Interest tests serve effectively in guidance programs in schools and colleges. Where these programs are understaffed, so that only a small amount of
time may be given to each individual, the interest test reduces the importance of intensive interviewing in the majority of cases. Every student may
be helped to select a course suited to his interests on the basis of a group
interest test. Attention is drawn to cases in which the interest scores do not
correspond to the student's professed aims, so that more careful counseling
may be used to clarify the ambiguity.

An example of this use of interest tests is a freshman enrollment plan used
at a Western college. Every freshman takes the Kuder test, together with
academic classification tests, during the first day of registration. The test
scores, together with the student's transcript and answers to a questionnaire
about his plans, are given to the faculty member who will plan the student's
program. When the student and adviser confer, the interests shown on the
test are compared with expressed vocational plans, and discrepancies are
clarified or noted for later attention. Courses are then selected to permit the
student an opportunity to explore and develop his major interests, while
meeting general freshman requirements. This plan avoids the difficulty that

freshmen, asked to state their field of interest in college, frequently give an inadequately considered answer and begin concentration in a major field that later proves not to satisfy their real interests.

Interest tests are often useful in a guidance program as a means of opening counseling. Where counselors are available to give general or specialized assistance, it is sometimes difficult to reach those who should be helped. Some students are unready to unveil their problem to an unknown counselor, and others, while wishing to obtain help, feel their problem to be too minor to warrant seeking out a counselor. By offering interest tests to those who wish them, it is possible to attract to the counseling office many who would not otherwise come but who need assistance. In a sense, it seems naïve that anyone should wish to take a test "to find out what his interests are," but appetite for such tests is widespread, and those who take the tests welcome an interpretation of their scores. Because they come voluntarily, many of the usual problems of rapport in counseling are avoided. Interest tests have the advantage over other psychological tests that they have a high degree of face validity, and can be interpreted without oversimplification or distortion. The results of interest tests rarely threaten the ego, whereas in many cases it would be damaging to offer to interpret intelligence tests or adjustment inventories to the client without careful preparation in advance. The counselor will of course find many openings in the discussion of the interest test to probe areas where more complete counseling is appropriate, and may wish to introduce other tests later. The interest inventory is largely self-explanatory, so that the counselor can lead the student to reach his own decisions on pertinent questions. This conforms to the current belief that decisions the person makes for himself are likely to be effective and more lasting than those imposed by another's authority.

Interests and Personality

In adjustment inventories the subject frequently conceals his attitudes and feelings. The person is usually pleased with and proud of his interests, however. Especially where it is understood that the tests will be used to provide the person with activities which will interest him, there is likelihood of honest self-report. Interests give clues regarding adjustment and personality.

Interests may be scored for masculinity-femininity by noting if one enjoys the activities normal to his sex group. The woman with strongly masculine interests, or the man with strongly feminine interests, may have found difficulty in adjusting to normal roles. Mollie Adams likes masculine clothes, affects a terse style of speech, and looks to activities like bowling and sporting events for recreation. Behind this lies a childhood in which her pleasantest moments were spent with her father, who supervised her development and encouraged her to be as rough and ready as the boys of her neighborhood. Being somewhat insecure in the "ladylike" atmosphere that surrounded the adolescent girls' first parties, Mollie accentuated her interest in the less gracious activities where she felt superior and at ease. Other girls may take on masculine attitudes because of a desire to prove that they are not mentally inferior, because of hidden aggression against men which leads to a desire to defeat them, or because of feared inability to compete for the attentions of men. Analogous motivations frequently account for excessively feminine interests among men.

Some interests indicate withdrawing tendencies, and may suggest shyness and feelings of social inadequacy. Isolative hobbies, though meritorious and often helpful to adjustment, may be of diagnostic significance. Highly intellectual interests or concentration in some field where one has developed unusual competence may be an attempt to withdraw from fields where one cannot be sure of superiority. It can be said that extreme concentration on any interest is symptomatic of need to overdevelop that aspect of satisfaction.

Some persons with conflicts arising from self-criticism find unusual satisfaction in activities which others find monotonous. Mathematical and clerical work, for example, appeals to some workers who need to be sure that what they do is right. Having added a column of figures and checked themselves, they can feel an assurance they could never have after writing a story, or planning a party, or some other activity where "rightness" is less objective. There are others who can be satisfied only when imposing their own individuality upon their work, perhaps out of some fear of losing status if they are like others. Such people frequently dislike routine or stereotyped activities, but respond eagerly to artistic tasks where originality is essential.

This use of interest tests is an attempt to go behind the interests to determine what type of personality would be conducive to such interests. Because it relies on the insight of the interpreter, it is open to error.

SUGGESTED READINGS

Darley, John G. "Counseling on the basis of interest measurement: general principles," in *Clinical aspects and interpretation of the Strong Vocational Interest Blank*. New York: Psych. Corp., 1941, pp. 26–32.

Paterson, Donald G. "Vocational interest inventories in selection." *Occupations*, 1946, 25, 152–153.

Strong, Edward K., Jr. "Interpretation of interest profiles" and "Use of interest and aptitude tests in counseling," in *Vocational interests of men and women*. Stanford Univ.: Stanford Univ. Press, 1943, pp. 412–482.

Super, Donald E. "The Kuder Preference Record in vocational diagnosis." *J. consult. Psychol.*, 1947, 11, 184–193.

REFERENCES

1. Buros, Oscar K. (ed.). *The 1940 mental measurements yearbook*. Highland Park, N.J.: The Mental Measurements Yearbook, 1941.
2. Buros, Oscar K. (ed.). *The third mental measurements yearbook*. New Brunswick: Rutgers Univ. Press, 1948.
3. Canning, L., and others. "Permanence of vocational interests of high school boys." *J. educ. Psychol.*, 1941, 32, 481–494.

4. Carter, Harold D. "Vocational interests and job orientation." *Appl. Psychol. Monogr.*, 1944, No. 2.
5. Cook, Walter W., and Leeds, Carroll H. "Measuring the teaching personality" *Educ. psychol. Measmt.*, 1947, 7, 399–410.
6. Crosby, R. C., and Winsor, A. L. "The validity of students' estimates of their interests." *J. appl. Psychol.*, 1941, 25, 408–414.
7. Darley, John G. *Clinical aspects and interpretation of the Strong Vocational Interest Blank.* New York: Psych. Corp., 1941.
8. Davis, Frederick B. *Utilizing human talent.* Washington: Amer. Council on Educ., 1947.
9. Detchen, Lily. "The effect of a measure of interest factors on the prediction of performance in a college social sciences comprehensive examination." *J. educ. Psychol.*, 1946, 37, 45–52.
10. Dunlap, J. W. *Dunlap Academic Preference Blank, manual of directions.* Yonkers: World Book Co., 1940.
11. Estes, S. G., and Horn, D. "Interest patterns as related to fields of concentration among engineering students." *J. Psychol.*, 1939, 7, 29–36.
12. Flanagan, John C. *Measuring interests.* Advisory Service Bull. No. 4. New York: Coop. Test Service, 1940.
13. Gordon, H. C., and Herkness, W. W. "Pupils appraise vocational interest blanks." *Occupations*, 1941, 20, 100–102.
14. Kogan, L., and Gehlmann, F. "Validation of the simplified method for scoring the Strong Vocational Interest Blank for Men." *J. educ. Psychol.*, 1942, 33, 317–320.
15. Laleger, G. E. *The vocational interests of high-school girls.* New York: Teachers Coll., Columbia Univ., 1942.
16. Lindgren, Henry C. "A study of certain aspects of the Lee-Thorpe Occupational Interest Inventory." *J. educ. Psychol.*, 1947, 38, 353–362.
17. Mosier, C. I. "Factors influencing the validity of a scholastic interest scale." *J. educ. Psychol.*, 1937, 28, 188–196.
18. Paterson, Donald G. "Vocational interest inventories in selection." *Occupations*, 1946, 25, 152–153.
19. Ryan, T. A., and Johnson, B. R. "Interest scores in the selection of salesmen and servicemen: occupational vs. ability-group scoring keys." *J. appl. Psychol.*, 1942, 26, 543–562.
20. Segel, David. "Differential prediction of scholastic success." *Sch. & Soc.*, 1934, 39, 91–96.
21. Strong, Edward K., Jr. *Vocational interests of men and women.* Stanford Univ.: Stanford Univ. Press, 1943.
22. Strong, Edward K., Jr. "Weighted vs. unit scales." *J. educ. Psychol.*, 1945, 36, 193–216.
23. Super, Donald E. "The Kuder Preference Record in vocational diagnosis." *J. consult. Psychol.*, 1947, 11, 184–193.
24. Traxler, A. E., and McCall, W. C. "Some data on the Kuder Preference Record." *Educ. psychol. Measmt.*, 1941, 1, 253–268.
25. Triggs, Frances O. "A study of the relation of Kuder Preference Record scores to various other measures." *Educ. psychol. Measmt.*, 1943, 3, 341–354.
26. Wittenborn, J. R., and others. "A comparison of interest measurement by the Kuder Preference Record and the Strong Vocational Interest Blanks for men and women." *Educ. psychol. Measmt.*, 1943, 3, 239–257.
27. Young, C. W., and Estabrooks, G. H. "Report on the Young-Estabrooks Studiousness Scale for use with the Strong Vocational Interest Blank for Men." *J. educ. Psychol.*, 1937, 28, 176–187.

CHAPTER 16

The Use of Test Results in Counseling

At this point in our consideration of tests, we have examined all the types generally used for educational and vocational guidance. Tests to be considered in subsequent chapters are most widely used in research and in clinical diagnosis, although in time they may be more used for counseling. This is therefore a convenient point to examine the problems that arise in the application of tests in counseling.

RESPONSIBILITY OF THE COUNSELOR

Special problems arise when tests are used in case work which are not important in military screening, employee selection, or research. In most psychological activities the main responsibility of the tester is to learn the truth. The test of a counselor, on the other hand, is whether he promotes the welfare of the client. Even if a counselor uses perfectly truthful techniques, his net effect is harmful if his truth leaves the client permanently less happy. In using tests for counseling, the psychologist must be aware of their special limitations in case work.

Unreliability in Individual Prediction

Even an unreliable test gives results better than chance—in a group. But in the individual case, the investigator has only one chance to predict, and one error may influence the life of the client drastically. Suppose it has been found that an IQ of 115 is needed for probable success in a profession. Even if 70 people out of 100 having IQ 110 fail in this field, one cannot make a clear prediction for Walter, IQ 110. Perhaps he would do better if tested again. Perhaps other qualities unknown to us make Walter one of the 30 who would succeed, rather than of the 70 who fail. Rarely are our tests so valid that a prediction about a single case is certainly true.

The counselor who is conscious of unreliability adopts many precautions to reduce its ill effects. He checks each test result against the case history for consistency. In case of doubt, he confirms any significant test findings by a second comparable test. He examines his case for special factors, such as language difficulty, which might make the test invalid. Most important, he thinks of a test performance as placing the subject in a probable range of scores, rather than as pegging him firmly at a particular percentile. Tests rarely miss fire in stating that a child is "somewhat, but not extremely, below average in scholastic aptitude." The statement that "this child's IQ is 87" is almost certainly untrue, in the sense that further data would not precisely confirm it.

Misuse of Test Information by Laymen

Whereas the psychologist can qualify scores as demanded by their invalidity and unreliability, few laymen have this training. They frequently overrate the power of psychological tools and misinterpret test reports. Both clients and such professional workers as teachers, physicians, and social workers may place false reliance on test data. Even when the tester's report is carefully qualified, the person receiving the report is likely to remember only portions of it. A parent, learning that a child's IQ is 87, may forget the tester's cautions about what the test does and does not measure, the possibility of growth or decline in IQ, and the approximate nature of predictions from it. Instead, the figure itself may be carried sharply in mind for years and used as a basis for rejecting the child or for making significant decisions.

Gross fallacies are often present in lay thinking about tests. There is the ever present belief that the IQ measures native intelligence. There is the misquotation that any child of IQ 140 is a genius. Percentiles are misread as percents. Norms—what the average sixth-grader *does* do—are misinterprete as standards—what every sixth-grader *should* do. Most psychologists now make it a practice never to give any client or co-worker a test score unless he can interpret that score so that the person will understand it.

Information as a Source of Maladjustment

Test results have emotional significance for the individual. While the scientist, on his side of the test paper, is being impartial and judicious, the client, on his side, is reacting with fear, pride, and worry. To the counselor, a score at the 75th percentile may look "good." To the college student who has viewed himself all his life as an exceptional person, at the top of the superior group, this same finding may be shattering. The psychologist may feel he is doing a service by telling a mother that her child cannot hope to become a doctor like his father. To the parents, his statement can be a threat of loss of face for having a not-superior child, an accusation of somehow having failed as parents, and a deathblow to plans they have been living out for 10 years. The counselor may be correct in attempting to give clients realistic ideas, but when he unleashes emotional forces, he must accept the responsibility of helping to resolve the conflicts aroused.

The counselor who reasons that the truth can do no harm neglects to consider that the client often distorts the truth to suit his needs. Selective memory is commonly noted. Given a large body of facts, the client forgets many, but recalls those which have emotional significance for him. Sometimes he suppresses and forgets those which are unwelcome, whereas in other cases he forgets favorable comments while remaining concerned about some minor defect in his record. Rationalization is also common. Given a test score which is not what he would like to hear about himself, the subject may invent and believe excuses for the score rather than treating it as a fact.

Taking a test is itself an emotional experience. This is shown by the evidence of stress found in Binet and Rorschach protocols, and by experimental measures of emotion during tests (8). Most people seek counseling because they are uncertain about their ability or adjustment. If they take a test, they expect it to give an answer to these doubts, for better or worse. A person who fears that he lacks mental ability cannot be expected to face possible proof of that fact calmly. Similar tensions are present when a test indicates fitness for a vocation or degree of personality adjustment. In taking most tests, there are moments of failure. These arouse emotion. Many subjects who can do well and whose scores are high relative to the group are upset and discouraged at the end of a test because they are conscious of their errors and failures. This is a necessary consequence of tests designed so that the average person will miss or fail to complete many items.

Unfortunately, problems are not eliminated by reassurance. The tester who tells the subject that he has done well does not remove doubts from his mind. If a subject has a thoroughly integrated feeling of inferiority, change in his attitudes must come through his readjustment, rather than through the assurance that an outside authority thinks him good. Because feelings of insecurity have usually been present for years, perhaps stemming from a felt lack of acceptance in infancy, they are not to be removed by a single "fact."

The problems stated in this section define the responsibilities of the counselor. There is no clear set of rules for avoiding the difficulties suggested. The counselor who is aware of the pitfalls may use tests more wisely in a particular situation.

1. Discuss the advantages and disadvantages of telling parents the intelligence test scores of their first-grade children.
2. Discuss the advantages and disadvantages of telling college freshmen their standings on the American Council Psychological Examination.
3. Discuss the advantages and disadvantages of giving the Bernreuter Personality Inventory to a college psychology class and permitting each person to score his own paper.
4. In each of the above cases, if it were decided to give out the information, what precautions would be helpful?

NON-DIRECTIVE OR CLIENT-CENTERED COUNSELING

The Non-Directive Point of View

In earlier days of psychological service, the counselor was often viewed as an expert passing judgment, as an engineer would inspect a bridge or a physician prescribe for a disease. More recently attention has been drawn to a counseling relation in which the counselor does not decide, direct, or advise, but rather helps the client think for himself. In extremely directive or prescriptive counseling, the "expert" obtains facts, decides, and tells the client what to do. More client-centered counseling stresses the importance of the client's making his own decisions and accepting himself and his characteristics. The client-centered point of view proposed by Rogers (5) has been a controversial topic, but most counselors have found his suggestions acceptable and desirable at least in part.

Rogers' basic view is that the important goal is the growth of the client toward maturity and adjustment. A person who has learned to face his problems and rely on his own judgment has been helped more than one who must seek advice in each new crisis.

Expert advice often fails to remove problems because psychological problems are entangled in emotional attitudes. The true problem is often not the surface problem voiced to the counselor. Suppose Stan Howard, an employee on a finishing machine, comes to inquire why he was not promoted to foreman. The directive personnel worker might give him the facts, based on tests and ratings, which "prove" that Howard would be a poor foreman. He may even give Howard a pep talk on how well he produces, about the chance of raising his pay as a workman, and about the undesirability of seeking a job where he would fail. Howard is likely to nod his head and leave. But he may be far from convinced he should not be a foreman. He may now, in fact, quit and go to another company where he'll "have a chance." He may have failed to state, or even recognize, that he is anxious to be a foreman solely because his brother-in-law is a foreman and he wishes equal status. Similar "irrelevant, non-objective" factors often lie behind the student who studies inadequately, the aircrewman who strives to be a pilot, the mother who overrates her child's ability, or the unpopular girl. Even when he seeks counseling, the client phrases his problem to protect the tender spots of his ego. The counselor who "solves" a surface problem may be helping the client to avoid facing his real conflicts.

The methods suggested by Rogers help the client face his true feelings. The counselor listens, accepts, and reflects the client's feelings by rephrasing what the client has said: "You think you'd rather be a foreman than a machine operator"; "It's discouraging when a man who came after you did is promoted over you"; "You feel that the management doesn't trust you." By accepting the feelings instead of trying to prove them false, Rogers finds himself able to promote ultimate adjustment. The client, freed from need to justify and apologize for his attitudes, gains insight into himself. Decisions made at this level stick because the client believes them.

The client is made responsible for the treatment. He asks the questions, limits the area discussed, makes the judgments, and decides when to terminate the counseling. If the counselor proposes a test, or suggests that poor reading may be a source of difficulty, or lays down alternative solutions, he is taking responsibility. The rejection of these methods is Rogers' most novel and most crucial point.

5. To what extent are these statements non-directive (insofar as can be judged without knowing the client's preceding remark)?
   a. Tell me about your background so I can understand this better.
   b. Here is a list of books from which you may wish to read something on your problem.
   c. You would like to get the opinion of another person. It seems too important to risk a wrong decision.
   d. Fortunately your previous record shows that you can do this well.
   e. I'll be free tomorrow at 10 if you wish to come in again.

Tests in Non-Directive Counseling

To a large extent tests, which are designed to help the tester be wise, become of secondary importance because they do not center on the feelings of the client. Says Rogers (6, p. 140):

"The counseling process is furthered if the counselor drops all effort to evaluate and diagnose and concentrates solely on creating the psychological setting in which the client feels he is deeply understood and free to be himself. It is unimportant that the counselor know about the client. It is highly important that the client be able to learn himself. (Not to learn *about* himself, but to learn and accept his own self.) In making use of these principles the counselor examines his own attitudes and techniques and endeavors to refine his procedures so as to eliminate all which are not in accord with the basic principles. Thus questions are eliminated from the interview because they invariably direct the conversation, advice is eliminated because it assumes the counselor to be the responsible person, diagnosis and evaluation are put aside because it has been learned that even when they are not voiced they tend to distort the counselor's responses in subtle ways and to break down his full acceptance of client attitudes."

Tests are not abandoned by this outlook. Instead of becoming ways of diagnosing the client, learning the answers so we can tell him, they become ways of helping him find out about himself. In non-directive counseling, *tests enter only when the client asks for them.* The client who comes in with the statement, "I'm worried because it takes me so long to learn an assignment," is not immediately seated before a battery of tests. Instead, counseling may go through to completion with no use of tests. Perhaps, in the course of examining his difficulties, he says, "I've often worried about whether I'm as bright as these students I compete with. I thought you people had some tests that would tell about that." Then the counselor can supply him with the means of measuring himself, since he has apparently reached the maturity required to face his question honestly.

It is the repeated experience of counselors trying this technique that when tests are delayed, problems come to light which would otherwise never have been voiced. A student may come to request an intelligence test. If given the test, told that his score is normal, and dismissed, he has been reassured but not necessarily helped. In taking the test he may have reduced his tension temporarily, but may have failed to solve the basic conflict that set him wondering about intelligence. Perhaps he was worrying about changing his major, or perhaps he is concerned because his grades in college are lower than in high school. Or the problem may be as remote from that stated as a worry because his wife's family considers his pronunciation peculiar. Insofar as the counselor avoids methods which bring the conference to a head, give an answer, and terminate it, he permits the client to dig into what really concerns him.

Most counselors compromise with the non-directive approach to some degree because of administrative conditions or other reasons. Even where the approach is not purely non-directive, emphasizing the client's responsibility is a helpful technique. Thus Bordin and Bixler place on the client the responsibility of choosing the tests to be taken. In contrast to establishing a standard battery of tests to be taken, they answer questions about tests by discussing at length the sorts of tests available. They neither recommend a particular test nor limit their descriptions to the tests the client asks about. After hearing what tests can be had, the client takes the initiative in deciding what to find out about himself (2).

Interpreting Tests Non-Directively

Decisions made by the counselor are apparently less effective for most clients than those they make themselves. The counselor who knows what test results imply can help the client most if he helps him learn their meaning and reason out his own decision, rather than following the medical practice of writing a prescription but concealing the diagnosis. Bixler and Bixler have made numerous suggestions for applying the client-centered point of view to test interpretation (1).

The counselor avoids the giving of opinions. The counselor is always tempted to comment on the goodness or badness of scores, if only as a means of giving confidence or of emphasizing the seriousness of symptoms. Such evaluation comes between the client and the score and makes it harder for him to accept the score as a reality. Bixler urges a statistical prediction, in such form as "Eighty out of one hundred students with scores like yours succeed in business." This is easier for the client to interpret than merely, "You are at the sixty-fourth percentile." The writer has found it an even better device to show college freshmen a scatter diagram plotting the test scores and grade averages of hundreds of cases. The client can judge the "success" of previous students by looking at the column of the chart where scores equal to his are plotted. The graph may show some cases making A's and some making failures. He can see for himself whether with his score he is likely to attain his aspiration. This procedure also reinforces the concept of unreliability in prediction. The scatter of cases makes it clear that his fate is not certain.

Bixler's second suggestion is that the counselor should be frank, although using general terms rather than specific scores. Low scores must be faced honestly, if the client is to gain in self-knowledge. But this can only come when he expresses readiness for the knowledge.

Personality tests are used primarily as a basis for helping the individual view his own feelings. Instead of, "Your home adjustment is low," Bixler says, "You seem to feel that you have more difficulties at home than in your social living." This invites the client to respond with more expression and recognition of feeling, rather than taking the score as a terminal diagnosis. It is especially necessary not to label a client maladjusted or neurotic or introvert. Such a label is threatening and carries no implications for constructive decisions.

The client must always feel free to reject any interpretation. He must be able to say that, though his score is low, he expects to succeed. He must be able to reject his own interest test score by insisting that he really likes engineering despite a low computational interest. It is only when he learns that he need not argue with the counselor that he feels free to examine himself non-defensively.

The counselor must be aware of and help the client recognize his emotional reactions to the test scores. It is emotional reactions that block rational thinking, so that the client can use the scores wisely only after he has come to an understanding of his emotions.

These points are illustrated in the following dialog published by Bixler from a case record (1, pp. 151–152):

"*Counselor*—Sixty out of one hundred students with scores like yours succeed in engineering. About eighty out of one hundred succeed in the social sciences. . . . The difference is due to the fact that study shows the college aptitude test to be important in social sciences, along with high school work, instead of mathematics.

"*Student*—But I want to go into engineering. I think I'd be happier there. Isn't that important too?

"*C*. You are disappointed with the way the test came out, but you wonder if your liking engineering better isn't pretty important?

"*S*. Yes, but the tests say I would do better in sociology or something like that. (Disgusted)

"*C*. That disappoints you, because it's the sort of thing you don't like.

"*S*. Yes. I took an interest test, didn't I? What about it?

"*C*. You wonder if it doesn't agree with the way you feel. The test shows that most people with your interests enjoy engineering and are not likely to enjoy social sciences—

"*S*. (Interrupts) But the chances are against me in engineering, aren't they?

"*C*. It seems pretty hopeless to be interested in engineering under these conditions, and yet you're not quite sure.

"*S*. No, that's right. I wonder if I might not do better in the thing I like—Maybe my chances are best in engineering anyway. I've been told how tough college is, and I've been afraid of it. The tests are encouraging. There isn't much difference after all—Being scared makes me overdo the difference."

6. What further insights might the client gain from continuing the conversation? What would be a suitable client-centered remark for the counselor to make next?

7. Which of the following statements would it have been legitimate for a non-directive counselor to make?
   a. It's probably better for you to work in an area you like than to follow these tests strictly.
   b. Studies show most people develop an interest in areas they do well; you probably would learn to like social science if you tried it.
   c. If you stay in engineering, you should plan to take a course in remedial mathematics.
   d. It seems to you that it's wisest to work in the field where your chances are best.
8. Reread the counselor's remarks carefully. Did he at any time suggest what he thought was right, or what he approved of? Did he disapprove of any idea of the client?

PRESCRIPTIVE COUNSELING

The Directive Point of View

Although emphasis has been placed on permissive counseling above, it should not be assumed that prescriptive methods are obsolete. They are widely used under many circumstances. Some counselors prefer them. Administrative requirements often force a counselor to be the responsible person, as when a veterans' counselor is required by law to approve the vocational plans of certain men. When a case is referred for counseling, rather than coming in voluntarily, the counselor cannot apply client-centered methods fully. Cases in which the client is incapable of self-direction, as in psychosis and severe neurosis, must also be prescribed for.

Those using tests directively emphasize the importance of "objective facts" as a basis for rational decision, in contrast to Rogers' emphasis on the emotional meaning of the "facts." The directive counselor often thinks of the client as leaning on someone for support, and considers tests an especially sound basis for giving the direction sought; in other cases, the counseling is viewed as a problem of convincing the client that his plans should be changed, and tests are regarded as a forceful type of evidence (7). The counselor who wishes to bring his client to face the facts takes a stand similar to John Dewey's (paraphrased here from a passage dealing with children) (3, pp. 84–85):

> The suggestion upon which clients act must in any case come from somewhere. It is impossible to understand why a suggestion from one who has a larger experience and a wider horizon should not be at least as valid as a suggestion arising from some more or less accidental source. It is possible of course to abuse the office, and to force the activity of the young into channels which express the counselor's purpose rather than that of the client. But the way to avoid this is not for the counselor to withdraw entirely. . . . The counselor's suggestion is not a mold for a cast-iron result but is a starting point to be developed into a plan through contributions from the experience of all engaged in the counseling process.

Prescriptive counselors generally organize their work to obtain as wide a variety of information about the client as possible, make a wise interpretation, and bring the client to base his action on this information. While they respect the right of the client to choose between alternatives of merit and do not force even a wise course of action upon him, their emphasis is on keeping the client from making errors. Says Williamson, who represents a "human engineering" point of view (9, pp. 134–138):

"The effective counselor is one who induces the student to want to utilize his assets in ways which will yield success and satisfaction. . . . Ordinarily the counselor states his point of view with definiteness, attempting through exposition to enlighten the student. . . . In respect to no student's problem does the counselor appear indecisive to the extent of permitting loss of confidence in the authority of his information. . . . If it is true that the counselor should not make the student's decision, it is equally true that someone must render this very service until some students are able, intellectually and emotionally, to think for themselves."

Test Batteries for Preliminary Diagnosis

Some testers have a battery of tests which serves as their first method of getting acquainted with the client. For Veterans Administration counseling centers a common battery consists of a short ability test, such as Otis Gamma, an achievement measure for those considering further schooling, the Kuder or Strong interest tests, and the Bell Adjustment Inventory (Adult). For those who are concerned with mechanical occupations, the Bennett test and various pencil-paper and dexterity tests may be used. Upon completion of the first tests and perhaps a preliminary interview, further tests may be called for, such as a reading measure, a Wechsler test, or aptitude tests. Final decision is based on a case history and a consideration with the client of his record. The program aims to provide the veteran with advice from a trained person who knows the wide range of occupations, the possibilities of further schooling and of psychological assistance, and the ways of diagnosing abilities and problems. The counselor is a skilled teacher, who must help the client acquire needed information as well as emotional attitudes.

In contrast to the standard-battery approach to diagnosis, many counselors feel that the best use of tests is to make a careful preliminary survey of the problem, before choosing particular tests to answer questions specific to the case. Thus one mental test might be chosen for one case, and not used again in months of counseling. Doll makes this comment regarding clinical diagnosis (4, p. 168):

"Every case study originates in some social situation. This is commonly referred to as the immediate problem or the 'complaint.' Sound casework requires that this immediate problem be formulated as explicitly as possible, and that it be verified in fact as may be practicable by objective procedures before proceeding with the clinical analysis of the problem. The delineation and verification of the initial problem requires a review of the individual's history in all aspects and this review is most serviceable when obtained prior to the use of test procedures. One of the most serious errors in current clinical-psychological practice is to proceed with test devices long before the immediate problem is specifically assured and before the antecedent history of the individual has been adequately explored. . . . The only sound position that can be taken by any competent clinician is to hold fire on test procedures until these preconditions of a satisfactory mental diagnosis are well established. Only by this approach can the clinician decide which tests are relevant in a given case and how many or of what variety. Only under these circumstances can he economically and quickly determine the direction of test analysis. And only from this base can he properly interpret the data derived from applying clinical-psychological test procedures with assurance of a harmonious coordination of these data with the entire clinical picture."

9. In each of the following situations, discuss the advantages and disadvantages of a standard battery given before the interview, compared to tests chosen on the basis of preliminary study of the case.
   a. A school psychologist works with children of junior-high-school age referred by their teachers as problem cases. The psychologist is to recommend suitable ways of dealing with the child.
   b. A clinical psychologist is to examine all men reporting to a veteran's counseling center who are suspected of serious emotional disturbances.
   c. A remedial-reading instructor in a college makes a study of all cases requesting help to determine if a reading difficulty is present.
   d. A vocational adviser is employed by a small city school system to test all pupils and make information regarding their aptitudes and interests available to the teachers who will do the counseling.
10. In the following situations, decide whether the welfare of the client would be promoted by giving him the information that tests could provide.
   a. High-school records of a college freshman suggest that he is probably so lacking in scholastic aptitude that he is more likely to fail than not.
   b. An engineering student seeks advice because of his poor grades. A telephone call to his instructor discloses a probable deficiency in arithmetic.
   c. A worker protests his non-promotion to foreman. Test records on file show that his intelligence is below that of successful foremen.

CAUTIONS IN COUNSELING

In helping the client make decisions, the counselor, whatever his technique, wishes the client to have a basis for optimism regarding the future. The non-directive counselor would prefer that this come through insight, whereas the directive counselor tends to give direct encouragement. In either case, however, the client should leave the counseling with a positive plan for action, rather than merely the knowledge that his former plan was inadequate. Similarly, he must have a feeling that he has some strong qualities, rather than a total feeling of failure because tests have brought to light only weaknesses. In every test performance, there are some praiseworthy aspects. The counselor who wishes to give support will call attention to such features as accuracy, originality, or persistence, in addition to giving the client facts about his score. Nearly all counselors working with normal late adolescents and adults agree in giving the client the facts on which recommendations (if any) are based. The counselor who refuses to give scores, even in general form, sets up a fear in the client that he was not told because his scores were too poor.

The most helpful single principle in all use of testing is that test scores are merely data on which to base further study. They must be coördinated with background facts, and they must be verified by constant comparison with other available data. This is the reason that continued counseling by an adviser over a year is more effective than "one shot" counseling, where an answer is given to each new specific problem by a different adviser. The test score helps the counselor by warning him to look in the record for further symptoms of a particular problem. The score, and study of items within the tests, suggest topics to probe by interview methods. While sometimes it is necessary to act on a problem immediately, it is sound practice to defer a final decision as long as possible, meanwhile seeking confirmation of tentative diagnoses.

Wherever possible, test results should be a starting point for action. They should not be an end in themselves. There is some satisfaction in being diagnosed and evaluated, but counseling is helpful only when behavior is changed. Test results may be used to encourage analysis of study habits, vocational exploration, or activities leading to personality development. Tests, at their most effective, are ways of helping people live more happily.

11. Discuss the advisability of delaying final decision in each of these situations. What supplementary information should be sought to confirm the tentative conclusions?
   a. A college student who is failing in engineering at midterm seeks a more suitable vocational goal. Aptitude and interest tests suggest journalism.
   b. An engaged couple, after a quarrel, seeks the help of a marital counselor. A personality test intended to predict marital adjustment (validity .50) shows that their score as a pair is low, in the range where there is an even chance of divorce.
   c. Students applying to enter a graduate school for social work are tested routinely. A girl shows severe neurotic signs on both self-report and the Rorschach test (Chap. 20).

SUGGESTED READINGS

Bixler, Ray H., and Bixler, Virginia H. "Test interpretation in vocational counseling." Educ. psychol. Measmt., 1946, 6, 145–155.
Bordin, Edward S., and Bixler, Ray H. "Test selection: a process of counseling." Educ. psychol. Measmt., 1946, 6, 361–373.
Combs, Arthur W. "Non-directive techniques and vocational counseling." Occupations, 1947, 25, 261–267.
Rogers, Carl R. "Psychometric tests and client-centered counseling." Educ. psychol. Measmt., 1946, 6, 139–144.
Williamson, E. G. "Counseling and the Minnesota point of view." Educ. psychol. Measmt., 1947, 7, 141–155.

REFERENCES

1. Bixler, Ray H., and Bixler, Virginia H. "Test interpretation in vocational counseling." Educ. psychol. Measmt., 1946, 6, 145–155.

2. Bordin, Edward S., and Bixler, Ray H. "Test selection: a process of counseling." *Educ. psychol. Measmt.,* 1946, 6, 361–373.
3. Dewey, John. *Education and experience.* New York: Macmillan, 1938.
4. Doll, Edgar A. "The social basis of mental diagnosis." *J. appl. Psychol.,* 1940, 24, 160–169.
5. Rogers, Carl R. *Counseling and psychotherapy.* Boston: Houghton Mifflin. 1942.
6. Rogers, Carl R. "Psychometric tests and client-centered counseling." *Educ. psychol. Measmt.,* 1946, 6, 139–144.
7. Staff, Advisement and Guidance Service, Veterans Administration. "The use of tests in the Veterans Administration counseling program." *Educ. psychol. Measmt.,* 1946, 6, 17–23.
8. Waite, William H. "The relationship between performances on examinations and emotional responses." *J. exp. Educ.,* 1942, 11, 88–96.
9. Williamson, E. G. *How to counsel students.* New York: McGraw-Hill, 1939.

CHAPTER 17

Self-Report Techniques: Attitudes

ATTITUDE SCALES AND OPINION SURVEYS

Political and social beliefs have been an important subject for investigation by psychologists and sociologists. Some studies have been primarily concerned with surveying the opinions of the public in general or of special groups. Opinion surveys such as the Gallup poll place little or no emphasis on reliable measurement of individuals. In contrast, attitude scales attempt to describe reliably the attitude of each individual, although they may also be helpful for group surveys. Polls are most often conducted by interviewing, whereas the attitude scale is a paper-pencil test. Where opinion surveys may deal with miscellaneous questions, asking only one question on each topic, attitude scales usually concentrate on one issue or group of issues. Like other tests, the attitude scale combines many questions measuring the same factor in order to obtain a reliable score. Opinion surveys try to report political and business trends for the guidance of policy makers.

Attitude scales have generally been used for more intensive research. The large number of questions makes the scale less satisfactory for widespread and practical use. The refined measurement permits one to correlate individual attitude scores with other factors and to detect small shifts in score. Attitude scales are suited to testing the effect of education or propaganda upon beliefs. The wide range of use of attitude scales is suggested by the variety of attitudes measured with scales now in existence. These include scales dealing with Russia, Negroes, communism, birth control, conservative vs. untraditional educational practice, labor unions, and satisfaction in one's job.

1. Design an experiment to test whether newspaper editorials change the beliefs of a community toward the United Nations. How would the procedures of obtaining data be changed if an attitude scale were used for measurement rather than a single-question opinion survey?
2. Discuss whether an opinion survey or an attitude scale would be more suitable for investigating each of these problems.
   a. A motion-picture producer wishes to know which of two titles will be most appealing to the public.
   b. A manufacturer wishes to know whether the majority of his men favor a group medical insurance plan.
   c. An investigator wishes to compare the attitude toward free enterprise of students majoring in different college departments.
   d. A social service administrator wishes to determine the attitudes of his staff

toward certain social groups as a basis for assigning them to duties in various sections of a large city.

ATTITUDE-TESTING TECHNIQUES

The Thurstone Method

The majority of attitude scales represent either the Thurstone or the Likert method of scale construction. The Thurstone method is important both because of its wide use and because it represents a major advance in test theory. Prior to the development of Thurstone's technique in 1928, attitude "measurement" had been largely confined to simple questionnaires. Among the weaknesses of such procedures was the lack of evidence that the separate questions measured the same attitude, and the arbitrary units of measurement employed.

While one could obtain numerical scores by counting answers, there was no assurance that the differences between scores 40 and 50, say, represented the same differences in attitude as the difference between scores 70 and 80. Thurstone's method, derived from psychophysical techniques, sought to arrange people on a continuous scale having equal-appearing units. Then, if Charles had a score midway between Alfred and Bill, one could say that his attitude was midway between the other two. Thurstone conceived of attitudes toward any object as being arranged on a single continuum, from highly favorable toward the object to highly unfavorable. An ideal scale would indicate just how favorable or unfavorable each subject is.

A Thurstone attitude scale consists of 20 or more statements representing all degrees of opinion. The subject indicates with which statements he agrees. Each statement has been assigned a scale value, ranging from 0.0 for the most extreme statement possible in an unfavorable direction, through 5.5 for neutral statements, to 11.0 for the most extremely favorable statement possible (33). Representative statements, with their scale values, from the scale for measuring attitude toward communism[1] are as follows:

Communism is the solution to our present economic problems (9.1).
Give Russia another twenty years or so and you'll see that communism can be made to work (8.4).
Workers can hardly be blamed for advocating communism (7.0).
Both the evils and benefits of communism are greatly exaggerated (5.4).
I am not sure that communism solves the problems of capital and labor (4.7).
If a man has the vision and the ability to acquire property, he ought to be allowed to enjoy it himself (3.3).
Police are justified in shooting down communists (0.3).

The score for the subject is the median scale value of the statements he checks.

In effect, the subject matches his opinion with the scale of opinions, select-

---

[1] Publisher: Univ. of Chicago Press.

ing his own position in the way that he might match a sample of gray paper with a series of samples ranging from black to white. This, at least, is the theory, but in practice few attitudes are as pure as the black-white continuum. As Murphy, Murphy, and Newcomb state (23, p. 897):

"No scale can really be called a scale unless one can tell from a given attitude that an individual will maintain *every* attitude falling to the right or to the left of that point (depending on how the scale is constructed). . . . If we have a genuine scale of attitudes toward compulsory military service, it is necessary to assume that every person favoring compulsory military service should also favor military service for persons conscientiously opposed to such service; the former proposition presupposes the latter. . . . As a matter of fact there is every reason to believe that none of the rather complex social attitudes . . . will ever conform to such rigorous measurement."

Guttman has developed a statistical theory for devising true scales, provided that the attitudes under study admit of such treatment (15). His method has so far had only limited application.

3. Interpret the following responses to the Thurstone scale on "attitude toward capital punishment." (Under the directions most often used, subjects check a larger number of statements than indicated here.)
   a. Mr. Adams checks statements with scale values 6.2, 7.2, 7.3.
   b. Mr. Brown checks statements with scale values 7.3, 8.4, 9.0, 9.4.
   c. Mr. Clark checks statements with scale values 5.3, 5.4, 5.7, 7.2.
   d. Mr. Dean checks statements with scale values 2.0, 6.2, 7.2, 7.3.
4. Prepare a set of seven statements reflecting approximately equally spaced positions along the attitude continuum for "traveling by commercial airlines" (as opposed to other modes of transportation).
5. Do the following constitute a true scale? "I favor no compulsory military training"; "I favor one year of compulsory military training"; "I favor two years of compulsory military training." Could a man logically favor two years of training but disapprove of one year of it?

There are three steps in Thurstone's technique of scaling: preparation of possible items, sorting by judges, and testing for relevance. Possible items are obtained by collecting opinions from writers and laymen reflecting all shades of belief. Each item is placed on a slip of paper. The entire pack of slips is then given to a judge who places the slips in eleven piles, ranging from one extreme to the other in approximately equal steps. This sorting is repeated by 50 or more judges. The equal intervals in the final scale are differences in attitude that appear equal to the judges. After a statement has been scaled by a number of judges, it is discarded if judges disagreed markedly in sorting it. For statements retained, the scale value is the median position assigned by the judges.

Statements chosen are now placed in a preliminary check list. This list is given to subjects as a means of checking the relevance of items. The method used resembles the internal-consistency test described on p. 78. The scores of those who check a given item are tabulated. If these persons generally have the attitude represented by the item, it is a good item. But if a favorable statement about communism is checked by many people whose general attitudes are unfavorable, the item does not measure the same factor as the rest of the test. The statement, "Communism has done many valuable things for the Russian people," might be checked by some who oppose communism. The statement perhaps measures "attitude toward communism for the Russians," where the rest of the scale emphasizes "attitude toward communism for this country." Items which are frequently checked by people whose attitude score is far from the scale value of the item are discarded. The final scale consists of items which have passed the tests for ambiguity and relevancy. Final items are selected to represent the entire range of attitudes.

Remmers has devised a generalized scale to avoid the labor of testing items each time a new scale is desired. He constructs a single scale for measuring "attitude toward any race" or "attitude toward any institution." Such statements as "This race has contributed a great deal to human progress," or "This race is no more deceitful than other people" can be scaled as usual. The resulting scale, with appropriate directions, measures attitude toward Germans, Chinese, or any other group. Substantially the same results are obtained with Remmers' scales as with scales constructed about a specific topic (26). Some of the generalized scales lead to absurdities when applied uncritically. One reviewer points out that the statement, "This institution does not consider individual differences," becomes meaningless when the institution being rated is marriage (21, p. 305).

Thurstone-type scales are reliable, with coefficients of equivalence generally near .85. This is quite high for such brief tests. Subjects are consistent in their self-reports. This consistency is present even when the specific statements are changed from form to form.

Stability of scores is not so high. Corey found that college students, retested after one year, changed in score considerably. The correlations between first and second test ranged for .28 to .61 (median .49). Coefficients of equivalence (split-half) for the first testing were between .35 and .82 (median .71) (8).

6. The split-half coefficients reported by Corey are much smaller than those found by other workers for the same scales. What factors might account for this?
7. If a test validly measures attitudes, should scores obtained a year apart have high correlations?

The Likert Technique

The Likert procedure for constructing attitude tests is increasing in use. The Likert-type scale resembles simple questionnaires, except that more refined techniques of item selection improve the instrument (19). Each scale is a series of statements, ranging from as few as 18 items to as many as 200. Each statement in a Likert scale is either definitely favorable or definitely unfavorable to the object of the scale. The subject indicates his reaction to each statement, usually on a five-point scale: strongly agree, agree, undecided, disagree, strongly disagree. These answers are credited 5, 4, 3, 2, and 1, respectively, for favorable statements; and 1, 2, 3, 4, and 5, respectively, for unfavorable statements. A favorable attitude is shown in a high score. Scores are interpreted on a relative basis since there is no absolute system of units such as Thurstone's.

The first step in the Likert procedure is the collection of possible statements. These are administered as a trial test to many subjects. These papers are scored and each item is correlated with the total test. If an item is not correlated with the total scale, it is discarded. This internal-consistency procedure eliminates ambiguous items and those not of the same type as the rest of the scale.

One widely known Likert-pattern scale is the Minnesota Survey of Opinion (which is *not* an opinion survey of the type described on p. 368). This is a set of six scales devised to study morale during the depression of the 1930's (28). Each statement in the scale reflects an optimistic or pessimistic outlook, the separate sections dealing with morale, inferiority feelings, family adjustment, attitude toward the law, economic conservatism, and attitude toward education. Items from the respective scales include:

SA A U D SD   It is difficult to think clearly these days.
SA A U D SD   It is difficult to say the right thing at the right time.
SA A U D SD   A man should be willing to sacrifice everything for his family.
SA A U D SD   A person should obey only those laws which seem reasonable.
SA A U D SD   Legislatures are too ready to pass laws to curb business freedom.
SA A U D SD   A man can learn more by working four years than by going to high school.

The coefficients of equivalence of the scales ranged from .79 to .85. Darley found that the coefficients of stability were lower—around .60 when the tests were given about nine months apart (10).

Several sets of tests have dealt with conservative-liberal opinions on prominent issues. The Scale of Beliefs of the Progressive Education Association measures high-school students' reactions to issues dealing with labor, economic policies, race, nationalism, militarism, and democratic practices (29, pp. 203–244). These scales had coefficients of equivalence (Kuder-Richardson) ranging from .79 to .86 for high-school groups, with a coefficient of .95 for the total Liberalism score. The Scale of Beliefs includes a device for measuring the consistency of attitudes. Each liberal statement in the test deals with the same issue as one conservative statement elsewhere in the test. One such pair is:

A U D   We should buy foreign products only when American goods are not available.
A U D   In this day of economic interdependence, it is desirable that we buy goods from other nations.

The Consistency score is the total number of times the student gives the same answer (i.e., consistently liberal or consistently conservative) on both items of a pair. A low Consistency score is found when responses are influenced by plausibility and appeal of verbal symbols rather than by well-formulated and consistent beliefs. Like other investigations, work with the Scale of Beliefs indicates that conservatism on one problem is highly correlated with conservatism regarding other issues.

Comparison of Testing Techniques

Several studies have tried to establish the comparative merits of the Thurstone and Likert techniques. Since corresponding scales of the two types have high correlations, there is little difference except in convenience. For most purposes, it matters little which method is used. In one study, comparable scales were constructed by both techniques. The correlation between them was as high as .92, which shows them to be practically interchangeable (12).

The time required to construct a Thurstone-type scale is a drawback. Careful construction of a Likert-type scale requires about half the time needed for the Thurstone procedure (12).

The two scales have established comparable reliabilities. Likert and others found that Thurstone scales yielded substantially higher reliabilities when rescored by the Likert method. For several scales and several groups, the Thurstone scales had split-half coefficients from .42 to .87, but when rescored with the Likert procedure the coefficients ranged from .67 to .95 (20). There is no evidence, however, that this higher reliability produces higher validity.

The factors which make for invalid self-report are equally present in both tests. The Likert method permits response sets to influence the score, which might lower validity. Where directions for the Thurstone scale require one to check, say, the six statements with which he most agrees, no response sets affect the score.

The Likert test is more diagnostic than the Thurstone method. Every subject responds to every item, so that item analysis gives a picture of reactions to specific issues. In scales measuring morale, several investigators have made item analyses to show just what hopes and fears were most common in particular groups (6, 9).

8. What advantages and disadvantages would you expect from directions, on Thurstone scale, to check each opinion statement "yes" or "no," rather than marking just the six statements one most accepts?
9. List the response sets to which the Likert method is susceptible.
10. Do reliability coefficients for attitude scales appear to be high enough for the uses to which they are most often put?

Other Techniques

Some instruments have sought to get beneath verbal abstractions by asking the subject what he would do in a particular case (24). Thus, in 1940, one

Fig. 79.   Photographs used to measure prejudice against Negroes (16).

investigation asked subjects what they would do to encourage war if Hawaii or California were threatened by an enemy (1). These predictions were thought to be a better reflection of tendency to act than mere expressions for or against war in the abstract.

Horowitz departed from the purely verbal method by presenting photographs of pleasant boys, both white and Negro. He used such directions as: "Pick out the one you like best, next best, etc. Show me all those that you want to sit next to you on a street car." The test appears to obtain more discriminating reactions from boys than verbal instruments where they respond to general symbols (16). Expressions of approval or disapproval of pictured incidents (race riots, fights between strikers and police) were used in another study to measure reactions to real events rather than verbal labels (22).

Bogardus' "social distance" method has been used to study race preferences. The subject shows the distance at which he keeps the race by stating whether he approves their entering his country, entering his vocation, and so on up the scale to marrying into his family (4). The method is primarily of value for measuring group differences rather than for obtaining reliable individual scores.

A particularly sound technique, the paired-comparison method, has received less use than it deserves. The subject is confronted with paired terms, such as Germans-Italians, French-Russians, Germans-Swedes, etc., each term being paired with another term. The subject marks the preferred member of each pair. From these judgments, one can reconstruct with great reliability the rank order of nationality preferences and can determine a scale value or acceptance score for each group (32). Typical results from the method are shown in Figure 80. Paired comparisons have the advantages of being precise, free from response sets, and relatively hard to falsify, since each item demands a response. The weaknesses of the method are that it is time-consuming, and it does not measure what each person believes about each stimulus, as it measures relative preferences only. For example, if a certain course made men more tolerant of all races, the paired-comparison technique might show no change in ranks of particular races. Suitable adaptation of the method might overcome this difficulty. The possibility of studying relations between competing attitudes seems promising. Attitude to universal military training might be studied more fruitfully than the usual scale permits, if subjects indicated their choice between u.m.t. and lowered taxes, u.m.t. and an additional year of college for qualified youth, u.m.t. and an expanded standing army, etc.

PROBLEMS OF ATTITUDE TESTING

Validity

Attitude tests have been severely criticized because they have been used without their validity having been established (21). The failure to demonstrate that they are valid measures of belief is in part due to the difficulty of finding criteria. Attitude tests were designed, not to replace less convenient ways of measuring attitudes, but to fill the need for any sort of measuring device. We know little about a man's attitude except what he tells us, so that there is no sure way of comparing his self-report, his "public" attitude, with his true private beliefs.

Some investigators have limited their purpose to determining the subject's publicly verbalized opinions. If that is the purpose of measurement, the self-report test has, by definition, a high degree of validity.

To determine whether verbal expressions of attitude are honest and "real," it is necessary to compare them with outside criteria. That they have some relation to behavior is shown by comparison of test scores of groups having known attitudes. Thurstone and Chave determined the test scores of church members and non-church members, with the results shown in Table 65. If what people do reflects their beliefs, the attitude test measures belief in the church. But even if a test is valid in comparing groups, scores of individuals may not all be valid. Just as there are hypocrites who profess socially approved opinions, there are those who join groups even though they do not believe in the objectives of the groups. Such a person might praise prohibition and join a temperance organization, while privately drinking, and owning distillery stock.

11. Some church members, according to Thurstone's data, have less favorable attitudes toward the church than some non-churchgoers. Is this possible if statements on the attitude scale represent true private attitudes?
12. Outline a procedure for testing the validity of a scale to measure attitude toward college fraternities, by comparing groups whose probable attitude is known.
13. Do the same for a scale intended to measure attitude toward chain stores.

Table 65. Percentage Distributions of Scores on Thurstone-Chave Scale for Selected Groups (33)

Attitude	Score	Divinity Students (N = 103)	Attend Church Frequently (N = 678)	Do Not Attend Church Frequently (N = 692)	Active Church Members (N = 581)	Not Active Church Members (N = 781)
Favorable	0–1	—	—	—	—	—
	1–2	17	18	1	18	2
	2–3	50	42	6	42	10
	3–4	23	23	11	20	14
	4–5	5	10	14	10	14
Neutral	5–6	4	4	17	6	14
	6–7	1	2	21	3	18
	7–8	—	1	14	1	15
	8–9	—	1	12	—	11
	9–10	—	—	3	—	3
Antagonistic	10–11	—	—	—	—	—

Stouffer validated a Thurstone-type scale on prohibition in 1929 by obtaining 238 autobiographies from college students. The case history included self-reports on significant experiences with drinking. The agreement between test scores and judges' ratings of attitude from the case histories was very high, the correlation being .81 (.86 when corrected for unreliability of judges) (31).

The Scale of Beliefs was validated by comparing it with teachers' judgments of pupils. Agreement was claimed in 90 percent of the cases (29, p. 227). Similar agreement was reported between the test and careful studies of 18 pupils through interviews and records of points of view expressed in classwork. Evidently the tests do represent fairly the public, verbal opinions of students.

A more penetrating attack upon the validity of attitude expressions studies the behavior of subjects. If one's attitude is his tendency to react favorably or unfavorably to an attitude object, a valid test should predict his reactions. Reactions are difficult to observe. They, too, are influenced by the desire to make a good impression on others. For many attitude objects, there are few daily circumstances where one can act out his attitudes.

One of the successful attempts to measure actual behavior was Corey's study of attitude toward cheating (7). A college psychology class took a Thurstone-type scale regarding cheating, which was unsigned but secretly identified by the instructor. The group stated that they approved of honesty. Actual behavior was then studied experimentally. A regular course examination was given each Friday. On Monday, papers were distributed to their owners to be graded in class. There was ample opportunity to change answers while scoring. Cheating was measured by comparing the score after class correction with a score recorded secretly by the instructor before returning the papers. Under these conditions cheating was found, despite the professed attitude. There was a correlation of only .02 between attitude and actual amount of cheating.

LaPiere's findings on verbal attitudes and behavior were similarly negative. Traveling with two Chinese companions, he found them refused service in hotels, restaurants, and auto camps only once in 251 times. Six months later he questioned each establishment by mail as to its policy. Over 90 percent of the respondents said that they would not serve Chinese. Says LaPiere, "Those factors which most influenced the behavior of others toward the Chinese had nothing to do with race. Quality and condition of clothing, appearance of baggage, cleanliness and neatness were far more significant for person to person reaction in the situations I was studying than skin pigmentation, straight black hair, slanting eyes, and flat noses" (17, p. 232).

These findings indicate that it is necessary to be skeptical of self-report attitude scales. They are useful only when one emphasizes that they represent publicly stated reactions to symbols. Such opinions are often important, especially if a group or individual states socially disapproved opinions. For example, a high-school teacher should try to increase the tolerance of a class professing intolerance. On the other hand, one could not conclude that a group giving "tolerant" answers was free from prejudice. An interviewer finds that uneducated adults report more premarital intercourse than educated adults; this does not prove that their conduct is different privately, but it does show a difference in the standards they apply in deciding what to tell. Shifts in overt verbal attitudes are important. If racial prejudice scores rise, this may be a mere bringing to the surface of antagonisms already present. But the fact that this antagonism is expressed or repressed shows significant social change.

Attitude tests are most likely to be valid when the subject has no motive to conceal his attitude. Attitude objects toward which there is no "right" behavior are more likely to elicit truthful self-report than those which involve prestige and group approval. The conditions of testing may affect responses, as shown by an experiment of Robinson and Rohde (27). They used the single-question interview, sometimes with non-Jewish and sometimes with identifiably Jewish interviewers. To the question, "Do you think the Jews have too much power?" percentage of "yes" responses was as follows:

With non-Jewish interviewer	24.3%
With Jewish interviewer	15.6%
With Jewish interviewer, using Jewish name	5.8%
With non-Jewish interviewer, non-Jewish name	21.4%

A significant limitation peculiar to attitude tests is that they readily become obsolete. Social issues change, and opinions that are radical in one generation become conventional in another. Statements may take on new meaning with changing events, even when the words remain unaltered. Thus, reactions to a scale regarding censorship no doubt change when public controversy centers around "subversive" books and movies, rather than around "obscenity." Certainly an old attitude scale must be scrutinized with care before use. Statements must be checked for obsoleteness, and the key must be checked to make sure that opinions once thought "liberal" are still so classifiable. Even with the Thurstone judging procedure, the scale value of items on attitude toward war changed markedly from 1930 to 1940 (13).

14. In Corey's study, what factors prevent one from assuming that amount of change in score is a completely valid measure of attitude on cheating?
15. What conclusions are warranted by each of the following findings?
    a. After a course in philosophy of education, a class of prospective teachers is much more favorable to "democratic classroom practices" than at the beginning of the course.
    b. Pupils in school A have a higher average score than pupils in school B, on a scale measuring the extent to which pupils feel that they are treated fairly by their teachers.
16. Would you expect true or false self-reports on a signed attitude test dealing with each of the following topics?
    a. Child-rearing practices.
    b. Tax reduction.
    c. Racial segregation.

Intensity of Attitude

Attitude scales do not show the intensity with which people hold a favorable or unfavorable opinion. Three people may show the same critical attitude toward communism. One may have chosen that opinion after little thinking and information and be open to conviction in either direction by any new argument. The second person may have reached the same opinion after careful study and may be difficult to convert to any other attitude. The third opinion may be based on conditioning and intense emotion. The only device so far used to measure intensity has been to ask subjects how strongly they believe a given opinion. There is no evidence that such statements are valid.

Neutral scores on scales have been difficult to interpret. If a person's score falls midway between the two extremes he may be unacquainted with the attitude object, he may be genuinely indifferent, or he may have conflicting feelings for and against which cancel out on the scale. As in personality tests, extreme scores are likely to be meaningful, whereas all we can say about a person falling near the middle of the scale is that his beliefs are not consistently extreme.

Complexity of Attitude Objects

A persistent problem in attitude testing is definition of the attitude object. The scale is best considered as measuring response to a verbal symbol, rather than to what the symbol stands for. Stagner tested attitude toward fascist practices in a test where the word "fascism" was not mentioned. Persons quite unfavorable to the symbol "fascism" were willing to endorse principles enunciated by Hitler and Mussolini. Stagner therefore considers the usual scale, in which the attitude object is overtly named, as merely a measure of verbal conditionings to the stereotyped meaning of the word used (30).

In real life, on the contrary, behavior is not based on verbal labels, as this comment shows (18): "The question 'What would you do if you met your friend Wang Chi, the Chinese, dressed in his best and beaming with good humor, on the corner of Sacramento Street and Grant Avenue, the day before New Year, when you were alone and in no hurry?' might constitute a symbolization of an actual situation. The question, typical of 'attitudinal' questionnaires, 'Do you consider that Chinese make good American citizens?' presents a vague symbolization of an exceedingly vague situational abstraction. What is a Chinese? What is an American citizen? What is good?"

Attitudes toward general concepts may not extend to specific instances. Inconsistency of attitudes is shown when those who orate about "freedom of speech" attempt to restrict certain groups which they consider subversive. Attitude scales rarely measure attitudes toward specific objects; rather, they concern "education," "the church," or "labor unions." Yet one is likely to react differently toward different churches or different unions. One can, in Thurstone's scale, react to the church in terms of its influence on society, in terms of the logic of its theology, in terms of its satisfyingness as a social center, and so on. A person may approve the social influence of the church and enjoy it as a social meeting place, without himself believing in religion. A deeply religious person might have doubts about some social practices of the church. It would be unwieldy to construct separate scales for each aspect of an attitude object. The justification for grouping many aspects is the statistical tendency for attitudes toward the various aspects to be similar. One cannot reason from a general attitude that an individual holds the same opinion regarding all phases of the attitude object.

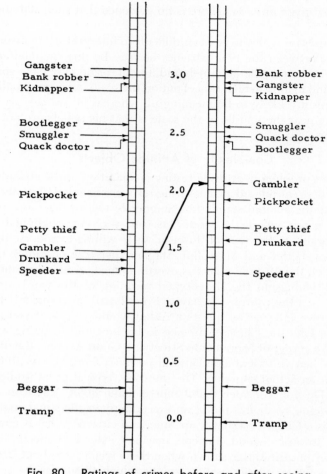

Fig. 80. Ratings of crimes before and after seeing
the movie "Streets of Chance" (25).

In studies of morale in particular, one must be wary of placing too much emphasis on general level of score. Such composite scores conceal variations in morale regarding specific aspects of the situation. A worker may have quite different attitudes toward the work itself, his foreman, opportunity for promotion, management, etc. (14). In wartime, morale regarding the chances of victory may be high; at the same time morale may be low regarding the effect of the war on the standard of living, or one's danger as a civilian from enemy bombing (19). Diagnostic morale scales are needed for full insight into significant grievances, anxieties, and sources of satisfaction.

17. From the statements listed on page 369, what aspects are included in the scale measuring attitude toward communism?

18. Show that a person could, without contradicting himself, mark statements having quite different scale values in the communism scale.
19. Show that "attitude toward compulsory military training" may be considered as a composite of reactions to many more specific attitude objects.

APPLICATIONS OF ATTITUDE TESTS

If attitude tests were completely valid indices of belief, they would have great practical significance. A typical practical question where a measure of true private attitudes would have untold value is in monitoring the new education program in Germany and Japan to determine if democracy is really being learned. In the absence of unqualified validity, many investiga-

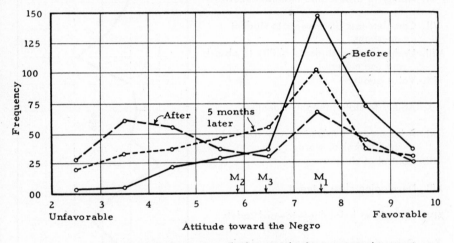

Fig. 81.   Attitudes toward Negroes before and after seeing the movie
Birth of a Nation (**25**).

tors have nevertheless applied attitude scales to research on the professed attitudes of pupils, voters, and workers.

Much attention has been given to determining how attitudes can be changed. One series of studies investigated the influence of motion pictures upon attitudes of youth (25). A typical finding was that after seeing a motion picture "Street of Chance" students ranked gambling a more serious crime, as shown in Figure 80. The effect of seeing "Birth of a Nation" on attitudes toward the Negro was also marked (Fig. 81).[2] Other studies of attitudes have proved definitely that appropriate educational procedures produce marked shifts (23, pp. 946 ff.).

In schools, attitude scales have been used for evaluation, particularly in the field of citizenship education. A major purpose of teaching is to form

[2] Figs. 80 and 81 from Peterson and Thurstone, *Motion pictures and the social attitudes of children.* Copyright, 1933, by The Macmillan Company and used with their permission.

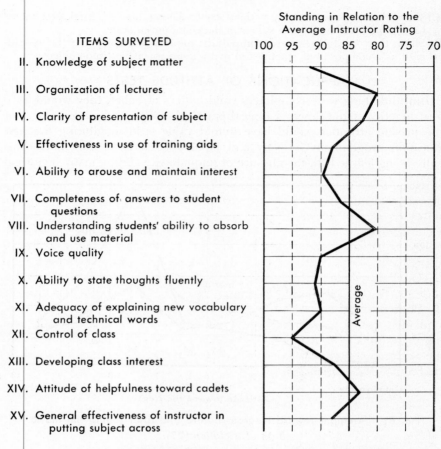

Fig. 82.   Profile chart for a navigation instructor (5, p. 100).

attitudes: appreciation of literature, scientific open-mindedness toward debatable questions, or interracial tolerance. The school must measure these attitudes if it wishes to be sure it is accomplishing its purpose. Testing of attitudes draws attention to individuals with undesired attitudes, so that special effort can be made to change them. Attitude tests also direct the pupil's attention to the fact that the school is concerned with more than factual learnings.

Attitude tests are effectively used in civilian and military schools to determine students' opinions on the training. The AAF navigation training program devised a Survey of Student Opinions covering many aspects of the training. Scores could be compared from instructor to instructor and from month to month, calling attention to weak points in the program (5, pp. 97, 168 ff.). Such information can be very constructive when used as a basis for self-improvement but is damaging to instructor morale when it brings criticism from his superiors or a threat of discharge.

In industry, scales measuring attitude toward the job have been applied to compare plants, departments, and groups of workers (3). Items from a scale by Bergen include the following (scale values in parentheses) (2):

On the whole, the company treats us about as well as we deserve (6.6).
In my job I don't get any chance to use my experience (3.2).
I think the company's policy is to pay employees just as little as it can get away with (0.8).

Such surveys are especially helpful if they are made the basis for correcting sore spots. Item analysis of the questionnaire is a starting point toward noting grievances, and interviewing employees often gives further insight into causes of dissatisfaction. Morale-measuring techniques are most helpful when representatives of the workers have a hand in planning the investigation.

Attitude scales have been adapted to studies of morale. The effect of the depression upon the confidence and optimism of adults was studied by Rundquist and Sletto (28). Similar measures were used to study the development of morale during wartime by a number of investigators. Attempts were made to identify the background factors related to good and poor morale. The general finding was that age, sex, occupation, and racial background were less effective in determining morale than the emotional adjustment of the person to his individual hardships (6, 9).

SUGGESTED READINGS

Briggs, T. H, and others. *The emotionalized attitudes.* New York: Teachers Col., Columbia Univ., 1940.

Newcomb, Theodore M. "Problems of method and validity," in Murphy, Gardner, and others, *Experimental social psychology.* New York: Harper, rev. ed., 1937, pp. 889–912.

Stagner, Ross, "Attitudes," in Monroe, W. S. (ed.), *Encyclopaedia of educational research.* New York: Macmillan, 1941, pp. 69–75.

Tiffin, Joseph. "Attitudes and morale," in *Industrial psychology.* New York: Prentice-Hall, 2nd ed., 1947, pp. 455–479.

REFERENCES

1. Allport, F. H., and Hanchett, Gertrude A. "The war-producing behavior of citizens." *J. soc. Psychol.,* 1940, 11, 447–490.
2. Bergen, Harold B. "Finding out what employees are thinking." *Conference Board Management Record,* April, 1939.
3. Bergen, Harold, and Harris, C. E. "Employer-employee relations in the office." *American Manufacturers' Association, Management Series,* 1939, No. 89, pp. 3–21.
4. Bogardus, E. L. "A social distance scale." *Sociol. and soc. Res.,* 1933, 17, 265–271.

5. Carter, Launor F. (ed.). *Psychological research on navigator training*. AAF Aviation Psychol. Prog. Res. Rep. No. 10. Washington: Govt. Printing Off., 1947.
6. Conrad, H. S., and Sanford, R. N. "Some specific war-attitudes of college students." *J. Psychol.*, 1944, 17, 153–186.
7. Corey, Stephen M. "Professed attitudes and actual behavior." *J. educ. Psychol.*, 1937, 28, 271–280.
8. Corey, Stephen M. "Changes in the opinions of female students after one year at a university." *J. soc. Psychol.*, 1940, 11, 341–351.
9. Cronbach, Lee J. "Exploring the wartime morale of high school youth." *Appl. Psychol. Monogr.*, 1943, No. 1.
10. Darley, J. G. "Changes in measured attitudes and adjustments." *J. soc. Psychol.*, 1938, 9, 189–199.
11. Edwards, Allen L. "A critique of 'neutral' items in attitude scales constructed by the method of equal appearing intervals." *Psychol. Rev.*, 1946, 53, 159–169.
12. Edwards, Allen L., and Kenney, Kathryn C. "A comparison of the Thurstone and Likert techniques of attitude scale construction." *J. appl. Psychol.*, 1946, 30, 72–83.
13. Farnsworth, Paul R. "Shifts in the values of opinion items." *J. Psychol.*, 1943, 16, 125–128.
14. Geiger, H. E., and others. "Apprentices' attitudes toward their training and the construction of a diagnostic scale." *J. appl. Psychol.*, 1938, 22, 32–41.
15. Guttman, Louis, "A basis for scaling qualitative data." *Amer. sociol. Rev.*, 1944, 9, 139–150.
16. Horowitz, E. L. "The development of attitude toward the Negro." *Arch. Psychol.*, 1936, 28, No. 194.
17. LaPiere, R. T. "Attitudes vs. actions." *Social Forces*, 1934, 13, 230–237.
18. LaPiere, R. T. "The sociological significance of measurable attitudes." *Amer. sociol. Rev.*, 1938, 3, 175–182.
19. Likert, Rensis. "A technique for the measurement of attitudes." *Arch. Psychol.*, 1932, 22, No. 140.
20. Likert, Rensis, and others. "A simple and reliable method of scoring the Thurstone attitude scales." *J. soc. Psychol.*, 1934, 5, 228–238.
21. McNemar, Quinn. "Opinion-attitude methodology." *Psychol. Bull.*, 1946, 43, 289–374.
22. Murphy, Gardner, and Likert, Rensis. *Public opinion and the individual*. New York: Harper, 1938.
23. Murphy, Gardner, and others. *Experimental social psychology*. New York: Harper, rev. ed., 1937.
24. Pace, C. R. "A situations test to measure social-political-economic attitudes." *J. soc. Psychol.*, 1939, 10, 331–344.
25. Peterson, Ruth C., and Thurstone, L. L. *Motion pictures and the social attitudes of children*. New York: Macmillan, 1933.
26. Remmers, H. H. "Generalized attitude scales—studies in social-psychological measurements," in *Studies in higher education*, 26. Lafayette, Ind.: Purdue Univ., 1934, pp. 7–17.
27. Robinson, Duane, and Rohde, Sylvia. "Two experiments with an anti-Semitism poll." *J. abnorm. soc. Psychol.*, 1946, 41, 136–144.
28. Rundquist, E. A., and Sletto, R. F. *Personality in the depression*. Minneapolis: Univ. of Minnesota Press, 1936.
29. Smith, Eugene R., Tyler, Ralph W., and others. *Appraising and recording student progress*. New York: Harper, 1942.

30. Stagner, Ross. "Fascist attitudes: their determining conditions." *J. soc. Psychol.*, 1936, 7, 438–454.
31. Stouffer, Samuel A. An experimental comparison of statistical and case history methods of attitude research. Unpublished Doctor's thesis, Univ. of Chicago, 1930.
32. Thurstone, L. L. "The method of paired comparison for social values." *J. abnorm. soc. Psychol.*, 1927, 21, 384–400.
33. Thurstone, L. L., and Chave, E. J. *The measurement of attitude.* Chicago: Univ. of Chicago Press, 1929.

CHAPTER 18

Observation of Behavior in Normal Situations

The preceding chapter concluded the discussion of self-report techniques. In the present chapter and the two following, attention is shifted to determination of typical behavior by direct observation. Observation methods can be highly valid when proper precautions are taken, but adequate observation is difficult and laborious. In the present chapter, we consider methods of obtaining data by observing the subject in such natural situations as school, playground, and shop.

Observation in normal or field conditions and observations in test situations, to be considered later, are distinguished in terms of whether we provide fixed test stimuli to which the subject responds. Field observations are often relied on merely because data of this type are readily obtainable. There are times, however, when they are used in preference to more standardized procedures and test stimuli. Many investigators feel that it is impossible to know personality unless we watch the subject react to the conditions that are most significant for him. Yet different stimuli provoke the most revealing behavior for different people. Test situations, unless unusually fortunate in their choice of stimuli, are not as likely to demonstrate the important behavior patterns of all subjects as are the normal conditions under which they live. The difficulty lies in seeing enough of the person's normal behavior, and of obtaining dependable records of that behavior.

DIFFICULTIES OF FIELD OBSERVATION

Sampling Error

Whenever one wishes to know the typical behavior of an employee, a student, or a patient, the most direct way to find out is to observe him in normal situations. If he does not know that we are watching him, we obtain a truthful picture of his characteristics, limited only by our skill as observers. This is our usual basis for judging associates and friends. Judgments based upon observation, however, are likely to be completely untrustworthy owing to sampling errors and observer errors.

To know the "typical" behavior of an individual, it is necessary to know how he characteristically acts in a particular situation. But situations change from day to day, and from moment to moment. If we observe the attentiveness of an employee before lunch, we may get a different impression from the one we get if we observe in midafternoon. If we observe cheerfulness or politeness when he is worried, our impression may be unfair. The only way to be even moderately certain that the behavior is typical is to study the subject on many occasions of the type about which we wish to generalize. This is usually expensive, and one cannot acquire a fair picture in a short time. In practice, it is usual to compromise between perfect sampling and economy.

A second difficulty of inference about individual differences arises from the fact that one can never observe two individuals in the same situation. Even when the situation is externally similar, previous conditions cause people to behave differently. Two children, side by side in a classroom, are exposed to much the same stimuli. When Jimmy fidgets more than John, one is likely to infer that Jimmy is "restless," "nervous," or "jumpy." If that impression is confirmed by repeated observations, one might be tempted to consider this difference in behavior fundamental. But if Jimmy usually comes to school without breakfast, if he expects to be criticized by the teacher for poor work, or if he is large for the chairs provided, the difference in activity may tell nothing about the boys' basic restlessness. In fact, if conditions were reversed, Johnny might be more restless than Jimmy is now. At best, comparative observations show how different people act under their present conditions but do not guarantee that these differences would persist if background conditions changed.

Observer Error

Whenever a person observes an event, he notices some happenings and ignores others. This is a necessary difficulty, since any activity has too many aspects for the human mind to attend to at once. Especially in social situations, where behavior observations are most needed, the complexity of interaction prevents exhaustive reporting. If errors in observing were merely random omissions, they would be unimportant. But observers make systematic errors, overemphasizing some types of happenings and failing to report other types.

Viewing the identical scene, observers give widely different reports. The following reports were written by four observers, each of whom saw the same motion-picture scene of about ten minutes' duration (from the film "This Is Robert"). The scene was shown twice without sound, and they were directed to note everything they could about one boy, Robert. The scene, in a first-grade classroom, showed several activities which revealed much of Robert's personality. Numbers in these accounts, referring to scenes in the film, were inserted in order to permit comparison of different accounts. Parentheses are a device used by the observers to set apart any inferences or interpretations.

Observer A: (2) Robert reads word by word, using finger to follow place. (4) Observes girl in box with much preoccupation. (5) During singing, he in general doesn't participate too actively. Interest is part of time centered elsewhere. Appears to respond most actively to sections of song involving action. Has tendency for seemingly meaningless movement. Twitching of fingers, aimless thrusts with arms.

Observer B: (1) Looked at camera upon entering (seemed perplexed and interested). Smiled at camera. (2) Reads (with apparent interest and with a fair degree of facility). (3) Active in roughhouse play with girls. (4) Upon being kicked (unintentionally) by one girl he responded (angrily). (5) Talked with girl sitting next to him between singing periods. Participated in singing. (At times appeared enthusiastic.) Didn't always sing with others. (6) Participated in a dispute in a game with others (appeared to stand up for his own rights). Aggressive behavior toward another boy. Turned pockets inside out while talking to teacher and other students. (7) Put on overshoes without assistance. Climbed to top of ladder rungs. Tried to get rung which was occupied by a girl but since she didn't give in, contented himself with another place.

Observer C: (1) Smiles into camera (curious). When group breaks up, he makes nervous gestures, throws arm out into air. (2) Attention to reading lesson. Reads with serious look on his face, has to use line marker. (3) Chases girls, teases. (4) Girl kicks when he puts hand on her leg. Robert makes face at her. (5) Singing. Sits with mouth open, knocks knees together, scratches leg, puts fingers in mouth (seems to have several nervous habits, though not emotionally overwrought or self-conscious). (6) In a dispute over parchesi, he stands up for his rights. (7) Short dispute because he wants rung on jungle gym.

Observer D: (2) Uses guide to follow words, reads slowly, fairly forced and with careful formation of sounds (perhaps unsure of self and fearful of mistakes). (3) Perhaps slightly aggressive as evidence by pushing younger child to side when moving from a position to another. Plays with other children with obvious enjoyment, smiles, runs, seems especially associated with girls. This is noticeable in games and in seating in singing. (5) Takes little interest in singing, fidgets, moves hands and legs (perhaps shy and nervous). Seems in song to be unfamiliar with words of main part, and shows disinterest by fidgeting and twisting around. Not until chorus is reached does he pick up interest. His especial friend seems to be a particular girl, as he is always seated by her.

1. What do you think really happened in scene (4)? Which observer came closest to adequate reporting of it?
2. Which of the numbered scenes appears to give the most significant information about Robert? How many of the observers reported that information?
3. To what extent have the observers succeeded in identifying and marking all their judgments and hypotheses?
4. Do the observers ever disagree, or are the differences entirely due to omissions and oversights?

All observers tend to be biased witnesses. The foreman, for example, is more likely to note an error made by a worker of whom he is critical than the same error made by one of his favorites. It is usual for us to form impressions of those we meet, so that we would willingly describe them if asked to. Having made a judgment, we are then prone to note and remember those events which support that judgment.

Every observer is more sensitive to some types of behavior than others. How does he regard nail biting, failure to look one in the eye, or profanity? If he considers these significant, he will be careful to note them and base his impression on them. In the same situation, another observer might give greatest attention to voice modulation, careful use of grammar, or friendliness of conversation. Ideally, an observer would base his impression on every revealing act, but when he is looking for one thing, he necessarily overlooks something else. One famous psychologist used to demonstrate this to his classes by requiring them to attempt to report "everything" he did in a short period. He then ostentatiously lifted a piece of apparatus above his head and manipulated it. The class, observing, always failed to report that during this process his "idle" hand unbuttoned his coat, removed his watch and laid it on the table, and took a cigarette from his case.

Observers interpret what they see. If they recorded only objective facts, others studying the data might reach quite different interpretations. Since people always try to give meanings to what they see, they find it difficult to avoid assuming meanings which may be untrue. Some time ago, the writer fell victim of this error in the following way. While lecturing to a new class, he noted repeatedly one student shaking his head from side to side. This, apparently coming just at the end of an explanation, caused the writer to restate his material, attempting to be more clear. With luck, there would be no head-shaking, and the instructor would go on to another point, but time after time the head-shaking appeared, causing him to go back over material, attempting to remove whatever confusion was causing the student to disagree so constantly. After two sessions of this backing and filling, the head-shaker came to the instructor after class to explain that he was not disagreeing, but was afflicted with an uncontrollable nervous tremor. Knowing this, the writer later noticed that the head-shaking was present many times when it could not be interpreted as a sign of disagreement. When we make an interpretation, we tend to overlook facts which do not fit the interpretation, and may even invent facts needed to complete the event as we interpreted it.

All observer errors are heightened when memory is permitted to operate. We tend to remember things which fit our impressions and biases, and events which are dramatic, but we forget many events that did not impress us deeply. In most non-scientific work, opinions of people are based on memory rather than careful records. When a vacancy occurs the boss promotes the worker whom he remembers as showing the best qualities. Another worker, who performed equally well, may not be recalled as favorably. Errors of memory even distort reports of characteristics such as height and punctuality which can be observed objectively.

5. A clinical psychologist asks a parent how well his six-year-old child gets along with other children. Illustrate how each of the following errors might operate.
   a. The observer has not observed an adequate sample for judging typical behavior.

b. The observer notices events which fit his preconceived notions.
c. The observer is most likely to note the behaviors he considers significant, and to ignore others of equal importance.
d. The observer may give a faulty interpretation to an event.

REDUCING ERRORS OF OBSERVATION

Time Sampling

If observations are made only as opportunity suggests, there is a strong probability of faulty sampling. One of the best ways of obtaining data which permit precise comparison of different individuals is time sampling. In time sampling, a set schedule of observations is planned in advance. Since it is usually not possible to observe every subject at the same time, the schedule is randomized so that each subject is seen under comparable conditions. In one study of social contacts of preschool children, for example, a schedule of one-minute observations was drawn up. After the observer watched a child for one minute, noting all social interaction, he wrote down a full record. Chil-

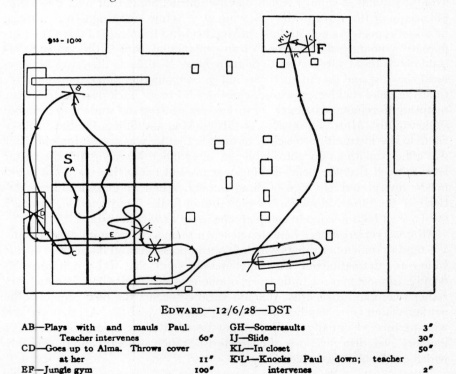

EDWARD—12/6/28—DST

AB—Plays with and mauls Paul.		GH—Somersaults	3″
Teacher intervenes	60″	IJ—Slide	30″
CD—Goes up to Alma. Throws cover		KL—In closet	50″
at her	11″	K¹L¹—Knocks Paul down; teacher	
EF—Jungle gym	100″	intervenes	2″

Fig. 83. Record obtained in a five-minute observation of a preschool child (31, p. 43). The diagram shows the nursery school play yard and traces Edward's movements. Letters mark the start and finish of each activity.

dren were watched in a predetermined order, which was altered from day to day. During the study, each child was observed an equal number of times during the first five minutes of the free-play hour, during the second five minutes, and so on (5, pp. 509–525).

The advantages of short, well-distributed time samples is that the cumulative picture is likely to be far more typical than an equal amount of evidence obtained in a few longer observations. Moreover, errors of memory are reduced, since the observer can make full notes during or just after observing. Time samples are especially suitable for recording specific facts that can be expressed numerically, such as the number of social contacts between children. A slightly more elaborate record shows the complete activity pattern during the observation period. The record shown in Figure 83 reports the behavior of Edward during a five-minute period. It indicates what he did, for how long, and where.

6. Why might an unfair picture of a child's behavior be obtained if he were always observed during the first five minutes of the play period and never during the second five minutes?
7. What sorts of information about Edward's personality could be obtained from a cumulation of records such as Figure 83?
8. What sorts of information about Edward's behavior are discarded, in making an objective record such as Figure 83?

Photographic and Phonographic Recording

Many of the errors in observing have been minimized by replacing the human observer. Unlike a human observer, mechanical recording devices can record several events occurring simultaneously, can watch several people at once, and can remain "on the job" continuously for as long as needed. A motion-picture camera sees virtually everything the eye can observe, and records it with no significant error. Sound recording under adequate acoustic conditions can fix for later reference all the conversation and other sounds the observer would notice. Recording therefore eliminates need for an expert observer at the scene of action.

Because the record notes, within limits, everything that happens, it is especially valuable in noting significant facts that an observer might miss. Events that seem trivial when they happen may become important in the light of later events. Thus, an observer is often puzzled when a subject loses his temper or behaves erratically for no apparent cause. A record permits one to retrace the preceding events to detect probable causes.

Recording has limited use because it is expensive, but it will probably become more feasible as technical improvements are made. Recent devlopments have reduced costs and provided equipment that can be operated easily. The motion picture especially is costly, and can rarely be used in typical situations. Some recent studies have substituted still photographs taken automatically at intervals such as fifteen seconds. While these films do not show motion, they are adequate for most events. Records of this type for a preschool group, for example, can be analyzed to determine which children play together and for how long. One of the greatest problems with recording devices is the difficulty of utilizing the records obtained. Even a fairly brief recording session produces a huge mass of film or sound recording which can only be reduced to convenient form by careful and well-planned analysis. Any analysis must discard some of the information recorded, to center attention on the most significant data.

Among the uses to which photography has been put are the following. Behavior of visitors to a museum exhibit has been recorded by a concealed camera taking photographs at frequent intervals (23). The records showed the time spent at each exhibit, the order in which the exhibits were approached, and other facts of value in exhibit planning. In aviation research, a motion picture of the pilot's head and shoulders, made by a camera mounted in the cockpit, recorded his behavior during landing. Direction of glance was studied as a means of improving landing technique (32). In gunnery training and evaluation of combat performance, cameras were synchronized with gun triggers used by aerial gunners (13). As the shot was fired, the camera made a record of the point of aim. The film yielded an accuracy score and permitted analysis of such causes of misses as inadequate lead.

Sound recording on disks has been expensive and usually required the constant services of a technician. Wire recorders and tape recorders have now been improved so that they are adequate for most observations. With a concealed microphone, records one hour or more in duration can be made at low cost and with little attention. Such records have been used to evaluate and train counselors and classification interviewers (7, 25). If a human observer were in the room, a counselor could probably not do typical work because of his client's consciousness of the observer. This factor is greatly reduced by automatic recording, although even so the counselor may perform differently because he knows of the microphone. Recordings of radio and battlephone communications have been used to study the performance of military personnel. The records permit analyzing clarity of speech and skill with which tactical duties are performed (6).

In addition to direct records of behavior, a few devices have been tried for recording the results of a person's actions. Thus, a "ride-recorder" was tried as a basis of objectively recording pilot performance. As the pilot executed standard maneuvers, the recording instrument noted changes in heading, tilt, and altitude of the plane (33).

9. Discuss the advantages and disadvantages of still pictures taken in sequences about one second apart, as compared with a human observer for each of the following purposes.
   a. A city engineer wishes to study the traffic patterns at an intersection to determine what difficulties cause traffic jams.

    b. In a study of rat performance, it is important to note both time and specific errors made in maze running.

10. Discuss the advantages and disadvantages of sound recordings as compared with a human observer for each of the following purposes.

    a. An investigator wishes to measure the skill with which different teachers handle discipline problems.

    b. A teacher of dramatics wishes to judge her students' ability to read a dramatic selection.

11. Sound recordings of group discussions are often used to study individual differences in dominance, leadership, and other traits. What types of observable information about personality could not be obtained from the sound record?

Training of Observers

Most people form their impressions of others haphazardly and inaccurately. They are misled by prejudices, and they draw conclusions from single events which are unwarranted. Observers should receive training, directed particularly to making them self-critical and objective. Training for interviewers is a well-developed practice in industrial personnel work. Foremen are receiving training in many industries to assist them in judging the men under them. Teachers receive special training in observation of children. All such programs improve the quality of resulting data.

DATA YIELDED BY OBSERVATIONS

Objective Data

An observer may record, free-style, what he sees, or he may record certain specific items to which his attention is directed. Standardization of observations is greatly increased if every observer notes a limited number of specific, countable behaviors, as in the time-sampling method. Objectivity of observations is obtained by defining carefully what is to be noted and providing a check list, schedule, or recording form for uniform data.

The extent to which factory workers attend to their work may be described by a time record which notes the exact moments when they are at work, and the time spent in looking around, obtaining tools, and visiting. The causes of distractions can also be noted. Such records for different workers and departments can be analyzed both for judging the workers and for planning rest periods or improved tool distribution. Morrison has used similar methods for recording the study habits of high-school students (20). Such records as shown in Figure 84 not only supply precise estimates of time spent in study but provide a basis for discussion with the pupil of ways of improving his efficiency and of recording improvement. Child development has been studied through records of social contacts, play activities, speech, and other objectively defined behaviors (5, pp. 509 ff.; 31). Such precise reports are especially useful for measuring changes, since the observer's memory is

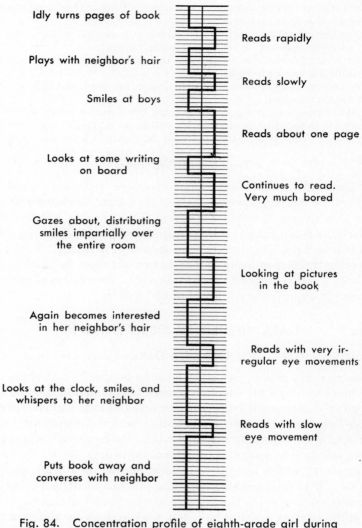

Idly turns pages of book

Reads rapidly

Plays with neighbor's hair

Reads slowly

Smiles at boys

Reads about one page

Looks at some writing on board

Continues to read. Very much bored

Gazes about, distributing smiles impartially over the entire room

Looking at pictures in the book

Again becomes interested in her neighbor's hair

Reads with very irregular eye movements

Looks at the clock, smiles, and whispers to her neighbor

Reads with slow eye movement

Puts book away and converses with neighbor

Fig. 84.   Concentration profile of eighth-grade girl during
20-minute study period (**20**).

an untrustworthy basis for comparing performance now with performance several months earlier.

Check lists and schedules are also used to systematize observation records. The check list used in observing ability (see p. 296) generally lists the correct actions and the significant errors to be noted. For observing typical behavior, a more flexible system is often required. The check list for such work may provide a series of categories for classifying acts. Quite different specific acts may be recorded rapidly with considerable objectivity. This procedure is il-

lustrated in the studies of Anderson and his associates, who observed teachers
to determine their tendency to domination or "integration" in leadership. The
observer checked the frequency of incidents in 28 categories and sub-cate-
gories such as the following (3):

DC   Domination with evidence of conflict
DC-3   Relocates child (e.g., changes his seat)
DC-5   Disapproval, blame or shame directed toward child as a person
DN   Domination with no evidence of conflict
IT   Integration with evidence of working together
IT-16   Approval of self-initiated behavior of child

Experienced observers, simultaneously recording over 600 incidents, agreed
closely in their reports (3, pp. 43 ff.).

12. What advantages and disadvantages would a check list or schedule have for
    each of the following purposes, compared to a one-paragraph descriptive
    report?
    a. A social agency wishes its visitor to report the condition of homes of its
       clients, including furnishings, conveniences, and neatness.
    b. A department store sends shoppers to be served by its clerks and observe
       their procedure and manner.
    c. A state requires an observation of the applicant's driving before issuing
       a license to drive.
13. An investigator wishes to measure punctuality, for research purposes. He
    stations himself where he can observe the arrival of each student attending
    a particular class. Number of minutes early or late is recorded for each person.
    Records are made on several days (10). What assumptions are involved in
    using the average of these records as an index of punctuality?

If observers record their opinions merely as descriptive statements, it becomes very difficult to compare one subject with another. In order to permit
routine processing of data or statistical analysis, the opinions are frequently
reduced to ratings on one or more traits. This method is so widely used, and
presents such a variety of problems, that it will be treated separately in a
later section.

Anecdotal Records

In marked contrast to numerical records and ratings are anecdotal records.
Anecdotal records are an attempt to escape the bleakness and narrowness of
quantitative methods, to obtain a full and lifelike picture of the subject. The
observer is free to note any behavior that appears significant, rather than
having to concentrate on the same traits for all subjects. Often the anecdotes
are reports of incidents noted by a teacher or supervisor in daily contacts,
rather than obtained by a special observer.

In an anecdotal record, the observer describes exactly what he observed,
avoiding mixing interpretation and fact. The record is made as soon after the
action as possible, to eliminate errors of recall. Cumulated over a period of
time, the descriptions of incidents provide a richer picture of behavior than

any other equally simple technique. The following are typical anecdotal reports:

"Paul, after projecting the film for the class, took it back to the office (where I happened to be) to rewind. He is not very skilled, and missed his timing, so that much of the film cascaded onto the floor instead of going onto the takeup reel. John came up just then and said something sarcastic about Paul's clumsiness. Paul gave no answer, but kept on at work with no change of manner and a stolid face. Richard, who had been watching Paul, turned on John, told him to 'shut up and give Paul a chance,' and muttered something about 'some of these kids make me sick.' [Paul seems to suppress emotion; he certainly heard John's very unpleasant tone.]"

"Joan spent the entire science period wandering from group to group instead of helping Rose as she was expected to. She interrupted many of the others, telling them they were doing the work wrong. She asked a lot of [foolish] questions ('Does filter paper make certain things go through or just keep certain things out?') and was teased a good deal by the boys. By the time Rose was finished she returned; Rose was quite angry, but they made up and Joan helped put things away. But on her first trip to the storeroom she stayed to plate a gold ring with mercury, while Rose made repeated trips with the equipment."

The observer has two responsibilities for making useful anecdotal records: he must select incidents worth reporting, and he must be objective. Two types of incidents are especially helpful: those which are characteristic of the person and those which are striking exceptions to his normal conduct. The typical incidents are helpful because they provide a more individualized picture of the typical behavior than the hackneyed trait names that would otherwise be used—friendly, showing initiative, rude, and so on. Exceptional actions are rarely reported in ratings and general impressions. But they too are characteristic of the person. A single incident showing interest in the company's welfare from a man known as a troublemaker, or a sign of enthusiasm for learning on the part of a boy who has been rebellious toward school may be the key which will open a new and successful method of dealing with the person.

Objective reporting of anecdotal material requires the same caution as any other type of scientific observation. The observer must weed out value judgments and interpretations, attempting rather to report the exact occurrences, including the significant preceding events and environmental conditions. Although the ideal anecdote would report "everything" about the incident, this can never be attained. The reporter selects for his record the facts he considers relevant.

Single anecdotes tell little about a person. As anecdotes accumulate, however, they begin to fill in a picture of his habits. If a particular response is typical, it will recur. An effective method of determining personality characteristics is to search through the anecdotes regarding a particular case to detect repetitions. A summary based on these recurring patterns usually requires confirmation by further directed observation.

14. Examine the first and second of the anecdotal reports given above, and indicate types of data that may have been discarded by the observer.
15. What information does the second anecdote give that would not be conveyed by ratings on attentiveness, responsibility, coöperation, and sociability?

RATING SCALES

Rating scales serve not only as a means of summarizing direct observations, but also as a device for obtaining descriptions of the subject from judges who have been familiar with his typical behavior in the past. Ratings are employed as criteria and as basic sources of data for many types of research, and are used practically in selecting workers, choosing workers to be promoted, admitting students to college, etc. Ratings are popular because they can be treated numerically and are superficially uniform from judge to judge. Descriptive statements by interviewers, observers, and acquaintances are hard

Table 66. Intercorrelations of Ratings Given 1100 Industrial Workers (11)

Traits	Safety	Knowledge of Job	Versatility	Accuracy	Productivity	Over-All Job Performance	Industriousness	Initiative	Judgment	Coöperation	Personality	Health
Safety	.35[a]	.61	.52	.63	.55	.60	.49	.54	.62	.61	.55	.25
Knowledge of job	.61	.46	.81	.85	.79	.82	.78	.78	.80	.67	.67	.52
Versatility	.52	.81	.47	.80	.72	.80	.71	.78	.82	.68	.63	.50
Accuracy	.63	.85	.80	.45	.81	.67	.80	.78	.84	.74	.70	.84
Productivity	.55	.79	.72	.81	.46	.86	.86	.80	.81	.81	.73	.45
Over-all job performance	.60	.82	.80	.67	.86	.46	.85	.83	.88	.80	.74	.60
Industriousness	.49	.78	.71	.80	.86	.85	.47	.82	.84	.80	.67	.53
Initiative	.54	.78	.78	.78	.80	.83	.82	.48	.86	.72	.72	.77
Judgment	.62	.80	.82	.84	.81	.88	.84	.86	.45	.76	.75	.43
Coöperation	.61	.67	.68	.74	.81	.80	.80	.72	.76	.37	80	.52
Personality	.55	.67	.63	.70	.73	.74	.67	.72	.75	.80	.39	.71
Health	.25	.52	.50	.84	.45	.60	.53	.77	.43	.52	.71	.36

[a] Italicized figures show correlations of two raters' judgments on each worker, i.e., reliability of judging.

to compare because of variations in style of writing. It is impossible at present to apply statistical methods to most qualitative reports of behavior. Rating scales are commonly used to reduce impressions to manageable form. Rating scales generally consist of a list of traits to be rated, the judge being asked to indicate the extent to which each behavior is characteristic of the subject.

All rating schemes are subject to severe observer errors. One error, the *halo effect*, has received a great deal of attention. Observers form a general opinion of a person, and the ratings they give him on specific traits are influenced by this general feeling of favorableness or unfavorableness. Even such an objectively measureable trait as productivity of a worker may be rated erroneously, if a poor worker has a pleasing personality. Table 66 gives convincing evidence of halo. This table shows the correlation of ratings given

1100 industrial employees. Ratings on quite dissimilar traits show a marked general factor, apparently corresponding to the foreman's opinion of the man's industriousness and productivity. A factor analysis shows two other factors, skill and health. This scale might as well be reduced from twelve traits to two, a general factor and a skill factor. The health rating is too unreliable to be depended upon (11).

Generosity error is also common. Whenever possible, raters tend to give subjects the benefit of the doubt. It is common to find 60 to 80 percent of an unselected group rated "above average" because of the urge to speak favorably if possible.

Among the many rating procedures in existence, the *descriptive graphic rating scale* seems to have particular usefulness. From the cumulated experience of years of use of rating methods, certain principles for preparing or criticizing scales have emerged:

1. The judge should be asked to rate only those traits which are essential for the purpose involved; rarely more than five to seven. As more traits are added, judges give less serious consideration to each, and rely more upon the "halo."

2. The judge should be urged to indicate which traits he has inadequate data for rating. Where a judge is directed to mark every trait, some ratings are little better than guesses. Conrad directed judges to star ratings of traits which they regarded especially important in the child's personality. Interjudge correlations on all traits ranged from .67 to .82. But for the traits which three judges agreed in starring, the correlations of ratings rose as high as .96 (9).

3. Each trait should be judged along a scale, rather than on an all-or-none basis. The judge will rarely report that an acquaintance is discourteous or unpunctual on a yes-or-no choice, but he may check such a statement as "sometimes forgets courtesy" or "is less punctual than the average." In general, five- to seven-point scales seem to serve adequately. Under very favorable conditions for rating, much finer subdivisions of the scale prove profitable (8).

4. Traits and scale positions should be described as unambiguously as possible. Different words have different meanings for judges, but if ratings are to be comparable they must be based on a uniform question. "Leadership" may suggest to one judge conscious wielding of authority, crisp decisions, and general dominance. A subject rated high by this judge would receive a lower rating from a judge who stresses encouragement of subordinates, leading a group to coöperative decisions, and subordinating the leader's desires to the decision of the group. Such words as "average" and "excellent," used in defining the scale of judgment, are even more indefinite in meaning. They should be replaced by specific descriptions of behavior.

A good example of the descriptive rating scale is the American Council on Education Personality Report, shown in Figure 85. This form is principally used to obtain ratings of high-school graduates for use by college admissions

Name of student...

		Please record here instances on which you base your judgment.
A—How are you and others affected by his appearance and manner?	☐ Sought by others ☐ Well liked by others ☐ Liked by others ☐ Tolerated by others ☐ Avoided by others ☐ No opportunity to observe	
B—Does he need frequent prodding or does he go ahead without being told?	☐ Seeks and sets for himself additional tasks ☐ Completes suggested supplementary work. ☐ Does ordinary assignments of his own accord ☐ Needs occasional prodding ☐ Needs much prodding in doing ordinary assignments ☐ No opportunity to observe	Please record here instances on which you base your judgment.
C—Does he get others to do what he wishes?	☐ Displays marked ability to lead his fellows; makes things go ☐ Sometimes leads in important affairs ☐ Sometimes leads in minor affairs ☐ Lets others take lead ☐ Probably unable to lead his fellows ☐ No opportunity to observe	Please record here instances on which you base your judgment.
D—How does he control his emotions?	☐ Unusual balance of responsiveness and control ☐ Well balanced ☐ Usually well balanced ☐ Tends to be unresponsive ☐ Tends to be over emotional ☐ Unresponsive, apathetic ☐ Too easily depressed, irritated or elated ☐ No opportunity to observe	Please record here instances on which you base your judgment.
E—Has he a program with definite purposes in terms of which he distributes his time and energy?	☐ Engrossed in realizing well formulated objectives ☐ Directs energies effectively with fairly definite program ☐ Has vaguely formed objectives ☐ Aims just to "get by" ☐ Aimless trifler ☐ No opportunity to observe	Please record here instances on which you base your judgment.

Fig. 85. The American Council on Education Personality Report, Form B.

officers. Another widely known form is the Haggerty-Olson-Wickman Behavior Rating Schedule. Questions are illustrated in Figure 86. This scale is used for recording opinions about the behavior and adjustment of children. Unlike purely descriptive scales, this is scored to yield a measure of behavior difficulties. Weights were determined by identifying the frequency of each rating in groups of children known to have behavior problems. Both of the scales shown require rating exactly at one of five positions. A graphic scale permits the judge to place checks anywhere along the scale.

Is he abstracted or wide awake?

| Continually absorbed in himself (5) | Frequently becomes abstracted (4) | Usually present-minded (2) | Wide-awake (1) | Keenly alive and alert (3) |

Is he shy or bold in social relationships?

| Painfully self-conscious (4) | Timid, Frequently embarrassed (2) | Self-conscious on occasions (1) | Confident in himself (3) | Bold, Insensitive to social feelings (5) |

How does he accept authority?

| Defiant (5) | Critical of authority (4) | Ordinarily obedient (3) | Respectful, Complies by habit (1) | Entirely resigned, Accepts all authority (2) |

Fig. 86. Items for the Haggerty-Olson-Wickman Behavior Rating Schedule.[1]

16. In the American Council rating scale, the trait scale for leadership (C) is defined by five specific phrases. What advantage does this scale have over a set of adjectives such as "Excellent," "Good," "Average," "Poor," "Unsatisfactory"?

17. Why might keenly alive children have more behavior problems than those rated as wide-awake? Would "keenly alive and alert" ordinarily be considered a sign of poor mental hygiene?

18. The phrase "very favorable conditions for rating" was used in paragraph 3 above. What type of conditions (apart from the scale itself) influence the precision and validity of ratings?

The *forced-choice* technique applied to rating scales is similar to the forced choice found helpful in self-report tests. It asks the judge to choose which of two equally favorable adjectives best applies to the subject. No matter what halo or generosity effects enter the judge's thinking, such a question forces him to consider the subject in regard to the specific trait in question. After deciding whether Jones is more calm than cautious, more friendly than intelligent, more creative than painstaking, and so on, the judge has provided the best picture his knowledge permits of the characteristics of the subject. This does not, however, yield a score on general merit, since every subject is marked on every pair of items. The device was used by the Army in scales not released for publication (28). The forced-choice scale was supplemented

[1] Reprinted by special permission from Haggerty-Olson-Wickman Behavior Rating Schedules. Copyright by World Book Company.

by a single general rating scale asking for the judges' opinion on the over-all merit of the person rated. Such scales were used experimentally to place men in assignments. Point scores were obtained by weighting the adjectives in each pair according to their correlation with success in a given job.

THE SOCIAL MATURITY SCALE

One tool of importance in evaluating normal behavior is the Vineland Social Maturity Scale.[2] This is ordinarily used as an adjunct to the clinical interview, rather than as a means of summarizing field observations. It is a standardized list of behaviors which permits a quite objective comparison of the subject's behavior with a norm. It is an age scale, somewhat analogous to the Binet test, listing behaviors characteristic of ages from birth to adulthood. The scale seeks to measure degree of maturation of social competence, shown in personal responsibility and social participation. Items from two of the age levels are as follows:

"Age II-III
"Asks to go to toilet.
"Initiates own play activities.
"Removes coat or dress.
"Eats with fork.
"Gets drink unassisted.
"Dries own hands.
"Avoids simple hazards.
"Puts on coat or dress unassisted.
"Cuts with scissors.
"Relates experiences.
"Age X-XI
"Writes occasional short letters.
"Makes telephone calls.
"Does small remunerative work.
"Answers ads; purchases by mail."

In using the scale, the examiner interviews an informant who is thoroughly acquainted with the child's performances, and marks the scale accordingly. A total score is computed which is called a "social age," corresponding to the "mental age" of Binet-type scales. A social quotient (SQ) may be derived. The tool is useful in research on social development under various kinds of environment, and is helpful in clinical analysis at all ages.

PROBLEMS OF RELIABILITY

Observations by impartial observers are generally accepted as valid if they can be made reliable. Observations are more often used as criteria than as predictors, and empirical studies of their validity are uncommon. The logical validity of observation data is easily accepted if errors of measurement

[2] Publisher: Educ. Test Bureau.

are eliminated. Tendency to quarrel is surely measured by observed incidence of quarreling. Tendency to seek solitary activities is validly revealed by a full record of how one spends his free time. The questions that may be asked regarding observations in normal situations reduce to three: How close is the agreement of different judges making the same observation? How great is the correspondence between observations in "similar" situations? How long must the person be observed to obtain a reliable measure?

Reliability of a Judge

The reliability of an observer hinges on the method of controlling observation and the method of reporting. Errors occur in observing through inattention of the judge or his selection of things to observe. Errors in reporting are at a minimum when he has made objective notes on specific facts observed. Errors rise when he makes judgments, as in a rating scale.

Ratings casually obtained are notoriously unreliable, as judges are inconsistent in repeated ratings and disagree with each other. Many prediction studies have been unable to obtain high validity coefficients even with good predictors, when ratings were used as criteria. The reliability coefficients for judgments based on general acquaintance are frequently .40 or .50, as is illustrated in Table 66. Single unconfirmed ratings should never be depended upon. Ratings may be made more reliable by combining the opinions of several judges. Symonds estimates that the correlations of average ratings can reach .90, when the average is based on eight judges (30). It is rarely possible, however, to obtain so many judges who know the person well.

The reliability of rating is greatest for those behaviors which can be objectively observed and which do not involve interaction with others. Traits reliably rated include originality and energy. Reliability is least for general attributes, especially in the field of character, and for traits dealing with interpersonal relations. Traits which are unreliably rated include integrity, coöperativeness, and kindness (14).

Although ratings based on incidental impressions are quite untrustworthy, judgments can be very reliable when based on systematic observation. Newman reports reliability coefficients for combined ratings by three trained observers ranging from .74 to .90 (22, p. 30). Similarly high correspondence was obtained by Conrad and by Anderson, referred to earlier.

19. Why might integrity, coöperativeness, and kindness be especially hard to rate reliably?
20. Which of the following traits would probably be hardest to rate reliably after observations: talkativeness, freedom from tension, freedom from anxiety, leadership, and sensitivity to others' opinions (14, p. 32)?
21. The Spearman-Brown formula used for estimating the reliability of lengthened tests (see p. 61) may also be applied to predict the reliability of combined judgments of several equally competent raters. Apply the formula to determine the reliability to be expected if the ratings of health and initiative

(Table 66) had been based on the average of three reports, instead of only one.

22. Ratings on leadership made at Officer Candidate School correlated only .15 with ratings on efficiency of combat leadership by superior officers in the field after the men had been observed in combat (15, p. 72). How can the smallness of the correlation be accounted for?

Consistency of Performance

There is no universal answer as to when observations in different situations will give similar pictures of the individual. Studies of personality assume that there is an underlying unity which causes a person's behavior to be consistent in similar situations. One must be cautious in assuming that situations which look comparable are really the same for the subject. Situations which seem to relate to the same trait may actually call forth very different behaviors from the same person.

The best evidence on this problem is Newcomb's observation of boys in a summer camp (21). Daily records were made of many particular responses, such as coöperation in after-meal work, fighting with other boys, and persistence in morning activities. When these day-to-day records were studied, most boys were found to be inconsistent, in the sense that they acted in an extrovert fashion half the time, and in an introvert fashion on the other occasions. As Newcomb points out, the situations are only superficially alike. "Whether or not Johnny engages in a fight may depend on whether or not he thinks he can 'lick' his opponent" (21, p. 39). The apparent inconsistency of Johnny's action, from an observer's frame of reference, may be highly consistent from Johnny's point of view. Correlations were computed between observed behaviors which were supposed to represent single traits, such as showing off or dominance over peers. Behaviors grouped within one of these supposed traits correlated little higher than obviously dissimilar behaviors. Another study found only trivial correlations (median .20) between punctuality observed in different situations. When scores were grouped in broad categories, some consistency between situations was found, but too little for refined prediction (9).

It is clear that conclusions about a person formed in one situation—even on the basis of many cumulated observations—are valid only for that situation. Inference as to how he would act in another situation is warranted only when responses under the two conditions have been shown to be correlated, or when observation yields so much understanding of his underlying personality structure (*his* frame of reference) that we can see what a new situation means to him.

Sampling Required

Symonds has commented emphatically on the need for adequate sampling (30, p. 5): "A single observation is unreliable, a single rating is unreliable, a single test is unreliable, a single measurement is unreliable, a single answer to a question is unreliable. Reliability is achieved by keeping up observations, ratings, tests, questions, measures. . . . If you ask one teacher for her judgment of a boy's trustworthiness, you obtain what she has been able to observe in those few narrow classroom situations that appeared when her attention was particularly directed to some act involving honesty. An adequate rating, on the other hand, requires the judgment of several raters in several situations at several different times. Reliable evidence is multiplied evidence."

The extreme variation in performances is suggested by the data in Table 67, based on observations of airplane landing. These data were gathered dur-

Table 67.   Reliability of Observations of Airplane Landing (29)

	N	Zone of Landing	Landing Attitude	Dropped or Bounced
Correlation of observers viewing same landing	304	.83	.79	.88
Correlation between two landings on same day	340	.12	.32	.32
Correlation between two landings on different days	340	.02	.04	.00

ing a test of ability, rather than observation under normal flying motivation. If the test motivation has any effect, however, it should be to increase consistency of performance by raising each man near to his maximum. The observer rated each landing on place of landing, attitude of plane (three-point or wheels first), and dropping or bouncing. Different observers agreed well in making the records required. Retests, however, showed almost no consistency of performance, and this consistency dropped even lower when tests were made on different days. The investigators blame part of the erratic changes on variations in wind, turbulence, and other external conditions. A single measure of landing behavior, no matter how reliably judged, gives little or no information of real value.

How many observations are required to obtain reliable data depends on the problem studied. The experimenter can measure reliability of sampling by correlating ratings from "odd" with "even" observations. By this means, it was determined that 24 or more five-minute time samples permitted "reasonably stable" estimates of individual differences in preschool children—except for a few children where unusual conditions altered behavior during some observations (4). Such studies do not permit a general statement as to the number of observations required. They do, however, show that several observations of each person are needed, and that many short observations are superior to a few longer samples of behavior.

23. How many landings must a man make, on a given day, to yield a "zone of landing" score having a reliability of .70? (Apply Spearman-Brown formula.)
24. As a criterion in selection research, would it be better to test every flier with repeated landings on the same day or with a similar number of landings spread over several days?

INCIDENTAL SOURCES OF DATA

Personal Records

In addition to observation, students of personality have been able to rely on evidence of typical behavior from incidental sources, such as personal records and products. As a person goes through life, he leaves behind him a trail of objective data which tell much about his personality and habits. With effort, the investigator can often unearth such records and use them as indices of typical behavior. These records are impartial, quantitative, and usually highly valid measures of the behavior they reveal. In industry, time cards punched routinely form an index of punctuality and absenteeism. Records of the nurse provide information on frequency of accidents. Production records often indicate both the quantity of output and the percentage of output rejected by inspectors. Obviously such data are less biased than the subjective reports of foremen. An example of the use of production data is the work of Roethlisberger and Dickson (26). To test the effect of experimental working conditions, each worker in the test group assembled relays as usual, except for the changes in ventilation, motivation, etc. being studied. The output of each worker, instead of going into a pool of finished parts, went into an identified box. The number of rejects and the number of satisfactory relays provided important data on the behavior of the workers (cf. p. 310).

Outside the job, the citizen tells about himself in his record of traffic citations and accidents, of payment of bills, and of marriage and parenthood. These data are rarely as useful as those gathered under uniform conditions for all people, but they are at times important. Accident records, for example, have been important criteria in studies of driving safety. School records are rich in data: records of absences, of extracurricular participation, disciplinary referrals, assignments completed, and so on. Such data also provide information about the typical behavior of teachers. If an investigator finds that Miss Franklin gives twice as many A's as Mr. Park, and that Mr. Park refers twice as many children to the principal, important hypotheses may be formed. The validity of objective data can generally be accepted, but one must avoid over-interpretation.

25. A traffic policeman writes 40 percent more tickets than normal for the force during a year's work. What factors might make it impossible to draw conclusions from this regarding his alertness or severity?
26. On what traits might a man's checkbook stubs provide data?

Personal Products

A man's habits are revealed in the objects he leaves behind him. The manuscripts of composers (and the music itself) reveal the temperaments of the artists, Beethoven's stormy impulsiveness appearing in bold, irregular pages,

Mozart's delicate spontaneity appearing in neat, vivacious strokes (34). The notches on the gun of the frontiersman report not only that he accounted for so many Indians, but also that he considered it important to record the number. Examining the personal products of the subject provides evidence of characteristics from quality of handwriting to schizophrenia. Because these data have usually been produced for purposes quite unrelated to the subject of investigation, they are generally good indicators of typical behavior. When produced under special test motivation, they indicate maximum ability instead.

Graphology, the study of handwriting, is receiving increasing attention (2). It is one of the few techniques which can be used to study the past personality of subjects, since samples of handwriting can usually be obtained for the subject at all stages in his development.

Personal products may be collected in school situations very easily. Themes, artistic productions, and answers to essay examinations are usually available. The wise teacher of grammar judges her success by studying the papers her pupils write for other teachers, where they are trying to express ideas rather than impress the English teacher. If observation is impracticable, one can judge a teacher far better from her lesson plans than from her answer to a question about how one should teach. Techniques of work in shop and art are frequently judged by the product. Although this source of evidence has not received widespread use because of the scarcity of data, it is of potential value for evaluating habits of neatness, accuracy, problem solving, and many other educational objectives. Outside the school, relatively little use has been made of products, although documents such as diaries, letters, and other papers are sometimes helpful to the psychologist (1). Procedures for improving the rating of products have been discussed in Chapter 12.

The use of personal products for insight into personality is a relatively new technique. It has become increasingly important as teachers, employers, social workers, and therapists have sought to understand the motivations that lie beneath symptomatic behavior. Virtually every act a man performs bears the imprint of his unique personality. Wolff, in his experimental depth psychology, has established significant relations between personality and handwriting, gait and voice (34). Artistic productions express feelings and action patterns; valid analysis has been made of products ranging from masterpieces of famous artists to the casual doodling of the common man. As in the projective techniques to be discussed in Chapter 20, it is important that the products to be studied should have been the free responses of the subject. If one is given a rigidly specified task to perform, he has little opportunity to impress his personality upon its design or execution. Insofar as he is free to choose what he wishes to produce, he gives the analyst more information.

The analysis of personal products follows closely the procedures and theories used in projective techniques. Here it will suffice to mention that study may be made of content, style, and method of attack. Interpretation for a specific purpose may stop at superficial description of such traits as neatness, or it may set up hypotheses based on psychoanalytic or other theories of personality.

27. What assumption is made when an English teacher judges the typical grammatical habits of her pupils from their papers in science and social studies classes?
28. A talented seven-year-old taking a special art class has produced the following set of spontaneous drawings over a period of several weeks. Quotation marks indicate his comments about them.

   Out West. "All the Indians are dead. The cowboys are raising the flags. The cows are dead, too."
   Man and King. "The last man wants to be king so he is kicking the king in the pants."
   End of the Birds. Boat, with hunters shooting birds.
   The Fish and All. Fish, bubbles, turtles, etc.
   The Clown. "The clown is selling balloons and lollipops. He is hungry too."
   Gas Station. Gas station with man and cars.
   Ford Station. Ford assembly plant with cars and ramps.
   Kottonton. Religious story. Shows little Kottonton chasing Satan, who calls for help.
   King. "Fat king has a rake in his hand to chop up everyone. But he is afraid of them."

   a. What ideas or themes seem to recur in these pictures? Which pictures seem to be most highly individual in content, unlike those of other seven-year-olds?
   b. What do these titles and comments suggest regarding the content of his mind?

STUDIES OF REPUTATION

Important data on reputation—how others view an individual—are obtained by sociometric techniques. These methods are neither observations nor self-reports. They resemble most closely the rating technique, but reports are made by the subject's peers rather than his superiors. One of the simplest sociometric methods is the "Guess Who" device. This was first used by Hartshorne and May with school children. The test consists of descriptions of roles played by children. Each child in the group responds to each description by naming any child he thinks that description fits. How other children view Walter is indicated by the description to which Walter's name is repeatedly matched. Typical descriptions are (12, p. 88):

Here is the class athlete. He (or she) can play baseball, basketball, tennis, can swim as well as any, and is a good sport.
This one is always picking on others and annoying them.

No one assumes that reputations are true reports of personality. How one's associates view him is itself significant even when they misjudge him. Reputations do in general correspond to behavior. Correlations, corrected for unreliability, between reputations among adolescents and careful observations of corresponding behaviors range from .45 to .70 (22, p. 39).

The *sociogram* is a device for studying the social structure of groups. Characteristics of an individual, including his popularity, may be studied by the Guess Who method, but the sociogram gives further insight by identifying cliques, hierarchies of leadership, and other social groupings. The sociogram was developed by Moreno (19). Although the technique has been amended in various ways which sacrifice effectiveness for convenience, the best procedure is to request members of a group to indicate their choices for companions in a particular activity. Jennings cites these illustrative directions to be used by a group leader for obtaining sociometric data (16):

"Each of you knows best whom you would enjoy being with in the same group at our community center for the times you will be working and playing together. No one can know this as well as yourself. We shall be arranging our new schedule for groups next Monday. As today is Friday, I can figure out the membership in groups by Monday if you would like to choose associates today. We will keep the same people we choose today for eight weeks, and then have a chance to choose again. Keep in mind all the boys and girls you have come to know here whether they are absent today or not. Let's give three choices, or four if you like. Wherever possible, I'll arrange the groups so that the individual gets all his choices. But is is very difficult to give all people all their choices because lots of people might choose one person."

While the wording is varied, effective directions deal with a real group, who make choices which will be followed up. The data are not obtained in a test setting; instead, they are obtained as a means of dealing with the group. If data are obtained from a less real question, such as "Who are your friends?" there is more likelihood of answers given to make a good impression. Subjects must know that their reports will be treated confidentially. The sociometric data should be used as promised, to set up work groups, committees, homeroom seating, or whatever; this permits one to obtain coöperation when the technique is used again at a later date.

When the choices are obtained, they are plotted in a sociogram. Figure 87 is the sociogram of a class of fourth-grade girls early in the school year. Pupils indicated not more than three choices, and were also permitted to list any whom they would not choose. This sociogram reveals several patterns often encountered. There are two groups or cliques. In one Emily is the most sought-after person, with Jane, Lenora, Caroline, Rhoda, and Louise as accepted members. In the other group, Agnes is the key figure, with Lurline, Patricia, and Ann as members. Patricia, one notes, is not thoroughly integrated with the clique; while accepted by Agnes, she is also reaching toward Emily in the other group, rather than Lurline or Ann. Agnes, who might be a popular leader of all the girls, instead shows considerable hostility, rejecting three popular girls. Ella is a fringer, not chosen by any of the others. Tess is even more isolated.

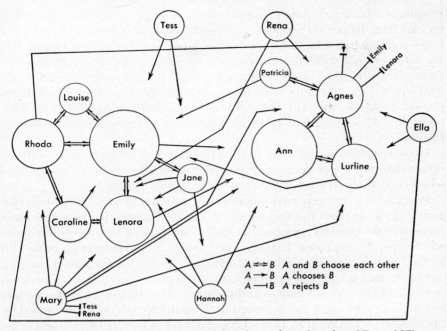

Fig. 87.   Sociogram for a class of fourth-grade girls (after **27**, p. 297).

29. What children besides Tess and Ella are fringers?
30. What interpretations of Agnes' hostility can be suggested?
31. Prior to this study, the teacher had characterized Tess as hard working, interested in accomplishing tasks, "fits in nicely with the group." Tess helps others with their sewing, at which she is superior. How would the teacher's outlook and treatment of Tess be affected by the information from the sociogram?
32. Plot a sociogram using the following choices made in a group of tenth-graders. Discuss the interactions shown.
    Shirley chooses Charles, Jim, and Sam.
    Charles chooses Shirley, Sam, and Jim; rejects Tom.
    Phil chooses Jim, Charles, and Shirley; rejects Wallace and Tom.
    Wallace chooses Phil, and Jack; rejects Tom.
    Jim chooses Jack, Sam, Charles, and Shirley; rejects Tom.
    Jack chooses Jim and Tom; rejects Phil.
    Shirley is chosen by several girls whom she does not mention. Sam and Tom were absent.
33. How does the sociometric method differ from the common secret popularity ballot?

The sociogram obtained differs when different questions are asked. For example, if sorority girls are asked to indicate their choice for roommates, and their choice of persons with whom to study, the sociometric patterns will differ. A best friend may be thought of as too noisy or untidy for a good roommate, and a girl quite unpopular in these respects may be regarded as an excellent helper on school assignments. Basic social configurations are fairly stable when different questions are used, but one cannot assume that the interpersonal structure of a group is the same under all conditions. The sociometric structure also changes with time. By December, Agnes was a "star" in her group, along with Rhoda and Emily. The cliques had disappeared, thanks to the skill of the teacher. Ann and Lurline still chose each other, but Agnes now turned her back on them, ignoring Ann and rejecting Lurline.

Social structure may also be studied by observing contacts and rejections, rather than reports of peers. This is especially helpful at the preschool level where verbal choices are difficult to obtain (18).

Sociograms have been used practically in a variety of ways. Roethlisberger and Dickson applied the technique to organize factory workers into more congenial and effective groups. The AAF formed teams by sociometric methods to operate airplanes. Teachers have found the sociogram an important method of understanding relations among pupils so that the school can promote activities which will broaden contacts between children, develop leadership, and break down cliques and isolation (25). Moreno used the method to assign girls in small living groups in an institution for girls committed by the Children's Courts (19). In the OSS, sociometric methods were used in assessment. Groups of candidates undergoing study lived and worked together for three days. After that close association, each man rated and described his fellows. These data gave evidence of ability to inspire confidence and friendship which would be crucial in many of the assignments to be given accepted men (24).

34. When sociograms were made of squadrons of Navy fliers on combat duty, it was found that the "administratively designated leaders" were often not the "natural leaders" in the group, i.e., the ones most chosen as work leaders (17, p. 133). What practical suggestions follow from this finding?
35. In a group of sorority girls, the sociometric question, "Whom would you choose as a roommate?" is asked; will results be the same if the question is changed to, "With whom would you choose to go on a double date?"

SUGGESTED READINGS

Biber, Barbara, and others. "Recording spontaneous behaviors," in *Child life in school*. New York: Dutton, 1942, pp. 33–53.

Dorcus, Roy M. "Methods of evaluating the efficiency of door-to-door salesmen of bakery products." *J. appl. Psychol.*, 1940, 24, 587–594.

Jennings, Helen, and others. *Sociometry in group relations*. Washington: Amer. Council on Educ., 1948.

Jones, Harold E. "Frames of observation of social behavior," and Newman, Frances B., "The development of methods in the adolescent growth study," in Newman, Frances B., "The adolescent in social groups." *Appl. Psychol. Monogr.*, 1946, No. 9, pp. 9–29.

Staff, Division on Child Development, Amer. Council on Educ. "Studying the interaction of children in groups," in *Helping teachers understand children*. Washington: Amer. Council on Educ., 1945, pp. 275–363.

REFERENCES

1. Allport, Gordon W. *The use of personal documents in psychological science*. New York: Soc. Sci. Res. Coun., 1942.
2. Allport, Gordon W., and Vernon, Philip E. *Studies in expressive movement*. New York: Macmillan, 1933.
3. Anderson, Harold H., and Brewer, Joseph E. "Studies of teachers' classroom personalities, II." *Appl. Psychol. Monogr.*, 1946, No. 8.
4. Arrington, Ruth E. "Time-sampling studies of child behavior." *Psychol. Monogr.*, 1939, 51, No. 2.
5. Barker, Roger B., and others (eds.). *Child behavior and development*. New York: McGraw-Hill, 1943.
6. Berry, R. N., and others. *A system of automatic devices for the detection and recording of errors in a 105 mm Howitzer battery*. O.S.R.D. Rep. No. 5313, 1945; Publ. Bd. No. 20288. Washington: U.S. Dep. Commerce, 1946.
7. Campbell, Ronald K. A study of interviewing techniques. Information Memorandum No. 3, Applied Psychology Panel, Natl. Def. Res. Comm., Project N116a. Stanford University, Calif., 1945.
8. Champney, Horace, and Marshall, Helen. "Optimal refinement of the rating scale." *J. appl. Psychol.*, 1939, 23, 323–331.
9. Conrad, Herbert S. "The validity of personality ratings of nursery-school children." *J. educ. Psychol.*, 1932, 23, 671–680.
10. Dudycha, George J. "An objective study of punctuality in relation to personality and achievement." *Arch. Psychol.*, 1936, No. 204.
11. Ewart, Edwin, and others. "A factor analysis of an industrial merit rating scale." *J. appl. Psychol.*, 1941, 25, 481–486.
12. Hartshorne, Hugh, and May, Mark A. *Studies in service and self-control*. New York: Macmillan, 1929.
13. Hobbs, Nicholas (ed.). *Psychological research on flexible gunnery training*. AAF Aviation Psychol. Prog. Res. Rep. No. 11. Washington: Govt. Printing Off., 1947.
14. Hollingworth, H. L. *Judging human character*. New York: Appleton-Century, 1922.
15. Jenkins, William O. "A review of leadership studies with particular reference to military problems." *Psychol. Bull.*, 1947, 44, 54–79.
16. Jennings, Helen H. "How we get together," *Survey*, 1948, 84, 41–44.
17. Kelley, George A. (ed.). *New methods in applied psychology*. College Park: Univ. of Maryland, 1947.
18. Moreno, Florence B. "Sociometric status of children in a nursery school group." *Sociometry*, 1942, 5, 395–411.
19. Moreno, J. L. *Who shall survive?* Washington: Nerv. and Ment. Dis. Publ. Co., 1934.
20. Morrison, Henry C. *The practice of teaching in the secondary school*. Chicago: Univ. of Chicago Press, rev. ed., 1931.
21. Newcomb, Theodore M. *The consistency of certain extrovert-introvert behavior patterns in 51 problem boys*. New York: Teachers Coll., Columbia Univ., 1929.
22. Newman, Frances B. "The adolescent in social groups." *Appl. Psychol. Monogr.*, 1946, No. 9.

23. Nielsen, L. C. "A technique for studying the behavior of museum visitors." *J. educ. Psychol.*, 1946, 37, 103–110.
24. OSS Assessment Staff. *Assessment of Men.* New York: Rinehart, 1948.
25. Porter, Elias H. "The development and evaluation of a measure of counseling interview procedure." *Educ. psychol. Measmt.*, 1943, 2, 105–126, 215–238.
26. Roethlisberger, Fritz, and Dickson, W. J. *Management and the worker.* Cambridge: Harvard Univ. Press, 1939.
27. Staff, Division on Child Development, Amer. Council on Educ. *Helping teachers understand children.* Washington: Amer. Council on Educ., 1945.
28. Staff, Personnel Research Section, Personnel Research and Procedures Branch, AGO. "The forced choice technique and rating scales." *Amer. Psychologist,* 1946, 1, 267.
29. Staff, Psychological Research Project (Pilot). "Psychological research on pilot training in the AAF." *Amer. Psychologist,* 1946, 1, 7–16.
30. Symonds, Percival M. *Diagnosing personality and conduct.* New York: Appleton-Century, 1931.
31. Thomas, Dorothy S., and others. *Some new techniques for studying social behavior.* New York: Teachers Coll., Columbia Univ., 1929.
32. Tiffin, Joseph, and Bromer, J. *Analysis of eye fixations and patterns of eye movement in landing a Piper Cub J-3 airplane.* Washington: CAA, 1943.
33. Viteles, Morris S., and Backstrom, Oscar, Jr. *An analysis of graphic records of pilot performance obtained by means of the R-S Ride Recorder, Part I.* Washington: CAA, 1943.
34. Wolff, Werner. *The expression of personality.* New York: Harper, 1943.

CHAPTER 19

Observation in Test Situations

GENERAL CHARACTERISTICS OF SITUATIONAL TESTS

Comparison with Other Methods

The assessment of typical behavior by self-report tests and by field observations has not been entirely satisfactory. Most self-report tests must assume, however dubiously, that the subject describes himself honestly. The strictly empirical self-report test escapes this limitation, but even here variation in frankness introduces a variable error of measurement. Moreover, the empirical test does not describe the subject, and may be used only for the limited purpose for which it has been validated.

Observation in normal situations escapes the errors of self-report, only by introducing marked observer errors. Field observation is frequently impractical because of the large amount of observing required for reliability, and has the great disadvantage that it is impossible to compare subjects on traits not normally evidenced in their daily activities. If, for example, an investigator intends to study individual differences in behavior after long periods of wakefulness, he can gather little evidence by field observation of workers or students. Only by setting up an artificial situation in which each person is kept awake for a long time can he observe how the person reacts to such fatigue.

Observation during test situations has advantages over both the other methods. This technique has been illustrated frequently in earlier chapters, since one of the major advantages of any individual test is the opportunity it affords for studying individual modes of reaction. Whereas, with the Binet and similar tests, observation is incidental, the "situational tests" discussed in this chapter are designed primarily to provide opportunity for observation. The significant features of a situational test are as follows:

1. The person is subjected to a stimulus situation which is made as nearly uniform as possible for all subjects.

2. The situation is designed to permit variation in those types of behavior which the tester wishes to observe.

3. The test is so designed that the subject believes one characteristic is being tested, whereas the observer is actually observing some other aspect of performance.

4. The observer, or a recording device, makes careful records of the subject's method of performance, rather than noting only the amount performed.

Not every situational test utilizes all these features.

An illustration of the technique is the Observational Stress Test of the AAF, used to assess men entering pilot training on their ability to resist distraction and confusion under pressure. An apparatus test is administered in such a way that each candidate is subjected to standardized stress-producing stimuli. The apparatus consists of a set of seven controls (foot pedal, throttle, stick, and various levers) which the examinee has to reset continually as signal lights change and buzzers sound. The total time required to react to each signal is recorded electrically. The examinee is told that he will be observed by a concealed observer "just as a check-pilot will rate you in flying." The administration of the test is standardized: one minute of rest and anticipation, one minute of directions regarding signals and controls, and three short test periods. In each period, the examinee is given a set of increasingly reproving "stress directions" while he is busily moving levers. The patterns of signals are made more complex. In test period C, the pattern of lights changes six times, after intervals of 15, 20, 15, 15, 10, and 40 seconds, while the examiner is delivering the following speech in an urgent manner: "Don't make lights flicker on and off. Be steady. . . . Quit making errors. You aren't moving fast enough. . . . More speed. . . . Hurry and stop the clock. . . . Last chance. . . . Set controls quickly. . . . You are still making errors." The concealed observer, meanwhile, makes extensive ratings of behavior considering general manner (poised, blocked, confident, etc.), reactions to criticism (obedient, ignores it, annoyed, etc.), and other characteristics. In addition, a thumbnail sketch of behavior is written, and objective clock scores showing performance for the successive periods are recorded. A final clinical rating, arrived at from all these data, correlated .35 with success in pilot training (cf. Table 49). Evidence is incomplete whether the clock scores, an objective measure of performance under stress, are a better or poorer predictor than the clinical assessment (5, pp. 660–663).

The greatest advantage of the test observation is that it makes possible the observation of characteristics which appear only infrequently in normal activities—characteristics such as bravery, reaction to frustration, and dishonesty. A single situational test may reveal more about such a trait than weeks of field observation. Second, the subject's desire to make a good impression does not invalidate the test. In fact, just because he is anxious to make a good impression, he reveals more about his personality than would normally appear. It is necessary, however, to take this motivation into account in interpreting results. The third advantage of the situational test is that it comes closer than other techniques to a standardized measure of typical behavior. Some tests place great reliance on the objective results, whereas others are used more as a basis for clinical and impressionistic evaluation. In either case, the test observation gives a better basis for comparing individuals than observations in which different subjects are seen in different situations. Errors of observation and sampling are still present, however.

Uses of Situational Tests

The principal uses of situational tests have been for research in character, frustration, and similar characteristics that are difficult to observe. Practical use has been limited because such tests are difficult to design and administer, but they have been found helpful in several types of military assessment. German military psychologists emphasized situational tests heavily, and such tests were adopted by the American Office of Strategic Services to select personnel for military intelligence duties. Use in other branches of the service was slight. Clinicians have adopted many tests primarily because of the observations they permit; such tests are especially helpful in studying thinking habits and reaction to emotion-producing situations.

Structured and Unstructured Situations

The principal difference between observational tests and tests for other purposes is that the former are more unstructured. This distinction is especially important in connection with projective tests (Chap. 20). Structuration is a helpful concept, if not taken too literally; most situations are somewhat unstructured, and no rigid classification can be made. A situation is structured if it has for all subjects a definite meaning. An unstructured situation presents so few cues to the subject that he can give it almost any meaning he wishes. "No Admittance" on a door is structured, if one knows English; the phrase suggests a definite response. If the same words were written in Chinese they would give the person almost no cue to guide his actions. A familiar unstructured stimulus is the strange sound in the night. Is it the wind? a burglar? the cat? water dripping? The interpretation we make is strongly influenced by our interests, by fears conscious and unconscious, and, of course, by learned background. In a structured situation, the subject knows just exactly what he is expected to do and how he is expected to do it. In the unstructured situation, we see how he behaves when he is permitted, even forced, to guide himself. The more ambiguous the situation, the more opportunity the subject has to reveal his own individual method of interpretation and performance. An example of the extremely unstructured situation is Waehner's procedure for studying personality. She observed her subjects' behavior and products after turning each one loose in a studio equipped with all types of art media and materials, with little more instruction than "You may do anything you like with these" (20). The stress test for pilots was more structured, since the man knew much of what he was to do; but he was left free to show confusion or emotion, since he did not know that these were being considered in evaluating him.

Highly structured situations are excellent as measures of ability, just because they force everyone to perform the same task. When a test of ability permits variation in work methods, observations become more informative but scores become less valuable, since subjects' scores change under different work methods.

Projective situations, at the opposite extreme from tests of ability, use almost totally unstructured stimuli. The projective test is so named because it permits the subject to project into the situation his own behavior tendencies, and to reveal his unconscious thoughts, wishes, and fears (3). Thus the householder who interprets the creak in the dark as a burglar may be revealing that he is more anxious than another man who interprets the same stimulus as a natural phenomenon and goes back to sleep.

1. In each of the following situations, discuss whether it would be preferable to employ observations in natural conditions, or standardized observations where conditions are fixed in advance, identical for all subjects.
   a. The telephone company wishes to rate its operators on courtesy and clarity of speech. It is able to tap conversations and make recordings.
   b. It is desired to screen Navy personnel for tendency to panic under conditions of extreme noise, as in amphibious landings.
   c. An investigator wishes to study the habitual recklessness of seven-year-old boys in climbing and jumping.
2. Discuss to what extent each of the following may be considered an unstructured stimulus situation.
   a. A teacher, during a test, glances up from her desk and barely observes a hasty movement of one boy who is pulling his hand into his lap from the aisle.
   b. A group of college students are appointed by the instructor as a committee to prepare a panel discussion on compulsory military training and present it to the class.
   c. A group of people play duplicate bridge, the same set of hands being played at each table.
   d. A questionnaire is designed to obtain information about age, income, education, etc. All possible answers are anticipated and presented on the blank in multiple-choice form.
3. Discuss to what extent each of the following is unstructured. If the situation is at all unstructured, discuss whether that characteristic is an advantage or a disadvantage.
   a. Stanford-Binet test, Memory for sentences.
   b. Stanford-Binet test, Picture interpretation (Fig. 20).
   c. A test of addition which presents in random order the combinations up to 9 + 9, the pupil being directed to do as many items as he can in the time allowed.
   d. In the Porteus test (Fig. 1), the subject is to solve a maze. The time it takes him to trace the correct path with his pencil is scored.

PROCEDURES STRESSING QUANTITATIVE MEASUREMENT

Numerous tests investigating typical behavior have been strictly objective in conception, yielding a numerical score representing the behavior in question. These may be contrasted with tests leading to qualitative evaluation of personality, which are discussed separately.

Tests of Character

The most widely known objective measures of typical performance are the tests designed for the Character Education Inquiry of Hartshorne and May (7, 8, 9). The tests in this series represent the only extended effort to evaluate personality by strictly quantitative and objective means. The measures

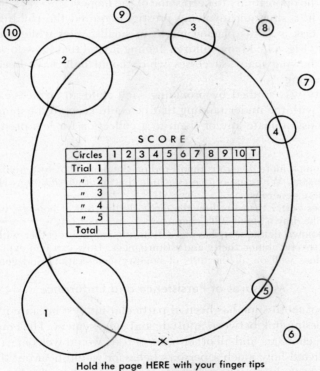

CIRCLES PUZZLE
First Trial

Wait for the signal for each trial. Put the point of your pencil on the cross at the foot of the oval. Then when the signal is given shut your eyes and put a small cross, or X in each circle, taking them in order.

Hold the page HERE with your finger tips

Fig. 88. An "improbable achievement" test of character (7, p. 62).

were designed for an investigation of the nature and development of character, and have been more important as a research method than in practical applications.

Character traits are those in which society judges one type of response as more ethical than another. In view of the sanctions surrounding such behavior, different individuals can be validly compared only by subjecting them to equal temptation in a situation where they believe they can violate standards without detection. Corey's measure of cheating (p. 377) is an example of such a technique, adapted from the C.E.I. procedures. Other traits studied by Hartshorne and May include truthfulness, honesty with money, persistence, coöperativeness, and generosity.

Honesty with money was tested in children by presenting arithmetic problems in which each pupil manipulated a set of coins to obtain the answers. One box of coins, secretly identified, was provided for each pupil, and at the end of the work each pupil placed his own box in a pile in front of the room. Since pupils were unaware that boxes could be identified, many took advantage of the opportunity to keep some of the money.

Honesty in a situation involving prestige required the children to do an impossible task, such as placing marks in small circles while keeping their eyes closed (Fig. 88). Many children, feeling it vital that they do well, turned in papers showing many successes which could only have been obtained through cheating.

Generosity was studied by providing each child an attractive, well-filled pencil box, with the understanding that he could keep all the items, or could inconspicuously donate any of them to a collection for less privileged children.

4. Harry is much more generous than Fred on the pencil-box test, giving up nearly all the objects. Why cannot one conclude that in other situations Harry would also be more generous?
5. If Bill does better than Fred on the circle-dotting test of honesty, what conclusions can be drawn about Bill's character?
6. Joe is a known delinquent, having gotten into trouble together with a gang of boys for several minor thefts and disturbances. How can you explain the fact that he does well on all the tests of honesty, coöperation, and generosity?

Measures of Persistence and Endurance

Strength of motivation has been of particular interest because it is thought of as the missing link between aptitude and achievement. The employer, the teacher, the clinician, and all other users of tests would welcome a technique which predicted how much a person's behavior would bear out the promise shown in tests of ability. Although tests of motivation have not been adequate to meet this need, a few tests have explored possible techniques.

Many measures of persistence have been devised for use in laboratory investigations. The usual technique is to establish a situation in which the subject is permitted to work as long as he will. If, after he has solved one or two puzzles, a subject is presented one which is difficult or impossible, the time he spends at work on it may be taken as an index of persistence. The limitation of such a measure is that its meaning is unclear. Does a low "persistence" score indicate indolence, realistic recognition of one's own limitations, or lack

of confidence? Does a high score indicate praiseworthy industry, slavish obedience, or unintelligent perseveration?

A similar method is the story test of Hartshorne and May (8, pp. 292 ff.).
The pupils read a story which builds to a climax: "Again the terrible piercing
shriek of the whistle screamed at them. Charles could see the frightened face
of the engineer. . . ." Here the examiner directs them that to learn the end-
ing they must read the difficult printed material that follows:

CHARLESLIFTEDLUCILLETOHISBACK"PUTYOURARMSTIGHT
AROUNDMYNECKANDHOLDON

. . . .

NoWhoWTogETBaCkoNthETREStle.HoWTOBRingTHaTErrIfIEDBURDeN
OFACHiLDuPtO

. . . .

fiN ALly tAp-taPC AME ARHYTH Month e BriD GeruNNing fee Tfee Tcom
ING[1]

The pupil separated each word with a vertical mark as he deciphered it; the
amount deciphered became an index of persistent effort.

The Downey Will-Temperament Test[2] was an early and ambitious attempt
to test personality by a series of tasks related to handwriting. The test in
its present form has been found unreliable and quite inadequate to reveal
the basic temperamental qualities of the individual. For less ambitious
purposes, some of the techniques may be useful. The "motor inhibition" test
is one related to voluntary effort; the subject is to write, as slowly as he
possibly can, the phrase "United States of America." Some subjects, highly
motivated, can stretch out this simple act to three-quarters of an hour, without interrupting their writing.

7. The test illustrated in Figure 89 is a test of self-control, requiring the pupil to
   work in the presence of attractive distractions. Does this measure the same moti-
   vational factors as the story-completion test of persistence?

A different technique for studying motivation is the test of resistance to
pain. In tests of this type, subjects are subjected to unpleasant stimuli, such as
a gradually increasing electrical stimulation (10). The subject is told that
his ability to endure pain is being tested, and that he can have the current
cut off whenever it becomes unbearable. This becomes a measure of how
much a subject wants to do well, since the pain in such studies is kept below the level where serious physical damage would result. The test is unstructured only in that the subject has no way of knowing how the pain he
is experiencing compares to that other men were willing ("able") to tolerate.
He therefore is faced with the problem of interpreting for himself whether he

---

[1] From Hartshorne and May, *Studies in deceit.* Copyright, 1928, by The Macmillan
Company and used with their permission.

[2] Publisher: World Book Company

FORM C-2

Fig. 89. A test of self-control, or resistance to distraction (**8**, p. 308).

has performed respectably and can ask to have the pain ended without seeming cowardly. Measures of this sort were tried for pilot selection, but proved too unreliable for use.

Frustrability

Quantitative measurement of reaction to frustration has been less widely applied than qualitative assessment under frustrating conditions. Nevertheless, a few objective, quantitative methods have been tried (21). The common procedure is to measure the subject's ability to perform some type of task such as cancellation or addition under normal test motivation. He is then exposed to a standardized stimulus expected to induce frustration. Unsolvable problems may be presented. Or a test may be given on which the subject expects and hopes to do well, such as an intelligence test, and after the paper has been scored, the tester tells him that his score was low. A second test is then given, similar to the one first given before frustration. A marked rise or decline in score from the original test is taken to indicate response to frustration.

General Findings from Quantitative Tests

Evidence from many studies with all the above techniques seem to confirm four generalizations:

1. Quantitative situation tests can be highly reliable, as measured by correlations between trials in the same series.
2. Irrelevant ability factors affect test scores and reduce validity unless partialed out.
3. Tests presumed to be equivalent, in the sense that they seek to measure the same trait, frequently have low or negligible correlations.
4. There is no possibility of assuming, without direct validation, that a test measuring trait X will predict behavior in a different situation where trait X is considered important.

The Hartshorne-May studies with character were particularly illuminating, because it had been assumed until that time that character was a unit, something predisposing to generally good or bad behavior, and that generalized "character training" would be effective. They found that character traits could indeed be dependably measured; correlations between deception tests of the same type were .62 to .87, when the deception scores were corrected for differences in ability. Moreover, the estimates were stable: tests of cheating showed self-correlations of .75 to .79 when retests were given six months apart (7, II, pp. 88–89). Jones has added the interesting finding that when adults are tested for honesty, their scores correlate .37 with the scores they had earned as adolescents (12). On the other hand, Hartshorne and May found that these excellent measures of deception did not correlate with each other; or, more precisely, the correlations between tests permitting cheating with different sorts of material were too low (.40 to .00) to warrant the conclusion that the various tests measured the same trait. The correlation between cheating on a classroom test and on a coördination test (Fig. 88) was only .50 even after correction for all errors of unreliability. These data exploded the notion that honesty was a general trait which would be measured by any situation permitting dishonesty. Further correlations, between different character tests, were so low as to prove untenable the notion of a generalized character accounting for all desirable traits. Intercorrelations of honesty, persistence, coöperation, and so on were positive, but averaged only .24. This is evidence that the "general factor" in character is of negligible size and has little relation to specific behaviors (9).

Similar evidence was obtained by Thornton with tests alleged to measure persistence (19). He found that tests supposed to relate to persistence actually measured three different personality factors. One factor was willingness to endure discomfort or pain, found in the shock test and in another test requiring one to grip a dynamometer as long and as firmly as possible. An entirely separate factor was found in tests of what he called "plodding," the keeping on at a task when no special immediate discomfort was involved. Tests showing this factor included the story test of Hartshorne and May and Downey's test of enforced slowness in writing. Interestingly, three self-report questionnaires alleged to obtain descriptions of persistence showed negligible relations with the actual persistence and endurance factors. Instead, they seemed to measure an entirely different factor of their own, presumably "tendency to claim to be persistent." Thornton's study supports the belief that there is a general tendency to persistence ("plodding"), but that some tests supposed to measure the factor actually do not. Moreover, in any single test of persistence, there is a large unique factor.

It is not difficult to understand why different tests of a trait like honesty have low correlations. Some people need to do well on school tasks, because that is an area where their aspiration is high and where they expect approval. The same persons may find no reason to cheat on a coördination test, which does not "mean anything to them." Even within the same stimulus-type, generalization is difficult. If we leave a dollar bill on a desk, Jones may take it, and Smith may not. Jones succumbed to that particular temptation more readily, but we may not conclude that he is less honest regarding money. Perhaps he needed money more, so that the temptation was not psychologically equal. If the amount had been twenty dollars, perhaps Jones would have left it on the table because of a realization that this would be a serious loss to the owner of the money, whereas Smith would have given in to the larger temptation. If it is impossible to generalize even from one controlled test to another of a similar type, it is clearly impossible to generalize that a pupil honest in tests will show good character in adult business dealings, or that a pupil caught in a petty theft will be untrustworthy in other matters. Similar cautions extend to all measures of generalized personality traits.

The experimenter who wishes to employ measures of specific traits encounters difficulties when he wishes to treat scores numerically. In a measure of cheating, the person who earns a high score without cheating will have little motive to cheat. In persistence tests, the measure is at best a composite of motivation and ability. Thornton found that physical strength was a major factor permitting some subjects to earn higher scores than others in motor and endurance tasks. Logical analysis is quite important in interpreting tests supposed to measure traits.

It should not be concluded that tests of specific traits have no place. They are invaluable for many research purposes, and the findings of such research may have practical significance. Maller is authority for the statement that the Hartshorne-May findings on the nature and development of character led one national agency working with youth to revise its program completely. One stimulus to the revision was the finding that those who had received most recognition in the agency's character-building activities were on the average *most* likely to cheat (11, p. 201). This again is not hard to explain when we consider that striving for recognition in a competitive program, and need to obtain high scores even in a puzzle test, may stem from the same basic insecurity and feeling of personal inadequacy.

Symonds, in 1931, concluded that performance tests of conduct are so specific that they permit only four possible actions (15, pp. 352–354):

1. They may be discarded as too specific to be practically useful.
2. Tests may be devised to correspond exactly to the situation where they will be used.
3. An estimate of a general trait, such as honesty, may be based on a large number of tests which are specific but have some intercorrelation.
4. Performance tests may be used empirically to predict any behavior with which they correlate.

8. Analyze the story-completion test of persistence, identifying all the factors which might cause one fifth-grader to earn a higher score than another.
9. Children from homes with low socio-economic status cheated more on achievement tests than other children ($r = .49$) (7). What factors must be taken into account before concluding that these children are more apt to violate standards of good conduct?

PROCEDURES LEADING TO QUALITATIVE EVALUATION

The Concept of the Indivisible Personality

In the field of personality, the tests just discussed are analogous to the measures of ability used by Binet's predecessors. The first stage in psychological measurement, it will be recalled, was to try to isolate specific abilities which could be precisely estimated, in the hope that a combination of these would reveal the significant features of man. In the trait approach to personality, investigators have sought to find a limited number of elements which could be used to map out and predict typical behavior. Except for limited types of prediction and research this approach has been found futile, because behavior seems to draw upon an almost limitless number of specific traits. Behavior in any given situation is determined by the combination of features in that situation, not by general habits. Even Guthrie, sympathetic to the conception of personality as habit, comments, "The search for universal traits, or traits that attach to all of an individual's behavior, is mistaken in its conception and bound to fail" (11, p. 63). Traits being specific, the trait method of measurement can only be useful for specific predictions.

Investigators of personality have had higher ambitions, and rightly so, since the clinician, the educator, and others dealing with people must predict their behavior in the wide range of life situations they daily encounter. A conception stemming from the work of Freud offers promise of accurate and useful analysis of personality. This point of view is referred to under a variety of names: "psychodynamics," "study of the personality as a whole," "depth psychology," and so on. It is complex, and cannot be adequately treated here. Probably the most adequate account for the person otherwise unacquainted with clinical literature is the summary by Mowrer and Kluckhohn (11, pp. 69–135).

The dynamic approach insists that personality is more than a collection of specific conditionings to situations. Instead, it is believed that the many specific behaviors exhibit an underlying unity. This unity is thought of in terms of "needs," "complexes," and other emotional forces. What the person does at any time can theoretically be predicted from his needs and a knowledge of the forces in the field where he acts. In one situation he may be dependent, to escape criticism from a superior; in another, he may be dominant, to avoid exposing his insecurity to a subordinate; in a third, he may be coöperative and non-assertive, because he feels secure with that group of companions. The dynamic approach assumes that inconsistencies in behavior have consistent causes, whereas the trait approach must consider inconsistencies as errors.

The dynamic approach is frankly qualitative, although scores are often employed in an intermediate stage of interpretation. The dynamic approach assumes that personality is constantly developing, and seeks to predict how it will change, rather than to assume that future behavior will be closely similar to behavior today. The approach further postulates that one trait can only be understood in relation to all other traits, and looks toward a synthesis of all types of evidence. Since both inference and synthesis are necessary in going from evidence of behavior to a description of personality dynamics, the method is subjective. The quality of the results depends upon the ability and effort of the analyst to a degree not found in other tests. This is a tremendous disadvantage, since even if the method is good, it is good only in the hands of a user with "clinical insight." And who is to judge which psychologists possess this intuition, and on what days it is functioning at its best? While the tests used in dynamic analysis are frequently standardized, the interpretation process is relatively uncontrolled. Different workers trained in the same theory do reach similar conclusions on most cases, but the process is definitely open to subjective errors.

The process of dynamic analysis begins with some type of evidence about the person's behavior. The evidence may be from a clinical interview, from a self-report test (cf. pp. 323 ff.), from personal products and documents, from observation in daily activities, or from specially planned test observations and projective tests. The data are related by the interpreter to everything else known about the subject, and an interpretation is made. The interpretative description is considered adequate when it is internally consistent and not contradicted by any of the data available, and when it conforms to the analyst's theory of personality. A description is sometimes limited to a particular segment of behavior, such as how the subject reasons or how he will function on a particular job. Sometimes it tries to describe him completely, as he is now. The most ambitious and most widely useful analysis not only considers the present but seeks to explain how the personality developed, from infancy onward. Interpretations are of course treated as tentative, except where a definite decision must be made immediately. The accuracy of the analysis is reviewed where possible in the light of subsequent evidence.

Tests usable in making a clinical evaluation of personality range from the commonest measures of intellect and psychomotor functions to highly complex observational tests of ability to work with others. Observation in connection with tests of ability has been discussed at length in earlier chapters. In the following sections, the reader will be introduced to tests of concept formation, reaction to frustration, and social behavior. These are representative of the situational tests now in use. In Chapter 20, projective tests will be discussed.

Tests of Concept Formation

Intellectual processes are commonly thought of as abilities, and in most mental tests the subject does try to do as well as he can. But mental performance has an important qualitative aspect, since people of similar ability attack problems in entirely different fashions. The way a person uses his intelligence, given a problem that permits varied attack, may be more significant clinically than a precise IQ. A few tests have been designed to identify the typical ways in which a person uses his mind. These tests have a close relation to tests of ability, and might well have been considered in Part II of the book; but their use is almost exclusively in connection with the clinical study of personality.

The most prominent tests of this type are the concept formation tests of Vigotsky, Hanfmann-Kasanin, and Goldstein-Scheerer-Weigl.[3] The Hanfmann-Kasanin[4] may be taken as an example. Twenty-two wooden blocks of several colors, shapes, heights, and sizes are placed on the table before the subject. On the hidden underside of each block is printed a nonsense syllable. The syllable defines a type of block (all *mur* blocks are small and tall). The examiner tells the subject that the blocks are of four different kinds, one of which is named *mur*, and that he is to find the four kinds and sort the blocks. The subject is then free to proceed as he likes to discover the classification, except that he may not invert the blocks to see the name. After each trial sorting, the examiner points out one mistake and requires the task to be repeated. This goes on until the problem is solved and the principle of classification is stated. Observation shows whether the subject uses a logical hypothesis ("perhaps all *mur* are triangles"), an arbitrary hypothesis, or pure guessing. The degree to which he can form an abstract concept from experience on successive trials is noted. One can observe ability to profit from a correction, ability to discard a false set and take on a new one, bizarre procedures and verbalizations, and so on. The test yields a numerical score, but more significant is the character of insight and conceptual thinking displayed. The test is based on the theory that schizophrenics are unable to think abstractly but must respond to each object in the environment as a separate individual thing. Preliminary results show marked differences between schizophrenics, normals, and cases of organic damage (6). Tests of this nature have not been employed as yet to assess the thinking habits of persons of normal mentality.

10. Which tests of the Stanford-Binet and Wechsler series are particularly suited to making observation of typical mental processes?
11. Are any personality characteristics other than intellectual habits likely to be brought to light in the Hanfmann-Kasanin test?

Reaction to Frustration; Stress Situations

Two techniques of studying reaction to frustration or emotional stress have been described earlier in the chapter, the Observational Stress Test of the Air Force and the measurement of change in test score before and after frustration. Both of these methods permit either quantitative or qualitative scoring. Several other methods for studying stress have been devised, this problem having attracted widespread attention for a number of reasons. Most of the significant problems in the field of personality relate to emotion, and one of the surest ways of inducing emotion is to frustrate the subject. Differences in emotional behavior are highly important in clinical diagnosis. And in practical selection, one of the important questions when filling

[3] Publisher: Psych. Corp.
[4] Publisher: C. H. Stoelting Co.

responsible positions is: How can this candidate cope with pressure, criticism, and obstacles?

Frustration methods have produced considerable understanding of development of aggression and other emotional responses in young children (2). A common situational test is to permit the child to play with moderately attractive toys for a period of time. He is then given a brief opportunity to play with a set of "magnificent" toys, far superior to the first set. When these are removed and placed behind a barrier, behavior of different children varies widely. Some sulk, some claw at the barrier, some peacefully return to the former toys. In playing with those toys, variation from the earlier play can be seen. Regression to a more immature form of play is especially common. Lerner has applied this method and games involving obstacles, to make clinical analysis of personalities of young children (14).

Only three controlled attempts to use stress methods in selection have been reported to date: the Air Force tests, a test given to prospective police officers (4), and the assessment program of the OSS (16). Presumably the method will be given further practical trial in civilian situations.

12. What practical difficulties may be anticipated if one introduces frustration tests like that of the Air Force into an industrial selection program?
13. Can one assume that the same frustrating situation is equally frustrating to all subjects?
14. Justify Freeman's statement that investigation of stress tests for possible industrial use must be done in real employment situations, since laboratory trials of the method are not comparable to the selection situation.

Tests of Social Behavior

If one had information about the intellectual processes, the emotional reactions, and the social behavior of a person, he would know about the most significant areas of personality. It is the third of these factors that is tapped by tests of leadership, coöperation, reaction to authority, and so on. Tests of interpersonal behaviors have become increasingly significant as psychology has extended its interest to the psychology of the group. In addition to the research interests of social psychology, tests of social behavior have major importance for selecting leaders in all fields. Military psychology has pioneered in these techniques.

A device for studying social behavior in perhaps its least complex form is a German test for leader selection, developed before World War II. A special apparatus is used, consisting of two pairs of shears, linked by rods so that they must move in unison. While one shear is opening, the other is closing. Each subject operates one pair of shears, cutting a series of increasingly complex patterns from a sheet of paper. The shears are so arranged that if one man goes directly and forcefully at his task, the shears of the other man move in a rhythm which makes accurate cutting almost impossible. By means of observation, automatic recording, and inspection of the product, the tester looks for evidence of initiative, dominance, and co-operation which is used with other data in assessing workers or soldiers (13).

More complex are the OSS leadership tests, based on German and British methods. In one, a group of candidates for the intelligence service are directed to move a heavy eight-foot log, and themselves, over two walls ten feet high, eight feet apart, and separated by an imaginary bottomless chasm. Observers note which men take initiative and leadership, how they direct others, how they accept directions, and other characteristics (16, 1).

The OSS program, of which this test is representative, is the most thoroughgoing attempt yet made to assess personality for practical purposes (as distinguished from clinical or research work). The problem was important, since men selected would take responsibility for security of vital information, for the safety of units of the underground behind enemy lines, or similar duties. Candidates for assignment were drawn from the military services and from civilian positions. They were tested in small groups, each group undergoing "testing" for three days. Testing included ability measures, a continuous observation by the psychological staff, interviews, group discussions, and situational tests. At the end of the testing, each man was judged on the basis of his total personality, or as much of it as could be brought to the surface by highly skilled observers using test situations as varied as they could invent.

One test likely to have widespread importance is the *psychodrama*. This method, which is also being applied to therapy, requires the subject to assume a role and play out a scene before an audience. In OSS testing, each man was assigned a role which might shed light on some facet of character about which the interviewers and observers felt they needed further data (18). A few of the themes used as a basis for psychodramas were:

Personal criticism—
    failure to send liquor to cocktail party
    making a poorly protected bank loan
Interpersonal conflict—
    competition in running dance halls
    differences of opinion on location of a hospital
Authority-subordination—
    sergeant reporting bread riot to a major
    motion-picture producer securing permission from censor to show a
      picture

In each drama, the two or more men are given their respective assignments and a sketch of the situation, but the dialog and outcome are left to develop in the discussion. While research reports on the technique are lacking, it is claimed that the man reveals much of his own character and of his insight into others.

Perhaps the high point of ingenuity in situation testing to date has been the OSS construction test (16, pp. 102 ff.). This device is thought of as a leadership test. The subject is assigned to build a five-foot cube with a sort of super-Tinkertoy. Poles and spools must be fitted together, and since the test is too large to be managed by one man, two helpers are assigned. After giving directions, the tester ostentatiously clicks his stop watch and retreats. What the subject does not know is that his helpers are highly trained "stumblebums." Kippy is negative, indolent, a drawback. Buster is an eager beaver, ready to do all manner of things, mostly wrong, and also primed to needle the candidate with personal criticism. This is reported as a typical dialog (1, p. 95):[5]

> "*Candidate*: Well, let's get going.
> "*Buster*: What is it you want done, exactly? What do I do first?
> "*Candidate*: Well, first put some corners together—let's see, make eight of these corners and be sure you pin them like this one.
> "*Buster*: You mean we both make eight corners or just one of us?
> "*Candidate*: You each make four of these, and hurry.
> "*Kippy*: Whacha in, the Navy? You look like one of them curly-headed Navy boys all the girls are after.
> "*Candidate*: Er, no, I'm not in anything.
> "*Kippy*: Just a draft dodger, eh?
> "*Candidate*: Let's have less talk and more work. You build a square over here and you build one over there.
> "*Kippy*: Who are you talking to—him or me? Why don't you give us a number or something—call one of us number one and the other number two?
> "*Candidate*: I'm sorry. What's your name?
> "*Buster*: Mine's Buster and his is Kippy. What's yours?
> "*Candidate*: You can call me Slim.
> "*Buster*: Not with that shining head of yours. What do they call you, Baldy or Curly? Did you ever think of wearing a toupee?
> "*Slim*: Come on, get to work.
> "*Kippy*: He's sensitive about being bald.
> "*Slim*: Just let's get this thing finished. We haven't much more time. Hey, there, you, be careful. You knocked that pole out deliberately.
> "*Kippy*: Who me? Now listen to me, you —, if this — thing had been built right from the beginning, the poles wouldn't come out. For —, they send a boy out here to do a man's job. . . ."

Kippy and Buster are psychologists, and are in a position to make an excellent report on the man's reaction.

VALIDITY OF SITUATIONAL TESTS

The validity of situational tests is in some respects not open to question. The man is placed in a standard situation, and how he reacts is unimpeachable evidence of honesty, frustrability, thinking methods, and so on at that

---

[5] Reprinted from the March, 1946, issue of *Fortune* Magazine by special permission of the Editors.

time, in that situation. The difficulty lies in inferring how he will act on other occasions and in other situations.

Systematic studies of the sampling reliability of situational tests are few. The evidence to date indicates that repeated measures on different occasions are highly correlated, provided that the tests on each occasion are fairly long. But there is little evidence on the reliability of frustration tests, which might be susceptible to the day-to-day variation in irritability of the subject.

The first assumption needed to compare individuals is that the stimulus situation is constant. But failing on a puzzle means more to some men than others, and produces unequal frustration. Some people are wounded by failure, but others are unconcerned about puzzle solving and are unmoved by failure on such a task. In stress situations, threat of failure may well be great for a man to whom getting into the Air Force is very important; he may show more emotionality than another man who doesn't care much. In combat, the qualities that made for a poor score in the Observational Stress Test may lead to superior devotion to duty, whereas the man who didn't care may lack motivation in the field. If qualitative evaluation is made, it is unnecessary to assume that the situation was identical for all persons. Instead, one may note that the subject displayed great emotion, which means either low tolerance of frustration or strong motivation to do well in this test. The advantage of qualitative interpretation is that every behavior can be studied in its context, which quantitative methods do not readily permit.

It is then necessary to make inferences from the observed behavior, which involves many sources of error. If the test is objective and quantitative, one has the burden of demonstrating that the test behavior is related to some external situation. If the procedure is qualitative, one must find means of minimizing subjective errors. The OSS used numerous interpreters, who agreed on the final assessment in conference, after all had become acquainted with the candidate. This is a costly method, but it may be essential to reach sound judgments.

The fact that assessors observing candidates in different situations were able to agree on the final assessment suggests that the OSS method must be getting at some truth about personality. Attempts to validate the method were not successful, on the whole. It was virtually impossible to obtain a dependable criterion for comparing men, since the assessees were assigned to different theaters of war, to perform different duties under different superiors. Ratings made under those conditions could scarcely be predicted even with the most superb psychological insight into each man. The correlations of assessment ratings with criterion ratings mean very little. One representative figure is the correlation of .39 between assessment ratings from the three-day testing and ratings made in the field, for men whose job overseas was the same one for which they were assessed (16, p. 427). A more clinical validation was made by comparing sketches written during assessment with descriptions of how the men performed in the field, for 36 cases. Staff members judged that in 24 of the cases, diagnosis and prognosis were essentially correct, and in only 5 cases was either essentially incorrect (16, p. 437). This type of judgment is too much open to bias to be considered final evidence of validity.

At this time, it is impossible to make a general evaluation of the validity of situational tests. So long as they are treated only as objective measures of limited traits, few questions arise. Evidence is quite inadequate to support any contention for or against their validity as measures of the total personality. As predictors, they seem to have promise, according to military experience. Presumably, when analysts can study the personality with many tests and arrive at a coherent and consistent picture of the individual, the individual tests must be sound. But there is no criterion to show whether a test has correctly laid open the inner personality structure of the subject. And even within a sound and useful test, such as the Hanfmann-Kasanin, there is little evidence to show which of the many interpretations the test leads to are sound, or to show which types of evidence and inference from the test are untrustworthy.

We must necessarily await further research before generalizing about observations in test situations. Situational and projective tests may be the only truly valid testing approach to personality. But they are too recent to be validated, since one must learn how to use a test before he can prove that his method of using it is valid.

15. If Corey's experimental test of cheating in a psychology class were repeated with the same students in a history class, what factors might cause different students to be identified as cheaters?
16. A personnel manager wishes to judge six college seniors as prospective branch managers. He brings the group together and leads them to discuss problems related to the position, such as current labor relations. He lets the men do the talking, merely keeping the conversation going. After the conference, he examines a recording made by a concealed microphone to determine how each man participated. What assumptions is he making if he hires the man who contributed most to the solution of the problems discussed?
17. If two psychologists, observing the situation testing of a subject, reach different interpretations regarding his personality, how could one determine which opinions are erroneous?
18. If one desires to institute an OSS-type program for the selection of personnel, stressing situational tests and qualitative evaluation of the total personality, how should the psychologists to conduct the program be selected?

SUGGESTED READINGS

Anon. "A good man is hard to find." *Fortune*, 1946, 33, 92–95 *et. seq.*
Lerner, Eugene. "Experiments in active play techniques," in Lerner, Eugene, and Murphy, Lois B. (eds.), "Methods for the study of personality in young children." *Monogr. Soc. Res. Child Developm.*, 1941, 6, No. 4, pp. 159–210.

REFERENCES

1. Anon. "A good man is hard to find." *Fortune,* 1946, 33, 92–95 *et. seq.*
2. Barker, Roger, and others. "Frustration and regression: an experiment with young children." *Univ. Ia. Stud. Child Welf.,* 1941, 18, No. 1.
3. Frank, L. K. "Projective methods for the study of personality." *J. Psychol.,* 1939, 8, 389–413.
4. Freeman, G. L., and others. "The stress interview." *J. abnorm. soc. Psychol.,* 1942, 37, 427–447.
5. Guilford, J. P. (ed.). *Printed classification tests.* AAF Aviation Psychol. Prog. Res. Rep. No. 5. Washington: Govt. Printing Off., 1947.
6. Hanfmann, Eugenia, and Kasanin, Jacob. "Conceptual thinking in schizophrenia." *Nerv. ment. Dis. Monogr. Ser.,* 1942, No. 67.
7. Hartshorne, Hugh, and May, Mark A. *Studies in deceit.* New York: Macmillan, 1928.
8. Hartshorne, Hugh, and May, Mark A. *Studies in service and self-control.* New York: Macmillan, 1929.
9. Hartshorne, Hugh, and May, Mark A. *Studies in the organization of character.* New York: Macmillan, 1930.
10. Howells, T. H. "An experimental study of persistence." *J. abnorm. soc. Psychol.,* 1933, 28, 14–29.
11. Hunt, J. McV. (ed.). *Personality and the behavior disorders.* New York: Ronald Press, 1944.
12. Jones, Vernon. "A comparison of certain measures of honesty at early adolescence with honesty in adulthood—a follow-up study." *Amer. Psychologist,* 1946, 1, 261.
13. Kunze, Bruno. "Proben für die Zusammenarbeit von Menschen und deren Wechselwirkung." *Industr. Psychotech.,* 1931, 8, 147–159.
14. Lerner, Eugene, and Murphy, Lois B. (eds.). "Methods for the study of personality in young children." *Monogr. Soc. Res. Child Developm.,* 1941, 6, No. 4.
15. Murray, Henry A., and Stein, Morris. "Note on the selection of combat officers." *Psychosom. Med.,* 1943, 5, 386–391.
16. OSS Assessment Staff. *Assessment of men.* New York: Rinehart, 1948.
17. Symonds, Percival M. *Diagnosing personality and conduct.* New York: Appleton-Century, 1931.
18. Symonds, Percival M. "Role playing as a diagnostic procedure in the selection of leaders." *Sociatry,* 1947, 1, 43–50.
19. Thornton, George R. "A factor analysis of tests designed to measure persistence." *Psychol. Monogr.,* 1939, 51, No. 3.
20. Waehner, Trude S. "Interpretation of spontaneous drawings and paintings." *Genet. Psychol. Monogr.,* 1946, 33, 3–72.
21. Zander, Alvin F. "A study of experimental frustration." *Psychol. Monogr.,* 1944, 56, No. 3.

CHAPTER 20

Projective Techniques

The preceding chapter ended on a note of uncertainty: that situational tests leading to qualitative, dynamic analysis of personality are a promising technique but must undergo extensive development and refinement. Projective techniques, being an extension and higher development of the same method, present similar problems. The projective test uses a stimulus even more unstructured than the situational test—if possible, one so novel that the subject can bring to it no specific knowledge of how to respond. White provides an apt summary of the strength and the weakness of the method (21, p. 215):

"Since little external aid is provided from conventional patterns he [the subject] is all but obliged to give expression to the most readily available forces within himself. It is further characteristic of projective methods that the subject does not know what inferences the experimenter intends to make; his attention is focussed on the play or task in hand, and it is well-nigh impossible for him to guess at its more remote psychological meaning. Favorable conditions are thus created for unselfconscious revelation from the hidden regions of personality.

"From the nature of the material sought and from the unavoidable indirectness of the seeking it is obvious that the interpretation of imaginative productions will offer great scientific difficulties. Even a short segment of imaginative behavior contains items, patterns, and trends in bewildering variety; intuition can seize upon clues, but it is no easy matter to establish reliability, observer agreement, and validity. This atmosphere of guesswork is highly uncongenial to the psychologist who prefers his science in relatively finished form. To a certain extent, however, it arises from the novelty of the problems and the recency of the attack upon them; pathways to a greater certainty are . . . already beginning to show themselves."[1]

Projective tests come nearer to grasping "the whole person" at once than any other testing technique. Even the complex situational tests must focus on segments of the personality, such as leadership behavior or response to stress, and many such tests must be combined to arrive at a whole analysis. A single projective test, however, will often yield a tentative portrait of the entire personality. Self-report tests were characterized earlier as a standardized clinical interview; in many ways, projective tests resemble a standardization of the dream interpretation that Freud introduced. The two most widely used projective tests, the Rorschach and the Thematic Apperception

---

[1] J. McV. Hunt (ed.), *Personality and the behavior disorders*. Copyright, 1944, The Ronald Press Company.

Test, will be described here, together with a brief summary of other techniques.

THE RORSCHACH TEST

History

The Rorschach inkblot test is the invention of Hermann Rorschach, a Swiss psychiatrist. As one of many studies of mental patients, he designed what he called "an experimental investigation in form-perception." This led first to the finding that schizophrenics, manics, hysterics, and other clinical groups had different characteristic ways of perceiving. He also learned to analyze these perceptual characteristics as an indication of the personality make-up of subjects, normal and abnormal. He published his *Psychodiagnostics*, giving the complete outline of his procedure and theory, in 1921, shortly before his death at the age of 37. In this, together with a posthumously published extension of his hypotheses, he outlined the test and its interpretation substantially as it is used today.

Marked interest in Rorschach work in the United States is usually dated from the appearance in 1937 of a monograph by Beck, based on his trials of the technique in a Boston hospital. The other major leader in America has been Klopfer, who elaborated Rorschach's original method. The Rorschach procedure was tested with many clinical groups prior to the recent war. During the war it was used experimentally and practically by all armed services especially in connection with neuropsychiatric problems. Success in these trials has stimulated widespread attempts to apply the procedure to children and college students, industrial employees including executive personnel, and all types of clinical groups. Recent methods of administering the Rorschach as a group test have increased the use of the test, though research on group methods is inadequate.

Acceptance of the Rorschach test has been retarded by the "cult" atmosphere said to surround it. In part this arises from its origin in clinical practice. Clinicians who tried the test and were impressed by its frequent successes in individual cases rarely had systematic research to support their convictions. Traditional experimental psychologists and psychometric investigators were not inclined to study the test, because one to two years of study were considered necessary to learn the test, and because it was said to be based on "insightful interpretation" rather than upon the objective scoring conventional in American testing. Recent data (28) indicate that objective analysis can be made of test responses, although many test users are not willing to so limit themselves. Another stumbling block to use of the test was the development of two systems of interpretation. Minor differences were emphasized, and divisions among Rorschach users were established which are only now dying out. A further problem in the acceptance of the Rorschach techniques is that a new vocabulary has been developed to discuss the information it brings to light. The report of a Rorschach analysis is likely to contain words like "inner life," "introversive," "experience balance," and "constriction"—terms which have little meaning to the person who has not made a detailed study of the test or psychiatric theory. Such terms are not conveniently definable, which makes the test harder to study than most, although it will be recalled that even so conventional a word as "intelligence" can be interpreted only in the light of much study of the test used in its measurement.

Test Procedure

The Rorschach test is an experiment, an attempt to see how the subject responds to a standardized stimulus. It differs from other experiments in the wide latitude of response open to the subject. The subject sits with his back turned to the experimenter. After establishing rapport, the investigator gives

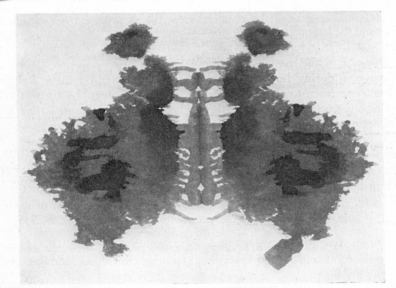

Fig. 90.   An inkblot of the Rorschach type.

him a card, with approximately the following instructions: "People see all sorts of things in these ink-blot pictures; now tell me what you see, what it might be for you, what it makes you think of" (25, p. 32).

The same procedure is followed for each card, the subject being permitted to respond as long as he desires. There are ten cards, which vary from V, a fairly good black-and-white representation of a bat, to IX, a vague mass of irregularly blended green, orange, and pink. The inkblots were selected by Rorschach from experimental trial of hundreds of blots. "Parallel" sets of cards have been prepared by Harrower, and Behn. Figure 90 shows an ink-blot of the Rorschach type.

In addition to transcribing as completely as possible the remarks of the subject, the experimenter notes, without the subject's awareness, how long it takes him to respond to each card, whether his average time per response is high or low, the extent to which he turns the card, and other behaviors.

1. An unstructured situation is one a person may interpret as he sees fit. What questions about the task must the person answer for himself in taking the Rorschach test?
2. Considering the Rorschach test solely as a sample of problem-solving behavior in a test situation, what hypotheses about the subject could be based on such data as the following.
   a. J. S. gives about twice as many responses as the average subject.
   b. H. G. takes an exceptionally long time per response.
   c. F. F. does not turn the black-and-white cards, but he repeatedly turns the colored cards, where he has difficulty finding possible answers.
3. What information might be obtained from the way the subject expresses his ideas and the language he uses?

The Integrative Analysis

Before considering how the responses are treated, it will be helpful to examine a specimen Rorschach report to see what is meant by the test's claim to describe the total personality. Although the test yields quantitative scores, the fullest outcome of the analysis is a description of the person, embracing his abilities, interests, motivation, and social attributes. Such a description, if complete and valid, would necessarily give a unique report for every person, corresponding to our knowledge that all people are really different.

Descriptions of cases may be brief or extensive, depending on their intended use. Each of the following paragraphs is a description of a college student, where the aim was a brief characterization (28, pp. 22–23):

"Immature, expansive girl. Unsystematic, rather careless, probably socially oriented and not much interested in studies. Moderate intelligence, warm, lively, but rather superficial."

"Constricted personality, emotional responsiveness deeply repressed. Very eager for approval and prestige, but fundamentally detached in human relationships and pedantic in approach to ideas. Conscientious, over-systematic, with rigid ideals and undue concentration on learned detail at the expense of independent or imaginative thought. Need for routine and exactness, with fear of freedom. Difficulty in meeting new situations or protracted situations of uncongenial nature. External adjustment as student likely to be satisfactory, but with very stubborn limitations."

In contrast to the above, which is nearly the minimum that the integrative approach to the Rorschach can provide, thorough analyses are often several pages long. Sample interpretations appear in the books by Beck and Rorschach, who include records of scholars, psychotics, feeble-minded persons, and children (5, p. 37). Among the questions the test can answer, at least in some records, are the following: What is this person's characteristic attack on problems? How great are his intellectual resources, including precision of observation, ability to organize, and originality? How hard does he drive himself; does he make the most of his ability? What emotional factors account for any gap between ability and quality of production? Has he any special interests? Does he enjoy social intercourse and can he adapt to other people? Is he at ease internally? Does he habitually express his emotions impulsively, repress them rigidly, or use them to enrich social relations?

4. For each of the above questions, what test or tests discussed in earlier chapters (if any) would give the same information?
5. Which of the above questions would it ordinarily be important to answer in each of the following situations?
   a. In guiding a college student having scholastic difficulty.
   b. In determining whether a disturbed person is under strain severe enough to cause a breakdown.
   c. In selecting a personnel manager.

Scoring Procedure

The first step in summarizing a Rorschach performance is to "score" each response. The scorer classifies each answer in three ways: according to location, determinant, and content. This scoring is guided by directions and scoring samples such as those for the Stanford-Binet test. Hertz has found that trained scorers, using the same system, agree on 93 percent of scorings on principal factors (17). Before a tester can score Rorschach responses dependably he must have studied the test and practiced analysis of records under supervision. For this reason, no attempt is made to teach the scoring procedure here. Just enough information is given to show how the test operates.

The scoring of four responses will illustrate the procedure. Suppose that on Card X, which is a mixture of bright-colored forms, we have these responses:

1. A big splashy print design for a summer dress.
2. Enlarged photograph of a snowflake (refers to a large crab-shaped area).
3. Two little boys blowing bubbles. You just see them from the waist up.
4. Head of a rabbit.

The scoring[2] of these responses (based in part on supplementary information obtained by inquiry) is:

Response	Location	Determinant	Content	
1.	W	CF+	Art,	Cg
2.	D	F−	N	
3.	D	M+	Hd	
4.	D	F+	Ad	P

[2] This discussion is based on the Beck system because of its greater simplicity and objectivity.

Locations are scored according to the area of the blot used in the response. Categories are W (whole), D (commonly perceived subdivisions), and Dd (unusual details). "Dress design" referred to all of the blot, and is scored W. The others are detail responses, scored D.

In scoring determinants, the scorer identifies the elements in the blot which led the subject to see what he did. Careful supplementary questioning is needed to make certain of this scoring. The principal determinants are form, color, movement, and shading. Most responses are dependent upon the shape of the blot (F). Responses which fit the blot are scored $F+$; those

Table 68.   Determinants Scored in Rorschach Systems

Determinant	Typical Response	Beck Symbol[a]	Klopfer Symbol[a]	Related to
Form				
Shape of blot	Cat face; totem pole	F	F	Awareness of reality
Movement				
Human seen in action	Men fighting	M	M	Poise, fantasy
Animal in action	Bird flying	—	FM	Less mature use of imagination
Inanimate force	Explosion	—	m	Inner conflict
Color				
Color of blot	Red butterfly, fire	C	C	Social-emotional response, impulsiveness
Shading				
Perspective	Landscape	V	FK	Feeling of inferiority
Texture	Fur rug	Y	c	Tact, shyness, caution
Hazy forms	Cloud; smoke	Y	K	Anxiety
Hazy quality differentiated	X-ray; relief map	Y	k	Anxiety
Achromatic color	Black cat; white sail	Y	C'	Depression or elation
Position				
Response to place on card	"Heart, because in center"	Po	Po	Irrationality

[a] Where two or more determinants affect the response, a combined symbol is used, e.g., CF, Fc, YF.

which are arbitrary in form are scored $F-$. Responses involving color also involve form in most cases. Where two or more determinants affect the response, they are combined. FC is a response, such as "yellow lion," in which the form is crucial. In CF responses such as "dress design," almost any shape of blot would be equally appropriate to the answer. Movement is of course not actually in the blot. A response seeing a human in movement indicates that the subject has imaginatively added something to the static form of the blot. Human or human-like action is scored M. A summary of all determinants is given in Table 68.

Content scoring uses such categories as humans (H), parts of humans (Hd), animals (A), parts of animals (Ad), objects (Ob), etc. "Snowflake" was scored nature (N). "Dress design" was scored Art and Clothing (Cg). An additional score, P, applies to certain popular responses which are often given. Original responses are scored O.

Content should be analyzed for "thematic material," in which the subject is using an inkblot to tell a story drawn from his own subconscious. One can note tentatively the possibility that a remark like the following reveals the subject's attitude toward his life:

(To Card VI.) "This is a cutworm. This is a section of a field and the cutworm is going up the row charging out leaving nothing behind but ground and desolation. Probably this would represent feelers, groping as it goes along. He's finding it pretty fruitless up here—this (behind him) has been better."

The scoring of responses is summarized by counting the number of times each symbol was used.

6. Score the following responses to Card X as well as you can without benefit of inquiry or access to the inkblot itself.
   a. A collection of brightly colored insects, mounted.
   b. A cow jumping through the air.
   c. A rough piece of pink coral.
   d. A tiny horse.

Meaning of Scores

Interpretation of Rorschach scores is difficult to learn. While trait names are associated with the various symbols, the full meaning of the test behaviors is oversimplified by the trait names. Caution must also be exercised because the same score has different meaning in different records. Any one score must be related to the total pattern. For example, a person who is forcing to obtain a large number of responses is more likely to have $F-$ responses than one who is less productive but has equal ability.

As a problem-solving situation, the test reveals much about the intellect and drive of the person. Form quality is dependent on self-criticism. $F-$ responses suggest lack of accuracy and are common in feeble-minded and psychotic performances. An extremely high percentage of $F+$, on the other hand, indicates very cautious self-criticism. The number and quality of responses is a measure of intellectual output. Quality of output is shown in precision of ideas, complexity of organization, and originality.

Location reveals the subject's problem-solving attack. Emphasis on W indicates an effort to solve the problem in a hard but complete way, and is associated with intellectual ambition, interest in systematically organized ideas and theoretical matters. The D approach, breaking a total problem into more meaningful sections, is thought of as a "common-sense" attack, one which must be used in practical affairs. Breaking the blot into tiny or unusual areas must represent some special drive. Sometimes it is a demand for perfect correspondence of blot with idea which can only be attained by matching some tiny form with an idea. Persons using many tiny details are often, in their daily lives, preoccupied by trivial and practically insignificant matters.

Hunter finds a correlation between Rorschach estimate and measured IQ of .78[3] (22). In a group of young children varying widely in age, several Rorschach scores correlate .60–.70 with Binet MA (11). But the Rorschach is less a measure of "how much intelligence?" than of how it functions. It may indicate that a person is not using his potential because of lack of drive or because of neurotic clinging to "certainties" which inhibits creativeness. It may indicate a good ability which breaks down under emotional stress. It may reveal a need for achievement that produces impressive results by sheer effort toward quantity rather than superior insight or ability to organize.

Content is a sign, as Beck puts it, of the person's "mental furniture." Special interests or preoccupations are significant.

Study of emotional make-up is based chiefly on determinants. A logical answer to "What do you see in the blot?" is one determined by form. One who uses form as a determinant similarly tends to base actions on reasoning or knowledge of facts. A person who acts on logic and logic alone is quite rigid. Modifications of a purely rational approach are seen in responses using color, shading, or movement.

In one of the most astonishing features of the inkblot test, response to color is found to be an index of affective response. The colored cards seem to be emotionally stimulating. The effect is that of introducing an irrelevant, irrational, but exciting factor into an already difficult intellectual assignment. This is not unlike having to make a life adjustment in which people are involved. Some subjects ignore the color—they would also be expected to disregard the emotions of others, to be formal and controlled. "Color shock" is frequent, in which the force of the color upsets the person's ability to produce good responses. Persons who are friendly and socially adaptive produce many FC responses. CF responses are associated with emotional instability, egocentricity, and excitability; pure C responses, with uncontrolled emotionality.

The shading responses are not fully understood. They seem to represent a hesitant taking-everything-into-account which may be related to tact and caution in dealing with people. In other responses, shading seems to be associated with anxiety and depressive mood.

Movement responses are considered an expression of the subject's inner impulses. A high M score is associated with rich imaginativeness and fantasy. Absence of M suggests inhibition of spontaneous ideas. The M score may therefore be considered as representing self-acceptance and internal security.

Rorschach characterized people by a ratio usually called the experience type. This is the balance between use of movement and use of color. Those with large amounts of movement are called introversive. This is not the same as the neurotic introversion of self-report tests. The introversive person finds much satisfaction in his "inner life," and is more creative, but is less responsive to others. The extratensive, or color-emphasizing, person is more

---

[3] This is a "contingency coefficient"; in this problem, perfect correspondence would yield a coefficient of .89 instead of 1.00.

responsive and more oriented to stimulation from without. People who avoid both *M* and *C* are referred to as constricted. These are not rigid types, since the factors may be present in any proportion.

7. Why might a "perfect" accuracy score, 100 percent *F* +, indicate an undesirable personality pattern for many situations?
8. Do the Rorschach scores related to quality of output reveal maximum ability or typical behavior? How does the Rorschach compare with the Binet test in that respect?

Scoring is objective. In addition to the determination of scores, however, the trained scorer looks for many cues in the interrelation of responses. The analyst tries to observe how well the subject recovers from emotional shock, how he copes with blocking or failure, whether he is in conflict about sex. Following scoring, the tester makes an interpretation of the total pattern of the subject. Hertz makes this statement regarding the objectivity of the process (18, p. 538):

"It should be noted that the final analysis in the procedure of the interpretation in terms of other clinical and test data defies standardization, as Rorschach originally contended. The information gleaned from the Rorschach material is projected against family background, education, training, health history, past life, qualitative judgments of the examiner and of other people, and other clinical and test data. This is then interpreted in terms of the examiner's experimental knowledge of the dynamics of human behavior. Final conclusions are made by inference and analogy depending upon the experience, ingenuity, the fertility of insight, and, not to be forgotten, the common sense of the examiner. Prolonged and extensive experience is necessary, not only with human personality but with all kinds of clinical problems. This last step by definition, therefore, is personal to the examiner and subjective in view. It permits no norms, and it eludes all standardization."

Despite the importance of the personal skill of the analyst, and despite differences in scoring systems, different users of the test can reach comparable conclusions. This is best demonstrated in a study where one record was interpreted by Hertz, Beck, and Klopfer. The three summaries agreed in all significant respects (20).

Group Procedures

The application of the Rorschach method to groups takes two forms. The Group Rorschach is administered by means of slides. It permits less adequate inquiry than the individual test but otherwise is satisfactory for intelligent adolescents and adults. Munroe has developed a short scoring procedure for use in screening (28). This procedure yields a single numerical index of adjustment.

A multiple-choice Rorschach has also been tried. Validation studies indicate that the procedure is valueless in its present form.

Validity

Description

The Rorschach, in attempting to describe the total individual, presents again the problem of what to use as a criterion. One satisfactory method is the comparison of a *blind diagnosis,* made from the test record alone, with a report from one who knows the patient well. These blind analyses are often striking in their close correspondence to facts about the person. Table 69

Table 69. Partial Comparison of Blind Rorschach Analysis and Case History of a Negro Girl **(8)**

Rorschach Interpretation	Case History
Considerably above average in intelligence	IQ 109
Cultural opportunity meager	Restricted environment
Into things which are viewed in a practical way by others she introduces new elements out of her fantasy. The danger here is that the element she introduces may be not only original but, to others at least, extraneous.	A great capacity for confusing fantasy with reality. She did not think it was peculiar that the dead should visit the living.
She is very critical, and her stubborn insistence on seeing things her own way very likely brings her into conflict with persons in positions of greater authority.	Maintained a superior attitude on the ward. Usually sarcastic and snappy. Always very definite and positive in her attitudes. Did not hesitate to voice her opinions.
Insecurity and fantasy going in the direction of phobia	Screaming at night, continually afraid of men, dogs, automobiles.

compares parts of a blind analysis and a case history, written independently, describing a 16-year-old Negro girl (8). In another study, analyses were made of 20 records of problem children. Judges were asked to match the Rorschach reports with case abstracts, five pairs at a time. There were 84 percent correct matchings (26). Hertz lists 20 studies reporting generally successful blind analyses of Rorschach records for various pathological cases (18, p. 546).

One of the few systematic comparisons of test results with behavior descriptions for many cases deals with adolescent problem children at a camp. The writers conclude (49, p. 93): "Although inconsistent in many details, the Rorschach test in most cases gave a total personality picture not inconsistent with . . . observations of behavior. . . . Certainly in this study, successful evaluation of behavior tendencies could only be arrived at through careful analysis of the total configuration. Single determinants and simple relations in the Rorschach psychogram were of little prognostic value."

There has been no systematic validation of the test, score by score or trait by trait. Accumulated blind descriptions show that on the whole the test does much better than chance; there is less evidence that each specific determinant, such as texture, is correctly interpreted. Until this evidence is provided, probably the test will lead to some invalid inferences from scores.

Clinical Diagnosis

The test has been widely used to classify abnormal subjects. It is most useful as part of a systematic diagnostic procedure, the test indications being confirmed by other methods. Evidence of abnormality is to be found in many specific signs in the test, as well as in the general quality and character of thinking. Beck summarized studies of hundreds of schizophrenics in part as follows—first in terms of scores, then in terms of the parallel traits (4, pp. 106–107):

"F + is low; color nuance tends in the direction of pure color, or C; Dd is high; sequence, or order, tends toward the confused; DW (wholes suggested by a minor part) is the most characteristic method of approach by a patient to his problems. . . .

"They misinterpret their world. . . . His willingness to be inaccurate is indifference to the world's opinion of his percepts. It is a lack of self-regard. Primitive, instinctual forces dominate schizophrenic personalities; when they are sensitive to the world's opinions, passions still rock them. They pay attention to and see meaning in insignificant, irrelevant material within their field of perception, material their healthier fellows neglect. . . . They are not orderly or logical, by the world's standards."

For detecting neurosis, the "signs" of Miale and Harrower-Erickson have been widely used. They found certain score patterns especially frequent in neurotics, and infrequent among comparable normals. The signs are listed in Table 70. Any subject showing five or more signs is likely to be neurotic

Table 70.   Rorschach Signs of Neurosis (13)

Sign	Percentage of Subjects Showing Each Sign	
	Neurotics N = 74	Normals N = 385
25 or fewer responses	97	62
Not over 1 M	72	32
More FM than M	86	57
Color shock—indication of emotion or blocking on colored cards	46	6
Shading shock—emotion or blocking on shaded cards	59	5
Refusal to respond, on any card	65	12
Over 50% F responses	57	19
Over 50% A and Ad responses	57	22
Not over 1 FC	79	29

(13). Kelley has written at length of the characteristics associated with organic defects, feeble-mindedness, convulsive states, depression, alcoholism, and so on (25). The studies on which clinical classification is based are rarely systematic investigations. Cumulative experience with cases of a given type has led to generalizations, but it is rarely possible to find validity coefficients or other evidence of the degree of confidence to be placed in a Rorschach interpretation.

Benjamin and Ebaugh found agreement between Rorschach diagnosis and clinical diagnosis to be between 85 and 98 percent, for 50 varied cases (6). Rapaport made an unusual statistical study, in which small, carefully diagnosed groups were compared on each Rorschach score. He found statistically significant differences, generally in the direction predicted by Rorschach theory. Although his study makes it undeniable that there are correspondences between Rorschach performance and abnormalities, he does not validate any mechanical system of signs for classification. He emphasizes that clinical diagnosis by Rorschach must be based on a study of the dynamics of test performance rather than on signs alone (33, p. 367).

Screening

Like pencil-and-paper tests, the Rorschach has been used to detect abnormal subjects in general populations. The test is fairly effective in screening neurotics. A cutting score of five neurotic signs identified 80 percent of Harrower's neurotics, at a cost of 15 percent false positives (13). Ross, however, found that the same signs segregated people of low socio-economic status who were not neurotic (39). He considers the signs to be measures of insecurity, not neurosis. Much remains to be done to clear away similar fallacies in other Rorschach assumptions.

Munroe applied her inspection technique to freshmen at Sarah Lawrence College to identify possible problem cases. She rated 348 girls on a four-point scale as to adjustment, after a quick study of their Group Rorschach protocols. She placed 185 girls in the two "best" categories, and 163 she rated as having moderate or severe problems. Ratings of emotional maladjustment based on teachers' observations and need for psychiatric services during two years showed 147 of the "good" group and only 52 of the "poor" group to be adequately adjusted (28).

Prediction

Use of the Rorschach for predicting academic and vocational success is just beginning. One line of evidence on its potentialities for vocational guidance comes from records of those who are successful in a line of work. There is no one personality most common in any one vocational group, according to studies of artists, pharmacists, and accountants (23, 35). In one study Roe did find a rather homogeneous "occupational personality" among paleontologists (34).

Evidently in most vocations people of very different natures can achieve success. There are different ways of succeeding in a profession—a doctor may be adept at building patients' confidence, at making accurate diagnoses, or at dexterously manipulating instruments. Such a point of view would stress use of the Rorschach in guidance for description of the subject, rather than in any quantitative application. There is no justification for use of the method as a mechanical selection test, unless each record is clinically evaluated. Even the clinical method is inadequately validated.

Munroe's adjustment rating was successful in predicting college freshman grades, a corrected coefficient of .49 being obtained. A similar coefficient for the American Council test of general ability was only .39. Rorschach was far more successful in identifying probable failure than ACE. There is need for evidence of the predictive value of the Rorschach in more typical colleges than Sarah Lawrence, which has a select student body and uses "progressive" educational methods.

Success of therapy can be predicted, according to several studies. For example, the success of insulin treatment was predicted on the basis of Rorschach records of schizophrenics before treatment. Of 47 cases where improvement was predicted, 44 did improve. Of 13 where failure was predicted, 9 did not improve (32).

9. How might people with different personalities achieve success in pharmacy in different ways?
10. How might the Rorschach test be used in a college program, so long as its predictive validity is no higher than .50?
11. Munroe found that some people with poor adjustment did superior college work. How can this be explained?

Stability of Rorschach Performance

Adequate reliability coefficients on the Rorschach test are hard to obtain. Split-half coefficients are technically unjustified. Retesting is usually of uncertain meaning because of memory. Kelley and others overcame this problem by testing 12 cases before and after mild electroshock, which wipes out memory for the first test but does not change personality. They report that "in general, in every test, the psychogram produced was essentially unchanged . . . and the diagnosis was in exact accord with the clinical impression" (24, p. 36). Some single scores, however, shifted considerably, which emphasizes the importance of studying patterns of scores. Percentage scores based on short records were notably undependable.

Troup obtained retest data for identical twins, with a six-month interval between tests. Correlations of main scores were fairly high ($W\%$, .82; $M\%$, .79). Judges were able to match the two tests for each person in 92 percent of the cases. That Rorschach patterns are highly individual is shown by the difficulty the judges had in trying to match the test of each subject with that of his identical twin. Success was little better than chance (46).

Application of the Rorschach Method

The Rorschach is widely used clinically to understand the characteristics of patients and problem cases. It yields an unusual amount of information in a short time. It indicates quickly whether a criminal or a delinquent, for example, should probably be examined further for psychotic trends or is functioning normally. It supplements Binet results for poor learners by suggesting whether low scores represent lack of mental power or inhibitions which prevent use of that power. Physicians, social workers, teachers, and counselors now frequently refer cases for Rorschach diagnosis.

As a prediction or screening device applied to normals, the test has excited much interest; but research on normals is scanty. Its peculiar claims should make it useful for identifying problem students and employees before overt trouble develops. It may lead to prevention of psychosis by identifying cases for treatment in a pre-psychotic stage. It may help in identifying the peculiar temperamental assets which make a productive genius, an inspiring leader, or an insightful counselor. If any of these prospects is borne out by adequate research, use of the test with normals will be highly significant.

The test will never be a tool for use by every tester. Because the flexibility of the test eludes those with superficial training, the test must be given by one who has specialized in it. Business firms and schools have found it desirable to turn over Rorschach testing to consulting psychologists with adequate experience.

Among the sorts of research to which the test is adapted, special mention should be made of developmental and intercultural comparisons. The emergence of personality can be studied by administering the test to children of different ages. The test has been used with some success on preschool children (11). Hertz has reported on differences between early and late adolescents (19). Causal factors may be studied by comparing records before and after therapy or other events (5, pp. 336 ff.). The fact that the test is thought to be equally valid in any culture has made it useful to cultural anthropologists. Differences between societies in temperament, reflecting different patterns of upbringing of children, are revealed objectively by the test. DuBois took records of the Alorese, on a Pacific island, and had blind interpretations made by Oberholzer in Switzerland (10). The results were in close correspondence to the analysis of personality trends based on observation of the islanders.

THE THEMATIC APPERCEPTION TEST

Description

In 1938, Murray and co-workers published probably the most elaborate systematic study of personality to date, after studying a group of subjects by many methods (30). Among the major tools developed was the Thematic Apperception Test. The test requires the subject to interpret a picture by telling a story about it—what is happening, what led up to the scene, and what will be the outcome.

Like the Rorschach, the TAT is an unstructured experiment. The pictures are chosen to allow varied interpretation. Apparently the responses are dictated by the past experiences, conflicts, and wishes of the subject. Essentially the person projects himself into the scene, identifying with a character just as he vicariously takes the place of a movie star when he sees a photoplay. Unlike the Rorschach, the major analysis is based on the content of responses rather than formal aspects. The TAT, more than the Rorschach, identifies the subject's drives, conflicts, and attitudes toward self.

The TAT consists of 20 pictures, somewhat different pictures being used for men and women. The subject is led to believe that his imagination is being tested. Two one-hour sessions are used for obtaining stories. In addition to the stories themselves, the observer notes behavior during the test: evidence of emotion, bizarre language, and habits of attack on problems.

Analysis of Responses

The performance of the subject is evaluated in both objective and subjective ways. The general quality of thinking—originality, logic, and so on—may be judged. The ability to maintain control under emotional stress is revealed, since usually some cards shock the individual by picturing problems similar to his own. Language and expression may show attempts to appear intellectual, schizophrenic lack of self-criticism, or other significant trends.

Murray scored responses in terms of "press" and "need." A press is a force acting on the individual; a need is something he seeks. Every act reported in the story may inferentially be classified as resulting from a press or a need. The following story analyzed by Sanford illustrates the procedure and some of the categories used in scoring need (n) and press (p). The picture used shows a man clinging to a dangling rope. A 13-year-old girl gave the following story (3, pp. 567–590):

"This bandit (n Acquisition and n Aggression) got put in jail (p Dominance, p Aggression, and p Blame), and he kept trying to get away (n Autonomy, and n Blamescape). They made harder rules and gave him less freedom and less comfort (p Dominance, p Aggression, and p Retention). The monotony was making him mad (p Lack, p Affliction). He had rather be shot than live in this awful dungeon (p Noxiance, p Disorderly Surroundings, and n Autonomy, n Abasement). He was going to try to anyway (n Autonomy and n Inviolacy). He got a rope (n Acquisition) and started to climb up the wall of the prison (n Autonomy). There was a big searchlight and when it was turned off him he started up (n Seclusion and n Autonomy). Then it turned and they saw him—all the jailers were after him (p Knowledge, p Dominance, and p Aggression). He was crafty. He kept dodging and they couldn't shoot him (n Seclusion and n Harmavoidance). Finally they shot the rope (p Aggression) and he fell and was killed on the cement floor. (Bad outcome: Death)."[4]

The final interpretation is no set of scores on traits, but a consideration of the interaction of needs and of themes of individual stories. In the stories,

---

[4] By permission from *Child behavior and development*, by Roger G. Barker, Jacob S. Kounin, and Herbert F. Wright. Copyrighted, 1943, by McGraw-Hill Book Co., Inc.

one looks for the hero with whom the subject identifies and tries to discover the real-life counterparts of the other characters of the story. No interpretation of a single story is dependable, but the story given above might well be that of a girl trying to establish independence of a family she considers autocratic. It is significant that she feels that if the hero (herself) tries to escape, he can't win.

Although the Murray method has been helpful in many studies, it is complex and can be used precisely only after training and experience. Most clinical workers now place emphasis on the study of content rather than on scores. It is possible to shorten the test by selecting just those pictures presenting conflicts suspected of having significance for a particular case.

Other Thematic Picture Tests

Standardization is less important in the TAT than in the Rorschach because treatment of results is less objective. Many workers have completely abandoned Murray's pictures, using other sets more suitable to their subjects.

Henry tested Indians with pictures of Indian life. He based his analysis on the following aspects of performance: mental approach, creativity, behavioral approach (ideas about peer, adult, school, and other daily relations), family dynamics, inner adjustment and defense mechanisms, emotional reactivity, and sexual adjustment (14).

It is possible to adapt the picture technique to testing of a specific attitude or problem—anti-Semitism, family relations, etc. The selection of pictures to probe a particular area is a powerful addition to the method which is only beginning to be explored.

12. Of the seven factors studied by Henry, which would also be described by the Rorschach test?
13. Describe two possible stimulus pictures for studying each of the following problems.
    a. Attitudes of workers toward management and its practices.
    b. Feelings of teachers about problem children.
    c. Attitudes of college students toward their studies.

Validity and Reliability

Objective treatments of TAT performance are disappointingly unreliable. Sanford and associates made a variety of such checks. Need scores assigned by four judges for the same test records had an average correlation of only .57. Correlations between scores obtained at separate times were low. Even split-half coefficients were, at best, around .48 for need scores (41, pp. 262–263). Scores on needs expressed in fantasy were correlated with ratings of needs indicated in overt behavior, carefully observed. But these correlations were so small (average, .11) that need scores cannot be used to predict behavior. If the test users are correct in saying that people often have needs which they cannot express in their overt behavior, this evidence does not prove the test to be worthless. But a test which purports to reveal "subconscious" factors can be validated only by an equally "subconscious" criterion.

Such a validation is often sought by comparative projective interpretations with each other. Workers have repeatedly commented on the consistency of the pictures of personality derived from different sources, but there have been few attempts sufficiently well controlled to evaluate the degree of dependability of any one test. Henry compared his picture-test records with Rorschach, life history, and other data, concluding that in 451 comparisons on specific descriptions there was essential agreement between TAT and at least one other source in 83 percent. There was definite disagreement in only 2 percent (14, p. 71). Separate case analyses for eight girls were made on TAT, Rorschach, life history, and a battery of pencil-and-paper emotional and character tests. One judge was able to match all 32 descriptions in sets, while other judges matched 18 and 15 correctly (14, p. 56). Some aspects of the interpretation were more thoroughly confirmed than others. Harrison obtained similar success for a point-by-point comparison of TAT with case histories of patients. He claimed 82.5 percent confirmations. IQ guessed from the test correlated .78 with Binet IQ. Attempts to classify patients by psychiatric categories were correct in 77 percent of the cases (12). Neither Henry nor Harrison used the Murray method of scoring.

A study by Murray and Stein attempted to predict military leadership from responses to selected pictures in a group test. The rank-correlation of test results with ratings of ROTC men by their superiors was .65 (31). Although no validated results are yet available, work by Henry on the personality of business executives (15) promises that the test will be useful on many practical prediction problems that have been impervious to other tests.

OTHER PROJECTIVE TESTS

While the Rorschach and TAT have the prestige associated with wide application, projective testing is a general technique, rather than a name given to a few tests. There are a large number of tests classified as projective, a few of which are listed in Table 71. Few of these tests, however, appear likely to be standardized and used as routine testing procedures. The reason is that the projective technique can be applied to any subject matter, so that each investigator and clinician uses what fits most easily into his immediate needs.

Nearly any situation in the person's life permits sufficient variety of interpretation to be used as a projective test. The analysis of personality trends in the Binet and Wechsler tests is essentially a projective method. Systematic observation of playground activities permits similar inferences about drives, habits, and tensions. The only unique characteristic of projective tests, so-called, is that the stimulus materials are designed to evoke revealing responses. There is no limit to suitable material. Experiments with preschool children have shown all these methods to have value (27):

Table 71.   Representative Projective Techniques

Test and Publisher	Stimulus Material	Age Range	Special Features	References
Mosaic test	Colored geometric shapes to make a pattern	Adults	Studies quality and process in thinking	9, 48
Picture-Frustration Test	Cartoons with unfinished dialog	Children, adults	Studies reaction to frustration	38
Rorschach (Grune and Stratton)	Inkblots	Age 2 to adult	Relatively objective. Extensive research available	5, 25, 37
Sentence completion (Psych. Corp.)	Unfinished sentences	Children, adults		36
Spontaneous paintings	Art materials to be used as subject wishes	Preschool to adult		1, 47
Szondi (Grune and Stratton)	Photographs of psychotics			44
Thematic Apperception Test (Harvard)	Pictures	Children, adults	Detects specific needs and conflicts	2, 30, 33, 40, 41, 45
Verbal summator	Recorded vowel sounds which resemble unclear speech	Adults		42
Word association	Neutral and emotionally weighted words	Children, adults	Relatively objective	33
World test (play technique)	Toy objects, sufficient to build a city, farm, etc.	Children, adults		7

Finger painting. The child is given "colored mud" and is allowed to make designs or pictures, or just to enjoy manipulating it.

Cold cream. The child is given a jar of cold cream, placed on a floor covered with oilcloth, and permitted to do anything with it he wishes.

Sticks. A frustration test (see p. 427).

Balloons. The child plays with many balloons with the understanding that they may be broken.

Toys. The child is given toys from which he may construct a home and people as he wishes. Dramatic play follows.

The application of these methods to many children is shown in a series of films produced by Vassar College (43). The situations bring to the surface a variety of attitudes: fear of criticism, acceptance of own impulses, suppressed aggression, feelings of rejection by the parents, rebellion against restriction, and so on.

Projective methods have special strengths which make them essential in modern research and applied psychology. They stress personality as an interrelated whole, rather than as a random mixture of isolated traits. They permit every person to have a different final analysis, corresponding to our knowledge that each person is unique. They tap forces which underlie overt behaviors and are otherwise not observable, and tendencies which will break forth under future stress though they are not yet apparent.

The disadvantages of projective methods are marked. They are far from fully objective. Their validity is probably less than perfect, and there is no present way of knowing just where a given analysis is incorrect. Responses are distorted if subjects know much about the test and how it is used. Projective methods are time-consuming and cannot be used without special training. No satisfactory method for objectively summarizing a group of records has been developed. Even the greatest enthusiast for projective methods would agree that they provide an excellent illustration of the principle that a test, good in one situation, may not be satisfactory for another purpose.

14. How might individual differences in personality be revealed in each of the following?
   a. Playing poker.
   b. Cooking dinner for one's family.
   c. Writing a book review.
15. What advantages might be expected in each of the five projective tests for preschool children that the other tests would not have?
16. Under what circumstances would a slightly valid self-report test be preferable to a highly valid projective test of emotional adjustment?

EVALUATION OF PERSONALITY TESTING

The many techniques for studying personality have now been presented, together with what evidence there is on their validity. Evaluation is now in order, although it must be recognized that any summation is risky in an area where so many new developments are emerging. In fact, the most certain statement that can be made about personality testing is that it is in a state of flux. That is in itself a great advance. In the 20 years between Woodworth's first inventory and World War II, the progress in practical testing of personality was negligible. Useful tests of attitudes and interests were designed, but in the more general aspects of personality only ingenious research studies on a small scale relieved the scene. Testers generally were immersed in self-report tests which had not been validated, and which in some cases had been shown to be completely invalid.

In the surge of interest and ingenuity in testing which broke through in time to receive a practical trial during the war, enough fertile ideas appeared to warrant great optimism. Not all the techniques which were labeled "promising" in this book will prove to be sound, but somewhere in this territory there must be gold. Tentative research suggests that the most promising areas for further exploration are:

the strictly empirical self-report test (e.g., Strong Vocational Interest, Minnesota Multiphasic, Classification Inventory),
the self-report descriptive test using forced choice (Kuder Preference),
the situational test (Observational Stress Test, OSS leadership tests),
and projective techniques (Rorschach, TAT).

Field observations, situational tests "measuring" limited traits, observation incidental to intelligence tests, and conventional adjustment questionnaires will all continue to be used, but it is less probable that they will undergo extensive improvement.

For the tester who must deal with personality now, rather than after years of further research, it is important to compare the techniques as they now stand. Under present conditions, all techniques have their uses. Self-report tests are the only method that can be administered briefly, though the better-designed personality questionnaires require about as much of the subject's time as the projective tests. Projective tests, however, require more time for scoring, and usually must be given individually. Observation in the field is rarely practical save for research; a total of two hours of observing per subject is generally required to estimate even one trait accurately. Ratings are convenient enough, but of dubious value unless raters are carefully trained and have good opportunity to observe.

In mass processing for screening of employees or students, the choice lies between empirically validated self-report tests and the Group Rorschach. The former have demonstrated value—provided that the particular test chosen has been validated in the specific situation in which it is being used. The Group Rorschach must certainly be validated where it is applied; Munroe's single study in college prediction is favorable, but shows only that this technique is worthy of trial by other personnel workers. Imperfect techniques may be tolerated in selection if they improve the quality of the group screened. They may be tolerated in psychiatric screening only if test indications are carefully verified.

In guidance and clinical work, a test with low validity can do great damage. Self-report tests can be trusted only as guides to interviewing, never as a basis for decision. The only present methods which offer promise of substantial validity are behavior observations, and of these, projective tests have the advantage because they can be most easily administered. It can only be concluded that there is at present no method of firmly established validity capable of measuring or describing personality. It is probable that situational tests and projective tests will be made valid and practical, but research must demonstrate where they are valid and where they err.

A change in personality tests is their increasing length. Very brief questionnaires had real value in military screening, with a draft population. But the questionnaires which seem to offer the greatest individual validity (Strong, Kuder, Multiphasic, Humm-Wadsworth, etc.) are extremely long, running toward 500 items. Short situational tests have been reliable, but to obtain a valid estimate of any moderately generalized trait it is often necessary to combine six to ten tests using different stimuli. Projective tests usually require around an hour to give, and the interpreter must work for a much longer time to dig the full meaning from the responses. The capstone is Murray's OSS method. Here the investigators needed a dependable measure of all aspects of personality and were willing to spend the time needed to get it. The time for each man—three days and nights. Obviously, measurement of personality is no simple matter.

BROAD ISSUES IN TESTING

This book was organized by separating tests of ability from tests of typical behavior. That division served to permit a systematic attack on the mountain of tests to be studied, but it has long since become obscured by the numerous tests that crowd the border line. The Wechsler test of ability turns out to be a major clinical method for studying the personality of abnormals, and perhaps of normals. The Rorschach test of personality proves to be especially useful as an indication of intellectual functioning. Such contradictions doom conventional thinking about ability and personality as separate entities. Intelligence, instead of being an inborn fixed quality, is increasingly found to be a growing, changing process, molded by anxiety, emotion, security, and other feelings. While a theory of hereditary capacity is still tenable, no theory of operating intelligence can pretend to isolate it from emotional factors. As clinical and experimental studies capitalize on new techniques for studying how intellects function, the separate aspects of ability and behavior will increasingly merge into a concept of the person as a whole.

Changing psychological theory and problems will influence testing. The industrial tester and the educational tester will still need tests of single variables for particular predictions. The clinician is moving rapidly toward tests of complex and interacting functions. The battle between those who wish their tests pure, quantitative, and precise and those who want their tests practical is still going on. Practical experience with tests of single isolated abilities and of specific quantitatively measured personality traits is unencouraging to the single-trait emphasis. For general intelligence, motor behavior, and personality, the tests which serve practically are usually those which resemble human functioning in life situations. And that functioning is invariably complex. It may be that further research will permit the factorially pure test and the single-trait test to fulfill practical needs of the clinician, educator, and industrial psychologist. That day seems likely to be remote.

The conflict between objectivity and subjectivity is another matter. So far, subjective tests can do things no objective method can. But subjectivity implies error, and it would be regrettable to conclude that errors cannot be reduced. In any variable, subjective recognition of differences must precede objective measurement. The present emphasis on subjective analysis of personality may well be a primitive stage, which can be largely objectified through further research. Objectivity must not be attained through discarding valid types of information. But neither may clinicians rest content with what Wechsler has called "inspired guesswork." As the subjective interpreter can reduce his processes to objective form, he reduces the possibility of error, makes it easier to train additional interpreters, and increases the value of his procedures. The statistician and psychometrician has a similar responsibility, to broaden his methodology to attack the variables of greatest significance in analyzing human behavior. Murphy places the conflict in perspective as follows (29, p. 668):

"The impression has got abroad that there is an antithesis between personality measurement and an approach in terms of structure. Yet measurement supports rather than negates the emphasis upon wholeness. When concerned with structure, we wish, of course, to observe structural relations long and carefully before we attempt to decide what is to be measured and in what way. How far we can go with measurement is always an empirical question. We are between Scylla and Charybdis; for the people who love to analyze and measure, who give us the beautiful factorial analyses of 'persistence,' 'radicalism,' etc., are seldom interested in the mode of articulation between traits—mostly the measurers get stuck in measuring—and the structuralists are too enamored of relationships to bother with *precise* measurements, however quantitative their statements may be implicitly."

All in all, psychological testing is an accomplishment its developers may well boast of. Errors of measurement have been reduced year by year, and the significance of tests has been increased, until today all facets of American society feel the impact of the testing movement. The school has perhaps been most radically affected. But industry, marriage, governmental policy, and character-building agencies have all been studied or directly improved by means of tests. Testers are daily making the lives of people better by guiding a man into a suitable lifework, by placing an adolescent under therapy which will avert mental disorder, or by detecting causes of a failure in school which could turn a child into a beaten individual. Methods are now available which, if used carefully by responsible testers, can unearth the talents in the population and can identify personality aberrations which would cause those talents to be wasted. Building on these techniques, we are in a position to capitalize as never before on the richness of human resources.

SUGGESTED READINGS

Hertz, Marguerite R. "Rorschach: twenty years after." *Psychol. Bull.*, 1942, 39, 529–572.

Meehl, Paul E. "Schizophrenia, catatonic form," in Burton, Arthur, and Harris, Robert E. (eds.), *Case histories in clinical and abnormal psychology*. New York: Harper, 1947, pp. 71–83.

Munroe, Ruth. "Use of the Rorschach method in college guidance." *J. consult. Psychol.*, 1943, 7, 89–96.

Munroe, Ruth. "Three diagnostic methods applied to Sally." *J. abnorm. soc. Psychol.*, 1945, 40, 215–227.

Schachtel, Anna H. "The Rorschach test with young children," and Murphy, Lois B., "Personality development of a boy from age two to seven." *Amer. J. Orthopsychiat.*, 1944, 14, 1–16.

White, Robert W. "Interpretation of imaginative productions," in Hunt, J. McV.

(ed.), *Personality and the behavior disorders.* New York: Ronald Press, 1944, pp. 214–251.

REFERENCES

1. Alschuler, Rose H., and Hattwick, LaBerta W. *Painting and personality.* Chicago: Univ. of Chicago Press, 1947.
2. Balken, Eva Ruth, and Vander Veer, Adrian H. "The clinical application of a test of imagination to neurotic children." *Amer. J. Orthopsychiat.*, 1942, 12, 68–80.
3. Barker, Roger G., and others. *Child behavior and development.* New York: McGraw-Hill, 1943.
4. Beck, Samuel J. "The Rorschach test in psychopathology." *J. consult. Psychol.*, 1943, 7, 103–111.
5. Beck, Samuel J. *Rorschach's test. I: Basic processes. II: A variety of personality pictures.* New York: Grune and Stratton, 1944, 1945.
6. Benjamin, John D., and Ebaugh, Franklin G. "The diagnostic validity of the Rorschach test." *Amer. J. Psychiat.*, 1938, 94, 1163–1178.
7. Bolgar, Hedda, and Fischer, Liselotte K. "Personality projection in the World Test." *Amer. J. Orthopsychiat.*, 1947, 17, 117–128.
8. Clapp, Hazel S., and others. "Clinical validation of a Rorschach interpretation." *Rorschach Res. Exch.*, 1938, 2, 125–163.
9. Diamond, Bernard L., and Schmale, Herbert T. "The Mosaic test. I. An evaluation of its clinical application." *Amer. J. Orthopsychiat.*, 1944, 14, 237–250.
10. DuBois, Cora. *The people of Alor.* Minneapolis: Univ. of Minnesota Press, 1944.
11. Ford, Mary. *The application of the Rorschach test to young children.* Minneapolis: Univ. of Minnesota Press, 1946.
12. Harrison, Ross. "Studies in the use and validity of the Thematic Apperception Test with mentally disordered patients: II. A quantitative validity study." *Character & Pers.*, 1940, 9, 122–133.
13. Harrower-Erickson, M. R. "The value and limitations of the so-called 'neurotic signs.'" *Rorschach Res. Exch.*, 1942, 6, 109–114.
14. Henry, William E. "The Thematic Apperception technique in the study of culture-personality relations." *Genet. Psychol. Monogr.*, 1947, 35, 3–135.
15. Henry, William E. "The business executive: a study in the psychodynamics of a social role." *Amer. J. Sociol.*, 1949, 54, 286–291.
16. Hertz, Marguerite R. "The reliability of the Rorschach ink-blot test." *J. appl. Psychol.*, 1934, 18, 461–477.
17. Hertz, Marguerite R. "Scoring the Rorschach ink-blot test." *J. genet. Psychol.*, 1938, 52, 15–64.
18. Hertz, Marguerite R. "Rorschach: twenty years after." *Psychol. Bull.*, 1942, 39, 529–572.
19. Hertz, Marguerite R. "Personality patterns in adolescence as portrayed by the Rorschach ink-blot method: I. The movement factors. II. The color factors." *J. gen. Psychol.*, 1942, 27, 119–188; 1943, 28, 3–61.
20. Hertz, Marguerite R., and Rubenstein, Boris B. "A comparison of three 'blind' Rorschach analyses." *Amer. J. Orthopsychiat.*, 1939, 9, 295–315.
21. Hunt, J. McV. (ed.). *Personality and the behavior disorders.* New York: Ronald Press, 1944.
22. Hunter, Mary. "The practical value of the Rorschach test in a psychological clinic." *Amer. J. Orthopsychiat.*, 1939, 9, 287–295.

23. Kaback, Goldie R. *Vocational personalities*. New York: Teachers Coll., Columbia Univ., 1946.
24. Kelley, Douglas M., and others. "The stability of the Rorschach method as demonstrated in electric convulsive therapy cases." *Rorschach Res. Exch.*, 1941, 5, 35–43.
25. Klopfer, Bruno, and Kelley, Douglas M. *The Rorschach technique*. Yonkers: World Book Co., 1942.
26. Krugman, Judith I. "A clinical validation of the Rorschach with problem children." *Rorschach Res. Exch.*, 1942, 6, 61–70.
27. Lerner, Eugene, and Murphy, Lois B. (eds.). "Methods for the study of personality in children." *Monogr. Soc. Res. Child Develpm.*, 1941, 6, No. 4.
28. Munroe, Ruth L. "Prediction of the adjustment and academic performance of college students by a modification of the Rorschach method." *Appl. Psychol. Monogr.*, 1945, No. 7.
29. Murphy, Gardner. *Personality*. New York: Harper, 1947.
30. Murray, Henry A., and others. *Explorations in personality*. New York: Oxford Univ. Press, 1938.
31. Murray, Henry A., and Stein, Morris. "Note on the selection of combat officers." *Psychosom. Med.*, 1943, 5, 386–391.
32. Piotrowski, Zygmunt A. "The Rorschach method as a prognostic aid in the insulin shock treatment of schizophrenics." *Psychiat. Quart.*, 1941, 15, 807–822.
33. Rapaport, David, and others. *Diagnostic psychological testing*. Chicago: Year Book Publishers, 1945, Vol. II.
34. Roe, Anne. "A Rorschach study of a group of scientists and technicians." *J. consult. Psychol.*, 1946, 10, 317–327.
35. Roe, Anne. "Painting and personality." *Rorschach Res. Exch.*, 1946, 10, 86–100.
36. Rohde, Amanda R. "Explorations in personality by the Sentence Completion method." *J. appl. Psychol.*, 1946, 30, 169–181.
37. Rorschach, Hermann. *Psychodiagnostics*. Translated by Paul Lemkau and Bernard Kronenberg. Berne: Hans Huber, 1942.
38. Rosenzweig, Saul. "The picture-association method and its application in a study of reactions to frustration." *J. Pers.*, 1945, 14, 3–23.
39. Ross, W. Donald. "The contribution of the Rorschach method to clinical diagnosis." *J. ment. Sci.*, 1941, 87, 331–348.
40. Rotter, Julian B. "Thematic apperception tests: suggestions for administration and interpretation." *J. Pers.*, 1946, 15, 70–92.
41. Sanford, R. Nevitt, and others. "Physique, personality and scholarship." *Monogr. Soc. Res. Child Develpm.*, 1943, 8, No. 1.
42. Shakow, D., and Rosenzweig, S. "The use of the tautophone (verbal summator) as an auditory apperceptive test for the study of personality." *Character & Pers.*, 1940, 8, 216–226.
43. Stone, L. J. (ed.). "Studies of normal personality development: I. Finger painting. II. Balloons. III. Frustration play techniques. IV. This is Robert" (16 mm. films). New York: New York Univ. Film Library, 1941, 1942.
44. Szondi, L. *Experimentelle Triebdiagnostik*. New York: Grune and Stratton, 1948.
45. Tomkins, Silvan S. *The Thematic Apperception Test*. New York: Grune and Stratton, 1947.
46. Troup, Evelyn. "A comparative study by means of the Rorschach method of personality development in twenty pairs of identical twins." *Genet. Psychol. Monogr.*, 1938, 20, 461–556.

47. Waehner, Trude S. "Interpretation of spontaneous drawings and paintings." *Genet. Psychol. Monogr.*, 1946, 33, 3–72.
48. Wertham, Frederic, and Golden, Lili. "A differential diagnostic method of interpreting mosaics and colored block designs." *Amer. J. Psychiat.*, 1941, 98, 124–131.
49. Young, Robert A., and Higginbotham, Sibley A. "Behavior checks on the Rorschach method." *Amer. J. Orthopsychiat.*, 1942, 12, 87–94.

APPENDIX A. REVIEWS OF STUDIES OF TESTING

Brady, M. B. "A survey of the results of intelligence tests in psychosis." *Brit. J. med. Psychol.*, 1942, 19, 215–261.

Goodenough, Florence L. "The measurement of mental growth in childhood," in Carmichael, Leonard E. (ed.), *Manual of child psychology*. New York: Wiley, 1946, pp. 450–475.

Cattell, Raymond B. "The measurement of adult intelligence." *Psychol. Bull.*, 1943, 40, 153–193.

Wolfle, Dael. *Factor Analysis to 1940*. Chicago: Univ. of Chicago Press, 1940.

Bennett, George K., and Cruikshank, Ruth M. *A summary of manual and mechanical ability tests*. New York: Psych. Corp., 1942.

Borow, Henry, and Whittaker, Betty A. *Tests in industry*. State College, Pa.: Extension services, Pennsylvania State Coll., 1943.

Kandel, I. L. *Professional aptitude tests in medicine, law, and engineering*. New York: Teachers Coll., Columbia Univ., 1940.

Long, W. F., and Lawshe, C. H., Jr. "The effective use of manipulative tests in industry." *Psychol. Bull.*, 1947, 44, 130–148.

Stead, William H., and others. *Occupational counseling techniques*. New York: American Book Co., 1940.

Traxler, Arthur E., and Townsend, Agatha. "Another five years of research in reading." *Educ. Rec. Bull.*, 1946, No. 46.

Ellis, Albert. "The validity of personality questionnaires." *Psychol. Bull.*, 1946, 43, 385–440.

Ellis, Albert, and Conrad, Herbert S. "The validity of personality inventories in military practice." *Psychol. Bull.*, 1948, 45, 385–426.

Maller, J. B. "Personality tests," in Hunt, J. McV. (ed.), *Personality and the behavior disorders*. New York: Ronald Press, 1944, pp. 170–213.

Newcomb, Theodore M. "Measurement of the adult personality," in Murphy, Gardner, and others, *Experimental social psychology*. New York: Harper, rev. ed., 1937, pp. 769–888.

Patterson, Cecil H. "The relationship of Bernreuter scores to parent behavior, child behavior, urban-rural residence, and other background factors in 100 normal adult parents." *J. soc. Psychol.*, 1946, 24, 3–50.

Super, Donald E. "The Bernreuter Personality Inventory: a review of research," *Psychol. Bull.*, 1942, 39, 94–125.

Symonds, Percival M. *Diagnosing personality and conduct*, New York: Appleton-Century, 1931.

Carter, Harold D. "Vocational interests and job orientation," *Appl. Psychol. Monogr.*, 1944, No. 2.

Beery, John R., and Bare, Thurman H. "The measurement of attitudes," in Briggs, T. H., and others, *The emotionalized attitudes*. New York: Teachers Coll., Columbia Univ., 1940, pp. 1–17.

Deri, Susan, and others. "Techniques for the diagnosis and measurement of intergroup attitudes and behavior." *Psychol. Bull.*, 1948, 45, 248–271.

McNemar, Quinn. "Opinion-attitude methodology." *Psychol. Bull.*, 1946, 43, 289–374.

Newcomb, Theodore M. "Social attitudes and their measurement," in Murphy,

Gardner, and others, *Experimental social psychology.* New York: Harper, rev. ed., 1937, pp. 887–1046.

Arrington, Ruth E. "Time sampling in studies of social behavior." *Psychol. Bull.,* 1943, 40, 81–124.

Scheerer, Martin. "Problems of performance analysis in the study of personality." *Ann. N.Y. Acad. Sci.,* 1946, 46, 653–675.

Hertz, Marguerite R. "Rorschach: twenty years after." *Psychol. Bull.,* 1942, 39, 529–572.

Sargent, Helen. "Projective methods: their origin, theory, and applications in personality research." *Psychol. Bull.,* 1945, 42, 257–293.

Tomkins, Silvan S. *The Thematic Apperception Test.* New York: Grune and Stratton, 1947.

White, Robert W. "Interpretation of imaginative productions," in Hunt, J. McV. (ed.), *Personality and the behavior disorders.* New York: Ronald Press, 1944, pp. 214–254.

APPENDIX B. PRINCIPAL TEST PUBLISHERS AND DISTRIBUTORS

Association Press, 347 Madison Avenue, New York 17, New York.

California Test Bureau, 5916 Hollywood Boulevard, Los Angeles 28, California.

Educational Test Bureau, 720 Washington Avenue, S.E., Minneapolis 14, Minnesota.

Educational Testing Service, 15 Amsterdam Avenue, New York 23, New York.[1]

C. A. Gregory, 345 Calhoun Street, Cincinnati, Ohio.

Grune and Stratton, 381 Fourth Avenue, New York 16, New York.

Houghton Mifflin Company, 2 Park Street, Boston 7, Massachusetts.

Doncaster G. Humm Personnel Service, P.O. Box 1433, Del Valle Station, Los Angeles 15, California.

Marietta Apparatus Company, Marietta, Ohio.

University of Minnesota Press, Minneapolis, Minnesota.

National Institute for Industrial Psychology, Aldwych House, London, W. C. 2, England.

Psychological Corporation, 522 Fifth Avenue, New York 18, New York.

Public School Publishing Company, 509 North East Street, Bloomington, Illinois.

Science Research Associates, 228 South Wabash Avenue, Chicago 4, Illinois.

Sheridan Supply Company, P.O. Box 837, Beverly Hills, California.

Stanford University Press, Stanford University, California.

C. H. Stoelting Company, 424 North Homan Avenue, Chicago 24, Illinois.

Teachers College, Columbia University, New York, New York.

Williams and Wilkins Company, Baltimore, Maryland.

World Book Company, Yonkers 5, New York.

---

[1] Handles most tests originated by American Council on Education, College Entrance Examination Board, Cooperative Test Service, and Progressive Education Association.

Author Index

Subject Index

Absolute measure, 20–21
Acceptability of tests, 47
Accomplishment quotient, 282
Achievement in school, and intelligence, 180
  prediction of, 130, 182, 209–210, 267, 333, 350–351
    See also College, success in
Achievement tests, 180, 270–300
  as criteria, 259–260
  historical development of, 272–273
  in employee selection, 298
  in school programs, 270–273, 281–283, 299–300
  summary tables, 286, 292–293
Adaptability Test, 6, 72
Adjustment, 17
  See also Personality
Administration of tests, 45, 84–96, 173, 221–222
Adults, ability of, 36, 119, 142
  intelligence tests for, 140–142
Age, basal, 109, 118
  chronological, 119
  educational, 282
  mental, 118–120
Age scale, 134
Agree-disagree item form, 50, 372
Aiming tests, 217–219, 221
Aircrew, selection of, 3, 6–8, 73, 215, 219–221, 249, 252–253, 261, 333, 351, 414
Air Force, U.S., 199, 200, 210–211, 404, 410
Algebra, prediction of success, 210, 249–250, 264
Allport Ascendance-Submission Test, 326
Allport-Vernon Study of Values, 323, 326
Alpha, Army, 104–105, 174, 244
Ambiguity, 78, 433
American Council on Education Personality Report, 399
American Council on Education Psychological Examination, 58, 90, 174, 180, 185–186
Anecdotal records, 395–396
Application of principles, 226, 276, 284–285

Aptitude Index, 334
Aptitude tests, 17
  algebra, 264
  art, 227–229
  clerical, 215, 265, 267
  dentistry, 214, 218, 267
  engineering, 52, 214, 226, 265
  foreign language, 264, 266
  law, 58, 265, 267
  mechanical, 216–227
  music, 231, 267
  nursing, 259, 265
  science, 52, 265
  stenography, 244–247
Arithmetic tests, for employee selection, 298
Army Alpha, 104–105, 174, 244
Army Beta, 58, 187
Army, British, 253–254
Army General Classification Test, 86, 174, 181
Art, 210, 226–229, 406, 415
Arthur Performance Scale, 162
Ascendance-Submission Reaction Study, 326
Assembly tests, 201, 202, 226, 248, 253
Ataxiameter, 217
Atkins Object Fitting Test, 114
Attitude tests, 17, 50, 193, 368–383
  pictorial, 374, 448
Audiogram, 231
Ayres Handwriting Scale, 74

Basal age, 109, 118
Batteries, achievement, 286
  diagnostic, 233–234
  in multiple correlation, 248–249
Behavior during tests, *see* Observation
Behavior Rating Schedule, 130
Bell Adjustment Inventory, 72, 75, 318, 326, 331, 332
Bellevue Scale, *see* Wechsler-Bellevue Intelligence Scale
Bennett Test of Mechanical Comprehension, 28, 58, 76, 225–226, 253
Bernreuter Personality Inventory, 72, 74, 314–319, 327, 329, 332, 335
Beta, Army, 58, 187